THE WRITINGS

OF

JOHN BRADFORD, M.A.,

MARTYR, 1555.

The Parker Society.

Instituted A.D. M.DCCC.XL.

For the Publication of the Works of the Fathers and Early Writers of the Reformed English Church.

THE WRITINGS

OF

JOHN BRADFORD, M.A.,

FELLOW OF PEMBROKE HALL, CAMBRIDGE,

AND PREBENDARY OF ST PAUL'S,

MARTYR, 1555.

CONTAINING

SERMONS, MEDITATIONS, EXAMINATIONS, &c.

EDITED FOR

𝕮𝖍𝖊 𝕻𝖆𝖗𝖐𝖊𝖗 𝕾𝖔𝖈𝖎𝖊𝖙𝖞,

BY

AUBREY TOWNSEND, B.D.,

OF TRINITY COLLEGE, DUBLIN, CURATE OF ST MICHAEL'S, BATH.

WIPF & STOCK · Eugene, Oregon

Wipf and Stock Publishers
199 W 8th Ave, Suite 3
Eugene, OR 97401

The Writings of John Bradford
Containing Sermons, Meditations, Examinations
By Bradford, John and Townsend, Aubrey
ISBN 13: 978-1-5326-0955-8
Publication date 10/21/2016
Previously published by Cambridge University Press, 1853

CONTENTS.

		PAGE
Preface of the Editor	. . . . . .	ix

I. Two Prefaces by Bradford, 1548.
    Preface to Artopœus on the Law and Gospel . . 5
    Preface to Orations of Chrysostom on prayer . . 13

II. Preface to Melancthon on Prayer, 1553 . . 19

III. Sermons on Repentance and the Lord's Supper, &c.
    Sampson to the Christian reader . . . 29
    Bradford to the Christian reader 38
    Sermon on repentance, 1553 43
    Sermon on the Lord's supper 82
    Bradford preaching before the court of Edward VI. 111

IV. Godly Meditations on the Lord's Prayer, Belief, and Ten Commandments, with other Exercises.
    Advertisement to the reader, 1562 . . . 115
    Instructions concerning Prayer 116
    Meditation on the Lord's Prayer . . . 118
    Meditation on the Belief 140
    Meditation on the Ten Commandments . . 148
    Meditation on prayer 173
    Paraphrase of the Lord's Prayer . . . 180
    On the second coming of Christ 185
    On the sober use of the body 187
    On the pleasures of life 188
    On true mortification 190
    On the Providence of God 191
    On the presence of God 193
    On the power and goodness of God . . . 194
    On Death 195
    On the passion of Christ 196
    A general Supplication 200
    A Confession of sins 202
    A prayer for the mercy of God 203
    A thanksgiving in the time of persecution . . 205

[BRADFORD.]

CONTENTS.

	PAGE
† A prayer on the work of Christ	206
A prayer for Faith	209
A prayer for Repentance	210
Dialogue between Satan and Conscience	210
A treatise on Election and Free-will	211
A brief sum of Election	219

V. PRIVATE PRAYERS AND MEDITATIONS, &c.

Prayer on the wrath of God against sin	224
When you awake out of your sleep, pray	230
When you behold the day-light, pray	231
When you arise, pray	231
When you apparel yourself, pray	232
When you are made ready to begin the day, pray	232
Cogitations meet to begin the day with	233
When you go forth of the doors, pray	234
When you are going any journey, pray	235
When you are about to receive your meat, pray	236
In the meal-time, pray	237
After your meat, pray	237
Cogitations for about the mid-day time	238
When you come home again, pray	238
At the sun going down, pray	239
When the candles be light, pray	240
When you make yourself unready, pray	240
When you enter your bed, pray	241
When you feel sleep to be coming, pray	242
Prayer for divine protection	242
A thanksgiving, being a godly prayer for all times	245

VI. MEDITATIONS FROM THE AUTOGRAPH OF BRADFORD IN A COPY OF THE NEW TESTAMENT OF TYNDALE.

* The second Birth	250
* On following Christ	252
* On Affliction	253

† The larger part of the 'prayer on the work of Christ' is now first printed from a MS. in Emmanuel College, Cambridge.

* The articles marked with an asterisk are now, it is believed, printed for the first time.

CONTENTS. vii

	PAGE
* The life of Faith	253
* On the conflict of Faith	254
* On a good Conscience	255

VII. MEDITATIONS AND PRAYERS FROM MSS. IN EMMANUEL COLLEGE, CAMBRIDGE, AND OTHER SOURCES.

* Meditation on the Lord's supper	260
Admonition written in a New Testament	264
* Prayer for the presence of God	264
A sweet contemplation of Heaven	266
Place and joys of the life everlasting	269
Felicity of the life to come	273
* Prayer for deliverance from trouble	276
* Prayer in the time of persecution	278
* Paraphrase of Psalm lxxix.	282
Prayer of one standing at the stake	292

VIII. FIVE TREATISES.

The old man and the new	297
* The flesh and the spirit	300
Defence of Election, Dedication	307
. . . . . Part I.	310
. . . . . Part II.	318
Against the fear of Death	332
The Restoration of all things	351

IX. TEN DECLARATIONS AND ADDRESSES.

Declaration concerning religion, 1554	367
Exhortation to Patience	375
Letter to men who relieved the prisoners	379
* Address on Constancy	385
Letter on the Mass, to Hopkins, &c., at Coventry, 1554	389
Declaration on the Reformation, 1554	399
Letter to the Queen and Parliament, 1554	401
Supplication to the King, Queen, and Parliament, 1554	403
* Remarks on a memorable trial	405
Admonition to lovers of the Gospel, 1555	407

X. Exhortation, 1554—5; and Farewells, 1555.

Exhortation to the brethren in England	414
Farewell to the city of London	434
Farewell to the university and town of Cambridge	441
Farewell to Lancashire and Cheshire	448
Farewell to the town of Walden	455

XI. Examinations and Prison-Conferences, 1555.

The first examination	465
The second examination	473
The last examination	482
Talk with Hussey and Seton	493
Talk with Bp. Bonner	496
Conference with Willerton	497
Talk with Cresswell and Harding	500
Conferences with Adn. Harpsfield	502
Talk with Clayden and others	515
Conference with Abp. Heath and Bp. Day	518
Conference with Alphonsus a Castro	530
Conference with Weston	538
Conference with Pendleton	541
Conferences with Weston, and Reasons against Transubstantiation	544
Talk with a Servant	553

Appendix.

Prefaces by Dr Wilkinson and Dr Harris, Oxford, 1652	558
Preface by Lever, 1567	565
Meditation on the tenth commandment, by Lever	569
Prayer for the afflicted in France, 1562	571
Ludovici Vivis Preces et Meditationes diurnæ	572
Prayer compiled by R. P.	578
Institutio contra vim Mortis, Bradfordo authore	581
Preface by Bp. Ironside, 1688	583
Officium et Sententia contra Johannem Bradford, 1555	585

Notes 588

PREFACE OF THE EDITOR.

This volume contains a large portion of the doctrinal and devotional writings of the martyr Bradford; including sermons, meditations, prayers, treatises, public addresses, examinations, and prison-conferences. These are collected and arranged from a variety of sources in print and manuscript.

Fourteen pieces, and parts of others, are now for the first time published. The three Prefaces, p. 5—24, are also first reprinted since the sixteenth century. It is hoped that the text presented throughout the volume is pure and correct. Fifty-one MSS., some in the autograph of Bradford, and some very early transcripts, varying severally in length from one to twenty-nine pages of this book, have been collated. The first editions of Bradford's works are exceedingly scarce: some do not exist in our public libraries: and the copies used were obtained after much research. Every reference has been verified; and the originals are quoted in the notes.

Some important pieces have usually been printed in the collection of his Letters[1]: but, as they are more properly public addresses than private epistles, they are classed in this volume as distinct treatises. Such are the following:

'The old man and the new,' p. 297—300: the 'Defence of election,' p. 310—18: 'The restoration of all things,' p. 351—64: the 'Exhortation to patience,' and 'Letter to men who relieved the prisoners,' p. 375—84: the Letter 'on the mass,' p. 389—99, and 'to the queen and parliament,' p. 401—3: the 'Admonition to lovers of the Gospel,' p. 407—11: the 'Exhortation to the brethren in England,' and 'Four farewells,' p. 414—60.

Further particulars with regard to the contents of this volume are supplied in the editorial prefaces, pp. 3, 16, 28, 112, 223, 248, 258, 294, 305, 331, 350, 366, 412, 463.

[1] Foxe, Acts and monuments, 1583, p. 1624—65; Bp. Coverdale, Letters of the martyrs, 1564, p. 251—489, 650—2.

The remaining letters of Bradford, about eighty-four in number, some of which have not hitherto been printed, will appear in the concluding portion of his works. That volume will also include the 'Hurt of hearing mass,' the translations from Chrysostom, Artopœus, and Melancthon, some minor pieces, a short memoir of Bradford, and an Index to both volumes.

The writings of Bradford, as a chaplain and friend of Bishop Ridley[1], are of interest to all churchmen; and they embrace topics of deep import, which have more or less exercised the minds of devout believers in every period of the church of Christ. They fully justify the encomium of Foxe: 'Sharply he opened and reproved sin; sweetly he preached Christ crucified; pithily he impugned heresies and errors; earnestly he persuaded to godly life[2].' They shew, 'how godly he occupied his time, being prisoner; what special zeal he bare to the state of Christ's church; what care he had to perform his office; how earnestly he admonished all men; how tenderly he comforted the heavy-hearted; how fruitfully he confirmed them whom he had taught[3].'

Such considerations encourage the hope, that the blessing of Almighty God may attend this endeavour to present to the public the entire remains of one, whom Bishop Latimer publicly designated 'that holy man[4];' and of whom Bishop Ridley, within three years after admitting him to the order of deacon, wrote: 'In my conscience I judge him more worthy to be a bishop, than many of us that be bishops already to be a parish-priest[5].' Strype describes him as 'a man of great learning, elocution, sweetness of temper, and profound devotion toward God;... of whose

[1] "I thank God heartily that ever I was acquainted with him, and that ever I had such a one in my house."—Bp. Ridley, Lett. to Bernhere, Works, p. 380, Parker Soc. See also p. 331—7, 363—9, 377—91, of Works of Bp. R.; and p. 82, 464 of this volume.
[2] Foxe, Acts, &c. 1583, p. 1603.
[3] Id. ibid. p. 1624.
[4] Protest of Bp. Latimer, A.D. 1554, Works, II. 258, Parker Soc.
[5] Bp. Ridley, Lett. to Gate and Cecil, Works, p. 337, Parker Soc.

worth the papists themselves were so sensible, that they took more pains to bring him off from the profession of religion, than any other[6].' That impartial historian also refers to 'Bradford' in conjunction with 'Latimer, Cranmer, and Ridley, as four prime pillars of the reformed church of England[7].'

It is the editor's welcome duty to return his best thanks, in behalf of the Parker Society, to the Reverend the Librarians of the Bodleian, Oxford, and the Cambridge University Library, and to the Reverend the Masters and Fellows of Emmanuel, and of Gonville and Caius College, Cambridge, for the privilege of access to manuscript remains of Bradford. The Society are also greatly indebted to the late O. H. Williams, Esq. of Ivy Tower near Tenby, for allowing a transcript to be taken of the Meditations in the autograph of Bradford, now first printed, p. 248—57.

Sincere thanks are likewise due to the Rev. Canon Havergal, the Rev. W. Maskell, and the Rev. P. Hall, for the use of early editions of the writings of this martyr; to the guardians of Archbishop Harsnett's Library, Colchester, for lending the *Excitationes animi in Deum*, by Ludovicus Vives, *Lugduni* 1558; to J. G. Mansford, Esq. for the loan of the rare first English edition, 1563, of the 'Acts and monuments' of Foxe; and to the Rev. W. Goode, for the use of the scarce Latin edition of Foxe, the *Rerum in ecclesia gestarum commentarii, Basil.* 1559.

The editor has much pleasure, in conclusion, in expressing his obligation to Dawson Turner, Esq. F.R.S., J. Bruce, Esq. F.S.A., and G. Offor, Esq.; and he desires, in particular, to record his very grateful sense of the assistance rendered by his esteemed and lamented friend, the late George Stokes, Esq., the founder of the Parker Society.

[6] Strype, Ecc. Mem. III. i. 363—4.   [7] Id. ibid. 423.

ERRATA.

p. 83, note 4, *instead of* p. 1780, *read* 1583, p. 1604.

p. 315, instead of note 2, read [² 'heirs,' MS.: ' heirs ; for if we be heirs of God, then are we fellow-heirs,' 1562, 1564.]

p. 316, note 3, line 3, *instead of* p. 327, l. 35, *read* p. 325, l. 37.

PREFACES
TO
TRANSLATIONS
FROM
ARTOPŒUS AND ST CHRYSOSTOM,
BY
JOHN BRADFORD.

1548.

The diuily=
on of the places of the lawe
and of the Gospell, gathered owt of the hooly scriptures by Petrum Arto‑ poeum: wher unto is added two orations of Prayeng to God made by S. John Chriso‑ stome, no lesse necessa‑ ry then lerned. Trā‑ slated into En‑ glish.

❡ Math. xxvi. ❜

Watche and pray that you fal not in to temptation.

❡ Imprinted by my[1] Gwalter Lynne. Anno. M.D. xlviii.

[From a copy in the Library of the Rev. W. Maskell, Broadleaze, Devizes.]

[1 Misprint for 'me'.]

[THE Translations from Artopœus and Chrysostom will appear in the following collection of the Writings of Bradford, after his Letters.

The Prefaces are now reprinted, first, since 1548: and, as the earliest compositions of Bradford, known to have been published by himself, are placed at the beginning of this volume.

The name of the translator is not supplied in the original edition: but the initials "J. B." occur at the end, above the colophon. Bishop Bale (*Catalogus*, 1557, VIII. 87.) states, *Bradfordus transtulit in Anglicum sermonem Artopœum de lege et evangelio, lib.* I, [*et*] *Chrysostomum de Oratione, lib.* I. Bishop Tanner (*Bibliotheca*, 1748) adds to the entry of Bale the first words of the *title*, and of the printed version of Artopœus, and of the Preface to that of Chrysostom, with the date, London, 1548.

Bradford, also, in a Letter "from the Temple, this 12th of May, 1548," addressed to Traves, speaks of Translations executed by himself: "Hereafter, and that shortly, by God's grace, I will send you, *primitiæ laborum meorum*, a work or two, which I have translated into English, so soon as they be printed, which will be afore Whitsontide[2]." Bradford writes in another Letter, "This Book, which I have sent, take it in good part. It is the first; I trust, it shall not be the last God hath appointed me to translate. The print is very false; I am sorry for it. I pray you, Be not offended at my babbling in the Prologues, &c[3]."]

[2 It will be remembered, that Edward VI. had come to the throne, Jan. 28, 1547. Bradford was entered at the Inner Temple, in London, the following 8th of April. The Order of Communion was printed March 8, 1548. The Preface of Bradford to Chrysostom on prayer is dated at the end, May 16, 1548: (vide p. 15.) and *Whitsunday*, 1548, fell on May 20: (vide tables in Sir H. Nicholas' Chronol.) Bradford went to Cambridge about the ensuing midsummer. The first Book of Common Prayer of Edward VI. was set forth by authority in 1549.—The dates in this and other notes are (unless the contrary be noted,) according to our present reckoning.]

[3 Foxe, Acts &c. (ed. 1583) 1661: or (ed. 1847) VII. 281—2.]

PREFACE TO THE PLACES OF ARTOPŒUS.

Here hast thou, good reader, the Division of the Places of the Law and of the Gospel, gathered out of the holy scriptures by the godly learned man master Petrus Artopeus: which (the Places of the Law and Gospel, I mean) whoso truly understandeth, cannot by any man's doctrine be seduced from the truth, or read the scriptures but to edify both himself and others: whereas he that is ignorant of the same cannot, though he were a great doctor of divinity, and could rehearse every text of the bible without book, but both be deceived, and deceive others; as the experience hereof (the more pity) hath taught, nay, seduced the whole world. For how can it be, that such as find no terror of conscience, and see not their just damnation in the law of God, which commandeth things impossible to man's nature and power; how can it be, I say, that such should find sweetness in the gospel of Christ? How can the benefit of Christ shew itself to him that needeth it not? What needeth the whole man the physician? "The law," saith St Paul, "was our schoolmaster unto Christ." But unto such as perceive and feel not the law, how is it a schoolmaster unto Christ? How is the law a schoolmaster unto such as will not learn? How have they learned, which think the law not to be impossible for man to fulfil? Or else, if they had looked on it, which is a spiritual doctrine, with spiritual eyes, would they have stirred any time contentions about the justification of faith? Would they have taught any satisfactions, which man can do, towards God, if they had learned the law? [Matt. ix.] [Gal. iii.]

It appeareth, therefore, by these things, that either the law hath not been their schoolmaster; or else, that they have been negligent, forgetful, or proud and disdainful scholars. For they have not applied free pardon of sins to Christ, as all the world knoweth. But if they were brought to him, they would grant him to be a perfect workman: they would be ashamed to say or think Christ to be but a patcher. Yet it appeareth (though openly in words they will not say so;

for that all christian hearts would abhor: it appeareth, I say), that they believe so.

<small>An objection.
Matt. vii.
Rom. ii.</small>

Yea, sir, will they say, why judge you so? Judge not, saith Christ: and, wherein you judge another, saith Paul, therein you condemn yourself. It seemeth, you speak of malice, and declare yourself to be but a railer.

No, sir, herein I do not slander you, nor do none otherwise than Christ himself teached: "You shall know the tree," saith he, "by his fruit." If I see a man rob his neighbour, do I evil, if I think him to be a thief? If I see a man lie with his neighbour's wife, do I evil, if [I] judge him to be a fornicator? If I hear a man unadvisedly (as not called in judgment) to swear by the mighty and most reverend name of God, do I naught, if I judge him to be a blasphemer?

<small>Objection.</small>

Nay, you will say, what is this to the excusing of your rashness and uncharitableness in judging us? For, though you belie us, yet we trust to be saved by Christ our Saviour.

<small>Answer.</small>

You say well, sir: I would your doings agreed to your sayings, and then were I a liar. But if you do so, let other men judge. Wherefore, I pray you, say you mass? Is not the mass, as you have taught and as you say it, a sacrifice propitiatory to take away sins, both of the quick and dead? Where is this taught you? Doth this law bring to Christ? Yea, you will say, for we offer there Christ. And

<small>Heb. vii.</small>

St Paul saith, "Christ offered himself once for all." But, I pray you, look on the nature of the law, which is, by

<small>The nature of the law.</small>

God's teaching and speaking, to open to man the poison of his own heart: the law will not leave man in arrogancy or presumption, but will rather bring him to desperation. The law pulleth man down, and leadeth him into hell's mouth, as

<small>Psal. xxx.
[Wisd. xvi. 13.]</small>

it is written, "Thou art he that leadest to hell," &c. The law filleth man full of grief and heaviness; and, if succour come not from heaven, full of blasphemy even against God and his ordinances, as the history of Job, well weighed of a godly wit, will declare. Thus, you see, the law, where she is schoolmaster, bringeth man into all humbleness of mind at the least.

<small>Note.</small>

Therefore, ye offerers, (for you say ye offer Christ,) what humbleness of mind is in you (if a man should grant you offered Christ), when you will offer that thing that no angel, no saint, no patriarch, no prophet, no man might or could offer? Are you not good scholars, when you are taught to be humble, and yet extol yourselves above angels? I say, none could be found meet in heaven nor in earth to offer that offering, wherewith God's wrath, deserved by our sins, was appeased and extinct, but even he that was of both natures, both God and man, Jesus Christ. He was the sacrificer and the sacrifice: he was the offerer and the lamb slain: slain, I say, for our sins. Alas, that ever such arrogancy should be crept into man's heart, not only to spoil Christ of his most glorious office, but to extol yourselves above angels, and to make yourselves check-mate with[1] Christ! *Note.*

The law, I say, never taught you this horrible presumption. No, say ye, Christ taught us. Did Christ teach you? When, or where? I provoke ye all to answer. Ye can never find it, I must needs still say, till I see you write it or speak it, out of the scripture, that you have authority to offer. In the mean time, I beseech you, good brethren, to leave off your arrogant presumption, and repent, and give to our good Christ his due honour and dignity.

Mark, also, doth not your offering, as you would have it, make, as I said, Christ a patcher? St Paul saith, "By one offering he hath made perfect them which are sanctified for ever." How say you to this? Doth not your offering make the offering which Christ made imperfect? For whatsoever is added to a perfection doth imply an imperfection. Take heed, good reader, therefore, if thou be sanctified, purged from thy sins, anointed with the Holy Ghost, and made the child of God, it is done all by that one oblation of Christ's body on the cross, brought in to thee by the faith that thou hast in the same oblation. Or, if that thou be not now sanctified, if ever thou look to be sanctified or saved, it must be only by this work, wrought of CHRIST in his own person. *Heb. x.* *Mark this.*

[1 i.e. to conquer, to take prisoner, to put an end to. Vide Todd; Nares, v. *mate;* Richardson. So in Marshall's Primer, 1535, "Neither is it meet to make them check with our Saviour Christ, much less then to make them checkmate."—Three Primers, Oxf. (1834) 8. So too Bp. Coverdale, "Therefore would not Josue that any thing should be set checkmate with the cross and oblation of Jesus Christ, but that all honour of cleansing and forgiveness of sins should be ascribed only unto him."—Bp. C., Works (Parker Soc.) The Old Faith, 50.]

Yet a little more. Where learned you to apply the mass for the sins of the quick and dead? Yea, even the bread and wine afore the words of consecration, as you call them, when you say, *Suscipe sancta Trinitas*[1], is applied for the salvation of the quick and the rest of the dead.

Scripture never teacheth you this word of application, nor giveth you this authority to apply the sacrifice of Christ's body, as you say, to whom you will. You will make Christ, to whom the Father hath given "all power in heaven and earth," under your power and your bondman, to serve as it pleaseth you, to whom, when, where, and how much shall be your will. So may you set Cain, if any man would give you a groat, out of hell. So may you falsify the true history of the rich glutton. You have not learned this of the law. For the law bringeth to Christ: but you bring from Christ. Leave off and cease your application therefore. Repent, and embrace by faith that only sacrifice which Christ himself made once for all: or else, I will be so bold to say, you shall never be saved. Thus you see, I judge you not amiss.

<small>Note well.
Matt. xxviii.

Gen. iv.
Luke xvi.

Heb. ix.</small>

Hereby it is evident, that these men, for all their great learning (as some of them have had), that yet they did never understand the law of God. For they never found sweetness in the gospel of Christ. Hath there not been great learned men, think you, that, besides this, have taught abstaining from certain kinds of meat, auricular confessions, worshipping of images, creeping to the cross, holy water, holy bread, pilgrimages, pardons, and I cannot tell what, necessary to salvation? And this verily hath come hereof, that they have not known the law nor the gospel, though they could both preach, and teach, and say all the bible without book. For he that feeleth the law working in his heart, can never be satisfied, but despair, except the gospel and joyful tidings of Christ be brought unto him.

In this book, therefore, thou hast the places of the Law and the Gospel divided, wherein I exhort thee to prove thy-

[[1] Suscipe, sancta Trinitas, hanc oblationem quam ego indignus peccator offero in honore tuo, beatæ Mariæ, et omnium sanctorum tuorum pro peccatis et offensionibus meis, et pro salute vivorum et requie omnium fidelium defunctorum.—Missale ad vs. Eccl. Sar. 1555. Ordin. Miss. fol. CL; Ancient English Liturgy, Maskell (1844) 22, or (1846) 56.]

self. For though thou learnest them by heart, yet that is not the thing which maketh thee happy: for so the other men which make Christ but a party[2] saviour, could do. But if thou wilt profit, it behoveth thee to have experience and practice of them. Prove, therefore, thyself in the law: see if the texts and sentences of the law do fear thee, make thee dread, yea, tremble and quake at the justice of God: for God himself hath spoken it, and his word must needs be true, "Heaven and earth shall pass, afore one tittle or iota of the law be unperformed." For in whose heart the law worketh no fear, yea, horrible fear of God's wrath, surely they are in an evil case. Unto such the doctrine is no law, nor God is no God: their hearts be hardened, God unto them seemeth false: for if they knew, that God would damn all such as walk not in his ways, they would not do as they do; they would not only leave off their wickedness, but also in looking in the law they would horribly fear the vengeance of God for transgressing the law. *Matt. v.*

But, alas! it is to be pitied, it is to be lamented: we ought to fear the plagues of God hanging over our heads. For notwithstanding God's most abundant mercy upon us, which should provoke us to repentance, when or where was there more security, and less fear of God, than is even in this realm of England at this day?

The laws of God were never more plentifully nor more plainly set forth amongst any other people, than they be amongst us. The commandments of God are continually, in the ears of all people, read openly in the churches, yea, written upon the walls, so that all men know them: yet is there none amendment. "Who shall I speak unto," saith the prophet Hieremy, "whom shall I warn, that he may take heed? Their ears are so uncircumcised, that they may not hear. Behold, they take the word of God but for a scorn, and have no lust thereto." *Jer. vi.*

It is true, say these our carnal gospellers, these papists will never have lust unto God's word, they will never look upon the Testament. Mary[3], saith the papists, these fellows of this new learning, see how they live; they read the scriptures, and they are worse than all other, they will swear

[2 i. e. in part.]

[3 An oath, meaning, By the Virgin Mary: corrupted afterward into *marry*.—Nares.]

wounds, heart, sides, &c.[1] The scripture would make us heretics: we will not be like these knaves, &c.

Note well this. ☞ Look, I pray you, what hatred is betwixt these two kinds of people: the one loveth the other so well, that, as the saying is, they would eat the other's heart[2] in garlick. Yet, for all this envy and malice, (which God of his gracious mercy reform!) mark, and you shall, I warrant you, see them agree both against God, even as the Pharisees and Sadducees, notwithstanding their contrary religions, agreed against Christ.

Deut. v. Do not you both hear and read, ☞ "Thou shalt not take the name of God in vain, for the Lord will not hold him guiltless, that taketh his name in vain?" Again,

Ecclus. xxiii. do you not hear, "The man which useth swearing shall be filled with iniquity, and the plague shall not depart from his house?" What think you, is there a God? You tear a-pieces his most holy name in your mouths: for "By God," is a most common oath with you both. What, do you think in deed, that God is true? I am sure you do not: for then were you worse than devils, for the devil feareth God; but you do not, seeing you know God saith, that his plague shall not depart from that man which useth swearing, and yet continue still to blaspheme that most holy, reverend, and terrible name of God. But unto you which yet continue to swear by God,

[Psal. viii.] it is not so. "O Lord," saith David, "how wonderful reverend is thy name in all the earth!" Alas! why do you then make so light a thing of it? For in all your talks, at every word's end almost, you rap out, as irreverently as you can, that most honourable and fearful name of God.

Lev. xxiv. ☞ Do you not read, that God commanded him which
Objection. blasphemed his name to be stoned to death? Yea, you will say, to swear by God is not to blaspheme God's name: the
Answer. story saith, he blasphemed and cursed by that name. Yes, to swear by God is to blaspheme God, as may be proved by the very text: for some texts have for *blasphemavit*[3], *diserte*

[1 Vide "A christen exhortacion vnto customable swearers," attributed by Bp. Tanner (*Bibliotheca*) to Bp. Coverdale; without date, N. Hyll, signature A ii.]

[2 An ancient expression of hatred: vide Hom. Il. Ω. 212.]

[3 *Et nuncupavit* (*explanavit*, Chald. vers. *exsecrans*, Jun. et Trem. *expressit*, Pagnin. Syriac. Tigurin. *diserte*, Tigurin.) *nomen, et maledixit*, Ar. Montan. Samarit. Pagnin. (vel, *despexit*, Oleast. Tigurin. vel, *blasphemavit*, Chald. Syriac. Jun. et Trem.).—Poli Synops. in Levit. xxiv. 11.]

expressit nomen illud, et vilipendit: "he did plainly express that glorious name, and set nought by it," as you all do, that so swear. I pray you, mark the history, and know, that it is written to be your warning and for your doctrine; as, if you repent not, you shall feel it: for God hateth the blaspheming his holy name as much now as he did then; and the longer he suffereth, the greater, if we repent not, will be our punishment. 1 Cor. x.
Rom. xv.

If a man blame a papist now for swearing by God, Oh, saith he, I will be no loller[4]: you may see I remember him. Blame a carnal gospeller for swearing, and he will say, No, I will be no papist. Alas! whose heart shaketh not for fear of God's vengeance? For, as God is above all things, so is "By God" the greatest oath, and the greatest sin next unto idolatry. Say not but ye be warned. Note.

I cannot leave it, saith another; howbeit I think none evil. O thou man, that sayest so, thou haddest most need to tremble: for upon thee God hath already poured his most horrible plague. Yea, sayest thou, how so? I feel no sickness, pocks, plagues, &c. No, no, man, the horriblest plague of God is, to be given up of God, as thou art that sayest, thou canst not leave it: for thou despisest God, and nothing regardest his threats. And yet thou canst leave from speaking that which the king enacteth for treason. But God hath enacted, "Thou shalt not swear at all: for whatsoever is more than Yea, yea, or Nay, nay; cometh of naught." And yet thou regardest not that. Say not but thou art warned. The greatest plague of God.

Again, what malice, hatred, envy, whoredom, uncleanness, lechery, divorcements, bribing, theft, ravin, slanders, filthy talk, pride, covetousness, gluttony, drunkenness, lying (and who can tell all?) is amongst us! Surely, the most horrible plagues of God, that ever were upon any nation, are upon us (us Englishmen, I say), except we earnestly repent.

Thus it is manifest, the law of God is not feared; so is not God feared, which proveth there is no faith: for how canst thou believe that God will perform his promise to thee, when thou fearest not his truth to perform his word and threat? God is no liar. Deceive not thyself, therefore: but prove whether thou be in faith. For except thou Note.

2 Cor. xiii.

[4 i. e. Lollard.]

Who hath faith. tremble and quake at God's justice in the law, thou hast no faith, but art an hypocrite: for faith is not, where the fear of God is not; and the fear of God is not, where God's law is not believed. Therefore, I say, take to thee the glass of God's law; look therein, and thou shalt see thy just damnation, and God's wrath for sin, which, if thou dreadest, will drive thee not only to an amendment, but also to a sorrow and hatred of thy wickedness, and even to the brim of despair, out of which nothing can bring thee but the glad tidings of Christ, that is, the gospel: for as God's word doth bind thee, so can nothing but God's word unbind thee; and until thou comest to this point, thou knowest nothing of Christ. Therefore, exercise thyself in this book. Make unto thee a sure foundation; begin at the Law: and if it fear thee, and bring thee to hell's mouth in consideration of thy sin and sinful nature, then come to Christ, come to the gospel: then shalt thou be a good scholar, and praise thy schoolmaster: then shalt thou feel the benefit of Christ; then shalt thou love him, and thy neighbour for his sake. Then will it make thine ears to glow, and thy heart to bleed, to hear or see any thing set in Christ's place. Then shalt thou look for the coming of thy Lord, and weep to hear his name evil spoken of. The which thing he grant for his mercy's sake .
AMEN.

TO THE READER,

GRACE AND PEACE, &c.

FORASMUCH, good reader, as the Almighty Lord, of his secret wisdom and mere goodness, hath so liberally, so fatherly, so lovingly, so mercifully visited us most unworthy wretches, and of all nations the most abominable sinners, with his most gracious blessing of his precious, sacred, holy word and gospel, in such abundance and plenteousness, as no people heretofore hath had or now hath such cause and so great occasion (if we will ponder the same) to be thankful, as we have: It is our duties again to kiss and embrace the Son, lest the Lord be angry, and so we perish from the right way. Psal. ii. It is our duties to arise forth of sleep, and to know the time Rom. xiii. of our visitation. It is our duties to bring honour and praise unto the Lord, well worthy his name, to bring forth gifts, Psal. xcvi. and come into his temple. Let the manifold examples of ingratitude and unthankfulness, and of God's vengeance for the same, both in the old Testament and in the new, be a warning unto us. Let the examples of late days, as well in this realm as in other countries, be monitions and lessons for us. God is the same God now he always hath been. And as much doth our sins, our obstinacy, and our wanton receiving of God's holy gospel, kindle the wrath of that patient and long-suffering Lord against us, as did the wickedness of others, upon whom, for our example, he hath taken punishment already. Let us learn, that "the long sufferance of God doth draw us to repentance" and to amendment of life: beware, lest we harden our hearts, and heap against and upon ourselves "the just judgment of God, the treasure of his wrath, against the day of vengeance," when his righteousness shall be opened, and he shall "reward every man according Rom. ii. to his deeds." How long shall God thus cry unto us: O ye Englishmen, "How long will you blaspheme mine honour? Psal. iv. Why have ye such pleasure in vanity, and follow lies?" "Let us," I say, therefore, which have been drowned in darkness, and now come into the sunshine of God's most glorious gospel, "cast away the works of darkness, and put on the armours of light; let us walk honestly as in the day time." Let us with all humbleness bewail our wickedness, our obstinacy, and resisting God's truth, our wanton carnal gospelling: and let us embrace it, let us follow it, let us not only be hearers, but also doers of the word. It crieth for amendment of living: let us therefore give it his due honour. God regardeth more obedience than sacrifice. If we will obey him, we shall eat the good things of the land. Let us, therefore, get up, and arise with the lost son, and say unto him, "Father, we have sinned against heaven, and before thee," &c. Let us fall before the throne of his mercy, and beg of him, by continual prayer, a thankful and an obedient heart, and therein to exercise our faith. For "this kind of devils is not cast out, but by prayer and fasting." Yea, faithful prayer is the only mean, whereby through Christ we both obtain all things necessary and convenient, and also retain and keep still the grace of God given unto us.

Now, seeing that amongst the many good and godly travails taken by divers men, as well in compiling as in translating into this our English tongue sundry learned and profitable books, there is but little of this most necessary exercise of faith, true prayer I mean; (for in all the external worshippings of God there is none so difficile and hard:) therefore I have thought necessary to translate something of the same; whereby we might learn, as well what true prayer is, as also the dignity and worthiness thereof. Which thing once known may give occasion and spur (if I may say so) to the slothful and negligent, to be more earnest therein; and also may instruct others which have continually exercised themselves, as they think, in true prayer, to be no longer vain mumblers, but true worshippers of God in spirit and verity; for God requireth such.

But, forasmuch as the most part of this sort, of a blind zeal, but not according to knowledge, seeking to establish their own righteousness, and not that which cometh only by Christ, despise and may not abide the names and works of godly men of this late time, whom they call new fellows, which most fruitfully, as of other matters, so no less godly have written of this; but do take all that they say to be rank heresy: to the intent these men, also, might by some means come into the knowledge of their abuses in prayer, wherein they put too much confidence and trust; I have, therefore, according to my little power and knowledge, wherewith I desire to edify, though most rudely, yet truly and plainly, translated these two notable Orations or Homilies of the most eloquent learned doctor, St John Chrysostom, which he entitled, Of praying to God. The which Homilies, being diligently read and weighed, shall, I doubt not (obstinacy put aside), cause thee, O good reader, to give thanks to that Spirit, which moved, yea, wrote herein, by that doctor; and also give thee occasion, not only to love prayer the better, but also to exercise thyself more earnestly in the true worshipping of God, and in exhorting and giving good example to all others to be the like, to the praise of God's most holy name. Which thing the most merciful Father grant through his dearly beloved Son, our Lord and Saviour Jesus Christ, which reigneth with him and the Holy Ghost for ever.

AMEN.

xvi. May. M.D.xlviii.

[The Translation from Melancthon will appear in the present collection of the Writings of Bradford (with those from Artopœus and Chrysostom), after his Letters.

The Preface is taken from the edition, without a date, by John Wight[1]. The volume of which it is a part probably was printed in July or August, 1553; because the Preface, which, from internal evidence, certainly was written at that time, speaks of the Treatise, as being then "putte foorth[2]" It is placed here, both on account of connection, in point of time, with the Sermon on Repentance, which it mentions to be "presently put foorth[2]"; and as probably published, as well as written by Bradford.

This short Address (not, I believe, reprinted hitherto in our day,) is of interest, in shewing the feeling entertained in England, by the faithful worshippers, during the brief period[3] between the decease of Edward VI. and the imprisonment of the godly Protestant Bishops and other Clergy.]

[1 He printed books, from 1551 to 1589.—Herbert, (Typogr. Antiq. II. 779, *et seq.*)
Maunsell, (Catal. 1595) 86, mentions "Phil. *Melangton*, his treatise of praier, translat. by Ioh. *Bradford.* prin. by Rob. Walg. in 12." The entry of Maunsell is repeated by Herbert (Typ. Ant. II. 1145), among the works issued by Robert Waldegrave, who began to print books about the year 1578.]

[2 p. 20.]

[3 Edward VI. died July 6, 1553. The Preface to Bradford's Sermon on Repentance is dated July 12. Queen Mary was proclaimed July 19, and came to London, August 3. Bradford saved the life of Bourne August 13, and was committed to the Tower, "within three days after."—Foxe, Acts, &c. (ed. 1583) 1409, 1604, or (ed. 1846) VI. 392, VII. 144, 145; Strype, Mem. (Oxf.) III. 1. 3, 20, 26, 32.]

PREFACE

TO A

TRANSLATION FROM MELANCTHON

BY

JOHN BRADFORD.

1553.

¶ A Godlye

treatyse of Prayer, translated into Englishe, By John Bradforde.

)∴(

¶ James. iiii.

You aske and receaue not, because you aske amisse, euen to consume it vpon youre voluptuousnesse.

¶ John. xvi.

Hytherto you haue asked nothinge in my name: aske and you shal receaue it that your ioye maye be full.

[The colophon is as follows:]

Imprinted at London in Paules Church yearde, at the sygne of the Rose, By John Wight.

[From a copy in the Library of the late George Stokes, Esq., Cheltenham.]

UNTO THE CHRISTIAN READER,

JOHN BRADFORD WISHETH THE TRUE KNOWLEDGE OF JESUS CHRIST.

In this book following thou hast, good reader, a godly piece of work made by the godly learned man, Master Philip Melancthon, concerning prayer. The which as he lamenteth to be either too little or too corruptly spoken of among many writers; even so do I lament the too little and too corruptly using of it in these days with many Englishmen, notwithstanding the same be very diligently and godly set forth by public authority, by private writings, by diligent preaching and exhortations. Whereunto, in that on all sides, spiritually and corporally, publicly and privately, these perilous days of necessity so nip us and provoke us to pray, and by prayer to fetch down help from above, that if now we will not with diligence use it, watching thereunto with all sobriety, surely we needs must feel that which we cannot be able to bear. For already God's anger is set on fire, as once it was against the Israelites, and hath begun to burn in the camp of God's church in England: I mean it not so much concerning the body, as concerning the head, even concerning king Edward the sixth, our late lord and most dear king. So that I fear me, it will go on forwards: for we have few Moses' and Aarons, which stand as gaps between God and us. And when God's judgment beginneth at such dear children of God as our most precious pearl and king was, I cannot believe it will stay there. Though he was Adam's child, (for who may say, 'My heart is pure from sin?') yet am I persuaded that it was not his but our sins which hath procured God to take him away from us, before he began to reform his commonweal, as graciously he had well begun and gone forwards in the reforming of the church, for that part which concerneth doctrine and the ceremonies of the same.

Num. xvi.

Prov. xx.

Discipline we want yet.

We never did know what a benefit of God he was unto us; and therefore we were unthankful, and that most impiously: wherethrough we have provoked God to take him away, that by the want of his benefit we should be brought to the feeling of our unthankfulness and impiety; but to this end, surely, that we might repent, ask mercy, pardon, and truly to turn to the Lord, that he might cause his striking angels to put up his sword, and eftsones[1] yet bless us far above our expectation, (if, I say, we will now lament our unthankfulness, sorrowing our sinful life, and with earnest prayer beg as well mercy for that which is past, as also grace hereafter for that which is to come,) by lightening the light of his holy countenance upon us.

2 Sam. xxiv.

But if we, seeing now God's anger thus kindled against us, and daily more and more sending out great smokes, which commonly do immediately precede great flames; as the tumults almost every where presently do shrewdly prognosticate: If, I say, we seeing this will not repent us of our unthankfulness and monstrous sinfulness, "seeking the Lord whilst he may be found," "in the day of our trouble calling upon him," as he commandeth us, not without a promise that also he will hear and help us; assuredly the ears of them that be to be born will tingle at the hearing of the great wrath that God will shew upon us. To the intent therefore that God might turn his favourable countenance towards us; in that the means thereunto is hearty repentance and prayer; because I cannot be every where to stir up men thereunto by preaching, I have thought it my duty to signify my good-will by writing that, which something God might use as a mean to help thereunto.

Psal. l.

Unto a Sermon therefore of Repentance, which even presently I have put forth, I have also put forth this Treatise of Prayer, the which hath been a good space translated; as a good part more of the Common-places of this Master Melancthon, which one day may fortune to come abroad, if I shall perceive any commodity by this to come to the church of Christ. Not that I stand in doubt whether the Common-places be profitable or not: but because I stand in doubt of my unfitness and unableness exactly and plainly to play the translator. This Treatise of Prayer might and should have had more labour and diligence on my part, if that the present time of itself had not even, as it were, enforced me to send it forth presently; that thereby in time some that should read it or hear it read might be taught, or at least occasioned,

[1 i. e. soon afterward.]

the more truly and diligently to pray to the God of mercy, that he would mitigate his anger justly conceived against us, and, as the prophet prayeth, "in his anger to remember his mercy." _{Hab. iii.}

It is enough, O Lord! and a plague most heavy, that we have lost our good king: but indeed we have deserved it; and with him that thou shouldest take also as well the benefit of tranquillity and politic peace, as also thy holy gospel and true religion. For never was there nation that so horribly abused thy gospel and contemned this as we have done. Yea, alas, Lord! presently we do it: so that righteous art thou if thou take it away, and give it to a nation that will bring forth the fruits of it. This three years, O Lord, _{Luke xiii.} yea, and three too, hast thou come to look for fruit: but thou findest none, save only leaves. Nay, Lord, no leaves dost thou find: for all our wickedness is so manifest that all nations see now to our shame, that we never received thy gospel but to cloak our covetousness, ambition, and carnality. Dear Father, yet cut us not down: let the sweet figs of thy sweet gospel tarry with us: and dig thou about us, and lay thy dung about us: so shall we, I trust, bring forth fruit to the praise of thy name. Let not now the wicked people say, "Where is their God?" Thou "our God art in heaven, and canst do whatsoever thou wilt:" do thou turn us to thee. O Lord, save us, and continue thy gospel and religion among us, for thy Son's sake, our Saviour Jesus Christ. Say 'Amen,' good reader, and use this book thereafter.

It teacheth thee what God thou shouldest call upon: it teacheth thee wherefore he heareth thee: it teacheth thee wherefore thou shouldest call upon him: it teacheth thee what things thou shalt ask, and in what order: it teacheth thee how to honour the saints, and what is their worship. It teacheth thee to be thankful, and giveth thee occasion to be thankful, if thou wilt read it, weigh it, carry it away, and practise that which it teacheth.

Go to therefore, take this book in thy hand to stir thee up to prayer; remember thine own weakness and need, as well in soul as in body; I will not say in thy goods, name, family, vocation, &c. Remember the state of God's church, of the commonweal, of thy friends, parents, &c. Remember that Satan sleepeth not, but as a roaring lion seeketh our destruction publicly and privately, spiritually and corporally. Remember how many have stand both before God and man as surely as thou dost, and yet have fallen and have been overthrown horribly. Remember how that the children of God have been diligent in prayers always from the beginning, as well in their needs corporal as spiritual. Remember that their prayers have not been in vain, but graciously have they obtained their requests as well for themselves as for others. Remember that God is now the same God, and no less rich in mercy and plentiful to them that truly call upon him: and therefore in very many places doth he command us to call upon him: so that except we will heap sin upon sin, we must needs use prayer. His promises are both universal towards all men, and most free without respect of our worthiness, if so be we acknowledge our unworthiness, and make our prayers in the faith and name of Jesus Christ; who is our Mediator, and sitteth on the right hand of his Father, praying for us, being the same Christ he hath been in times past, and so will be unto the end of the world, to help all such as come to him.

Only in thy prayer away with the purpose of sinning, for he that prayeth with a purpose to continue in any sin cannot be heard; his own conscience presently condemneth him; he can have no true testimony or assurance of God hearing him. For even as in vain he that hath a wound desireth the healing of the same, so long as in the wound there remaineth the thing that is the cause of the wound, as a knife, a pellet, a dart, or a shaft-head, &c.: even so in vain is the prayer of him that retaineth still the purpose to continue in sin; for by it the soul is no less wounded than the body with a sword or any such instrument. As therefore to the healing of the wound in a man's body this is first gone about, that the knife or iron which is in it be first pulled out, so do thou in prayer away with purposing to continue in sin. God condemned in the old law all spotted sacrifices: away therefore with the spots of purposing to continue in sin. Bid adieu, when thou goest to prayer, bid adieu, I say, and farewell to thy covetousness, to thy uncleanness, swearing, lying, malice, drunkenness, gluttony, idleness, pride, envy, garrulity, slothfulness, negligence, &c. If thou feelest thy wilful and perverse will

Levit. xxii.

unwilling thereunto, out of hand complain it to the Lord, and for his Christ's sake pray him to reform thy wicked will, put him in remembrance of his promise sung by the angels, *Hominibus bona voluntas*, that by Christ it should be to his glory to give "to men a good will," to consent to his will, and therein to delight night and day. The which is that happiness which David singeth of in his first Psalm: therefore more earnestly crave it, and cease not till thou get it: for at the length the Lord will come in an acceptable time, I warrant thee, and give it thee, and whatsoever else thou shalt also ask to his glory, in the name and faith of his dear Christ, who is "the door of the tabernacle" whereat the acceptable sacrifices to God were offered, as this book doth well teach thee if thou wilt diligently mark it. Luke ii.
And in his law he will delight night and day, &c.
Levit. xvii.

Therefore to it I will now refer thee, beseeching the everliving God of mercy to endue thee and me and all other his children with the Spirit of grace and prayer, that we may diligently use this sacrifice of "the calves of our lips," which is not abrogate with the old sacrifices of the old Testament: that we may use it, I say, diligently every day, not only "at evening and morning," as the old law used to teach us, in the beginning and ending of all things we go about, to seek for God's help; but also, as David saith, *meridie* ["at noon"] even in the midst of all our works, yea, in all parts of our works, at all times, as Christ teacheth us "always to pray and never to be weary." Not that I mean this so, as though I would have any to follow the Psallians or Euchites[1], which, to obey this commandment of Christ for praying always, did nothing else night and day but recite psalms and certain prayers, thinking him most holy which had read and rehearsed most psalms and prayers: but that I would have us to have our affections upon God, and our desire for his help ("for without him can we do nothing") not quenched or pressed down by oblivion or forgetfulness of God, which is the worm and moth of a christian conscience. And whereunto we shall be holpen, if that we do often ejaculate, and, as it were, send out of our hearts and lips some short sighs and words for God's help, as we read of good and holy men that were accustomed so to do. Amongst whom Hos. xiv.
Heb. xiii.
Num. xxviii.
Ps. cxix. [62. lv. 17.]
John xv.

[1 Vide Mosheim, Eccl. Hist. cent. IV. II. v. 24.]

was great care and diligence of perseverance in prayer, as the history of St. James (whose knees by kneeling in prayer was as hard as though they had been of a camel rather than of any man[1]) and of many other doth teach us.

God open our eyes to see our great need and
his great mercies and ready help: and then
doubtless we will be as diligent as
heretofore we have been negli-
gent, and yet are. The
Lord amend us.
Amen.

[1 Μόνος εἰσήρχετο εἰς τὸν ναόν· ηὑρίσκετό τε κείμενος ἐπὶ τοῖς γόνασι, καὶ αἰτούμενος ὑπὲρ τοῦ λαοῦ ἄφεσιν· ὡς ἀπεσκληκέναι τὰ γόνατα αὐτοῦ δίκην καμήλου, διὰ τὸ ἀεὶ κάμπτειν ἐπὶ γόνυ προσκυνοῦντα τῷ Θεῷ, καὶ αἰτεῖσθαι ἄφεσιν τῷ λαῷ.—Hegesipp. in Euseb. Ecc. Hist. II. xxiii. ed. Vales. Paris. 1659, p. 63—4.]

TWO SERMONS

ON

REPENTANCE

(1553)

AND ON

THE LORD'S SUPPER

BY

JOHN BRADFORD.

A Sermon

of repentaunce, made by John Bradforde.

(-)

Luke xiii.
Excepte you repent you shall all lykewyse peryshe.

Apoc. ii.
Remembre whence thou arte fallen, and repent thee.

[Title-page of the first edition of 1553.]

¶ Two notable Sermons,

Made by that worthy Martyr of Christ Maister Iohn Bradford, the one of Repentance, and the other of the Lordes supper neuer before imprinted

(☞)

¶ Perused and allowed according to the Queenes Maiesties Iniunction.

(∗)

1574

¶ Imprinted at London by Iohn Awdeley, and John Wyght.

[The Sermon on Repentance, with a Letter from Bradford 'to the Christian Reader', was originally published in 1553. Bradford, in the Preface dated July 12 of that year, says, "I...have now caused this Sermon to be printed[1]:" and he observes in the Preface to the Translation from Melancthon, which certainly was written and probably was printed in July or August 1553, "Unto a sermon of repentance, which even presently I have put forth, I have also put forth this treatise of prayer[2]." And Sampson states[3], that Bradford "in his life time" "did both preach and publish" that on Repentance.

The Two Sermons were published together in one volume in 1574, with a Preface by Sampson describing the character and life of Bradford. More than one impression of this book, closely alike in type, signatures, and catchwords, were printed in that year. That which the editor conceives to be probably the earliest of these (from a very few errata corrected in another impression of 1574) may be known by not having side-notes or references on signatures B i recto, B iii recto, B v recto, C i reverse, among others. A copy is in the collection of the late George Stokes, Esq., of Cheltenham.

The Sermon on Repentance, in the present reprint, follows the text of an imperfect copy of the very rare edition of 1553[4], in the possession of the editor, formerly the property of the late Archdeacon Pott, the last two pages being taken from an impression of 1574 also belonging to the editor, free from the errata referred to above. The text of 1553 has been closely compared with that of 1574, and occasionally with the editions of 1581, 1599, 1617, 1619, and 1652.

The Sermon on the Lord's Supper was first published[5] in 1574. The present reprint follows the text (unless where otherwise noted) of a MS. in the Library of Emmanuel College, Cambridge, which supplies twelve lines now printed, at p. 90, for the first time. That MS. has been collated throughout with the edition of 1574 used for the Sermon on Repentance, and has been sometimes compared with 1581, 1599, and 1617; and the chief respects in which the MS. differs from 1574 have been noted.

There is reason to believe that the Sermon on the Lord's Supper was revised by Bishop Ridley: see p. 82, note 1.]

[1 p. 42.]   [2 p. 20.]   [3 p. 29.]
[4 A copy, imperfect, was formerly in the possession of Herbert (*Typogr. Antiq.*, III. 1572): and there was a copy also not perfect (possibly that which Herbert once had) in the library of the Duke of Roxburghe, 1812, noted (in Supplem. to Catal. 597), "Bradforde's Sermon on Repentance, imp. 1553."]
[5 Vide black letter title (1574), p. 27, and statement of Sampson, p. 29.]

TO THE CHRISTIAN READER,

THO. SAMPSON[1] WISHETH THE FELICITY OF SPEEDY AND FULL CONVERSION TO THE LORD.

GODLY learned men do write and publish books to profit the age in which they do live, and the posterity. This desire was in the author of this Treatise, Master John Bradford, who was the preacher and publisher of this Sermon of Repentance. And now, to the end that we which do live in earth after him, and are the posterity, may take as much or more profit by it than they did to and for whom, in his lifetime, he did both preach and publish it, the same his labour is by new imprinting published again. Nothing is added to this Sermon or altered in it; only to the Sermon of Repentance before printed is added another Sermon of the Lord's Supper which he also made, and was never printed before. And aptly shalt thou see, good reader, these two Sermons joined together. For, in diligent perusing of the last, thou shalt see how necessarily he draweth the doctrine of repentance to them all which do with due preparation receive the holy sacrament of Christ. I do not know which of the ser-

[1 Was ordained Deacon by Abp. Cranmer, assisted by Bp. Ridley, 1549. Rector of Alhallows, Bread St. 1551. Dean of Chichester, 1552. A chief translator of the Bible, 1560, Geneva. Refused the Bishoprick of Norwich, 1560. Dean of Christ Church, Oxford, 1561; but (refusing to wear the appointed habits) was deprived by special order from the Queen, 1565. Prebendary of St Paul's, 1570. Published "these remarkable memorials of this heavenly confessor and martyr" (Strype, Ann. III. i. 102) in 1574. Master of Whittington College, London; Master of the Hospital of William de Wygston, at Leicester. Died, April 9, 1589, aged 72.—Vide Strype, Cranmer, Oxf. 1812, I. 273, 356, 419, Parker, I. 368, Annals, I. ii. 150, 151; Wood, Athenæ Oxon. Bliss, I. 548; Newcourt, Repertorium, 196, 246; Life of Bp. Ridley, by Ridley, 302; Zurich Letters, Parker Soc. see index; Anderson, Annals, Eng. Bible, 1845, II. 321.]

mons I should most praise: I wish that by reading both thou mayest make thy great profit. In both these sermons thou shalt read Bradford preaching repentance with his own pen.

They are counted the most profitable teachers, which have themselves good experience by practice in themselves of that which they do teach to others; such as may safely say, "Brethren, be ye followers of me, and look on them which walk so as ye have us for an example." And surely such a pattern was Master Bradford in his lifetime, of this doctrine of repentance which in both these sermons he teacheth, that I which did know him familiarly must needs give to God this praise for him, that among men I have scarcely known one like unto him. I did know when and partly how[1] it pleased God, by effectual calling, to turn his heart unto the true knowledge and obedience of the most holy gospel of Christ our Saviour; of which God did give him such an heavenly hold and lively feeling, that, as he did then know that many sins were forgiven him, so surely he declared by deeds that he "loved much." For where he had both gifts and calling to have employed himself in civil and worldly affairs profitably; such was his love of Christ and zeal to the promoting of his glorious gospel, that he changed not only the course of his former life, as the woman did (Luke vii.), but even his former study, as Paul did change his former profession and study.

Touching the first, after that God touched his heart with that holy and effectual calling, he sold his chains, rings, broaches, and jewels of gold, which before he used to wear, and did bestow the price of this his former vanity in the necessary relief of Christ's poor members, which he could hear of or find lying sick or pining in poverty. Touching

[1 "Sampson...studied the municipal laws in one of the Temples, where being converted to the Protestant religion, did shortly after, as 'tis said, convert John Bradford the martyr."—Wood, Athenæ Oxon. Bliss, I. 548—9.]

Phil. iii. 17.

Luke vii.

the second, he so declared his great zeal and love to promote the glory of the Lord Jesus, whose goodness and saving health he had tasted, that to do the same more pithily he changed his study; and being in the Inner Temple in London at the study of the common laws, he went to Cambridge to study divinity; where he heard Doctor Martin Bucer diligently, and was right familiar and dear unto him. In this godly course he did by God's blessing so profit, that that blessed martyr, Doctor Ridley, then Bishop of London[2], did as it were invite him and his godly companion, Master Thomas Horton, to become Fellows of Pembroke Hall, in Cambridge: and afterwards the said Doctor Ridley called our Bradford to London, gave him a prebend in Paul's church, lodged him in his own house there, and set him on work in preaching. And besides often preaching in London, and at Paul's cross, and sundry places in the country, and specially in Lancashire; he preached before king Edward the sixth, in the Lent, the last year of his reign, upon the second Psalm: and there in one sermon, shewing the tokens of God's judgment at hand for the contempt of the gospel, as that certain gentlemen upon the Sabbath-day going in a wherry to Paris Garden[3], to the bear-baiting, were drowned; and that a dog was met at Ludgate carrying a piece of a dead child in his mouth; he with a mighty and prophetical spirit said, 'I summon you all, even every mother's child of you, to the judgment of God, for it is at hand:' as it followed shortly after in the death of king Edward. In which

[2 "Dr Nicholas Ridley...was not then Bishop of London, as Bradford's friend mistakes, being Bishop of Rochester from near a twelvemonth before Bradford went to the University [which last took place about midsummer 1548] to the beginning of the year 1550, (Godwin de Præsul. Angl. et Rymeri Fœd. Tom. xv. p. 164, 222) and also Master of Pembroke Hall."—Biogr. Britann. II. 1748, art. Bradford.]

[3 "The famous bear-garden on the Bankside in Southwark, contiguous to the Globe theatre. So called from *Robert de Paris*, who had a house and garden there in the reign of Richard II." Nares, Glossary. Vide Brand, Pop. Antiq. Ellis, II. 285.]

state and labour of preaching he continued till the cruelty of the papists cut him off, so as thou mayest read in the history of his life and death compiled by that faithful servant of the Lord Jesus, Master John Fox[1].

Indeed he had many pullbacks, but God still helped forward his chosen servant in that trade of life to which he had called him; in which he ran forward so happily that he did outrun me and other his companions. For it pleased God with great speed to make him ready and ripe to martyrdom, in which through Christ he hath now gained the crown of life. But in all stops and stays he was much helped forward by a continual meditation and practice of repentance and faith in Christ, in which he was kept by God's grace notably exercised all the days of his life. Even in this mean time he heard a sermon which that notable preacher Master Latimer made before king Edward the sixth, in which he did earnestly speak of restitution to be made of things falsely gotten: which did so strike Bradford to the heart for one dash with a pen, which he had made without the knowledge of his master[2] (as full often I have heard him confess with plenty of tears), being clerk to the treasurer of the king's camp beyond the seas[3], and was to the deceiving of the king, that he could never be quiet till, by the advice of the

[1 Acts, &c. 1583, p. 1603—1623, or ed. 1847, VII. 143—194.]

[2 Sir John Harrington of Exton in Rutlandshire. It is only right to place beside the above the words of Bradford in his last Examination before Bp. Gardiner: "My lord, I set my foot to his foot, whosoever he be, that can come forth and justly vouch to my face that ever I deceived my master. And as you are chief justicer by office, in England, I desire justice upon them that so slander me, because they cannot prove it."—Exam. of Bradford, London, Griffith, 1561, signature a vi. Vide also Foxe, Acts, &c. ed. 1583, p. 1610, or ed. 1847, VII. 162. The subject will receive further notice in this collection of the Writings of Bradford.]

[3 At Boulogne. Vide Foxe, Acts, &c. ed. 1583, p. 1603, or ed. 1847, VII. 143: and see A. D. 1544, et seq., in Grafton, Chron. 1569, p. 1273; in Holinshed 1587, II. 964; in Stow ed. 1615, p. 587; in Speed, Hist. 1623, p. 1050; and in Carte 1752, III. 179: and see Playfair, Baronetage, I. 72.]

same Master Latimer a restitution was made. Which thing to bring to pass, he did willingly forbear and forego all the private and certain patrimony which he had in earth[4]. Let all bribers and polling[5] officers, which get to themselves great revenues in earth by such slippery shifts, follow this example, lest, in taking a contrary course, they take a contrary way, and never come where Bradford now is.

But besides this, our Bradford had his daily exercises and practices of repentance. His manner was, to make to himself a catalogue of all the grossest and most enorme sins, which in his life of ignorance he had committed; and to lay the same before his eyes when he went to private prayer, that by the sight and remembrance of them he might be stirred up to offer to God the sacrifice of a contrite heart, seek assurance of salvation in Christ by faith, thank God for his calling from the ways of wickedness, and pray for increase of grace to be conducted in holy life acceptable and pleasing to God. Such a continual exercise of conscience he had in private prayer, that he did not count himself to have prayed to his contentation, unless in it he had felt inwardly some smiting of heart for sin, and some healing of that wound by faith, feeling the saving health of Christ, with some change of mind into the detestation of sin, and love of obeying the good will of God. Which things do require that inward entering into the secret parlour of our hearts of Matt. vi. which Christ speaketh; and is that smiting of the breast which is noted in the publican; and is the same to the which the Psalmist exhorteth those men loose in sin: (Psalm iv. 4.) "Tremble ye, and sin not; speak in yourselves;" that is, enter into an account with yourselves: "when you are on your couches;" that is, when ye are solitary and alone: "and

[4 The letter of Bradford to Traves, of May 12, 1548, and those which begin, severally, "*Gratia, misericordia*. If mine heart," and "The selfsame mercy," seem to lead to a different conclusion.—Foxe, Acts, &c. 1583, p. 1661—4, or ed. 1847, VII. 277—285.]

[5 i. e. plundering.]

[BRADFORD.]

3

be quiet or silent;" that is, when ye have thus secretly and deeply considered of your case and dealing, ye shall cease to think, speak, and do wickedly. Without such an inward exercise of prayer our Bradford did not pray to his full contentation, as appeared by this: he used in the morning to go to the common prayer in the college where he was, and after that he used to make some prayer with his pupils in his chamber; but not content with this, he then repaired to his own secret prayer and exercise in prayer by himself, as one that had not yet prayed to his own mind: for he was wont to say to his familiars, 'I have prayed with my pupils, but I have not yet prayed with myself.'

Let those secure men mark this well, which pray without touch of breast, as the Pharisee did; and so that they have said an ordinary prayer, or heard a common course of prayer, they think they have prayed well, and, as the term is, they have served God well; though they never feel sting for sin, taste of groaning, or broken heart, nor of the sweet saving health of Christ, thereby to be moved to offer the sacrifice of thanksgiving, nor change or renewing of mind: but as they came secure in sin and senseless, so they do depart without any change or affecting of the heart; which is even the cradle in which Satan rocketh the sins of this age asleep, who think they do serve God in these cursory prayers made only of custom, when their heart is as far from God as was the heart of the Pharisee. Let us learn by Bradford's example to pray better, that is, with the heart and not with the lips alone; *Quia Deus non vocis, sed cordis auditor est*[1], as Cyprian saith: that is, "Because God is the hearer of the heart and not of the voice:" that is to say, not of the voice alone without the heart, for that is but lip-labour. This conscience of sin and exercise in prayer had Bradford, clean contrary to that cursed custom of those graceless men, which do joy to make large and long accounts of their lewdness,

[1 Cyprian. de Orat. Domin. Op. Oxon. (1688) 140.]

and glory therein, so feeding their delights with their lives past, as a dog returneth to smell to his cast gorge, and the horse to his dung: such as the prophet Esay (iii. 9) saith, "They declare their sins as Sodom, they hide them not: woe be to their souls!" It goeth with them as in the days of Jeremiah it went with those, "Thou haddest a whore's forehead; thou wouldest not be ashamed." God give these men better grace; else let them be assured they shall find woe, woe to their very souls. Jer. iii. 3.

Another of his exercises was this: he used to make unto himself an ephemeris or a journal, in which he used to write all such notable things as either he did see or hear each day that passed. But whatsoever he did hear or see, he did so pen it that a man might see in that book the signs of his smitten heart. For if he did see or hear any good in any man, by that sight he found and noted the want thereof in himself, and added a short prayer, craving mercy and grace to amend. If he did hear or see any plague or misery, he noted it as a thing procured by his own sins, and still added, *Domine, miserere mei,* "Lord, have mercy upon me." He used in the same book to note such evil thoughts as did rise in him; as of envying the good of other men, thoughts of unthankfulness, of not considering God in his works, of hardness and unsensibleness of heart when he did see other moved and affected. And thus he made to himself and of himself a book of daily practices of repentance.

Besides this, they which were familiar with him might see how he, being in their company, used to fall often into a sudden and deep meditation, in which he would sit with fixed countenance and spirit moved, yet speaking nothing a good space. And sometimes in this silent sitting[2] plenty of

[[2] "In the midst of dinner he used often to muse with himself, having his hat over his eyes, from whence came commonly plenty of tears dropping on his trencher."—Foxe, Acts &c. ed. 1583, p. 1604, or ed. 1847, VII. 145.]

tears should trickle down his cheeks. Sometime he would sit in it and come out of it with a smiling countenance. Oftentimes have I sitten at dinner and supper with him in the house of that godly harbourer of many preachers and servants of the Lord Jesus, I mean Master Elsyng[1], when, either by occasion of talk had, or of some view of God's benefits present, or some inward cogitation and thought of his own, he hath fallen into these deep cogitations: and he would tell me in the end such discourses of them that I did perceive that sometimes his tears trickled out of his eyes, as well for joy as for sorrow. Neither was he only such a practiser of repentance in himself, but a continual provoker of others thereunto, not only in public preaching, but also in private conference and company. For in all companies where he did come, he would freely reprove any sin and misbehaviour which appeared in any person, especially swearers, filthy talkers, and popish praters. Such never departed out of his company unreproved. And this he did with such a divine grace and christian majesty, that ever he stopped the mouths of the gainsayers. For he spake with power, and yet so sweetly, that they might see their evil to be evil and hurtful unto them, and understand that it was good indeed to the which he laboured to draw them in God.

To be short: as his life was, such was his death. His life was a practice and example, a provocation to repentance: at his death (as the foresaid history witnesseth), when he was burned in Smithfield, and the flames of fire did fly about his ears, his last speech publicly noted and heard was this: REPENT, ENGLAND[2]! Thus was our Bradford a

[[1] A Letter from Bradford, inscribed " To my dear friends and brethren, R. and E. with their wives and families," i.e. "to two faithful friends of his, one Royden and Elsing" (*Foxe*), is given in Bp. Coverdale, Letters of the Martyrs (1564) 338, and in Foxe, Acts &c. 1583, p. 1642, or ed. 1847, VII. 235.]

[[2] Foxe, Acts &c. 1583, p. 1623, or ed. 1847, VII. 194.]

preacher and an example of that repentance which he did preach. Jonas preached to Ninive repentance; and all Ninive, the king, princes, people, old and young repented. To England Bradford did preach, and yet doth preach repentance. And surely England hath now much more cause to repent than it had when Bradford lived and preached repentance; for all states and sorts of persons in England are now more corrupt than they were then.

Let therefore now Bradford's Sermon, his life, his death, move thee, O England, to repent, at thy peril. I wish and warn that as in Ninive, so in England all from the highest to the lowest do unfeignedly repent; they which are of the court, they which are of the church, they which are of the city, they which are of the country, princes, prelates, and people. Let all and every one repent, and depart from that evil which he hath in hand, and turn wholly to the Lord. And I do humbly beseech thy Majesty, O glorious Lord Jesus, which didst come to bless Israel, turning every one of them from their sins, to work now by thy Spirit in our hearts the same sound repentance which thy holiness did preach to men, when thou saidest, "Repent, for the kingdom of God is at hand." This work in us, O gracious God our Saviour. Amen.

And now, reader, I leave thee to the reading and practising of that repentance which Bradford here teacheth.

TO THE CHRISTIAN READER,

JOHN BRADFORD WISHETH THE TRUE KNOWLEDGE AND PEACE OF JESUS CHRIST, OUR ALONE AND OMNISUFFICIENT SAVIOUR.

GREAT and heavy is God's anger against us, as the most grievous plague of the death of our late king (a prince of all that ever was sithen[1] Christ's ascension into heaven, in any region, peerless) now fallen upon us doth prognosticate. For, when God's judgment hath begun with his child thus, our dear darling, let other men think as they can, I surely cannot be persuaded otherwise but that a grievous and bitter cup of God's vengeance is ready to be poured out for us Englishmen to drink of. The whelp God hath beaten, to fray the bandog. "Judgment is begun at God's house." In God's mercy to himwards he is taken away, that his eyes should not see the miseries we shall feel. He was too good to tarry with us, so wicked, so froward, so perverse, so obstinate, so malicious, so hypocritical, so covetous, unclean, untrue, proud, carnal, &c., a generation. I will not go about to paint us out in our colours. All the world which never saw England by hearsay seeth England. God by his plagues and vengeance, I fear me, will paint us out and point us out. We have so mocked with him and his gospel, that we shall feel it is no bourding[2] with him.

Of long time we have covered our covetousness and carnality under the cloak of his gospel, so that all men shall see us to our shame. When he shall take his gospel away, and give it to a people that will bring forth the fruits of it, then shall we appear as we be. To let his gospel tarry with us he cannot: for we despise it, contemn it, are glutted with

1 Pet. iv.

Heb. xi.

[1 'Sith' occurs in the authorised version of Ezek. xxxv. 6. Vide, in Tooke, I. 267, or Richardson, Dict. v. sin, the derivation of 'since.']

[2 Bourding: jesting.]

it. We disdain his manna: It is but a vile meat, think we.
We would be again in Egypt, and sit by the greasy fleshpots,
to eat again our garlic, onions, and leeks. Sithen God's
gospel came amongst us, we say now, we had never plenty:
therefore again let us go and "worship the queen of heaven." Jer. xliv.
"Children begin to gather sticks, the fathers kindle the fire, Jer. vii.
and the women make the cakes, to offer to the queen of
heaven, and to provoke the Lord to anger." The earth cannot abide now the words and sermons of Amos; the cause of Amos vii.
all rebellion is Amos and his preaching. It is Paul and his Acts xvii.
fellows that make all out of order. *Summa*, the gospel is
now πάντων περίψημα and κάθαρμα τοῦ κόσμου· the outcast [1 Cor. iv. 13.]
and curse of the realm; and so are the preachers: therefore
out of the doors with them. So that, I say, God cannot let
his gospel tarry with us, but must needs take it away, to do
us some pleasure therein. For so shall we think for a time,
as the Sodomitanes thought when Lot departed from them; Gen. xix.
as the old world thought when Noe crept into his ark; as Gen. vii.
the Jerosolomitanes thought when the apostles went thence
to Peltis³. Then were they merry, then was all pastime:
when Moses was absent, then went they "to eating and drink- Exod. xxxi.
ing, and rose again to play:" then was all peace, all was
well, nothing amiss. But, alas! suddenly came the flood and
drowned them, the fire and burnt them up, Titus and besieged them⁴; God's wrath waxed hot against them. Then
was welaway⁵, mourning, and woe: then was crying out,
wringing of hands, renting of clothes, sobbing and sighing
for the miseries fallen out of the which they could not
escape. But, O you mourners and cryers out, ye renters of
clothes, why mourn you? what is the cause of your misery?
The gospel is gone, God's word is little preached, you were⁶
not disquieted with it: Noe troubleth you not, Lot is departed, the apostles are gone. What now is the cause of
these your miseries? Will you at the length confess it is

[³ Vide Euseb. Eccl. Hist. III. v. ed. Vales. Paris. 1659, p. 75: and also annot. Vales.]

[⁴ The last ten words are omitted in all editions after 1553.]

[⁵ i. e. 'woe on woe,' or 'alas, alas,' from the Anglo-Saxon *welawa*, or *walawa*. Vide Johnson, Nares, Richardson, v. 'welaway.']

[⁶ So 1553, 1574, 1581: 'are,' 1599.]

your sins? Nay, now it is too late. God called upon you, and you would not hear him; therefore yell and cry out now, for he will not hear you. You bowed your ears from hearing of God's law; therefore your prayer is execrable.

But, to come again to us Englishmen. I fear me, I say, for our unthankfulness' sake, for our impiety and wickedness, as God hath taken away our king, so will he take away his gospel. Yea, so we would have it: then should all be well, think many. Well, if he take that away, for a time perchance we shall be quiet, but at length we shall feel the want to our woe: at length he will have at us, as at Sodom, at Jerusalem, and other places. And now he beginneth to brew such a brewing, wherein one of us is like to destroy another[1], and so make an open gap for foreign enemies to devour us and destroy us. The father is against the son, the brother against the brother: and, Lord, with what conscience!

O be thou merciful unto us, and in thine anger remember thy mercy; suffer thyself to be entreated; be reconciled unto us; nay, reconcile us unto thee. O thou God of justice, judge justly. O thou Son of God, which camest to destroy the works of Satan, destroy his furours[2] now smoking, and almost set on fire in this realm. We have sinned; we have sinned: and therefore thou art angry. O be not angry for ever. Give us peace, peace, peace in the Lord. Set us to war[3] against sin, against Satan, against our carnal desires; and give us the victory this way.

1 John iii.

This victory we obtain by faith. This faith is not without repentance, as her gentleman usher[4] before her: before her, I say, in discerning true faith from false faith, lip-faith, Englishmen's faith: for else it springs out of true faith.

[1 Lady Jane Grey having been proclaimed July 10, 1553, four days after the death of Edward VI.—This preface is dated July 12: and Queen Mary was proclaimed July 19.—Strype, Mem. Oxf. III. i. 4, 21.]

[2 Vide Richardson, v. fury.]

[3 So 1553, 1574: 'work,' 1581, 1599, 1617.]

[4 "Faith is a noble duchess: she hath ever her gentleman usher going before her, the confessing of sins: she hath a train after her, the fruits of good works, the walking in the commandments of God."—Bp Latimer, 7th Serm. before Edw. VI. ed. 1578. sig. L viii: ed. Parker Soc. i. 237.]

This usher then, of repentance, if we truly possessed, we should be certain of true faith, and so assured of the victory over death, hell, and Satan. His works then, which he hath stirred up, would quail. God would restore us politic peace. Right should be right, and have right. God's gospel should tarry with us: religion should be cherished, superstition suppressed; and so we yet something happy, notwithstanding the great loss of our most gracious liege sovereign lord. All these would come to pass, you see, if the gentleman usher I spake of (I mean Repentance) were at inn with us: as, if he be absent, we may be certain that lady Faith is absent. Wherefore we cannot but be vanquished of the world, the flesh, and the devil: and so will Satan's works prosper, though not in all things to blear our eyes, yet in that thing which he most of all desireth. Therefore to repentance for ourselves privately, and for the realm and church publicly, every one should labour to stir up both ourselves and others.

This to the end that for my part I might help, I have presently put forth a Sermon on Repentance, which hath lien by me half a year at the least, for the most part of it. For the last summer, as I was abroad preaching in the country, my chance was to make a Sermon of Repentance, the which was earnestly of divers desired of me, that I should give it them written, or else put it forth in print. The which thing to grant as I could not, (for I had not written it,) so I told them that had so earnestly desired it. But when no way would serve but I must promise them to write it as I could, I consented to their request that they should have it at my leisure. This leisure I prolonged so long, that as I ween I offended them, so did I please myself as one more glad to read other men's writings, than in such sort to publish my writings for other men to read. Not that I would others not to profit by me; but that I, knowing how short my *supellex*[5] and store[6] is, would be loth for the enemies to have just occasion of evil speaking and wresting that which simply is spoken. But when I considered this present time to occasion men now to look upon all things in such sort

[5 i. e. furniture.]
[6 'slender my store' 1574 and after editions.]

as might move them to godliness, rather than to any curious questioning, I for the satisfying of my promise, and profiting of the simple, ignorant, and rude, have now caused this Sermon to be printed[1]. The which
I beseech God for his Christ's sake to
use as a mean whereby of his mercy
it may please him to work in
me and many others true
hearty repentance for
our sins, to the
glory of his
name.

Thus fare thou well in the Lord. The 12th of July, Anno M.D.LIII.

[1 Vide p. 28 above.]

A SERMON OF REPENTANCE

MADE BY JOHN BRADFORD.

THE life we have at this present is the gift of God, "in whom we live, move, and are:" and therefore is he called Jehovah[1]. For the which life as we should be thankful, so we may not in any wise use it after our own fantasy, but to the end for the which it is given and lent us; that is, to the setting forth of God's praise and glory, by repentance, conversion, and obedience to his good will and holy laws: whereunto his long-suffering doth, as it were, even draw us, if our hearts by impenitency were not hardened. And therefore our life in the scripture is called a "walking:" for that as the body daily draweth more and more near his end, that is the earth, even so our soul draweth daily more and more near the death, that is salvation or damnation, heaven or hell. *Acts xvii. Exod.iii.[vi.]*

Of which thing in that we are most careless, and very fools, (for we, alas! are the same to-day we were yesterday, and not better or nearer to God, but rather nearer to hell, Satan, and perdition, being covetous, idle, carnal, secure, negligent, proud, &c.;) I think my labour cannot be better bestowed than with the Baptist, Christ Jesus, and his apostles, to harp on this string, which of all other is most necessary, and that in these days most specially. What string is that? saith one. Forsooth, brother, the string of Repentance, the which Christ our Saviour did use first in his ministry; and as his minister at this present I will use unto you all:

"Repent; for the kingdom of heaven is at hand." Matt. iii.

This sentence thus pronounced and preached by our Saviour Jesus Christ, as it doth command us to repent, so to the doing of the same it sheweth us a sufficient cause to stir

[1 Nomine enim יְהֹוָה a verbo הָיָה *fuit*, ducto, significari censebant Deum *æternum, immutabilem*, qui nunquam non idem futurus sit.—Gesen. Lex.]

us up thereunto : namely, for that "the kingdom of heaven," which is a kingdom of all joy, peace, riches, power, and pleasure, "is at hand" to all such as do so, that is as do repent. So that the meaning hereof is as though our Saviour might thus speak presently : "Sirs, for that I see you all walking the wrong way, even to Satan and unto hell-fire, by following the kingdom of Satan which now is coloured under the pilled[1] pleasures of this life and foolishness of the flesh, most subtilely, to your utter undoing and destruction, behold and mark well what I say unto you, 'The kingdom of heaven,' that is another manner of joy and felicity, honour and riches, power and pleasure, than you now perceive or enjoy, is even 'at hand,' and at your backs; as, if you will turn again, that is 'repent you,' you shall most truly and pleasantly feel, see and inherit. Turn again therefore, I say, that is, 'Repent:' for this joy I speak of, even 'the kingdom of heaven, is at hand.'"

Here we may note, first, the corruption of our nature, in that to this commandment, "Repent you," he addeth a cause, "for the kingdom of heaven is at hand." For, by reason of the corruption and sturdiness of our nature, God unto all his commandments commonly either addeth some promise to provoke us to obedience, or else some such sufficient cause as cannot but tickle us up to hearty labouring for the doing of the same : as here to the commandment of doing penance he addeth this ætiology or cause, saying, "For the kingdom of heaven is at hand."

Again, in that he joineth to the commandment the cause, saying, "For the kingdom of heaven is at hand," we may learn that of "the kingdom of heaven" none to whom the ministry of preaching doth appertain can be partaker but such as repent and do penance. Therefore, dearly beloved, if you regard "the kingdom of heaven," in that you cannot enter therein except you repent, I beseech you all of every estate, as you would your own weal, to repent and do penance. The which thing that you may do, I will do my best now to help you, by God's grace.

[1] i. e. 'bare, as if picked or stripped,' Nares, Gloss. So the word 'peeled' in Isai. xviii. 2, 7, 'a nation scattered and peeled:' *expilatam*, Jun. et Trem.—1574 and after editions read 'vain.']

But first, because we cannot well tell what repentance is through ignorance and for lack of knowledge, and false teaching, I will, to begin withal, shew you what repentance is. Repentance or penance is no English word, but we borrow it of the Latinists, to whom penance is a forthinking[2] in English; in Greek a being wise afterwards; in Hebrew a conversion or turning[3]. The which conversion or turning, in that it cannot be true and hearty, unto God especially, without some good hope or trust of pardon for that which is already done and past, I may well in this sort define it, namely, That penance is a sorrowing or forthinking[2] of our sins past, an earnest purpose to amend or turning to God, with a trust of pardon.

This definition may be divided into three parts: that penance or repentance should contain[4], First, a sorrowing for our sins: Secondly, a trust of pardon, which otherwise may be called a persuasion of God's mercy by the merits of Christ for the forgiveness of our sins: and Thirdly, a purpose to amend, or conversion to a new life. The which third or last part cannot be called properly a part; for it is but an effect of penance, as towards the end you shall see by God's grace. But lest such as seek for occasion to speak evil should have any occasion, though they tarry not out the end of this sermon, I therefore divide penance into the three foresaid parts; Of sorrowing for our sins: Of good hope or trust of pardon; and, Of a new life.

Thus you now see what penance is, a sorrowing for sin, a purpose to amend, with a good hope or trust of pardon.

[I.] This penance not only differeth from that which men commonly have taken to be penance, in saying and doing our enjoined Lady Psalters[5], seven Psalms[6], fastings,

---

[2 i. e. regret, repentance: see Nares, v. 'for' and 'forthink.']

[3 Pœnitentia: μετάνοια שׁוּבָה (Is. xxx. 15), or נחֵם (Hos. xiii. 14). Vide Gesen. Lex.]

[4 The last six words only occur in 1553.]

[5 See note A.]

[6 Ps. vi. xxxii. xxxviii. li. cii. cxxx. cxliii: Horæ beat. V. Mar. ad leg. Sarisb. Eccl. rit. Paris. 1519, fol. cx. "These Psalms were very

pilgrimages, almose[1] deeds, and such like things; but also from that which the more learned have declared to consist of three parts, namely contrition, confession, and satisfaction[2].

Contrition they call a just and a full sorrow for their sin. For this word, just and full, is one of the differences between contrition and attrition[3].

Confession they call a numbering of all their sins in the ear of their ghostly father. For as, say they, a judge cannot absolve without knowledge of the cause or matter, so cannot the priest or ghostly father absolve from other sins than those which he doth hear[4].

Satisfaction they call amends-making unto God for their sins[5] by their 'undue works', *opera indebita*[6], works more than they need to do, as they term them.

This is their penance which they preach, write, and allow. But how true this gear is, how it agreeth with God's word, how it is to be allowed, taught, preached, and written, let us a little consider.

If a man repent not until he have a just and full sorrowing for his sins, dearly beloved, when shall he repent? For inasmuch as hell-fire and the punishment of the devils is a

---

anciently selected, and known by name as the *seven Psalms*, or *Penitential*."—Monum. Rit., Maskell, 1846, II. 78.]

[1 i. e. alms.]

[2 Sunt... quasi materia hujus sacramenti, ipsius pœnitentis actus, nempe Contritio, Confessio, et Satisfactio: qui, quatenus in pœnitente ad integritatem sacramenti, ad plenamque et perfectam peccatorum remissionem ex Dei institutione, requiruntur, hac ratione partes Pœnitentiæ dicuntur.—Concil. Trident. Sess. IV., Jul. Tert. ann. 1551, cap. III. Antv. 1564, fol. 66. Vide Thom. Aquin. Summ. Theol. Pars III. Quæst. xc. Art. 2, Colon. 1622, p. 207.

The subject is elaborately treated upon by Hooker, Ecc. Pol. VI.: and by Willet, Synopsis Papismi, 1600, contr. XIV. See also Bp. Taylor, Dissuasive from Popery, I. II. and II. I. 11; and Bp. Burnet on Art. XXV., Ch. of Eng.]

[3 Attritio significat in spiritualibus quandam displicentiam de peccatis commissis, sed non perfectam: Contritio autem perfectam.— Thom. Aquin. Summ. Theol. Partis III. Suppl. theol. Lovan. Quæst. I. Art. ii. Colon. 1622, p. 3.—Concil. Trid. ibid. cap. IV. fol. 66.]

[4 See note B.]

just punishment for sin; inasmuch as in all sin there is a contempt of God which is all goodness, and therefore there is a desert of all illness; alas, who can bear or feel this just sorrow, this full sorrow for our sins, this their contrition, which they so do discern from their attrition? Shall not man by this doctrine rather despair than come by repentance?

If a man repent not until he have made confession of all his sins in the ear of his ghostly father; if a man cannot have absolution of his sins, until his sins be told by tale and number in the priest's ear; in that, as David saith, none can understand, much less then utter all his sins, *Delicta quis intelligit?* "Who can understand his sins?" in that David of himself complaineth elsewhere how that his "sins are overflowed his head, and as a heavy burden do depress him;" alas, shall not a man by this doctrine be utterly driven from repentance? Though they have gone about something to make plasters for their sores of confession or attrition to assuage this gear, bidding a man to hope well of his contrition though it be not so full as is required, and of his confession though he have not numbered all his sins, if so be that he do so much as in him lieth: dearly beloved, in that there is none but that herein he is guilty, (for who doth as much as he may?) trow ye that this plaster is not like salt for sore eyes? Yes, undoubtedly, when they have all done they can for the appeasing of consciences in these points, this is the sum, that we yet should hope well, but yet so hope that we must stand in a mammering[5] and doubting whether our sins be forgiven. For to believe *remissionem peccatorum*, that is, to be certain of 'forgiveness of sins,' as our creed teacheth us, they count it a presumption. O abomination! and that not only hereat, but in all their penance as they paint it.

As concerning satisfaction by their *opera indebita*, 'undue works,' that is, by such works as they need not to do but of their own voluntariness and wilfulness, (wilfulness indeed!) who seeth not monstrous abomination, blasphemy, and even open fighting against God? For if satisfaction can be done by man, then Christ died in vain for him that so satisfieth: and so reigneth he in vain; so is he a bishop and a priest

Psal. xix.
Psal. xxxviii.

[5 Mammering: hesitation.]

in vain. God's law requireth love to God with all our heart, soul, power, might, and strength; so that there is nothing can be done to God-ward which is not contained in this commandment; nothing can be done over and above this. Again Christ requireth that to man-ward "we should love one another as he loved us:" and trow we that we can do any good thing to our neighbour-ward which is not herein comprised?

Yea, let them tell me when they do any thing so in the love of God and their neighbour but that they had need to cry, *Dimitte nobis debita nostra*, "Forgive us our sins:" so far are we off from satisfying. Doth not Christ say, "When you have done all things that I have commanded you, say that you be but unprofitable servants?" "Put nothing to my word," saith God. 'Yes, works of supererogation'[1] (superabomination!) say they. "Whatsoever things are true," saith the apostle St Paul, "whatsoever things are honest, whatsoever things are pure, whatsoever things are convenient, whatsoever things are of honest report, if there be any virtue, or if there be any praise, have you them in your mind, and do them, and the God of peace shall be with you." I ween this well looked on will pull us from popish satisfactory works which do deface Christ's treasures and satisfaction.

In heaven and in earth was there none found that could satisfy God's anger for our sins, or get heaven for man, but only the Son of God, Jesus Christ, the Lion of the tribe of Juda, who by his blood hath wrought the work of satisfaction, and alonely is "worthy all honour, glory, and praise," for he hath "opened the book with the seven seals."

Dearly beloved, therefore abhor this abomination, even to think that there is any other satisfaction to God-ward for sin

[1 Ratio quare [indulgentiæ] valere possint, est unitas corporis mystici, in qua multi in operibus pœnitentiæ supererogaverunt ad mensuram debitorum suorum, et multas etiam tribulationes injustas sustinuerunt patienter, per quas multitudo pœnarum poterat expiari, si eis deberetur: quorum meritorum tanta est copia, quod omnem pœnam debitam nunc viventibus excedunt, et præcipue propter meritum Christi.—Thom. Aquin. Summ. ibid. Quæst. xxv. Art. 1. p. 32. Vide Hooker, Ecc. Pol. VI. v. 9, ed. Keble; Willet, Synopsis, 662, 917, 1089; Field, Of the Church, III. app. 13 (1635) 331; Bennet, Conf. Popery, 1701, II. 19; Bp. Burnet on Art. XIV., Ch. of Eng.]

than Christ's blood only. Blasphemy it is, and that horrible, to think otherwise. "The blood of Christ purifieth," saith St John, "from all sin." And therefore he is called "the Lamb slain from the beginning of the world;" because there was never sin forgiven of God, nor shall be, from the beginning unto the end of the world, but only through Christ's death: prate the pope and his prelates as please them with their pardons[2], purgatory[2], purgations[3], placebos[4], trentals[5], diriges[4], works of supererogation, superabomination, &c. *Rev. xiii.*

"I am he," saith the Lord, "which put away thine offences, and that for mine own sake, and will no more remember thine iniquities. Put me in remembrance, for we will reason together; and tell me what thou hast for thee to make thee righteous. Thy first father offended sore," &c. And thus writeth St John: "If any man sin, we have an advocate," saith he, "with the Father, even Jesus Christ the righteous, and he is the propitiation (or satisfaction) for our sins:" as in the fourth chapter he saith that "God hath sent his Son to be a propitiation" or mean for the taking away of[6] our sins, according to that which Paul writeth, where he calleth Christ "a merciful and faithful priest to purge the people's sins." So that blind buzzards and perverse papists they be, which yet will prate our merits or works to satisfy for our sins, in part or in whole, before baptism or after. For, to omit the testimonies I brought out of John and Paul, which the blind cannot but see, I pray you remember the text out *Isai. xliii.* *1 John ii.* *Heb. ii.*

[2 See note C.]

[3 "Our Saviour Christ by his own blood purged both body and soul. But the bishop of Rome, to make himself also a mediator with Christ, hath taken upon him to purify the soul and conscience with holy water, holy salt, and other his holy creatures of his own devising, to the intolerable injury of Christ's blood which only hath the effect."—Abp. Cranmer, Answ. to the Devon. rebels, Remains, Oxf. II. 226; or Parker Soc. II. 177. Vide Becon, "Reliques of Rome," 1563, fol. 158, ch. "Of holy water."]

[4 See note D.]

[5 'Trental' or 'month's mind': an office of thirty masses said on thirty different days for a person deceased. Vide Du Cange, Gloss., v. *tricenarium*; Becon, "Reliques of Rome," 1563, fol. 207, ch. "Of trentals;" Brand, Pop. Antiq. ed. Ellis, 1813, II. 213, et seq.]

[6 'mean for the taking away of' 1553: 'satisfaction for' 1574, and after editions.]

[BRADFORD.]

of Esay which even now I rehearsed, being spoken to such as were then the people of God and had been a long time, but yet were fallen into grievous sins after their adoption into the number of God's children. "It is for mine own sake," saith God, "that I put away thy sins." Where is your parting of the stake now? If it be for God's own sake, if Christ be the propitiation, then recant, except you will become idolaters, making your works God and Christ. Say as David teacheth, "Not to us, Lord, not to us, but to thy name be the glory."

And it is to be noted that God doth cast in their teeth even the sin of their first father, lest they should think that yet perchance for the righteousness and goodness of their good fathers their sins might be the sooner pardoned, and so God accept their works.

If they had made[1] 'satisfaction' for that which is done to the congregation publicly by some notable punishment, as in the primitive church was used to open offenders[2], sparkles whereof and some traces yet remain, when such as have sinned in adultery go about the church with a taper in their shirts[3]; or if they had made 'satisfaction' for restitution to man-ward of such goods as wrongfully is gotten, the which true penance cannot be without; or if by satisfaction they had meant a new life to make amends to the congregation thereby, as by their evil life they did offend the congregation, in which sense the Apostle seemeth to take that which he writeth, 2 Cor. vii., where the old interpreter calleth ἀπολογίαν 'satisfaction[4],' which rather

[1 'taken' 1574 and after editions.]

[2 Vide Bingham, Orig. Eccl. xviii. ii. 1726, II. 210; Nicholls, Comm. (1712), and Wheatley, Illustr., on Ash-Wednesday, and on the Commination Service.]

[3 "In the case of incest, or incontinency, the sinner is usually enjoined to do a public penance in the cathedral or parish-church, or public market, bare-legged and bare-headed, in a white sheet, and to make an open confession of his crime in a prescribed form of words." But the penance "may be totally altered by a commutation."—Burn, Eccles. Law, v. *Penance*. Vide Remains of Abp. Grindal, Parker Soc. 455; Bp. Gibson, Codex, Oxf. 1761, tit. XLVI. c. II.; Orig. Liturg., Palmer, 1846, ch. xxiii. on "public and private penitence."]

[4 *Sed defensionem*. Quidam habent, sed excusationem: in Græco autem ἀπολογίαν, id est satisfactionem præcepti, scilicet dicit.—Hieron. Op. V. col. 1025, ed. Bened. Par. 1693—1706, comm. incerti auctoris in epist. II. ad Cor. cap. vii.]

signifieth a 'defence' or 'answering again:' If, I say, they had taken 'satisfaction' any of these ways, then they had done well, so that the satisfaction to God had been left alonely to Christ.

Again, if they had made 'confession,' either for that which is to God privately, either for that which is to the congregation publicly, either for that which is a free consultation with some one learned in God's book and appointed thereunto, as first it was used, and I wish were now used amongst us[5], either for that which is a reconciliation of one[6] to another, it had been something. Yea, if they had made it for faith, because it is a true demonstration of faith, as in Paul we may see, to the Romans the tenth and to the Hebrews[7], when he calleth Christ the captain " of our confession," [Heb. iii.] that is of our faith; and so confessors were called in the primitive church, such as manfully did witness their faith with the peril of their lives: if, I say, they had taken it thus, then had they done right well.

And so 'contrition:' if they had left out their subtle distinction between it and 'attrition' by this word just or full, making it a hearty sorrow for their sins, then we would never have cried out against them therefor. For we say, penance hath three parts[8]: contrition, if you understand it for a hearty sorrowing for sin; confession, if you understand it for faith of free pardon in God's mercy by Jesus Christ; and satisfaction, if you understand it not to God-wards (for that only to Christ must be left alone), but to man-ward in restitution of goods wrongfully or fraudulently gotten, of name hindered by our slanders, and in newness of life: although, as I said before and anon will shew more plainly by God's grace, that this last is no part of penance indeed, but a plain effect or fruit of true penance.

I might here bring in examples of their penance, how perilous it is to be embraced: but let the example of their grandsire Judas[9] serve, in whom we see all the parts of their penance as they describe it, and yet notwithstanding was

[5 Vide Bp. Jewel. Defence, part II. Works (1609) 141; Bp. Ridley, Works, Parker Soc. 338; Hooker, Ecc. Pol. VI. iv. 14, ed. Keble.]
[6 'one' 1553: 'of one' 1574 and after editions.]
[7 The last nine words occur only in 1553.]
[8 Vide Hooker, Ecc. Pol. VI. iii. 5, Keble.]
[9 Vide Homily of Repentance, Part II. Ch. of England.]

4—2

he damned. He was sorry enough, as the effect shewed; he had their contrition fully, out of the which he confessed his fault, saying, "I have betrayed innocent blood;" and thereunto he made satisfaction, restoring the money he had received. But yet all was but lost; he hanged up himself, his bowels burst out, and he remaineth a child of perdition for ever. I would wish that this example of Judas, in whom we see the parts of their penance, 'contrition, confession, and satisfaction,' would move them to penance, and to describe it a little better, making hope or trust of God's free mercy a piece thereof; or else with Judas they will mar all.

Perchance these words, 'contrition, confession, and satisfaction,' were used as I have expounded them at the first[1]. But in that we see so much danger and hurt by using them without expositions, either let us join to them open expositions always, or else let us not use them at all, but say as I write, that penance is a hearty sorrow for our sins, a good hope or trust of pardon through Christ, which is not without an earnest purpose to amend or a new life. This penance is the thing whereto all the scripture calleth us. This penance do I now call you all unto. This must be continually in us, and not for a Lent season, as we have thought; this must increase daily more and more in us: without this we cannot be saved.

Search therefore your hearts all: all swearers, blasphemers, liars, flatterers[2], idle talkers, jesters, bribers, covetous, drunkards, gluttons, whoremongers, thieves, murderers, slanderers, idle livers, negligent in their vocation, &c. All such and all other as lament not their sins, as hope not in God's mercy for pardon, as purpose not heartily to amend, to leave their swearing, drunkenness, whoredom, covetousness, idleness, &c.; all such, I say, shall not nor cannot enter into God's kingdom, but hell-fire is prepared for them, weeping, and gnashing of teeth. Whereunto, alas! I fear me, very many will needs go, in that very many will be as they have been, let us even to the wearing of our tongue to the stumps preach and pray never so much to the contrary, and that even in the bowels of Jesus Christ: as now I

[1 See Hooker, Ecc. Pol. VI. iv. 13, ed. Keble; Bingham, Orig. Eccl. XVIII. iii. 1726, II. 215.]

[2 Two words of the original are omitted.]

beseech you all, all, all, and every mother's child, to repent and lament your sin, to trust in God's mercy, and to amend your lives.

Now, methinks, ye are somewhat astonied; whereby I gather that presently you desire this repentance, that is, this sorrow, good hope, and newness of life. The which that you may the rather attain and get to your comforts, as I have gone about to be a mean to stir up in you[3] by God's grace this desire of repentance, so through the same grace of God will I go about now to shew you how you may have your desire in this behalf.

And first, concerning this part, namely, sorrow for your sins and hearty lamenting of the same; for this, if you desire the having of it, you must beware that you think not that of yourselves or of your own free-will by any means you can get it. You may easily deceive yourselves and mock yourselves, thinking more of yourselves than is seemly. "All good things," and not pieces of good things, but "all good things," saith St James, "cometh from God the Father of light." If therefore penance be good, as it is good, then the parts of it be good: from God therefore do they come, and not of our free-will. "It is the Lord that mortifieth, that bringeth down, that humbleth," saith the scripture in sundry places. "After thou hadst stricken my thigh," saith Jeremy, "I was ashamed." Lo, he saith, "After thou hadst stricken me;" and therefore prayeth he even the last words almost he writeth, "Turn us, Lord, and we shall be turned:" the which thing David useth very often. *James i.* *1 Sam. ii.* *Jer. xxxi.* *Lam. v.*

Wherefore, first of all, if thou wouldest have this part of penance, as for the whole, because it is God's gift, so for this part go thou unto God and make some little prayer, as thou canst, unto his mercy for the same, in this or like sort: *Acts xi.* *2 Tim. ii.* *Acts v.*

'Merciful Father of our Saviour Jesus Christ, because I have sinned and done wickedly, and through thy goodness have received a desire of repentance, whereto this long sufferance doth draw my hard heart, I beseech thy mercy[4] in Christ to work the same repentance in me; and by thy Spirit, power and grace, to humble, mortify, and fear my conscience

[3 'stir up' 1553: 'stir up in you' 1574 and after editions.]
[4 'beseech thee for thy mercy's sake' 1574 and after editions.]

for my sins to salvation, that in thy time thou mayest comfort and quicken me again, through Jesus Christ, thy dearly beloved Son. Amen.'

After this sort, I say, or otherwise as thou thinkest good, if thou wilt have this first part, contrition or sorrow for thy sins, do thou beg it of God through Christ. And when thou hast asked it, as I have laboured to drive thee from trusting in thyself, so now I go about to move thee from flattering of thyself, from sluggishness and negligence, to be diligent to use these means following.

Unto prayer, which I would thou shouldest first use as thou canst, secondly, get thee God's law as a glass to toot[1] in; for in it and by it cometh the true knowledge of sin, without which knowledge there can be no sorrow. For how can a man sorrow for his sins, which knoweth not his sins? As when a man is sick, the first step to health is to know his sickness; even so to salvation, the first step thereto is to know thy damnation due for thy sins.

The law of God therefore must be gotten and well tooted in; that is, we must look in it spiritually, and not corporally or carnally as the outward word or letter doth declare and utter. And so our Saviour teacheth us in the fifth of Matthew, expounding the sixth and seventh commandments, not only after the outward deed, but also after the heart; making there the anger of the heart a kind of murder, lusting after another man's wife a kind of adultery.

And this is one of the differences between God's law and man's law, that of this (man's law, I mean) I am not condemnable so long as I observe outwardly the same. But God's law goeth to the root and to the heart, condemning me for the inward motion, although outwardly I live most holily. As for example: if I kill no man, though in my heart I hate, man's law condemneth me not, but otherwise doth God's law. And why? For it seeth the fountain whence the evil doth spring. If hatred were taken out of the heart, loftiness in looks, detraction in tongue, and murder by hand could never ensue. If lusting were out of the heart, curiosity in countenance, wantonness in words, then[2] boldness in body, would not appear.

In that therefore this outward evil springs out of the in-

[1 Toot: search, look.]   [2 A word of the original is omitted.]

ward corruption, seeing God's law also is a "law of liberty," as saith St James, and "spiritual," as saith St Paul, perfectly and spiritually it is to be understand, if we will truly come to the knowledge of our sins: for of this inward corruption reason knoweth but little or nothing. "I had not known," saith Paul, "that lusting" (which to reason, and to them which are guided only by reason, is thought but a trifle,) "I had not known," saith he, "this lusting to have been sin, if the law had not said, *Non concupisces*, Thou shalt not lust."

James ii.
Rom. vii.
Rom. vii.

To the knowledge therefore of our sin, without which we cannot repent or be sorry for our sin, let us, secondly, get God's law as a glass to toot in; and that not only literally, outwardly, or partly, but also spiritually, inwardly, and throughly. Let us consider the heart, and so shall we see the foul spots we are stained withal at least inwardly, whereby we the rather may be moved to hearty sorrow and sighing. For, as St Austin saith, "It is a glass which feareth nobody; but even look what a one thou art, so it paints thee out[3]"

In the law we see it is a foul spot not to love the Lord our God, with all (I say) our heart, soul, power, might, and strength, and that continually.

In the law it is a foul spot not only to make to ourselves any graven image or similitude, to bow thereto, &c., but also not to frame ourselves wholly after the image whereto we are made, not to bow to it, to worship it.

In the law we see that it is a foul spot not only to take God's name in vain, but also not earnestly, heartily, and even continually to call upon his name only, to give thanks unto him, to believe, to publish, and to live[4] his holy word.

In God's law we see it is a foul spot to our souls not only to be an open profaner of the Sabbath-day, but also not to rest from our own words and works that the Lord might both speak and work in us and by us; not to hear his holy word, not to communicate his sacraments, not to give occasion

[3 Proferatur speculum scripturæ divinæ. Speculum hoc neminem palpat: qualis es, talem te tibi demonstrat.—August. Serm. de Temp. Barbar. cap. iii. Op. VI. col. 609, ed. Bened. Par. 1679—1700: and vide tom. IV col. 1131, enarr. in Ps. ciii. serm. I. 4.]

[4 So 1553, 1574: 'live in' 1581 and after editions.]

to others to holiness by our example in godly works, and reverent esteeming of the ministry of his word.

In God's law we see it a foul spot to our souls not only to be an open disobeyer of our parents, magistrates, masters, and such as be in any authority over us; but also not to honour such even in our hearts, not to give thanks to God for them, not to pray for them, to aid, to help or relieve them, to bear with their infirmities, &c.

In God's law we see it a foul spot in our souls not only to be a man-queller[1] in hatred, malice, proud looks, brags, backbiting, railing, or bodily slaughter; but also not to love our neighbours, yea, our enemies, even in our hearts, and to declare the same in all our gestures, words, and works.

In God's law we see it a foul spot to our souls not only to be a whoremonger in lusting in our hearts, in wanton looking, in unclean or wanton talking, in actual doing unhonestly with our neighbour's wife, daughter, servant, &c.; but also not to be chaste, sober, temperate in heart, looks, tongue, apparel, deeds, and to help others thereunto accordingly, &c.

In God's law we see it is a foul spot to our souls not only in heart to covet, in look or word to flatter, lie, colour, &c., in deed to take away any thing which pertaineth to another; but also in heart, countenance, word, and deed, not to keep, save, and defend that which pertaineth to thy neighbour, as thou wouldest thine own.

In God's law we may see it a foul spot not only to lie or bear false witness against any man, but also not to have as great care over thy neighbour's name as over thine own.

Sin in God's law it is, we may see, and a foul spot, not only to consent to evil lust or carnal desires; but even the very natural or carnal lusts and desires themselves (for so I may call them, nature[2] itself being now so corrupted,) are sin, as self-love, and many such-like.

By reason whereof, I trow, there is none that tooteth well herein, but though he be blameless to the world and fair to the shew, yet certainly inwardly his face is foul arrayed, and so shameful, saucy, mangy, pocked, and scabbed, that he cannot but be sorry at the contemplation thereof; and

[1 Man-queller: murderer.]
[2 So 1574: 'natural' 1553.]

that so much more, by how much he continueth to look in this glass accordingly.

And thus much concerning the second mean to the stirring up of sorrow for our sin, that next unto prayer we should toot in God's law spiritually. The which tooting if we use with prayer, as I said, let us not doubt but at the length God's Spirit will work, as now to such as believe; for to the unbelievers all is in vain, their eyes are stark blind, they can see nothing; to such as believe (I say) I trust something is done even already.

But if neither by prayer, nor by tooting in God's law spiritually, as yet thy hard unbelieving heart feeleth no sorrow nor lamenting for thy sin; thirdly, look upon the tag tied to God's law. For as to man's law there is a tag tied, that is, a penalty; so is there to God's law a tag tied, that is, a penalty, and that no small one, but such a great one as cannot but make us to cast our currish tails between our legs, if we believe it; for all is in vain, if we be faithless not to believe before we feel.

This tag is God's malediction or curse: *Maledictus omnis*, Gal. iii. saith it, *qui non permanet in omnibus quæ scripta sunt in libro legis, ut faciat eam.* ["Cursed is every one who continueth not in all things that are written in the book of the law to do it."] Lo, "accursed," saith he, "is all," no exception, "all," saith God, "which continueth not in all things:" "for he that is guilty of one is guilty of the whole," saith St James: "in all things" therefore, saith the Holy Ghost, "which are written in the book of the law to do them." He saith not, to hear them, to talk of them, to dispute of them; but "to do them."

Who is he now that doth these? *Rara avis*[3], 'few such birds,' yea, none at all. For "all are gone out of the way," though not outwardly by word or deed, yet inwardly at the least by default and wanting of that which is required: so that a child of one night's age is not pure, but by reason of birth-sin in danger of God's malediction: much more then we which, alas! have "drunken in iniquity as it were water," Job xv. as Job saith. But yet, alas! we quake not.

Tell me now, good brother, why do you so lightly consider God's curse, that for your sins past you are so careless, as

[3 Juvenal. Sat. vi. 164.]

though you had made a covenant with death and damnation, as the wicked did in Esay's time? What is God's curse? At the pope's curse with book, bell, and candle[1], O how trembled we which heard it but only, though the same was not directed unto us but unto others! But to this God's curse, which is incomparably more fell and importable, and is directed, yea, hanging over us all by reason of our sins, alas, how careless are we! O faithless hard hearts! O Jezebel's guests, rocked and laid asleep in her bed! O wicked wretches, which being come into the deep of sin do contemn the same! O sorrowless sinners, and shameless, shrinking harlots!

<small>Rev. ii.</small>

Is not the anger of a king death? And is the anger of the King of all kings a matter to be so lightly regarded as we do regard it, which for our sins are so retchless that we slug[2] and sleep it out? "As wax melteth away at the heat of the fire," saith David, "so do the wicked perish at the face (or countenance) of the Lord." If, dearly beloved, his face be so terrible and intolerable for sinners and the wicked, what trow we his hand is? At the face or appearing of God's anger the earth trembleth. But we, earth, earth, yea, stones, iron, flints, tremble nothing at all. If we will not tremble in hearing, woe unto us! for then we shall be crashed a-pieces in feeling. If a lion roar, the beasts quake; but we are worse than beasts, which quake nothing at the roaring of the lion: I mean the Lord of hosts. And why? Because "the curse of God, hardness of heart," is already fallen upon us; or else we could not but lament and tremble for our sins, if not for the shame and foulness thereof, yet at the least for the malediction and "curse of God" which hangeth over us for our sins.

<small>Psal. lxviii.</small>

<small>Lam. iii.</small>

Lord, be merciful unto us for thy Christ's sake, and spare us. In thine anger remember thy mercy towards us. Amen.

And thus much for the third thing to the moving of us to sorrow for our sins, that is, for the tag tied to God's law; I mean for the malediction and curse of God. But if our

---

[1 Vide Foxe, Acts, &c., 1583, p. 1038, or ed. 1846, v. 20; Beeon, "Reliques of Rome," 1563, fol. 237, ch. "the general sentence or curse;" Monumenta Ritualia, Maskell, 1846, I. 226, *ordo excomm.*, and diss. on occas. offices, sect. xii.]

[2 Slug: are lazy, dull.]

hearts be so hard that through these we yet feel not hearty sorrow for our sins, let us, fourthly, set before us examples past and present, old and new, that thereby the Holy Spirit may be effectual to work in his time this work of sorrowing for our sin.

Look upon God's anger for sin in Adam and Eve, for eating a piece of an apple. Were not they, the dearest creatures of God, cast out of paradise? Were not they subject to mortality, travail, labour, &c.? Was not the earth accursed for their sins? Do not we all, men in labour, women in travailing with child, and all in death, mortality, and misery, even in this life feel the same? And was God so angry for their sin, and he being the same God, will he say nothing to us for ours, alas! much more horrible than the eating once of one piece of an apple?

In the time of Noe and Lot God destroyed the whole world with water, and the cities of Sodoma and Gomorrah, Zeboim and Admah, with fire and brimstone from heaven for their sins; namely for their whoredoms, pride, idleness, unmercifulness to the poor, tyranny, &c.; in which wrath of God even the very babes, birds, fowls, fishes, herbs, trees, and grass, perished: and think we that nothing will be spoken to us much worse and more abominable than they? For all men may see, if they will, that the whoredoms, pride, unmercifulness, tyranny, &c., of England, far passeth in this age any age that ever was before[3]. Lot's wife looking back was turned into a salt stone: and will our looking back again, yea, our running back again to our wickedness, do us no hurt? If we were not already more blind than beetles, we would blush. Pharaoh his heart was hardened so that no miracle could convert him. If ours were any thing soft, we would begin to sob.

Of six hundred thousand men alonely but twain entered into the land of promise, because they had "ten times sinned

Gen. vii. xix.
[Deut. xxix. 23.]

Gen. xix.

Josue and Caleb.
Numb. xiv

[3 Vide Sermon of Gilpin before Edward VI. 1552, in Life of Gilpin, 1753; Sermons of Bp. Latimer, Parker Soc. *passim*; Works of Bp. Ridley, Parker Soc. 59, 60; Strype, Mem. II. ii. 131, *et seq.*, ann. 1553, 'view of the manners of all sorts of men in these times, nobility, gentry, yeomanry, judges, the poor, the clergy;' Nares, Life of Burghley, I. 497, *et seq.*; Haweis, Sketches, &c. 1844, ch. vii., 'state of public morals under Edward.']

against the Lord," as he himself saith. And trow we that God will not "swear in his wrath that we shall never enter into his rest," which have sinned so many "ten times" as we have toes and fingers, yea, hairs of our heads and beards, I fear me; and yet we pass[1] not?

<small>Levit. xxiv. Numb. xv.</small>
The man that sware and he that gathered sticks on the sabbath-day were stoned to death. But we think our swearing is no sin, our bibbing, rioting, yea, whorehunting on the sabbath-day, pleaseth God; or else we would something amend our manners.

<small>1 Sam. iii.</small>
Helias' negligence in correcting his sons nipped his neck in two. But ours, which pamper up our children like puppets, will put us to no plunge. Helias' sons, for disobeying their father's monition, brought over them God's vengeance: and will our stubbornness do nothing?

<small>1 Kings xxi. xxii. 2 Sam. xxi. 2 Kings x.</small>
Saul his malice to David, Ahab's displeasure against Naboth, brought their blood to the ground for dogs to eat: yea, their children were hanged up and slain for this gear. But we continue in malice, envy, and murder, as though we were able to wage war with the Lord.

<small>2 Sam. xi. xii. xiii. xiv. xv.</small>
David's adultery with Bethsabe was visited on the child born, on David's daughter defiled by her brother, and on his children, one slaying another, on his wives defiled by his own son, on himself driven out of his realm in his old age, and otherwise also, although he most heartily repented his sin. But we are more dear unto God than David, which yet was a man after God's own heart; or else we could not but tremble and begin to repent.

<small>Luke xvi.</small>
The rich glutton's gay paunch-filling, what did it? It brought him to hell. And have we a placard[2] that God will do nothing to us?

<small>Josh. vii.</small>
Achan's subtle theft provoked God's anger against all Israel; and our subtilty, yea, open extortion, is so fine and politic that God cannot espy it.

<small>2 Kings v. Acts i.</small>
Giezi his covetousness, brought it not the leprosy upon him and on all his seed? Judas also hanged himself. But the covetousness of England is of another cloth and colour. Well, if it were so, the same tailor will cut it accordingly.

<small>Acts v.</small>
Anania and Sapphira by lying linked to them sudden

[[1] Pass: care, regard.]
[[2] Placard: edict, notification.]

death. But ours now prolongeth our life the longer, to last in eternal death.

The false witnesses of the two judges against Susanna lighted on their own pates; and so will ours do at length. Hist. Sus.

But what go I about to avouch ancient examples, where daily experience doth teach? The sweat the other year[3], the storms the winter following[4], will us to weigh them in the same balances. The hanging and killing of men themselves, which are, alas! too rife in all places, require us to register them in the same rolls. At the least in children, infants, and such like, which yet cannot utter sin by word or deed, we see God's anger against sin in punishing them by sickness, death, misshape, or otherwise, so plainly that we cannot but groan and grunt again, in that we a little more[5] have gushed out this gear gorgeously[6] in word and deed.

And here with me a little look on God's anger, yet so fresh that we cannot but smell it, although we stop our noses never so much: I pray God we smell it not more fresh hereafter. I mean it forsooth (for I know you look for it) in our dear late sovereign lord the king's majesty. You all know he was but a child in years: defiled he was not with notorious offences. Defiled! quoth he? Nay, rather adorned with so many goodly gifts and wonderful qualities as never prince was from the beginning of the world. Should I speak of his wisdom, of his ripeness in judgment, of his learning, of his

[3 "The 15th of April [1551], the infectious sweating sickness began in Shrewsbury. In London, in few days, nine hundred and sixty gave up the ghost: people being in best health were suddenly taken and dead in four and twenty hours, and twelve or less. Seven honest householders did sup together, and before eight of the clock in the next morning six of them were dead. This sickness followed Englishmen. in strange countries. Wherefore this nation was much afeard of it, and for the time began to repent and remember God; but as the disease relented, the devotion decayed."—Stow, Annals (1615), 605; Holinshed 1587, III. 1066; Grafton (1569), 1315; Carte 1752, III. 259; Edward VI., Diary in Bp. Burnet, Reform. Records.]

[4 "In this year [1551—2] the sea brake in at Sandwich, insomuch that it did overflow all the marshes thereabout, and drowned much cattle, to the great loss both of the town and the country."—Fabian, Chron., contin. (ed. 1559), 556.]

[5 'a little more' only in 1553.]

[6 'more abundantly' 1574 and after editions.]

godly zeal, heroical heart, fatherly care for his commons, nursely solicitude for religion, &c.? Nay, so many things are to be spoken in commendation of God's exceeding graces in this child, that, as Sallust writeth of Carthage[1], I had rather speak nothing than too little, in that too much is too little.

This gift God gave unto us Englishmen before all nations under the sun, and that of his exceeding love towards us. But alas and welaway[2]! For our unthankfulness' sake, for our sin's sake, for our carnality and profane living, God's anger hath touched not only the body, but also the mind[3], of our king by a long sickness; and at length hath taken him away by death; death! cruel death! fearful death, death! &c.

Oh, if God's judgment be begun on him, which, as he was the chiefest, so I think the holiest and godliest in the realm of England; alas, what will it be on us whose "sins are overgrown so our heads" that they are climbed up into heaven! I pray you, my good brethren, know that God's anger for our sin towards us cannot but be great, yea, too fell, in that we see it was so great that our good king could not bear it. What followed to Jewry after the death of Josias? God save England, and give us repentance! My heart will not suffer me to tarry longer herein. I trow this will thrust out some tears of repentance.

If therefore to prayer for God's fear, the tooting in God's glass and the tag thereto will not burst open thy blockish heart; yet I trow the tossing to and fro of these examples, and specially of our late king, and this troublesome time, will tumble some tears out of thine heart, if thou still pray for God's Spirit accordingly. For who art thou, think always with thyself, that God should spare thee more than they whose examples thou hast heard? What friends hast thou? Were not of these, kings, prophets, apostles, learned,

Ps. xxxviii.

[1 De Carthagine silere melius puto quam parum dicere, quoniam alio properare tempus monet.—Sallust. Bell. Jugurth. xxii., ed. Wasse, Cantabr. (1710) 288.]

[2 i. e. 'woe on woe,' as above, p. 39. 'Alas,' 1617, 1619, 1652.]

[3 Haweis conceives that Bradford probably alludes to the will of the late King, whereby Edward left the crown to the heirs of the Duchess of Suffolk.—Sketches of the Reformation (1844), 293. Vide letter of Bradford to Sir James Hales, in Foxe, Acts, &c. 1583, p. 1637, or ed. 1847, VII. 223.]

and coming of holy stocks? I deceive myself, think thou with thyself, if I believe God, being the same God that he was, will spare me whose wickedness is no less but much more than some of theirs. He hateth sin now as much as ever he did. The longer he spareth, the greater vengeance will fall: the deeper he draweth his bow, the sorer will the shaft pierce.

But if yet thy heart be so hardened that all this gear will not move thee, surely thou art in a very evil estate, and remedy now know I none. What, said I none? know I none? Yes; there is one which is suresby [4] (as they say) to serve if any thing will serve. You look to know what this is. Forsooth the passion and death of Jesus Christ. You know the cause why Christ became man, and suffered as he suffered, was the sins of his people, that he might save them from the same. Consider the greatness of the sore, I mean sin, by the greatness of the surgeon and of the salve. Who was the surgeon? No angel, no saint, no archangel, no power, no creature in heaven nor in earth, but only he by whom all things were made, all things are ruled also, even God's own dearling and only beloved Son becoming man.

O what a great thing is this that could not be done by the angels, archangels, potestates, powers, or all the creatures of God, without his own Son; who yet must needs be thrust out of heaven, as a man would say, to take our nature and become man! Here have ye the surgeon: great was the cure that this mighty Lord took in hand.

Now what was the salve? Forsooth dear gear and of many compositions. I cannot recite all, but rather must leave it to your hearty considerations. Three and thirty years was he curing our sore; he sought it earnestly by fasting, watching, praying, &c. The same night he was betrayed, I read how busy he was about a plaister in the garden, when he lying flat on the ground, praying with tears, and that of blood, not a few, but so many as did flow down on the ground again, crying on this sort, "Father," saith he, "if it be possible, let this cup depart from me." That is, 'If it be possible else mankind's sins can be taken away, grant that it may be so. Thou heardest Moses crying for the idolaters; thou heardest Lot for the Zoarites; Samuel, David, and many other, for the

<small>Matt. xxvi.
Luke xxii.</small>

[4 i. e. to be surely depended upon.]

Israelites; and, dear Father, I only am "thine own Son," as thou hast said, "in whom thou art well pleased." Wilt thou not hear me? I have by the space of three and thirty years done always thy will; I have so humbled myself that I would become an abject amongst men to obey thee. Therefore, dear Father, if it be possible, grant my request, save mankind now without any further labour, salves, or plaisters.' "But yet," saith he, "not as I wilt, but as thou wilt."

But, sir, what heard he? Though he sweat blood and water in making his plaister for our sore of sin, yet it framed not. Twice he cried without comfort. Yea, though to comfort him God sent an angel, we yet know that this plaister was not allowed for sufficient until hereunto Christ Jesus was betrayed, forsaken of all his disciples, forsworn of his dearly beloved, bound like a thief, belied on, buffeted, whipped, scourged, crowned with thorns, derided, crucified, racked, nailed, hanged up between two thieves, cursed and railed upon, mocked in misery, and had given up the ghost. Then "bowed down the head of Christ," that is, God the Father which is "the head of Christ:" then allowed he the plaister to be sufficient and good for the healing of our sore which is sin. Now would God abide our breath, because the stink, that is, damnation or guiltiness, was taken away by the sweet savour of the breath of this Lamb thus offered once for all.

1 Cor. xi.

So that here, dearly beloved, we as in a glass may see, to the bruising of our blockish hard hearts, God's great judgment and anger against sin. The "Lord of lords," the "King of kings," "the brightness of God's glory," the Son of God, the dearling of his Father, "in whom he is well pleased," hangeth between two thieves, crying for thee and me and for us all, "My God, my God, why hast thou forsaken me?" O hard hearts that we have, which make tuts for sin! Look on this: toot in the very heart of Christ pierced with a spear, wherein thou mayest see and read God's horrible anger for sin. Woe to thy hard heart that pierced it!

Ps. xxii.

And thus much for the first part of repentance: I mean, for the means of working contrition. First use prayer; then look on God's law; thirdly see his curse; fourthly set examples of his anger before thee[1]; and last of all set before thee the death of Christ. From this and prayer cease not till thou

[[1] 'before thee' 1574: not in 1553.]

feel some hearty sorrow for thy sin: the which when thou feelest, then labour for the other part, that is, Faith, on this sort.

[II.] As first, in contrition, I willed thee not to trust to thy free-will for the attaining of it, so do I will thee in this. Faith is so far from the reach of man's free-will, that to reason it is plain foolishness. Therefore thou must first go to God, whose gift it is; thou must, I say, get thee to the Father of mercy, whose work it is; that, as he hath brought thee down by contrition, and humbled thee, so he would give thee faith, raise thee up, and exalt thee. *John vi.* *Col. ii.*

On this manner therefore, with the apostles, and the poor man in the gospel that cried, "Lord, increase our faith;" "Lord, help my unbelief," pray thou and say:

'O merciful God, and dear Father of our Lord and Saviour Jesus Christ, in whom as thou art well-pleased, so hast thou commanded us to hear him; forasmuch as he often biddeth us to ask of thee, and thereto promiseth that thou wilt hear us, and grant us that which in his name we shall ask of thee; lo, gracious Father, I am bold to beg of thy mercy, through thy Son Jesus Christ, one sparkle of true faith, and certain persuasion of thy goodness and love towards me in Christ, wherethrough I being assured of the pardon of all my sins, by the mercies of Christ thy Son, may be thankful to thee, love thee, and serve thee in holiness and righteousness all the days of my life.'

On this sort, I say, or otherwise as God shall move thee, pray thou first of all, and look for thy request at God's hand without any doubting, though forthwith thou feelest not the same; for oftentimes we have things of God given us, long before we feel them as we would do.

Now unto this prayer use thou these means following:

After prayer for faith, which I would should be first, secondly, because the same springeth out of the hearing, not of masses, matins, canons, councils, doctors, decrees, but out of the hearing of God's word; get thee God's word; but not that part which serveth specially to contrition, that is, the law; but the other part which serveth specially to consolation and certain persuasion of God's love towards thee, that is, the gospel or publication of God's mercy in Christ, I mean the free promises.

[BRADFORD.]

But here thou must know that there is two kinds of promises; one which are properly of the law, another which are properly of the gospel. In the promises of the law we may indeed behold God's mercy, but so that it hangeth upon the condition of our worthiness; as, 'If thou love the Lord with all thy heart, &c., thou shalt find mercy.' This kind of promises, though it declare unto us God's love which promiseth where he needeth not, yet unto him that feeleth not Christ, which is the end of the law, they are so far from comforting, that utterly with the law they bring man to great despair; so greatly we are corrupt; for none so loveth God as he ought to do. From these therefore get thee to the other promises of the gospel, in which we may see such plenty and frank liberality of God's goodness, that we cannot but be much comforted, though we have very deeply sinned.

For these promises of the gospel do not hang on the condition of our worthiness, as the promises of the law do; but they depend and hang on God's truth; that, as God is true, so they cannot but be performed to all them which lay hold on them by faith, I had almost said, which cast them not away by unbelief.

Mark in them therefore two things, namely, that as well they are free promises without any condition of our worthiness, as also that they are universal, offered to all; all, I say, which are not so stubborn as to keep still their hands, whereby they should receive this almesse[1] in their bosoms, by unbelief. As concerning infants and children you know I now speak not, but concerning such as be of years of discretion. And now you look that I should give you a taste of these promises, which are both free and universal, excepting none but such as except themselves. Well, you shall have one or two for a say.

In the third of John saith our Saviour, "So God the Father loved the world, that he would give his dearling, his own only Son, that all that believe in him should not perish, but have everlasting life." Lo, sir, he saith not that some might have life, but "all" saith he. And what "all"? "all" that love him with all their hearts? "all" that have lived a

[1 i. e. alms.]

godly life? Nay, "all that believe in him." Although thou hast lived a most wicked and horrible life, if now thou believe in him thou shalt be saved. Is not this sweet gear?

Again saith Christ, " Come unto me, all you that labour and are laden; and I will refresh you." Let us a little look on this letter: " Come unto me." Who should come, Lord? priests, holy men, monks, friars? Yea, cobblers, tinkers, whores, thieves, murderers also, if they lament their sins. " Come unto me," saith he, "all ye that labour and are laden;" that is, which are afraid for your sins. And what wilt thou do, Lord? "And I will refresh you," saith he. *Matt xi.*

O what a thing is this! "And I will refresh you." Wot you who spake this? He that never told a lie: he is "the truth:" there "was never guile found in his mouth." And now will he be untrue to thee, good brother, which art sorry for thy grievous sins? No, forsooth! "Heaven and earth shall pass and perish; but his word shall never fail." *1 Pet. ii.* *Matt. xxiv.*

St Paul saith, "God would have all men saved;" (lo, he excepteth none;) and to Titus, "The grace of God bringeth salvation to all men." As from Adam all have received sin to damnation, so by Christ all have grace offered to salvation, if they reject not the same. I speak not now of infants, I say; nor I need not to enter into the matter of predestination. In preaching of repentance, I would gather where I could with Christ. *1 Tim. ii.* *Tit. ii.*

"As surely as I live," saith God, "I will not the death of a sinner." Art thou a sinner? Yea. Lo, God sweareth he will not thy death: how canst thou now perish? Consider with thyself, what profit shouldest thou have to believe this to be true to others, if not to thyself also? Satan doth so. Rather consider with Peter, that the promise of salvation pertaineth not only to them which are nigh, that is, to such as are fallen a little; but also "to all whom the Lord hath called, be they never so far off." *Ezek. xxxiii.* *Acts ii.*

Lo, now by me the Lord calleth thee, thou man, thou woman, that art very far off. The promise therefore pertaineth to thee: needs must thou be saved, except thou with Satan say, God is false: and yet, if thou do so, God "is faithful, and cannot deny himself;" as thou shalt feel by his plagues in hell, for so dishonouring God to think that he is not true. *2 Tim. ii.*

Will he be found false now? The matter hangeth not on thy worthiness, but it hangeth on God's truth. Clap hold on it; and I warrant thee Christ is " the propitiation of our sins, yea, for the sins of the whole world." Believe this, man: I know thou believest it. Say therefore in thy heart still, *Domine, adauge mihi fidem.* " Lord, increase my faith ;" "Lord, help my unbelief." "Blessed are they which see not" by reason this gear, "but yet believe." Hope, man, past all hope, as Abraham did.

<small>Luke xvii.
Mark ix.
John xx.

Rom. iv.</small>

And thus much for a taste of these promises, which are every where not only in the new Testament, but also in the old. Read the last end of Leviticus xxvi.; the prophet Esay xxx, where he saith, " God tarrieth, looking for thee, to shew thee mercy;" also the fortieth, and so forth to the sixtieth[1]. Read also[2] the 2nd Samuel xxiv.; Psal. xxxiv.; Joel ii.; &c.[3]

Howbeit, if this gear will not serve, if yet thou feelest no faith, no certain persuasion of God's love, then unto prayer and diligent considering of the free and universal promises of the gospel; thirdly set before thee those benefits which God hath tofore given thee, and presently giveth thee. Consider how he hath made thee a man or a woman, which might have made thee a toad, a dog. And why did he this? Verily, because he loved thee. And trowest thou that, if he loved thee when thou wast not, to make thee such a one as he most graciously hath made thee; will he not, trowest thou, now love thee being his handy-work? Doth he hate any thing that he made? Is there unableness with him? Doth he love for a day, and so farewell? No, forsooth, " he loveth to the end :" " his mercy endureth for ever." Say therefore with Job, *Operi manuum tuarum porrige dexteram :* that is, " To the work of thy hand put thy helping hand."

<small>John xiii.
Psal. cxviii.
[Job xiv. 15.
Vulgate.]</small>

Again, hath he not made thee a christian man or woman, where, if he would, he might have made thee a Turk or

---

[1 So 1574: 'Leviticus xxvi., the prophet Esay from the fortieth chapter: in the thirtieth saith he, God tarrieth. mercy' 1553.]

[2 'also' 1574: not in 1553.]

[3 The references in this sentence, having been according to the Vulgate, have here, as in other places, been altered in form, to accord with the authorised English Bible.]

paynim? This thou knowest he did of love. And dost thou think his love is lessened, if thou lament thy sin? Is his hand shortened for helping thee? "Can a woman forget the child of her womb? And though she should do it, yet will not I forget thee," saith the Lord. He hath given thee limbs, to see, hear, go, &c.: he hath given thee wit, reason, discretion, &c.: he hath long spared thee, and borne with thee, when thou never purposedst to repent. And now, thou repenting, will he not give thee mercy? Wherefore doth he give thee to live at this present, to hear me to speak this, and me to speak this, but of love to us all? O therefore let us pray him that he would add to this, that we might believe these love-tokens, that he loveth us: and indeed he will do it. Lord, open our eyes in thy gifts to see thy gracious goodness. Amen.

But to tarry in this I will not. Every man let him consider God's benefits past and present, public and private, spiritual and corporal, to the confirming of his faith concerning the promises of the gospel, for the pardon of his sins.

I will now go to shew you a fourth mean to confirm your faith of this gear, even by examples. Of these there are in the scriptures very many, as also daily experience doth diversely teach the same, if we were diligent to observe things accordingly: wherefore I will be more brief herein, having respect to time which stealeth fast away.

Adam in paradise transgressed grievously, as the painful punishment which we all as yet do feel proveth, if nothing else. Though by reason of his sin he displeased God sore, and ran away from God, (for he would have hid himself, yea, he would have made God the causer of his sin, in that he gave him such a mate, so far was he from asking mercy;) yet, all this notwithstanding, God turned his fierce wrath, neither upon him nor Eve (which also required not mercy), but upon the serpent Satan; promising unto them a seed, Jesus Christ, by whom they at the length should be delivered. In token whereof, though they were cast out of paradise for their nurture, to serve in sorrow, which would not serve in joy; yet he made them apparel to cover their bodies, a visible sacrament and token of his invisible love and grace concerning their souls. If God was so merciful to Adam, which so sore brake his commandment, and rather blamed God than asked mercy; trowest thou, O man, that

Gen. iii.

he will not be merciful to thee, which blamest thyself, and desirest pardon?

To Cain he offered mercy, if he would have asked it. "What hast thou done?" saith God: "The voice of thy brother's blood crieth unto me out of the earth." 'O merciful Lord,' should Cain have said, 'I confess it!' But, alas! he did not so; and therefore said God, "Now," that is, in that thou desirest not mercy, "now," I say, "be thou accursed." Lo, to the reprobate he offered mercy; and will he deny it thee which art his child?

Noah did not he sin and was drunk? Good Lot also both in Sodom dissembled a little with the angels, prolonging the time, and out of Sodom he fell very foul; as did Judas and the patriarchs against Joseph. But yet, I ween, they found mercy. Moses, Miriam, Aaron, though they stumbled a little, yet received they mercy: yea, the people in the wilderness often sinned and displeased God, so that he was purposed to have destroyed them. "Let me alone," saith he to Moses, "that I may destroy them:" but Moses did not "let him alone," for he prayed still for them; and therefore God spared them. If the people were spared through Moses' prayer, they not praying with him, but rather worshipping their golden calf, eating, drinking, and making jolly good cheer; why shouldest thou doubt whether God will be merciful to thee? having, as indeed thou hast, one much better than Moses to pray for thee and with thee, even Jesus Christ, "who sitteth on the right hand of his Father and prayeth for us," being no less faithful in his Father's house, the church, than Moses was in the synagogue.

David, that good king, had a foul foil when he committed whoredom with his faithful servant's wife Bethsabe; whereunto he added also a mischievous murder, causing her husband, his most faithful soldier Ury, to be slain with an honest company of his most valiant men of war, and that with the sword of the uncircumcised.

In this his sin though a great while he lay asleep, (as many do now-a-days, God give them wyn[1] waking!) thinking that by his sacrifices he offered all was well, God was content; yet at length, when the prophet by a parable had

[1 i. e. joy; the Anglo-Saxon *wyn*, 'gaudium,' from whence 'winsome,' merry, cheerful. Vide Jun. Etymol. Angl. ed. Lye, Oxon. 1743, v. 'wune.' 'Wynne' 1553: 'good' 1574, and after editions.]

opened the poke[2], and brought him in remembrance of his own sin in such sort that he gave judgment against himself, then quaked he. His sacrifices had no more taken away his sins, than our sir John's[3] trentals[4] and wagging of his fingers over the heads of such as lie asleep in their sins; out of the which when they are awaked, they will well see that it is neither mass nor matins, blessing nor crossing, will serve. Then, I say, he cried out, saying, *Peccavi, Domine:* " I have sinned," saith he, 'against my Lord and good God which hath done so much for me: I caused indeed Ury to be killed: I have sinned, I have sinned: what shall I do? I have sinned, and am worthy of eternal damnation.' But what saith God by his prophet? *Dominus*, saith he, *transtulit peccatum tuum: non morieris.* " The Lord hath taken away thy sins: thou shalt not die." O good God, he said but *Peccavi;* " I have sinned;" but yet from his heart, and not from his lips only, as Pharaoh and Saul did; and incontinently he heareth, " Thou shalt not die: the Lord hath taken away thy sins;" or rather hath laid them upon another, yea, translated them upon the back of his Son Jesus Christ, who bare them; and not only them, but thine and mine also, if that we will now cry but from our hearts, *Peccavimus:* " We have sinned," good Lord, "we have done wickedly:" "enter not into judgment with us," but "be merciful unto us after thy great mercy, and according to the multitude of thy compassions do away our iniquities," &c. For indeed God is not the God of David only: *idem Deus omnium:* " he is the God of all." So Rom. x. that *quicunque invocaverit nomen Domini salvus erit:* "he or she, whosoever they be that call upon the name of the Lord, shall be saved." In confirmation whereof this history is written, as are also the other I have recited, and many moe which I might recite; as of Manasses, that wicked king which slew Esay the prophet[5], and wrought very much

[2 Poke: a bag or sack. 'Opened the poke,' a proverbial expression. Vide Ray, and Fuller, Proverbs, and Bailey, Dict.]

[3 See note E.]

[4 Vide p. 49 note 5, above.]

[5 "The tradition of the Jews, that Isaiah was put to death by Manasseh, is very uncertain; and one of their principal Rabbins (Aben Ezra, Com. in Isai. i. 1.) seems rather to think that he died before Hezekiah; which is indeed more probable." Bp. Lowth on Isaiah, p. 225, ed. 1825.]

wickedness, yet the Lord shewed mercy upon him, being in prison, as his prayer doth teach us. Nabucodonozar, though for a time he bare God's anger, yet at the length he found mercy. The city of Niniveh also found favour with God, as did many other which I will omit for time's sake, and will bring forth one or two out of the new Testament, that we may see God to be[1] the same God in the new Testament he was in the old.

[marginal: 2 Kings xxi. 2 Chron. xxxiii. 18, 19.] Dan. iv.]
[marginal: Jonah iii.]

I might tell you of many, if I should speak of the lunatic, such as were possessed with devils, lame, blind, dumb, deaf, lepers, &c.; but time will not suffice me: one or two therefore shall serve.

Mary Magdalene had seven devils; but yet they were cast out of her; and of all others she was the first that Christ appeared unto after his resurrection.

Thomas would not believe Christ's resurrection, though many told him which had seen and felt him; by reason whereof a man might have thought that his sins would have cast him away. "Except I should see and feel," saith he, "I will not believe." Ah wilful Thomas! "I will not," saith he: but Christ appeared unto him, and would not leese[2] him: as he will not do thee, good brother, if that with Thomas thou wilt keep company with the disciples, as Thomas did.

[marginal: John xx.]

Peter his fall was ugly: he accursed himself if ever he knew Christ, and that for fear of a girl; and this not once, but even three divers times, and that in the hearing of Christ his Master: but yet the third time Christ looked back and cast on him his eye of grace, so that he went out and wept bitterly; and after Christ's resurrection not only did the angels will the women to tell Peter that Christ was risen, but Christ himself appeared unto him severally, such a good Lord is he.

[marginal: Matt. xxvi. Luke xxii.]

The thief hanging on the cross said but this: "Lord, when thou comest into thy kingdom, remember me." And what answer had he? "This day," saith Christ, "shalt thou be with me in paradise."

[marginal: Luke xxiii.]

[1 'to be' 1574: not in 1553.]
[2 "The word occurred in our authorised version of the Bible, 1 Kings xviii. 5, 'that we leese not all the beasts'; but is one of those readings which have been tacitly changed in the modern editions." Nares, Glossary.]

What a comfort is this! in that he is now the same Christ to thee and me and us all, if we will run unto him; for he is the same Christ to-day and to-morrow, until he come to judgment. Then indeed he will be inexorable; but now is he more ready to give, than thou to ask. If thou cry, he heareth thee, yea, before thou cry. Cry therefore, be bold, man: he is not partial. "Call," saith he; "and I will hear thee." "Ask, and thou shalt have; seek, and thou shalt find;" though not at the first, yet at the length. If he tarry awhile, it is but to try thee. *Nam veniens veniet, et non tardabit.* "He is coming, and will not be long." Heb. xiii. Jer. xxxiii. Matt. vii. Heb. x.

Thus have you four means which you must use to the attaining of faith, or certain persuasion of God's mercy towards you, which is the second part of penance; namely prayer, the free and universal promises of God's grace, the recordation of the benefits of God past and present, the examples of God's mercy. Which although they might suffice, yet will I put one moe to them, which alonely of itself is full sufficient; I mean the death of the Son of God, Jesus Christ; which if thou set before the eyes of thy mind, it will confirm thy placard[3]; for it is the great seal of England, as they say, yea, of all the world, for the confirmation of all patents and perpetuities of the everlasting life whereunto we are all called.

If I thought these which I have before recited were not sufficient to confirm your faith of God's love towards such as do repent, I would tarry longer herein. But because both I have been long, and also I trust you have some exercise of conscience in this daily (or else you are to blame), I will but touch and go.

Consider with yourselves what we are, misers[4], wretches, and enemies to God. Consider what God is; even he which hath all power, majesty, might, glory, riches, &c., perfectly of himself, and needeth nothing, but hath all things. Consider what Christ is: concerning his Godhead, co-equal with his Father, even he by whom all things were made, are ruled and governed; concerning his manhood, the only darling of his Father, in whom is all his joy. Now, sir, what a

[3 See p. 60, note 2, above: 'assurance' 1617, 1619, 1652.]
[4 i.e. unhappy ones.]

love is this, that this God which needeth nothing would give wholly his own self to thee his enemy, wreaking his wrath upon himself in this his Son, as a man may say, to spare thee, to save thee, to win thee, to buy thee, to have thee, to enjoy thee for ever! Because thy sin had separated thee from him, to the end thou mightest come eftsoons into his company again, and therein remain, he himself became, as a man would say, a sinner, or rather sin itself, even a malediction or a curse; that we sinners, we accursed by our[1] sin, might, by his[2] oblation or offering for our sins, by his curse, be delivered from sin and[3] from malediction. For by sin he destroyed sin, killing death, Satan, and sin, by their own weapons; and that for thee and me, man, if we cast it not away by unbelief. O wonderful love of God! Who ever heard of such a love? The Father of heaven for us his enemies to give his own dear Son Jesus Christ! and that not only to be our brother, to dwell among us, but also to the death of the cross for us! O wonderful love of Christ to us all, that was content and willing to work this feat for us! Was there any love like to this love?

Rom. v.

God indeed hath commended his charity and love to us herein, that when we were very enemies unto him, he would give his own Son for us. That we, being men, might become, as you would say, gods, God would become man. That we, being mortal, might become immortal, the immortal God would become mortal man. That we, earthly wretches, might be citizens of heaven, the Lord of heaven would become, as a man would say, earthly. That we, being accursed, might be blessed, God would be accursed[4]. That we, by our father Adam being brought out of paradise into the puddle of all pain, might be redeemed and brought into paradise again God would be our Father, and an Adam thereunto. That we

[1 'his' 1553: 'our' 1574.]

[2 'might by his' 1574: 'that by his,' and 'might' after 'by his curse', 1553.]

[3 'and' 1574: not in 1553.]

[4 A passage very like the above occurs near the end of the Homily on the Nativity, in the second book of Homilies, which Bp. Burne states (on Article xxxv.) as it "was not finished till about the time of King Edward's death, so it was not published before Queen Elizabeth's time:" "O how much are we" "at God's hands."]

having nothing might have all things, God having all things would have nothing. That we, being vassals and slaves to all, even to Satan the fiend, might be lords of all and of Satan, the Lord of all would become a vassal and a slave to us all, and in danger of Satan,

O love incomprehensible! Who can otherwise think now but, if the gracious good Lord disdained not to give his own Son, his own heart's joy, for us his very enemies, tofore we thought to beg any such thing at his hands, yea, tofore we were; who, I say, can think otherwise but that with him he will give us all good things? If, when we hated him and fled away from him, he sent his Son to seek us; who can think otherwise than that now we loving him, and lamenting because we love him no more, but that he will for ever love us? He that giveth the more to his enemies, will not he give the less, trow you, to his friends? God hath given his own Son, than which thing nothing is greater, to us his enemies: and, we now being become his friends, will he deny us faith and pardon of our sins? which, though they be great, yet in comparison they are[5] nothing at all. Christ Jesus would give his own self for us, when we willed it not: and will he now deny us faith, if we will it? This "will" is Phil. ii. his earnest that he hath given us truly to look in deed for the thing willed. And look thou for it in deed; for as he hath given thee "to will," so will he give thee "to do."

Jesus Christ gave his life for our evils, and by his death delivered us. O then, in that he liveth now and cannot die, will he forsake us? His heart's blood was not too dear for us when we asked it not: what can then be now too dear for us asking it? Is he a changeling? is he mutable as man is? can he repent him of his gifts? Did he not foresee our falls? Paid not he therefore the price? Because he saw we should fall sore, therefore would he suffer sore. Yea, if his sufferings had not been enough, he would yet once more come again. God the Father, I am sure, if the death of his Son incarnate would not serve, would himself and the Holy Ghost also become incarnate, and die for us. This death of Christ therefore look on as the very pledge of God's love towards thee, whosoever thou art, how deep soever thou hast sinned. See, God's hands are nailed, they cannot strike thee; his feet also, he cannot run from thee: his arms are wide open

[5 'they are' 1574: not in 1553.]

to embrace thee: his head hangs down to kiss thee: his very heart is open! So that therein see, toot[1], look, spy, peep; and thou shalt see nothing therein but love, love, love, love to thee. Hide thee therefore, lay thy head there, with the evangelist.

This is the clift of the rock wherein Elias stood: this is the pillow of down for all aching heads. Anoint thy head with this oil: let this ointment embalm thy head and wash thy face. Tarry thou here, and cock-sure thou art, I warrant thee. Say with Paul, "What can separate me from the love of God?" Can death, can poverty, sickness, hunger, or any misery persuade thee now that God loveth thee not? Nay, nothing can separate thee from the love wherewith God hath loved thee in Christ Jesus. Whom he loveth "he loveth to the end." So that now, where abundance of sin hath been in thee, the more is the abundance of grace.

But to what end? Forsooth that, as sin hath reigned to death, as thou seest, to the killing of God's Son, so now grace must reign to life to the honouring of God's Son, who is now alive and "cannot die any more:" so that they which by faith feel this cannot any more die to God, but to sin, whereto they are dead and buried with Christ. As Christ therefore liveth, so do they, and that to God, to righteousness and holiness. The life which they live is *in fide Filii Dei;* "in the faith of the Son of God."

[III.] Whereby you see that now I am slipped into that which I made the Third part of penance, namely, newness of life; which I could not so have done, if that it were a part of itself indeed, as it is an effect, a fruit of the second part, that is, of faith or trust in God's mercy.

For he that believeth, that is, is certainly persuaded sin to be such a thing that it is the cause of all misery, and of itself so greatly angereth God, that in heaven nor in earth nothing could appease his wrath, save alonely the death and precious blood-shedding of the Son of God, in whom is all the delight and pleasure of the Father; he, I say, that is persuaded thus of sin, the same cannot but in heart abhor and quake to do or say, yea, to think any thing willingly which God's law teacheth him to be sin.

Again he that believeth, that is, is certainly persuaded

[1 See p. 54, note 1, above.]

God's love to be so much towards him, that, where through sin he was lost and made a firebrand of hell, the eternal Father of mercy, which is the omnisufficient God, and needeth nothing of us, or of any thing that we can do, to deliver us out of hell and to bring us into heaven, did send even his own most dear Son out of his bosom, out of heaven, into hell, as a man would say, to bring us, as I said, from thence into his own bosom and mercy, we being his very enemies; he, I say, that is thus persuaded of God's love towards him, and of the price of his redemption by the dear blood of the Lamb immaculate, Jesus Christ, the same man cannot but love God again, and of love do that and heartily desire to do better, the which might please God.

Trow you that such a one, knowing this gear by faith, will willingly walter[2] and wallow in his wilful[3] lusts, pleasure, and fantasies? Will such a one, as knoweth by faith Christ Jesus to have given his blood to wash him from his sins, play the sow, to walter[2] in his puddle of filthy sin and vice again? Nay, rather than he will be defiled again by wilful sinning, he will wash often the feet of his affections, watching over the vice still sticking in him, which as a spring continually sendeth out poison enough to drown and defile him, did not the sweet water of Christ's passion in God's sight wash it, and his blood satisfy the rigour of God's justice due for the same.

This blood of Christ shed for our sins is so dear in the sight of him that believeth, that he will abhor in his heart to stamp it and tread it under his feet. He knoweth now by his belief that it is too much, that hitherto he hath set too little by it, and is ashamed thereof. Therefore the residue of his life he purposeth to take better heed to himself than tofore he did: for, because he seeth by his faith the grievousness of God's anger, the foulness of sin, the greatness of God's mercy and of Christ's love towards him, he will now be heedy[4] to pray God to give him his grace accordingly; that as with his eyes, tongue, hands, feet, &c., he hath displeased God, doing his own will, even so now with the same eyes, tongue, ears, hands, feet, &c., he may displease his own

[2 i. e. lie grovelling.]
[3 'woeful' 1553: 'wilful' 1574.]
[4 i. e. careful.]

self and do God's will. Willingly will he not[1] do that which might renew the death of the Son of God. He knoweth he hath too much sin unwillingly in him, so that thereto he will not add willing offences.

This willing and witting offending and sinning, whosoever doth flatter himself therein, doth evidently demonstrate and shew that he never yet indeed tasted of Christ truly: he was never truly persuaded or believed how foul a thing sin is, how grievous a thing God's anger is, how joyful and precious a thing God's mercy in Christ is, how exceeding broad, wide, high, and deep Christ's love is. Perchance he can write, prate, talk, and preach of this gear; but yet he in heart[2] by faith never felt this gear: for, did he once feel this gear indeed, then would he be so far from continuing in sin willingly and wittingly, that wholly and heartily he would give over himself to that which is contrary, I mean to a new life, "renewing his youth even as the eagle doth."

Psal. ciii.

For as we, being in the servitude of sin, demonstrate our service by giving over our members to the obeying of sin, from iniquity to iniquity; even so we, being made free from sin by faith in Jesus Christ, and endued with God's Spirit, a Spirit of liberty, must needs demonstrate this freedom and liberty by giving over our members to the obedience of the Spirit; by the which we are led and guided from virtue to virtue, and all kind of holiness. As the unbelievers declare their unbelief by the working of the evil spirit in them outwardly the fruits of the flesh; even so the believers declare their faith by the working of God's good Spirit in them outwardly the fruits of the Spirit. For, as the devil is not dead in those which are his, but worketh still to their damnation; so is not God dead in them which be his, but worketh still to their salvation: the which working is not the cause of the one or the other being in any, but only a demonstration, a sign, a fruit of the same; as the apple is not the cause of the apple-tree, but a fruit of it.

2 Cor. iii.

Ephes. ii.
Gal. v.

Thus then you see briefly, that newness of life is not indeed a part of penance, but a fruit of it, a demonstration of the justifying faith, a sign of God's good Spirit possessing

[1 'now', a misprint, 1553: 'not' 1574.]
[2 So 1553, 1574, 1652: 'part,' an early impression of 1574 (vide p. 28 above), 1581, 1599, 1617, 1619.]

the heart of the penitent; as the old life is a fruit of impenitency, a demonstration of a lip-faith or unbelief, a sign of Satan's spirit possessing the heart of the impenitent, which all those be that be not penitent; for mean I know none. He that is not penitent, that same is impenitent: he that is not governed by God's Spirit, the same is governed by Satan's spirit; for all that be Christ's are governed with the Spirit of Christ, which Spirit hath her fruits. All other that be not Christ's are the devil's: "he that gathereth not with Christ scattereth abroad." Rom. viii.
Gal. v.

Therefore, dearly beloved, I beseech you to consider this gear, and deceive not yourselves. If you be not Christ's, then pertain you to the devil: of which thing the fruits of the flesh doth assure you, as whoredom, adultery, uncleanness, wantonness, idolatry, witchcraft, envy, strife, contention, wrath, sedition, murder, drunkenness, gluttony, blasphemy, slothfulness, idleness[3], slandering, &c. If these apples grow out of the apple-trees of your heart, surely, surely the devil is at inn[4] with you, you are his birds, whom when he hath well fed, he will broach[5] you and eat you, chaw[6] you and champ[7] you; world without end, in eternal woe and misery. But I am otherwise persuaded of you all: I trust you be all Christ Jesus his people and children, yea, brethren by faith.

As ye see your sins in God's law, and tremble, sigh, sorrow, and sob for the same; even so you see his great mercies in his gospel and free promises; and therefore are glad, merry, and joyful, for that you are accepted into God's favour, have your sins pardoned, and are endued with the good Spirit of God, even the seal and sign manual of your election in Christ before the beginning of the world. The which Spirit, for that he is the Spirit of life, given to you to work in you, with you, and by you, here in this life, sanctification and holiness, (whereunto you are called that ye might be holy, even as your heavenly Father is holy;) I beseech you all by admonition and warning of you, that you would stir up the gifts of God given to you, generally and particu- 2 Cor. i.

1 Thess. iv.
1 Pet. i.

2 Tim. i.

[3 Two words of the original are omitted.]
[4 i. e. his lodging, or abode. See Nares, Glossary.]
[5 i. e. transfix, pierce through.]
[6 i. e. grind with teeth.]
[7 i. e. bite, devour.]

larly, to the edifying of his church: that is, I pray you that you would not molest the good Spirit of God, by rebelling against it when it provoketh and calleth you to go on forwards, that he which is holy might yet be more holy, he which is righteous might be more righteous; as the evil spirit moveth and stirreth up the filthy to be yet more filthy, the covetous to be more covetous, the wicked to be more wicked.

<small>Ephes. iv.</small>

<small>Rev. xxii.</small>

Declare you now your repentance by works of repentance: bring forth fruits, and worthy fruits. Let your sorrowing for your evils demonstrate itself by departing from the evils you have used. Let your certainty of pardon of your sins through Christ and your joy in him be demonstrated by pursuing of the good things which God's word teacheth you. You are now "in Christ Jesus God's workmanship, to do good works, which God hath prepared for you to walk in." "For the grace of God, that bringeth salvation unto all men, hath appeared, and teacheth us that we should deny ungodliness and worldly lusts, and that we should live soberly, righteously, and godly in this present world, looking for that blessed hope and glorious appearing of the mighty God and of our Saviour Jesus Christ, which gave himself for us to redeem us from all unrighteousness, and to purge us a peculiar people unto himself, fervently given unto good works." Again (Titus iii.), "For we ourselves also were in times past unwise, disobedient, deceived, serving lusts and divers pleasures, living in maliciousness and envy, full of hatred, and hating one another. But, after that the kindness and love of God our Saviour to man-ward appeared, not by the deeds of righteousness which we wrought, but of his mercy he saved us, by the fountain of the new birth, and with the renewing of the Holy Ghost; which he shed on us abundantly through Jesus Christ our Saviour; that we, once justified by his grace, should be heirs of eternal life through hope. This is a true saying."

<small>Ephes. ii.</small>

<small>Titus ii.</small>

But I will make an end, for I am too tedious.

Dearly beloved, repent your sins: that is, be sorry for that which is past; believe in God's mercy for pardon, how deeply soever you have sinned; and both purpose and earnestly pursue a new life, bringing forth worthy and true fruits of repentance. As you have given over your members from sin to sin to serve the devil; your tongues to swear, to lie, to flatter, to scold, to jest, to scoff[1], to vain jangling, to boasting, &c.; your hands to picking, groping, idleness, fighting, &c.; your feet to skipping, going to evil, to dancing, &c.; your ears to hear fables, lies, vanities, and evil things, &c.; so now give over your members to godliness, your tongues to speak, your ears to hear, your eyes to see, your mouths to taste, your hands to work, your feet to go about such things as may make to God's glory, sobriety of life, and love to your brethren; and that daily more and more diligently: for in a stay to stand you cannot; either better or worse you are to-day than you were yesterday. But better I trust you be, and will be, if you mark well my theme, that is, "Repent you."

The which thing that you would do, as before I have humbly besought you, even so now yet once more I do again beseech you, and that for the tender mercies of God in Christ Jesus our Lord: "Repent you:" "repent you; for the kingdom of heaven" (that is, a kingdom full of all riches, pleasures, mirth, beauty, sweetness, and eternal felicity) "is at hand." The eye hath not seen the like, the ear hath not heard the like, the heart of man cannot conceive the treasures and pleasures of this kingdom, which now "is at hand" to such as repent; that is, to such as are sorry for their sins, believe God's mercy through Christ, and earnestly purpose to lead a new life. 1 Cor. ii. Isai. lxiv.

The God of mercy, through Christ his Son, grant us his holy Spirit, and work in our hearts this sorrow, faith, and new life, which through his grace I have spoken of, both now and for ever. Amen.

[[1] Three words of the original are omitted.]

A SERMON OF THE LORD'S SUPPER[1].

JESUS EMMANUEL.

MS. 1. 2. 8. no. 11. Emman. Coll. Cambridge[2].

Two Sermons by Bradford, Awdeley and Wight 1574, and after editions.

THERE are two sacraments in Christ's church: one of initiation, that is, wherewith we be enrolled, as it were, into the household and family of God, which sacrament we call baptism; the other wherewith we be conserved, fed, kept, and nourished to continue in the same family, which is called the Lord's supper, or the body and blood of our Saviour Jesus Christ, broken for our sins and shed for our transgressions.

Two Sacraments in Christ's Church.

Of the former sacrament, that is, of baptism, to speak now I am not purposed, because occasion and time serve not so thereto. Of the second therefore will I speak something by God's grace, if that you remember this, that baptism in Christ's church now sithen Christ's death is come in place of circumcision in the same church afore Christ's coming: whereby we may see that christian parents seem to be no less bound to offer their infants and babes to be baptized, that they may be taken and accounted of us as members of Christ's mystical body, wherein they are received and sealed, than were the Hebrews their children to be circumcised and so to be[3] taken as pertaining to the covenant and league with God,

Baptism is in place of circumcision.

Christian men's children ought to be baptized.

[1 Bp. Ridley, in a letter to Bradford, 1554, writes: "Dearly beloved, I wish you grace, mercy and peace. According to your mind I have run over all your papers; and what I have done, which is but small, therein may appear. In two places I have put in two loose leaves: I had much ado to read that was written in your great leaves, and I ween somewhere I have altered some words, because I could not read perfectly that which was written. Blessed be God that hath given you liberty ., that you may use your pen to his glory, and to the comfort, as I hear say, of many."—To this Foxe annexes the following side note: "This was a treatise of the Lord's Supper, with other things, which Master Bradford sent to him to peruse and to judge thereof."—Foxe, Acts, &c. 1583, p. 1725, or ed. 1843—8, VII. 426.]

[2 This MS. is followed, unless where otherwise noted. The latter part of the Sermon, from p. 102, l. 28 ('the gravity and grievousness of sin') to the end, is also contained in a MS. in the autograph of Bradford, 2. 2. 16. no. 20. in Emmanuel College, Cambridge. This MS. has supplied two lines at p. 107: MS. 1. 2. 8. no. 11. generally agrees with it closely.]

[3 'Circumcised   be', MS. 1. 2. 8: not in 1574.]

wherein they were engraffed, alonely the circumstance of the Gal. iv. eighth day, not necessary to be observed, being now abrogate.

But to come again. Of the Lord's supper I am purposed presently to speak through the help of God, because we are assembled in Christ, I hope, to celebrate the same[4].

Now that the things which I shall speak may be better observed and carried away of you, I will tell you how and in what sort I will speak of it. Three things would I have marked, as the principles and scope whereto I will refer all that I shall at this time speak thereof. They are these: *Who, what,* and *wherefore.* That is, to make it more plain, Who did institute this thing which we are about to celebrate: *Quis:* this is the First. The Second is, What the thing is which is *Quod: Cur.* instituted. And the Last is, Wherefore, and to what end it was instituted, whereby we shall be taught how to use it.

[I.] For the First, Who did institute this sacrament and supper.

Who did institute this Sacrament.

You all do know that[5] things are more esteemed sometime for the dignity and authority of the person, sometime for the wisdom of the person, sometime for the power and magnificence of the person, sometime for the holiness of the person[6], and sometime for the tender love and kindness of the person. If need were, I could by examples set forth every one of these; but I hope it is not necessary.

Now then, how can the thing which we be aboutward to celebrate but be esteemed of every one highly, in that the Author of it doth want no dignity, no authority, no wisdom, no power, no magnificence, no holiness, no tender love and kindness, but hath all dignity, authority, wisdom, power, magnificence, holiness, tender love, mercy, glory, and all that can be wished, absolutely? He is God eternal, co-equal and consubstantial with the Father and with the Holy Ghost,

[4 Foxe states that, while Bradford was in prison in the King's Bench and the Counter in the Poultry, he preached twice a day continually . also the sacrament was often ministered; and through his means (the keepers so well did bear with him) such resort of good folks was daily to his lecture, and to the ministration of the sacrament, that commonly his chamber was well nigh filled therewith. Acts, &c. p. 1780.]

[5 'it,' MS. 1. 2. 8: 'that' 1574.]

[6 The last seven words occur in MS. 1. 2. 8, but are not given in 1574 and after editions.]

6—2

"the image of the substance of God," the Wisdom of the Father, "the brightness of his glory," by whom all things were made, are ruled, and governed. He is the King of all kings, and the Lord of all lords. He is the Messias of the world, our most dear and loving Brother, Saviour, Mediator, Advocate, Intercessor, Husband, Priest: so that the thing which cometh from him cannot but be esteemed, loved, and embraced. If dignity like us; if authority like us; if wisdom like us; if power like us; if glory like us; if goodness and[1] mercy like us; yea, if any thing that can be wished like us, then cannot this which our Lord did institute but like us; and that so much the more, by how much it is one of the last things which he did institute and command.

God open our eyes to see these things accordingly! so shall we come with more reverence to this table of the Lord: which thing he grant for his mercy's sake. Amen.

And thus much for the first, who did institute this sacrament.

What the Sacrament is.

[II.] Now to the Second, What the sacrament is.

If we shall ask our eyes, our nose, our mouth, our taste, our hands, and the reason of man, they will all make a consonant answer, that it is bread and wine: and verily therein they speak the truth and lie not, as by many things may be proved, although the papists prate their pleasure to the contrary.

And here, my dearly beloved, I think I shall not be either tedious or unprofitable unto you, if that I tarry a little in shewing this verity, that the substance of bread and wine remaineth in the sacrament after the words of consecration (as they call them) be spoken. Whereby we may learn how shameless beasts they be which would enforce men to believe transubstantiation, which is an error whereupon in a manner

Transubstantiation is the foundation of all popery.

dependeth all popery; for it is the stay of their priesthood, which is neither after the order of Aaron, nor after the order of Melchisedec, but after the order of Baal: which thing is something seen by their number; for false prophets and priests of Baal were always many moe in number when the wicked were in authority, than true priests and prophets of the Lord, as the holy histories of the bible do teach. Read 1 Kings xviii.

That in the supper of the Lord, or in the sacrament of Christ's body, which the papists call 'the sacrament of the altar'

[1 'goodness and' 1574: not in MS. 1. 2. 8.]

as though that were Christ's sacrament, which thing they can never prove; (for it, being perverted and abused to a contrary end, as of sacrificing propitiatorily for the sins of the quick and of the dead, of idolatry by adoring or worshipping it with godly honour, &c., is no more Christ's sacrament but an horrible profanation of it: and therefore, as Christ called "God's temple," which was "called a house of prayer," for the abusing and profaning of it by the priests, "a den of thieves;" so this which the papists call 'the sacrament of the altar' full truly may we call an abominable idol: and therefore I would all men should know that 'the sacrament of the altar' as the papists now do abuse it, omitting certain substantial points of the Lord's institution, and putting in stead thereof their own dregs and dreams, is not the sacrament of Christ's body, nor the Lord's supper; whereof when we speak reverently, as our duty is, we would not that men should think we speak it of the sacrament [of] the popish mass:) That, I say, in the supper of the Lord, or in the sacrament of Christ's body, there remaineth the substance of bread and wine, as our senses and reason doth teach, these many things also do teach the same. *The sacrament of the popish mass is not the sacrament of Christ's body.*

First, the Holy Ghost doth plainly tell us, by calling it often "bread" after the words of consecration, as 1 Cor. x., "Is not the bread which we break a partaking of the body of Christ?" saith Paul. Lo, plainly he saith, "the bread which we break," not only calling it 'bread,' but addeth thereto 'breaking;' which cannot be attributed either to Christ's body whereof no bone was broke, either to any accident, but must needs be of substance: which substance, if it be not Christ's body, cannot be but bread; as in the eleventh chapter four times he plainly calleth it, 'He that eateth of this bread, he that receiveth this bread,' &c. And in the Acts of the apostles we read how that (in speaking of the communion) they "met together to break bread," &c. So that it is plain, the substance of bread and wine doth remain in the supper after the words of consecration; as also may appear plainly by Christ's own words, which calleth that which he gave them in the cup "wine" or "the fruit of the vine," as both Matthew and Mark do write: whereby we see that there is no transubstantiation of the wine; and therefore may we also see that there is no transubstantiation of the bread. *First reason against transubstantiation.*

As for the papists' cavilling, how that it hath the name of *An answer to the papists'* bread because it was bread, as Simon the leper was called still leprous though he was healed, or as Moses' rod being turned into a serpent was called a rod still, it[1] proveth nothing; for there was in the one a plain sight, and the senses certified that Simon was no leper, and in the other plain mention that the rod was turned into a serpent. But concerning the sacrament, neither the senses see any other thing than bread, neither is there any mention made of turning: and therefore their cavil is plainly seen to be but a cavil and of no force.

cavil for the foresaid reason. Matt. xxvi. Exod. vii.

But to come again, to bring more reasons against transubstantiation: secondly, that the substance of bread remaineth still, the very text doth teach; for the evangelists and the apostle St Paul do witness that Christ gave that to his disciples, and called it his body, which he took, on which he gave thanks, and which he brake. But he "took bread," "gave thanks" on bread, and "brake" bread: *ergo* he gave bread, and called bread "his body," as he called the cup "the new Testament." So that it followeth by this, that there is no transubstantiation. And this reason I myself have promised in writing to prove by the authority of the fathers; namely Irenæus, Tertullian, Origen, Cyprian, Epiphanius, Hieronymus, Austin, Theodoret, Cyril, Bede[2]; if so be I may have the use of my books[3].

Second reason. Matt. xxvi. Mark xiv. Luke xxii. 1 Cor. xi.

To M. Willerton. To M. Weston. To M. Pendleton.[3]

Third reason.

Thirdly, that in the sacrament there is no transubstantiation of the bread, by this reason I do prove. Like as by our Saviour Christ the Spirit of truth spake of the bread, "This is my body;" so saith the same Spirit of truth of the same bread, that "we many are one body and one bread," &c. So that, as it appeareth the sacrament not to be the church by transubstantiation, even so it is not Christ's natural body by transubstantiation.

1 Cor. x.

Fourth reason.

Fourthly, I prove that there is no transubstantiation by Luke and Paul's words spoken over the cup. For no less are they effectual to transubstantiate the cup, than their words spoken of the bread are operatorious and mighty to transubstantiate the bread: for, as they say of the bread, "This is my body," so say they of the cup, "This cup is

[1 'it' 1574: not in MS. 1. 2. 8.]   [2 See note F.]
[3 See the 'prison-conferences' of Bradford, as referred to on the margin above. A like declaration is made by Bp. Ridley in his Disputation at Oxford, April 1554, Works, Parker Soc. 203.]

the new Testament:" which thing is absurd to be spoken or thought[4] either of the cup or of the thing in the cup by transubstantiation. Yea, rather in saying these words, "This cup is the new Testament," we are taught by their coupling this word "cup" to the demonstrative "this," how we should, in these words, "This is my body," know that this word "this" doth there demonstrate bread.

Fifthly, that the substance of bread remaineth in the sacrament, as the reasons before brought forth do prove, so doth the definition of a sacrament; for the fathers do affirm it to "consist of an earthly thing and of an heavenly thing[5]," of "the word and of the element[6]," of "sensible things and of things which be perceived by the mind[7]." But transubstantiation taketh clean away 'the earthly thing, the element, the sensible thing;' and so maketh it no sacrament. And therefore the definition of a sacrament full well teacheth that bread, which is 'the earthly thing, the sensible thing, and the element,' remaineth still, as St Austin saith, "The word cometh to the element[6];" (he saith not, 'taketh away the element;') and so it is made a sacrament.

Fifth reason.

Irene.
Austin.
Chrysostom.

Sixthly, the nature and proportion of a sacrament teacheth this also which I have affirmed. For, as Cyprian writeth that "sacraments bear the name of the thing which they signify[8];" so doth St Austin teach that, "if sacraments have

Sixth reason.
Cypr. in Serm. de Chrismat.

August. ad Bonifacium.

[4 'taught,' MS.: 'thought' 1574.]

[5 .. εὐχαριστία, ἐκ δύο πραγμάτων συνεστηκυῖα, ἐπιγείου τε καὶ οὐρανίου....—Iren. Cont. Hær. Lib. Quinq. IV. xviii. (olim xxxiv.) 5. Op. I. 251, ed. Bened. Venet. 1734.]

[6 Accedit verbum ad elementum, et fit sacramentum etiam ipsum tanquam visibile verbum.—August. In Johann. Evang. xv. Tract. LXXX. 3. Op. III. II. col. 703, ed. Bened. Par. 1679—1700.]

[7 . ἐν αἰσθητοῖς τὰ νοητά σοι παραδίδωσι. Chrysost. In Matt. Hom. LXXXII. (al. LXXXIII.) Op. VII. 787, ed. Bened. Par. 1718—38. divina autem illum sanctificante gratia, mediante sacerdote, liberatus est quidem ab appellatione panis, dignus autem habitus Dominici corporis appellatione, etiamsi natura panis in ipso permansit.—Id. Ep. ad Cæsar. Monach. Op. III. 744; and in Routh, Script. Eccl. Opusc. II. 127, Oxon. 1840. See the remarkable history of this treatise in connexion with Abp. Cranmer and Peter Martyr, in Cave, Hist. Liter. Oxon. 1740, I. 315.]

[8 .. ut. significantia et significata eisdem vocabulis censerentur, ut sacramentum et res sacramenti, veritas et figura, usque adeo individualsam haberent efficientiam.—Arnold. Abbat. Bonæ-vall. De unct. chrism. in Cypr. Op. Oxon. (1682.) Append. p. 48.]

not some signification with the thing whereof they be sacraments, then are they no sacraments[1]." Now in the Lord's supper this similitude is, first, in nourishing, that, as bread nourisheth the body, so Christ's body broken feedeth the soul: secondly, in bringing together many into one, that, as in the sacrament many grains of corn are made "one bread," many grapes are made one liquor and wine; so the multitude which worthily receiveth the sacrament are made "one body" with Christ and his church: last of all, in one unlikely likeliness or similitude, that, as bread eaten turneth into our nature, so we rightly eating the sacrament by faith turn into the nature of Christ. So that it is plain to them that will see, that to take the substance of bread away is clean against the nature and proportion of a sacrament.

I will speak nothing how that this their doctrine of transubstantiation, besides the manifold absurdities it hath with it (which to rehearse I omit), it utterly overthroweth the use of the sacrament, and is clean contrary to the end wherefore it was instituted; and so is no longer a sacrament but an idol, and is the cause of much idolatry; converting the people's hearts from an heavenly consideration to an earthly, and turning the communion into a private action, and a matter of gazing and piping, of adoring and worshipping the work of men's hands. For the living God which "dwelleth not in temples made with men's hands," much less lieth he in pyxes[2] and chests, whose true worship is "in spirit and verity:" which God grant us all to render unto him continually. Amen.

Seventh reason.

The sacrament of baptism doth also[3] teach us, that, as the substance of the water remaineth there, so in the Lord's supper remaineth the substance of bread after consecration: for, as by baptism we are engraffed into Christ, so by the supper we are fed with Christ. These two sacraments the Apostle gladly coupleth together, 1 Cor. x. and xii.: "We are baptized into one body," saith he, "and have drunk all of one Spirit," meaning it by the cup, as Chrysostom[4] and

1 Cor. x. & xii.

[1 Si enim sacramenta quandam similitudinem earum rerum quarum sacramenta sunt non haberent, omnino sacramenta non essent.—August. Epist. xcviii. ad Bonifac. sect. 9. Op. II. col. 267]

[2 'pyx,' from the Latin 'pyxis,' the box in which consecrated wafers were kept for the sick.—Vide Du Cange, Gloss.]

[3 'also' 1574: not in MS. 1. 2. 8.]

[4 Τουτέστι, πρὸς τὴν αὐτὴν ἤλθομεν μυσταγωγίαν, τῆς αὐτῆς ἀπο-

others, great learned men, do well interpret it. As therefore in baptism is given unto us the Holy Ghost and[5] pardon of our sins, which yet lie not lurking in the water; so in the Lord's supper is given unto us the communion of Christ's body and blood, that is, grace, forgiveness of sins[6], innocency, life, immortality, without any transubstantiation or including of the same in the bread. By baptism "the old man is put off," and "the new man put on," yea, "Christ put on," but without transubstantiation of the water: and even so it is in the Lord's supper. We by faith spiritually in our souls feed on Christ's body broken, do eat his flesh, and drink his blood, do dwell in him and he in us, but without transubstantiation. *Gal. iii.*

As for the cavil they make, that "we are baptized into one body," meaning thereby the mystical body and not the natural body of Christ; whereby they would enforce that we are fed with the natural body of Christ, but we are not engrafted into it but into the mystical body, and so put away the reason aforesaid: as for this cavil, I say, we may soon avoid it, if so be we will consider how that Christ, which is the head of the mystical body, is not separate from the body. And therefore to be engraft to the mystical body is to be engraft to the natural body of Christ, to be a "member of his flesh," and bone "of his bones;" as pope Leo full well doth witness, in saying, that *corpus regenerati fit caro crucifixi*[7]: "The body," saith he, "of the regenerate is made the flesh of Christ crucified." And hereto I could add some reasons for the excellency of baptism. I trow it be more to be begotten than to be nourished. As for the excellent miracle of the patefaction[8] of the Trinity, and the descent of the Holy Ghost in baptism in a visible form, the *Answer to the cavil against the seventh reason.*

λαύομεν τραπέζης πνεῦμα εἰπών, ἀμφότερα ἐδήλωσε, καὶ τὸ αἷμα καὶ τὴν σάρκα· δι' ἀμφοτέρων γὰρ ἐν πνεῦμα ποτιζόμεθα. Ἐμοὶ δὲ δοκεῖ νῦν ἐκείνην λέγειν τοῦ πνεύματος τὴν ἐπιφοίτησιν. τὴν ἀπὸ τοῦ βαπτίσματος καὶ πρὸ τῶν μυστηρίων ἐγγινομένην ἡμῖν.—Chrysost. In Epist. I. ad Cor. Hom. xxx. Op. X. 270, ed. Bened. Par. 1718—38.]

[5 'and' 1574: not in MS. 1. 2. 8.]

[6 'forgiveness of sins' 1574: not in MS. 1. 2. 8.]

[7 ... susceptus a Christo, Christumque suscipiens, non idem sit post lavacrum, qui ante baptismum fuit; sed corpus regenerati fiat caro crucifixi.—Leon. Magni Serm. LXIII. de Pass. Dom. XII. cap. vi. Op. I. col. 246, Venet. 1753—57.]

[8 Patefaction: disclosure, manifestation.]

like whereto was not seen in the Lord's supper, I will omit to speak hereof further than I would you should know how that it were no mastery to set forth the excellency of this sacrament, as well as of the supper.

We may in no case condemn them that were before Christ's incarnation, neither our infants which die before the receipt of the supper; as doubtless they must needs be condemned if that they be not insert and engrafted into the very true body and natural body of our Saviour Christ: which thing they are not but by baptism, if the papistical doctrine be received concerning the necessity of this sacrament; for this sentence remaineth true still, "Except you shall eat the flesh of the Son of man, and drink his blood, you cannot have life:" which thing our infants want, if by baptism it be not conferred unto them.

Eighth reason.

But enough of this: now to the eighth reason[1].

It is a plain sign of antichrist, to deny the substance of bread and wine to be in the Lord's supper after consecration. For in so doing and granting transubstantiation the property of the human nature of Christ is denied; for it is not of the human nature, but of the Divine nature, to be in many places at once: as Didymus *de Spiritu Sancto* doth prove thereby the divinity of the Holy Ghost[2]. Now grant transubstantiation, and then Christ's natural body must needs be in many places: which is nothing else but to confound the two natures in Christ, or to deny Christ's human nature, which is the self-same that St John saith, to deny "Christ to be come in the flesh:" and this whoso doeth, by the testimony of St John, is "an antichrist" in his so doing, whatsoever otherwise they do prate. Read St Austin in his epistle to Dardanus[3], and his fiftieth[4]

[1 This line and the preceding paragraph are supplied by MS. 1. 2. 8, being omitted in 1574 and the after editions.]

[2   Spiritus autem sanctus, cum in pluribus sit, non habet substantiam circumscriptam.—Did. Alex. De Spirit. Sanct. Lib. I. 6, Hieron. interpr. in Hieron. Op. II. col. 112, stud. Vallars. Veron. 1734—42.]

[3 Una enim persona Deus et homo est, et utrumque est unus Christus Jesus; ubique per id quod Deus est, in cœlo autem per id quod homo.—August. Liber ad Dardan. seu Ep. clxxxvii. 10. Op. II. col. 681, ed. Bened. Par. 1679—1700.]

[4 Secundum præsentiam majestatis semper habemus Christum: secundum præsentiam carnis, recte dictum est discipulis, 'Me autem non semper habebitis.—Id. In Johann. Evang. XII. Tract. L. 13. Op. III. II. col. 634.]

and thirtieth[5] treatise upon St John: and easily you shall see how that "Christ's body must needs be in one place, (*Oportet in uno loco esse;*) but his truth is in all places."

If there be no substance of bread in the sacrament, but transubstantiation, then Christ's body is received of the ungodly and eaten with their teeth: which is not only against St Austin calling this speech, "Except you eat the flesh of the Son of man," &c. to be "a figurative speech[6];" but also against the plain scriptures, which affirm them to dwell in Christ and Christ in them, and they to have everlasting life that eat him; which the wicked have not, although they eat the sacrament. "He that eateth of this bread," saith Christ, "shall live for evermore." Therefore they eat not Christ's body, but, as Paul saith, "they eat judgment and damnation;" which I trow be another manner of thing than Christ's body. And this doth St Austin affirm, saying, "None do eat Christ's body, which is not in the body of Christ;" that is, as he expoundeth it, "in whom Christ dwelleth not, and he in Christ[7]:" which thing the wicked do not, because they want faith and the Holy Spirit, which be the means whereby Christ is received.

Ninth reason.

To the things which I have here brought forth to improve[8] transubstantiation, I could bring the fathers to confirm the same, which succeeded continually many hundred years after Christ. Also I could shew that transubstantiation

[5 Corpus enim Domini in quo resurrexit uno loco esse potest: veritas ejus ubique diffusa est.—Id. In Johann. Evang. VII. Tract. XXX. 1. Op. III. II. col. 517.]

[6 'Nisi manducaveritis,' inquit, 'carnem Filii hominis et sanguinem biberitis, non habebitis vitam in vobis.' Facinus vel flagitium videtur jubere: figura est ergo, præcipiens passioni Dominicæ communicandum, et suaviter atque utiliter recondendum in memoria, quod pro nobis caro ejus crucifixa et vulnerata sit.—Id. De Doctr. Christ. Lib. III. 24. Op. III. I. col. 52.]

[7   recte intelligunt non dicendum esse eum manducare corpus Christi, qui in corpore non est Christi. Ipse dicens, 'Qui manducat carnem meam et bibit sanguinem meum in me manet, et ego in eo,' ostendit quid sit non sacramento tenus, sed re vera corpus Christi manducare et ejus sanguinem bibere. . Sic enim hoc dixit, tanquam diceret, Qui non in me manet, et in quo ego non maneo, non se dicat aut existimet manducare corpus meum, aut bibere sanguinem meum. —Id. De Civit. Dei, Lib. XXI. cap. xxv. 3, 4. Op. VII. col. 646, 7: and vide In Johann. Evang. VI. Tract. XXVI. 18. Op. III. II. col. 501.]

[8 Improve: disprove.]

is but a new doctrine, not established before Satan, which was tied for a thousand years, was letten loose. Also I could shew that ever hitherto, since it was established, in all times it hath been resisted and spoken against. Yea, tofore this doctrine the church was nothing so endowed with goods, lands, and possessions, as it hath been since: it hath brought no small gain, no small honour, no small ease to the clergy; and therefore no marvel though they strive and fight for it. It is their *Maozim*[1]: it is their Helena[2]. God destroy it with the breath of his mouth, as shortly he will, for his name's sake. Amen.

<small>Rev. xx.</small>

If time would serve, I could and would here tell you of the absurdities which cometh by this doctrine; but for time's sake I must omit it. Only for God's sake see this, that this their doctrine of transubstantiation is an untruth, as already I have proved: and forget not that it is the whole stay of all papacy and the pillar of their priesthood, whereby Christ's priesthood, sacrifice, ministry, and truth is letted[3], yea, perverted and utterly overthrown. God our Father, in the blood of his Son[4] Christ, open the eyes and minds of our magistrates and all other that bear the name of Christ[5], to see it in time to God's glory and their own salvation. Amen.

<small>What the sacrament is.</small>

Now, to return to the second matter, what the sacrament is, you see that to the senses and reason of man it is bread and wine; which is most true[6], as by the scriptures and otherwise I have already proved: and therefore away with transubstantiation.

But here, lest we should make it no sacrament (for a sacrament consisteth of two things), and lest a man should by this gather that we make it none other thing but bare bread and[7] a naked sign, and so rail at their pleasure on us, saying, 'How can a man be guilty of the body and blood of

---

[1 i. e. guardian deities. מָעֻזִּים Vide Dan. xi. 38, marginal reading, authorised version; Mede, Apostasy of the latter times, I. xvi, xvii, Works, 1672, p. 667, et seq.]

[2 i. e. ground of contention; in allusion to the Trojan war. Vide Calv. Instit. IV. xviii. 18. Op. IX. I. 387, Amst. 1667—71.]

[3 Letted: hindered.]

[4 'Son' 1574: not in MS. 1. 2. 8.]

[5 The last nine words in 1574: not in MS. 1. 2. 8.]

[6 'truth,' MS. 1. 2. 8: 'true' 1574.]

[7 'and' 1574: not in MS. 1. 2. 8.]

Christ by unworthy receiving it, if it be but bare bread?' and so forth; for this purpose I will now speak a little more hereabout by God's grace, to stop their mouths, and stir up your good hearts more to the worthy estimation and perception of this holy mystery.

When a loving friend giveth to thee a thing, or sendeth to thee a token (as, for an example, a napkin [8] or such like), I think thou doest not as thou shouldest do, if that with the thing thou considerest not the mind of thy friend that sendeth or giveth thee the thing, and according thereto to esteem and receive it. And so of this bread think I that, if thou do [9] not rather consider the mind of thy lover Christ than the thing which thou seest, yea, if thou do not altogether consider Christ's mind, thou dealest unhonestly and strumpetly with him: for it is the property of strumpets to consider the things given and sent them, rather than the love and mind of the giver and sender; whereas the true [10] lovers do not consider in any point the things given or sent, but the mind of the party. So we, if we be true lovers of Christ, must not consider barely [11] the outward thing which we see and our senses perceive; but rather altogether we must and should see and consider the mind of Christ, and thereafter and [12] according to it to esteem the sacrament.

But how shall we best know the mind of Christ? Forsooth, as a man's mind is best known by his word, so by Christ's words shall we know his mind. Now his words be manifest and most plain. "This" saith he, "is my body:" therefore accordingly should we esteem and take and receive it. If he had spoken nothing, or if he had spoken doubtfully, then might we have been in some doubt. But in that he speaketh so plainly, saying, "This is my body," who can, may, or dare be so bold as to doubt of it? He is "the truth" and cannot lie: he is omnipotent and can do all things: therefore it is his body. This I believe, this I confess, and pray you all heartily to beware of these and such like words, that it is but a sign or a figure of his body; except you will

[[8] 'and,' MS.: 'or' 1574.]
[[9] 'do' 1574: not in MS. 1. 2. 8.]
[[10] 'true' 1574: not in MS. 1. 2. 8.]
[[11] 'in any point,' MS. 1. 2. 8: 'barely' 1574.]
[[12] 'and' 1574: not in MS. 1. 2. 8.]

Two kinds of signs. discern betwixt signs which signify only, and signs which also do represent, confirm, and seal up, or (as a man may say) give with their signification. As for example, an ivy-bush is a sign of wine to be sold[1]: the budding of Aaron's rod did signify Aaron's priesthood allowed of the Lord: the reservation of Moses' rod did signify the rebellion of the children of Israel: the stones taken out of Jordan, Gideon's fleece of wool, and such as these, be signs significative, and shew no gift. But in the other signs, which some call exhibitive, is there not only a signification of a thing, but also a declaration of a gift, yea, in a certain manner a giving also: as baptism signifieth not only the cleansing of the conscience from sin by the merits of Christ's blood, but is also a very cleansing from sin; and therefore it was said to Paul, that he should "arise and wash away his sins," and not that he should arise and take only a sign of washing away his sins. In the Lord's supper the bread is called "a partaking of the Lord's body," and not only a bare sign of the body of the Lord.

This I speak, not as though the elements of these sacraments were transubstantiate (which I have already impugned); either as though Christ's body were in the element, either were tied to the element otherwise than sacramentally and spiritually; either that the bread, water[2], and wine may not and must not be called sacramental and external signs; but that they might be discerned from significative and bare signs only, and be taken for signs exhibitive and representative.

By this means a christian conscience will esteem and call the bread of the Lord as 'the body of Christ;' for it[3] will never esteem the sacraments of Christ after their exterior appearance, but after the words of Christ: whereof it cometh that the fathers, as Chrysostom and others, do speak with so full a mouth when they speak of the sacrament; for their respect was to Christ's words. If the schoolmen which followed them had had the same spirit as they had, then would they never have consented to transubstantiation. For with great admiration some of the fathers do say that the bread is changed or

[1 See Bp. Ridley on the Lord's Supper, Works, Parker Soc. 10; Nares, Glossary.]
[2 'water,' MS. 1. 2. 8: not in 1574.]
[3 'they,' MS. 1. 2. 8: 'it' 1574.]

turned into the body of Christ, and the wine into his blood, meaning it of a mutation or changing, not corporal, but spiritual, figurative, sacramental, or mystical; for now it is no common bread nor common wine, being ordained to serve for the food of the soul. The schoolmen have understand it as the papists now preach, of a substantial changing; as though it were no great miracle that common bread should now be assumed into that dignity that it should be called 'Christ's body,' and serve for celestial food, and be made a sacrament of his body and blood.

As before I have spoken, I would wish that this sacrament should be esteemed and called of christian men, after Christ's words, namely 'Christ's body,' and the wine 'Christ's blood,' rather than otherwise. Not that I mean any other presence of Christ's body than a presence by grace, a presence by faith, a presence spiritually, and not corporally, really, naturally, and carnally, as the papists do mean; for in such sort Christ's body is only in heaven, 'on the right hand of God the Father Almighty,' whither our faith in the use of the sacrament ascendeth, and receiveth whole Christ accordingly. *Christ's presence in the supper.*

Yea, but one will say, that to call the sacrament on this sort is to give an occasion of idolatry to the people, which will take the sacrament they see simply for Christ's body, as by experience we are too well taught: and therefore it were better to call it 'bread,' and so less harm should be, especially in this age. *An objection as touching the calling of the sacrament.*

To this objection I answer, that indeed great idolatry is committed to and about this sacrament, and therefore men ought, as much as they can, to avoid from occasioning or confirming it: but, inasmuch as the Holy Ghost is wiser than man, and had foresight of the evils that might be, and yet notwithstanding doth call it 'Christ's body,' I think we should do evil if we should take upon us to reform his speech. If ministers did their duties in catechising and preaching, then doubtless to call the sacrament 'Christ's body,' and to esteem it accordingly, could not give occasion to idolatry, and confirm it. Therefore woe unto them that preach not! *An answer. [1574.]*

There are two evils about the sacraments, which to avoid the Holy Ghost hath taught us. For, lest we should with the papists think Christ's body present in or with the bread *Two evils about the sacrament.*

really, naturally, and corporally, to be received[1] with our bodily mouth (where there is no other presence of Christ's body than spiritually and to the faith), in many places he keepeth still the name of "bread;" as in the [first] epistle to the Corinthians, the tenth and eleventh chapters[2]. And lest we should make too light of it, making it a bare sign and no better than common bread, the Holy Ghost calleth it "Christ's body:" whose speech I wish we would follow, and that not only as well to avoid the evil which is now-a-days most to be feared concerning the sacrament (I mean it of contemning it), as also for that no faithful man cometh to the sacrament to receive bread simply, but rather, yea, altogether to communicate with Christ's body and blood; for else "to eat and drink," as Paul saith, they "have houses" of their own.

The contempt of the sacrament in the days of king Edward hath caused these plagues upon us presently. The Lord be merciful unto us! Amen.

And thus much for the objection of calling the sacrament by the name of Christ's body.

Another objection of Christ's presence in the sacrament.

'Why,' saith one, 'to call the sacrament Christ's body, and to make none other presence of Christ than by grace or spiritually and to faith (which is "of things hoped for and of things which" to the bodily senses "do not appear"), is to make no presence at all, or to make him none otherwise present than he is in his word when it is preached: and therefore what need we to receive the sacrament, inasmuch as by this doctrine a man may receive him daily in the field, as well and as much as in the church in the celebration and use of the sacrament?'

An answer how Christ is present in the sacrament.

To this reason I first answer, that indeed neither the scripture nor christian faith will give us leave to make any carnal, real, natural, corporal, and such gross presence of Christ's natural body in the sacrament, (for it is in heaven, and "the heavens must have it," as saith Peter, till Christ's coming to judgment;) except we would deny the humanity of Christ, and the verity of man's nature in him. The presence therefore which we believe and confess is such a presence as reason knoweth not and the world cannot learn, nor any that looketh in this matter with other eyes, or heareth with other

[1 'perceived,' MS. 1. 2. 8: 'received' 1574.]
[2 So 1574: '10 and 11' MS. 1. 2. 8.]

ears, than with the ears and eyes of the Spirit and of faith. Which faith, though it be of "things hoped for," and so of things absent to the corporal senses, yet this absence is not an absence indeed but to reason and to the old man; the nature of faith being a "possession of things hoped for." Therefore to grant a presence to faith is not to make no presence at all but to such as know not faith.

And this the fathers taught, affirming Christ to be present by grace; and therefore not only a signification, but also an exhibition and giving of the grace of Christ's body; that is, of "life and of the seed of immortality[3]," as Cyprian writeth. We "eat life and drink life[4]," saith St Austin. We feel a presence of the Lord "by grace" or "in grace[5]," saith Chrysostom. We receive "the celestial food that cometh from above[6]," saith Athanasius. We receive "the property of the natural conjunction and knitting together[7]," saith Hilarius. We perceive "the nature of flesh, the blessing that giveth life[8]," in bread and wine, saith Cyrillus: and elsewhere he

How the doctors call the sacrament.

[3 immortalitatis alimonia datur, a communibus cibis differens. ...Panis iste communis, in carnem et sanguinem mutatus, procurat vitam et incrementum corporibus.—Arnold. Abbat. Bonæ-vall. De Cœn. Dom. in Cypr. Op. Oxon. 1682. Append. p. 39, 40.]

[4 Illud manducare refici est: ... illud bibere quid est nisi vivere? Manduca vitam, bibe vitam: habebis vitam, et integra est vita.—August. Serm. cxxxi. de verb. Evang. Johan. vi. i. Op. V. col. 641, ed. Bened. Par. 1679—1700.]

[5 σχῆμα πληρῶν ἕστηκεν ὁ ἱερεύς, τὰ ῥήματα φθεγγόμενος ἐκεῖνα· ἡ δὲ δύναμις καὶ ἡ χάρις τοῦ Θεοῦ ἐστι.—Chrysost. De prodit. Judæ, Hom. I. Op. II. 384, ed. Bened. Par. 1718—38.

Bp. Ridley, Works, Parker Soc. 201, attributes the sentiment to Eusebius Emissenus; and the words, "ut.. perennis victima illa viveret in memoria, et semper præsens esset in gratia," occur in Euseb. Emiss. in Corp. Jur. Canon. Decret. Gratian. Decr. Tert. Pars, De Consecr. Dist. ii. can. 35, Paris. 1618, p. 419.]

[6 .. καὶ λοιπὸν τὴν εἰρημένην σάρκα βρῶσιν ἄνωθεν οὐράνιον καὶ πνευματικὴν τροφὴν παρ' αὐτοῦ διδομένην μάθωσιν.—Athan. Epist. iv. ad Serap. 19. Op. I. II. 710, ed. Bened. Par. 1698.]

[7 tanquam nobis. . nulla per sacramentum carnis et sanguinis naturalis communionis proprietas indulgeretur: cum . . et per manentem in nobis carnaliter Filium, et in eo nobis corporaliter et inseparabiliter unitis, mysterium veræ ac naturalis unitatis sit prædicandum.—Hilar. De Trin. viii. 17. Op. col. 957, ed. Bened. Par. 1693.]

[8 Εἰ διὰ μόνης ἀφῆς τῆς ἁγίας σαρκὸς ζωοποιεῖται τὸ ἐφθαρμένον,

[BRADFORD.]

saith that with the bread and wine "we eat the virtue of Christ's proper flesh[1]," life, grace, and the property of the body of the only-begotten Son of God, which thing he himself expoundeth to be "life." Basilius saith that we by the sacrament receive "the mystical advent of Christ[2];" "grace, and the virtue of his very nature," as Ambrose saith; that we receive "the sacrament of the true body[3]." Epiphanius saith, we receive "the body" or "grace[4]." And Jerome saith that we receive "spiritual flesh," which he calleth "other flesh than that which was crucified[5]." Chrysostom saith that we receive "influence of grace and the grace of the Holy Ghost[6]." St Austin saith that we receive grace and verity, "the invisible grace[7]" and holiness of the members of Christ's body[8].

All the which sayings of the fathers do confirm this our faith and doctrine of the sacrament; we granting in all things herein unto them, and they in like manner unto us. And

πῶς οὐχὶ πλουσιωτέραν ἀποκερδανοῦμεν τὴν ζωοποιὸν εὐλογίαν, ὅταν αὐτῆς καὶ ἀπογευσώμεθα;—Cyril. Alex. In Joann. IV. ii. Op. IV 361, Lut. 1638.]

[1 Οὐκοῦν ὁ τρώγων τὴν ἁγίαν σάρκα Χριστοῦ ζωὴν αἰώνιον ἔχει.—Id. ibid. 363.]

[2 σάρκα γὰρ καὶ αἷμα πᾶσαν αὐτοῦ τὴν μυστικὴν ἐπιδημίαν ὠνόμασε. —Basil. Epist. viii. 4. Op. III. 84, ed. Bened. Par. 1721—30.]

[3 ideo in similitudinem quidem accipis sacramentum, sed vere naturæ gratiam virtutemque consequeris.—Ambros. De Sacram. VI. i. Op. II. col. 380, ed. Bened. Par. 1686—90. Cave and Oudinus consider this treatise spurious.—Cave, Hist. Liter. I. 263, Oxon. 1740; Oudin. Comm. de script. eccles. I. col. 659—65, Lips. 1722.]

[4 ἠθέλησεν χάριτι εἰπεῖν, Τοῦτό μου ἐστί τόδε .—Epiphan. Ancorat. 57. Op. II. 60, Par. 1622.]

[5 Dupliciter vero sanguis Christi et caro intelligitur, vel spiritualis illa atque divina, de qua ipse dixit, 'Caro mea vere est cibus, et sanguis meus vere est potus;' vel caro et sanguis quæ crucifixus [crucifixa, ed. Bened.] est, et qui militis effusus est lancea.—Hieron. Comm. in Epist. ad Ephes. Lib. I. cap. i. Op. VII. col. 553, stud. Vallars. Veron. 1734—42.]

[6 ἱερέα παρεστῶτα, καὶ Πνεῦμα μετὰ πολλῆς τῆς δαψιλείας τοῖς προκειμένοις ἐφιπτάμενον.—Chrysost. In Ep. I. ad Cor. Hom. XXIV. Op. X. 218, ed. Bened. Par. 1718—38.]

[7 Moyses visibilibus sacramentis per ministerium suum, Dominus autem invisibili gratia per Spiritum sanctum, ubi est totus fructus etiam visibilium sacramentorum.—August. Quæst. in Heptateuch. III. 84. Op. III. 1. col. 524, ed. Bened. Par. 1679—1700.]

[8 This paragraph is closely similar to a passage in the Disputation of Bp. Ridley, 1554, Works, Parker Soc. 201, 202.]

therefore the lying lips which both belie the doctors, as though they granted a carnal and real presence of Christ's body, naturally and corporally, after the papists' declaration and meaning; and which belie us also, as though we denied all presence of Christ, and so made it but a bare sign; these lying lips the Lord will destroy, if they repent not, and with us teach not the truth, that the sacrament is a food of the soul, a matter of faith, and therefore spiritually and by faith to be talked of and understand. Which faith they want, and therefore they err so grossly, in that they would have such a presence of Christ as is contrary to all the scriptures, and to our christian religion: whereby cometh no more commodity to the receiver than by our spiritual presence which we teach, and according to God's word do affirm; for what profit cometh by their doctrine, which ours hath not[9]?

We teach these benefits to be had by the worthy receiving of the sacrament, namely, that we abide in Christ, and Christ in us; again that we attain by it a celestial life, or a life with God; moreover that by faith and in spirit we receive not only Christ's body and blood, but also whole Christ, God and man. Besides these we grant, that by the worthy receiving of this sacrament we receive remission of our sins and confirmation of the new Testament. Last of all by worthy receiving we get by faith[10] an increase of[11] incorporation with Christ and amongst ourselves which be his members: than which things what more can be desired? Alas! that men consider nothing at all, how that the coupling of Christ's body and blood to the sacrament is a spiritual thing; and therefore there needs no such carnal presence as the papists imagine. Who will deny a man's wife to be with her husband one body and flesh, although he be at London and she at York? But the papists are animal men, guided by carnal[12] reason only: or else would they know how that the Holy Ghost because of our infirmity useth metaphorically the words of abiding, dwelling, eating, and drinking of Christ, that the unspeakable conjunction of Christ with us might something be known.

The profit of this doctrine.
1
2
3
4
5

God open their eyes to see it! And thus much for this.

Now to that part of the objection which saith, that we

[9 'what profit . hath not,' MS. 1. 2. 8: not in 1574.]
[10 'by faith,' MS. 1. 2. 8: not in 1574.]
[11 'an increase of' 1574: not in MS. 1. 2. 8.]
[12 'carnal' 1574: not in MS. 1. 2. 8.]

teach Christ to be none otherwise present in the sacrament than in his word. I would that the objectors would well consider, what a presence of Christ is in his word. I remember that St Austin writeth how that Christ's body is received sometime "visibly," and sometime "invisibly[1]:" the "visible" receipt he calleth that which is by the sacraments; the "invisible" receipt he calleth that which by the exercise of our faith with ourselves we receive. And St Jerome, in the third book upon Ecclesiastes, affirmeth that "we are fed with the body of Christ, and we drink his blood, not only in mystery, but also in knowledge of holy scripture[2]:" where he plainly sheweth that the same meat is offered in the words of the scriptures, which is offered in the sacraments; so that no less is Christ's body and blood offered by the scriptures, than by the sacraments. Upon the hundred and forty-seventh Psalm he writeth also, that "though these words, 'he that eateth my flesh, and drinketh my blood,' may be understand in mystery, yet," saith he, "it is more[3] true to take Christ's body and his blood for the word of the scriptures and the doctrine of God[4]." Yea, upon the same Psalm he saith plainly, that "Christ's flesh and blood is poured into our ears by hearing the word, and therefore great is the peril if we yield to other cogitations while we hear it[5]." And therefore, I trow, St Austin saith that "it is no less peril to hear God's word negligently than so to

[1 .. ut scilicet quotidianum panem simul petamus et necessarium corpori, et sacratum visibilem, et invisibilem [Sic plerique MSS. At editi, 'et sacramentum visibile et invisibile *annot. ed. Bened.*] verbi Dei.—August. In Serm. Dom. in Monte, II. vii. Op. III. II. col. 211, ed. Bened. Par. 1679—1700.]

[2 hoc solum habemus in præsenti seculo bonum, si vescamur carne ejus, et cruore potemur, non solum in mysterio, sed etiam in scripturarum lectione.—Hieron. Comm. in Eccles. cap. III. Op. III. col. 413, stud. Vallars. Veron. 1734—42.]

[3 'now,' MS. 1. 2. 8: 'more' 1574.]

[4 . quando dicit, 'qui non comederit carnem meam, et biberit sanguinem meum,' licet et in mysterio possit intelligi, tamen verius corpus Christi, et sanguis ejus, sermo scripturarum est, doctrina divina est.—Id. Breviar. in Psalt. Psal. cxlvii Op. VII. Append. col. 385. The commentary on the Psalms attributed to Jerome is considered spurious: vide Cave, Hist. Liter. I. 273. Oxon. 1740.]

[5 Si quando audimus sermonem Dei, et sermo Dei et caro Christi et sanguis ejus in auribus nostris funditur, et nos aliud cogitamus, in quantum periculum incurrimus!—Id. ibid.]

use the sacrament[6]." But hereout may no man gather that therefore it needeth not to receive the sacrament; or to affirm that a man may as much by himself meditating the word in the field receive Christ's body, as in the[7] church in the right use of the sacraments: for Christ ordaineth nothing in vain or superfluously; he ordaineth nothing whereof we have not need; although his authority is such that without any questioning his ordinances are to be obeyed.

Again, though in the field a man may receive Christ's body by faith, in the meditation of his word; yet deny I that a man doth ordinarily receive Christ's body, by the only meditation of Christ's death or hearing of his word, with so much light and by such sensible assurance (whereof, God knoweth, our infirmity hath no small need), as by the receipt of the sacrament. Not that Christ is not so much present in his word preached, as he is in or with his sacrament; but because there are in the perception of the sacrament more windows open for Christ to enter into us, than by his word preached or heard. For there (I mean in the word) he hath an entrance into our hearts, but only by the ears through the voice and sound of the words; but here in the sacrament he hath an entrance by all our senses, by our eyes, by our nose, by our taste, and by our handling also: and therefore the sacrament full well may be called seeable, sensible, tasteable, and touchable words. As therefore when many windows are opened in a house, the more light may come in than when there is but one opened; even so by the perception of the sacraments a christian man's conscience hath more help to receive Christ, than simply by the word preached, heard, or meditated. And therefore, methinks, the apostle full well calleth the sacraments obsignations or "sealings" of God's promise. Read Romans the[7] fourth, of circumcision.

And thus much for the answer to the objection aforesaid.

Now to return from whence[8] we came, namely to the consideration of the second thing, what the sacrament is; *What body and blood of Christ we receive.*

[6 non minus reus erit qui verbum Dei negligenter audierit, quam ille qui corpus Christi in terram cadere negligentia sua permiserit.—August. Serm. supposit. ccc. 2. (al. Homil. quinquag. XXVI.) Op. V Append. col. 504, ed. Bened. Par. 1679—1700.]

[7 'the' 1574: not in MS. 1. 2. 8.]

[8 'thence,' MS. 1. 2. 8: 'whence' 1574.]

I have told you that it is not simply bread and wine, but rather Christ's body, so called of Christ and so to be called and esteemed of us. But here let us mark what body and what blood Christ called it. The papists still babble, "This," "this is my body, this is my blood:" but what body it is, what blood it is, they shew not. Look therefore, my dearly beloved, on Christ's own words; and you shall see that Christ calleth it "his body broken" and "his blood shed." Mark, I say, that Christ calleth it "his body which is broken," "his blood which is shed" presently; and not 'which was broken' or 'shall be broken,' 'which was shed' or 'shall be shed,' but "which is shed," "which is broken" presently[1], as the Greek texts[2] do plainly shew: thereby teaching us, that as God would have the passover called, not 'which was the passover,' or 'which shall be the passover,' but plainly "the passover," to the end that in the use of it 'the passing over' of the striking angel should be set before their eyes as present; so in the celebration of the Lord's supper the very passion of Christ should be as present, beholden[3] with the eyes of faith: for which end Christ our Saviour did especially institute this supper, saying, "Do you this in remembrance of me;" or, as Paul saith, "Shew you the Lord's death till he come."

The supper of the Lord then is not simply Christ's 'body and blood,' but Christ's "body broken and his blood shed." Wherefore broken? wherefore shed? Forsooth that teacheth Christ himself, saying, "broken for you," and "shed for your sins and for the sins of many." Here now then we have occasion, in the use of this sacrament, to call to mind the gravity and grievousness of sin, which could not be taken away by any other means than by the shedding of the most precious blood, and breaking of the most pure body of the only-begotten Son of God, Jesus Christ, by whom all things were made, all things are ruled and governed. O who considering this gear shall not be touched[4] to repent? Who, in receipt of this sacrament, thinking that Christ saith to him, 'Take, eat, this is my body which is broken for thee, This is my blood

The sacrament teacheth repentance.

[1 The last eight words in MS. 1. 2. 8.: not in 1574.]
[2 Τοῦτό μου ἐστὶ τὸ σῶμα τὸ ὑπὲρ ὑμῶν κλώμενον.—1 Cor. xi. 24.
Τοῦτο γάρ ἐστι τὸ αἷμά μου, τὸ τῆς καινῆς διαθήκης, τὸ περὶ πολλῶν ἐκχυνόμενον.—Matt. xxvi. 28; Mark xiv. 24; and see Luke xxii. 20.]
[3 'beholding it,' MS. 1. 2. 8.: 'beholden' 1574.]
[4 'teached' MS. 2. 2. 16.: 'taught,' MS. 1. 2. 8.: 'touched' 1574.]

which is shed for thy sins,' can but tremble at the grievousness of his sins, for the which such a price was paid? If there were no plague at all else to admonish man of sin, how grievous a thing it is in God's sight, surely that one were enough. But, alas, how bewitched are our hearts through Satan's subtleties and the custom of sin, that we make sin a thing of nothing!

God open our eyes in time and give us repentance; which we see this sacrament doth, as it were, enforce us unto in the reverent and true use of the same.

Again, in hearing that this which we take and eat is Christ's 'body broken for our sins' and his 'blood shed for our iniquities,' we are occasioned to call to mind the infinite greatness of God's mercy and truth, and of Christ's love towards us. For what a mercy is this, that God would for man, being[5] lost through his own wilful sins, be content, yea, desirous to give his own only Son, "the image of his substance, the brightness of his glory," "being in his own bosom," to be made man for us, that we men by him might be, as it were, made[6] gods! What a mercy is this, that God the Father so should tender[7] us, that he would make this his Son, being[8] co-equal with him in Divinity[9], a mortal man[10] for us, that we might be made immortal by him[11]! What a kindness is this, that the Almighty Lord should send to us his enemies his dear darling to be made poor, that we by him[11] might be made rich! What bowels of compassion is this, that the omnipotent Creator of heaven and earth would deliver his own only beloved Son for us creatures, to be not only flesh of our flesh and bone of our bones, that we might by him through the Holy Ghost be made one with him and so with the Father, by taking of him[12] the merits of his flesh, that is, righteousness, holiness, innocency, and immortality; but also to be a slain sacrifice for our sins, to satisfy his justice, to convert or[13] turn

The sacrament teacheth faith.

Heb. i.
John i.

Rom. v.
2 Cor. viii.

Eph. v.

[5 'being,' MS. 2. 2. 16. and 1574: not in MS. 1. 2. 8.]
[6 'made' 1574: not in MS. 1. 2. 8.]
[7 Tender: regard or treat with tenderness.]
[8 'being' 1574: not in MS. 1. 2. 8.]
[9 'in Divinity' 1574: not in MS. 1. 2. 8.]
[10 'mortal,' MS. 1. 2. 8.: 'a mortal man' 1574.]
[11 'by him' 1574: not in MS. 1. 2. 8.]
[12 'taking of him,' MS. 2. 2. 16.: 'communicating,' MS. 1. 2. 8. and 1574.]
[13 'and,' MS. 1. 2. 8.: 'or' 1574.]

death into life, our sin into righteousness, hell into heaven, misery into felicity for us[1]! What a mercy is this, that God would raise up this his Son Christ, not only to justify and regenerate us, but also in his person to demonstrate unto us our state which we shall have! for in his coming "we shall be like unto him." O wonderful mercy of God, which would assume this his Christ, even in human[2] body, "into the heavens," to take and keep there possession for us, to "lead our captivity captive," to appear before him always praying for us, to make the throne of justice a throne of mercy, the seat of glory a seat of grace! so that with boldness we may come and appear before God, to ask and "find grace in time convenient." Again what a verity and constant truth in God is this, that he[3] would, according to his promise made first unto Adam and so to Abraham and others, in his time accomplish it by sending his Son so graciously! Who would doubt hereafter of any thing that he hath promised?

And as for Christ's love, O whose heart can be able to think of it any thing as it deserveth? He being God would become man: he being rich would become poor: he being Lord of all[4] the world would become[5] a slave to us all: he being immortal would become mortal, miserable, and taste of all God's curses, yea, even of hell itself for us! His blood was nothing too dear, his life he nothing considered, to bring us from death to life. But this his love needeth more hearty weighing than many words speaking: and therefore I omit and leave it to your consideration.

So that in the receipt of this supper, as I would you would tremble at God's wrath for sin; so would I have you to couple to that terror and fear true faith, by which ye might be assuredly[6] persuaded of God's mercy towards you and Christ's love, though all things else preached the contrary.

Surely do every of you think, when you hear these words, 'Take, eat, this is my body broken for your sins: Drink, this is my blood shed for your sins;' that God the

[1 So 1574: MS. 1. 2. 8. has 'death into life, to make sin unto us grace, hell to us heaven, misery felicity!']

[2 'human' 1574: not in MS. 1. 2. 8.]

[3 'he' 1574: not in MS. 1. 2. 8.]

[4 'all,' MS. 2. 2. 16.: not in MS. 1. 2. 8. or 1574.]

[5 'would become,' MS. 2. 2. 16.: 'became,' MS. 1. 2. 8. and 1574.]

[6 So 1574: 'faith which might assuredly be,' MS. 1. 2. 8.]

eternal Father embraceth you, Christ calleth and clepeth[7] you most lovingly, making himself one with you, and you one with him, and one with another amongst yourselves. You ought no less to be certain now that God loveth you, pardoneth your sins, and that Christ is all yours, than if you did hear an angel from heaven speaking so unto you. And therefore rejoice and be glad, and make this supper *eucharistiam,* 'a thanksgiving[8],' as the fathers named it. Be no less certain that now[9] Christ and you are[10] all one, than you are[10] certain the bread and wine is one with your nature and substance after you have eaten and drunken it. Howbeit in this it differeth, that you by faith are, as it were, changed[11] into Christ, and not Christ into you, as the bread is[12]; for by faith he dwelleth in us, and we in him.

God give us faith in the use of this sacrament to receive Christ, as he giveth us hands to receive the element, symbol, and visible sacrament! God grant us, not to "prepare our teeth and belly" (as St Austin saith[13]), but rather of his mercy he prepare, and give us true and lively faith to use this and all other his ordinances to his glory and our own comforts. He sweep the houses of our hearts, and make them clean, that they may be a worthy harborough[14] and lodging for the Lord. Amen.

[III.] Now let us come and look on the Third and last thing, namely, Wherefore the Lord did institute this sacrament.

<small>3 Wherefore the sacrament was instituted.</small>

Our nature is very oblivious of God and of all his benefits: and again it is very full of dubitation and doubtings of God's love and of his kindness. Therefore to the end these two things might be something reformed and holpen in us, the Lord hath instituted this sacrament; I mean that we might

[7 i. e. nameth, calleth.]

[8 'a thanksgiving' 1574: not in the MSS.]

[9 'now,' MS. 2. 2. 16.: not in MS. 1. 2. 8.]

[10 'are,' MS. 2. 2. 16.: 'be,' MS. 1. 2. 8. and 1574.]

[11 'are, as it were, changed,' MS. 1. 2. 8. and 1574: 'pass,' MS. 2. 2. 16.]

[12 'is' 1574 'doeth,' MS. 1. 2. 8.]

[13 Utquid paras dentes et ventrem? Crede, et manducasti.—August. In Joann. Evang. vi. Tract. xxv. 12. Op. III. ii. col. 489, ed. Bened. Par. 1679—1700.]

[14 i. e. harbour, station.]

have in memory the principal benefit of all benefits, that is, Christ's death; and that we might be on all parts assured of communion with Christ, of all kindness the greatest that ever God did give unto man.

The former to be the end wherefore Christ did institute this sacrament, he himself doth teach us, saying, "Do you this in remembrance of me." The latter the apostle doth no less set forth in saying, "The bread which we break, is it not the partaking (or communion) of the body of Christ? Is not the cup of blessing which we bless the partaking (or communion) of the blood of Christ?" So that it appeareth, the end wherefore this sacrament was instituted was and is for the reformation and help of our oblivion of that which we should never forget, and of[1] our dubitations of that whereof we ought to be most certain.

<small>What commodities we have of our communion with Christ.</small>

Concerning the former, namely of the memory of Christ's death, what commodity it bringeth with it, I will purposely for time's sake omit. Only a little will I speak of the commodities coming unto us by the partaking and communion we have with Christ. First, it teacheth us that no man can communicate with Christ but the same must needs communicate with God's grace and favour, wherethrough sins are forgiven. Therefore this commodity cometh herethrough, namely, that we should be certain of the remission and pardon of our sins: the which thing we may also perceive by the cup, in that it is called "the cup of the new Testament," to which new Testament is properly attributed on God's behalf oblivion or "remission of our sins." First, I say therefore, the supper is instituted to this end, that he which worthily receiveth should be certain of the remission and pardon of his sins and iniquities, how many and great soever they be. How great a benefit this is, only they know which have felt the burden of sin, which of all heavy things is the most heavy.

Again, no man can communicate with Christ's body and blood but the same must communicate with his Spirit; for Christ's body is no dead carcase. Now he that communicateth with Christ's Spirit communicateth, as with holiness, righteousness, innocency, and immortality, and with all the merits of Christ's body; so doth he with God and all his glory, and with the church, and all the good that ever it or any member

[1 'of,' MS. 2. 2. 16. and 1574: 'for,' MS. 1. 2. 8.]

of it had, hath[2], or shall have; for which causes' sake, the supper used to be called of the fathers *eucharistiam*, 'a thanksgiving[3].' This is 'the communion of saints' which we believe in our creed, which hath waiting on it 'remission of sins, resurrection of the flesh, and life everlasting.'

Note. Though I apply this thus, yet I would not that any man should think that communionem sanctorum *in the creed is not set forth there for the better explication of that which precedeth it; namely what the holy catholic church is.*

To the end that we should be most assured and certain of all these, Christ our Saviour did institute this his supper; and therefore would have us to use it. So that there is no man, I trow, which seeth not great cause of giving thanks to God for this holy sacrament of the Lord: whereby, if we worthily receive it, we ought to be certain that all our sins, whatsoever they be, are pardoned clearly; that we are counted for God's children[4]; that we are regenerate and "born again into a lively hope, into an inheritance immortal, undefiled, and which can never wither away;" that we are in the fellowship of God the Father, the Son, and the Holy Ghost; that we are God's temples, one with God, and God one with us; that we are members of Christ's church, and fellows with the saints in all felicity; that we are certain of immortality in soul and body, and so of eternal life: than which things what can be more demanded? Christ is ours, and we are Christ's: he dwelleth in us, and we in him. O happy eyes that see these things; and most happy hearts that feel them!

1 Pet. i.
1 John i.
1 Cor. vi.
2 Cor. vi.

My dearly beloved, let us pray unto the Lord to open our eyes to see these wonderful things, to give us faith to feel them. Surely we ought no less to be assured of them now in the worthy receipt of this sacrament, than we are assured of the exterior symbols and sacraments. If an angel should come from heaven[5] and tell you these things, then would you rejoice and be glad. And, my dear hearts in the Lord, I even now, though most unworthy, am sent of the Lord to tell you no less but that you, worthily receiving this sacrament, shall receive remission of all your sins, or rather certainty that they are remitted; and that you are

[2 'have,' MS. 1. 2. 8.: 'hath' 1574.]

[3 The last sixteen words occur only in the autograph MS. 2. 2. 16. no. 20. in Emmanuel College, Cambridge.]

[4 'that we are counted for God's children' is only found in the autograph MS. 2. 2. 16. no. 20.]

[5 So MS. 2. 2. 16.: 'from heaven should come,' MS. 1. 2. 8. and 1574.]

even[1] now God's darlings, temples, and fellow-inheritors of all the good that ever he hath. Wherefore see that you give thanks unto the Lord for this his great goodness, and praise his name for ever.

An objection of unworthy receiving. Oh, saith one, I could be very glad indeed and give thanks from my very heart, if that I did worthily receive this sacrament. But, alas! I am a very grievous sinner, and I feel in myself very little repentance and faith: therefore I am afraid that I am unworthy.

The answer. To the answering of this objection, I think it necessary to speak something of the worthy receiving of this sacrament, in as great brevity and plainness as I can.

The apostle willeth all men to prove and "examine themselves before they eat of the bread and drink of the cup; for they that eat and drink unworthily eat and drink damnation:" therefore this probation and examination is necessary. If men will try their gold and silver, whether they be copper or no, is it not more necessary that men should try their consciences? Now how this should be, the papists teach amiss, in sending us to their auricular confession, and to the numbering of their sins[2], which is impossible.

Of the trial of ourselves before the Lord's supper. The true probation and trial of a christian conscience consisteth altogether in faith and repentance. Faith hath respect to the doctrine and articles of our belief: repentance hath respect to manners and conversation. Concerning the former (I mean of faith) we may see the apostle teacheth us, 1 Cor. xi. Concerning the latter, for our conversation, those sins which are called commonly mortal or deadly are to be removed. These sins are discerned from other sins by the apostle (Rom. vi.), in saying, "Let not sin reign and bear a *Deadly sin, what it is.* swing in your mortal bodies:" for truly then we sin deadly, when we give over to sin and let him have the bridle at his liberty, when we strive not against it, but allow it and consent unto it. Howbeit, if we strive against it, if it displease us, then truly, though sin be in us (for we ought to obey God without all resistance or unwillingness), yet our sin is not of those sins which do separate us from God, but for Christ's sake shall not be imputed unto us believing.

Therefore, my dearly beloved, if that your sins do now

[1 'even,' MS. 2. 2. 16. and 1574: not in MS. 1. 2. 8.]
[2 The last seven words in MS. 1. 2. 8., but not in 1574.]

displease you; if you purpose unfeignedly to be enemies to sin in yourselves and in others, (as you may during your whole life if you hope in Christ for pardon;) if you believe according to the holy scriptures and[3] articles of the christian faith set forth in your creed; if, I say, you now trust in God's mercy through Christ's merits; if you repent and earnestly purpose before God to amend your life, and to give over yourselves to serve the Lord in holiness and righteousness all the days of your life, (although before this present you have most grievously sinned;) I publish unto you that[4] you are worthy guests for this table, you shall be welcome to Christ, your sins shall be pardoned, you shall be endued[5] with his Spirit, and so with communion with him and the Father, and with[6] the whole church of God: Christ will dwell in you, and you shall dwell in him for evermore.

Wherefore behave yourselves accordingly with joyfulness and thanksgiving. Do you now appear before the Lord, make clean your houses, and open the doors of your hearts by repentance and faith, that "the Lord of hosts, the King of glory," may "enter in": and for ever hereafter beware of all such things as might displease the eyes of his majesty. Fly from sin as from a toad: come away from popery and all antichristian religion. Be diligent in your vocations, be diligent and earnest in prayer, hearken to the voice of God in his word with reverence, live worthy your profession. "Let your light in your life so shine, that men may see your good works, and glorify your[7] Father which is in heaven." As you have been darkness, and followed "the works of darkness;" so now henceforth be "light in the Lord," and have society with the works of light.

Now hath God renewed his covenant with you: in God's sight now are you as clean and healed from all your sores of sins. Go your ways, "sin no more lest a worse thing happen unto you." See that your house "being new swept be furnished" with godliness and virtue; and beware of idleness, lest the devil come "with seven spirits worse than

[3 'holy scriptures and' 1574: not in MS. 1. 2. 8.]
[4 'that' MS. 2. 2. 16. and 1574: not in MS. 1. 2. 8.]
[5 So 1574: 'you shall be endued' after 'of God,' in MS. 1. 2. 8.]
[6 'with,' MS. 2. 2. 16.: not in MS. 1. 2. 8. or 1574.]
[7 'the,' MS. 1. 2. 8.: 'your,' MS. 2. 2. 16. and 1574.]

himself," and so take his lodging; and then your latter end will be worse than the first.

God our Father, for the tender mercy and merits of his Son, be merciful unto us, forgive us all our sins, and give us his holy Spirit, to purge, cleanse, and sanctify us, that we may be holy in his sight through Christ; and that we now may be made ready and worthy to receive this holy sacrament with the fruits of the same, to the full rejoicing and strengthening of our hearts in the Lord.
To whom be all honour and glory,
world without end.
Amen.

To God be all praise for ever[1].

JOHN BRADFORD.

[The following is the colophon of the edition of Two Sermons by Bradford, 1574, which has been collated: vide p. 27, 28, above.]

Imprinted at
London by Iohn Awdeley, and John wyght.
The. xxx. of September.
Anno Domini.
1574

[1 This line occurs in the autograph MS. 2. 2. 16. no. 20, but apparently in a different, though contemporary hand: it is also in 1574, but not in MS. 1. 2. 8.]

BRADFORD PREACHING BEFORE THE COURT

OF

EDWARD VI.

[The following account of the faithfulness of John Bradford in rebuking the worldliness of the courtiers of Edward VI.[1] is supplied by Knox the Scottish Reformer in his 'Godly Letter to the faithful in London, Newcastle, and Berwick,' &c. 1554.]

... Master Bradford (whom God for Christ's his Son sake comfort to the end) spared not the proudest; but boldly declared that God's vengeance shortly should strike those that then were in authority, because they loathed and abhorred the true word of the everlasting God; and amongst many other[3] willed them to take ensample by the late duke of Somerset, who became so cold in hearing God's word, that, the year before his last apprehension, he would go to visit his masons, and would not dingy[4] himself from his gallery to go to his hall for hearing of a sermon. *Harl. MSS. 416. no. 30. fol. 50—1. British Museum.* *Letter to the faithful, &c., by Knox, Singleton 1554: signature A viii.[2]*

'God punished him,' said that godly preacher, 'and that suddenly: and shall he spare you that be double more wicked? No, he shall not. Will ye or will ye not, ye shall drink the cup of the Lord's wrath. *Judicium Domini, judicium Domini!* The judgment of the Lord, the judgment of the Lord!' lamentably cried he with a lamentable voice and weeping tears[5].

[1 Bradford had been appointed one of the six chaplains to the king, Dec. 18, 1551.—Edward VI. Diary in Bp. Burnet, Reform. Records. Vide also Strype, Mem. II. i. 522—4, Cranmer, I. 432; Mc Crie, Life of Knox 1812, p. 68.]

[2 Copy, British Museum, professedly printed at Rome, but has the device of Singleton: vide Herbert, Typogr. Antiq. II. 741.]

[3 'amongst many other,' a MS. quoted by Mc Crie, in his own possession, ibid. Append. p. 435: not in the Harl. MS.]

[4 Dingy: 'vex' or 'trouble.' Vide Jamieson, Suppl. to Dict. v. 'ding,' who however explains the word 'dingyie' in the passage above by 'deign.' 'Danger' Harl. MS.: 'disease,' ed. Singleton 1554: 'dingyie,' the MS. quoted by Mc Crie, ibid.]

[5 Compare the testimony to the preaching of Bradford given by Bp. Ridley, Works, Parker Soc. 59, 331. A description like that of Knox, which may possibly refer to the same occasion, occurs in the Preface of Sampson, p. 31 above.]

[The following " Godly Meditations with other exercises," "gathered by John Bradford in the time of his imprisonment," which occupy p. 116—220 of the present volume, were, for the most part, "first printed"[1] by Hall 1562, and are now republished, with the exceptions hereafter mentioned, from a copy of that impression belonging to the editor.

The greater part of the 'prayer on the work of Christ' (entitled in the Meditations 1562, 'a prayer for deliverance from sin and to be restored to God's grace and favour again') is now printed for the first time from a MS. in the Library of Emmanuel College, Cambridge.

Various prayers and meditations in the following series follow the text of MSS. also in Emmanuel College (as noted in the margin of each), and have been collated with the printed edition of 1562.

The following memorandum is printed in a copy of the Meditations of 1562, in the collection of the late George Stokes, Esq., on a separate paper, evidently belonging to that book, and annexed to signature I iii, after the meditation on the ninth commandment:

"¶ Through unperfectness of copies his doing upon the tenth commandment is not yet come to light: therefore take this in good part till God send the rest."

Lever "added his endeavour to supply that lack," in the collection of Meditations and other pieces by Bradford, printed by Seres 1567, (of which the title is supplied further on in this volume;) of which he speaks with much humility in a preface which, with the meditation he furnished, is printed in the Appendix to this volume, from a copy which had belonged to the late Rev. Legh Richmond, now in the possession of the Rev. J. Ayre.

The meditation on the tenth commandment given in the present volume follows the text of a copy of the "Godly Meditations" of Bradford, Allde 1604, in the University Library, Cambridge.

The "Godly Meditations," 1562, have been occasionally compared with a copy of the edition of Allde 1578, belonging to the Rev. W H. Havergal, Prebendary of Worcester, and with 1604, 1607, 1614, and 1621; as also with 1567 in the meditations on the Lord's prayer, belief, commandments, and on prayer. The text of 1604 in the tenth commandment has been collated with 1607, 1614, and 1621.

The 'meditation on the Lord's Prayer,' from p. 118 to 126 line 16, and that 'on the belief,' p. 140—8, have also (as noted on the margin of each) been collated with MSS. in Emmanuel College, Cambridge, with which the printed text of 1562 generally agrees closely.

The variations however are only noted in special cases.

The portion of the 'Defence of election' given in the collection of 1562 is printed further on in the present volume, together with its other parts, as a separate treatise, as found in a MS. in the Bodleian Library, Oxford.]

[1 See title of that edition, p. 114 of this volume.]

GODLY MEDITATIONS

ON THE

LORD'S PRAYER, BELIEF,

AND

TEN COMMANDMENTS,

WITH OTHER EXERCISES,

BY

JOHN BRADFORD.

GODLIE
meditations vpon
THE LORDES PRAYER, THE
beleefe, and ten commaundementes, with other comfortable meditations, praiers and exercises.
Whereunto is annexed a defence of the doctrine of gods eternall election and predestination, gathered by the constant martyr of God John Bradford in the tyme of his imprisonment.

The contentes wherof appeare in the page nexte folowyng.

DARK.   P O S T   NES,

T E N E B R A S

AFTER   L V X   LIGHT.

Nowe fyrst prynted by Rouland Hall, dwellyng in gutter lane at the signe of the halfe Egle and key, the. 12. of October 1562.

TO THE READER[1].

HERE hast thou, good reader, such godly meditations, prayers, and other exercises of that worthy witness of God, John Bradford, as God by his singular providence hath hitherto preserved, and now at the length brought to light, for thy comfort and commodity. Daily and hourly was this his exercise, to talk with God by faithful and hearty meditation and prayer, with power piercing the heavens: and many such godly exercises did he leave behind him, which either time hath consumed, or else such as keep them in store to their own private use do little consider what benefit they withhold from the church of God; which if they shall yet brotherly communicate, there shall not lack good will and diligence to set them abroad. In the mean season, let us with thankfulness receive, read, and practise these, as means to quicken our spirits, to stir up our dull hearts to a more fervent invocation of God's holy name: which, how far it is from that it should be in us, and what need we have thereof, if our dead senses cannot feel, here may we see and perceive. Here may we learn to flee unto God by prayer, that we run not on still with this unthankful world into forgetfulness of his great benefits poured upon us, especially for the liberty of his gospel which we (in much mercy restored now unto us again) so unthankfully receive, so ungodly neglect, so wickedly abuse. God grant us his good Spirit to work in us this good work, to look about us in time; to consider our state past and present, as indeed we have great cause to do; and so with hearty prayer flee unto God to prevent the plagues that are at hand; lest with double woe we find the latter end worse than the beginning.

[1 This advertisement 'to the reader' was prefixed first to the 'Godly Meditations' of Bradford, Hall 1562, and was reprinted in various after editions.]

INSTRUCTIONS

TO BE OBSERVED CONCERNING PRAYER.

THERE be nine things that pertain to the knowledge of true prayer. First, to know what prayer is. Secondly, how many sorts of prayer there be. Thirdly, the necessity of prayer. Fourthly, to whom we ought to pray. By whom we must pray. Where to pray, and what to pray. The excellency of prayer. What we must do, that our prayers may be heard.

[1] What prayer is.

Prayer is a simple, unfeigned, humble, and ardent opening of the heart before God, wherein we either ask things needful, or give thanks for benefits received. Paul, in the first to Timothy and second chapter, calleth it by four sundry names in one sentence, to wit, " prayer, supplication, intercession, and thanksgiving ;" in Latin, *deprecatio, obsecratio, intercessio, et gratiarum actio*. Whereof the first is for the avoiding and preventing of evil; the second is an earnest and fervent calling upon God for any thing; the third is an intercession for other; the fourth is a praising of God for things received.

2. There be two manner of ways how we should pray.

First publicly, and that is called common prayer; and privately, as when men pray alone, and that is called private prayer: and how both these two are allowed before God, the scripture beareth testimony by the example of all the holy men and women before and after Christ.

3. Of the necessity of prayer.

There be four things that provoke us to pray: first the commandment of God; secondly, sin in us, which driveth us of necessity to God for succour, life, and mercy; thirdly, our weak nature being unable to do any good requireth prayer to strengthen it, even as a house requireth principal pillars for the upholding of it; fourthly, the subtlety of the enemy (who privily lurketh in the inward parts, waiting to overthrow us, even in those things which we think to be best done) stirreth us vehemently thereunto.

4. To whom we ought to pray.

Three things pertain to him that must be prayed unto: first, that he have such ears as may hear all the world at once; secondly, that he be in all places at once; thirdly, that he have such power that he may be able to help, and such mercy that he will deliver.

5. By whom we should pray.

Christ only is "the way" by whom we have free access unto the Father, and for whom our prayers are accepted, our infirmities notwithstanding: without whom all our prayers are abominable.

6. 7. Where to pray, and what to pray.

As touching the place where we should pray, seeing all places are one, there is none forbidden: only the common prayer must be made in what place soever the congregation of Christ doth assemble.

What to pray, lieth in the necessity of every man: and forasmuch as we need both spiritual and corporal things, we may boldly ask them both; for, as to ask spiritual gifts it is profitable and commanded, so to ask corporal it is necessary and allowed.

8. Of the excellency of prayer.

The worthiness of prayer consisteth in two things; in the dignity of the commander who is God, the fountain of all goodness, who also commandeth only good things; and in the effect that followeth it, which is the obtaining of whatsoever we desire faithfully according to the will of God.

9. What to do that we may be heard.

First we must put off our own righteousness, pride, and estimation of ourselves, and "put on Christ" with his righteousness: secondly, an earnest faith and fervent love, with the putting off all rancour, malice, and envy, is required: finally true repentance knitteth up the knot, for in it are contained all the virtues aforenamed.

J. BRADFORD.

A MEDITATION
OF THE
LORD'S PRAYER.[1]

OUR FATHER.

<small>Meditations of Bradford, Hall 1562, and after editions.</small>

<small>MS. 1, 2, 8. No. 77. Emmanuel College, Cambridge[2].</small>

<small>Gen. i. iii. xii. xxii. xxiii. xxiv. xxv. Exod. xiii. xiv. xv. &c. xix. xx. Heb. i. 1 Cor. xv. Rom. v.</small>

<small>Matt. i. Luke i.</small>

<small>Gen. iii. xii. xxvi. xxviii. Psal. lxxxix.</small>

<small>2 Sam. vii. Luke i. Psal. cx.</small>

<small>Rom. viii.</small>

THOU, good Lord, which madest heaven and earth, the sea, and all that is therein, together with thy dearly beloved Son Jesus Christ, and with thy holy Spirit; thou, the same God which openedst thyself to Adam by thy promise; thou, "the God of Abraham, Isaac, and Jacob;" thou which "broughtest thy people of Israel forth of Egypt with a mighty hand and a stretched-out power;" thou which gavest thy law upon mount Sinai; thou which spakest by thy prophets, and last of all "in these latter days" by thy dearly beloved Son Jesus Christ, (whom thou wouldest should be made a second Adam, that as by the first we are "children of wrath," carnal, and full of concupiscence, so by him we might be made 'children of grace' and spiritual, by communicating with him the quality, merits, virtues, and grace of his flesh, through the operation of the Holy Spirit, as he communicated with us the substance of our flesh in the womb of the virgin Mary, by the operation of the same Holy Spirit; being that blessed Seed which was promised to Adam, Abraham, Isaac, Jacob, David, which should "bruise the serpent's head," which should bring "the blessing on all nations," which should reign over thy house for ever, and mightily overcome thine and our enemies; as indeed he did by his incarnation, nativity, circumcision, exile, baptism, fasting, temptation, doctrine, deeds, miracles, workings, agonies, bloody prayer, passion, death, resurrection, and ascension; and yet he still doth by his mediation and interces-

[1 The meditation 'on the Lord's Prayer,' p. 118—39; 'on prayer,' p. 173—80; and on 'the second coming of Christ,' p. 185—7; after appearing in the 'Godly Meditations' of Bradford, Hall 1562, were printed in the 'Christian Prayers,' &c. collected by Henry Bull, Powell (probably 1565, see ref. to 'Ludlowe's prayers,' which are part of that collection, in Herbert, Typogr. Antiq. II. 735), and Middleton 1570: vide Parker Soc. edition, p. 9—41, 1—9, and 98—101.]

[2 This MS. has on a blank leaf the words prefixed, "Familiaris meditatio in Orationem Dominicam per dominum Joannem Bradfordum."]

sion for us; and at the length he will on all parts fully accomplish by his coming to judgment, which will be suddenly, "in the twinkling of an eye," "in the blast of a trumpet," and "shout of an archangel;" when he shall be seen "with thousands of saints" and "innumerable thousands of angels," all the whole world being on fire, and all people that ever were, are, or shall be, then standing before his tribunal or "judgment-seat," to render an account of that they have done in this body, be it good or bad:) thou, I say, this God which art holy, righteous, true, wise, pure, chaste, mighty, "merciful, good, gracious," a hater of sin, an avenger of unrighteousness, &c., wouldest that I, which am "born in sin and conceived in iniquity," which by nature am a "child of wrath," (for my heart is so unsearchably evil, that out of it springeth corrupt concupiscence, so that the inclination thereof is prone to evil always even from my youth up; as is my understanding and mind so darkened that I cannot perceive those things that be of God of myself, and by all[3] the wisdom which I receive from Adam naturally, or otherwise attain by labour or study before regeneration: I cannot think a good thought, much less wish it or consent unto it, and least of all do it[4]:) thou, I say, yet wouldest that I being such a one in whom dwelleth continual "enmity against thee," that I which am nothing but sin, and one that doeth evil always before thee, should call thee and believe thee, this God and Father of our Lord and Saviour Jesus Christ, to be in very deed my Father.

  That is, thou wouldest I should be most assured that thou of thine own good will which thou barest to me-wards before I was, yea, before the world was, hast in Christ chosen me to be thy child, and through him art become my most loving Father; from whom I should look for all good things, and be most certainly persuaded that, look how much thou art more than man, so much thy love and fatherly providence towards me passeth the love and providence of any father towards his child, in loving me, caring how to help me, providing for me, nurturing me, and helping me in all my needs. So certain thou wouldest have me to be of this, that to doubt of it doth most displease thee and dishonour thee, as either thou wert

Matt. xxiv.
1 Cor. xv.
1 Thess. iv.

2 Cor. v.

Exod. xxxiii. xxxiv.
Psal. v.
Joel ii.
Psal. li.
Eph. ii.
Gen. vi. viii.
Jer. xvii.

1 Cor. ii.
2 Cor. iii.

Rom. viii.

When and wherefore God is become our Father.
Eph. i.

We should be certain and without doubt that God is our Father.

The greatest dishonour to God, is to doubt.

[3 'and all' 1562: 'and by all' 1578, 1614.]
[4 So 1562, 1578, 1614: the last eight lines ('my heart is so' 'least of all do it') are printed on the margin of 1567, and are omitted in 1607.]

not true or not able to do these things, or else becamest not my Father in respect of thine own goodness in Christ only, but also in respect of my worthiness and deserts.

<small>Causes to confirm our faith that God is our Father.</small>

And that I should not waver or doubt of this, that thou art my dear Father, and I thy child for ever through Jesus Christ, it is required in the first commandment which saith, "I am the Lord thy God; thou shalt have none other gods but me." Again, thy Son doth here command me to call thee by the name of "Father." Moreover in the first article of my belief I profess the same in saying, 'I believe in God the Father Almighty.' Besides this, there are many other things to confirm me herein, as the creation and government of the world generally, and of every creature particularly; for all is made and kept for man, and so for me, to serve me for my commodity, necessity, and admonition. Again, the creation of me, in that thou hast made me after thy image, having a reasonable soul, body, shape, &c., where thou mightest have made me a toad, a serpent, a swine, deformed, frantic, &c.; moreover thy wonderful conservation, nourishing, and keeping of me hitherto in my infancy, childhood, youth, &c.; all these, I say, should confirm my faith of thy fatherly love.

But of all things, the opening of thyself by thy word and promise of grace made after man's fall, first to Adam, then to Abraham, Isaac, Jacob, and so to other, being published by the prophets from time to time, and last of all accomplished by thy dear Son Jesus Christ, in whom thy

<small>2 Cor. i.</small>

"promises are yea and Amen;" the opening of thyself thus, I say, in and by Christ, is the most chief and sure certificate that thou art my Father for his sake, and I thy dear child, although of myself I am most unworthy. For thou accord-

<small>John iii.</small>

ing to thy promises hast not spared thy dear Son Jesus Christ, but given him to the death of the cross for my sins. Thou wouldest he should be made flesh of our flesh and blood of our blood, in the womb of the virgin Mary, by

<small>Eph. v.</small>

the operation of the Holy Spirit, that we by the working of the same Spirit, through the merits of his flesh and blood, might be made flesh of his flesh and blood of his blood: that is, as he hath the substance of our flesh and blood, even so we might have and for ever enjoy in him and through him the qualities, virtues, and gifts of righteousness, holiness, innocency, immortality, and glory, wherewith he hath endued our nature in his own person for us all; that as now in faith and hope we have the same, so in his coming we might fully enjoy them in very deed, for then shall "our bodies, now vile, be like to his glorious body." Phil. iii.

[He]rein appeareth thy love, "not that we loved thee, but that thou lovedst[1] us," and hast given thy Son for us. Herein dost thou "commend unto us thy love, that when we were yet sinners, Christ thy dear Son died for us;" so that nothing "should separate us from thy love in Christ Jesus, neither death, nor hunger," &c. "For if, when we were enemies, we were reconciled unto thee by the death of thy Son, much more we being reconciled shall be saved by his life." 1 John iv. Rom. v. Rom. viii. Rom. v.

And that I should not doubt hereof, but certainly be persuaded all things to pertain to me; where I might have been born of Turks, lo, thou wouldest I should be born of christian parents, brought into thy church by baptism, which is the sacrament of adoption, and requireth faith, as well of remission of my sins, as of sanctification and holiness to be wrought of thee in me by thy grace and holy Spirit: where I might have been born in an ignorant time and region, thou wouldest I should be born in this time and region, wherein is more knowledge revealed than ever was here, or in many places is: where I might have been of a corrupt judgment, and entangled with many errors, lo, thou of thy goodness, as thou hast reformed my judgment, so dost thou keep it, and now for the same judgment's sake dost vouchsafe somewhat by the cross to try me. What baptism is and what it requireth.

By all which things I should confirm my faith of this, that thou always hast been, art, and wilt be for ever my dear Father: in respect whereof I should be, as certain of salvation and of the inheritance of heaven for ever, so be thankful, cast my whole care on thee, trust on thee, and call on thee, with comfort and certain hope for all things that I want. For, in that thou hast given to me this benefit, to be thy child, undeserved, undesired on my behalf, simply and only in respect of thine own goodness and grace in Christ, lest at any time I should doubt of it; how should I but hope certainly that nothing profitable to me can be denied, in that thy power is infinite? For, as thy good will is declared in What is the effect or fruit that cometh of this certain persuasion, that God is our Father.

[[1] So 1562 corrected in the list of errata, 1567, 1607, 1614: 'lovest' 1578.]

adopting me, so nothing can be finally wanting me which may make for my weal; for that should improve thy power to be almighty, in that thy will is so bounteously already declared; whereas my belief requireth to believe in thee 'the Father Almighty.'

In consideration whereof I should in all things behave myself as a child, rejoice in thee, praise thee, trust in thee, fear thee, serve thee, love thee, call upon thee, &c. But, alas, how heavy-hearted am I! how unthankful am I! how full of unbelief and doubting of this thy rich mercy! how little do I love thee, fear thee, call upon thee! &c.

O be merciful unto me, forgive me, good Father, for thine own sake, and grant me the Spirit of thy children to reveal thyself unto me, and Jesus Christ thy dear Son our Lord, by whom we are made thy children; that I may truly know thee, heartily love thee, faithfully hang upon thee in all my needs, with good hope call upon thee, render faithfully this honour to thee that thou art my God and Father, and I thy dear child through thy grace in Christ; and so always be endued with an assured hope of thy goodness, and a faithful obedient heart in all things to thy holy will. At thy hands and from thee as I must look for all things, so come I unto thee, and pray thee to give me these things which thy dear children have and thou requirest of me, that I might come and ask them of thee, as now I do through Jesus Christ our Lord.

As by this word "Father" I am taught to glory of thee and in thee, and all that ever thou hast, (for thou art wholly mine, my Lord, my God, and my Father;) so by this word "our" I am taught to glory of all the good that all and every of thy servants that ever were, are, or shall be, had, have, and shall have: for now I am taught to believe that thou hast called me into the communion of thy church and people, whom hereby I perceive thou hast commanded to be careful for me as for themselves, and in all their prayers to be as mindful of me as of themselves. Again, as by this word "Father" I am taught to remember and render my duty I owe to thee-wards, faith, love, fear, obedience, &c., so by thy word "our" I am taught my duty towards thy people, to be careful for them, and to take their sorrow, poverty, and affliction, &c., as mine own; and therefore to labour to help them in heart and hand after my vocation and ability, utterly abhorring all pride, self-love, arrogancy, and contempt of any.

By reason whereof I have great cause to lament and to rejoice: to lament, because I am so far from consideration, much more from doing my duty to thy people in thoughts, words, or deeds; to rejoice, because I am called of thee, and placed in the blessed society of thy saints, and made a member and citizen of "the heavenly Jerusalem;" and because thou hast given in commandment to all thy church to be as careful for me as for themselves. But, alas, how far am I herefrom! As I am guilty of unthankfulness for this thy calling me into the blessed communion of thy dear Son and church, yea, of thyself; so am I guilty of self-love, unmercifulness, pride, arrogancy, forgetfulness, contempt of thy children; for else I could not but be otherwise affected and otherwise labour than I do.

O be merciful unto me, good Father, forgive me, and grant for Christ's sake that, as my tongue soundeth this word "our," so I may in heart feel the true joy of thy blessed communion, and the true love and compassion which thy children have and feel towards their brethren; that I may rejoice in all trouble, in respect of that joyful communion; that I may deny myself to honour thy children upon earth, and endeavour myself to do them good for thy sake, through Jesus Christ our Lord. I come only to thee to give me that which I cannot nor must not elsewhere have; and thou requirest it of me, that therefore I should as thy child come and crave it to thy glory.

WHICH ART IN HEAVEN.

As by these words "Our Father," I am taught to glory and rejoice for the blessed communion which I am called to with thee, dear Father, with thy Christ, and with thy holy church; so also am I here taught by these words, "which art in heaven," to rejoice in respect of the place and blessed joys whereunto at the length in thy good time I shall come: for now I may perceive that as heaven is thy home, so is it mine also, being as I am thy child through Christ, although here for a time I am bodily on earth and in misery.

Again by these words, "which art in heaven," I am admonished not only to discern thee from earthly fathers, and to know how that thou art almighty, present in all places, and of most purity, to confirm thereby my faith, to be provoked the more to fear thee, to reverence thee, &c.; but also I am admonished to judge of thy fatherly love by heavenly benefits, and not by corporal simply and alonely; for oftentimes the wicked prosper more in the world, and have more worldly benefits, than thy children. So that by this I see thou wouldest pull up my mind from earth and earthly things to heaven and heavenly things; and that I should see further by corporal benefits thy heavenly providence for me. For if thou place me thus on earth, and thus bless me as thou dost and hitherto hast done from my youth up, in that thou art nothing so careful for my body as for my soul, how should I but think much of thy providence for it in thy home, where is such glory as the "eye hath not seen," &c.? of which things these corporal benefits of thine given me on earth should be as it were inductions, and the taking of them away admonitions to be more mindful of permanent things, and less mindful of transitory things.

By reason hereof I have great cause to lament and to rejoice: to lament, because I am so earthly-minded, so little desirous of my home, so unthankful for thy providence and fatherly correction here on earth; to rejoice, because of my home and the great glory thereof, because thou dost so provide for me here, because thou dost so correct and chasten me, &c. But, alas! I am altogether a wretch, earthly, and unthankful not only for these corporal benefits, health, riches, friends, fame, wisdom, &c., for thy fatherly correction, sickness, temptation, &c., but also for thy heavenly benefits, for Christ Jesus, for the promise of thy Spirit, for thy gospel, &c.; yea, even for heaven itself and thy whole glory; as the Israelites were for the land of Canaan, and therefore never enjoyed it, but perished in the wilderness. I am proud in prosperity, and forget thee, waxing secure and careless, &c.: I am impatient in the cross, and too much consider worldly discommodity.

O dear Father, forgive me for thy Christ's sake all mine unthankfulness, love of this world, contempt and oblivion of thy heavenly benefits; and grant me thy holy Spirit to illuminate the eyes of my mind with the light and lively knowledge of thy presence, power, wisdom, and goodness in thy creatures, but specially in Christ Jesus thy Son; and so by the same Spirit inflame mine affections, that I may desire nothing in earth but thee, and to be present with thee, that my "conversation may be in heaven (continually): from whence" Col. iii. grant me still to "look for the Lord Jesus, to make this my Phil. iii. vile body like unto his own glorious (and immortal) body, according to his own power by which he is able to do all things." As thou hast given me to be thy child, so I pray thee give me these things which be the properties of thy children given from thee in thy good time.

HALLOWED BE THY NAME.

Thy name is that whereby thou art known; for names serve to discern and know one thing from another. Now though thou art known by[1] thy creatures, yet in this our corrupt estate they serve but to make us "excuseless." There- Rom. i. fore properly, most lively, and comfortably thou art known by thy holy word, and specially by thy promise of grace, and freely pardoning and receiving us into thy favour for Christ Jesus' sake: for the which goodness in Christ "thou art praised and magnified according to thy name:" that is, Psal. xlviii. so much as men know thee in Christ, they magnify thee and How God's praise thee; which here thou callest "hallowing" or sanctify- lowed. ing. Not that thou art the more holy in respect of thyself, but in respect of men, who the more they know thee, the more they cannot but sanctify thee: that is, they cannot but as in themselves by true faith, love, fear, and spiritual service, honour thee, so also in their outward behaviour and words they cannot but live in such sort as other seeing them may in and by their holiness and godly conversation be occasioned, as to know thee, so to sanctify thy name accordingly. And therefore thou settest forth here unto me what is the chief and principal wish and desire of thy children and people; The chief desire of God's namely, that thou in Christ mightest be truly known and children. honoured both of themselves and of others, inwardly and outwardly. By reason whereof easily a man may perceive by the contrary, that the greatest sorrow and grief thy The greatest grief of God's people have is ignorance of thee, false service or religion, and people. wicked conversation: against the which they pray and labour diligently after their vocations, as they, for the obtaining of

[[1] i. e. by means of.]

the others both to others and to themselves, do take no small pains in prayer, study, and godly exercise.

Our ignorance.
By reason hereof I see that I am far from this desire and lamentation, which is in thy children. I see mine ignorance of the true knowledge of thee and thy name; for else it had not needed thee so by thy word to have revealed thyself: I see also mine ignorance of the excellency of the same; for else wouldest thou not have told me that the sanctifying of thy name is the chiefest thing thou requirest of every man.

Our great need.
Again, I see my great want of holiness; for else thou needest not to teach me to seek and pray for that I want not.

Our perversity.
Moreover I see my great perversity, which would not seek at thy hands for sanctification, although I see my need thereof; for else thou wouldest not have commanded me to pray for it, if I seeing my want would have prayed unto thee therefor.

God's love.
Last of all I see thy wonderful goodness, which wilt undoubtedly give unto me sanctification and holiness; for thou wouldest not that I should ask for that thing that thou wilt not give me.

So that I have great cause to lament and rejoice: to lament, because I am so far from this desire and lamentation, which thy children have; also because of my ignorance, poverty, perversity, unthankfulness, &c., but most of all because thy holy name, word, and religion, is so blasphemed both in doctrine and living of many, especially in this realm. To rejoice I have great cause for thy exceeding goodness and mercy, which wouldest so disclose thyself by thy works, word, and gospel, which wouldest open these things thus unto me, and also give unto me and others sanctification in thy sight by faith, and in the sight of men by pureness of life and godly conversation. But, alas! I do heartily neither the one nor the other, that is, lament and rejoice, as thou, Father, which searchest my heart, dost right well know.

O be merciful unto me, and forgive me: yea, give me of thine own pity thy holy Spirit to reveal and open to my mind effectually my miserable estate and condition, my ignorance, perversity, and my carelessness for thy true honour and dishonour, in such sort that I may heartily lament these evils, and have them pardoned and taken from me through Jesus Christ our Lord. Again, good Father, give me the same thy holy Spirit to reveal to me thy name, word, and gospel, that I may lively know thee, unfeignedly love thee, heartily obey thee, and above all things desire and labour by all means lawful, that all godliness in doctrine and conversation may be exercised both in me and in all others, for whom thou wouldest I should pray.

Here think upon the state of religion and the life of the professors of the gospel, that you may lament some, pray for some, and give thanks for some.

LET THY KINGDOM COME.

THY kingdom is in two sorts to be considered, universally and particularly: universally, according to thy power, wherewith thou governest all things every where, in earth, heaven, hell, devils, angels, men, beasts, fowls, fishes, and all creatures, animate and inanimate, sensible and insensible: of this kingdom spake David, when he said, "Thy kingdom ruleth over all." Particularly thy kingdom is to be considered according to thy grace, wherewith thou reignest only in thy church and elect people, ruling and governing all and every member of thy church to thy glory and their eternal comfort: not that out of this church I exclude thy power; for as therewith thou defendest thy people, so thou punishest thine enemies; but because thy grace is specially considered, being, as it were, the very keeper that keepeth and guideth thy people. *[margin: God's kingdom in respect of his power. Psal. cliii. God's kingdom in respect of his grace.]*

The time will be when this kingdom of grace and power, now being as distinct, shall be united and made one kingdom of glory; which will be when Christ shall give up his kingdom into thine hands; that is, in the resurrection when "death the last enemy shall be subdued," and thou shalt be "all in all." In the mean season this kingdom of grace is miraculously and mightily propagated, enlarged, and governed by the true ministry of thy word and sacraments, through the working of thy holy Spirit: and this is the mean and way, whereby as thou didst first plant, so dost thou enlarge, amplify, and preserve the same. This kingdom of grace begun, continued, and enlarged by the true preaching of thy gospel and ministration of thy sacraments, is the thing which Christ teacheth here thy children to pray for, that it might come; that is to say, that thy gospel might so mightily, purely, and plenteously be preached (maugre the head of *[margin: God's kingdom in respect of his glory. How God's kingdom here is conserved and enlarged.]*

all thine enemies), that the number of thine elect might be brought in, and so the kingdom of thy glory might appear.

So that as I see thy children desire, pray, and labour, that thy gospel might be truly preached, heard, and lived in themselves, and in others; so they lament the not preaching and refusing, the not living and unbelieving thy gospel: yea, they lament the lingering of the coming of thy Christ; for in his coming they know they shall be "like unto him;" and "having this hope, they purify themselves as he is pure."

<small>1 John iii.</small>

By reason hereof I see, first, that I am far from this desire and lamenting which thy children have. I see my ignorance of thy kingdom and power every where, of thy grace only in thy church, and of thy glory when all the enemies of thy grace shall be cast down, and thy glory and power shall embrace each other. I see my ignorance how acceptable a service to thee is the true preaching and the hearing of thy gospel; for else thou hadst not needed to have placed this petition next to the petition of the sanctifying of thy name. Again I see here my unableness to enter into thy kingdom, and to attain to it; for else what need should I have to pray for that to come from thee which otherwise may be achieved? Thirdly, I see also my perversity and contempt of thy kingdom and grace: for although I see my want, yet I would not desire thy kingdom to come, if thou didst not command me to pray so; for if I would have prayed for it, thou wouldest not have commanded me. Last of all I see thy goodness, which wilt bring thy kingdom, and that, as generally by sending forth ministers to preach truly, so particularly by regenerating me more and more, and by giving me as grace here so glory elsewhere; for thou wouldest not I should pray for that which thou wilt deny.

<small>Our ignorance.</small>

<small>Our need.</small>

<small>Our perversity.</small>

<small>God's goodness.</small>

So that I have great cause to lament and rejoice: to lament because of my miserable estate and condition, because of my sin, ignorance, rebellion, perversity, Satan's power, contempt of thy grace, thy gospel, and ministry, here or elsewhere; to rejoice because of thy goodness and great mercy, which hast brought me into thy church, keepest me in it, and wilt do so still; also because of the ministry of thy word and sacraments, by which the Holy Ghost is and will be effectual; and finally because of that great glory whereunto thou hast called me, and now wilt give unto me asking the same.

But, alas! how unthankful I am and sorrowless, Lord, thou knowest; for my heart is not hid from thee, &c.

O be merciful unto me, and forgive me, good Father, and grant the Spirit of thy children, to reveal unto me my ignorance of thy kingdom, my poverty and perversity, that I may lament the same, and daily labour for thy help and thy holy Spirit, to suppress the kingdom of sin in myself and in others. Again grant me that same thy holy Spirit, to reveal to me thy kingdom of power, grace, and glory; to kindle mine affections; to regenerate me more and more; to reign in me as in a piece of thy kingdom; to give to me to desire, to pray, and to labour for thy kingdom, both to myself and to others, effectually to thy glory; and to assure my conscience of thy goodness that thou wilt give me grace and glory, &c.

Here call to mind the state of the ministry and ministers, the light and life of gospellers, the errors and heresies which men be entangled withal.

THY WILL BE DONE.

As thy power is infinite, so is thy wisdom accordingly. Whereby as we may perceive that nothing is or can be done against thy power, or otherwise than by it; so is there not, nor cannot be, any thing done against or otherwise than by thy omnipotent and secret will; which is always, as thou art, good, holy, and just, how far soever it seem otherwise to our foolish reason and judgment. And therefore here we are taught to pray, that thy will may be done here without sin on man's behalf, as it is on the angels' behalf in heaven. *God's omnipotent will unknown and unrevealed.*

Again, forasmuch as thou art incomprehensible of thyself, as well concerning thy power as concerning thy wisdom, we may not according thereto search thee, but rather adore and worship thy majesty, and tremble at thy judgment and works; and therefore pray always that we may be content with thy will, and be buxom[1] thereto. And forasmuch as thou hast revealed to us so much of thy will in thy word written, as is necessary for us in this life to know, yea, as we can attain unto, and a little further; we ought to take all things done thereagainst as sin and transgression, although thou canst *God's will revealed and known.*

[1 i.e. obedient.]

use the same sin to serve thy providence: of the which providence we cannot nor may not judge further than thou hast and shalt open it unto us. So that this petition, "Thy will be done," is not simply to be understand concerning thy omnipotent will unrevealed, against the which nothing is nor can be done; but rather concerning thy will revealed in thy law and gospel; the which thou here teachest me, that we should desire not only to know it, but also to do it, and that in such perfection and willingness as it is in heaven. The which thing I perceive hereby that thy children do desire daily in and for themselves and others, and do lament the contrary in whomsoever it be; so that often their "eyes gush out with rivers of tears, because men keep not thy laws."

Psal. cxix.

By reason hereof I see that I am far from the signs and tears of thy people. I see my ignorance of thy will, if thou hadst not opened the same by thine own mouth; I see my ignorance how acceptable a service obedience to thy will is: and therefore dost thou place this petition amongst the first and continual desires of thy children. Again I see my poverty in godly obedience, which had need to be taught to pray for it, thereby to signify unto me my want and inability to attain it but by thy gift. Thirdly I see my disobedience; for else never wouldest thou have commanded me to have prayed for the doing of thy will, if I, seeing my want, would have prayed so. Last of all I see thy goodness, which wilt give to me and others to obey thy will; that is, to love thee with all our hearts, to love our neighbour as ourselves, to die to ourselves, to live to thee, to take up our cross, and to follow thee, to believe, to repent, &c.; for else thou wouldest never have bidden us to pray for a thing which we should not look for.

Our ignorance.

Our need.

Our disobedience.

God's goodness.

So that I have great cause to lament and rejoice: to lament because of my miserable state and condition, because of my sin, ignorance, poverty, and perversity; also because thy will is everywhere either not known or contemned, and Satan's will, the will of the world and of the flesh, readily obeyed. To rejoice I have great cause, for that thou hast opened thyself and will unto mankind; for that also thou peculiarly hast taught me these things, and because also thou wilt grant me grace to do the same. But, alas! how unthankful I am, and how hard-hearted, thou Lord dost know.

O be merciful unto me, and forgive me. I pray thee, gracious God, grant me thy holy Spirit to reveal to me my ignorance of thy will, my poverty and perversity, that I may heartily bewail it, &c.; and by thy help and working of the same Spirit may suppress the will of the flesh. Again grant me thy holy Spirit to reveal to me thy will declared in thy law and gospel, that I may truly know the same; and inflame so my affections, that I may will and love the same in such sort that it may be my meat and drink to do thy will.

Here call to mind the ten commandments of God, particularly or generally, what therein he requireth; and pray for the same particularly as you see your need, and that not only for yourself but also for other. Pray for patience to suffer what cross soever God shall lay upon you, and pray for them that be under the cross that they may be patient. Pray for spiritual wisdom in every cross, peculiarly or publicly, that you may see and love God's will.

GIVE US THIS DAY OUR DAILY BREAD.

By "bread," the food of the body, are[1] understand all *Bread.* things necessary for this corporal life, as meat, drink, health, success in vocation, &c. By this word "give" we should *Give.* understand that not only spiritual things but also corporal benefits are God's free gifts, and come not for our worthiness or travail taken about the same, although our travails be oftentimes means by the which God doth give corporal things. By "daily" is understand the contented minds of thy *Daily.* children with that which is sufficient for the present time, as having hope in thee that they shall not want, but daily shall receive at thy hands plenty and enough of all things. By this word "our" is as well understand public benefits, as peace *Our.* in the commonweal, good magistrates, seasonable weather, good laws, &c., as particular benefits, as be children, health, name, success in the works of our vocation, &c.: and besides this, by it we should see the care even for corporal things, which thy children have for others as well as for themselves.

So that here I may learn how far I am from that I should be, and I see thy children are come unto. I see my ignorance also, how that, as spiritual things do come from

[1 'are' 1562 corrected in the list of errata, 1567, 1607, and 1614: 'is' 1578.]

thee, so do temporal things; and as they come from thee, so are they conserved and kept of thee: and therefore thy children are thankful, and look for them as thy mere gifts, notwithstanding the means which they use, if they have them: howbeit they use them but as means; for except thou work therewith, all is in vain. Again here I am taught to be content with sufficient for the present time, as thy children be, which have the shortness of this life always before their eyes; and therefore they ask but for daily sustenance, knowing this life to be compared to a day, yea, a watch, a sound, a shadow, &c. Moreover I may learn to see the compassion and brotherly care thy children have one for another. Last of all here I may see thy goodness, which, as thou wilt give me all things necessary for this life (or else thou wouldest not bid me ask, &c.), so thou commandest all men to pray and care for me, and that bodily: much more then, if they be able, they are commanded to help me both in body and soul.

Psal. cxxvii.

By reason whereof I have great cause to lament and rejoice: to lament, because I am not so affected as thy children be, because of my ignorance, my ingratitude, my perversity, and contempt of thy goodness, and of the necessity of thy people, which, alas! be in great misery, some in exile, some in prison, some in poverty, sickness, &c. To rejoice I have great cause because of thy goodness in teaching me these things, in commanding me to ask whatsoever I want, in giving me so many things unasked, in keeping the benefits given me, in commanding men to care for me, to pray for me, to help me, &c. But, alas! how far I am from true lamentation and rejoicing, Lord, thou knowest.

O be merciful unto me and help me, forgive me, and grant me thy holy Spirit to reveal to me my need, ignorance, great ingratitude and contempt of thy mercies and thy people; and that in such sort that I might heartily lament and bewail my misery, and through thy goodness be altered with thy people to mourn for the miseries of thy children as for mine own. Again reveal to me thy goodness, dear Father, even in corporal things, that I may see thy mercy, thy presence, power, wisdom, and righteousness, in every creature and corporal benefits; and that in such sort, that I may be throughly affected truly to reverence, fear, love, obey thee, hang upon thee, to be thankful to thee, and in all my need to come unto thee, not only when I have ordinary means by the which thou commonly workest, but also when I have none; yea, when all means and helps are clean against me.

Here remember the state of your children and family; also your parents, neighbours, kinsfolks; also your friends, country, and magistrates, &c. as you shall have time thereto, and by God's good Spirit shall be provoked.

FORGIVE US OUR DEBTS, AS WE FORGIVE THEM THAT ARE DEBTORS UNTO US.

By our "debts" are understand not only things we have done, but the omission and leaving undone of the good things we ought to do. By "our" is not only understand the particular sins of one, but also generally the sins of all and every one of thy church. By "forgiveness" is understand free pardon and remission of sins by the merits and deserts of thy dear Son Jesus Christ, who gave himself a ransom for us. By our forgiving of other men's offences to us-ward is understand thy good will; not only that it pleaseth thee that we should live in love and amity, but also that thou wouldest have us to be certain of thy pardoning us of our sins: for as certain as we are that we pardon them that offend us, so certain should we be that thou dost pardon us, whereof the forgiving our trespassers is, as it were, a sacrament unto us. *Debts.* *Our.* *Forgiveness.* *As we forgive, &c.* *The forgiving of such as offend us is as a sacrament to assure us that our sins are pardoned. [1567.]*

So that by this petition I am taught to see that thy children, although by imputation they be pure from sin, yet they acknowledge sin to be and remain in them; and therefore do they pray for the remission and forgiveness of the same. Again, I am taught hereby to see how thy children do consider and take to heart not only the evils they do, but also the good they leave undone; and therefore they pray thee heartily for pardon.

Moreover I am here taught to see that thy children are careful for other men and for their trespasses, and therefore pray that they might be pardoned, in saying "our sins," and not my sins. Besides this I am taught here to see how thy children not only forgive all that offend them, but also pray for the pardoning of the offences of their enemies, and such as offend them; so far are they from maliciousness, pride, revengement, &c. Last of all I am taught to see how merciful thou art, which wilt have me to ask pardon: whereof thou wouldest that we should in no point doubt, but be most assured that for Christ's sake thou hearest us, and that not only for ourselves but also for many others; for thou dost not command us to ask for any thing thou wilt not give us.

By reason whereof I have great cause to lament and rejoice: to lament because of my miserable estate, which am so far from these affections that are in thy children, which am so ignorant and careless of sin, not only in leaving good undone, but also in doing evil, and that daily in thought, word, and deed, &c. I speak not of my carelessness for other folk's sins, as of my parents, children, family, magistrates, &c., neither of the sins of them to whom I have given occasion to sin. To rejoice I have great cause because of thy mercy in opening to me these things, in commanding me to pray for pardon, in promising me pardon, and in commanding others to pray for me. I ought surely to be persuaded of thy mercy, though my sins be innumerable; for I see, not only in this but in every petition, how that every one of thy church prayeth for me: yea, Christ thy Son, who sitteth on thy right hand, prayeth for me, &c.

O dear Father, be merciful unto me, and forgive me all my sins; and of thy goodness give me thy holy Spirit to open mine eyes that I may see sin, the better to know it, the more truly to hate it, and most earnestly to strive against it, and that effectually both in myself and others. Again grant me the same thy holy Spirit to reveal unto me the remedy of sin by Christ only, and to work in me by faith to embrace the same thy Christ and mercies in him; that I may henceforth be endued with thy holy Spirit, more and more to begin and obey thy good-will continually, and to increase in the same for ever.

Pray for them to whom you have given any occasion of sin. Here call to mind the special sins you have committed heretofore. Remember, if you have occasioned any to sin, to pray for them by name. Remember that God's law should be so near unto us, that the breaking thereof in others should be an occasion to make us to lament with tears, &c.

LEAD US NOT INTO TEMPTATION.

BECAUSE of our continual and great infirmities, because of the great diligence and subtleties of our enemies, and *The greatest punishment.* because thou art wont to punish sin with sin, which of all punishments is the greatest and most to be feared; in this petition thou wouldest have thy children to have the same in remembrance; and for a remedy hereof thou hast appointed prayer.

Remedy against evil, is prayer.

So that the only cause why any are overcome and led into temptation is, for that they forget what they desire in the petition going before this, which should be never out of their memory, to provoke them to be more thankful to thee, and more vigilant and heedy hereafter for falling into like perils: for which to be avoided, thou dost most graciously set forth a remedy in commanding us to pray, after pardon for our sins past, for thy grace to guide us, so that we be not led into temptation, but might be delivered from evil. And because thou wouldest have all thy children to hang wholly upon thee, to fear thee only, and only to love thee, thou dost not teach them to pray, 'Suffer us not to be led,' but, "Lead us not into temptation;" that, I say, they might only fear thee, and certainly know that Satan hath no power over so much as a pig but whatsoever thou givest unto him, and of thy secret but most just judgment dost appoint him to use, not as he will (for then we were all lost), but as thou wilt, which canst will nothing but that which is most just; as, to give them to the guiding of Satan, which will not be guided by thy grace, as thou didst Saul, &c.

Our sins should not be forgotten of us, if we would have them forgotten with God. Commodities coming by remembering our sins be thankfulness, vigilancy, and gentleness to offenders.

Why we pray not, 'Suffer us not to be led,' &c.

Matt. viii.

Occasions to evil are in two sorts; one by prosperity and success, another by adversity and the cross, &c. The evils coming of success commonly are unthankfulness, pride, security, and forgetting ourselves, forgetting of others, forgetfulness of God, of our mortality, &c. The evils coming of adversity commonly are impatience, murmuring, grudging, despairing, contemning of God, flattering of men, stealing, lying, &c., with many other evils, whereto temptations will entice a man that is left to himself: whereas to one that is guided with God's Spirit temptations are but trials to the glory of God, comfort of the tempted, and edifying of thy church. But, as I said, if a man be left alone, temptations entice even to the devil himself; and therefore thy children pray to be delivered from evil, (understanding thereby Satan himself the sower and supporter of all evil;) and this thy children do as well for others as for themselves.

Occasions to evil in two sorts.

What temptations are to the godly, and what they are to the wicked.

So that I may learn hereout many good things. First, to remember often our infirmity and weakness, and the dangerous state we stand in, in the respect of our flesh, of the world which is full of evil, of Satan which seeketh to sift us, and as a roaring lion to destroy us, and of our sins which deserve all kinds of punishments and correction; that I might with thy children fear thee, watch, pray, and desire the day of redemption from all evils.

Again I may learn here, that to avoid all dangers and evils is not in the power of man, but only thy work: by reason whereof I should consider thy great goodness, which hitherto hast kept me from so many evils, both of soul and body, yea, of name, goods, &c.; as thou hast done in my infancy, childhood, youth, middle age, &c.

Thirdly I may learn here, that I should be careful for others, both that they might be delivered from their evils, and that they might be preserved from temptation, and from being overcome in the same: and therefore thou teachest me to pray, not 'Deliver me from evil' simply, but "Deliver us from evil."

Last of all I am taught hereby to see thy goodness towards me, which wilt deliver me from evil, and from being overcome in temptations; (for thou wouldest not have me to ask for that which I should not look for at thy hands certainly:) by reason whereof thou wouldest have me to be in a certainty of salvation for ever; for else I cannot believe my prayer to be heard, if that finally I should not be delivered from evil. And therefore thou joinest hereto a giving of thanks, which with thy church I should say: "For thine is the kingdom, thine is the power, thine is the glory for ever."

Thine is the kingdom, &c.

By reason whereof I have great cause to lament and to rejoice: to lament because of my corruption, infirmity, weakness, oblivion and carelessness for thy people, ingratitude, &c.; because of Satan's power, vigilance, and prudence, which hath overcome most grave, wise, and holy men, whereof some never recovered, as Cain, Cham, Ahithophel, Saul, Judas, &c.: to rejoice because of thy goodness, which teachest me this, and shewest me the remedy, commandest all thy church to pray for me, and wilt at length deliver me from all evil, and give me glory. But, alas! I am altogether careless and miserable.

O be merciful unto me, dear Father, and for Christ's sake forgive me all my sins. Grant me thy holy Spirit to reveal to me mine infirmities, weaknesses, perils, dangers, &c., in such sort that as I may heartily lament my miseries, so I may ask and obtain thy grace to guide me from all evil for evermore. Again grant me the same thy holy Spirit to reveal to me thy love and kindness towards me, and that in eternity, in such sort that I may be thoroughly persuaded of the same; become thankful unto thee; and daily expect and look for the revelation of thy kingdom, power, and glory, as one that for ever shall have the fruition of the same, through thine own goodness and mercy in Christ prepared for me before the beginning and foundation of the world was laid.

Here call to mind our security, Satan's vigilancy, our negligence, his diligence, our infirmity, his ability, our ignorance, his craftiness and subtlety. Item, call to mind how that he hath overthrown for a time many of the dear saints of God, to whom we are to be compared in nothing; as Adam, Eve, Lot, Judas, Tamar, Moses, Aaron, Miriam, Sampson, Gideon, Eli, David, Solomon, Hezekias, Josias, Peter, Thomas, and innumerable moe.

Item, call to mind the goodness of God and of our Shepherd Christ, which hath kept us hitherto, keepeth us still, and teacheth us here to know that he will keep us for ever; for he would not have us to ask for deliverance from evil, if that he would not we should certainly look for the same. If thou doubt of final perseverance, thou dishonourest God. Be certain therefore, rest in hope, be still in his word. See also how he hath commanded his whole church and every member thereof to pray for thee as well as for themselves, in these and all other things.

Now and then go about to reckon how many and divers kinds of evils there be, that thereby, as you may know you are delivered from none but by God's great goodness, so you may see that the number of evils that you have are nothing to be compared to the multitude of evils wherewith, if your Christ were not, the devil would all-to[1] bewray[2] and dress[3] you.

But what are all the miseries and evils that can be, to be

[1 i. e. altogether. So in the authorised version of Judges ix. 53, "all—to brake his scull."]

[2 i. e. defile: Richardson, Dict.]

[3 So 1562 corrected in the list of errata, and 1578: 'bewray you, infect and corrupt you,' 1567, 1604, and 1607: 'bedaub and dress you, infect and corrupt you,' 1614 and 1621.]

compared to the least joys prepared for us in heaven! O think of those joys, and pray that, when the tide of death cometh, we may hale forth[1] of the haven of this flesh and this world joyfully.

In praying this petition, call to mind the evils you have been in, the evils you are in, and the evils you may fall in, if God should not preserve you; that you might be stirred up the more to thankfulness, to prayer, to trust in God, to modesty, &c.

FOR THINE IS THE KINGDOM, THINE IS THE POWER, THINE IS THE GLORY FOR EVER.

As in the beginning of this prayer by these words, "Our Father which art in heaven," thy children are excited and stirred up to a full confidence of obtaining the petitions following and all things necessary; so in the latter end thou hast added for the same purpose these words, "For thine is the kingdom, thine is," &c.; wherein I am taught these many things. First, that in prayer I should have such consideration of thy kingdom, power, glory, and eternity, that my mind should be stricken with an admiration of the same. Secondly, that I should so consider them especially in prayer, that I should not doubt but that thou workest, rulest, and governest all things everywhere, in all persons and creatures, most wisely, justly, and mercifully. Thirdly, that in prayer all my petitions should tend to the setting forth of thy power, of thy kingdom, and of thy glory. Last of all, that in prayer I should in no wise doubt of being heard, but be assured that thou which hast commanded me to pray, and hast promised to hear me, dost most graciously for thy mercy's sake and truth's sake hear my petitions according to thy good will, through Jesus Christ thy dear Son, our Lord and only Saviour.

We may not doubt but that he which hath commanded us to pray, and promised to hear us, will also hear our prayer. [1567.]

By reason whereof I have great cause to lament and rejoice; to lament, because I consider not these things in prayer in such sort as should move me to admiration and gratitude; because I consider not thy power and wisdom generally in all things; because I am so careless for thy kingdom, and because I am so full of dubitation and doubting of thy goodness. To rejoice I have great cause, because thou revealest these things unto me on this sort; because of thy power,

[¹ A nautical phrase, meaning 'pull forth.' Vide Encycl. Britann. vol. x. Edinb. 1823, v. 'hale.']

kingdom, and glory, which maketh to the hearing of my prayers and helping of me; because thou wilt use me as thine instrument to set forth thy kingdom, power, and glory; and because it pleaseth thee to hear my prayers, and assuredly wilt save me for ever. But, alas, how far am I from these lamentations and rejoicings! by reason whereof I deserve damnation.

O be merciful unto me, and forgive me, and of thy goodness grant me thy holy Spirit to reveal to me my blindness, oblivion, and contempt of thy kingdom, power, and glory, with the greatness of my doubtings; that I may heartily, as lament them, so have them pardoned and taken from me through the merits of Jesus Christ thy Son. Again, give me thy holy Spirit to reveal to me in such sort thy kingdom, power, glory, and eternity, that I may always have the same before mine eyes, be moved with the admiration thereof, labour effectually to set forth the same; and finally, as to have the fruition thereof after this life, so to increase in an assured, certain, and lively expectation of the same, that I may always and in all things rejoice in thee through Christ, and give lauds, thanks, and praises perpetually unto thy most holy name, O blessed Father, Son, and Holy Ghost, three persons and one God, to whom be all honour and glory world without end.

Here think, that if the kingdom, power, glory, and eternity be God's, which is our Father, what our dignity is which be his children. If the power be our Father's, of whom should we be afraid? If the devil be subject to the Lord's power and kingdom, as he is, how can the subject have power over us which be sons and heirs, in that he hath not power over porkets[2] without the providence and permission of God? Therefore full well should we pray, "Lead us not into temptation," rather than, 'Let us not be led into temptation;' for power is the Lord's, and the devil hath none but that he hath of God's gift. No; he were not of capacity to receive power, if God did not make him of capacity, although the execution of it is rather of God's permission.

Give all thanks, praise, and glory to God our Father, through Christ our Lord and Saviour. So be it.

[2 'a swine' 1578.]

A MEDITATION

UPON THE TWELVE ARTICLES OF THE CHRISTIAN FAITH.

I BELIEVE IN GOD THE FATHER, &c.

Meditations of Bradford, Hall 1562, and after editions.
MS. 1. 2. 8. No. 50. Emmanuel College, Cambridge[1].

THY people, O Lord God, the Father of our Saviour Jesus Christ, do here in saying this article, 'I believe in God the Father Almighty,' &c., by faith know that thou, together with Jesus Christ and the Holy Ghost, didst create all things that be in heaven and in earth; for by heaven and earth are understand all things therein. And as they know this, so they by the same faith do see thee the same God, the Father, the Son, and the Holy Ghost, to govern all things after thy great wisdom, power, righteousness, and mercy; using every creature they see as means to put them in remembrance of fearing, reverencing, trusting, and loving thee; for in every creature they behold thy presence, power, wisdom, and mercy.

Again by this word 'Father' they declare their belief how that they are not only thy creatures, and all that ever they have to be thy gracious gifts and blessings; but also how that they are thy children dearly beloved and cared for of thee through Jesus Christ. Wherethrough, notwithstanding their unworthiness, as they conceive a sure hope of thy goodness and fatherly love towards them in soul and body for ever, so are they thankful for their creation, and for that thou hast made them thy excellent creatures, lords of all: they are thankful for the creation of all creatures, and use the same with thankfulness as visible tokens of thy invisible love: they are thankful for thy conserving and keeping them, and for the governing them and all this world; lamenting that they are no more thankful, that they believe no deeper, that reason hath so great a swing with them in these matters.

But I, most gracious good Lord and Father, though I say, 'I believe in thee, my Father Almighty, Maker of heaven

[1 This MS. has on a blank leaf the words prefixed, "Secundum Spiritum sanctificationis, in Symbolum apostolicum familiaris meditatio per dominum Joannem Bradfordum." The MS. probably once belonged to Sampson (see p. 29, note 1, above), whose name is inscribed upon it.]

and earth,' yet thou knowest that I am full of much doubting, not only of this whether thou art my good, almighty, and most loving dear Father in Christ, (because I feel in myself such a conscience[2] of unworthiness, and so great want of those things which thou requirest of thy children, and so transfer the cause of my being thy child in part to myself, where it is due only and wholly always to thy mercy and grace in Christ;) but also thou knowest my doubting of my creation and governance, and of the creation and governance of all this world; as I declare by my unthankfulness for my creation, for mine adoption, for my gubernation[3], for thy providence for me. Or else, dear Father, I could not but heartily with thy children rejoice, and praise thy holy name, and that continually; being henceforth careful for nothing but how to please thee, and profit thy people, and that they might praise thy name in all things for evermore, desiring the sanctification of thy name, the coming of thy kingdom, the doing of thy will upon earth as it is in heaven.

Thou mightest have made me a dog, but of thy goodness hast made me a creature after thine image. Thou mightest have made me a Turk, a Jew, a Saracen; but thou hast made me a Christian, a member of thy church. Thou, after my birth, mightest have left me, and in all need have made no providence for me, as we sometimes see hath happened unto others; but yet thou never didst so with me: and yet I am of all others most unthankful.

Thy creatures I thankfully use not. Thy invisible love by thy manifold visible tokens I consider not; as now I should by this apparel of my body, by this corporal health, by this light, by this my hearing, seeing, feeling, memory, understanding, time, place, company, creatures, and benefits, as well in keeping innumerable evils from me both in soul and body, which else could not but come to me, as also in giving to me presently so many things as without thy especial grace and working I never could have had or presently could keep them. In thy creatures I see not thy power, for I fear thee not: I see not thy presence, for I reverence thee not: I see not thy wisdom, for I adore thee not: I see not thy mercy, for I love thee not: I praise thee not but in lips and tongue. And therefore, in that all thy creatures do teach me,

[2 i. e. consciousness.]   [3 i. e. government.]

cry out upon me to be thankful to thee, to love, fear, serve thee, and trust in thee, and that continually; in that I do not so, they cannot but cry out upon me and against me in thy sight, and in the day of judgment will weapon themselves against me.

O that I did now consider this! O that my blind eyes and my deaf ears were opened! O that my miserable and foolish heart were made wise and converted! This only thou canst do, which hast all men's hearts in thy hands, to bow them as pleaseth thee. "Bow my heart," good Lord, "into thy testimonies." "Open my eyes." Make me to hear for thy mercy's sake, that I may believe, and so love thee, be thankful to thee, amend in all things and serve thee; though not as thy dear servants do, yet at the least as other brute creatures do; that is, to obey thee, and to be profitable to others.

Ps. cxix.

Now, forasmuch as my sins let[1] this and all good things from me, I beseech thee pardon me all my sins according to thy gracious promise, for our Lord Jesus Christ's sake. Amen.

I BELIEVE IN JESUS CHRIST, HIS ONLY SON, &c.

THY servants, O Christ Jesu, and people, do know by faith that as thou art almighty and God with the Father, by whom all things were made and are ruled; (for thou art God eternal, co-equal and consubstantial with the Father and the Holy Ghost;) so thou art man, and hast taken our nature upon thee by the operation of the Holy Ghost in the womb of the virgin Mary, and art become the blessed "seed which hast bruised the serpent's head;" the blessed "seed in whom all nations are blessed;" the Prophet whom Moses did prophesy of; the sampler he saw in the mount; the truth and body of all the types, figures, and shadows of the old law; the Messias, Christ, and Saviour of thy people; the Advocate and Redeemer; the pacifier of God's wrath for sins, the opener of heaven, and giver of everlasting life.

Gen. iii.
Gen. xxii.
Deut. xviii.
Exod. xxv.

This they know thou broughtest to pass in thy human nature, by thy incarnation and nativity, by thy being here on earth, by thy living, teaching, fasting, praying; especially by thy suffering under Pontius Pilate, by thy death, burial, resurrection, ascension unto the heavens, and reigning on the

[1 i. e. hinder.]

right hand of the Father, from whence thou shalt come to judge both the quick and the dead. And as they know this, so by faith they apply it also to themselves, that for their sake thou wast made man, didst pray, fast, wast tempted, didst die, rosest again, and didst ascend into heaven; and there art set their Advocate, Bishop, and High-priest, always appearing in God's sight for them; from whence they look for thee, knowing that thou wilt not enter into judgment with them to damn them, which wouldest damn thyself for them. Hebr. ix.

Gal. iii.

By this faith they feel these affections in themselves, namely, the hatred of sin, the fear of God, the love of God, trust in thee, and love to thy church. The hatred of sin they feel, because it is so foul a thing as would not be washed away with any other thing than with thy precious blood-shedding; the fear of God, because his anger is so great against sin that no less price could pacify his wrath than thy most painful death; the love of God, because he hath so loved them, that he would not spare thee his dear Son for them, even when they were his enemies; trust in thee, because thou hadst no respect to thyself, but most willingly didst give thyself wholly to be our Saviour and servant; love to thy people and church, because generally and particularly in every member of the same they see how dear they are to thee, and therefore they cannot but be so to them. O how do they imitate and follow thy footsteps! how do they rejoice when they are in any thing by affliction made like to thee! O how do they lament their sins, ingratitude, unbelief; love thee, and wholly yield themselves unto thee! Whereas I, O gracious God and dear Saviour, Jesus Christ, though I say I believe in thee which wast conceived by the Holy Ghost, yet, alas! I do but babble this; for nothing is else in me but unbelief. Of thy power and love, of thine anger and mercy, I have but an opinion, as my insensibleness and unthankfulness doth declare.

If a man should shew me friendship but in a trifle, or suffer any thing at all for me, I could not but be thankful; and thou, besides my creation, hast redeemed me and brought me into the number of God's children, than which thing nothing is greater: and lo, I am unthankful.

Thou hast suffered much for me: from heaven thou camest into earth to fetch me into heaven: but I regard it not.

Thou barest my sins on thy back, suffering a most bitter death: but I am so far from thankfulness, that I still more and more loath thee.

Thou wouldest enter into a communion with me, taking my nature unto thee concerning the substance thereof, that I might enter into a communion with thee concerning the qualities wherewith in thyself thou hast endued it: but I consider it not.

Thou didst die to deliver me from death: but I still more and more give thee cause to die, so ungrateful am I.

Thou didst arise to justify me: but I with the Jews would still keep thee down, because I would not leave my wickedness.

Thou ascendedst to heaven to take possession for me there, to be always in the sight of thy Father for me, to send me down gifts, to pray for me: but I daily am pulling thee down again, as much as in me lieth; I am altogether earthly; I hide myself out of thy sight by forgetting thee; I reject and abuse thy gifts; I neglect prayer.

Thou art now in a readiness to come to judge both quick and dead: but I tremble not at this gear, nor beseech thee before thou come to be merciful unto me, and not to enter into judgment with me: yea, I think nothing at all of thy coming. *Mali non cogitant judicium:* 'The wicked' consider not the end, they 'think not on thy judgment.' [Prov. xxviii.]

Thou wouldest bring me to thy Father, that I might find grace: but I put this off, and therefore am worthy to feel thee a Judge, which refuse to feel thee a Saviour.

Now the cause of all these things is unbelief; the which though it be natural by reason of the corruption of our nature, yet I have augmented the same maliciously in not labouring thereagainst, and continuing in all sins and wickedness: by reason whereof I deserve most justly thy anger thereupon, even rejection from thy face for ever.

Long hast thou mourned even with displeasure and anger the incredulity of my heart, calling me therefrom, and offering me thy grace, which I have neglected and rejected, and therefore am never worthy to have it any more offered unto me: much more then I am unworthy to have grace given me to receive thy mercy.

Alas! what shall I do? Shall I despair, or, as long as

I can, keep me unmindful of my misery? O Saviour Christ Jesu, wilt not thou be merciful unto me? Thou didst die for me when I deserved it not: and now is thy mercy shortened? Wilt not thou give me thy grace, and take from my heart this horrible unbelief? Shall I never love thee? shall I never hate sin? shall I never, as with my mouth I say, 'I believe in Jesus Christ,' so in heart say the same? shall Satan possess me for ever? O Christ Jesus, which hast "led captivity captive," what, wilt not thou help me? Though I desire it not as I should, yet give me to desire when thou wilt. Ephes. iv.

Thou didst appear "to destroy the work of the devil:" thou seest his work in me: good Christ, destroy his work, but not thy work. Save me for thy great mercy's sake. Give me to believe in thee, in thy death, resurrection, and ascension. Pardon me my sins, and mortify now in me my corrupt affections. Raise me up and justify me. Regenerate me daily more and more. Give me faith of immortality, resurrection of this body. Give me faith to ascend into heaven, and to be certain that thou hast already taken possession for me there. Give me to look for thy coming, and to be ready in thy coming to find mercy to everlasting life, &c.

I BELIEVE IN THE HOLY GHOST, &c.

O HOLY Spirit, the third person in Trinity, which didst descend upon Christ our Saviour in his baptism in the likeness of a dove; thy children know that with the Father and Son thou madest and rulest all creatures, visible and invisible. They know thee in their redemption to be no less willing and loving than the Father and the Son; (for thou didst always declare Christ to be the Son of God, and gavest testimony inwardly in the hearts of thy elect to believe and embrace the same:) and outwardly by miracles and wonders they know thee to be "the Comforter" and Governor whom Christ did promise in his corporal absence should teach, rule, keep, comfort, and govern his church and people. John xvi.

Again, as in the former part of their belief they consider the works of creation and redemption, so in this part they consider the place where the same is most effectual and taketh place, even thy holy church, which is catholic, (that is, extending itself to all times, to all places, to all kinds of people;) for in this church only they know that, as all things were made, so the work of redemption was taken in hand, that thou, blessed Trinity, mightest in this church be praised, magnified, served, and worshipped for ever.

This church is nothing else but a communion and society of saints; that is, not only a society of all such as be, have been, or shall be thy people, but also a society or partaking of Christ Jesus, which is "the head" of the same; yea, by him of thee, O blessed Father which art "the head of Christ," and of thee, O Holy Ghost which now shadowest and sittest upon the same, to hatch and cherish it, as the hen her chickens, by the extending of thy wings; not only to defend them from their enemies, but also to cover their sins, and to remit them in this life; beginning also here the resurrection of the flesh and everlasting life, the which thou wilt in the end of the world consummate, so that they shall not need to be covered for sin; for then shall they be pure, and have glorious bodies, immortal and spiritual, the which shall have the fruition of eternal joy, life everlasting, and glory, such as "the eye hath not seen, the ear hath not[1] heard," nor the heart of man can conceive. For then Christ Jesus shall give up his kingdom to God the Father, that God may be "all in all" concerning the governance of it by the ministration of his word, and other means whereby now he governeth it, that it may be his Father's kingdom, we being become "like unto him:" that is, as to the manhood of Christ the Godhead is united, and is "all in all" without any other means; even so God shall be in us, assuming then not only in the person of Christ the human nature, but also all the human nature of his church which be members of Christ; the wicked and reprobate being separate then from this communion, and cast into eternal perdition with Satan and antichrist, there to be in torments and horror for ever.

By reason of this their faith they are thankful to thee, O Holy Spirit, which hast taught them this, and given them to believe it. By reason of this faith they singularly pray, love, and help thy church here militant, and labour to be

Phil. iii.

1 Cor. ii.

1 Cor. xv.

1 John iii.

[1 'not' 1567, 1614.: omitted in MS. 1. 2. 8. and in 1562 and 1578.]

holy, &c. By reason of this faith they confess themselves sinners, they desire and believe pardon of their sins, they are risen and rise daily concerning the inward man, and do feel the life eternal begun in them; more and more labouring, praying, wishing, and desiring for the same wholly and perfectly.

Whereas, O Lord God and most gracious Holy Spirit, thou knowest that it is otherwise with me. I do but babble with my lips in saying, 'I believe in the Holy Ghost;' for I am unthankful: to thee, O Holy Spirit, I am unthankful[2] for calling me into thy church: I do not live holily: I confess not, I lament not my sins, I pray not for remission of them, I stand in doubt thereof. As I feel not myself risen from a sinful life as I should be, or as I feel not life begun in me as it is in thy dear children, so do I doubt hereof whether I have pardon of my sins, whether I am regenerate, whether I feel truly everlasting life: the which thing doth most displease thee. And yet with my tongue I say, 'I believe in the Holy Ghost.'

Note here what great imperfections and dubitations the children of God feel and confess to remain in them. [1567.]

O, I beseech thee, good Holy Spirit, for thy love's sake which moved thee to agree and be willing to patefy[3] and open thy goodness, not only in the work of creation, (for thou didst lie upon the waters, and, as the hen her chickens, didst, as it were, hatch the work of creation,) but also in the work of redemption; and therefore didst ascend and abide not only upon Christ in his baptism, but also on the apostles and church in fiery tongues visibly, the fiftieth day[4] after Christ's resurrection; as now thou dost invisibly, generally and particularly, sit upon thy church and children, being the consolator, "the Comforter," the teacher and leader, the guider and governor of us all: for this thy love's sake, I say, I beseech thee to be merciful unto me, and forgive me my doubting, unbelief, ingratitude, and horrible monstrous uncleanness and sin, and utterly take them from me. Bring me into thy church which thou guidest: that is, guide me, make me holy, and by faith couple me to Christ, by charity

Gen. i.

Matt. iii.

Acts ii.

[² 'to thee, O Holy Spirit, I am unthankful,' MS. 1. 2. 8.: not in 1562, nor after editions.]

[³ i. e. disclose.]

[⁴ 'fyfte daye' 1562, 1567: 'fifty dayes 1578, 1607, 1614.]

to thy people: that is, give me the communion of saints with thy saints, overshadow my sins, raise me up to righteousness, begin in me everlasting life; and now more and more to expect and look for all these great mercies, and at length to possess eternal felicity with thee, O blessed Trinity, the Father, the Son, and the Holy Ghost, three persons and one almighty, eternal, most just, wise, and good God: to whom be all glory, power, and dominion, now and for ever.

A MEDITATION

UPON THE TEN COMMANDMENTS.

I AM THE LORD THY GOD, WHICH BROUGHT THEE OUT OF THE LAND OF EGYPT, &c.

Meditations of Bradford, Hall 1562, and after editions.

O GOOD Lord and dear Father, here thou wouldest I should know that thou, which broughtest thy people of Israel out of Egypt with a mighty hand and a stretched-out power; which gavest thy law upon mount Sinai in great thundering, lightning, fire; which spakest by the prophets, and didst send thy dearly beloved Son, Jesus Christ, co-equal and consubstantial with thee in power, majesty, and glory, to take upon him our nature by the operation of the Holy Ghost in the womb of the virgin Mary; of whose substance he was made and born man, but pure without sin, that we, by birth children of wrath, by him might be made thy children, children of grace, communicating with him righteousness, holiness, and immortality by the working of the Spirit, as he communicated with us flesh and blood, but not infected with sin as is ours, by the working of the same Holy Spirit; which Spirit, after his bitter death, resurrection, and ascension into the heavens, he sent plentifully and by a visible sign unto his apostles and disciples, by whom he published the gospel throughout the whole world; and so continually hath done from age to age, doth, and will do unto the end of the world, by the ministry of preaching: thou wouldest, I say, that we should know and believe that thou, this almighty Lord and God, which on this sort hast revealed and opened thyself, art the one alone, very true and eternal almighty God, which madest and rulest heaven and earth and all things visible and invisible, together with this thy dearly beloved Son Jesus Christ, and with the Holy Spirit, consubstantial and co-eternal with thee, dear Father.

Not only this, but also thou wouldest that I should know and believe, that by the same thy dearly beloved Son thou hast brought me from the tyranny and captivity of Satan and this sinful world, whereof the captivity of Egypt under Pharaoh was a figure. And in his blood shed upon the cross thou hast made a covenant with me, which thou wilt never forget, that thou art and wilt be my Lord and my God; that is, thou wilt forgive me my sins and be wholly mine, with all thy power, wisdom, righteousness, truth, glory, and mercy.

Wherefore, although I might confirm my faith by the innumerable mercies hitherto poured upon me most abundantly; (as thy children of Israel might have done, and did confirm their faith by the manifold benefits poured upon them in the desert;) yet specially the seal of thy covenant (I mean thy holy sacrament of baptism, wherein thy holy name was not in vain called upon me, O dear Father, sweet Son and Saviour Jesus Christ, and most gracious good Holy Ghost,) should most assuredly confirm, and even on all sides seal up my faith of this thy covenant, that thou art my Lord and my God; even as Abraham and thy people of Israel did by the sacrament of circumcision; which as the apostle calleth the "seal" or signacle "of righteousness," so dost thou call it; Rom. iv. being but the sign of thy covenant indeed, yet thy very covenant; because as thy word is most true and cannot lie, as thy covenant is a covenant of peace infallible and everlasting, even so the sacrament and seal of the same is a most true testimonial and witness thereof.

In consideration therefore of this, that thou, the almighty God, of thine own goodness hast vouchedsafe not only to make me a creature after thine own image and likeness, which mightest have made me a beast; to give unto me a reasonable soul endued with memory, judgment, &c., which mightest have made me an idiot without wit or discretion, &c.; to endue me with a body beautified with right shape, limbs, health, &c., which mightest have made me a cripple, lame, blind, &c.; graciously to enrich me concerning fortune, friends, living, name, &c., which mightest have made me a slave, destitute of all friends, and helpless[1] for this life; but also hast vouchedsafe that I, being a miser[2], "born in sin, conceived in iniquity," to whom nothing is due (more than to a Turk, Jew, or Saracen,) but eternal damnation, should be called into the number of thy people, enrolled in thy book, and now in thy covenant, so that thou, with all that ever thou hast, art mine; for which cause's sake hitherto thou hast kept me, cherished, defended, spared, and fatherly chastised me, and now graciously dost keep me and care for me, giving me to live, be, and move in thee, expecting also and "waiting how thou mightest shew mercy upon me:" in consideration, I say, of this, most justly and reasonably thou requirest that as thou art my Lord God, so I should be thy servant and one of thy people. As thou hast given thyself wholly unto me, to be mine, with all thy power, wisdom, &c.; (for he that giveth himself giveth all he hath;) so should I be wholly thine, and give over myself unto thee to be guided with thy wisdom, defended with thy power, holpen, relieved, and comforted by thy mercy.

Isai. xxx.

First therefore to begin withal, thou commandest "that I should have none other gods in thy sight." That is to say, as I should have thee for my Lord and God to look for all good things most assuredly at thy hands, and therefore I should put all my trust in thee, be thankful unto thee, love thee, fear thee, obey thee, and call upon thy holy name in all my needs; so should I give this faith, love, fear, obedience, thankfulness, and invocation or prayer, to none other (no, not in my heart), but only to thee, or for thee, where thou commandest.

All this to do, O Lord God, and that with most joyful heart, I have great cause; for what a thing is it, that thou, Jehovah, wouldest vouchsafe to make me, as thou hast done; to give thy Son for me, and to become my God! O what am I, that thou wouldest I should put my trust in thee! This thou doest, that I might never be confounded, but might be most happy. What am I, that thou wouldest I should fear thee! where the only cause why thou requirest this of me is, not only because thou hast power to cast both body and soul into

---

[1 'Helpless' 1562 corrected in the list of errata, and 1578: 'helps' 1567, 1607, and 1614.]

[2 i. e. unhappy one.]

hell-fire, and because they that fear thee not shall perish; but also that thou mightest give me thy wisdom, that it might go well with me in the evil day, that thou mightest reveal thy Son to me, and thy mercy might be upon me from generation to generation. O what am I, that thou wouldest have me to obey thee! not only that I never perish with the disobedient, but that thou mightest give me thy holy Spirit, and rewards innumerable. O what am I, that thou wouldest I should love thee! the which thing thou doest to this end, that I might fully and wholly enjoy and possess thee, according to the nature of love; and therefore dost thou require my whole heart, that I might dwell in thee, and thou in me. What am I, that thou wouldest I should call upon thee! verily, because thou wilt give me whatsoever I shall ask of thee in the name of thy dear child Jesus Christ: and even so wouldest thou have me thankful, that thou mightest pour out upon me yet more plentifully all good things.

So that great cause have I to put my trust in thee, to love, fear, and obey thee, to call upon thee, to be thankful unto thee; not only in respect of the hurt which else will ensue, but also in respect of the commodity that hereby cometh unto me; but most of all, yea, alonely for thy own sake, for thy goodness, wisdom, beauty, strength and power, truth and great mercies.

But, alas! dear Father, what shall I say? As in times past horribly I have broken this thy law in trusting in thy creatures, calling upon them, loving, fearing, and obeying many things besides thee and rather than thee; even so at this present I am a most miserable wretch. Blinded I am through unbelief and mine own wickedness; so that I see not firmly this thy power, wisdom, goodness, &c., but waver and doubt of it. I love little or nothing; I fear less; I obey least of all; thankfulness and prayer are utterly quenched in me: by reason whereof I am worthy of eternal damnation. If after thy justice thou shalt deal with me simply, I am, O Lord, damned and lost for ever, for I am very wicked.

But yet, inasmuch as thou hast given thy Son Jesus Christ to be a slain propitiatory sacrifice "for the sins of the whole world," so "that he which believeth in him shall not perish," but be saved (for so thou hast promised), thy truth now requireth to save me. Howbeit, here thou mayest say unto me that I do not believe; and therefore notwithstanding thy truth and promise, in that I believe it not, thou mayest most justly, after thy justice, damn me. O Lord God, to this I cannot otherwise answer (my unbelief is so great), but because thy mercy is above all thy works, and thy goodness and love is that which all creatures most highly commend and magnify as the thing whereof thou art called God; because thou art right good, and love itself; because of this thy mercy, gracious God, if thou wilt look thereon and couple thy truth therewith, then, good Lord, I shall be saved and praise thy name for evermore.

THOU SHALT NOT MAKE TO THYSELF ANY GRAVEN, &c.

As the first commandment teacheth me as well that thou art my God, as what God thou art; and therefore of equity I should have none other gods but thee; (that is, I should alonely hang on thee, trust in thee, love thee, serve thee, call upon thee, obey thee, be thankful to thee;) so because thou didst reveal thyself visibly that thou mightest visibly be worshipped, this commandment is concerning thy worship, that in no point I should follow in worshipping thee the device or intent of any man, saint, angel, or spirit; but should take all such as idolatry and image-service, be it never so glorious. And why? Forsooth, because thou wouldest I should worship thee as thou hast appointed by thy word; for if service be acceptable, it must needs be according to the will of him to whom it is done, and not of him which doeth it. But inasmuch as of man none knoweth the will and pleasure but his spirit, except he reveal by word or sign the same; much more of thee, O Lord, none doth know the[1] will but thy Spirit, and they to whom thou dost reveal the same. And therefore abominable even in thy sight are all those things which with men are in most force and estimation, because they are not after thy word.

So that the meaning of this precept is, that as in the first I should have none other gods but thee, so I should have no worship of thee but such as thou appointest. Hereby therefore I see great cause of thankfulness for this commandment, in that thou wouldest have mine outward service, and that after thy appointment, lest I should busy my brain how best to serve thee.

[[1] 'The' 1562 corrected in the errata, and 1614: 'thy' 1567, 1578, and 1607.]

Good Lord, thou needest not my service: perfect thou wast before I was: therefore it is for mine own commodity that thou commandest me, yea, even for mine own wealth. Thou mightest have letten me have stand all day idle; but such is thy love that thou wouldest I should go into thy vineyard, that with thy servants I might receive the hire of blessedness. And how great a benefit is it to deliver me of so great a burden, wherewith I should have been cumbered, if I should have served thee in any point after my wit and reason! But, alas! I not considering what a promotion thy service is, nor what an easy service it is and simple (for one may well know what to do and when he pleaseth thee, namely, when he serveth thee as thou hast appointed), as I am and always have been unthankful, so I am and always have been a grievous transgressor of this thy law. For as in times past, when I did not know this commandment, I was an image-worshipper of stocks, stones, &c., yea, bread and wine; so now I am a worshipper of mine affections, offering to them the service due unto thee, though not thereby to worship thee, as I thought when I kneeled to stocks and stones, bread and wine, &c., yet with no less transgression of thy law: for the which I have deserved and do deserve everlasting damnation. *Matt. xx.*

If we should serve God after man's device, the burden would be intolerable, for men's devices are infinite.

Of thy goodness and great mercy, dear Father, I beseech thee forgive me for Christ's sake, whom thou didst give to be the fulfilling of the law to all them that should believe. O Father, "I believe: help mine unbelief." As thou hast of thy goodness hitherto spared me, transgressing this thy holy precept; so of thy goodness forgive me as well mine idolatry done in times past, as that which of late time I have committed and do commit. And as thou by this commandment hast delivered me from the one, that is, bowing myself to stocks and stones, so, dear Father, deliver me from all other bowing myself after mine own will to mine own affections; that I may have none other God in heart but thee, nor do service to any other but only to thee, and for thee, after thy word as thou commandest. O open mine eyes to see thy will in this thy gracious precept. Give me a will to love it heartily, and a heart to obey it faithfully, for thy dear Son's sake, Jesus Christ our Lord. Amen. *Mark ix.*

THOU SHALT NOT TAKE THE NAME OF THE LORD THY GOD IN VAIN.

By this commandment I perceive, O Lord, that as in the first thou wouldest in the exterior service of thee I should utterly abandon mine own will and reason, and all the reasons or good intents of man, and wholly give myself to serve thee after thy will and word; so here dost thou begin to tell me how thou wilt have my tongue to be exercised in thy service: and therefore thou biddest me not to take thy name in vain, as by temerarious or vain swearing, by cursing, praying without sense, (as those do that pray in a tongue they know not, praying without faith or attent consideration of the thing desired, without hearty desire and certain expectation of obtaining that which is to thy glory and mine salvation;) also by jesting or foolish abusing, or negligent reading or hearing of thy holy word, by the which thou as by thy name art known; and in like manner by denying thy truth and word, or concealing it when occasion is offered to promote thy glory and confirm thy truth. By reason whereof I may well see that thou wouldest have me to use my tongue in humble confessing thee and thy word and truth, after my vocation; in praying heartily, and calling upon thy name; in reading and hearing thy word, and speaking thereof, with all reverence, diligence, and attention; in thanksgiving, and praising thee for thy great mercy; in instructing my brother, and admonishing him when he erreth, after my calling and vocation, with all humbleness, gentleness, and love.

Thus wouldest thou have me to exercise my tongue, and not to think that the exercising of it in this sort is a vain and unprofitable thing, but a thing that pleaseth thee and profiteth myself and other.

And forasmuch as thou knowest that our tongue is a slippery member, and we very negligent over it, and of the great commodity that might thereby come to us and other by using it in thy service accordingly; thou hast added a fearful and most true commination[1], that though men will find no fault or punish us therefor, yet wilt not thou hold him guiltless that taketh thy name in vain; as by many examples we are

Levit. xxiv.

[1 'communication' 1562: 'commination' 1567, 1578, 1607, 1614.]

taught, as in thy holy word, so by daily experience, if we would consider the same.

And therefore I have great cause to give praise and thanks to thy most holy name for many great benefits, which by this commandment I receive, and ought with thankfulness to consider. First, that it would please thee, not only to give me a tongue, where thou mightest have made me speechless; but also that thou wouldest have it sanctified to thy service. Again, that thou wouldest not only reveal thy name unto us, but also wouldest give me leave to call upon it, praise and publish it; yea, thou hast commanded me so to do, and not only commanded, but hast promised that thou wilt hear my prayer, and that my praising of thee and confessing thy word and truth shall not be in vain. Thirdly, that thou wouldest all men should use their tongue so that thereby I might be the better instructed, admonished, and occasioned to use myself well, and in the obedience of this thy holy precept. But what go I about to reckon by tale the causes of thanks for this commandment? seeing that they be innumerable, if a man should but look even upon thy very word, by the which as by thy name thou art most truly known: the which word thou commandest unto us in this commandment, &c., as thou dost preaching, private admonishing, thanksgiving, and prayer; than the which nothing is more profitable to us in this vale of misery.

But, gracious good Lord, I acknowledge myself not only to be a most unthankful wretch for this thy holy precept, and the great mercies which herethrough I perceive thou hast most graciously poured upon me, and dost yet still offer unto me; but also that I am a miserable transgressor of this thy most holy, good, and blessed commandment, as always I have been in times past. Horribly have I abused thy name in swearing, cursing, and jesting wickedly. I have called upon other names than thine, as the names of Peter, Paul, Mary, &c., yea, of some whose salvation is to be doubted of. I have foolishly prayed in such a tongue as I knew not what I prayed and said; with many other transgressions of this precept, wherein yet I am conversant, as in seldom praying; and when I pray, I am not attent, nor very desirous of the thing I ask with my tongue. After prayer I do not earnestly look for the good things asked and prayed for; and therefore when I obtain my request, I am most unthankful: thy word I read little and most negligently, forgetting forthwith what I read: I admonish not others when I hear them abuse thy holy word: I am afraid, for fear of loss of friends, name, or life, to confess thy truth, gospel, and name which was called upon me in baptism, and not in vain if I did not thus make it in vain. But, alas! I can in no wise comprehend the multitude of my transgressions concerning this thy law.

But this is a sin above other sins, that under thy name, word, and gospel, I play the hypocrite, having more care for mine own name than for thine: for if my name were evil spoken of, it would grieve me, and I would defend it; but, alas! I hear thine daily evil spoken of, and see it profaned by false doctrine and evil living, but it grieveth me not. After my vocation I seek not, nor do not go about to redress these things in myself and in others. And why? Because, good Lord, I love myself better than thee, and not thee with my whole heart. Thy first commandment hath no place with me, as it should have: it possesseth not my heart, mind, and will, as thou requirest most to mine own commodity: by reason whereof I am worthy of eternal damnation.

O what shall I do, gracious God, which not only have been so grievous and filthy a swearer, curser, &c., so great a caller upon dead creatures, and so heinous a transgressor of this law; but also at this present do so horribly and hypocritically offend thee, in taking thy name in vain, and that so many ways; in praying and not praying; in reading and not reading; in speaking and not speaking; and not confessing simply and from my heart thy doctrine, truth, and name; but regarding mine own name far above it? Shall I fly from thee? Then undoubtedly I am more guilty, and more shall disobey this thy holy precept, adding sin to sin: whereas thou wouldest I should call upon thy holy name, dear Lord, which hast given thy dear Son Jesus Christ to be a Mediator for us; that through him we might find not only grace for the pardon of our sins past, but also for the obtaining of thy holy Spirit; as well the better to understand, as also the better and more frankly to obey, this thy holy precept for ever.

For his sake therefore, dear God, pardon my sins past and present, whereof this law doth accuse me; and grant, most gracious Father, that I may be endued with thy holy Spirit, to know and love thy holy name, word, and truth in Jesus Christ; that I may be zealous, wise, and constant; and that my tongue may be sanctified henceforth, and guided with thy holy Spirit and grace, to publish, confess, and teach after my vocation to others, as occasion is offered, thy truth and gospel; to call upon thy name in all my need, to give thanks unto thee, praise thee, magnify thee, and to sanctify thy holy name, as a vessel of thy mercy, for ever and ever.

REMEMBER THAT THOU KEEP HOLY THE SABBATH DAY, &c.

AFTER thou hast told me how in the external service of thee, gracious Lord, thou wilt have my tongue used, so dost thou now teach me how thou wilt have mine ears and all my whole body occupied, namely in sanctification and holiness; that is, in those things which thou peculiarly hast appointed to be means immediately to help to that end; as in hearing thy word preached, and using the ceremonies of thee appointed, even as thou hast commanded: for the which things to be exercised of thy people thou at the first didst appoint a certain day, namely the seventh day, which therefore thou calledst thy sabbath, that thereby they with their children and family, resting from all exterior labour which hindereth the meditation of the mind, might not only be more able to go on through with their travail and labour (for without some rest nothing can endure, in respect whereof thou wouldest the very beasts which in labour were exercised should have the privilege of this sabbath), but also and much rather that thy people might with their family and children be instructed and taught; first by the ministry of thy word in preaching and catechising; secondly by the using of thy sacraments, appointed after thy commandment and institution, they might be assured of thy promises; thirdly by praying they might be augmented in all godliness; and last of all by their meeting together, and exercising all these thy works of sanctification, they might increase in love and charity one towards another, as members of one body, and fellows of one inheritance; and thus by meeting together, praying, and using thy sacraments, they might be instructed in thy law, and of that sabbath whereinto thou thyself didst enter after thou hadst made the world, ceasing from thy works, not of conservation, but of creation: into the which as after this life, and the works of this time, they should enter, so now they begin spiritually to enter, in resting from their own works which the old man moveth them unto.

Not that, good Lord, thou wouldest these works, appointed for the sabbath day, should not be exercised at any other time, but only on the seventh day; but because thou didst as well ordain them for a policy to endure till the coming of Christ, as also according to the revelation of thee in that time didst open thyself, beginning then in figures and shadows whose verities in thy time were to be opened, therefore it pleased thee to appoint then the seventh day: which seventh day, although by reason of the policy being by thee destroyed, and by reason of Christ the verity and body of all shadows, it be abrogate from us; yet standeth this commandment in force, as well for the works of sanctification, that is, for preaching thy word, coming to hear it, for praying, using thy sacraments, and coming together to that end; as also for those days which by common order and on good ground are ordained and received; howbeit with this liberty, that necessity of our faith and sanctification and charity may dispense therewith, occasion of wilful and witting offence being avoided, &c.

So that hereby I perceive thy will and pleasure to be, that I should at all times, as much as charity and necessity will permit, give over myself, and cause all other, over whom I have charge, so to do (especially on the Sundays and other holidays being received, and to that end appointed), to the resorting to the temple and places appointed to prayer; to hear with meekness thy holy word, and use thy sacraments and ceremonies as thou hast commanded; and to exercise all things which might be to the confirmation and propagation of thy holy religion, or make to the increase of love and charity; as giving to the poor, reconciling such as be in variance, visiting the sick, and even, as it were, beginning that sabbath whereof Esay speaketh.

Isai. lviii.

By reason whereof I have great cause to thank thee, most gracious Father, that thou wouldest appoint me to be in this time, wherein thou hast more plentifully revealed thyself than thou didst, not only before Christ's coming, but also since Christ's ascension. Never, since England was England, didst thou so manifestly reveal thy truth, as thou hast done in these days. Great cause I have to thank thee, that thou wouldest institute the ministry of thy word and sacraments, as means whereby thy holy Spirit is effectual to work in our hearts sanctification. Great cause have I to thank thee, that thou wouldest keep the books of the prophets and apostles until this time. Great cause have I to praise thee, that thou wouldest give me such knowledge in them as thou hast done of thy great mercy. Great cause have I to thank thee for the good and true ministers and preachers of thy word, which thou hast sent amongst us, and given me grace to hear them. Great cause have I to thank thee, that in this religion thou hast given so long quietness and harborough to thy church. Great cause have I to thank thee, for that thou wouldest make me such a man in whom thy holy Spirit might work. Great cause I have to thank thee, which wouldest call me into thine eternal sabbath and rest, full of all joy, such as "the eye hath not seen, the ear hath not heard." Great cause have I to thank thee, that so many days are appointed for this end, that we should meet together to hear thy word and receive thy sacraments. Great cause have I to thank thee for the institution of thy sacraments, which thou hast ordained as thy visible and palpable words, to the obsignation and confirmation of the faith of all such as use the same after thy commandments. But infinite are the causes for the which I ought to give thee thanks for this commandment.

But, alas! I am not only unthankful, but also a most miserable transgressor of it. I will not now speak of my transgressions past concerning this commandment: presently they are so many that I cannot; for thou knowest how I do not only at convenient times, on the work-days, keep myself away from common prayers in the congregation and assembly of thy people, and from hearing of thy word, but also on the sabbath-days. To ride or go about this or that worldly business I am very prest[1]: to sit down at this tavern, and to go to that man's table, I am ready at the first bidding: but, alas! to resort to the table of thy Son, and receive with thankfulness the sacrament of his body and blood, for confirmation of my faith; that is, to learn spiritually to taste Christ's body broken, and his blood shed,

[1 i. e. ready.]

for the remission of my sins; to do this, O how unwilling am I! To go to mass and sacrings[1], with such-like idolatry, I have been a great time more ready than now I am to hear thy word, and use thy sacraments, as I should do. Thy ministers I pray not for; thy church I am not careful for; no, not now, good Lord, when wicked doctrine most prevaileth, idolatry, superstition, and abomination aboundeth, the sacrament and sacrifice of thy dear Son Jesus Christ is blasphemously corrupted; when for preaching there is nothing but massing; for catechising, censing[2]; for reading of the scriptures, bell-ringing; for singing of psalms and godly songs to our edification, all is done in Latin, with such notes, tunes, ditties, and descants[3], that utterly the mind is pulled from the consideration of the thing (if men did understand it) unto the melody. All which my wickedness hath brought in, my profaning of this commandment, and my not praying.

This was his meditation in queen Mary's time. [1614.]

Now in the reign of queen Mary all papistry was brought again into England. [1567.]

Behold how the children of God accuse themselves, as well for general as particular plagues. [1567.]

Thy ministers are in prison, dispersed in other countries, spoiled, burnt, murdered: many fall for fear of goods, life, name, &c., from the truth they have received, unto most manifest idolatry: false preachers abound amongst thy people: thy people, dearly bought even with thy blood, are not fed with the bread of thy word, but with swillings[4]: antichrist wholly prevaileth: and yet for all this, alas! I am too careless, nothing lamenting my sins, which be the cause of all this.

O dear Father, forgive me for Christ's sake, and be merciful unto me; and as of thy mercy thou hast given[5] me time to repent, so give me repentance. Grant me thy holy Spirit to open to me this thy law; so that I may know thy will in it, love it, and always obey it. Thy good Spirit sanctify me, and work in me a true taste of eternal life, and pleasure in the meditation of it. Give me, gracious, good

[1 'sacre,' to consecrate: 'sacring,' technically, the elevation of the host, at which time the 'sacring bell' was rung. See Becon, Displaying of the Mass, Works, Parker Soc. III. 270; and a like passage in Abp. Cranmer, Works, Parker Soc. I. 229: see also Ancient English Liturgy, Maskell, ed. 1846, p. 93.]

[2 i. e. the perfuming with incense.]

[3 i. e. variations of an air in music.]

[4 i. e. food for swine.]

[5 'Hast given' 1562 corrected in the errata for 'didst give,' 1567, 1578, 1607, and 1614.]

Father, one little mouthful of the bread that thou feddest Eli withal: give me that with him I may come into mount Horeb. Help thy church, cherish it, and give it harborough here and elsewhere for Christ's sake. Purge thy ministry from corruption and false ministers; send out preachers to feed thy people; destroy antichrist and all his kingdom; give to such as be fallen from thy truth repentance; keep others from falling, and by their falling do thou the more confirm us. Confirm the ministers and poor people in prison and exile; strengthen them in thy truth; deliver them, if it be thy good will: give them that with conscience they may so answer their adversaries, that thy servants may rejoice, and the adversaries be confounded. Avenge thou thy own cause, O thou God of hosts; and help all thy people, and me especially, because I have most need.

1 Kings xix.

HONOUR THY FATHER AND MOTHER, THAT THOU MAYEST LIVE LONG, &c.

AFTER that thou hast told me, good Lord, thy will concerning the service which thou requirest inwardly and outwardly to be given unto thee, now dost thou begin to tell me what thy will is that I should do and leave undone for thy sake unto man. And first thou settest before mine eyes them whom thou for order's sake and the more commodity of man in this life hast set in degree and authority above me, comprehending them under the name of "father and mother," that I might know that as of thee they are commanded to bear towards me a fatherly[6] love and a motherly care, in the very names of father and mother, wherewith thou honourest them; so am I commanded of thee to do that which is most equal and just (as the very brute beasts do teach us), that with childly affection and duty I should behave myself towards them: that is, I should honour them, which comprehendeth in it love, thankfulness, reverence, and obedience; and that not so much because they be my parents, and in their offices are careful for me, (for it may be they will neglect the doing of their duties towards me,) but because thou commandest me so to do, howsoever they do.

So that by this commandment I perceive that thou

[6 'fatherly' 1562 corrected in the list of errata, 1567, 1578, 1607, and 1614.]

[BRADFORD.]

wouldest I should consider them whom thou hast placed in authority and superior degree, as parents, magistrates, masters, or such-like, and accordingly behave myself toward them, honour them, that is to say, love them, be thankful unto them, reverence them, and obey them, for thy sake, so long as they pass not their bounds; that is, so long as they require not otherwise than thou hast given them commission or permission to do.

And forasmuch as thou seest their care and office is great, and our corruption to obey is very much; as well to encourage them in their vocation to be diligent, as to inflame me to humble obedience unto them, therethrough to make them more willing to sustain cares for me; thou addest a promise, that is, long life, which, so far as it is a blessing from thee, thou wilt endue us withal. Whereby we may gather, that a civil[1] life doth much please thee, and receiveth here rewards, especially if we lead it for conscience to thy law: and, on the contrary part, a disobedient life to them that be in authority will bring the sooner thy wrath and vengeance in this life. All which worketh much to the commendation of the state of politic and civil magistrates.

By reason hereof, dear Father, I see myself much bounden to praise thee, and heartily to obey this thy commandment; for in it and by it thou declarest thy great love toward us, which even in this present life, our pilgrimage and passage to our home, wouldest have us to enjoy the benefit of peace, and most seemly quietness and order, and by this order so couple us that none should contemn or despise another, but even high and low to be and account themselves as parents and children.

Particularly, for my part, I cannot but say that I have most cause to thank thee for my parents, schoolmasters, and others, under whose tuition thou hast put me. No pen is able to write the particular benefits which I have hereby received in my infancy, childhood, youth, middle age, and always hitherto. O how good a Lord hast thou declared thyself to me! which in them and by them hast nourished, fed, instructed, corrected, defended, and most graciously kept me. I could reckon innumerable behind me, and but few before me, so much made of and cared for as I have been

[1 i. e. subject to human government.]

hitherto. No small token of thy love to me-ward is it, that thou wouldest engrave in their hearts, and command them under pain of damnation, to be careful over me, to do me good, and provide for me, as they have done, or rather thou by them.

Publicly also for the commonwealth, and such as thou hast placed in authority over me in both thy regiments[2], if I considered them that have been and them that be, I could not but praise thee, good Lord; for no less praiseworthy art thou for thus chastening us, and admonishing us now presently by them that be in authority of our ingratitude and unthankfulness, than by such as have been, for all kinds of good things. But infinite are the causes of thankfulness, which this commandment considered should stir up in me.

But, alas! most merciful Father, as I acknowledge myself most unthankful unto thee for all thy benefits poured upon me in this life by my parents, nurses, tutors, masters, magistrates, bishops, pastors, and good friends, even from my cradle unto this hour, so unto them have I always been and am in not loving them, as my coldness in praying for them and to my power in helping them declareth; and also my not reverencing them, my contemning them, and temerariousness[3] in my mistrusting, or too narrowly and too straitly looking at them and their duties, sheweth; and not obeying them (as by my contumacy appeareth,) not only when anything to me unpleasant or unprofitable, but also profitable and convenient is required. And yet I speak not of the evil and muttering reports, of the offences in transgressing the politic laws for apparel and meats, and other no small offences which I have committed and given. O this is a sin, dear Father, that I always have been a private more than a commonweal man: always I seek for mine own commodity, contemning that which maketh to the commodity of others. As for my disobedience and wicked behaviour towards my own parents and all others whom thou hast set over me, dear Father, no tongue can express it: and therefore I am worthy of damnation.

But, gracious good Lord and dear Father, I beseech thee for thy Christ's sake to have mercy upon me and pardon me, as of thy goodness it pleased thee to pardon the

[2 i.e. governments.]   [3 i.e. rashness.]

patriarchs. Thou hast given this commandment as thy holy law, to open to us how corrupt we are, and how much we swerve from the pattern whereafter we were first made, and once agreed thereto before Adam's fall; that we might loathe ourselves, and even thereby be driven to seek and set by thy sweet mercies in Jesus Christ; whom therefore thou didst send to fulfil the law in his flesh, that we might borrow of him the same by true faith: which of thy goodness work in us by thy holy Spirit, and open this law unto us, that we may more and more increase in the knowledge, love, and obedience of it, to thy glory and our salvation. Amen.

Dear Father, be merciful to our magistrates, especially the queen's highness, whose heart with the residue of her counsellors turn into thy testimonies: give them thy wisdom and a zeal to the truth according to knowledge, that they may use the power they have received of thee to the cherishing of thy church, that with us here thy word may have free passage, and thy true worship may be maintained; and not only here, but also every where amongst those whom thou wouldest we should pray for.

Be merciful to my poor parents, gracious Lord, with my brethren, sisters, wife, children, family, servants, kinsfolks, neighbours, as thou knowest they have all need. Give unto the hearts of all parents, magistrates, and such as be in authority here or elsewhere, that they may according to that thou hast put them in trust withal be faithful, diligent, careful, and happy. Grant unto children, servants, and subjects, that every one may render love, obedience, thankfulness, and reverence to all such as thou hast put in authority over them. Bless the church, and send it peace and harborough here or elsewhere. Bless the commonweal, and send us peace. Bless the dioceses and shires, and send them good bishops and justices. Bless every household and family, that thy peace may be in the same continually.

Finally write this law and all thy laws in our hearts, we beseech thee, that we may keep them. Amen.

THOU SHALT DO NO MURDER, &c.

As in the commandment going next before thou settest before me the personages of all such as thou for the commodity, order, and peace of man in this life hast placed in authority, accordingly of us for thy sake to be esteemed; so dost thou in this commandment set before us to look on the personages of all men generally, high and low, over whom thou givest us a charge that we shall not kill or murder them: in which word thou comprehendest all kind of hatred or malice, in word, thought, or deed, as thy dearly beloved Son, expounding this commandment, doth teach. Yea, because thou wouldest all men should be dear unto us, being all of one substance, of one similitude, coming of the same parents Adam and Eve, made of one God, redeemed of one Christ in whom we should be coupled as members of one body, and live to the aid, succour, and comfort one of another; because of this, I say, easily we may see that not only thou forbiddest here to beware of all kinds of displeasures, but also thou commandest us to bear and exercise all kind of love and favour in heart, word, and deed, and that for thy commandment's sake; for else towards our enemies our hearts would arise and be great, in that they, contemning their duties towards us, seem to deserve the like at our hands. _{Matt. v.}

By reason hereof I have great cause to thank thee, dear Father: for hereby I see how that thou dost much love my soul, which art so careful over my body; so that he which hurteth it displeaseth thee, and he that doth it good pleaseth thee, if so be he do it for thy sake. By this commandment now I see that it is thou that hast kept me from doing many evils, which else I should have outrageously done, and hast stirred me up to do good to my brethren, if at any time I have done any; even as thou hast also kept and dost keep presently others from doing me hurt, and hast and dost stir up those that do me good, to do so unto me. O how great is the multitude of thy benefits, good Lord, wherewith thou hast overwhelmed me, and the which through this commandment I perceive myself to have received, presently do receive, and so long as I live am like to receive! for thou commandest all men every where to do me good, love me, defend me, and cherish me; such is thy love to me in this present life, and that for my body. O how great is thy love then to me in everlasting life, and that for my soul! If in a strange country so great is thy protection, how great is it at home!

But, alas, dear Lord, how unthankful have I been, and am yet still, for these thy fatherly benefits! O mine ingratitude! Yea, Lord, horribly have I transgressed, and still do transgress this thy gracious precept, in pride, envy, disdain, malice, hardness of heart, unmercifulness, and contemning thy children, saints, and servants. Self-love altogether reigneth in me, and desire of praise, rule, and fame: I am so far from love and mercy in heart, good Lord, that no man can hear it in my tongue, nor see it in my works; but rather clean contrary, and that generally, and to them to whom I am most bound particularly. By reason whereof I have deserved everlasting damnation, and to be cast away from thy presence for ever.

O most gracious Father, forgive me for Christ's sake, I beseech thee: for to this end didst thou give this commandment, that I, seeing my corruption and depravate nature by sin, might come to thy mercy deserved by Christ, and through faith in him might find not only pardon of that which is past, but also thy grace and holy Spirit to begin in me the obedience to this and all other thy holy precepts for evermore. So be it.

For this thy Christ's sake, dear Father, I beseech thee therefore to take from me, and all other for whom thou wouldest that we should pray, all envy, pride, arrogancy, disdain, hatred, and all suspiciousness; and grant unto us bowels of mercy, humility, patience, meekness, long-suffering, gentleness, peace, charity, and all kind of brotherly love. Comfort the feeble, relieve the poor, help the fatherless, heal the sick, bless the afflicted: shew thy great mercy upon all poor prisoners, and deliver them in thy good time: remember thy pity toward strangers, captives, widows, and such as be oppressed.

THOU SHALT NOT COMMIT ADULTERY.

HERE, good Lord, thou goest about to command unto me, as love in the other, so pureness and chastity in this; and therefore thou sayest, I should "not commit adultery:" in the which word thy Son our Saviour Jesus Christ doth comprehend all uncleanness, yea, the very concupiscence and abusing of the heart in lusting after any man's wife, or otherwise unchastely. By the which, in that thou wouldest have us to love in ourselves and others purity and cleanness, that we might be holy as thou our God art holy, and our bodies being temples of thy holy Spirit might be kept pure and accordingly; easily we may see that, as thou forbiddest all unclean deeds, words, looks, and thoughts, so dost thou command us to love and exercise all purity, chastity, cleanness, sobriety, temperancy, &c.

By reason whereof I have great cause to be thankful unto thee, which not only for the help and commodity of man, but also for remedy of man's infirmity, hast made womankind, and ordained the state of matrimony, which in thy sight is so holy and pure that thou accountest the[1] state of matrimony to be an undefiled thing: and such care thou hast over the personages married and their condition, that unto damnation they sin, which not only go about to defile that bed, but within their hearts do wish or desire it; yea, which do not endeavour themselves with thought, word, and deed, to help that purity and cleanness between married folks be kept. But the great causes thou givest us to thank thee for this state and ordinance, and for thy defending us by this commandment, are innumerable.

Full well I see that it is thou which by this commandment not only refrainest me, but also keepest my wife from impurity, which else we might both commit. Great is thy love, O good Lord, and more than I am able to consider, which declarest thyself to be thus careful over me concerning the benefits which come unto me both for the mind, body, and goods, by sobriety and temperancy, which here thou requirest. Only this I cannot but see, that I have great cause to thank thee which art so careful over me, as by this commandment I well see.

But, alas! good Lord, what shall I say? which am and have been so far from thankfulness, that I am to be accounted amongst the most unthankful: yea, thou knowest it, good Lord. Filthily have I broken this law, and caused other so to do, of whose repentance I am uncertain; as also my tongue, alas! hath often been too shamefully exercised, mine eyes and my thoughts too wickedly abused. All this gear I have increased by mine intemperancy in eating, drinking, cherishing my body, &c. I have also hurt my bodily health, minished that which I and others should live on, and horribly hindered all good prayers and meditations: wherein, though I have time and place, yet, alas! I nothing exercise

[1 A few words of the original are omitted.]

myself as I should do. By reason whereof I have deserved everlasting damnation.

O good Lord and gracious Father, do thou for thy name's sake, and in Christ's blood, pardon me and forgive me, I beseech thee. And as thou hast most mercifully hitherto spared me, so of thy mercy put away my trespasses, and the transgressions of those whom I have caused to sin. Let that love which moved thee to pardon Judah, with Tamar, David, Bethsabe, and the great sinner of whom we read in St Luke, move thee to pardon and forgive me also. Thou gavest this commandment to this end, that I might know my sin and sinful nature, and so thereby be driven to thy Christ crucified, for whose sake I ask mercy; and also that thy good Spirit may be given unto me, to purify me, and work so in me and with me, that I may truly know, heartily love, and faithfully obey this thy holy precept, inwardly and outwardly, now and for ever. Amen.

<small>Luke vii.</small>

Gracious good Lord, grant to me and my wife, that we may dwell together according to knowledge, and may keep our vessels in holiness: grant, O Lord, that we may be pure and undefiled; and grant the same to all that be married: and to them which be unmarried grant that they may live a pure, chaste, and undefiled life; and, if they have not the gift of singleness of life, grant them such mates with whom they may live holily to thy praise. Dear Father, give me the gift of sobriety and temperancy, and, grant the same to all them whom thou wouldest I should pray for. As in times past I have used my tongue and other members evil, so now, good Lord, grant that I may use them well, chastely, and godly. This, I pray thee, grant through Jesus Christ: and finally, O Lord, both in soul and body sanctify me, and, as in thy temple, dwell in me now and for evermore. Amen.

THOU SHALT NOT STEAL.

Now that thou hast taught me the service required of thee for me to observe towards the personages of all men and women of every condition, thou beginnest to tell me what thou wouldest I should do concerning their goods: and, as in the next commandment before this thou didst command unto me sobriety and pureness, so dost thou in this justice and righteousness, forbidding me to steal; under the which word thou comprehendest all kinds of deceit. The which thing thou doest, because thou wouldest that I should give myself wholly to the study and exercise of justice; as in the precept next going before thou wouldest I should give over myself wholly to the keeping of sobriety and pureness: so that I see thy good pleasure herein is not that I should alonely abstain from all theft, but also from all fraud and craft in word or deed; yea, that I should earnestly follow and exercise all equity, truth, and justice.

By reason whereof I see myself much bound to praise thee, which art so careful over my goods and substance, that, if any man should go about to steal from me, or to defraud me in any thing, yea, whosoever goeth not about to keep and care for that I have as he would do for his own, the same displeaseth thee.

O Lord, if thou hast such care for my goods, cattle, and such pelf, how great is thy care for my soul! If this one commandment were not, I perceive, as I for my own part should have done and do much worse than I have done, so much worse had been done to me and mine than hath been. It is thou, good Lord, I perceive, that hast both given me all that I have, and also still conservest and keepest the same; and not my own policy, wisdom, and industry; for in vain were all this, except thou didst vouchsafe to use and take it as a mean to work by. There is nothing therefore that I have, but whensoever I look upon it, by this commandment I learn thy goodness, strength, and power; for, as thou givest it of thy mercy, so it speaketh to me that presently thou still dost keep it for me: so that exceeding great cause have I to thank thee for this precept, dear God and most gracious Lord.

But, alas! I am so far from thankfulness (as always I have been for all thy care for me, and for all that ever thou hast given unto me), that, as I have used subtlety and craft, yea, sometimes theft and bribery; so now, good Lord, I still, when occasion is offered, do exercise the same. I live also voluptuously of that thou hast given and lent me, and nothing consider what equity requireth, and what or how great the necessity of the poor is, whom I do thus defraud by excess and prodigality. That which I borrow I with unwillingness do repay: I use it more negligently than I would do mine own. Lack of excommunication, of justice, the great usury, robbery, oppression, and such-like wickedness as is exercised amongst us, I lament not, labour not after my vocation for the redress of the same; I pray not to thee thereabout, but neglect altogether. Yea, even those things wherewith I am put in trust, or am hired to do, those, I say, I do with great negligence: so that great is my sin herein, and worthy I am of damnation.

But, merciful God, I beseech thee for Christ's sake to have mercy upon me, and to pardon me my unthankfulness, thefts, frauds, deceits, avarice, negligences, and great carelessness for the lack of justice, and for the monstrous oppression, usuries, excess, riot, the which be horribly exercised in the commonweal. For thy mercy's sake in Christ Jesus, O Lord, whom thou hast given to fulfil the law for them that do believe, give me true faith and thy holy Spirit, to work in me the knowledge, love, and perpetual obedience of this thy holy precept and all other thy commandments for ever.

Dear Lord, give unto me, and to all whom thou wouldest I should pray for, the hatred of all craft, and love of all justice. Grant to the oppressed thy comfort; to wrongers repentance; to thieves and deceivers, that they may make restitution; to justices of peace, landlords, and the rich of the world, that they may have thee before their eyes, love their poor tenants and brethren; to labourers and artificers, that they may be diligent in their work and labour, and that wherewith they are put in trust.

THOU SHALT NOT BEAR FALSE WITNESS AGAINST THY NEIGHBOUR.

Now dost thou, most gracious Lord, instruct me in this commandment, how I should use my tongue towards my neighbour, and behave myself concerning his name, forbidding me to bear false witness; in the which thou forbiddest me all kinds of slandering, lying, hypocrisy, and untruth. And why? Because, as "members of one body," thou wouldest we should "speak truth one to another," and be careful every one to cover other's infirmity, and with our tongue defend the names of others, even as we would that other should defend ours: so that in this commandment, as thou forbiddest me all kind of evil, perilous, calumnious and untrue speaking, so dost thou command to me all kind of godly, honest, and true report and talk.

By reason whereof I have great cause to praise thee, in that I see thee to be so careful over my name, that all men are by thee commanded to defend the same. O precious God, great is thy care over my soul, I now perceive. If this commandment were not, I see, as I should have done and do much worse with my tongue to others than is happened, so should I have felt of others towards me. Besides this, no small commodity is it to me, that thou wouldest all men should use truth in all their words to me.

O how great a good thing is this unto me! If we consider the hurt that cometh by untruth, and by words wherethrough many are deceived, easily may we see a wonderful benefit and care of thee for us in this commandment.

But, gracious Lord, like as I acknowledge my unthankfulness to be monstrous and great, and always hath been hitherto, even so yet continue I in wonderful hypocrisy in all my conversation; often lying, and speaking, as vainly, so offensively, fleshly, subtlely, calumniously, and giving my ears to hear such things as be slanderously spoken; not repugning or admonishing other, as the slanderer to do as he would be done by, to tell his tale where he should tell it, neither admonishing the party slandered of that which is reported of him, thereby to take better heed; but rather I augment it. By reason whereof I have deserved eternal damnation.

But thou, good Lord, be merciful unto me, I beseech thee, for Christ's sake, whom thou hast ordained to be "the end of the law to all them that do believe," as well for pardon of that which is past, as for not imputing the imperfection that remaineth. In his name therefore, good Lord, I beseech thee to pardon me, and give me thy holy Spirit to open to me this law and all other thy precepts, so to understand them that I may heartily love them, and faithfully give myself to the obedience of them for ever. Grant me thy good Spirit to sanctify my tongue, that it may be kept from lying, slandering, and all such vices; and that it may be continually used in thy service, and speaking that which may be to edify to thy glory and praise, through Jesus Christ our Lord. Amen.

THOU SHALT NOT COVET THY NEIGHBOUR'S HOUSE, THOU SHALT NOT COVET THY NEIGHBOUR'S WIFE, NOR HIS SERVANT, NOR HIS MAID, NOR HIS OX, NOR HIS ASS, NOR ANY THING THAT IS HIS.

Meditations of Bradford, Allde 1604[1], and after editions.

HERE, O most gracious Lord God, thou givest me the last commandment of thy law who having taught me what outward actions I shall avoid, that I do not thereby offend or undo my neighbour, as murder, adultery, theft, and false witness, now thou teachest me a rule for my heart, to order that well, from the abundance whereof all our works and words proceed, that I shall not covet any thing that is my neighbour's.

I know hereby that, if he have a fairer house than I, I may not wish for it; if he have a more beautiful wife than I, I may not desire her; if he have an honest and a faithful servant, and such a one as helpeth to get his living, I must not think to myself I would I had him away from his master; I may not desire to take from him his ox, nor his ass, no, not his dog, no, not the meanest thing he hath in his possession. So that, in the other commandments[2] as thou hast forbidden all injuries and evil practice against my neighbour, so now thou chargest me to beware of thinking any evil thought against him.

By reason whereof I have great cause to praise thee, in that I see thee to be so careful over mine estate, my house, my wife, my servants, and the beasts that drudge for my service, that all men are by thee commanded not once to wish them from me. The apostle said well, when he taught us, saying, "Cast all your care upon God, for he careth for you." It is true, I find it true: thus thou "carest for us," and wouldest have us to "care one for another."

But, gracious Lord, I must needs confess that I have forgotten and broken this commandment, and do so still every day. I am wishing and woulding every minute of an hour: I have gone about to take my neighbour's house over his head: many times have I had unchaste thoughts in my heart touching his wife and children: I have gone about to inveigle and entice his servants from him: I could have been content to have wrought his beast and spared my own: I

[1 See prefatory note, p. 112 above.]
[2 So 1614: 'commandment' 1604, 1607.]

always thought he had too much, and I too little: and the dregs of these things, O Lord, are not quite out of my heart. By reason whereof I have deserved to have thy law executed upon me with all severity.

But thou, good Lord, be merciful unto me in this point also for Jesus Christ's sake; for otherwise I am of all men most miserable. Good Lord, pardon me; consider the frailty of my flesh, the corruption of my nature, the multitude of temptations, how of myself I am able to do nothing, how if I be left to myself I shall come to nothing.

Set my heart straight in the case of religion to acknowledge thee one God, to worship none other God, to reverence thy name, and to keep thy sabbaths. Set my heart right in matters of human conversation, to honour my parents, to obey rulers, and reverence the ministry of the gospel; to have hands clean from blood, true from theft, a body free from adultery, and a tongue void of all offence. But purge the heart first, O Lord, and then the hand, the eye, the tongue, the foot, and all the whole body will be the cleaner.

Write all these thy laws in my heart, O Lord, and in the hearts of all the faithful people; that we may believe them and keep them all the days of our lives, to thy glory and praise, through Jesus Christ our Saviour. Amen.

A MEDITATION
CONCERNING PRAYER[3].

THE mind of man hath so large room[4] to receive good things, that nothing indeed can fully fill it but only God; whom then thy mind fully possesseth, when it fully knoweth him, it fully loveth him, and in all things is framed after his will. They therefore, dear Lord God, that are thy children and have tasted somewhat of thy goodness, do perpetually sigh, that is, do pray, until they come thereto: and, in that they love thee also above all things, it wonderfully woundeth them that other men do not so, that is, love thee, and seek for thee

Meditations of Bradford, Hall 1562, and after editions.

[3 The heading in 1562 is, 'A meditation concerning prayer, with a brief paraphrase upon the petitions of the Lord's Prayer.']
[4 So 1567: 'roomth' 1562, 1578, 1604, 1607, 1614.]

with them. Whereof it cometh to pass, that they are inflamed with continual prayers and desires that thy kingdom might come every where, and thy goodness might be both known, and in life expressed, of every man.

And because there are innumerable many things, which as well in themselves as in others be against thy glory, they are kindled with continual prayer and desire, sighing unspeakably in thy sight for the increase of thy Spirit: and sometimes when they see thy glory more put back than it was wont to be, either in themselves or in any other, then are they much more disquieted and vexed. But because they know that thou dost rule all things after thy good will, and that none other can help them in their need, they oftentimes do go aside, all businesses laid apart, and give themselves to godly cogitations and talk with thee, complaining to thee as to their Father of those things that grieve them, begging thereto, and that most earnestly, thy help not only for themselves, but also for others, especially for those whom singularly they embrace in thee; and often do repeat and remember thy gracious benefits both to others and to themselves also: wherethrough they are provoked to render to thee hearty thanks; thereby being inflamed, as well assuredly to hope well of thy good will towards them, and patiently to bear all evils, as also to study and labour to mortify the affections of the flesh, and to order all their whole life to the service of their brethren and to the setting forth of thy glory.

This they know is that prayer thy Son Jesus Christ our Lord commanded to be made to thee "in the chamber, the door being shut." In this kind of prayer he himself did watch often even "all the whole night." Herein was Paul frequent, as all thy saints be. This kind of prayer is the true lifting up of the mind unto thee: this standeth in the affections in the heart, not in words and in the mouth. As thy children be endued with thy Spirit, so frequent they this talk with thee: the more thy Spirit is in them, the more are they in talk with thee.

O give me plentifully thy Spirit, which thou hast promised to "pour out upon all flesh," that thus I may with thy saints talk with thee night and day, for thy only beloved Son's sake, Jesus Christ our Lord. Amen.

Moreover thy saints, to provoke them to this kind of

prayer, do use, first, their necessity, which they consider in three sorts; inwardly concerning their souls; outwardly concerning their bodies; and finally concerning their names and fame, whereto they add the necessity of those that be committed to them, the necessity of thy church, and of the commonweal.

Secondly, they use thy commandments, which require them, under pain of sin, to pray to thee in all their need.

Thirdly, they use the consideration of thy goodness, which art naturally merciful to "young ravens calling upon thee;" much more then to them for whom ravens and all things else were made, for whom thou hast "not spared thy dear Son, but given him," &c.

Fourthly, they use thy most sweet and free promises made to hear and help "all them that call upon thee" in Christ's name.

Fifthly, they use examples how that thou, which art the God of all, and "rich unto all them that call upon thee" in Christ's name, hast heard and holpen others calling upon thee.

Sixthly, they use the benefits given them before they asked, thereby not only provoking them to ask more, but also certifying their faith that, if thou wast so good to grant them many things unasked, now thou wilt not deny them any thing they ask to thy glory and their weal.

Last of all, they use the reading and weighing of psalms and other good prayers, because they know thereby peculiarly (besides the other scripture) there is no small help; as may appear by Paul, where he willeth the congregation to use "psalms, hymns, and spiritual songs," but so that in the heart we should sing and say them: not that thy children do not use their tongues and words in praying to thee; for they do use their tongues, speech, and words, to stir up their inward desire and fervency of the mind; full well knowing that else it were a plain mocking of thee, to pray with lips and tongues only. *Ephes. v Col. iii.*

O that I might feel now thy Spirit so to affect me, that both with heart and mouth I might heartily and in faith pray unto thee!

Now, concerning the things that are to be prayed for, thy children know that the prayer taught by thy Son most lively and plainly doth contain the same: and therefore they often use it, first asking of thee their heavenly Father through Christ, that thy name might every where be had in holiness and praise; then that thy kingdom by regeneration and the ministry of the gospel might come; and so thirdly, that willingly, perfectly, and perpetually, they might study to do, yea, do indeed thy will, with thy holy and heavenly angels and spirits. These things they seek and pray for, namely thy kingdom and thy righteousness, before any worldly benefit. After which petitions, because all things, yea, even the benefits of this present life, do come from thee, they do godly desire the same under the name of "daily bread," being instructed of thy wisdom, that after small benefits to ask corporal is not unseemly to thy children, which know both spiritual and corporal to come from thy mercy. In the other petitions they pray for things to be taken from them, beginning with forgiveness of sins, which were impudently prayed for, if that their hearts were not so broken, that they could forgive all things to all men for their part: they add their profession, that is, charity, whereby they profess that they have forgiven all offences done to them. Howbeit, because it is not enough to have pardon of that which is past, except they be preserved from new offences, they pray thee not to lead them into temptations by permitting them to the perverse suggestion of Satan, but rather to deliver them from his importunity and power; by "evil" understanding Satan the author of all evil.

O, dear God, that thou wouldest endue me with thy Spirit of grace and prayer, with thy children accordingly to make this prayer always whensoever I do pray!

As for outward evils, so long as they do not, as it were, enforce thy people to sin, in that christian perfection[1] doth account them amongst thy benefits, thy Son hath not taught thy church to pray for the taking away of them in this prayer; for here he hath contained but those things, for the which all christians, generally and particularly, may of faith pray at all times. It often cometh to pass that exterior evils, because they be not evils indeed, that is, they are not against God's grace in us, therefore they cannot of faith be prayed for to be taken away; for thy children that have faith do always prefer thy judgment before their own: the which judgment when they know by that which happeneth to them, they submit themselves thereto wholly; although the Spirit make his "unspeakable groanings" to help their infirmities by

[[1] 'perfection' 1562 corrected in the list of errata, 1567, 1578, and 1607: 'profession' 1614.]

prayer, not to have them taken away, but that they might have strength and patience to bear the burden accordingly. Which burden, if it be too heavy in the bitter sense and feeling thereof, they in their prayers do complain something, rather than pray to have it taken away; as our Saviour did in the garden, when he added to his complaint, "Not my will, but thy will, be done." So do thy people in all their complaints add, 'Not as we will, but as thou wilt:' for they are taught by thy Spirit no otherwise to pray for the taking away of corporal evils, either from themselves or from others, unless they by the same Spirit do certainly see the same to make to thy glory; (as did thine apostles and servants, when absolutely and without condition they did ask health or miracle for any, when they healed or raised the dead by prayer;) for they know nothing can be better than when it is according to thy will. O that I might always know thy will in all things, and for ever apply myself thereto!

Hereof it cometh that thy saints and dear children, which love their neighbours as themselves, do yet notwithstanding in their prayers ask vengeance of some, as we may read in the psalms of David; because, in praying and talking with thee, they see by thy holy Spirit (for without it is no true prayer) sometimes thy judgments upon some which they perceive to "sin to death," and therefore ought not to be prayed for, but rather to be prayed against, because thy glory cannot be set forth as it should be without their destruction. Thy will is always best, and the thing whereto they frame all their desires. Therefore, when they perceive it decreed with thee, such and such by their destruction to set forth more mightily thy glory; how should they but desire and pray for the same, and write it as David hath done? that the godly in reading and weighing such prayers might receive comfort, and the ungodly be afraid. Else, when that they perceive not so manifestly the determined judgment of God, they in their prayers do most heartily pray for them, as Samuel did for Saul, Moses for the Israelites, Abraham for the Sodomites.

O good Father, for thy mercy's sake, give me the true love of mankind; but yet so that I may love man for thee and in thee, and always prefer thy glory above all things, through Christ our Lord.

[BRADFORD.]

Now, though thy children do know that thy will cannot but be done, and nothing can be done but that thou of thine own will hast determined to do (although no man should desire the same), yet are they earnest and frequent in prayer; first, to render obedience to thee, which requirest prayer as a spiritual service to thee; secondly, because thou hast ordained prayer to be as an instrument and mean by the which thou workest things with thee already decreed and determined.

Thy children do use prayer to offer thee their service, if it shall please thee to use the same. As they do eat and drink, which is a mean ordained of thee for the conservation of their life, not looking hereby to lengthen their days above their bounds which already thou hast appointed, but as becometh them to use thy means which thou hast ordained to serve thy providence; so do they herein (as men not curious to know thy providence further than thou revealest it) use prayer as a mean by the which thou art accustomed to work many of thy children's desires, that according to thy good will thou mayest use the same. They do not think a mutability in thee; (for thou art God, and art not changed, "with thee there is no variableness;") and therefore they pray, not as men which would have thy determinations and ordinances, which are in most wisdom and mercy, to be altered; but rather that they might submit their wills to thine, and make them more able to bear thy will and pleasure. They know thou hast promised to help them calling upon thee: wherefore they doubt not but thou so wilt do, and therefore pray accordingly.

They love thee heartily, and therefore they cannot but desire much to talk with thee, that is, to pray; even as a well-mannered and loving wife will not take upon her to ask any thing of her husband at all but that she hopeth he would take in good part, and do of his own free will, although she had spoken nothing thereof. When she knoweth what her husband's will is in things, she gladly talketh with him thereof; and, accordingly as she seeth he is purposed to do, she will often desire him to do it. Even so thy children, I say, which heartily love thee, in that they know thy wisdom and will is best, how can they but often talk with thee, and desire thee to do that which they know is best; which they know also thou wouldest do, if none should ask or pray for the same?

Thy children use prayer as a mean by which they see plainly thy power, thy presence, thy providence, mercy, and goodness towards them, in granting their petitions; and by prayer they are confirmed of them all. Yea, thy children use prayer to admonish them how that all things are in thy hands. In prayer they are, as it were, of thee put in mind of those things they have done against thee their good Lord: by reason whereof repentance ensueth, and they conceive a purpose to live more purely ever afterwards, and more heartily to apply themselves to all innocency and goodness.

Who now considering so many great commodities to come by reason of prayer would marvel why thy children are much in prayer, and in labouring to provoke others thereunto? For, as none that is a suitor to any other will use any thing which might offend or hinder his suit, so no man that useth prayer will flatter himself in any thing that should displease thee, to whom by prayer he moveth suit whensoever he prayeth: so that nothing is a more provocation to all kind of godliness than prayer is. And therefore not without cause we may see thine apostles and servants to labour so diligently, and desire that others might use prayers for themselves and others.

As concerning outward things which thy children pray for, although they know thy will and decree is not variable, and thy purpose must needs come to pass, yet do they receive by their prayer no small commodity. For either they obtain their requests, or no: if they do obtain them, then prove they by experience that thou doest the will of them that fear thee, and so they are more kindled to love and serve thee. And indeed for this purpose thou art wont, when thou wilt do good to any, to stir up their minds to desire the same good of thee, to the end that both thou and thy gifts may be so much more magnified and set by of them, by how much they have been earnest suitors and petitioners for the same: for how can it but inflame them with love towards thee, to perceive and feel thee so to care for them, hear them, and love them? If they do not obtain that they pray for, yet undoubtedly they receive great comfort to see that the evils which press them, and whereof they complain still, do not oppress and overcome them; and therefore they receive strength to bear the same the better.

O good Father, help me that I might heartily love thee, complain to thee in all my needs, and always by prayer to pour out my heart before thee. Amen.

A PARAPHRASE

UPON THE LORD'S PRAYER[1].

O ALMIGHTY and eternal God, "of whom all fatherhood in heaven and in earth is named," whose "seat is the heaven, whose footstool is the earth;" which of thy great clemency and unspeakable love hast not weighed nor considered our great unkindness and wilful disobedience, but according to the good pleasure of thy eternal purpose hast in thy well-beloved Son Jesus Christ chosen us out of the world, and dost accept us, far otherwise than we be in deed, to be called, yea, and to be indeed, thine adopted sons; and dost vouchsafe, O loving Father, that we, as it were heavenly children, should every one of us confess, declare, and call thee 'our heavenly Father;' *Hallowed be thy name.* grant, dear Father, that among us thy poor children, by pureness of mind and conscience, by singleness of heart, by uncorrupt and innocent life, and example of virtue and godliness, thy most holy "name may be sanctified;" and that so many of all other nations as thou hast thereunto chosen and predestinate, beholding our godliness and virtuous deeds that thou workest in us, may be the more stirred to hallow and glorify thy blessed name.

Thy kingdom come. O faithful Father, we beseech thee that the kingdom of thy holy Spirit, of grace and prayer, of thy loving kindness and mercy, and of all other thy holy virtues, and of thy holy and most blessed word, may continually reign in our hearts; so that thou wouldest vouchsafe thereby to make us worthy to be partakers of the realm and kingdom of thy glorious and blessed presence.

Thy will be done. O dear God and heavenly Father, we humbly desire thy goodness to bow our hearts unto thee, to make us humble of mind, to make us low in our own sight and obedient; that, like as thy dear Son, our only Saviour Jesus Christ, counted

[1 The heading in 1562 is, 'Another paraphrase or meditation upon the Lord's Prayer.']

his meat, works, praise, and life, to be only in obeying to thy most blessed will, wherein for our sakes "he became obedient to the death of the cross;" so we may, even unto the very death, in lowliness, in meekness, patience, and thankfulness, obey unto thy holy will; and not to murmur and grudge, nor refuse whatsoever thy fatherly pity shall think good to lay on us, be it poverty, hunger, nakedness, sickness, slanders, oppressions, vexations, persecutions, yea, or death itself, for well-doing; but in all things seek and labour to make these our earthly bodies serviceable to do thy will, and to refuse that thou wilt not; never to strive nor wrestle against thy holy will; but, with thy heavenly "citizens and household, builded upon the foundation of thy holy prophets and apostles, thy Son Jesus Christ being the head cornerstone," all self-will and controversy in opinions secluded, the lusts, desires, and affections of the flesh mortified, the flattering assaults of the vain world, the cruel and subtle layings await of the devil, overcome, agreeing together quietly, and united in spirit, we may freely obey unto thy most blessed will, therein to walk all the days of our life.

O dear God, give unto our needful bodies necessary sustenance, and take from us all love of worldly things, all carefulness and covetousness, that we may the more freely worship and serve thee. O merciful Father, we beseech thee to give unto us that heavenly "bread" to strengthen our hearts, (I mean the body of thy dear Son Jesus Christ, the very food and health of our souls;) that we may always with thankfulness firmly feed on him by faith, and utterly forsake and abhor all false doctrine and persuasions of men, and all lying spirits that shall persuade us any otherwise of him than thy holy word doth teach and assure us. Satisfy our hungry souls, dear Father, with the marrow and fatness of thy rich mercy, promised to us in the same thy Son, and of our eternal election, redemption, justification, and glorification in him. Make us, O gracious God, to contemn and despise this world with the vain things and pleasures thereof, and inwardly to hunger for thy blessed kingdom and presence: which do thou satisfy, good God, in thy good time, according to thy good will and pleasure. O most loving God, give us the "bread" of thy divine precepts, and make our hearts perfect, that we may truly and freely walk and live in them all the days of

Give us this day our daily bread.

our life. O dear and merciful Father, we beseech thee, give us the "bread" of thy lively and heavenly word, and the true understanding thereof; which is the "light of our paths," the food, strong tower, and sure defence of our souls; that we, being well fenced with this munition, fed and filled with this food, may be worthy guests at thy celestial feast and wedding, where we shall never hunger nor want.

And forgive us our trespasses. O most righteous and merciful God, Father and Governor of our life, we confess that we have grievously sinned against thee from our youth up until now, in ingratitude, in unthankfulness, wilfulness, disobedience, presumption, and innumerable our negligences and sins, which we from time to time most heinously have committed; whereby we have deserved not only sore and grievous plagues, but even eternal damnation, were it not that thou art the Lord of mercy, and hast power to shew mercy on whom thou wilt; wherein thou art rich and plentiful to all them that call upon thee faithfully.

Wherefore, dear Father, we, seeing our manifold and grievous sins which we have committed against thee, and also thy great mercy, loving-kindness, patience, and long-suffering towards us, are compelled not only to bear patiently and suffer our enemies when they rail on us, slander us, oppress us, vex us, or trouble us, curse, persecute, and kill us; but also to speak well of them, to instruct them, to pray for them, to do them good, to bless them, to clothe them, feed them, so "heaping coals" of thy charity and love upon them; and mercifully to "forgive them," even as thou, dear Father, for thy beloved Christ's sake "hast forgiven us."

Thus hast thou taught us, good Father, not as the hypocrites to look narrowly on our neighbours' faults, but diligently to examine our own consciences, wherein we have offended thee, and also what occasion of offence or falling we have given to our brethren in eating, drinking, going, apparel, speaking, dissolute or uncomely laughter, in bargaining, or by any means; and with all speed seek to reconcile ourselves to them, and to forgive unto other from the bottom of our hearts whatsoever they have offended us, and to do none otherwise than we wish and desire in our hearts that other should do to us; that so we may find thee, O Lord, in "forgiving us our trespasses," mild and merciful: which speedily do thou shew thyself unto us, for thy dear Christ's sake.

O Lord, thou God of the righteous, we feel the frailty of our nature to be so perverse and apt to sin, that, when thou by the gifts of thy holy Spirit dost move us, and as it were call us, yea, rather draw us unto thee, then are we drawn away and tempted of our own concupiscence and lust, beside the great and dangerous assaults of the world and devil: therefore, faithful Father, we thy poor children beseech thee to take from us all those evils and occasions that may draw us from thee. O dear God, protect, defend, and strengthen us against all the suggestions and assaults of our enemies, 'the world, the flesh, and the devil,' that neither in prosperity we wax haut[1] or high-minded, to say unthankfully, 'What fellow is the Lord?' nor yet in the abundance of temptations, anguish, vexation, tribulation, or persecution, to be oppressed with fear, nor deceived by flattery, nor yet to fall in despair, and so utterly perish. *(And lead us not into temptation.)*

But in all dangers and perils of temptations, and in the midst of the stormy tempests of tribulation, dear Father, make us, thy poor children, to feel the consolation of the certainty of our eternal election in Christ Jesus our Lord, and to perceive thy fatherly succour ready to help us; lest that we, being overcome with the wicked sleights and deceitful invasions of the enemies, should (as without thy grace and merciful protection we shall) be drawn into an obstinate mind; and so shut up the conduit that should lead thy gracious gifts and benefits unto us to our commodity and comfort, that thou mightest "lead us forth with the evildoers," and harden our hearts.

Therefore, O good God, give us these thy good gifts, namely strength, patience, and joyfulness of heart, to "rejoice in temptation," and assure us that it is "the trial of our faith;" that faith in us may "have her perfect work;" that, when we be well approved, and purged with the fire of temptations, we may finish our life in victory, and evermore live with thee in thy heavenly kingdom, where no temptation shall do us hurt.

Finally, most merciful Father, we humbly beseech thee to "deliver us" from this present evil world, from all human and worldly fear, from all infirmities of the flesh and mind, from false prophets and teachers, from false brethren, from traitors and tyrants, &c.: and, if it be thy good pleasure, and *(But deliver us from evil.)*

[1 'Haut' or 'haught:' haughty.]

may make most to the glory of thy name, "deliver us" from the hands of our enemies, and from all other evils present and to come, both of body and soul, that we, being by thy great mercy defended 'from all hurtful things,' may always use 'those things that be profitable for us,' 'devoutly given to serve thee in good works;' that, the yoke of our enemies and the bands of sin being shaken off, we may possess the inheritance of thy heavenly kingdom, which thy dear Son Jesus Christ hath with his precious blood purchased for thine elect "from the beginning of the world."

"For thine is the kingdom:" thou only hast the majesty, thou only art the God above all gods, King of all kings, and Lord of all lords; thou only hast the power and authority to "set up kings, and to put them down;" thou "liftest the poor out of the dust, and makest him to sit among the princes of thy people;" thou only "makest wars to cease," and "givest victory" to whom thou wilt. O dear God, there is neither majesty, rule, nor power, honour nor worship, dignity nor office, riches nor poverty, health nor sickness, plenty nor scarcity, prosperity nor adversity, war nor peace, life nor death, nor any other thing, but it is all thine: and thou both hast the power, and also wilt give it to whom it pleaseth thee in thy time and season, that all glory may be given to thee alone, for thou art worthy.

O dear Father, to thee we come therefore for help and succour, for without thee there is no help at all. O good Father, "deliver us" from all that is evil in thy sight, for thy own name's sake, and for thy dear Christ's sake; that we being armed with thy holy armour, and weaponed with thy blessed word, and instructed by thy holy Spirit, may, according to thy holy promise, "serve thee without fear all the days of our life," in such holiness and righteousness as is acceptable in thy sight.

To thee therefore, our dear Father, our Creator, feeder, protector, governor, and defender; and thy beloved Son Jesus Christ, our only peace, mercy-seat, Redeemer, justifier, and advocate; and thy holy Spirit, our sanctification, our wisdom, teacher, instructor, and Comforter, be all dominion, power, and glory, for ever and ever. Amen.

A MEDITATION

ON THE COMING OF CHRIST TO JUDGMENT, AND OF THE REWARD BOTH OF THE FAITHFUL AND UNFAITHFUL.

O Lord Jesus Christ, the Son of the everliving God, by whom all things were made, are ruled and governed; as of thy love for our redemption thou didst not disdain to be our Mediator, and to take upon thee our nature in the womb of a virgin, purely and without sin, by the operation of the Holy Spirit, that both thou mightest in thine own person wonderfully beautify and exalt our nature, and work the same in us also, first abolishing the guiltiness of sin by remission, then sin itself by death, and last of all death by raising up again these our bodies, that they may be "like unto thine own glorious (and immortal) body, according to the power wherewith thou art able to subject all things unto thee;" as, I say, of thy love for our redemption thou becamest man, and that most poor and afflicted upon earth, by the space of thirty-three years at the least, in most humility; and paidest the price of our ransom by thy most bitter death and passion, (for the which I most heartily give thanks to thee;) so, of the same thy love towards us, in thy good time thou wilt "come again in the clouds of heaven with power and great glory," "with flaming fire," "with thousands of saints," "with angels of thy power," "with a mighty cry, shout of an archangel," and "blast of a trump," suddenly "as the lightning which shineth from the east," &c. when men think least, "even as a thief in the night" when men be asleep. [Matt. xxiv.]

Thou wilt so come, I say, thus suddenly "in the twinkling of an eye," all men that ever have been, be, and shall be, with women and children, appearing before thy tribunal judgment-seat, to render an account of all things which they have thought, spoken, and done against thy law, openly and before all angels, saints, and devils; and so to receive the just reward of thy vengeance, if that they have not repented and "obeyed the gospel;" and so to "depart from thee to the devil and his angels," and all the wicked which ever have been, be, or shall be, into hell-fire, which is unquenchable and of pains intolerable, easeless, endless, hopeless, even from the face of thy glorious and mighty power.

But, if they have "repented and believed thy gospel," if they be found watching with their lamps and oil in their hands, if they be found ready apparelled with the "wedding-garment" of innocency; if they have not hardened their hearts, and "hoarded up their treasure of thy vengeance in the day of wrath to be revealed," but have used the time of grace, "the acceptable time, the time of salvation," (that is, the time of this life, in the which thou "stretchest out thy hand" and spreadest thine arms, calling and crying unto us to "come unto thee which art meek in heart and lowly, for thou wilt ease all that labour and are heavy laden;") if they have visited the sick and prisoners, comforted the comfortless, fed the hungry, clothed the naked, lodged the harbourless; if they have not "loaden their hearts with gluttony and surfeiting, and carefulness of this life;" if they have not "digged and hid their talent in the ground," doing no good therewith, but have been faithful to occupy thy gifts to thy glory, and here washen their garments in thy blood by hearty repenting them; then shall thy angels gather them together, not as the wicked which shall be collected as fagots and "cast into the fire," but as the good "wheat that is gathered into thy barn." Then shall they "be caught up to meet thee in the clouds," then shall their "corruptible body put on incorruption," then shall they be endued with immortality and glory, then shall they be with thee and "go whither thou goest," then shall they hear, "Come, blessed of my Father, possess the kingdom prepared for you from the beginning," &c. Then shall they be set on seats of majesty, "judging the whole world;" then "shall they reign with thee for ever;" then "shall God be all in all" with them and to them. Then shall they enter and inherit "heavenly Jerusalem" and the glorious restful land of Canaan, where is always day and never night, where is no manner of weeping, tears, infirmity, hunger, cold, sickness, envy, malice, nor sin; but always joy without sorrow, mirth without measure, pleasure without pain, heavenly harmony, most pleasant melody, saying and singing, "Holy, holy, holy, Lord God of hosts," &c.

Summa, "the eye hath not seen, the ear hath not heard, neither hath it entered into the heart of man," that they shall then inherit and most surely enjoy; although here they be tormented, prisoned, burned, solicited of Satan, tempted of the flesh, and entangled with the world; wherethrough they are enforced to cry, "Thy kingdom come:" "come, Lord Jesu," &c. "How amiable are thy tabernacles!" "Like as the hart desireth the water-brooks," &c. "Now let thy servant depart in peace:" "I desire to be dissolved, and to be with Christ." "We mourn in ourselves, waiting for the deliverance of our bodies," &c. *Rev. xxii. Psal. xlii. Rom. viii.*

O gracious Lord, when shall I find such mercy with thee, that I may repent, believe, hope, and look for this gear, with the full fruition of these heavenly joys which thou hast prepared for all them that fear thee; and so rest with thee for evermore?

A MEDITATION

CONCERNING THE SOBER USAGE OF THE BODY[1].

THIS our body, which God hath made to be the tabernacle and mansion of our soul for this life, if we considered accordingly, we could not but use it otherwise than we do; that is, we would use it for the soul's sake, being the guest thereof, and not for the body itself: and so should it be served in things to help, but not to hinder the soul. A servant it is, and therefore it ought to obey to serve the soul, that the soul might serve God; not as the body will, neither as the soul itself will, but as God will; whose will we should learn to know, and behave ourselves thereafter. The which thing to observe is hard for us now by reason of sin, which hath gotten a mansion-house in our bodies, and dwelleth in us, as doth the soul: to the which (sin I mean) we are altogether of ourselves inclined, because we naturally are sinners and born in sin; by reason whereof we are ready as servants to sin, and to use our bodies accordingly, making the soul to sit at reward[2], and pampering up the servant to our shame. *MS. 1. 2. 8. 22. Emman. Coll. Cambridge. Meditations of Bradford, Hall 1562, and after editions.*

O therefore, good Lord, that it would please thee to open this gear unto me, and to give me eyes to consider effectually this my body what it is, namely a servant lent for the soul to sojourn in, and serve thee in this life: yea, it is, by reason

[1 The heading in 1562 is, 'A meditation concerning the sober usage both of the body and pleasures in this life.']

[2 i. e. rereward, the rear.]

of sin that hath his dwelling there, become now to the soul nothing else but a prison, and that most strait, vile, stinking, filthy, and therefore in danger of miseries, to many in all ages, times, and places, till death hath turned it to dust; whereof it came, and whither it shall return, that the soul may return to thee from whence it came until the day of judgment come; in the which thou wilt raise up that body, that then it may be partaker with the soul, and the soul with it inseparably, of weal or woe, according to that is done in and by the same body here now in earth.

O that I could consider often and heartily these things! Then should I not pamper up this body to obey it, but bridle it that it might obey the soul: then should I fly the pain it putteth my soul unto by reason of sin and provocation to all evil, and continually desire the dissolution of it with Paul, and the[1] deliverance from it, as much as ever did prisoner his deliverance out of prison; for alonely by it the devil hath a door to tempt, and so to hurt me: in it I am kept from thy presence, and thou from being so conversant with me as else thou wouldest be: by it I am restrained from the sense and feeling of all the joys and comforts (in manner) which are to be taken as joys and comforts indeed. If it were dissolved, and I out of it, then could Satan no more hurt me; then wouldest thou speak with me face to face; then the conflicting time were at an end; then sorrow would cease, and joy would increase, and I should enter into inestimable rest.

O that I considered this accordingly!

Phil. i.

A MEDITATION

CONCERNING THE PLEASURES OF THIS LIFE[2].

Meditations of Bradford, Hall 1562, and after editions.

THE beginning of all evil in our kind of living springeth out of the depravation and corruptness of our judgment, because our will always followeth that which reason judgeth to be followed. Now that which every man taketh to be friendly and agreeing to his nature, the same doth he judge necessarily to be good for him, and to be desired. This is meat,

[1 'the' 1562: not in MS.]
[2 The heading in 1562 is, 'Another meditation to the same effect.']

drink, apparel, riches, favour, dignity, rule, knowledge, and such-like; because they are thought good and agreeing either to the body or to the mind, or to both; for they help either to the conservation or to the pleasure of man, accounted of every one amongst good things.

Howbeit, such is the weakness of our wit on the one part, and the blindness and too much rage of our lusts on the other part, that we being left to ourselves cannot but in the desire of things which we judge good and agreeing to our nature, by the judgment of our senses and reason, we cannot, I say, but overpass the bounds whereby they might be profitable unto us; and so we make them hurtful to us, which of themselves are ordained for our health. What is more necessary than meat and drink, or more agreeing to nature? but yet how few be there which do not hurt themselves by them! In like manner it goeth with riches, estimation, friends, learning, &c. Yea, although we be in these most temperate, yet when there wanteth the Spirit, our regenerator, we are so drowned in them, that we utterly neglect to lift up our minds to the good pleasure of God, to the end we might imitate and follow God our Maker, by yielding ourselves over duly to use his gifts to the common and private utility of our neighbours.

But now God only is life and eternity, and cannot but demand of us his handy-work, that we should render ourselves and all we have to the end wherefore we were made; that is, to resemble for our portion his goodness, as those which be nothing else but witnesses and instruments of his mercy. So that, when we wholly do naturally strive against that kind of life whereto he hath created us, by seeking always ourselves, what other thing ought to ensue but that he should again destroy us, and take away his notable gifts, wherewith he endued us that by all kind of well-doing we should resemble his image? Yea, what other thing may ensue, but that he should leave us, and that eternally? that we might feel and by experience prove how bitter a thing it is to leave the Lord, in whom is all goodness.

O that therefore I might find such favour in thy sight, dear Father, that thou wouldest work in me by thy holy Spirit a true knowledge of all good things, and hearty love to the same, through Christ Jesus our Lord and only Saviour. Amen.

A MEDITATION

FOR THE EXERCISE OF TRUE MORTIFICATION[1].

MS. 1. 2. 8. no. 25 Emman. Coll. Cambridge.

Meditations of Bradford, Hall 1562, and after editions.

HE that will be ready in weighty matters to deny his own will, and to be obedient to the will of God, the same had need to accustom himself to deny his desires in matters of less weight, and to exercise mortification of his own will in trifles: for, if that our affections by this daily custom be not as it were half slain, surely, surely, when the plunge shall come, we shall find the more to do. If we cannot "watch with Christ one hour," as he saith to Peter, we undoubtedly can much less go to death with him. Wherefore that in great temptations we may be ready to say with Christ, "Not my will, but thine be done," in that this commonly cometh not to pass but where the roots of our lusts by thy grace, dear Father, are almost rotten and rooted out by a daily denial of that they desire, I humbly beseech thee, for Christ's sake, to help me herein.

First pardon me my cherishing and, as it were, watering of mine affections, obeying them in their devices and superfluous desires: wherethrough in that they have taken deep root, and are too lively in me, I secondly do beseech thee to pull them up by the roots out of my heart, and so henceforth to order me, that I may continually accustom myself to weaken the principal root, that the by-roots and branches may lose all their power. Grant me, I beseech thee, that thy grace may daily mortify my concupiscence of pleasant things, that is, of wealth, riches, glory, liberty, favour of men, meats, drinks, apparel, ease, yea, and life itself; that the horror and impatiency of more grievous things may be weakened, and I made more patient in adversity. Whereunto I further do desire and pray thy goodness, dear Father, that thou wilt add this, namely, that I may for ever become obedient and ready to thy good will in all things, heartily and willingly to

[[1] The following meditations, 'on mortification,' 'on the providence of God,' 'on the presence of God,' 'on the power and goodness of God,' 'on death,' and 'on the passion of Christ,' and the larger part of the 'general supplication,' p. 190—202; and the 'prayer for the mercy of God,' the 'thanksgiving,' part of the prayer 'on the work of Christ,' and the prayers 'for faith' and 'repentance,' p. 203—210; after appearing in the 'Godly Meditations' of Bradford, Hall 1562, were printed in the 'Christian Prayers,' &c. collected by Henry Bull, Powell (see p. 118, note 1, above), and Middleton 1570: vide Parker Soc. edition, p. 96—8, 109—20, 136—41, 159—61, 188—9.]

serve thee, and do whatsoever may please thee. For doubtless, although we accustom ourselves in the pleasant things of this life to a mortification and denial of ourselves, yet we shall find enough to do when more bitter and weighty crosses come: for, if thy Son our Saviour, ever wont to obey thy good will, prayed so heartily and often, "Not my will, but thy will be done," (whereby he declareth himself to be very man;) how can it be but we, whose nature is corrupt, not only in nativity, but in the rest of our whole life also, shall find both our hands full, in great and grievous temptations, wholly to resign ourselves unto thee?

Grant therefore, dear Father, for thy Christ's sake, to me a most miserable wretch, thy grace and holy Spirit to be effectual in me, that daily I may accustom myself to deny my will in more easy and pleasant things of this life; that, when need shall be, I may come with Christ to thee with a resigned will, always steadfastly expecting thy mercy, and in the mean season continually obeying thee with readiness and willingness, doing whatsoever may most please thee, through Christ our Lord, which liveth with thee, &c.

JOHN BRADFORD[2].

A GODLY MEDITATION

AND INSTRUCTION OF THE PROVIDENCE OF GOD TOWARDS MANKIND.

THIS ought to be unto us most certain, that nothing is done without thy providence, O Lord; that is, that not nothing is done, be it good or bad, sweet or sour, but by thy knowledge, that is, by thy will, wisdom, and ordinance, (for all these knowledge doth comprehend in it;) as by thy holy word we are taught in many places, that even the life of a sparrow is not without thy will, nor any liberty or power upon a porket have all the devils in hell but by thy appointment and will: which will we always must believe most assuredly to be all just and good, howsoever otherwise it seem unto us; for thou art marvellous and not comprehensible in thy ways, and holy in all thy works.

Meditations of Bradford, Hall 1562, and after editions.

Strype, Ecc. Mem. III. ii. Doc. XXIX.

God worketh all in all marvellously, justly and holily. Matt. x. Matt. viii.

But hereunto it is necessary also for us to know no less certainly that though all things be done by thy providence, yet the same providence hath many and divers means to

[2 'John Bradford,' MS.: not in 1562.]

God worketh by means, without means, and against means. work by, which means being contemned, thy providence is contemned also: as for example, meat is a mean to serve thy providence for the preservation of health and life here; so that he which contemneth to eat because thy providence is certain and infallible, the same contemneth thy providence. Indeed, if that it were so that meat could not be had, then should we not tie thy providence to this mean, but make it free as thou art free, that is, that without meat thou canst help and give health and life; for it is not of any need that thou usest any instrument or mean to serve thy providence: thy power and wisdom is infinite, and therefore should we hang on thy providence, even when all is clean against us. But for our erudition and infirmities' sake, it hath pleased thee by means to work and deal with us here, to exercise us in obedience, and because we cannot else (so great is our corruption) sustain thy naked and bare presence.

Grant me therefore, dear Father, I humbly beseech thee for Christ's sake, that, as I something now know these things, so I may use this knowledge to my comfort and commodity in thee: that is, grant that in what state soever I be, I may not doubt but the same doth come to me by thy most just ordinance, yea, by thy merciful ordinance; for, as thou art just, so art thou merciful, yea, thy "mercy is above all thy works." And by this knowledge grant me that I may humble myself to obey thee, and look for thy help in time convenient, not only when I have means by which thou mayest work, and art so accustomed to do, but also when I have no means but am destitute: yea, when that all means be directly and clean against me, grant, I say, yet that I may still hang upon thee and thy providence, not doubting of a fatherly end in thy good time.

Again, lest I should contemn thy providence, or presume upon it by uncoupling those things which thou hast coupled together, preserve me from neglecting thy ordinary and lawful means in all my needs, if so be I may have them and with good conscience use them, (although I know thy providence be not tied to them further than pleaseth thee;) but grant that I may with diligence, reverence, and thankfulness use them, and thereto my diligence, wisdom, and industry in all things lawful, to serve thereby thy providence, if it so please thee; howbeit, so that I hang in no part on the means, or on my diligence, wisdom, and industry, but only on thy providence: which more and more persuade me to be altogether fatherly and good, how far soever otherwise it appear and seem, yea, is felt of me.

By this I being preserved from negligence on my behalf, and despair or murmuring towards thee, shall become diligent and patient, through thy mere and alone grace: which give and increase in me, to praise thy holy name for ever, through Jesus Christ our Lord and only Saviour. Amen.

A MEDITATION
OF THE PRESENCE OF GOD.

THERE is nothing that maketh more to true godliness of life than the persuasion of thy presence, dear Father, and that nothing is hid from thee, but all to thee is open and naked, even the very thoughts, which one day thou wilt reveal and open either to our praise or punishment in this life (as thou didst David's faults which he did secretly), or in the life to come; for "nothing is so hid that shall not be revealed:" therefore doth the prophet say, "Woe to them that keep secret their thoughts to hide their counsel from the Lord, and do their works in darkness, saying, Who seeth us?"

Grant to me therefore, dear God, mercy for all my sins, especially my hid and close sins: "enter not into judgment with me," I humbly beseech thee: give me to believe truly in thy Christ, that I never come into judgment for them; that with David I might so reveal them and confess them unto thee, that thou wouldest cover them. And grant further, that henceforth I always think myself continually conversant before thee; so that, if I do well, I pass not of the publishing of it as hypocrites do; if I do or think any evil, I may forthwith know that the same shall not always be hid from men. Grant me that I may always have in mind that day wherein hid works of darkness shall be illumined; and the sentence of thy Son, "Nothing is so secret which shall not be revealed." So in trouble and wrong I shall find comfort, and otherwise be kept through thy grace from evil: which do thou work, I humbly beseech thee, for Christ's sake. Amen.

Soli Deo honor et gloria: [To God alone be honour and glory.] 1554.   JOHN BRADFORD[1].

[1 These two lines occur only in Strype, who printed from a MS. which had once belonged to Foxe.]

A MEDITATION

OF GOD'S POWER, BEAUTY, GOODNESS, &c.

Meditations of Bradford, Hall 1562, and after editions.

BECAUSE thou, Lord, wouldest have us to love thee, not only dost thou will, entice, allure, and provoke us, but also dost command us so to do, promising thyself unto such as love thee, and threatening us with damnation if we do otherwise: whereby we may see both our great corruption and naughtiness, and also thine exceeding great mercy towards us.

First, concerning our corruption and naughtiness, what a thing is it that power, riches, authority, beauty, goodness, liberality, truth, justice, which all thou art, good Lord, cannot move us to love thee! Whatsoever things we see fair, good, wise, mighty, are but even sparkles of that power, beauty, goodness, wisdom, which thou art. For to the end thou mightest declare thy riches, beauty, power, wisdom, goodness, &c., thou hast not only made, but still dost conserve all creatures to be, as David saith of the heavens, declarers and setters-forth of thy glory, and as a book to teach us to know thee.

How fair thou art, the beauty of the sun, moon, stars, light, flowers, rivers, fields, hills, birds, beasts, men, and all creatures, yea, the goodly shape and form of the whole world, doth declare.

How mighty thou art, we are taught by the creation of this world even of nought, by governing the same, by punishing the wicked mighty giants thereof, by overthrowing their devices, by repressing the rages of the sea within her bounds, by storms, by tempests, by fires: these and such-like declare unto us thine invisible, almighty, and terrible power, whereby thou subduest all things unto thee.

How rich thou art, this world, thy great and infinite treasure-house, doth well declare. What plenty is there not only of things, but also of every kind of things; yea, how dost thou yearly and daily multiply these kinds! How many seeds dost thou make of one seed; yea, what great increase dost thou bring it unto! These cannot but put us in remembrance of the exceeding riches that thou hast; for if to thine enemies which love thee not (as the most part in this world be), if to them thou givest so plentifully thy riches here, what shall we think that with thyself thou hast laid up for thy friends!

How good thou art, all creatures generally and particularly do teach. What creature is there in the world which thou hast not made for our commodity? I will not say how that thou mightest have made us creatures without sense or reason, if thou hadst would. But, amongst all things, none doth teach us so thy great love towards us as doth the death of thy most dearly beloved Son, who suffered the pains and terrors thereof, yea, and of hell itself, for our sakes.

If this thy love had been but a small love, it would never have lasted so long, nor Christ should never have died.

A MEDITATION
OF DEATH, AND THE COMMODITIES IT BRINGETH.

WHAT other thing do we daily in this present life, than heap sin to sin, and hoard up trespass upon trespass? so that this day is worse always than yesterday, by increasing, as days, so sins, and therefore thy indignation, good Lord, against us. But when we shall be let go out of the prison of the body, and so taken into thy blessed company, then shall we be in most safety of immortality and salvation: then shall come unto us no sickness, no need, no pain, no kind of evil to soul or body; but whatsoever good we can wish, that shall we have, and whatsoever we loath shall be far from us.

MS. 1. 2. 8. no. 16. Emman. Coll. Cambridge[1]. Meditations of Bradford, Hall 1562, and after editions.

O, dear Father, that we had faith to behold these things accordingly! O that our hearts were persuaded thereof, and our affections inflamed with the desire of them! then should we live in longing for that which now we most loath. O help us, and grant that we, being ignorant of things to come, and of the time of our death which to thee is certain, may so live and finish our journey here, that we may be ready, and then depart, when our departing may make most to thy glory and our comfort through Christ.

What is this life but a smoke, a vapour, a shadow, a warfare, a bubble of water, a word, grass, a flower? Thou shalt die, is most certain; but of the time, no man can tell when.

[1] The name of 'Thomas Horton' (see p. 31, l. 11, above) is written upon this MS.]

The longer in this life thou dost remain, the more thou sinnest, which will turn to thy more pain.

By cogitation of death our minds be often in manner oppressed with darkness, because we do but remember the night of the body, forgetting the light of the mind, and of the resurrection. Thereto remember the good things that after this life shall ensue, without wavering, in certainty of faith; and so shall the passage of death be more desired. It is like a sailing over tho sea to thy home and country: it is like a medicine or purgation to the health of soul and body: it is the best physician: it is like to a woman's travail; for, as the child being delivered cometh into a more large place than the womb wherein it did lie tofore, so thy soul being delivered out of the body cometh into a much more large and fair place, even into heaven.

JOHN BRADFORD, out of L. Vives[1].

A GODLY MEDITATION
UPON THE PASSION OF OUR SAVIOUR JESUS CHRIST.

MS. 1. 2. 8.
no. 70. and
MS. 2. 2. 15.
no. 95. 2.
Emman. Coll.
Cambridge.

Meditations
of Bradford,
Hall 1562,
and after
editions.

O LORD Jesus Christ, the Son of the everliving and almighty God, by whom all things were made and be ruled and governed; thou "the lively image of the substance" of the Father, the eternal wisdom of God, "the brightness of his glory," 'God of God, Light of Light,' co-equal, co-eternal, and consubstantial with the Father; thou of the love thou hadst to mankind, that, when he was fallen from the fellowship of God into the society of Satan and all evil, didst vouchsafe for our redemption to become a mediator between God and man, taking to the Godhead our nature as concerning the substance of it, and so becamest man also, "the heir of all," and most merciful Messias; which by the power of thy Godhead and merits of thy manhood hast made purgation of our sins, even by thine own self, whilst thou wast here on earth; being now set on the right hand of thy Father even concerning our nature, for our behalf[2], in majesty, glory, and

[1 This line is in the MS., but not in 1562. The foregoing Meditation is mostly translated by Bradford from the *Excitationes animi in Deum*, by Ludovicus Vives, p. 149—50, ed. Lugdun. 1558: vide prefatory note, p. 223 in this volume.]

[2 'for us,' MS. 1. 2. 8: 'for our behalf,' MS. 2. 2. 15.]

power infinite; I beseech and humbly pray thy mercy to grant me at this present to rehearse some of thy passions and sufferings for mankind, and so for me[3], the last night thou wast here tofore thy death; that thy good Spirit might thereby be effectual to work in me as well faith for the forgiveness of my sins[4] by them, as mortification of mine affections, comfort in my crosses, and patience in afflictions. Amen.

In the midst of thy last supper with thy dear apostles, these things could not but be before thee, namely, that they all would leave thee, the most earnest would forswear thee, and one of the twelve should most traitorously betray thee; which were no small crosses unto thee: Judas was admonished of thee to beware; but when he took no heed, but wilfully went out to finish his work, contemning thy admonition and counsel, he[5] could not but vex thy most loving heart.

After supper there was contention amongst thy disciples who should be greatest after thee, yet dreaming carnally of thee and thy kingdom, and having this affection of pride and ambition busy among them, notwithstanding thy diligence in reproving and teaching them.

After thy admonition to them of the cross that would come, thereby to make them more vigilant, so gross were they that they thought they could with their two swords put away all perils; which was no little grief unto thee. After thy coming to Gethsemane, heaviness oppressed thee, and therefore thou willedst thy disciples to pray: thou didst tell to Peter and his fellows that thy heart was heavy to death: thou didst will them to "pray," being careful for them also lest they should "fall into temptation." After this thou wentest a stone's cast from them, and didst pray thyself, falling flat and grovelling upon the earth: but, alas! thou feltest no comfort, and therefore thou camest to thy disciples, which of all others were most sweet and dear unto thee: but, lo, to thy further discomfort, they pass neither of thy perils nor of their own, and therefore sleep apace. After thou hadst awaked them,

[3 'for me,' MS. 1. 2. 8: 'for mankind and so for me,' MS. 2. 2. 15.]
[4 'faith, as well of the pardon of my sins,' MS. 1. 2. 8: 'as well faith, for the forgiveness of my sins,' MS. 2. 2. 15.]
[5 'he,' 1562: not in MS. 1: 2. 8.]

thou goest again to pray: but thou foundest[1] no comfort at all, and therefore didst return again for some comfort at thy dearest friends' hands. But yet again, alas! they are fast asleep; whereupon thou art enforced to go again to thy heavenly Father for some sparkle of comfort in these thy wonderful crosses and agonies, or deadly pangs[2]. Now here thou wast so discouraged and so comfortless, that even streams of blood came running from thine eyes and ears and other parts of thy body. But who is able to express the infiniteness of thy crosses even at thy being in the garden? all which thou sufferedst for my sake, as well to satisfy thy Father's wrath for my sins, as also to sanctify all my sufferings the more gladly to be sustained of me.

After thy bloody prayer thou camest, and yet again foundest thy disciples asleep: and, before thou canst well awake them, lo, Judas cometh with a great band of men to apprehend thee as a thief, and so doth, leading thee away bound to the high bishop's house Annas, and so from him to Caiaphas. Here now to augment this thy misery, behold, thy disciples flee from thee, false witnesses be brought against thee, thou art accused and condemned of blasphemy. Peter, even in thy sight, forsweareth thee: thou art unjustly stricken for answering lawfully; thou art blindfolded, stricken, and buffeted all the whole night in the bishop Caiaphas' house of their cruel servants.

In the morning betimes thou art condemned again of the priests of blasphemy, and therefore they bring thee before the secular power to Pilate, by whom thou art openly arraigned in the moot-hall[3], as other thieves and malefactors were: when he saw that thou wast accused of malice, yet he did not dismiss thee, but did send thee to Herod, where thou wast derided shamefully, in coming and going to and from him, all the way wonderfully, especially after Herod had apparelled thee as a fool.

[1 'found,' MS. 1. 2. 8: 'foundest' 1562.]
[2 'or deadly pangs,' MS. 2. 2. 15: not in MS. 1. 2. 8, nor in 1562.]
[3 'Moot-hall': council-chamber, hall of judgment. 'Moot' or 'mote': a meeting or assembly, from the Anglo-Saxon *mot.* and *gemot.* Vide Skinner, Etymol. ling. Angl. Lond. 1671, v. 'mote;' and Todd's Johnson, Dict. v. 'mote' and 'moot-hall.' 'In the mote hall,' MS. 2. 2. 15: these words are scored across in MS. 1. 2. 8.]

Afore Pilate again therefore thou wast brought, and accused falsely. No man did take thy part, or speak a good word for thee. Pilate caused thee to be whipped and scourged, and to be handled most pitifully, to see if any pity might appear with the prelates: but no man at all pitied thee.

Barabbas was preferred before thee: all the people, head and tail, was against thee, and cried, 'Hang thee up.' Unjustly to death wast thou judged: thou wast crowned with thorns that pierced thy brains: thou wast made a mocking-stock: thou wast reviled, rebated[4], beaten, and most miserably handled.

Thou wentest through Jerusalem to the place of execution, even the mount of Calvary: a great cross to hang thee on was laid upon thy back to bear and draw, as long as thou wast able.

Thy body was racked to be nailed to the tree, thy hands were bored through, and thy feet also; nails were put through them to fasten thee thereon: thou wast hanged between heaven and earth, as one spewed out of heaven, and vomited out of the earth, unworthy of any place: the high priest laughed thee to scorn, the elders blasphemed thee and said, "God hath no care for thee:" the common people laught and cry out upon thee: thirst oppressed thee, but vinegar only and gall was given to thee to drink: heaven shined not on thee, the sun gave thee no light, the earth was afraid to bear thee, Satan did sore tempt and assault[5] thee, and thine own senses caused thee to cry out, "My God, my God, why hast thou forsaken me?"

O wonderful passions which thou sufferedst! In them thou teachest me, in them thou comfortest me; for by them God is my Father, my sins are forgiven: by them I should learn to fear God, to love God, to hope in God, to hate sin, to be patient, to call upon God, and never to leave him for any temptations' sake, but with thee still to cry, yea, even when very death shall approach[6], "Father, into thy hands I commend my spirit."

[4 Rebated: beaten back, beaten down. Vide Richardson, Dict.]
[5 'tempted,' MS. 1. 2. 8: 'did sore tempt and assault,' MS. 2. 2. 15.]
[6 'yea, even when very death shall approach,' is only in MS. 2. 2. 15.]

A GENERAL SUPPLICATION,

BEING A CONFESSION OF SINS AND PRAYER FOR THE MITIGATION OF GOD'S WRATH AND PUNISHMENT FOR THE SAME[1]

Meditations of Bradford, Hall 1562, and after editions.

O ALMIGHTY God, King of all kings, and Governor of all things, whose power no creature is able to resist, to whom it belongeth justly to punish sinners, and to be merciful unto them that truly repent; we confess that thou dost most justly punish us, for we have grievously sinned against thee: and we acknowledge that in punishing us thou dost declare thyself to be our most merciful Father, as well because thou dost not punish us in any thing as we have deserved, as also because by punishing us thou dost call us, and, as it were, draw us to increase in repentance, in faith, in prayer, in contemning of the world, and in hearty desiring for everlasting life and thy blessed presence. Grant us therefore, gracious Lord, thankfully to acknowledge thy great mercy, which hast thus favourably dealt with us, in punishing us not to our confusion but to our amendment. And seeing thou hast sworn that "thou wilt not the death of a sinner, but that he turn and live," have mercy upon us, and turn us unto thee for thy dearly beloved Son Jesus Christ's sake, whom thou wouldest should be made a slain sacrifice for our sins, thereby declaring thy great and unspeakable anger against sin, and thine infinite mercy towards us sinful wretches.

And, forasmuch as the dulness of our hearts, blindness, and corruption, is such that we are not able to arise up unto thee by faithful and hearty prayer, according to our great necessity, without thy singular grace and assistance; grant unto us, gracious Lord, thy holy and sanctifying Spirit to work in us this good work, with a pure and clean mind, with an humble and lowly heart, with grace to weigh and consider the need and greatness of that we do desire, and with an assured faith and trust that thou wilt grant us our requests, because thou art good and gracious even to young ravens calling upon thee, much more then to us for whom thou hast made all things, yea, and hast not spared thine own dear

[1 This prayer in MS. 1. 2. 8. no. 84. in Emmanuel College, Cambridge, somewhat abridged, has the title, "A confession which he used daily in his prayers." It is inscribed, in the 'Christian Prayers,' &c. of Bull (see p. 190, note 1, above), 'A prayer to be said of such as suffer any kind of trouble or cross, either private or common.']

Son; because thou hast commanded us to call upon thee; because thy throne whereunto we come is a throne of grace and mercy; because thou hast given us a mediator Christ, to bring us unto thee, being "the way" by whom we come, being "the door" by whom we enter, and being our "head" on whom we hang, and hope that our poor petitions shall not be in vain, through and for his name's sake.

We beseech thee therefore of thy rich mercy, wherein thou art "plentiful to all them that call upon thee," to forgive us our sins, namely our unthankfulness, unbelief, self-love, neglect of thy word, security, hypocrisy, contempt of thy long-suffering, omission of prayer, doubting of thy power, presence, mercy, and good-will towards us, insensibleness of thy grace, impatiency, &c. And to this thy benefit of correcting us, add these thy gracious gifts, repentance, faith, the spirit of prayer, the contempt of this world, and hearty desiring for everlasting life. Endue us with thy holy Spirit, according to thy covenant and mercy, as well to assure us of pardon, and that thou dost accept us into thy favour as thy dear children in Christ and for his sake, as to write thy law in our hearts, and so to work in us that we may now begin and go forwards in believing, living, fearing, obeying, praying, hoping, and serving thee; as thou dost require most fatherly and most justly of us, accepting us as perfect through Christ and by imputation.

And moreover, when it shall be thy good pleasure and most to thy glory, deliver us, we beseech thee, out of the hands of thine adversaries by such means, be it death or life, as may make to our comfort most in Christ. In the mean season and for ever save us and govern us with thy holy Spirit and his eternal consolation.

And concerning thine adversaries, which for thy sake are become our adversaries, so many of them as are to be converted, we beseech thee to shew thy mercy upon them and to convert them: but those that are not to be converted, which thou only dost know, most mighty God and terrible Lord, confound, and get thy name a glory over them; abate their pride, assuage their malice, bring to nought their devilish devices: and grant that we and all thine afflicted children may be armed with thy defence, weaponed with thy wisdom, and guided with thy grace and holy Spirit, to be preserved for ever from all giving of offences to thy people, and from all perils, to glorify thee, which art the only Giver of all victory, through the merits of thy only Son, Jesus Christ our Lord. Amen.

A CONFESSION OF SINS.

MS. 1. 2. 8. no. 83. Emman. Coll. Cambridge.

Meditations of Bradford, Hall 1562, and after editions.

Strype, Ecc. Mem. III. ii. Doc. xxx.

As David seeing thine angel with his sword ready drawn, most righteous Lord, to plague Jerusalem, cried out unto thee, "It is I, Lord, that have sinned, and I that have done wickedly: thine hand, Lord, be on me, and not on thy poor sheep;" wherethrough thou wast moved to mercy, and badest thine angel put up his sword, thou hadst taken punishment enough; even so we, gracious Lord, seeing thy fearful sword of vengeance ready drawn, and presently striking against this commonweal and thy church in the same, we, I say, are occasioned every man now to cast off our eyes from beholding and narrowly spying out other men's faults, and to set our own only in sight, that, with the same David thy servant, and with Jonas in the ship, we may cry, 'It is we, O Lord, which have sinned, and procured this thy grievous wrath.'

And this we now gathered together[1] in Christ's name do acknowledge, confessing ourselves guilty of horrible ingratitude for our good king, for thy gospel and pure religion, and for the peace of thy church, and quietness of the commonweal, besides our negligences and many other our grievous sins: wherethrough we have deserved not only these but much more grievous plagues, if that even presently thou didst not, as thou art wont, "remember thy mercy."

Hereupon (that thou "in thine anger rememberest thy mercy" before we seek and sue for it) we take boldness, as thou commandest us to do in our trouble, to come and call upon thee to be merciful unto us: and of thy goodness now we humbly in Christ's name pray thee to hold thy hand and cease thy wrath, or at the least so to mitigate it that this realm may be quietly governed, and the same eftsoons to be a harborough for thy church and true religion: which do thou restore to us again, according to thy great power and mercy, and we shall praise thy name for ever, through Jesus Christ our only Mediator and Saviour. Amen.

[1 See p. 83, note 4, above.]

A PRAYER

FOR THE MERCY OF GOD[2].

O LORD God and dear Father, what shall I say? that feel all things to be in manner with me as in the wicked. Blind is my mind, crooked is my will, and perverse concupiscence is in me as a spring or stinking puddle. O how faint is faith in me! how little is love to thee or thy people, how great is self-love, how hard is my heart! &c. by the reason whereof I am moved to doubt of thy goodness towards me, whether thou art my Father or no, and whether I be thy child or no. Indeed worthily might I doubt, if that the having of these were the causes, and not the fruits rather, of thy children.

Meditations of Bradford, Hall 1562, and after editions.

The cause why thou art my Father is thy mercy, goodness, grace, and truth in Christ Jesus, the which cannot but remain for ever: in respect whereof thou hast borne me this good-will, to accept me into the number of thy children, that I might be holy, faithful, obedient, innocent, &c. And therefore thou wouldest not only make me a creature after thy image, enduing me with right limbs, shape, form, memory, wisdom, &c., (where thou mightest have made me a beast, a maimed creature, lame, blind, frantic, &c.;) but also thou wouldest that I should be born of christian parents, brought into thy church by baptism, and called divers times by the ministry of thy word into thy kingdom, besides the innumerable other benefits always hitherto poured upon me: all which thou hast done of this thy good-will that thou of thine own mercy barest to me in Christ and for Christ before the world was made: the which thing as thou requirest straitly that I should believe without doubting, so in all my needs that I should come unto thee as to a Father, and make my moan without mistrust of being heard in thy good time, as most shall make to my comfort.

Lo, therefore to thee, dear Father, I come through thy Son our Lord, Mediator, and Advocate, Jesus Christ, who sitteth "on thy right hand making intercession" for me, and pray thee of thy great goodness and mercy in Christ to be merciful unto me, that I may feel indeed thy sweet mercy as thy child.

[[2] The heading in 1562 is, 'A prayer for the remission of sins.']

The time, O dear Father, I appoint not; but I pray thee that I may with hope still expect and look for thy help: I hope that, as for a little while thou hast left me, thou wilt come and visit me, and that in thy great mercy, whereof I have need by reason of my great misery. Thou art wont for a little season in thine anger to hide thy face from them whom thou lovest: but surely, O Redeemer, "in eternal mercies thou wilt shew thy compassions;" for, when thou leavest us, O Lord, thou dost not leave us very long, neither dost thou leave us to our loss, but to our lucre and advantage; even that thy holy Spirit with bigger portion of thy power and virtue may lighten and cheer us, that the want of feeling to our sorrow may be recompensed plentifully with the lively sense of having thee to our eternal joy: and therefore thou swarest, that "in thine everlasting mercy thou wilt have compassion on us." Of which thing to the end we might be most assured, thine oath is to be marked; for thou sayest, "As I have sworn that I will not bring any more the waters to drown the world; so have I sworn that I will never more be angry with thee, nor reprove thee. The mountains shall remove, and the hills shall fall down; but my loving-kindness shall not move, and the bond of my peace shall not fail thee." Thus sayest thou the Lord our merciful Redeemer.

Isai. liv.

Dear Father, therefore I pray thee, remember even for thine own truth and mercy's sake this promise and everlasting covenant, which in thy good time I pray thee to write in my heart, that I may "know thee to be the only true God and Jesus Christ whom thou hast sent;" that I may love thee with all my heart for ever; that I may love thy people for thy sake; that I may be holy in thy sight through Christ; that I may always not only strive against sin, but also overcome the same daily more and more, as thy children do; above all things desiring "the sanctification of thy name," "the coming of thy kingdom," "the doing of thy will here on earth, as it is in heaven," &c., through Jesus Christ our Redeemer, Mediator, and Advocate. Amen.

A THANKSGIVING

IN THE TIME OF PERSECUTION [1].

O GRACIOUS God, which seekest all means possible how to bring thy children into the feeling and sure sense of thy mercy, and therefore, when prosperity will not serve, then sendest thou adversity, graciously correcting them here [2] whom thou wilt shall with thee elsewhere live for ever; we poor misers [3] give humble praises and thanks unto thee, dear Father, that thou hast vouched us worthy of thy correction at this present, hereby to work that which we in prosperity and liberty did neglect: for the which neglecting and many other our grievous sins, whereof we now accuse ourselves before thee, most merciful Lord, thou mightest most justly have given us over, and destroyed us both in souls and bodies. But such is thy goodness towards us in Christ, that thou seemest to forget all our offences: and, as though we were far otherwise than we be indeed, thou wilt that we should suffer this cross, now laid upon us for thy truth and gospel's sake, and so be thy witnesses with the prophets, apostles, martyrs, and confessors, yea, with thy dearly beloved Son Jesus Christ; to whom thou dost now here begin to fashion us like, that in his glory we may be like him also.

O good God, what are we on whom thou shouldest shew this great mercy? O loving Lord, forgive us our unthankfulness and sins. O faithful Father, give us thy holy Spirit now to cry in our hearts, 'Abba, dear Father;' to assure us of our eternal elections in Christ; to reveal more and more thy truth unto us; to confirm, strengthen, and stablish us so in the same, that we may live and die in it as vessels of thy mercy, to thy glory and to the commodity of thy church. Endue us with the Spirit of thy wisdom, that with good conscience we may always so answer the enemies in thy cause, as may turn to their conversion or confusion, and our unspeakable consolation in Jesus Christ: for whose sake we beseech thee henceforth to keep us, to give us patience, and to will none otherwise for deliverance or mitigation of our

MS. 1. 2. 8. no. 83. 2. Emman. Coll Cambridge. Meditations of Bradford, Hall 1562, and after editions.

[1 The heading in 1562 is, 'Another prayer for remission of sins.']
[2 'here them,' MS.: 'them here' 1562.]
[3 See p. 73, note 4, above.]

misery, than may stand always with thy good pleasure and merciful will towards us.

Grant this, dear Father, not only to us in this place, but also to all other elsewhere afflicted, for thy name's sake, through the death and merits of Jesus Christ our Lord. Amen.

A MOST GODLY AND EARNEST PRAYER
UPON THE PASSION AND PAINFUL WORK OF OUR SAVIOUR CHRIST[1].

MS. 1. 2. 8. no. 71. Emman. Coll. Cambridge.

Meditations of Bradford, Hall 1562, and after editions.

O ALMIGHTY and everlasting Lord God, which hast made heaven, earth[2], &c.! O incomprehensible unity! O always to be worshipped, most blessed Trinity! I humbly beseech thee and pray thee, by the assumption and crucified humanity of our Lord Jesus Christ, that thou wouldest incline and bow down the great depth of thy Deity to the bottomless pit of my vility: drive from me all kind of vice, maliciousness[3], and sin, and "make in me a new and clean heart, and renew in me a right spirit," for thy holy name's sake.

O Lord Jesu, I beseech thy goodness, for that exceeding great love which drew thee out of thy Father's bosom into the womb of the holy virgin, and for the assumption of man's nature, wherein it pleased thee to save me and to deliver me from eternal death; I beseech thee, I say, that thou wouldest draw me out of myself into thee, my Lord God: and grant this thy love may recover again to me thy grace, that may make increase[4], and make perfect in me that which is wanting in me; may raise up in me that which is fallen, may restore to me that which I have lost, and may quicken in me that which is dead and should live; and so I to become conformable unto thee in all my life and conversation, thou dwelling in me and I in thee, my heart being suppled with thy grace, and settled in thy faith for ever. O thou, my God, loose and set at liberty my spirit from all inferior

[1 So the MS. The heading in 1562 is, 'A prayer for deliverance from sin, and to be restored to God's grace and favour again'.]

[2 'earth' 1562: not in MS.]

[3 'maliciousness,' MS.: 'wickedness' 1562.]

[4 'that may make increase,' MS.: 'to increase' 1562.]

things, govern my soul, and so work that both in soul and body I may be holy and live to thy glory, world without end. Amen.

[5] I humbly pray thee for thy holy nativity's sake, that thou wouldest sanctify my nativity, begin in me a new life and a godly, to thy praise for ever.

I beseech thee for thy holy poverty's sake, that thou wouldest make me rich with thy heavenly riches, and give me to contemn this world.

For thy holy circumcision's sake take from me the foreskin of my heart, and "circumcise me with circumcision not made with hands," that I may "put off the old man," and be made "a new creature," endued with thy righteousness, holiness, innocency and immortality.

For thy exile's sake grant me to take this life as an exile, and make me a citizen and home-dweller of thy kingdom in heaven; which grant me to aspire, and to long to come into the same, as thou art in it both soul and body.

For thy holy baptism's sake grant me the baptism of thy Spirit, that I may be anointed with thy holy anointment in such measure as may please thee, to thy glory and my endless comfort; that henceforth I may live a God's child, and be guided by the same Spirit for ever.

For thy fasting and temptation's sake grant me to mortify mine affections and carnality, and grace to stand against all the assaults of the adversary; whom as thou overcamest in thine own person, so I beseech thee do in me.

For thy holy conversation's sake grant me to follow thee as my pattern in all things effectually.

For thy holy doctrine's sake lighten the eyes of my mind that I may see, and inflame mine affections that I may love for evermore thy paths, going in the same purely to thy glory.

For thy holy miracles' sake miraculously convert my soul, heal my wounds, cure my diseases, restore to me life, give me inward sight, inward hearing, inward speech; cast out all evil in me, and come and dwell in me for ever.

For thy great humility's sake in washing thy disciples',

[5 The remainder of this prayer is now first printed from MS. 1. 2. 8. in Emmanuel College, Cambridge.]

even thine enemy's, feet, wash away from me all my filth of sin and all my readiness to do evil; mundify[1] the feet of my naughty affections, and keep them always clean from henceforth, that they never be defiled. And grant me always that I may be ready to humble myself by all means to serve my brother, even mine enemies, to their comfort in thee.

For thy holy preparation of the place for thee to sup in, and for the institution of thy holy supper, which thou hast instituted for the memory of thy death and passion, and of thy coming again, to confirm our faith of pardon of our sins, and communion with thee and all thy merit and glory, make good and prepare in me a meet and worthy place for thee to sup in; and feed me with thyself, that I may dwell in thee and thou in me by thy holy Spirit, to couple me unto thee, and so to thy Father.

O work in me by the same Spirit true love, that I may be linked to all thy people, being one with them also, &c.

For thy exceeding great lowliness' sake, which sufferedst thyself to be sold of thine own disciple, grant that I do never sell thee, my Lord God, for any worldly glory or gain, but may contemn all things, and even mine own self, for thy sake and for thy kingdom.

For thy wonderful heaviness, sorrow, dread, prayer, agony, and bloody sweat, which thou sufferedst in the garden for me, utterly forsaking thine own will, grant me to see and hate sin in myself and others, which was the cause of all this thine agony and torments. Grant me not to make a trifle of that which was so painful for thee to purchase. Grant that in all adversity I may deny myself utterly, and offer up myself wholly unto thee.

For that thy wonderful love, wherethrough thou didst permit thyself not only to be betrayed of Judas, but also to be delivered to thine enemies, grant that I never betray thee, either in myself or in any others, neither at any time do refuse to do my duty and the good I can, even to my very enemies.

For thy charity's sake, which made thee willing to be taken and bound of wicked and ungracious men, loose me from the bonds of all sins, and tie me in the strings of thy precepts and loving of thy holy will, that for ever hereafter

[[1] Mundify: make clean.]

I may persevere in thy service, and never have liberty or be loosed to follow the pleasure of the flesh at any time.

For thy most ardent compassion's sake, which moved thee to suffer for my sake many slanders, taunts, mockings, and cruel entertainments of thine adversaries, have mercy upon my sinful soul, and unlade her from the great load of sin laid upon her, wherewith, alas! I have defiled thy gracious image most shamefully, and done much wrong and contempt to thy holy name in myself continually.

O grant, dear Lord, that I may be ready for ever hereafter to suffer gladly all kind of taunts, injuries, contempts, and slanders, for thy name's sake.

For that love's sake, which made thee not to abhor for me to be most painfully whipped, scourged, and beaten, pardon and forgive me that I have so often, alas! beaten thee with my hands, scourged thee with my tongue, and punished thee with my feet and affections; but may henceforth as gladly suffer all kind of stripes for thee, and have mine affections, words, and deeds diverted and guided by thy grace to thy glory for ever.

For those most spiteful spittings and spewings of the Jews in thy face for my sake, dear Lord, forgive me that I have bespewed so my face and conscience (wherein thou wouldest dwell and have thy face to shine) with so many vile, filthy and wicked cogitations, and unclean desires; and thereto have altogether bewrayed[2] thy most holy body (which by faith I have received in hearing thy words and receiving thy sacraments) with most stinking gobbets[3] of phlegm; I mean, with most naughty, idle thoughts, words and deeds, &c.

JOHN BRADFORD.

A PRAYER

FOR THE OBTAINING OF FAITH.

O MERCIFUL God, and dear Father of our Lord and Saviour Jesus Christ, in whom as thou art well pleased, so hast thou commanded us to hear him; forasmuch as he often biddeth us to ask of thee, and thereto promiseth that thou wilt hear us,

Meditations of Bradford, Hall 1562, and after editions.

[2 Vide p. 137, note 2, above.]   [3 'Gobbets:' fragments, morsels.]

and grant us that which in his name we shall ask of thee; lo, gracious Father, I am bold to beg of thy mercy, through thy Son Jesus Christ, one sparkle of true faith and certain persuasion of thy goodness and love towards me in Christ; wherethrough I being assured of the pardon of all my sins, by the mercies of Christ thy Son, may be thankful to thee, love thee, and serve thee in holiness and righteousness all the days of my life. Amen.

A PRAYER
FOR REPENTANCE.

MOST gracious God and merciful Father of our Saviour Jesus Christ, because I have sinned and done wickedly, and through thy goodness have received a desire of repentance, whereto this long-suffering doth draw my hard heart; I beseech thee, for thy great mercy's sake in Christ, to work the same repentance in me; and by thy Spirit, power, and grace, to humble, mortify, and fear my conscience for my sins to salvation, that in thy good time thou mayest comfort and quicken me, through Jesus Christ, thy dearly beloved Son. So be it.

A DIALOGUE
OR COMMUNICATION BETWEEN SATAN AND OUR CONSCIENCE.

Satan. THOU hast sinned against God; therefore thou must die.

Conscience. Why then died Christ?

Satan. For sinners: but how knowest thou he died for thee?

Conscience. Because I am a sinner, and he is both able and willing to forgive me.

Satan. I grant that he is able to forgive thee: but how knowest thou he will?

Conscience. He would not surely have died, if he would not forgive.

Satan. But how knowest thou that he will forgive thee?

Conscience. Because I would fain be forgiven.

Satan. So would Judas as well as thou, and prevailed not.

Conscience. The scriptures went upon Judas' fact, which must needs be fulfilled: they never went upon mine. Again Judas bare a figure of the people of the Jews, which tribe only fell from Christ, when all other eleven tribes of the world did stick fast unto him. I am a poor sinner of the gentiles, of whom it is written, "I will be exalted in the gentiles."

Satan. If thou be a 'sinner of the gentiles,' yet thou must consider thy sin is great.

Conscience. I grant: but Christ's passion is greater.

Satan. O but thou hast sinned very often!

Conscience. Tell me not, Satan, what I have done, but what I will do.

Satan. Why, what wilt thou do?

Conscience. By God's grace my full purpose is hereafter to take better heed, and to amend my former life.

Satan. Is that enough, thinkest thou?

Conscience. What lacketh?

Satan. The favour of God, which hath clean forsaken thee.

Conscience. So God favoured and "loved the world," that he gave his own dear Son, that whosoever seeth him as the Israelites did the brasen serpent, they "shall not perish, but have life everlasting[1]."

A TREATISE

OF ELECTION AND FREE-WILL.

THAT there is and always hath been with God, even before the world was made, an election in Christ of all those that shall be saved, many places in the scriptures do teach; as to the Eph. i.; Rom. viii. ix. xi.; 1 Thess. i.; Matt. xx. xxii. xxiv.; Mark xiii.; Titus i.; Acts xiii.; Phil. ii.; Luke x. xviii.; Rev. iii. xiii. xvii. xxi. xxii.; John vi. viii. x. xiii. xvii.; and almost every where in the new Testament. In no case

MS. 1. 2. 8. no. 13. Emman. Coll. Cambridge.

Meditations of Bradford, Hall 1562, and after editions.

[1 Part of the 'Defence of election,' which appears subsequently in this volume, is printed after this 'Dialogue' in the 'Godly Meditations' of Bradford 1562, and after editions.]

therefore it may be denied of any that is godly, although he cannot attain to God's wisdom, justice, and mercy in it; for that were to see God's fore-parts. We must grant it therefore, because the word of God doth not only teach it, but also it standeth with the very nature of God, that to him not only men, but all things also that have been or shall be for ever in all creatures, are not only certain, but so certain that they cannot but be accordingly, and serve his providence; for else God were not God, if any thing were, hath been, or could be without his knowledge, yea, certain knowledge. Which knowledge in God may not be separated of any man from his wisdom, and so not from his will; except we would make two gods, as did the Manichees[1], one the author of all good, and another the author of all evil; both which, say they, were eternal and without beginning: which their opinion is devilish and against the word of God most manifestly, which affirmeth in many places that there is no more gods but one, or any other that have power to do good or evil absolutely or of themselves.

Exod. xxxiii.

But lest some men which are too curious should hereout gather, that then all things come by fatal necessity, as the Stoics thought, or by compulsion and coaction, as others think; and therefore, say they, all God's precepts requiring that which we cannot do are in vain; I think it good to speak something hereof.

Against the Stoics' fatal necessity.

First. The Stoics' opinion is to be condemned as concerning fatal necessity; for that it tieth and bindeth God to the second causes, and maketh him which is a most free agent bound and tied, so that he cannot work but as the second cause moveth him[2]. For they did imagine a perpetual connexion and knitting together of causes by a perpetual order which is contained in nature: whereas we should certainly know that it is God which is the ruler and arbiter of all things, which of his wisdom hath foreseen and determined all things that he will do, and now of his power doth in his time put the same in execution, according as he hath decreed with himself.

[1 Vide Mosheim. Eccl. Hist. cent. III. II. v. 2—10; Neander, Ch. Hist., Rose, sect. IV. ii. vol. II. 140—68, Lond. 1841—2.]

[2 Vide Cicero. De Natur. Deor. Lib. I. xv., De Fato Lib. Sing., Op. IV 408, 468 et seq. Lond. 1681; Cudworth, Intellect. System, ch. I. i. iii. ed. 1678.]

Herein to tarry any longer I need not, for that I think there be none now which be of this opinion to attribute things to fortune, a word unseemly for Christians.

Secondly. That all things are done by coaction or compulsion is false, and out of God's providence and predestination cannot be gathered or maintained; for there must be a difference put between necessity and constraint.

All and every thing that hath been done, is, or shall be, in consideration of God's providence as it is with God, are of necessity, but yet not of compulsion or constraint: as for example, you shall see that necessity is one thing, and constraint is another thing. God is good of necessity: but who now will say then that he is so by coaction, or enforced thereto? The devil is naught of necessity, but not by coaction: good men do well of necessity, but not by compulsion: wicked men do evil of necessity, but not of constraint. A thing that is done willingly is not to be said to be done by constraint. God is good willingly, but not by compulsion: the devil is naught willingly, but not of enforcing: good men do good willingly, but not constrainedly: wicked men do transgress willingly, but not compelled. So that it is plain, though all things be done of necessity, yet are they not of compulsion and enforcement.

By reason whereof, a man that will be diligent in looking hereon may see matter enough to purge God from being the author of all evil or of any evil, although he be the Author of all things and of all actions; which are to be construed according to the will of the doers: and so may we see one action to be both good and evil in respect of God's will and Satan's will. For, inasmuch as a thing is done according to God's will, the same is good, for his will is good; and, inasmuch as a thing is done according to Satan's will, it is evil, because his will is evil.

But now to the third thing, that is, whether God's precepts, requiring that which is not in our powers, be frustrate or no, although all things are done of necessity and by God's providence.

To the understanding hereof two things are to be considered: first, that we must think of God, not as he is in himself, but as by his word he teacheth us; secondly, the state of man before his fall is to be compared with the state of man presently, as he is now brought into this world.

For the first, although it be most true that to God all things are so certain as before is spoken; yet, in that God hath opened to us by his word so much of his will as we should with diligence search and observe, we may not think otherwise but that whatsoever is done against that word, the same is sin and evil in him whosoever he be that doth thereagainst; although the same transgression God doth and can use to serve his providence accordingly. Of which providence we may not otherwise judge, than his word giveth us leave: that is, we must do nothing to serve it but as his word teacheth. If Adam had been ruled hereby, then he had not eaten the apple; for, in that he obeyed not the word of God which he knew, easily we may perceive that he did not eat the apple to obey God's providence which he knew not. So that evident it is, Adam's fall to be sin and evil, and he himself with the serpent to be the author thereof; God not allowing or approving the evil, which is to be construed according to the will of the doer: which will in Adam was naught, although the action God turned to serve his providence, thereby[1] setting forth his wonderful wisdom, power, and goodness: whereat we ought rather with reverence to wonder, than by wandering further than beseemeth us to call into question why God did so. Which 'why' no man is able to understand, and therefore we should bid our busy brain sit down, and not to covet again to be like to God, as Adam did, and therefore he fell so foul as he did.

For the second (man's state I mean before his fall and his state now) thus let us think; namely, that God made man after his image, that is, endued man with a soul immortal, wise, righteous, and holy: for the image of God is not concerning the body which man hath[2] common with the beasts of the earth, but it is from above and[3] of God's breathing. So that Adam, transgressing God's precept, did not according as he should and might have done, but according as he should not have done, and might have avoided, if that he had not received the persuasion and counsel of the serpent: which

[1 'there,' MS.: 'thereby' 1562.]
[2 'had,' MS.: 'hath' 1562.]
[3 'it is from above, and' 1562: not in MS.]

God permitted him to do, thereby to declare that perfect justice, wisdom, and holiness is not nor cannot be in any creature which is not God also: and therefore Christ being God was made man, that in man there might be this perfection and justice which is in Christ our Lord, and in Adam we could never have had. Which wisdom of God we shall joyfully one day behold, if we will now restrain our busy brain and curiosity from searching further than we should do.

But to return again. Adam, I say, being made after God's image, (which he received for us all, to have derived the same unto us all by natural propagation,) by transgressing the commandments lost and mangled so the same image of God in himself and in us all, that for immortality came death, for wisdom came foolishness, for righteousness came unrighteousness, for holiness came corruption, concerning God's judgment and in God's sight; (although there remained in him, concerning man's judgment and the sight of the world, life, wisdom, righteousness, and holiness;) the which all we by propagation do from our mother's womb receive: so that we may well see our state now to be far from the state we had before Adam's fall. And therefore God's law requireth nothing of us but that which was in our nature before the fall, which we see is impossible for us to pay accordingly; and yet God not unjust, in that he asketh of us nothing thereby but the self-same thing which he gave us in our creation.

The law then and the precepts of God were given after the fall of man, not that man should thereby get life and the thing which was lost by sin, (for the blessed Seed was promised for the recovering hereof, and to him that[4] pertained;) but that man by it might know sin and what he had lost, thereby to desire more deeply the promised Seed, by whom as we be received, so our evils be not imputed; and that we, being renewed by his holy Spirit and new seed, should "as new-born babes" desire, and by will begin to do the law of God: which, after our deliverance forth of this corrupt body and "man of sin" by death, we shall without all let fully accomplish, and at the length receive the body to be "spiritual" (as Paul saith) and holy, ready to obey and serve the Spirit as an helper rather than an hinderer.

O happy day, when wilt thou appear?

[4 i. e. the recovering life and what was lost by sin.]

By this which I have already spoken, I think the diligent reader may see how that there is election of God's children, and how that God's providence stretcheth itself to all things; so that all things in respect thereof come of necessity, but yet nothing thereby to be done by constraint and enforcement: wherethrough God is seen to be the Author of all things, and yet of no evil or sin.

The state of man before his fall and after, with the cause of God's law and precepts given to man, I have briefly touched. Now it resteth that I should speak something of free-will, what it is, and how far we may grant that man hath free-will.

That this may be understand, as I would have the end wherefore God gave his law to be considered; (namely, not for man to get thereby eternal life, which appertained to the promised Seed[1], but to shew man what sin is and what by sin he lost, that he might by his inability be driven to desire of very necessity the promised Messias, and so by him to receive the Spirit; wherethrough being regenerate he might learn to love the law, to take it as a directory and rule to live by, and to hedge in his old man from controlling;) this gear, I say, as I would have it considered if we will understand man's free-will, so would I have this marked, namely the difference betwixt the life which we lost and had in our first creation, and now have by birth before regeneration.

In our first creation we had a life not only with the creatures, but also with God: which life utterly Adam lost, as he declareth by running away to hide himself from God; and this he lost for us also as well as for himself, in respect whereof the scripture calleth us "dead." Concerning this life therefore that is with God, we have no will at all, much less any free-will; for how can a dead man have any will? The will therefore we have is only for this life and with men: that is, it is not good and free but in respect of men and in this life. In respect of God and life with him all our will is as we are, even "dead." Yea, and the will we have for this present life, if a man will consider "the god of this world," and how we are his slaves by birth and continually till we be regenerate, and how ready our affections are to serve his

[1 'seed promised,' MS.: 'promised seed' 1562.]

purpose; I think none will say otherwise but that man's will unregenerate is none otherwise free than pleaseth his master, who must needs serve, spite of his head, our God; and therefore all to be done by God's providence, as I said before, without any imputation of evil to our good and most holy Father.

'Yea, but,' saith one, 'what free-will hath man that is regenerate?' This will I briefly shew, when that I have spoken of justification, the which precedeth regeneration, from whom we may discern it, but not divide it, no more than heat from the fire.

Justification in scripture is taken for the forgiveness of our sins, and consisteth in the forgiveness of our sins. This is only God's work, and we nothing else but patients[2] and not agents. After this work, in respect of us and our sense, cometh regeneration, which altogether is God's work also: for, as to our first birth we bring nothing, (bring, quoth I? yes, we bring to let it many things, but to further it nothing at all,) so do we bring nothing that can help to our justification; as St Austin full well saith, "He that made thee without thee, shall he not justify thee without thee?" which the papists have perverted, reading it affirmatively without interrogation[3], as though we brought something to

The papists read thus without interrogation, Qui fecit te sine te, non

[2 i. e. passive.]

[3 So the Benedictine edition, in which the argument of Augustine, on which the punctuation obviously must depend, is as follows:

totum ex Deo: non tamen quasi dormientes, non quasi ut non conemur, non quasi ut non velimus. Sine voluntate tua non erit in te justitia Dei. Voluntas quidem non est nisi tua, justitia non est nisi Dei. Esse potest justitia Dei sine voluntate tua, sed in te esse non potest præter voluntatem tuam Resurrexit propter justificationem nostram. Quid est, propter justificationem nostram? Ut justificet nos, ut justos faciat nos. Eris opus Dei, non solum quia homo es, sed etiam quia justus es. Melius est enim justum esse, quam te hominem esse. Si hominem te fecit Deus, et justum tu te facis; melius aliquid facis, quam fecit Deus. Sed sine te fecit te Deus. Non enim adhibuisti aliquem consensum, ut te faceret Deus. Quomodo consentiebas qui non eras? Qui ergo fecit te sine te, non te justificat sine te. Ergo fecit nescientem, justificat volentem. Tamen ipse justificat, ne sit justitia tua, ne redeas ad damna, ad detrimenta et stercora, invenire in illo non habens justitiam tuam, 'quæ ex lege est,' sed justitiam per fidem Christi, quæ est ex Deo.—August. Serm. clxix. 13. de verb. apost. Phil. III. Op. V. col. 815, Par. 1679—1700. Vide Fulke, Defence, Parker Soc. 386—7.]

our justifying: whereas it (I mean justification) is a much more excellent work than the work of our creation; and therefore too arrogant are they which will not give all to God in it, as they do in their creation.

justificabit te sine te 'He that made thee without thee, shall not justify thee without thee;' that is, without thy help, thy works, thy worthiness.

Good men fly from that pride, and are content to give no less to God justifying and regenerating them, than they do to their parents for their first generation. Afore we be justified and regenerated of God, we are altogether dead to God and to all goodness in his sight; and therefore we are altogether patients till God have wrought this his only work, justification and regeneration. Which work, in respect of us and our imperfection and falls, in that it is not so full and perfect but it may be more and more, therefore by the Spirit of sanctification (which we receive in regeneration as the seed of God) we are quickened to labour with the Lord, and to be more justified; that is, by faith and the fruits of faith, to ourselves and others to declare the same; and so to increase from virtue to virtue, from glory to glory, having always need to have our feet washed, although we be clean notwithstanding.

Now to the question. A man regenerate (which we ought to believe of ourselves, I mean that we are so by our baptism, the sacrament thereof requiring no less faith), a man, I say, regenerate, that is, "born of God," hath the Spirit of God. And, as a man born of flesh and blood hath the spirit thereof, whereby as he can stir up himself to do more and more the deeds of the flesh, so the other can, by the Spirit of God in him, stir up in himself the gifts and graces of God, to glorify God accordingly. Howbeit, here let us mark that as "the old man" is a perpetual enemy to the new-born man, so accordingly to his strength the works of "the new man" are letted and made ineffectual. Therefore God hath taught us to pray and promised his help, which he most commonly in manner giveth by the cross; whereby "the old man" is weakened, and the new receiveth strength more and more, desiring a dissolution and an utter destruction of "the old man" by death, that it might go to God from whence it came, and to his home, even heaven; where in the last day it shall receive the old Adam, now so schooled that it will never more be but a most faithful friend to serve and praise the Lord for evermore.

Thus have you now what free-will the regenerate children of God have, for whose sakes the gospel and sweet free promises are given: and to the regenerate "new man" they properly do pertain; as doth the law with all comminations, and the conditional promises (I mean promises hanging upon condition on our worthiness), pertain properly to the old and unregenerate man, so that, when he kicketh, he must by them be bridled and kept down. When the inward man would be comforted, he must not have the law, nor his comminations and conditional promises, but the gospel and her most sweet free promises. So shall we walk neither on the right nor on the left hand, but keep the right way to heavenward, even Christ our Lord and Captain, as his soldiers, servants, and lively members; neither despairing nor carnally living, but fearing and rejoicing as is appertaining: which God grant for his mercy's sake. Amen.

And thus, my dearly beloved, I have sent to you briefly my mind herein according to your desire. Because I have had little time and many other lets, I shall heartily pray you to take this in good part, and with the more indifferency and attention to read it; for my desire was to write fully and speedily. Therefore it perchance hath the more obscurity, and desireth a friendly reader, construing all to the best, and brotherly admonishing where cause may appear.

JOHN BRADFORD.

A BRIEF SUM
OF THE DOCTRINE OF ELECTION AND PREDESTINATION.

GOD's foresight is not the cause of sin or excusable necessity to him that sinneth: the damned therefore have not nor shall have any excuse, because God, foreseeing their condemnation through their own sin, did not draw them, as he doth his elect, unto Christ. But, as the elect have cause to thank God for ever for his great mercies in Christ, so the other have cause to lament their own wilfulness, sin, and contemning of Christ, which is the cause of their reprobation, and wherein we should look upon reprobation; as the only goodness of God in Christ is the cause of our election and salvation, wherein we should look upon God's election.

Meditations of Bradford, Hall 1562, and after editions.

He that will look upon God or any thing in God, simply and barely as it is in God, the same shall be stark blind. Who can see God's goodness, as it is in God? who can see his justice, as it is in him? If therefore thou wilt look upon his goodness, not only look upon his works, but also upon his word: even so, if thou wilt look upon his justice, do the like. Then shalt thou see that election is not to be looked on but in Christ, nor reprobation but in sin. When the second cause is sufficient, should not we think that they are too curious that will run to search the first cause, further than God doth give them leave by his word? the which first cause because they cannot comprehend, therefore do they deny it. God be merciful unto us for his name's sake, and give us to love and live his truth, to "seek peace and pursue it."

Because God of his goodness, for the comfort of his children and certainty of their salvation, doth open unto them something the first cause of their salvation, that is, his goodness before the beginning of the world, to be looked upon in Christ; a man may not therefore be so bold as to wade so in condemnation further than God revealeth it. And, forasmuch as he hath not revealed it but in sin, therefore let us not look on it otherwise.

Mark this well, and be not too curious.

Seek to be delivered from sin, and fear not reprobation: but if thou wilt not, thou shalt find no excuse in the last day. Say not but thou art warned.

[Note annexed to the first edition, 1562.]

To the former meditations and prayers, for your further comfort and godly exercise, you may join those most godly and comfortable meditations which are annexed to his book lately imprinted against the fear of death.

[Colophon.]

Printed at London
by Rouland Hall, dwelling in
gutter lane at the sygne of
the halfe Egle and Key.
1562.

PRIVATE PRAYERS AND MEDITATIONS,

WITH

OTHER EXERCISES,

BY

JOHN BRADFORD.

A Godlye

Medytacyon composed by the faithfull and constant seruant of God J. B. Precher who latlye was burnte in Smytfelde for the testimonie of Jesus Christe by the tyrannye of Antechriste in his fylthy members.

(∴)

¶ Psalme. lxxix.

O Lorde let the bengeaunce of thy seruauntes bloude that is shedde be openlye showed upon the ungodlye, in oure sight. O let the sorowful sighting of the prisoners come before thee: and accordinge to the greatnes of thy power preserbe thou those that are appoynted to dye.

[From a copy in the Bodleian Library, Oxford.]

[The following 'Private prayers and meditations with other exercises' were first printed by Copland, in a separate volume, March 15, 1559[1].

This series was republished by J. Allde 1578, together with the 'Godly Meditations' (which occupy p. 116—220 above) first printed by Hall 1562, the pagination being continued from that collection as reissued in 1578, but with separate title and signatures. The Meditations of 1559 were afterward reprinted by E. Allde, similarly appended, in 1604, 1607, 1614, 1622, and 1633.

The 'prayer on the wrath of God against sin,' p. 224—9, and some of the 'private prayers and meditations,' p. 232—4, 239—41, follow respectively (as noted on the margin of each) the text of MSS. in Emmanuel College, Cambridge, which have supplied various words, and occasionally two or three lines, not in the printed editions. These MSS. have been collated with a copy of the very rare edition of Copland 1559, in the Bodleian Library, Oxford; and the differences are noted wherever a deviation from the Cambridge MSS. occurs.

The remaining prayers and meditations in the following series observe the text of the edition of 1559, which has been compared occasionally with those of 1578, 1604, 1607, 1614, and 1622: but the variations from the edition of Copland are only noted in special cases.

The 'private prayers and meditations' were, for the most part, translated by Bradford from the *Excitationes animi in Deum* of Ludovicus Vives, a devout writer, and one of the chief restorers of learning, in the former part of the sixteenth century. The originals of Vives are reprinted in the Appendix to this volume from a copy of the *Excitationes*, Lugduni 1558, in the Library of Archbishop Harsnet, Colchester.

Several of the 'private prayers,' after appearing in the Meditations of Bradford 1559, were reprinted in the first edition of the 'Book of Christian Prayers,' ornamented with wood-cut borders, Day 1569, on signatures a ii to c iv. A copy of this edition, which is exceedingly scarce, is preserved in the archiepiscopal Library at Lambeth.

Many of the 'private prayers' (retranslated from Vives, and with extensive alterations) appeared in the after editions of that 'Book,' 1578, 1581, 1590, 1608, on signatures B i to D ii.

Various meditations also in the preceding series (p. 116—220) namely those ' on the second coming of Christ,' ' on the sober use of the body,' ' on mortification,' ' on the presence of God,' ' on the power and goodness of God,' ' on death,' and ' on the passion of Christ,' p. 185 —99, after appearing in the Meditations of Bradford, Hall 1562, were reprinted in the first edition of the 'Book of Christian Prayers,' signatures e ii, k ii, d iv, i ii, m ii, i iv, k iv. The meditation ' on mortification,' p. 190 above, also appeared in the after editions of that 'Book,' 1578— 1608, signature E e i; and that ' on death,' p. 195, above, was given in those later editions, signature H h i, in an altered form, being retranslated from Vives.]

[1 See the colophon at p. 247.]

PRAYER

ON THE WRATH OF GOD AGAINST SIN[1].

JESUS EMMANUEL.

MS. 1. 2. 8. no. 14. 2. Emman. Coll. Cambridge.
Meditations of Bradford, Copland 1559, and after editions.

O ALMIGHTY and everlasting Lord God, the dear Father of our Saviour Jesus Christ, "which hast made heaven and earth, the sea and all that therein is;" which art the only Ruler, governor, conserver and keeper of all things, together with thy dearly beloved Son Christ Jesus our Lord, and with "the Holy Ghost the Comforter;" O holy, righteous, and wise; O strong, terrible, mighty, and fearful Lord God, Judge of all men, and Governor of all the whole world; O exorable, patient, and most gracious Father, whose eyes are upon the ways of all men, and are so clean they cannot abide impiety; thou "searchest the hearts," and "triest the very thoughts and reins" of all men. Thou hatest sin and abhorrest iniquity: for sin's sake thou hast grievously punished mankind thy most dear creature, as thou hast declared by the penalty

Gen. iii.
of death laid upon all the children of Adam; by the casting out of Adam and his offspring forth of paradise; by the curs-
Gen. vii.
ing of the earth; by the drowning of the world; by the
Gen. xix. Exod. iv.
burning up of Sodom and Gomor; by the hardening of Pharaoh his heart, so that no miracle could convert him; by the
Exod. xiv.
drowning of him and his people with him in the Red Sea; by the overthrowing of the Israelites in the wilderness, so that of six hundred thousand alonely two did enter into
1 Sam. xiii.
the land of promise; by rejecting of Saul; by the great
2 Sam. xii.
punishments upon thy servant David notwithstanding his hearty repentance; by grievously[2] afflicting Solomon in

[1 This prayer, after appearing in the Meditations of Bradford, 1559, was printed in the 'Christian Prayers,' &c. collected by Henry Bull, Powell (see p. 118, note 1, above), and Middleton 1570: vide Parker Soc. edition, p. 78—83, where it has the following title: 'A form of prayer meet for our state and time, to move us to true repentance, and to turn away God's sharp scourges yet threatened against us.' The MS. has, after 'Jesus Emmanuel,' the words, 'A fruitful and most godly prayer,' in a separate line.]

[2 'grievous,' MS.: 'grievously' 1559.]

himself and in his seed; by the captivity of the ten tribes; 2 Kings xvii. and by the thraldom of the Jews, wherein until this present day they continue a notable spectacle of thy wrath to the world against and for sin.

But, of all spectacles of thine anger against sin, the greatest and most notable is the death and bloody passion of thy dearly beloved Son Jesus Christ. Great is thine anger against sin, when in heaven and earth nothing could be found which might appease thy wrath, save the blood-shedding of thy only and most dearly beloved Son, in whom was and is all thy delight. Great is the sore of sin that needed such a salve: mighty was the malady that needed such a medicine. If in Christ, in whom was no sin, thy wrath was so fierce for our sin that he was constrained to cry, "My God, my God, why hast thou forsaken me?" how great and importable[3] then is thine anger against us, which are nothing but[4] sinful!

They that are thy children, through the contemplation of thy anger against sin set forth most evidently in the bloody death of Christ, do tremble and are afraid, lamenting themselves upon him, and heartily cry for mercy: whereas the wicked are altogether careless and contemptuous[5], nothing lamenting their iniquities, or crying unto thee heartily for mercy and pardon: amongst whom we are rather to be placed than amongst thy children; for that we are so senseless for our sins, and careless for thy wrath; which we may well see to be most grievous against us, and evidently set forth in the taking away of our good king and thy true religion, in the exile of thy servants, prisonment of thy people, misery of thy children, and death of thy saints; also by the[6] placing over us in authority of thy enemies, by the success thou givest them in all they take in hand, by the returning again into our country of antichrist the pope. All these, as they do preach unto all the world, but specially unto us, thy grievous wrath, so do they set before our eyes our iniquities and sins which have deserved the same: for thou art just and holy in all thy works, "thy judgments are righteous" altogether; it is we, it is we that have sinned, and procured these plagues; we have

[3 'Importable:' insupportable.]
[4 'but,' MS.: 'nothing but' 1559.]
[5 'contemn,' MS.: 'contemptuous' 1559.]
[6 'the' 1559: not in MS.]

been unthankful wretches and most carnal gospellers. Therefore unto us pertaineth shame, and nothing else is due but confusion; for we have done very wickedly, we have heaped sin upon sin, so that the measure hath overflowed and ascended up to heaven, and brought these plagues, which are but earnest of greater to ensue. And yet, alas! we are altogether careless in manner. What shall we do? what shall we say? who can give us penitent hearts? who can open our lips, that our mouths might make acceptable confession unto thee?

Alas! of ourselves we cannot think any good, much less wish it, and least of all do it. As for angels or any other creatures, they have nothing but that which they have received, and[1] they are made to minister unto us; so that where it passeth the power of the master, the minister must needs want. Alas, then[2], what shall we do? Thou art holy, and we unholy; thou art[3] good, and we nothing but evil; thou art pure, and we altogether impure; thou art light, and we most dark darkness: how[4] then can there be any conveniency or agreement betwixt us? O what now may we do? Despair? No; for thou art God, and therefore thou art good; thou art merciful, and therefore thou forgivest sins; "with thee is propitiation, and therefore thou art worshipped."

[Ps. cxxx. 4. see Vulgate.]

When Adam had sinned, thou gavest him mercy tofore he desired it; and wilt thou deny us mercy, which now desire the same? Adam excused his fault, and accused thee; but we accuse ourselves, and excuse thee; and shall we be sent empty away? Noe found favour when thy fury abounded; and shall we, seeking grace, be frustrate? Abraham was pulled out of idolatry when the world was drowned therein; and art thou his God only? Israel in captivity in Egypt was graciously visited and delivered; and, dear God, the same good Lord, shall we always be forgotten? How often in the wilderness[5] didst thou defer and spare thy plagues at the requests of Moses, when the people themselves made no petition to thee at all! And seeing we not only now make our prayers unto thee through thy goodness, but also

[1 'and' 1559: not in MS.]
[2 'then' 1559: not in MS.]
[3 'art' 1559: not in MS.]
[4 'when,' MS.: 'how' 1559.]
[5 'desert,' MS.: 'wilderness' 1559.]

have a Mediator for us now far above Moses, even thy Son so dear Christ Jesus, shall we, I say, dear Lord, depart ashamed?

So soon as David had said, "I have sinned," thou didst forthwith answer to[6] him that he should not die, thou hadst "taken away his sins." And, gracious God, even the self-same God, shall not we which now with David gladly confess that we have sinned, (O pardon us!) shall we, I say, not hear by thy good Spirit that our sins are pardoned? O grant that with Manasses we may find favour and mercy. Remember that thou hast not spared thine own only Son so dear Jesus Christ, but given him for us all to die for our sins, to rise for our righteousness, to ascend for our possession-taking in heaven, and to appear before thee for us for ever, "a High Priest after the order of Melchisedec," that through him we might have free access to come to thy throne, now rather of grace than of justice[7]. Remember that thou by him hast bidden us "ask," and promised that we "shall receive," saying, "Ask, and you shall have; seek, and you shall find; knock, and it shall be opened unto you."

O then, dear God, and most meek and[8] merciful Father, we heartily beseech thee to be merciful unto us. For this thy Christ's sake, for his death's sake, for his resurrection's sake, for his mediation's sake[9], for thy promise, truth, and mercy's sake[10], have mercy upon us; pardon and forgive us all our sins, iniquities, and trespasses, whatsoever we have committed against thee, in thought, word, or deed, ever or at any time hitherto by any means. Dear Father, dear Father, have mercy upon us. Though we be poor, yet our Christ is rich; though we be sinners, yet he is righteous; though we be foolish, yet is he wise; though we be impure, yet he is pure and holy: for his sake therefore be merciful unto us. Call to mind how thou hast promised that thou "wilt pour out of thy clean waters, and wash us from our filth, and cleanse us from our evils;" forget not that thou hast promised to "take from us our stony hearts," and dost promise to "give us soft

[6 'to' 1559: not in MS.]
[7 'glory,' MS.: 'justice' 1559.]
[8 'and' 1559: not in MS.]
[9 The last eight words are in the MS., but not in 1559.]
[10 The last seven words are in 1559, but not in the MS.]

hearts, new hearts, and to put into the midst of us right spirits." Remember thy covenant, namely, how thou "wilt be our God, and we shall be thy people;" forget not the parts of it, that is, to "put out of thy memory for ever our unrighteousness," and to "write in our minds and hearts thy laws" and testimonies. Remember that thou dost straitly charge us to "have none other gods but thee;" saying, that thou art "the Lord our God."

O then declare the same to us all[1], we heartily now beseech thee. Forgive us our sins, forgive us our iniquities, cleanse us from our filthiness, wash us from our wickedness, pour out thy holy Spirit upon us. Take from us our hard hearts, our stony hearts, our impenitent hearts[2], our distrusting and doubtful hearts, our carnal, our secure, our idle and beastly, our foolish hearts, our impure, malicious, arrogant, envious, wrathful, impatient, covetous, hypocritical, and epicureal[3] hearts: and in place thereof give us new hearts, soft hearts, faithful hearts, merciful hearts, loving, obedient, chaste, pure, holy, righteous, true, simple, lowly, and penitent hearts; and give us hearts to fear thee, to love thee, trust in thee for ever. Write thy law in our hearts, graft it in our minds, we heartily beseech thee.

Give us "the Spirit of prayer," and make us diligent and happy in the works of our vocations: take into thy custody and governance for ever our souls and bodies, our life, and all that ever we have; tempt us never further than thou wilt make us "able to bear;" and whatsoever thou knowest we have need of, in soul or body, dear God and gracious Father, vouchsafe to give us the same in thy good time; and always as thy children guide us, so that our lives may please thee, and our deaths praise thee, through Jesus Christ our Lord: for whose sake we heartily pray thee to grant these things thus asked, and all other things necessary for our soul and body, not only to us, but to all others also for whom thou wouldest we should pray; especially for thy children that be in thraldom[4], in exile, in prison, in misery, in heaviness, poverty, sickness, &c.: amongst whom most specially

[1 So 1559: 'unto us the same, all,' the MS.]
[2 'our impenitent hearts' 1559: not in MS.]
[3 i.e. luxurious, sensual.]
[4 'in thraldom' 1559: not in MS.]

care for and keep N. N. with all others which for thy name's sake suffer any kind of persecution and trouble[5].

Be merciful to our king and queen with their whole council, to the nobility and magistrates of our realm: according to thy good will give them grace to repent, and after their vocations to seek and set forth thy glory. Be merciful to all the whole commonalty and subjects of our realm[6]: grant us all true repentance, and[7] mitigation of our miseries; and, if it be thy good will, send thy holy word and religion amongst us in our own realm and country[8] once again. Pardon our enemies, persecutors, and slanderers; and, if it be thy pleasure, turn their hearts. Be merciful unto our parents, brethren and sisters, friends and kinsfolk, families and neighbours, and such as by any means thou hast coupled and linked unto us by love or otherwise. And unto us poor sinners, here gathered together in thy holy name, grant thy blessing and holy Spirit to sanctify us, and dwell in us; and as thy children to keep us, this day and for ever, from all evil, to thine eternal glory, our everlasting comfort, and the profit of thy church, which mercifully maintain, cherish, and comfort: strengthen them that stand, so that they never fall; lift up them that be fallen; and keep[9] us from falling from thee, through the merits of thy dearly beloved Son Jesus Christ, our Lord and only Saviour, which liveth and reigneth with thee and the Holy Ghost, to whom be all praise and honour, both now and for ever[10]. Amen.

Per Joannem Bradford.

[5 The last twenty-four words, 'amongst whom. and trouble,' MS.: not in 1559.]

[6 The last five lines, 'our king and queen subjects of our realm,' MS.: 'all the whole realm of England' 1559.]

[7 'and' 1559: not in MS.]

[8 'in our own realm and country,' MS.: not in 1559.]

[9 'keep' 1559: 'keeping,' MS.]

[10 The last twenty-two words, 'which liveth. .for ever' 1559: not in MS.]

PRIVATE PRAYERS

FOR THE MORNING AND EVENING, AND FOR OTHER TIMES OF THE DAY[1].

WHEN YOU AWAKE OUT OF YOUR SLEEP, PRAY THUS:

<small>Meditations of Bradford, Copland 1559, and after editions.</small> O MOST dear Father of our Saviour Jesus Christ, whom none doth know but of thy gift, grant that to the manifold great benefits of thy goodness given to me this, which of all other is most, may be added; that, like as thou hast awaked my body from sleep, so thou wouldest throughly awake, yea, deliver my soul from the sleep of sin and darkness of this world; and that which now is awaked out of sleep thou wouldest, after death, restore to life; for that is but sleep to thee, which is death to us. Dear God, I most heartily beseech and humbly pray thy goodness to make my body such a companion, or rather a minister of godliness to my soul, in this present life, that in the life to come it may partake[2] with the same everlasting happiness by Jesus Christ our Lord.

<small>Ephes. v.</small> "Awake, thou that sleepest, and arise from the dead, and Christ shall shew light unto thee."

Occasions to meditate.

Here call to mind the great mirth and blessedness of the everlasting resurrection: also remember to muse upon that most clear light and bright morning, and new clearness of our bodies, after the long darkness it hath been in: all then shall be full of joy.

[1 The following 'Private prayers and meditations,' p. 230—42, after appearing in the Meditations of Bradford 1559, were reprinted in the 'Christian Prayers,' &c. collected by Henry Bull, Powell (see p. 118, note 1, above), and Middleton 1570: vide Parker Soc. edition, p. 60—77. The heading, 'Private prayers for the morning and evening, and for other times of the day,' is not in 1559, but is taken from the 'Prayers,' &c., Bull, 1570, p. 104.]

[2 'part take' 1559: 'take part with the same of,' Prayers, &c. Bull, 1570.]

SO SOON AS YOU BEHOLD THE DAYLIGHT, PRAY:

O LORD, thou greatest and most true light, whence this light of the day and sun doth spring! O Light, which dost lighten every man that cometh into this world! O Light, which knowest no night nor evening, but art always a midday most clear and fair, without whom all is most dark darkness, by whom all be most splendent! O thou Wisdom of the eternal "Father of mercies!" lighten my mind, that I may only see those things that please thee, and may be blinded to all other things. Grant that I may walk in thy ways, and that nothing else may be light and pleasant unto me.

"Lighten mine eyes, O Lord, that I sleep not in death, lest mine enemies say, I have prevailed against him."

Occasions to meditate.

Muse a little how much the light and eye of the mind and soul is better than of the body; also, that we care more for the soul to see well, than for the body. Think that beasts have bodily eyes, and therewith see; but men have eyes of the mind, and therewith should see.

WHEN YOU ARISE, PRAY:

OUR first father tumbled down himself from a most excellent, high, and honourable estate into the mire of misery and deep sea of shame and mischief: but, O Christ, thou putting forth thine hand didst raise him up: even so we, except we be lift up of thee, shall lie still for ever. O good Christ, our most gracious Redeemer, grant that as thou dost mercifully raise up[3] now this my body and burden, even so I beseech thee raise up my mind and heart to the light of the true knowledge of the love of thee, that my "conversation may be in heaven," where thou art.

"If thou be risen with Christ, think upon those things that be above."

Occasions to meditate.

Think something how foul and filthy that Adam's fall was by reason of sin, and so of every one of us from the height of God's grace: again think upon the great benefit of Christ, by whose help we do daily arise from our fallings.

[3 'us' 1559, a misprint for 'up:' omitted in 1578, 1604, 1614.]

WHEN YOU APPAREL YOURSELF, PRAY:

O Christ, clothe me with thine own self, that I may be so far from "making provision for my flesh to fulfil the lusts of it," that I may clean put off all my carnal desires, and crucify the kingdom of the flesh in me. Be thou unto me a weed[1] to warm me from catching the cold of this world. If thou be away from me, dear Lord, all things will be unto me forthwith cold, weak, dead, &c.; but if thou be with me, all things will be warm, lively, fresh, &c.[2] Grant therefore, that as I compass this my body with this coat, so thou wouldest clothe me wholly, but specially my soul, with thine own self.

"Put upon you as the elect of God, bowels of mercy, meekness, love, peace," &c.

Occasions to meditate.

Call to mind a little how we are incorporate into Christ; again, how he doth clothe us, nourish us under his wings, protection, and providence, preserve us, &c.

WHEN YOU ARE MADE READY TO BEGIN THE DAY WITHAL, PRAY:

MS. 2. 2. 15. 60. Emman. Coll. Cambridge.

Meditations of Bradford, Copland 1559, and after editions.

O Almighty God and most merciful Father, thou knowest, and hast taught us also something to know, that the weakness of man and woman is great, and that without thy grace they can neither do nor think any good thing: have mercy upon me, I humbly beseech thee, which am[3] thy most weak, frail, and unworthy child. O be gracious and tender towards me[4]: lighten my mind that I may with pleasure look upon good things only: inflame my heart with the love thereof, that I may carefully covet them; and at the last by thy gracious conducting may happily attain them through Jesus Christ our Lord.

[1 i. e. 'garment.' The editions 1578, 1604, 1614, have 'reed,' signifying 'thatch:' see Bailey, Dict., and Holloway, Provinc. Dict. 1838. The Latin of Vives is *indumentum*.]

[2 The last fourteen words occur in 1559, but are omitted in 1578, 1604, 1614.]

[3 'which am' 1559: not in MS.]

[4 'O be gracious and tender towards me' 1559: not in MS.]

I, distrusting altogether mine own weakness, commend and offer myself, both soul and body, into thy hands. "Thy loving Spirit lead me forth unto the land of righteousness." Ps. cxliii.

COGITATIONS MEET TO BEGIN THE DAY WITH.

THINK first that man consisteth of soul and body, and that the soul is from heaven, heavenly, firm, and immortal; but the body is from the earth, earthly, frail, and mortal.

[5] Again, think that though by reason of sin, wherein you are conceived and born, the parts of the soul which do understand and desire be so corrupt that, without special grace to both parts, you can neither know nor love any good thing in God's sight, much less then do that is good; yet this notwithstanding think that you are regenerate by Christ's resurrection, (which your baptism requireth you to believe;) and therefore have both those parts something reformed both to know and to love; and therefore to do also some good in the sight of God through Christ, for whose sake our poor doings are accepted for good, the evil and infirmity cleaving thereunto not being imputed through faith.

Think that by faith, which is God's seed (for "they which believe are born of God," and made God's children,) given to those that "be ordained to eternal life;" think, I say, that by faith you receive more and more the Spirit of sanctification, through the use of God's word and sacraments, and earnest prayer to illuminate your minds, understanding, judgment, and reason, and to bow, form, frame, and inflame your affections with love and power to that that good is; and therefore use you the means aforesaid accordingly.

Think that by this Spirit you are through faith coupled to Christ as a lively member, and so to God, and as it were made one with him; and by love which springeth out of this faith you are made one also with all that be of God; and so you have fellowship with God, and all good men that ever were or shall be, in all the good that God and all his saints have or shall have. Think that as by faith and love, through the Spirit of God, you are now entered into this communion, (the blessedness whereof no tongue can express,) so after this

[5 The remainder of this meditation does not occur in the *Excitationes animi* of Vives: see prefatory note, p. 223 above.]

life you shall first in soul, and in the last day in body also, enjoy for ever the same society most perfectly, which now is but begun in you.

Think then of your negligence, that doth so little care for this your happy estate; think upon your ingratitude to God for making you, redeeming you, calling you, and so lovingly adopting you; think upon your folly in fantasying so much earthly and bodily pleasures; think upon your deafness and blindness, which hear not God, nor see him, he calling you so diligently by his works, word, and sacraments; think upon your frowardness, which will not be led of God and his Spirit; think upon your forgetfulness and inconsideration of your heavenly estate, how "your body is the temple of the Holy Ghost," your members are "the members of Christ," the whole "world and all things therein are your own."

<small>1 Cor. vi.</small>

Therefore say unto your soul, 'O my soul, arise, follow God, contemn this world, purpose well, and pursue it, long for the Lord's coming, be ready and watch that he come not upon thee unawares.' And, forsomuch as you must live to God's pleasure, see the vocation and state of your life whereunto God hath called you; and pray to God for grace, knowledge, and ability to take the most profitable things in hand, well to begin, better to go on, and best of all to end the same to God's glory, and the profit of your brethren; and think that time lost, wherein you speak or do not, or (at the least) think not, something to God's glory and the commodity of your brethren.

WHEN YOU GO FORTH OF THE DOORS, PRAY:

<small>Meditations of Bradford, Copland 1559, and after editions.</small>

Now must I walk among the snares of death, stretched out of Satan and of his mischievous ministers in the world, carrying with me a friend to them both, and a foe to myself, even this body of sin and sinful flesh.

O grand captain Christ, lead me and guide me, I beseech thee; defend me from the plagues and subtleties whereof I am endangered; grant that I may take all things that hap as I should do: only upon thee set thou mine eyes, that I may so go on forwards in thy way, as by no things I be hindered, but rather furthered, and may refer all things to thee accordingly. "Shew me thy ways, O Lord, and teach me thy paths."

Consider how vainly the most part of men be occupied, how they do trouble and cumber themselves diversely, how they meddle with many things, thereby much alienating their minds from the knowledge and cogitation of that which they should most esteem, and so become a let and an offence to others. As in going abroad you will see that your apparel be seemly in the sight of men, so see how seemly you appear in the sight of God.

WHEN YOU ARE GOING ANY JOURNEY, PRAY:

THIS our life is a pilgrimage: from the Lord we came, and to the Lord we make our journey; howbeit, through thievish places, and painful, yea, perilous ways, which our cruel enemies have, and do prepare for us now more than stark blind by reason of sin.

O Christ, which art a most true lodesman[1] and guide, and thereto most expert, faithful, and friendly, do thou put out thine hand, "open mine eyes," make thy highways known unto me; which way thou didst first enter into out of this corruptible life, and hast fenced the same for us to immortality. Thou art "the way;" lead us unto the Father by thyself, that all we may be one with him, as thou and he together be one.

"Shew me the way that I should walk in, for I lift up my soul unto thee." Ps. cxliii.

Or pray thus:

Merciful Father, thou art wont to send to thy servants and men of simple hearts thine angels to be their keepers, and as it were guides, as elder brethren, to watch upon thy weak children: so didst thou to young Tobias, to Jacob, to Abraham's servant, to Joshua, &c. O good God, though we be much unlike unto them (so many are our sins), yet, for thine own goodness sake, send thine holy angels to pitch their tents about us, from Satan and his slaves to hide and defend, to carry us in their hands, that we come not into further danger than thou throughout wilt deliver us for thine own sake.

His angels "are[2] ministers for them that be heirs of salvation." Satan sleepeth not, but seeketh always to destroy us. Heb. i.

[1 i. e. leading man, a pilot.]
[2 'or' 1559, 1578: 'are' 1614.]

Think something how we are strangers from our country, from our home, from our original; I mean, from God. Again think upon your madness, that do linger and loiter so gladly in this our journey and pilgrimage; also, how foolish we are to fantasy things which we cannot carry with us, and to contemn conscience which will always be a companion to us, to our joy if it be good, but to our shame and sorrow if it be evil and corrupt; finally, how unnatural we are, that so little desire to be at our home, to be with our only Father, Master, fellows, and friends, &c.[1]

WHEN YOU ARE ABOUT TO RECEIVE YOUR MEAT, PRAY:

THIS is a wonderful mystery of thy work, O Maker and Governor of the world, that thou dost sustain the lives of men and beasts with these meats: surely this power is neither in the bread nor food, but in thy will and word, by which word all things do live and have their beings. Again, how great a thing is it, that thou art able yearly to give sustenance to so many creatures! This is spoken of by thy prophet in thy praises: "All things look up to thee, and thou givest them meat in due season; thou openest thine hand, and fillest with thy blessing every living thing." These doubtless are wonderful works of thine almightiness.

I therefore heartily pray thee, O most liberal Lord and faithful Father, that, as thou by meat through thy word dost minister life to these our bodies, even so by the same word with thy grace do thou quicken our souls, that both in soul and body we may please thee till this our mortal carcass shall put on immortality, and we shall need no more any other food, but thee only, which then wilt be "all in all."

"Taste and see how good the Lord is." "Bless the Lord, O my soul, which feedeth and filleth thy mouth with good things." Think a little how great God's power is, that made us; also think how great his wisdom is to preserve us; but most of all think how many things are given to our use, how wonderful it is to give us life, but most of all to propagate to immortality the life of the soul by his only beck.

[[1] The last ten lines are not in the *Excitationes animi* of Vives: see prefatory note, p. 223 above.]

Last of all think that God, by his providence for thy body, would have thee to confirm thy faith of God's providence for thy soul.

IN THE MEAL-TIME PRAY:

O MOST liberal distributor of thy gifts, which givest us all kind of good things to use, thou being pure givest pure things; grant to me thy grace, that I misuse not these thy gracious gifts given to our use and profits. Let us not love them because thou dost give us these things; but rather let us love thee because thou givest them, and for that they be necessary for us for a season till we come unto thee. Grant us to be conversant amongst thy gifts soberly, purely, temperately, holily, because thou art such a one: so shall not we turn that to the poison of our souls, which thou hast given for the medicine of our bodies; but, using thy benefits thankfully, we shall find them profitable both to soul and body.

Think that the meats and drinks set before you are given to you to use and not to abuse; think they are given to profit and not to hurt you; think that they are not given to you alone, but unto others also by you: in eating and drinking think that you do but feed the worms; remember the poor prisoners, sick, &c., as though you were in their case; think upon the food of your soul, Christ's "body broken," and his "blood shed." Desire "the meat that lasteth for ever;" John vi. "work for it." Christ's meat was to do his Father's will[2]. John iv.

AFTER YOUR MEAT PRAY THUS:

BY corporal meats thou dost sustain our corporal daily life (ready otherwise to perish), the which surely is a great work; but yet this is much greater, more profitable, and more holy, that thy grace, O Jesu Christ, doth keep away from us the death of the soul. For this life we ought much to thank thee; and because thou dost prolong it with thy good gifts, we most heartily praise thee: howbeit, this life is but the way to eternal life, which we beseech thee, for thy death's sake, that thou wilt give us; and so shall we not only give

[2 The last five lines are not in Vives.]

thee (as we can) thanks in time for temporal things, but also eternal thanks for eternal things. O grant to us these our desires for thy mercy's sake. Amen.

Think now that God hath given thee this his blessing of meat, &c., and thereto time that thou mightest, as repent, so seek his glory and the commodity of thy brethren. Therefore go thereabout; but first pray for grace well to begin: and again consider how thou hast been partaker of other men's labours, as of the husbandman's, the miller's, the baker's, the brewer's, the butcher's, the cook's, &c.[1] See therefore that thou be not a drone bee, but rather such a one as may help the hive.

If God have thus fed thy body, which he loveth not but for thy soul's sake, how can it be then but that he will be much more ready to feed thy soul? Therefore take a courage to thee, and go to him for grace accordingly.

COGITATIONS FOR ABOUT THE MID-DAY TIME.

As the body is now environed on all sides with light, so see that thy mind may be. As God giveth thee thus plentifully this corporal light, so pray him that he will give thee the spiritual light. Think that, as the sun is now most clear, so shall our bodies be in the day of judgment. As now the sun is come to the highest, and therefore will begin to draw downward; so is there nothing in the world so perfect and glorious, which, when it is at the full, will not decrease, and so wear away[2].

WHEN YOU COME HOME AGAIN, PRAY:

THERE is nothing, O Lord, more like to thy holy nature than a quiet mind. Thou hast called us out of the troublesome disquietness of the world into that thy quiet rest and peace, which the world cannot give, being such a "peace as passeth all men's understanding."

Houses are ordained for us, that we might get us into them from the injury of weather, from the cruelty of beasts,

[1 Four words in this sentence are omitted in 1578, 1604, 1614.]
[2 The last three paragraphs are not in Vives.]

from disquietness of people, and from the toils of the world. O gracious Father, grant that through thy great mercy my body may enter into this house from outward actions, but so that it may become buxom[3] and obedient to the soul, and make no resistance thereagainst, that in soul and body I may have a godly quietness, and peace to praise thee. Amen.

Peace be to this house, and to all that dwell in the same.

Think what a return, and how merry a return, it will be to come to our eternal, most quiet, and most happy home: then will be all grief gone away: whatsoever here is pleasant and joyful, the same is nothing but a very shadow in comparison, &c.

AT THE SUN GOING DOWN PRAY:

How unhappy are they, O Lord, on whom thy sun goeth down, and giveth no light! (I mean thy grace, which is always clear as the mid-day.) Dark night unto them is the mid-day, which depart from thee: in thee is never night, but always day-light most clear. This corporal sun hath his courses, now up, now down: but thou, dear Lord, if we love thee, art always one. O that this block and veil of sin were taken away from me, that there might be always clear day in my mind! *[MS. 2. 2. 15. 60. Emman. Coll. Cambridge. Meditations of Bradford, Copland 1559, and after editions.]*

Occasions to meditate.

Think that as we are not sorry when the sun goeth down, because we know it will rise again; even so we should not sorrow for death, wherethrough the soul and body do part asunder; for they shall eftsoons return, and come together again in most glorious wise.

So long as the sun is up, wild beasts keep their dens, foxes their burrows, owls their holes, &c., but when the sun is down, then come they abroad: so wicked men and hypocrites keep their dens in the gospel; but, it being taken away, then swarm they out of their holes like bees, as this day doth teach[4]. *[This is meant of the bloody time of queen Mary. [Bull, Christian Prayers, &c. 1570, p. 124.]]*

[3 i. e. compliant, obedient.]
[4 The last six lines are in 1559 and after editions, but not in the MS. Neither are they in Vives.]

WHEN THE CANDLES BE LIGHT, PRAY:

Most thick and dark clouds do cover our minds, except thy light, O Lord, do drive them away. Thy sun, O most wise worker, is, as it were, a firebrand to this world: thy wisdom, whereby light cometh to both soul and body, is a firebrand to the spiritual world. After day, when the night cometh, thou hast given for the remedy of darkness a candle: after sin, for the remedy of ignorance, thou hast given thy doctrine, which thy dear Son hath brought unto us. O thou, that art the Author and Master of all truth, and art "the true Light," make us so to see, that the dimness of our minds may be driven clean away. "Lift thou up the light of thy countenance upon us;" and send joy and gladness into our hearts.

"Thy word is a lantern to my feet and a light unto my paths."

Occasions to meditate.

Think that the knowledge which God giveth unto us by the candle-light (whereby we see those things in this night of our bodies, which are expedient for us) should make us to wish much more for this doctrine of God and spiritual light of our souls; and when we get it, the more to esteem it, and diligently to embrace it: again that, as all would be horror without candle-light, so there is nothing but mere confusion where God's word taketh not place[1].

WHEN YOU MAKE YOURSELF UNREADY, PRAY:

This our life and weak-knit body, by reason of sin, by little and little will[2] be dissolved, and so shall be restored to the earth from whence it was taken: then will be an end of this vanity, which by our folly we have wrought to ourselves.

O most meek Father, so do thou untie me[3], (for thou art he that hast knit these our weak members together,) that I may perceive myself to be loosed and dissolved, and so may remember both of whom I was made, and also whither I must go, lest I be had unprovided unto thy tribunal and judgment-seat[4].

[1 The last three lines are not in Vives.]
[2 'shall,' MS.: 'will' 1559.]   [3 'me' 1559: not in MS.]
[4 'and judgment' 1559: not in MS.]

Occasions to meditate.

"Put off the old man," with his lusts and concupiscence; Col. iii. be content with Joseph to put off thy prison-apparel, that thou Ephes. iv. Gen. xli. mayest put on new. Think that, as we do willingly put off our garments, because we shall receive them again when the night is past, so we should not unwillingly forsake our bodies when God by death shall call us, because we shall receive them again in "the resurrection of the just."

WHEN YOU ENTER INTO YOUR BED, PRAY.

The day now ended, men give themselves to rest in the night; and so, this life finished, we shall rest in death. Nothing is more like this life than every day; nothing more like death than sleep; nothing more like to our grave than our bed.

O Lord, our Keeper and Defender, grant that I now laying me down to rest, being unable to keep myself, may be preserved from the crafts and assaults of the wicked enemy: and grant further that, when I have run the race of this life, thou wouldest of thy mercy call me unto thee, that I may live and watch with thee for evermore. And now, gracious God, give me to take my rest in thee, and bring to pass that thy goodness may be, even in sleep, before mine eyes; that sleeping I be not absent from thee, but may have my dreams to draw me unto thee, and so both soul and body may be kept pure and holy for ever.

"I will lay me down in peace, and take my rest." Ps. iv.

Think that, as this troublesome day is now past, and night Meditations of Bradford, come, and so rest, bed, and pleasant sleep, which maketh most Copland 1559, and after excellent princes and most poor peasants alike; even so after editions. the tumults, troubles, temptations, and tempests of this life, they that believe in Christ have prepared for them an haven[5] and rest most pleasant and joyful. As you are not afraid to enter into your bed, and to dispose yourself to sleep, so be not afraid to die, but rather prepare yourself to it: think that now you are nearer your end by one day's journey, than you were in the morning.

[[5] 'heaven' 1559, 1578: 'haven' 1607, 1614, and Bull, Prayers, &c. 1570. The Latin of Vives is *portum*.]

[BRADFORD.]

WHEN YOU FEEL SLEEP TO BE COMING, PRAY.

O LORD Jesus Christ, my Watchman and Keeper, take me to thy care: grant that, my body sleeping, my mind may watch in thee, and be made merry by some sight of that celestial and heavenly life wherein thou art the King and Prince, together with the Father and the Holy Ghost; thy angels and holy souls be most happy citizens.

O purify my soul, keep clean my body, that in both I may please thee, sleeping and waking, for ever. Amen.

PRAYER FOR DIVINE PROTECTION[1].

1 Tim. ii.   "Pray in every place, lifting up pure hands."

O MIGHTY King, and most high Almighty God, the Father of our Lord Jesus Christ, which mercifully dost govern all things which thou hast made, look down upon the faithful "seed of Abraham," the "children of thy chosen Jacob," thy "chosen people" I do mean, consecrate unto thee by the anointing of thy holy Spirit, and appointed to thy kingdom by thy[2] "eternal purpose," free mercy, and grace, but yet as strangers wandering in this vile vale of misery, brought forth daily by the worldly tyrants "like sheep to the slaughter."

O Father of all flesh, who by thy Divine providence "changest times and seasons," and most wonderfully disposest kingdoms; thou hast destroyed Pharaoh, with all his horse and chariots, puffed up with pride against thy people, leading forth safely by the hands of thy mercy thy beloved Israel through the high waves of the raging waters. Thou, O God, the Lord of all hosts and armies, didst first drive away from the gates of thy people the blasphemous Sennacherib, slaying of his army fourscore and five thousand by thy angel in one night; and after by his own sons, before his own idols, didst kill the same blasphemous idolater, shewing openly to all heathen thy provident power towards thy despised "little ones."

[[1] 'A fruitful prayer for the dispersed church of Christ, compiled by R. P.' is printed in the Meditations of Bradford, Copland 1559, commencing on signature D i, before the 'prayer for Divine protection;' and in the after editions. The 'prayer compiled by R. P.' is supplied in the Appendix to this volume.]

[[2] 'the' 1559, 1607: 'thy' 1578, 1614.]

Thou didst transform and change proud Nabuchodonosor, the enemy of thy people, into a brute beast, "to eat grass" and hay, to the horrible terror of all worldly tyrants. And, as thou art "the Father of mercies and God of all consolation," so of thy wonderful mercy didst thou preserve those thy servants in Babylon, which with bold courage gave their bodies to the fire, because they would not worship any dead idol: and, when they were cast into the burning furnace, thou didst give them cheerful hearts to rejoice and "sing psalms," and savedst unhurt the very "hairs of their heads," turning the flame from them to devour their enemies.

Thou, O Lord God, by the might of thy right arm which governeth all, broughtest Daniel thy prophet safe into light and life forth of the dark den of the devouring lions, where by false accusations he was shut under the earth, of those raging beasts to be devoured; but thou turnedst their cruelty upon his accusers, repaying the wicked upon their own pates. Yea, Lord, which passeth all wonders, and is far above man's power to perceive therein thy working, thou didst cause the huge and great dragon of the seas, that horrible leviathan and behemoth, the main whale fish, to swallow up and devour thy servant Jonas, to keep him "three days and three nights" in the dungeon of his belly, the dark hell-like grave to a living man; thou didst cause that great monster to carry him to the place that thou hadst appointed, and there to cast him up safe, and able to do thy message.

Now also, O heavenly Father, beholder of all things, "to whom only belongeth vengeance," thou seest and considerest how thy holy name by the wicked worldlings and blasphemous idolaters is dishonoured; thy sacred word refused, forsaken, and despised; thy holy Spirit provoked and offended; thy chosen temple polluted and defiled: tarry not too long therefore, but shew thy power speedily upon thy chosen household, which is so grievously vexed and so cruelly handled by thy open enemies. Avenge thy own glory, and shorten these evil days "for thy elect's sake." Let thy kingdom come of all thy servants desired[3]. And though our livings hath offended thy Majesty, as we do confess unfeignedly, O Lord, that we have all sinned, our kings, princes, priests, prophets, and people, (all we, together with our parents, fathers, and mo-

[3 'thy desired' 1559: 'thy servants desired' 1614.]

thers, have most grievously, infinitely passing all measure and number, with our hard flintish hearts, our dissolute and careless life, without all shame and repentance for sin, offended, transgressed, trespassed, sinned, and committed most horrible wickedness, so that we have worthily deserved the uttermost of thy plagues and terrible vengeance;) yet for thine own glory, O merciful Lord, suffer not the enemy of thy Son Christ, the Romish antichrist, thus wretchedly to delude and draw from thee our poor brethren, for whom thy Son once died, that by his cruelty, after so clear light, they should be made captives to dumb idols and devilish inventions of popish ceremonies thereunto pertaining. Suffer him not to seduce the simple sort with his fond opinion that his false gods, blind mumbling, feigned religion, or his foolish superstition, doth give him such conquests, such victories, such triumph, and so high hand over us.

We know most certainly, O Lord, that it is not their arm and power, but our sins and offences, that hath delivered us to their fury, and hath caused thee to turn away from us. But turn again, O Lord, let us fall into thy hands otherwise: seeing thy justice must punish us, let us fall into thy hands (as David did choose) by dearth, famine, or pestilence, or what way thou likest; lest these vain idolaters do rejoice at the miserable destruction of those men whom they make proselytes, and from thy doctrine apostates.

But, O Lord, thy holy will be fulfilled! This is thy righteous judgment, to punish us with the tyrannical yoke of blindness, because we have cast away from us the sweet yoke of the wholesome word of thy Son our Saviour.

Yet consider the horrible blasphemies of thine and our enemies: they name a cake their God, their Christ, and altogether they know nothing of thy power: they say in their hearts, 'There is no God, which either can or will deliver us.'

Wherefore, O heavenly Father, the Governor of all things, the Avenger of the causes of "the poor, the fatherless, the widow, and of the oppressed," look down from heaven with the face of thy fatherly mercies, and forgive us all former offences; and for thy Son Christ's sake have mercy upon us, which by the force and cruelty of wicked and blasphemous idolaters, without causes approved, are haled and pulled from our own houses; are slandered, slain, and murdered as rebels and traitors, like persons pernicious, pestiferous, seditious, pestilent, and full of mortal poison, to all men contagious: where we do meddle no further but against the helly "powers of darkness," "against the spiritual craftiness in heavenly things[1]," which would deny the will of our God and the power of our Christ unto us. We do contend no further but only for our "Christ crucified," and the only salvation by his blessed passion, acknowledging[2] none other God, none other Christ or Saviour, but only thee the everliving Lord and our most merciful Father, and thy dear Son our Saviour, who is in the same glory with thee in the high heavens.

Therefore, O Lord, for thy glorious name sake, for Jesus Christ's sake by whom thou hast promised to grant all righteous requests, make the wicked idolaters to wonder and stand amazed at thy Almighty power; use thy wonted strength to the confusion of thine enemies, and to the help and deliverance of thy persecuted people.

All thy saints do beseech thee therefor. The young infants which have somedeal tasted of thy sweet word, "by whose mouths" thou hast promised to "make perfect thy praises," "whose angels doth alway behold thy face," who beside the loss of us their parents are in danger to be compelled and driven (without thy great mercies) to serve dumb and insensible idols, do cry and call to thee. Their pitiful mothers, with lamentable tears, lie prostrate before the throne of thy grace.

Thou "Father of the fatherless, Judge of the widows," and Avenger of the oppressed, let it appear, O Lord omnipotent, that thou dost hear, judge, avenge, and punish all wrongs offered to all thy "little ones that do believe in thee." "Do this, O Lord, for thy name's sake." "Arise up, O Lord, and thine enemies shall be scattered and confounded." So be it, O Lord most merciful, at thy time appointed.

A THANKSGIVING, BEING A GODLY PRAYER TO BE READ AT ALL TIMES.

HONOUR and praise be given to thee, O Lord God Almighty, most dear Father of heaven, for all thy mercies

[1 Eph. vi. 12, so rendered in the Bible printed by Grafton and Whitchurch 1539. Vide English Hexapla, London 1841.]

[2 'knowledging' 1559, 1578, 1607: 'acknowledging, 1614.]

and loving-kindness shewed unto us, in that it hath pleased thy gracious goodness, freely and of thine own accord, to elect and choose us to salvation before the beginning of the world: and even like continual thanks be given to thee, for creating of us after thine own image; for redeeming us with the precious blood of thy dear Son, when we were utterly lost; for sanctifying us with thy holy Spirit in the revelation and knowledge of thy holy word; for helping and succouring us in all our needs and necessities; for saving us from all dangers of body and soul; for comforting us so fatherly in all our tribulations and persecutions; for sparing us so long, and giving us so large a time of repentance.

These benefits, O most merciful Father, like as we do acknowledge that we have received[1] of thy only goodness, even so we beseech thee, for[2] thy dear Son Jesus Christ's sake, to grant us always thy holy Spirit, whereby we may continually grow in thankfulness towards thee, to be "led into all truth," and comforted in all our adversities. O Lord, strengthen our faith; kindle it more in ferventness and love towards thee, and our neighbours for thy sake.

Suffer us not, dearest Father, to receive thy word any more in vain: but grant us always the assistance of thy grace and holy Spirit, that in heart, word, and deed, we may sanctify and do worship to thy holy name; help to amplify and increase thy kingdom; and whatsoever thou sendest, we may be heartily well content with thy good pleasure and will. Let us not lack the thing, O Father, without the which we cannot serve thee; but bless thou so all the works of our hands, that we may have sufficient, and not to be chargeable, but rather helpful unto others. Be merciful, O Lord, to our offences; and, seeing our debt is great which thou hast forgiven us in Jesus Christ, make us to love thee and our neighbours so much the more. Be thou our Father, our Captain, and Defender in all temptations; hold thou us by thy merciful hand, that we may be delivered from all inconveniences, and end our lives in the sanctifying

[1 'knowledge to have received them' 1559: 'do acknowledge that we have received,' Bull, Christian Prayers, &c. 1570, p. 160.]

[2 'that for' 1559, 1578: 'for' 1607, 1614, and Bull, Prayers, &c. 1570.]

[3 The clauses of the Lord's Prayer in the side notes are from Bull, Prayers, &c. 1570, p. 161.]

and honour of thy holy name, through Jesu Christ our Lord and only Saviour. Amen.

Let thy mighty hand and outstretched arm, O Lord, be still our defence, thy mercy and loving-kindness in Jesu Christ thy dear Son our salvation, thy true and holy word our instruction, thy grace and holy Spirit our comfort and consolation unto the end and in the end. Amen.

O Lord, "increase our faith[4]."

Bradford's beads that he prayed on being in prison for the testimony of Jesus Christ, leaving them as necessary to be used of the faithful.

¶ "Blessed are the dead that die in the Lord: even so, saith the Spirit, that they rest from their labours, but their works follow them." Rev xiv

[Colophon.]

Imprinted at London in Saint Martins parishe in the vinetre, vpon the three Crane warfe, by wyllyam Coplande.

Anno. Do. M.D.LIX. the xv. daye of Marche.

[4 This prayer, after appearing in the Meditations of Bradford 1559, was appended with others to the Psalms in metre, Sternhold and Hopkins, printed by Day, 1566, from whence it was reprinted in the numerous subsequent editions of the 'Psalms,' which were very frequently bound with the 'Book of Common Prayer,' Ch. of Eng., though entirely distinct publications. It was republished in the Scottish 'Book of Common Order,' Edinburgh 1611, and Aberdeen 1633, among the prayers commonly used in private houses. It was given in the 'Christian Prayers,' &c. collected by Henry Bull, Powell (see p. 118, note 1, above), and Middleton 1570: vide Parker Soc. edition, p. 147, where it is entitled, 'A thanksgiving to God for his great benefit, and prayer for grace to confirm and increase the same.' It has also appeared in the 'Liturgical Services of the reign of Elizabeth,' Parker Soc. 1847, p. 264, being taken from the 'Psalms' 1566.]

[The following Meditations are now first printed from the autograph of Bradford in a copy of the New Testament of Tyndale, Jugge 1548, belonging to O. H. Williams, Esq., of Ivy Tower near Tenby, in whose family (which was connected by marriage at the time of the Reformation with that of Bishop Ferrar,[1]) the book has been handed down from about that period.

The initials 'I. B.' and 'I. H.' are written on the reverse of the last fly-leaf containing Bradford's autograph, and are also engraven in gilt letters on each side of the cover: and a few MS. lines on the reverse of the title of the Testament (which will appear hereafter among the letters of Bradford) dated February 8, 1555, are written to a lady whom Bradford addresses as 'mine own most dearly beloved sister in the Lord.'

It is not unlikely that the initials 'I. B.' and 'I. H.' may indicate John Bradford and Mistress Joyce Hales, (a daughter-in-law of Sir James Hales, Justice of the Common Pleas;) to whom the 'Defence of election' and the treatise on 'The restoration of all things,' in this volume, are respectively inscribed; and to whom two among the letters of Bradford[2] were written.

The Testament is in an ornamented binding, apparently of the reign of Elizabeth: the writing having been cut by the binder, it would seem that the book, after the death of Bradford, had been bound for Joyce Hales in memory of the martyr.]

[1 See the Gentleman's Magazine, July 1791, letter of W. Williams, Esq., vol. LXI. p. 608; and March 1848, p. 245—7.]
[2 That 'to Mistress I. H.' in Bp. Coverdale, Letters of the Martyrs 1564, p. 306; and that 'to a faithful woman in her heaviness and troubles,' in Bp. C. ibid. p. 322; and in Foxe, Acts, &c. 1583, p. 1640, or ed. 1843—8, VII. 230.]

MEDITATIONS

FROM THE AUTOGRAPH OF

JOHN BRADFORD,

IN A COPY OF

THE NEW TESTAMENT OF TYNDALE.

MEDITATIONS.

THE SECOND BIRTH[1]

<small>MS. in a copy of the New Testament, Jugge 1548, belonging to O. H. Williams, Esq. Original, Holograph.</small>
As the sense or affection of the flesh "neither it can be" or ever in this life will "be subject to the law of God," wherethrough the most holy on earth hath cause in consideration thereof continually to fight, seeing in himself not only one enemy but enmity itself against God; so the seed of God, which dwelleth in them that are "born of God," neither will nor can, nor never will nor can, trespass or sin against God: by reason whereof they that are "born of God" have great cause to rejoice, seeing in themselves, through God's goodness, not only a friend but friendliness itself towards and with God. For, though "in the flesh" and all they have concerning and from the first birth, so often as they consider it, they have great cause to tremble; yet, in respect of their second birth and the seed of God that dwelleth in them, they should much more rejoice, and be certain of eternal salvation, because "he is stronger that is in them than he that is in the world." For no less durable and mighty is the seed of God in his children regenerate, than the seed of the serpent in the unregenerate, to move and rule the will of man accordingly; for will followeth nature, corrupt nature hath corrupt will, pure nature hath pure will.

Now then, who doth not then know that the regenerate, in that and insomuch as they be regenerate, that, I say, they have pure will according to the nature of the Spirit of God regenerating them? So that, as their corrupt nature hath his corrupt affections, which never will "be subject nor can be to God's law," (wherethrough though the works of the Spirit in them be something spotted, yet is not that spotting imputed or laid to their charge for the covenant's sake, which God hath made with him in the blood of Christ, whereof they are and shall be assured by faith;) so the regenerate man hath his pure affection which never can nor will sin against God.

[1 The original of this meditation is on four fly-leaves prefixed to the New Testament 1548, described in the prefatory note, p. 248 above. The several headings in this series are not in the original.]

And hitherto appertaineth the saying of St John, how that the children of God "cannot sin," speaking not of the present time only, but finally and perpetually, no less attributing to God's seed (which, he saith, "doth abide in them that are born of God"), than to the seed of the devil in our corrupt nature and flesh. So that the children of God are always sinners and always righteous; sinners in respect of themselves, and of that they be of the first birth; righteous in respect of Christ, and of that they be of the second birth.

And thus we see what free-will man hath. In respect of his first birth his will is free to sin and nothing else: in respect of his second birth his will is free to do good and nothing else; by reason whereof we ought to be in most certainty of salvation. In confirmation whereof, to this of St John, (which is, "they which are born of God cannot sin,") we may look on other places of scripture confirming the same, as that God promiseth to make his people "a new heart;" item, that he promiseth he will bring it so to pass that they shall "walk in his laws;" item, that Christ promiseth his Spirit "shall be in him to whom he giveth it a spring of water running unto eternal life;" also, that he witnesseth "them which believe in him" already to be "passed" all doubt and death, and to be presently in "eternal life."

But you will say, perchance, that 'David a regenerate person not only would sin but could do it, and did it indeed, as Peter also and divers others: where was the seed of God in these men? Did not David pray God to give him [his] Spirit again? Therefore he had lost this seed: and so it followeth that no man is so certain, but that he may utterly lose the Spirit of God, and so perish.'

To answer this, consider David and Peter according to these two births, whereof the one is perfect (I mean it of that which is first); but the second is but begun, and not yet perfect until the soul be delivered out of the body by death, as the body out of the mother's womb by birth. No marvel then if we see "the old man" in the children of God oftentimes to do ill for a time, as in David and Peter, which proveth not yet that they had lost the Holy Ghost: for, as a sparkle of fire may be covered in the ashes though it appear not, even so I doubt not but that the seed of God was in these men though it appeared not. And as for David praying for the "renovation of a right spirit in him," [it] doth not fully prove an utter privation of the same; for the children of God do pray often after their sense rather than after the verity, as when Christ said, "My God, my God, why hast thou forsaken me?" which was not so indeed but to his sense. Yea, David prayed that God would "not take away his holy Spirit," whereby he knowledgeth no utter privation of the same: whereof we have a demonstration in his humble acception of Nathan reproving him, of acknowledging his fault, and humbling himself before the face of God, and praying for pardon. Came this of the seed of the flesh? Were not these evident signs of God's seed and holy Spirit, which kept so David that he "could not sin," that is, continue in it finally? though for a time God most justly did give power to the enemy to prevail, and, as it were, to triumph in David's fall.

Therefore, and in the sins of other the elect, we see that the seed of Satan sleepeth not in the most holy; whereby we should be stirred up more to vigilancy and prayer, that by our negligence it prevail not. We see also that, though for a time God suffer Satan to sift his children, yet his seed reviveth at the length, and getteth the upper hand, (for else they should lie still, and perish for ever:) wherethrough we are taught not to fall and abuse this to a carnality, but rather so to consider it, that in our falls we may arise, and in our standing we may stand still, and be thankful.

Indeed no man, I grant, is so certain as he should be: but that the child of God should not be certain, that I utterly deny. Rather let us a-knowledge our unbelief, and give God this honour, which of all other is most excellent, that he is merciful and true. He that giveth to God this testimony in his heart, and consenteth that God is merciful and kind unto him, and thereto true, the same doth honour him most highly.

ON FOLLOWING CHRIST[1]

Many would come to thee, O Lord, but few will come after thee. Many would have the reward of thy saints, but very

[1 The original of this meditation is written at the end of the 'office of all estates,' which is part of the New Testament 1548, described at p. 248 above.]

few will follow their ways: and yet we know, or at the least we should know, that the entrance to thy kingdom and paradise is not from a paradise, but from a wilderness; for we come not from pleasure to pleasure, but from pain to pleasure, or from pleasure to pain, as thy story of the rich glutton and Lazarus doth something set forth.

E carcere [from prison], 15 *Februarii*,
JOHN BRADFORD.

ON AFFLICTION[2].

ENEMIES to God are such as hate God. So that, when in thy- Ps. lxviii self thou seest not this hatred of God, think that the punishments, how great and grievous soever they be, thou hast, be not the punishments of enemies, but rather the fatherly castigations of children. Therefore be not dismayed, but take occasion as a child to go to God as to thy Father through Christ; and doubt not of love and friendship accordingly, how deeply soever thou hast deserved the contrary.

THE LIFE OF FAITH[3].

LABOUR for a lively sight and sense of heavenly things, and so shall no sight or sense of earthly things trouble your affections, further than you shall be able enough with ease and pleasure relinquish and forsake them, whensoever God's glory shall require. Now this sight and sense of heavenly things is not otherwise than by faith; which beginneth not but where reason faileth, or rather maketh an end. Therefore[4], in all matters of religion and concerning salvation, leave reason

[2 The original of this short meditation is written on the last page of the New Testament 1548, beneath the colophon.]

[3 The original of this meditation is written on a fly-leaf at the end of the Testament 1548. Twenty-four lines by Bradford in verse (which will appear in the concluding volume of his Writings) are prefixed to this meditation: these, with the ensuing meditations 'on the conflict of faith,' and 'on a good conscience,' occupy in the original six fly-leaves.]

[4 Here a blank occurs in the original, as if for the name, which Bradford may have deemed it prudent not to write.]

with Abraham's ass, and leave your corporal senses with his servants in the valley, to be occupied in civil things, if that you will climb up with Isaac into the hill of heaven; whither God our Father bring us for his mercy's sake.

J. B.

ON THE CONFLICT OF FAITH[1]

WHENSOEVER thou seest a blindness[2] in thy mind and a hardness in thine heart, and therefore art troubled, and something therethrough moved to waver and doubt of God's mercy towards thee, beware that thou be not unthankful to the Lord for the mercy which in this plague he sendeth, in that he suffereth thee not so much to see of thy blindness and hardness as it is: for, if this little piece which thou now dost something see do a little make thy faith to waver, O how much would thy faith waver if thou sawest the thing as it is! Therefore be thou thankful for not seeing so much of the evil thou hast, as it is[3].

God will never destroy any that is not his enemy: but none is his enemy that would be his friend; that is, that would amend, and do desire to do his will. Whensoever therefore thou dost see in thyself a will consenting to God's will and lusting to do it, never think that the plague poured out upon thee is to thy destruction, but to thy correction and weal[4].

If we ought to be patient when any man doth wrong us, much more then when God doth deal roughly with us, in that he cannot wrong us. God is patient: he then that is patient is common with God, or rather hath communion with God in this virtue: whereby it followeth that the patient man cannot perish, inasmuch as none having any communion with God can perish[5].

[1 Vide prefatory note, p. 248, and note 3 in the last page.]
[2 The last few words are rather doubtful, having been nearly cut off in the binding.]
[3 Here a blank of some lines occurs in the original.]
[4 The last six words are underscored in the original.]
[5 Here a blank of some lines occurs in the MS.]

This is the treasure of godly men, which the world is very ignorant of, namely, that all evil spiritual[6] and corporal happen to the good and weal of God's elect; item, that God is then nearest when he seemeth to be farthest; also, then he is most merciful and a sweet Saviour, when he seemeth to be most wroth and to destroy; moreover, that we then have eternal righteousness, which we look for by hope as a most certain possession, when we feel terror of sin and death. Item, then we are lords of all things when we be most wanting, as "having nothing and yet possessing all things."

As Moses lifting up his hands, the Israelites prevailed against the Amalekites, even so our souls lifting up their hands to God in earnest prayer, we shall prevail against our enemies: but, as it was needful for Moses to have his arms underpropped, so have we need of perseverance. Now perseverance is the true and proper daughter of faith; which faith is not without confession, as David and Paul doth witness when they say that they "believed and therefore did they speak," making speaking the demonstration of believing; and therefore Paul also, where [he] saith that the "belief of the heart and the confession of the mouth" doth justify and "save;" thereby shewing that saving faith is not without confession, and that in the very mouth, much more then in the life. The which confession in that very many now-a-day do want, not daring once to speak, [for] fear of losing that which they shall leave (will they, nill[7] they,) at the length; easily we may see that they want faith also, and so are in danger to "the wrath of God which abideth upon them that believe not;" that is, upon such as confess not the truth for fear of the wrath of the magistrates, which because they would avoid, they fall into "God's wrath," which is horrible.

JOHN BRADFORD.

ON A GOOD CONSCIENCE[8].

LEARN to let the world daily more and more to die unto you, before you die to it, lest death when it cometh will be more dangerous. When you depart hence, nothing in all this

[6 A pen-stroke is drawn in the original across the word 'spiritual.']
[7 i. e. be unwilling.]
[8 Vide prefatory note, p. 248, and p. 253, note 3.]

world will go with you: then will it and all things here make as though they never had known you: therefore esteem it not so much as many do, for you shall find no true friendship of it. Rather study to get and keep "a good conscience," which if you have at your departure, then are you happy. "A good conscience" I call a good purpose in all things to live after God's will. This is given "by the resurrection of Christ," that is, by knowing certainly, through faith, that Christ by his death hath made purgation of your sins past, and by his resurrection hath justified you and regenerated you; so that you, purposing to live as God shall teach you, have in God's sight "a good conscience," whose root you see is in faith: which God for his mercy's sake more and more increase in us. Amen.

See that thou let the world die to thee tofore thou die unto it, or else thou shalt die indeed, where otherwise thou shalt never die.

As Moses and Elias talked with Christ of his departing which he fulfilled at Jerusalem by death, so do they tell and talk with us that our departing is never fulfilled till death cometh: then both in body and soul we shall depart from this life, and go to God our Father.

As the original of your words and works is of the mind, and as it is, so be they constructed[1]; so the end of all your words and workings should be to the mind, that thou by it might be edified.

It is better for the truth's sake to suffer pain, than for flattery promotion to obtain: he that for fear of any power doth hide the verity, upon his own pate God's grievous vengeance falleth[2].

He that considereth God and his ways (I mean it concerning his mercies or displeasures) simply out of himself in others, surely the same shall feel little affection; that is, shall little fear or rejoice. Therefore, when you consider the judgments and mercies of God shewed upon others, see that by some means you apply the same in some part to yourself: so shall you find commodities.

[1 In the original, 'constrēd.']
[2 These last words are doubtful, having been somewhat cut in the binding.]

To fear God is "the beginning of wisdom;" for by it we "depart from evil," and so are more meet to receive God's grace and fellowship, which cannot be had of them that "walk in darkness." Therefore, inasmuch as this book[3] doth teach true wisdom, if that you will be a reader and student of it, see that you bring with you "the fear of God," for which you must pray heartily: and, that you may know when you "fear the Lord," mark how you "depart from evil" and flee from "the works of darkness." Which things if you do, then come a God's name, and with reverence read this book[3], knowing for certain that therein the Lord doth speak unto you.

Be not therefore an Eutychus, but rather a Thyophile[4]; [Acts xx. 9.] and God shall give you his blessing; which thing he do for his mercy's sake!

[3 The New Testament.]
[4 'Theophilus:' a person who loves God.]

[The ten following Meditations and Prayers are collected from various sources.

Five of these are now first printed from MSS. in Emmanuel College, Cambridge, namely the 'Meditation on the Lord's Supper,' p. 260—3; the 'Prayer for the presence of God,' p. 264—6; the Prayers 'for deliverance from trouble,' and 'in the time of persecution,' and the 'Paraphrase of Psalm LXXIX,' p. 276—91.

The short 'Admonition written in a Testament,' p. 264, is reprinted from Bishop Coverdale, 'Letters of the martyrs,' 1564.

The 'Sweet contemplation of heaven,' p. 266—9, is taken from the 'Godly Meditations' of Bradford, Allde 1604.

The meditations on the 'Place and joys of the life everlasting,' and on the 'Felicity of the life to come,' p. 269—75, are printed from a copy of the 'Christian Prayers,' &c. collected by Henry Bull, Middleton 1570[1], in the collection of the late George Stokes, Esq.

These two meditations also occur in the first edition of the ornamented 'Book of Christian Prayers,' Day 1569, signature F iii—I ii; but not in the after editions, 1578, 1581, 1590, 1608. Vide prefatory note, p. 223 above.

The 'Prayer of one standing at the stake' is printed from a MS. in Emmanuel College, Cambridge, 1. 2. 8. no. 92. which is inscribed, 'Bradford's prayer at the stake for Robert Harr'[ington][2]. It is also to be found in the 'Prayers,' &c. collected by Henry Bull, Middleton, n. d. p. 404, and Beale 1619, p. 266, with the title, 'A prayer which Master John Bradford said a little before his death in Smithfield.'

It is also given in Foxe, Acts, &c. 1570, p. 2002, or ed. 1843—8, VII. 686, between the account of the martyrdom and the letters of Adn. Philpot, as if written by that martyr, with the title, 'A prayer to be said at the stake of all them that God shall account worthy to suffer for his sake;' and it has been reprinted from Foxe, ed. 1597, in the 'Examinations,' &c. of Philpot, Parker Society, p. 162—4.

Its text in this volume has been collated with another MS. in Emmanuel College, 2. 2. 16. no. 6., which supplies the signature at the end, 'John Bradford:' but the variations are only noted where a deviation from MS. 1. 2. 8. is followed.]

[[1] This book is 'richly bound with embroidered covers by the Ferrars, of Little Gidding, [about A.D. 1630,] apparently as a present to the noble family of Vaughan.'—Preface to 'Christian Prayers,' &c. Bull, Parker Soc. p. VI, VII. Vide Memoir of Nicbolas Ferrar, London 1837, p. 117, 152; Wordsworth, Eccl. Biogr. IV. 186—7, 213, 232, Lond. 1839.

The two meditations 'of the life everlasting' and 'of the life to come,' p. 269—75, are also in the earlier edition of the 'Prayers, &c. by Bull, printed by Powell (see p. 118, note 1, above.) Vide Bull, 'Prayers,' &c. Parker Soc. p. 101—9.]

[[2] Robert Harrington was a younger son of Sir Robert H. of Exton in Rutlandshire, and an intimate friend of Bradford; to whom, under the name of 'Nathanael,' two among the letters of Bradford are addressed. Vide p. 32, notes 2 and 3, above; Bp. Coverdale, Letters of the martyrs, 1564, p. 414—8, and Foxe, Acts, &c. 1583, p. 1653—4, or ed. 1843—8, VII. 258—62; Betham, Baronetage, I. 107, Lond. 1801.]

MEDITATIONS

AND

PRAYERS

BY

JOHN BRADFORD,

FROM

MSS. IN EMMANUEL COLLEGE, CAMBRIDGE,

AND OTHER SOURCES.

MEDITATIONS AND PRAYERS.

MEDITATION

ON THE LORD'S SUPPER[1]

JESUS IMMANUEL.

MS. 2. 2. 16. no. 10. Emman. Coll. Cambridge. Original, Holograph.

THIS heavenly banquet (wherewithin thou dost witness thyself, O sweet Saviour, to be "the bread of life" wherewith our souls are fed unto true and eternal life and immortality) grant me grace so now to receive, as may be to my singular joy and comfort.

The signs and symbols be bread and wine, which are sanctified in thy body and blood, to represent the invisible communion and fellowship of the same. For, as in baptism thou, O God, dost regenerate us, and as it were engraft us into the fellowship of thy church, and by adoption make us thy children; so, as a good householder and Father, thou dost afterwards minister meat to nourish and continue us in that life whereunto thou "by thy word hast begotten us." And truly, O Christ, thou art the food of the soul: and therefore our heavenly Father giveth thee unto us, that we being refreshed in communicating of thee might be received into immortality.

Now, because this mystery is of itself incomprehensible, thou dost exhibit and give unto us a figure and image hereof in visible signs: yea, as though thou paidest down present earnest, thou makest us so certain hereof, as if with our eyes we saw it. And this is the end wherefore thou didst institute this thy supper and banquet, namely, that it

[1 This meditation is now printed for the first time.
Brackets are inserted in this series (as elsewhere in this volume), wherever a word or syllable has been supplied by the editor, to complete the sense of a passage otherwise imperfect.]

might confirm us, as of thy body once so offered for us that we may feed on it, and in feeding feel in us the efficacy and strength of thy one alone sacrifice; so of thy blood once so shed for us that it is unto us a continual potion and drink, according to the words of thy promise added there, "Take, eat, this is my body which is given for you." So that the body which was once offered for our salvation we are commanded to "take and eat," that, whiles we are partakers thereof, we might be most assured the virtue of thy lively death is of force in us: whereof it cometh that thou callest the cup "the testament (or covenant) in thy blood;" for the covenant which thou once hast stricken with us in thy blood, thou dost as it were renew the same as concerning the confirmation of our faith, so often as thou reach unto us this holy cup to drink of.

O wonderful consolation which cometh to the godly hearts by reason of this sacrament! For here we have assured witness that thou Christ art so coupled unto us, and we so engrafted in thee, that we are "one body" with thee; and whatsoever thou hast we may call it our own. Boldly therefore we may boast that "everlasting life," thine inheritance, is ours; that "the kingdom of heaven," whereinto thou art entered, can no more be taken away from us or we from it, than from thee or thou from it. Again, our sins can no more condemn us than thee; for thou would they should be laid to thy charge as though they were thine.

This is a wonderful change which thou makest with us of thy unspeakable mercy. Thou wast made "the Son of man" with us, that we with thee might be made "the sons of God:" thou camest down from heaven unto earth, to bring us from the earth into heaven: thou tookest upon thee our mortality, that thou mightest give us thy immortality: thou tookest upon thee our weakness, that thou mightest make us strong with thy strength: thou tookest on thee our poverty, to pour upon us thy plenty: thou tookest upon thee our unrighteousness, that thou mightest cloak us with thy righteousness.

O comfort of comforts! Of all these things we have so assured witness in this sacrament, that we ought without all wavering to be so sure that they are exhibit and given unto us, as if with our corporal eyes we did see thee, O sweet Christ, present in visible form, and with our very hands touched and handled thee; for this word cannot lure[1] or beguile us, "Take, eat, drink: this is my body which is given for you: this is my blood which is shed for the forgiveness of your sins."

In that thou biddest us "take," thou wouldest signify unto us that it is ours. In that thou biddest us "eat," thou wouldest we should know that it is made "one flesh" with us. In that thou sayest it is "thy body given for us," "thy blood shed for us," thou wouldest that we should learn both to be not only thine now, but also ours; for thou tookest and gavest both not for thy commodity but for ours.

Grant therefore, good Lord, that we may, as be thankful to thee for ever, so diligently always to mark that the chiefest and almost the whole pith of the sacrament consisteth in these words, " which is given for you," " which is shed for you:" for else it would little help us to have thy body and blood distributed now, except they had been given for our redemption and salvation. By the bread and wine therefore they are represented, that we might learn that they are not only ours, but also that they are destinate and appointed unto us for the seal of spiritual life.

Thus, good Lord, grant us thy grace to consider this sacrament, that we stick not in the corporal things, and things which are object to our eyes, hands, taste and feeling, as the papists teach the people; (whose eyes open, and turn their hearts according to thy good will!) but that we may arise to the consideration of spiritual things hereby accordingly. That is, grant that we may deeply consider, as bread nourisheth, sustaineth, and conserveth the life of this our body, so thy body, O Christ, is the only and alone food to quicken and make strong the soul; as wine nourisheth, refresheth, confirmeth, and cheereth the heart[2], so doth thy blood shed for us on[2] the cross to the souls of all faithful receivers and users of this most holy sacrament.

Grant, good Lord, therefore that I may truly consider and know the principal parts of the sacrament not to exhibit and give the body simply and without further consideration, but rather to obsign[3] and confirm that promise, wherein, as

[1 'Lure:' betray, deceive. Vide Bailey, Dict.]
[2 ' the heart' and 'for us on' are scored across in the original.]
[3 'Obsign:' seal, ratify.]

thou dost witness thy flesh to be food indeed, and thy blood to be drink indeed, by which we are fed unto everlasting life, so thou affirmest thyself to be "the bread of life, whereof whoso eateth shall live for ever."

And that this thing might be brought to pass, thy sacrament doth send us to thy cross, O Christ, where this promise indeed was performed, and most fully on all sides accomplished: for we cannot to salvation feed on thee or eat thee, O Christ, except thou hadst been crucified; and this we do when with lively sense we apprehend and catch hold on the efficacy of thy death. For, though thou call thyself the "bread of life," yet dost thou it not by reason of the sacrament, but because there was such a one given to us from the Father, and because thou didst give thyself such a one, by taking part with us in our mortal nature, to make us partakers of thy divine immortality; by offering thyself "a sacrifice for us," to take to thyself our malediction; and pitifully to pour on us thy blessing, by swallowing up death by thy death, and by raising up to glory and incorruption this our corruptible flesh which thou tookest on thee, through thy resurrection.

So then it remaineth that we should apply all this unto us: and this we do, as by thy gospel, so no less but rather more clearly by thy holy Supper, where, as thou offerest thyself unto us with all thy benefits, so we by faith receive the same.

Grant me therefore to mark well that this sacrament is not the thing that maketh thee to begin to be "the bread of life;" but that this maketh thee so to us, by making us to call to mind that thou wast made "the bread of life," for us continually to feed on; and by giving to us a taste and savour of that bread, that we might feel the virtue of the same bread.

A BRIEF ADMONITION

WRITTEN BY MASTER BRADFORD IN A NEW TESTAMENT OF A FRIEND OF HIS.

Bp. Coverdale, Letters of the martyrs, 1564, p. 687.

1 Cor. i.

This book is called *Sermo crucis*, 'the word of the cross,' because the cross doth always accompany it: so that, if you will be a student hereof, you must needs prepare yourself to the cross, which you began to learn before you learned your alphabet[1]: and Christ requireth it of every one that will be his disciple, therein not swerving from the common trade of callings or vocations, for no profession or kind of life wanteth his cross. So that they are far overseen which think that the profession of the gospel, which the devil most envieth, the world most hateth, and the flesh most repineth at, can be without a cross. Let us therefore pray that God would enable us to "take up our cross" by "denying ourselves."

E carcere [From prison], 18 *Februarii*, 1555.

JOHN BRADFORD.

PRAYER

FOR THE PRESENCE OF GOD[2]

WITH white garments of innocency and righteousness, and palms of victory in their hands.

MS. 2. 2. 15. no. 95. 3. Emman. Coll. Cambridge.

OH, happy is he that may have but a sight of the immortal and incorruptible inheritance which these thy people shall enjoy for ever[3]!

O that it please thee, O Father, as of thy mercy thou hast called me into thy company and communion [of[4]] thy saints, so of the same thy goodness thou wouldest give me to become like[wise[4]] affected, that in my heart I might cry as

[1 The figure of a cross was then and afterward prefixed to the alphabet for young persons. See, for instance, "The Primer in English moste necessary for the educacyon of chyldren," Wayland, n. d. (qu. 1539) signature A viii.; copy, British Museum: and vide Nares, Glossary, v. 'Christ-cross.']

[2 This prayer is now printed for the first time.]

[3 The preceding five lines are scored across in the MS.]

[4 The MS. torn.]

they do, and desire to be with thee, not simply because of this prison and exile that I am in presently, but rather only because of thee, and of love to thee: which love I humbly pray thee, that art love itself, that thou wouldest write in my heart, and graciously open thine ears to the words of my mouth at this present, which I have borrowed out of thy mouth by thy servants, saying, "Remember [me], O Lord, according to the favour that thou bearest unto thy people; O visit me with thy salvation; that I may see the felicity of thy chosen, and rejoice in the gladness of thy people, and give thanks with thine inheritance." O give me "the Spirit of wisdom and revelation by the knowledge of thyself." O "lighten the eyes of my mind, that I may know what the hope is whereunto thou hast called me, and how rich the glory is of thine inheritance upon thy saints, and what is the exceeding greatness of thy power to thy people-ward which believe." O make me "able to comprehend with thy saints what is the breadth, and length, depth and height," of thy sweet mercy; that is, that I may know the excellent love of the knowledge of Christ, that I may be fulfilled with all fulness that cometh of thee. O "lighten mine eyes that I sleep not into death;" but "send thy light to me, to lead and bring me into thy tabernacle," that I may "believe to see the goodness of thee in the land of the living." O give me "the spirit, not of the world, but which is of thee, that I may know the things that are given to us of God," which are such as "the eye hath not seen, nor the ear hath heard, nor the heart is able to conceive;" for "the light of the moon shall be as the light of the sun, and the light of the sun shall be sevenfold, even as the light of seven days, in thy blessed kingdom where and when thou wilt bind up the wounds of thy people and heal their plagues." O that I might have some lively sight hereof!

When shall I rejoice of an [exchange][5] for the immortal, the undefiled and the immarcescible[6] inheritance, whereto thou hast called me, and dost keep for me in heaven? When shall I hear the sweet songs of thy saved people, crying, "Salvation be to him that sitteth in the throne of our God and to the Lamb?" When shall I with the elders and the angels sing and say, "Lauds, and glory, and wisdom, and

[5 MS. torn.]   [6 'Immarcescible:' unfading, incorruptible.]

thanksgiving, and honour, and power, and might, be to thee our God for ever and ever?" When shall I be "covered with a white stole[1], and have a palm in my hand, to stand before the throne, night and day, to serve thee in the temple, and to have thee to dwell in me?" When shall I hear thy "great voice saying from heaven, Behold, the tabernacle of God is with men, and he will dwell with them, and they shall be his people, and God himself will be with them their God?"

O happy were they that now might have a little shew of thine "holy city, new Jerusalem, descending from heaven, prepared" of the gracious God, "as a bride decked for her husband," which thou shewedst thy servant St John. This should I see if I were with him "in the Spirit;" but this cannot be so long as I am "in the flesh." O that the time were come that I might then "put off this tabernacle" in thy mercy, that I might see this great sight which is felicity itself! But herein I must do, and will tarry, thy good pleasure. As I came not hither into this world when I would, but when thou wouldest; even so, not when I will, but when thou wilt, take me hence in thy mercy.

In the mean season as thy child conserve and keep me; and further grant to me, that being in this body yet I may live "not in the flesh but in the Spirit," now and then to have some little true taste of the pleasant dainties of thy house and sanctuary, that all worldly pleasures may be unpleasant and unsavoury, to my eternal comfort, through Christ our Lord. Amen.

A SWEET CONTEMPLATION
OF HEAVEN AND HEAVENLY THINGS.

Meditations of Bradford, Allde 1604, reverse of signature P v—ix.

O MY soul, lift up thyself above thyself; fly away in the contemplation of heaven and heavenly things; make not thy further abode in this inferior region, where is nothing but travail and trials, and sorrow, and woe, and wretchedness, and sin, and trouble, and fear, and all deceiving and destroying vanities. Bend all thine affections upward unto the

[[1] 'Stole:' robe, from the Latin *stola*.]

superior places where thy Redeemer liveth and reigneth, and where thy joys are laid up in the treasury of his merits which shall be made thy merits, his perfection thy perfection, and his death thy life eternal, and his resurrection thy salvation. Esteem not the trifling pleasures of this life to be the way to this wealth, nor thy ignominious estate here to be any bar to prevent thee from the full use and joyful fruition of the glory there prepared for thee.

I am assured that though I want here, I have riches there; though I hunger here, I shall have fulness there; though I faint here, I shall be refreshed there; and though I be accounted here as a dead man, I shall there live in perpetual glory.

That is the city promised to the captives whom Christ shall make free; that is the kingdom assured to them whom Christ shall crown; there are the joys prepared for them that mourn; there is the light that never shall go out; there is the health that shall never be impaired; there is the glory that shall never be defaced; there is the life that shall taste no death; and there is the portion that passeth all the world's preferment. There is the world that never shall wax worse; there is every want supplied freely without money; there is no danger, but happiness, and honour, and singing, and praise, and thanksgiving unto the heavenly Jehovah, "to him that sitteth on the throne," "to the Lamb" that here was led to the slaughter, that now "reigneth;" with whom I "shall reign" after I have run this comfortless race through this miserable earthly vale.

The honour in this earth is baseness; the riches of this world is poverty; the fulness of this life is want; the joys of this world's kingdom are sorrow, and woe, and misery, and sadness, and grief. And yet "the fool saith in his heart," 'There is no other heaven but this harmful deceiving world's happiness, no other hell but this world's bitterness, no better comfort than this world's cares, no further help than this world's wealth.'

Thus is man's wisdom made foolishness, and man's glory turned into shame, and man's power made of no force: and the faithful poor that are here despised, they are advanced, the sorrowful are comforted, and the castaways in this world are recei[ved] to this blessed being, that cannot be expressed with the tongue of man, nor conceived with the heart of man.

"O that I had wings," saith heavenly-hearted David, that I might fly away from this world's vanities, and possess heaven's happiness! "O that I were dissolved," saith blessed Paul, "that I might be with Christ!" O that I were in this place of such wished happiness, where I might rest from those worldly labours, and earthly miseries, and transitory vanities!

But be not heavy, O my soul, though thou must yet wade under the burden of these earthly troubles; for these heavenly mysteries are not seen of carnal eyes, nor can be obtained by carnal means; but through troubles, and afflictions, and dangers, and persecutions, they must be achieved: and none that are God's elected shall be free from this world's hatred. For such difference is there between earth and heaven, and between earthly and heavenly things, that whoso delighteth in the first shall be deprived of the latter; for we cannot have this world's heaven and "the heaven of heavens," the heaven of saints and angels, and cherubim and seraphim, where are all unspotted and all glorious, and all "in white robes" of sanctity, and where Christ the sacrificed Lamb is unto them "All in all."

Oh, blessed are all they that are thus assured; blessed are the poor that shall have this heaven's riches; blessed are the base that shall be thus advanced; blessed are the low that shall be thus raised; and blessed are the world's despised that shall have this heaven's happiness; yea, happy is this wretched world's unhappy man, for he shall be happy.

I will daily meditate of [the] greatness and majesty of this high heaven's blessed estate, where I shall one day bless my God with the company of his saints; and where I shall one day sit secure and free from the dangers and perils, and crosses, and afflictions, that now do assail me on the right hand and on the left, within me and without me; and am never free from one calamity or another.

But it is good for me to be here humbled, that I may be there advanced where I wish speedily to come: it is good that I were in want here, that I might seek heavenly necessaries: it is good that the world did discourage me, that I might fly to God that comforteth me: it is good that I am daily killed here, that I might live continually.

Now therefore, O my soul, stand up, fear not, faint not at this world's crosses; but give glory to this great God, praise this high and helping God, seek him "while it is day;"

drive not off to pray to this God, notwithstanding any hope thou hast in mortal men, but reject not his gracious means, who, in favour infinite and mercy endless, moveth the hearts of men in this life to do good unto such as he seeth distressed. He can find out and afford infinite means to succour them that are his, and will not leave them forsaken in danger; for he even here giveth me his blessings as pledges of his never-failing love, that, being visited in his mercy with timely comforts here, I may assure me of greater blessings in heaven, where they are prepared beyond all that I can ask or think.

" O Lord God of hosts, who is like unto thee," who hast "established thy kingdom with truth and equity, with mercy and judgment?" "Thou hast a mighty arm, strong is thine hand, and high is thy right hand:" whoso is under thy protection, he is safe; and " he that trusteth in thee, mercy embraceth him on every side."

O, blessed art thou, O my soul, if thou canst "rejoice in the Lord." He is thy Father, he is thy helper: walk therefore " in the light of his countenance," and be patient; wait in hope till these storms be past: and then shalt thou have that quiet rest that he hath prepared in heaven.

" Lord, increase my faith."

" Our conversation is in heaven, from whence also we look for the Saviour, even the Lord Jesus." Col. iii. 1, 2.

" If ye be risen with Christ, seek those things which are above, where Christ sitteth at the right hand of God."

" Set your affections on things which are above, and not on things which are on the earth."

A MEDITATION
OF THE LIFE EVERLASTING,
THE PLACE WHERE IT IS, AND THE INCOMPARABLE JOYS THEREOF.

THAT there is an everlasting life, none will deny but such as will deny God; for, if he be true and just (which he must needs be, or else he is not God), then can there not be but an eternal life. That he hath both spoken it and promised it, in Matt. xxv., 1 Cor. xv., Heb. iv. xi. xii., 1 Pet. i., it plainly Bull, Christian Prayers &c. Middleton 1570, signature N i—iv; and after editions.

appeareth, and elsewhere in very many places. So that to deny an everlasting life is to deny God, to deny Christ, and all that ever he did; also to deny all piety and religion; to condemn of foolishness all good men, martyrs, confessors, evangelists, prophets, patriarchs. Finally the denial of eternal life is nothing else but a denial of the immortality of the soul, and so a plain making of man nothing better than beasts.

<small>1 Cor. xv.</small> If it be so, "let us then eat and drink, for to-morrow we shall die." Lord, preserve us from this Sadduceal and epicureal impiety; and grant us for thy mercy's sake, dear God, that we may be assuredly persuaded that there is indeed an eternal life and bliss with thee for them that put their trust in thee; amongst whom account me for thy mercy's sake.

Again, this eternal life, and the place appointed for them that be thy servants, all men do grant to be with thee: albeit they do not think that, because thou art everywhere, therefore eternal life is everywhere; for they by thy word do know that, inasmuch as "no man can see thee and live," this <small>Where this eternal life is. John xiv.</small> eternal life and thy blessed presence is most pleasant and had in fruition after in another world, whereunto by corporal death they do depart, and are translated to a place <small>1 Tim. vi.</small> above them, where thou "dwellest in a light whereunto no man can approach." "Abraham's bosom," they read, was above, as the place for the wicked was alow and beneath. Elias was caught up "into heaven:" and thy Son our dear <small>John xvii.</small> Saviour prayed, "that where he is, those also might be which thou hadst given him, and might see his glory." Now he, dear Father, we learn by thy Spirit, was ascended and taken up in his very body "into heaven," whither Stephen looked up, and saw thy Christ "standing on thy right hand;" to <small>Acts vii.</small> whom he prayed, "O Lord Jesu, receive my spirit."

Grant, I beseech thee, gracious God and Father, that I may have "a clean heart" more and more to see thee, and so in spirit to see and look often upon this place; whither bring me at the length in body also, I humbly pray thee.

Now, what a thing this everlasting life is, no man is able to conceive, much less able to utter; for "the peace of God," <small>1 Cor. ii.</small> which is eternal life, "passeth all understanding." "The eye hath not seen, the ear hath not heard, neither can man's heart conceive those things, which thou," dear God, "hast prepared for them that love thee." Whatsoever therefore can be spoken or imagined of thy kingdom, of the clearness, joy, and felicity of the same, is nothing in comparison; as we may see by thy prophets, which (because they could not otherwise) under corporal things have shadowed the same: so that the confidence of eternal life, what a thing it is, can in no wise be told.

Howbeit, somewhat we may be brought into some sight of it by earthly things to think on this sort. If God hath given here so many things in a strange place, how many are the great good things that be at home! If in a prison are so many mercies, how many are they in the palace! If the wicked have so many benefits, what is the store prepared for thy servants, O Lord! If thy children find such comforts in the day of tears and mourning, what shall they find in "the day of the marriage!" If with beasts men being have the use of so innumerable blessings, O how many are the blessings which they shall enjoy with thy angels and with thyself, O dear God, when they shall "see thee," and have the fruition of thee, in whom is fulness without loathing of all good and fair things, so that nothing can be more desired, and that for evermore!

What knowledge may be had in this life of the life everlasting.

This thy children do not so see as they now believe it. I say that even in their bodies they shall see it for ever, as Job said. They believe that they "shall see thee, and their own eyes behold thee," when these our corporal eyes, our bodies being raised, shall do their duties. Such a knowledge of thee they believe to have, as shall not be only intellectual and by faith, as now it is; but even a full sight and fruition, yea, a conjunction and fellowship with thee. Now they "see but as in a glass, even in a dark speaking; but then they shall see thee face to face." For faith, though it be "the substance of things hoped for," and a certain dark sight of thee, yet it may not be compared to the reward of faith, and glorious sight which we shall see in the life to come, when faith and hope shall cease.

Job xix.
1 Cor. xiii.
[Gr. ἐν αἰνίγματι.]
Heb. xi.

Now thy children "know that they be thy sons, though it yet appear not what they shall be." "We know," say they, "that when our Christ," God and man, "shall appear, then shall we be like unto him, for we shall see him even as he is." O great prerogative, to see Christ as he is! which is not to be considered so much for the manhood, as for the God-

1 John iii.

head itself; as Paul doth also write, that "when all things are subject unto the Son, then shall he be subject unto thee," dear Father, also, "that God may be All in all." And therefore Christ our Saviour prayed for us, "that we might know thee the only true God:" not that our Christ thy Son is not with thee the true, co-equal, and substantial God, but that we might now know how that, after the judgment, such a mystery of his mediatorship shall not be in heaven as is now on earth.

<small>1 Cor. xv.</small>

Then thou, blessed Trinity, God the Father, God the Son, and God the Holy Ghost, shalt "be All in all." Thou shalt be the end of our desires; thou shalt be looked upon without end; thou shalt be loved without loathing; thou shalt be praised without weariness. Although loathsomeness be wont to follow fulness, yet our fulness in the contemplation of thy pleasures shall bring with it no kind at all of loathsomeness. Society of joys shall be in the beholding of thee. "Pleasures are on thy right hand for ever." "We shall be satisfied when we arise after thine image;" I mean in the resurrection.

<small>Psal. xvi.</small>
<small>Psal. xvii.</small>

O dear Father, shew thyself unto us, and we ask no more. O grant us with thy saints in everlasting life to praise with perpetual praises thy holy name. Happy then, and happy again were we, if that day were come, that we might sing with thy angels, elders, and innumerable thousands, a new song, and say, "Thou Christ Jesu, which wast slain, art worthy to receive power, and riches, and wisdom, and strength, and honour, and glory, and blessing." In this blessed life all kind of maladies, griefs, sorrows, and evils be far away, and all full of all kind of mirth, joy, and pleasure.

<small>Rev. v.</small>

O that we might see now a little with St John that "holy city, new Jerusalem, descending from heaven, prepared of God as a bride trimmed for her husband!" O that we might now something hear the great voice speaking out of the throne, "Behold, the tabernacle of God is with men, and he will dwell with them, and they shall be his people, and he shall be unto them their God: he will wipe away all tears from their eyes, and death shall be no more, nor weeping, nor crying, nor sorrow; for the former things are gone."

JOHN BRADFORD.

MEDITATION

OF THE BLESSED STATE AND FELICITY OF THE LIFE TO COME.

This body is but a prison, wherein the soul is kept; and that verily not beautiful nor bright, but most foul and dark, disquiet, frail, and filled up with much vermin and venomous vipers (I mean it concerning our affections), standing in an air most unwholesome, and prospect most loathsome, if a man consider the excrements of it by the eyes, nose, mouth, ears, hands, feet, and all the other parts: so that no Bocardo[1], no little-ease[2], no dungeon, no bishop's prison, no gatehouse, no sink, no pit, may be compared in any point to be so evil a prison for the body, as the body is for and of the soul; wherethrough the children of God have been occasioned to cry and lament their long being in it. 'O,' saith David, 'how long shall I lie in this prison?' "O wretch that I am!" saith Paul, "who shall deliver me out of this body of sin?" which is "an heavy burden to the soul," as the wise man saith. And therefore the godly cry, '"Now let thy servant depart in peace." O that I were dissolved, and had put off this earthly and frail tabernacle! Take me unto thee, and "bring my soul out of this prison, that it may give thanks unto thee," O Lord.' For so long as we be in this body, we cannot see the Lord: yea, it is as an heavy habitation, and depresseth down sore the spirit from the familiarity which it else should have with God.

This world and life is an exile, a vale of misery, a wilderness, of itself being void of all virtues and necessaries for eternal life, full of enemies, sorrows, sighings, sobbings, groanings, miseries, &c.; in danger to hunger, cold, heat, thirst, sores,

Margin notes: Bull, Christian Prayers, &c. Middleton 1570, signature N v—viii; and after editions. Rom. vii. [Wisd. ix. 15.] Luke ii. Ps. cxlii.

[1 'Bocardo:' the old north gate of Oxford used as a prison, in which Abp. Cranmer and Bps. Latimer and Ridley were confined before their martyrdom: it was taken down in 1771. The door of their cell is preserved at Oxford, in the parish-church of St Mary Magdalen, in the 'martyrs' aisle.' Vide Skelton, Oxon. antiq. restaur. Vol. II. plates 120—1, Oxf. 1823.]

[2 'Little-ease:' a stocks for the neck and feet, see Nares, Glossary: also, a cell in which the prisoner could not either stand or recline, vide Theatr. crudel. hæret. Verstegan. p. 72—3, Antverp. 1592.]

[BRADFORD.]

sickness, temptations, trouble, death, and innumerable calamities; being momentary, short, unstable, and nothing but vain; and therefore is compared to a warfare, a woman's travail, a shadow, a smoke, a vapour, a word, a storm, a tempest: in the which God's people feel great molestations, griefs and troubles, now of Satan himself, now of the world, now of their own flesh, and that so wonderfully, diversely, dangerously, and contrarily, that they are enforced to cry, 'O Lord, " when shall we come and appear before thee?" when shall this misery end? when shall we be delivered out of this vale of misery, out of this wilderness, out of these continual afflictions and most perilous seas?'

But where thou art, Lord and dear " Father of mercy," there is not only no prison, no dolours, no sorrow, no sighings, no tears, no sickness, no hunger, no heat, no cold, no pain, no temptations, no displeasure, no malice, no pride, no uncleanness, no contention, no torments, no horror, no sin, no filth, no stench, no dearth, no death, no weeping, no tears, no misery, no mischiefs; there is, I say, not only no such thing, or any evil, noisome, or displeasant thing, but all liberty, all light, all pleasantness, all joy, rejoicing, mirth, pleasure, health, wealth, riches, glory, power, treasure, honour, triumph, comfort, solace, love, unity, peace, concord, wisdom, virtue, melody, meekness, felicity, beatitude, and all that ever can be wished or desired, in most security, eternity, and perpetuity, that may be thought not only of man but of angels and archangels, yea, above all thoughts. The "eye hath not seen the like, the ear hath not heard, nor no heart is able to conceive" in any point any part of the blissful beatitude which is with thee, most dear Lord and Saviour, most gracious God and Comforter. Where thou art, O blessed God, the archangels, angels, thrones, powers, dominations, cherubim, seraphim, patriarchs, prophets, apostles, martyrs, virgins, confessors, and righteous spirits, cease not to sing night and day, " Holy, holy, holy, Lord God of hosts!" 'Honour, majesty, glory, power, empire, and dominion be unto thee, O God the Creator, O Lord Jesu the Redeemer, O Holy Spirit the Comforter!'

In recordation of this, O how thy children rejoice! How contemn they the pleasures of this world; how little esteem they any corporal grief or shame; how desire they to be with thee! "How amiable are thy tabernacles, O Lord God of hosts!" say they: "my soul hath a desire to enter into the courts of the Lord: my heart and my soul rejoiceth in the living God." "Blessed are they that dwell in thy house, they that may always be praising thee;" "for one day in thy courts is better than a thousand elsewhere. I had rather be a door-keeper in the house of my God, than to dwell in the tents of ungodliness; for the Lord God is a light and defence." And again, "Like as the hart desireth the water-brooks, so longeth my soul after thee, O God. My soul is athirst for God, yea, even for the living God: when shall I come to appear before the presence of God?" "My soul thirsteth for thee, my flesh also longeth after thee, in a barren and dry land where no water is." *[Psal. lxxxiv.] [Psal. xlii.] [Psal. lxiii.]*

They (thy children I mean, O Lord,) desire the day of that thy redemption. Still they cry, "Let thy kingdom come;" they cry, "Come, Lord Jesus." They "lift up their heads," looking for thy appearing, O Lord, which will make their "vile body like to thine own glorious (and immortal) body;" for, "when thou shalt appear, they shall be like unto thee." *[Rom. viii.] [Rev. xxii.] [Phil. iii.]*

Thy angels will gather them together, and they shall meet thee in the clouds, and be always with thee. They shall hear this joyful voice, "Come, ye blessed of my Father, possess the kingdom prepared for you from the beginning." *[Matt. xxv.]*

Then shall they be "like to thy angels." Then shall they be "like unto the sun in thy kingdom." Then shall they have crowns of glory, and be "endued with white garments" of innocency and righteousness, having palms of victory in their hands. Oh, happy is he that may but see that immortal and incorruptible inheritance, which they shall enjoy for evermore! Amen. *[Matt. xiii.] [Rev. vii.]*

J. BRADFORD.

PRAYER FOR DELIVERANCE FROM TROUBLE, BEING
A GODLY PRAYER MADE BY JOHN BRADFORD[1].

MS. 1. 2. 8. no. 81. Emman. Coll. Cambridge.

O ETERNAL, almighty, and most merciful God, which hast revealed thyself unto mankind, not only by the handywork of this world, and deliverance out of Egypt, but also (which is the greatest of all) by the sending of thy only-begotten Son our Lord Jesus Christ into this vale of misery, and by the gifts of thy holy Spirit wherewith thou hast adorned thy church; we humbly beseech thee, by thy dear Son Jesus Christ, that thou wouldest meekly open thy gracious ears to our complaints, and send down thy help and aid, not so much for our sakes, as for the glory of thy holy name. For, whereas man did lie, as thou knowest, altogether so overwhelmed in sin, that not only he was destitute of that righteousness he had of thy creation, but also in nowise could by any his powers or merits rise up to recover the same righteousness, and therefore of necessity the inheritor[2] of eternal punishment; yet thou, most merciful God, hadst mercy upon that our marvellous great misery, and therefore didst promise, and at length send unto us, thine only-begotten Son, that he might pay the ransom for our sins, and obtain by his obedience unto thee his dear Father, that so many as believed in him might be endued with his righteousness, to be reputed as just for his sake before thy tribunal-seat; that, although they want righteousness of their own, yet they might have the fruition of the righteousness of another, namely of the Lord Jesus Christ; whereby, as they might be made able to stand in thy judgment, so to be kindled in thy holy Spirit to the rendering of obedience to thee truly and from the very heart.

This is the doctrine of thy gospel, which thou at the first shewedst to the fathers, which thy prophets taught, which thy Son Jesus Christ declared unto us, which thy holy Spirit by the apostles hath published throughout the whole world: which doctrine in these our days thou hast notably set

[1 This prayer is now printed for the first time.]
[2 'The inheritor' is written in the MS. over the words 'the child.']

forth by thy servant king Edward in the book of Homilies appointed in his reign to be read in the churches. By this doctrine thou keepest thy church, not only in afflictions of this life, but also in the torments of death itself.

Now, dear and most meek Father, we humbly beseech thee to consider with thyself what wicked and cruel men think of this thy great benefit. Behold, we open before thy Majesty the articles of our bishops in their visitations, the statutes, laws, ordinances and injunctions of our parliaments and magistrates, and working of sophisters, wherewith the doctrine of thy Son our Saviour Jesus Christ concerning "the righteousness of faith" is so condemned that it is plainly accused of devilishness. Yea, Lord, so far forth do thy enemies now proceed, that, as tofore by slaughter they made havoc of thy sheep and church, even so now by all kinds of violence, cruelty, and injustice, they go about their impiety.

Therefore "arise, O Lord our God, defend thou thine own cause;" "forget not the blasphemies wherewith the wicked blaspheme thee;" deliver thy Christ from their presumption, which they by all means, and especially this parliament, seek utterly to condemn. Keep thy church which thine enemies desire to oppress and utterly to destroy: defend thy prisoned servants which at this present are in bonds for the defence of thy verity.

Indeed we confess frankly that we are grievous sinners, and in no point have been thankful unto thee for thy wonderful great benefits, which hitherto thou hast plentifully poured out upon us. But now, good Lord, we desire to repent and something lament our miserable and sinful life : we desire to embrace and heartily to believe the gospel of thy Son, that, because we are sinners, and cannot make amends for our sins in any point by any means or merits of our own, we may obtain free remission of our sins for and through Christ thy Son. And we pray thee further, that henceforth thou wilt govern our whole life by thy holy Spirit; wherethrough the remnants of our flesh may be mortified, and we may serve and sanctify thy holy name for ever.

As concerning thy adversaries, Lord, thou knowest, that although they would seem nothing less than persecutors of thy name and church, yet the thing itself declareth that they do persecute the true doctrine of the gospel of thy Son; and not only do not acknowledge their impiety, but also do defend it, and undertake so to do by all means they can. This is not their mind, that they might promote the glory of thy holy name; but that they might without blame live lord-like, after their lusts and beastly pleasures, satisfying their cruel and covetous desires and concupiscences. And wilt thou, O Lord our God, approve this their purpose? wilt thou help this their hope? No, no; thou wilt never do it: "for thou art not God that will iniquity; the wicked shall not dwell with thee; thou hatest all workers of wickedness; thou wilt destroy all that speak lies."

We indeed are unworthy to see thy glory; but yet thou art worthy that thy glory might be shewed to all the whole world. Wherefore we pray and earnestly beseech thee, in Christ's name, that thou wouldest witness publicly in these our days, how that thy will is such as "hateth iniquity," and "abhorreth these crafty and blood-thirsty men." For if thou shalt now leave us, dear Father, will not the world say, 'Where is their gospel? where is their Christ? Could Christ keep them in prison, preserve them in death?'

These blasphemies even now, dear Lord, we hear to walter[1] out of their hearts and lips. This thou knowest, O Lord, "the trier of the heart and reins." Let therefore, O good God, thy strength be magnified: and, as thou hast said, "Call upon me in the day of thy trouble, and I will deliver thee, and thou shalt honour me;" even so now hear us calling upon thy name through thy only begotten Son, our Saviour and Lord, Jesus Christ. Amen.

PRAYER

IN THE TIME OF PERSECUTION[2].

JESUS EMMANUEL.

MS. 2. 2. 16. no. 33. Emman. Coll. Cambridge.

O ALMIGHTY, everlasting, and most merciful Lord God, the dear Father of our Lord and Saviour Jesus Christ, and

[1 'Walter:' roll, tumble.]

[2 This prayer is now printed for the first time. The heading in the MS. is, 'A prayer made by Master Bradford for the faithful people in']

through him our most gracious good Father, whose providence is over us, whose wisdom and righteousness is seen over all, as thy mercy, even in the midst of most miser[ies[3]], is tasted of all; indeed we have deserved most horrible plagues by reason of our unthankfulness, contempt, and slanderous abusing thy most holy gospel, which most plentifully and purely thou didst give us with such a prince to propagate the same, as never, sithen England was christened, was known the like.

We, I say, have deserved not only the taking away of this our dear prince, and the benefit of the ministry of thy pure gospel, but also all other most terrible plagues that can be devised: for great and heinous are our offences, and therefore "just thou art, and righteous are thy judgments" if, as thou hast begun, thou shalt continue to pour out upon us thy fearful plagues and indignation. But, gracious Lord, [remit] thine anger, because thou art accustomed to remember mercy, and full well "knowest whereof we are made," and what we are able to bear. We beseech thee, which art "rich in mercy," and "plentiful to all them that call upon thee," that for thy name's sake through Christ thou wouldst correct us according to thy sweet mercy, and not in thy sour favour and indignation. Much better it is for us, dear Father, and more tolerable, that we should yield ourselves into thy hands to be chastised of thee, than to fall into the hands of thy enemies, as David prayed; for great is thy [mercy][4]. *Psal. ciii.* *Rom. x.* *Psal. vi.* *2 Sam. xxiv.*

"Against thee, against thee only have we sinned," and broken thy holy commandments. But, loving Lord and almighty God and Father, well thou knowest we have not sinned against the devil, the world, the pope and his prelates, neither against the queen's highness and politic magistrates of the realm: so that justly have they no right or power to punish us. Howbeit thou mayest justly use them as thy fierce rod against us. *Psal. li.*

But, good God and heavenly dear Father, against them have we not so behaved ourselves, that rightly and justly they can be thought to punish us. Yea, rather they wish that with them horribly we would displease and sin against thee; for nothing should it grieve them if we were horrible rebels against thee, blasphemers of thy name, idolaters, wor-

[[3] The MS. is here somewhat injured, and therefore not distinct.]
[[4] MS. torn.]

shippers of stocks and stones, false servers of thee, adulterers, thieves, drunkards, murderers, gluttons, oppressors, and altogether overwhelmed in mischief. But this is our sin and offence against them, because we preach, believe, and confess thee, God the Father, to be the true and only God, and Jesus Christ thy dear Son to be the only Lord, Saviour, Bishop, Priest, and Mediator; and the Holy Spirit to be the only Comforter, vivificator, counsellor, and master of all truth; and thy written word to be the "lantern to our feet," the sufficient doctrine to our salvation. This, dear Lord, is a sin against them, because we will not serve thee after the traditions of men, but as in thy word by thy Son and apostles thou hast taught us. Therefore are they much[1] wroth and persecute us.

If we would worship bread instead of Christ, cast off our hope[2] and creed of the satisfactory and propitiatory sacrifice which thy Son our Lord did make in his own body "himself once for all" to the "perfect sanctifying for ever" of all that shall be saved, and come, and buy their propitiatory sacrifices in that abominable idol the mass; if we would cast off thy commandments to follow good intents, to serve thee in a tongue we know not, to pray unto saints, to buy pardons, to run a pilgrimage gate-going[3], to offer candles and tapers to images, to buy trentals[4], diriges[5], to say as they say, and do as they do, submitting ourselves to the faith of the antichristian, popish, and devilish church, clean contrary from the faith of thy catholic and true church, (which is grounded and builded upon thy dear child Jesus Christ, who, as he is "the foundation," so is he "the fulness of all, whereof we all receive," and the very sinew which "coupleth and knitteth together" every one of us to grow and go forwards "into a perfect man," "being made of thee unto us wisdom, and righteousness, and sanctifying and redemption," that our rejoicing might be in him, which also "is our Head," from whom cometh our life by the working of his Spirit, which is kept always alive in us, so long as we suck of the blood and natural juice

[1 MS. torn.]
[2 This word is very faint, and therefore doubtful in the MS.]
[3 'Gate:' road. Todd's Johnson Dict.]
[4 See p. 49, note 5, above.]
[5 See note D.]

which descendeth from our Head into the members; that is to say, so long as we stick and abide by his written word and gospel, not suffering the same to putrefy and corrupt by admitting false glosses and expositions of men's own brains and devices, not contained in thy book of the Bible:) if, I say, dear Lord, we would do thus, leaving the water in the well of life, and drink of their dirty digged pits and cisterns, then should we have peace with them; then would not the devil rage; then would the world wrestle no more against us; then would the pope and his prelates promote us; then would the queen be merciful, and the magistrates our good masters, even as thy dear child saith, "If you were of the world, the world would love his own." *Jer. [ii.]*

John. [xv.] xvii.

Here therefore look down, a merciful Father towards us, and a fierce Judge towards all such our enemies as are not to be converted: for they are no less thine enemies than ours; so that in persecuting us and punishing us they persecute thee and punish thee: for this word which we preach, believe, and confess, is not our word, but thy word, and not our expositions or construings, but the expositions and construings of thy holy Spirit.

This gear the devil cannot abide, but would have thy place, and be to us a god. The pope and his prelates would reign in men's consciences; and for God's word they would have us to believe their stinking traditions, councils, decrees, and lies. The queen and magistrates in place of thy Son Jesus Christ would place their abominable idol of bread: in place of our "Priest after the order of Melchisedec" they would place priests after the order of Baal and antichrist: instead of Christ's sacrifice they would thrust out unto us an horrible sacrilege[6].

[6 'sacrilege and,' MS. which ends thus imperfectly.]

PARAPHRASE OF PSALM LXXIX[1].

JESUS EMMANUEL.

MS. 2.2.16. no. 38. Emman. Coll. Cambridge. Original, Holograph.

O GOD, the Father of our Lord and Saviour Jesus Christ, which of thine own mere goodness hast vouchedsafe to make an everlasting covenant with us, namely that thou wilt be our God, and we shall be thy people and inheritance; behold, as in times past "the heathen came into thine inheritance" of Israel, and "polluted thy holy temple" at Jerusalem, and also made the goodly city of "Jerusalem itself a heap of stones," devastating it; even so now very many heathen and limbs of antichrist, though outwardly they profess Christ, are come into thine inheritance and church which thou hast with us in this realm of England, and "have defiled thy holy temple," that is, the souls and bodies of many which have professed thee, in whom, as in thy temple, thou shouldest dwell: they have, I say, "defiled them," by enforcing them through tyrannical precepts and threats to resort to idololatrical and antichristian service, which thou by thy word didst never allow, but rather and utterly forbid: as is Latin service to them that understand not Latin, invocation to saints, adoration with godly honour of thy creatures of bread and wine, as though they were God, being but the sacraments of the body and blood of thy Son our Saviour Jesus Christ, which they utterly corrupt and horribly profane by presuming to offer up the same unto thy Majesty without any calling of them to that office by thee: in which doing, they do as much as in them is, to crucify Christ again, utterly denying his one and alone sacrifice offered up by himself to be omnisufficient, contrary to all thy holy scriptures.

That thy people should allow this kind of religion, dear Father, thou seest how these wicked heathen have prevailed, and "have defiled thy temple," making the face of thy church (once with us, in the time of thy dear servant king Edward the sixth, no less beautiful in thy sight by reason of pure

[1] This paraphrase is now printed for the first time. It must have been written subsequently to February 12, 1554, the day of the execution of Lady Jane Grey, mentioned in p. 283, and before February 4, 1555, the day of the martyrdom of Rogers, who is spoken of as still alive, p. 289.—Foxe, Acts, &c. 1583, p. 1422, 1493; or ed. 1843—8, VI. 424, 611.]

doctrine and the godly administration of thy sacraments, than was the city of Jerusalem which was a figure of thy church,) utterly defaced, devastated, and now nothing but a "heap of stones;" the congregation of the faithful, thy true church, being scattered abroad, driven into exile, and cast into prisons, temples of stones yet still remaining.

As once "the heathen gave the carcases of thy servants to be meat for the birds of the air," and as "they gave the flesh of thy holy ones to a prey for the beasts of the earth," when Antiochus and other tyrants oppressed the country of Jewry; even so now these limbs of antichrist with their parasites and sworn shavelings (except [thou] for thy mercy and truth's sake do let them) are purposed and fully determined to hang up and burn the bodies, flesh, and bones, of all that will persevere to worship thee after the verity and truth. In demonstration whereof they have cast of thy dearest saints no small number into exile and prison, utterly taking from them with all injustice all kind of comfort and equity. [Maccabees i. and ii.]

As in times past "the heathen poured out the blood of thy people like water round about Jerusalem, so that there was none to bury the dead;" even so these hell-hounds, limbs of antichrist, have done in times past in the slaughter of Frith, Barnes, Garret, Jerome, Lambert, Lacells[2], &c., and now lately have done by the cruel destroying of the good and innocent Lady Jane: as they thirstily gape to drink up more blood of thy slaughter-sheep which they have in prison, and keep for assoil[3] and cooling of their heat which will not be slaked until they have destroyed all thy seely[4] souls, or driven them out of England, except thou, good Lord, wilt for thy name's sake prevent them.

As once thy people complained to thee, that they "were made a reproach and by-word unto their neighbours, a laughing-stock and scorn to such as dwelled about them;" even so now, dear Father, we thy people at this present here in England cannot but complain, that "we are become a by-word to our neighbours, a mock and mowing[5] to those that dwell about us:" for everywhere now it is tauntingly spoken, 'Where

[2 Vide Foxe, Acts, &c. 1583, p. 1037, 1200, 1124, 1240; or ed. 1843—8, v. 18, 438, 236, 550.]

[3 'Assoil:' releasing, setting free.]

[4 'Seely:' simple, harmless.]

[5 'Mowing:' grimace, a look assumed in derision.]

are our protestants? where are these new gospellers? where is the new doctrine they taught?'

Therefore with thy people we are enforced to cry out, "How long, O Lord, wilt thou be angry?" The punishments we do not so much complain of, although they be painful, as do we thy displeasure which daily increaseth. But "how long, O Lord?" "Shall thy wrath," which we have wrought to work our woe, dear Lord, "burn for ever?" as now it beginneth even corporally to bring us into a servitude and captivity, to demonstrate the heinous captivity of soul many are caught in by idolatry and horrible abomination; whereto very many do consent against their conscience, outwardly allowing that which inwardly they detest, for fear of loss of life, lands, goods, liberty, friends, &c. "Shall," I say, "this wrath burn" and waste all "for ever?"

Alas, O Lord, who is able to bear thy wrath? O Lord, which art "a consuming fire," wilt not thou "in thine anger remember thy mercy?" Wilt not thou remember that we are as hay, dust, stubble, and straw, and cannot but "consume in thy displeasure?"

O "pour out thy wrath" and vengeance rather upon the wicked "which have not," nor will not "know thee, and upon the countries which call not" and will not call "upon thy name," but upon their avowries[1]; or trust in their own policy and power, and go about as they have done and will do, if thou let not, to "devour Jacob," thy church and poor people; and so also have not, do not, nor will not cease to destroy thy tabernacle, temple, worship, true religion, and service, with all them that love the same. To the Lord these caterpillars and Philistines are known. If there be any of them to be converted, those do thou convert, O Father: [upon] the residue which are not to be converted "pour out thy wrath" and heavy indignation, that we might praise thy holy name, and others might tremble at thy power, and sing praises unto thee, "in the day of thy visitation."

But methinks, we hear thee object unto us our monstrous ingratitude for thy word so plentifully preached, for thy

[1 'Avowry:' a guardian, a protector, (referring here to saint or angel worship,) from the Latin of the middle ages, 'advocaria,' i. e. 'protectio,' 'tutela.' Du Cange, Gloss. Compare Bp. Latimer, Works, I. 225, Parker Soc.]

sacraments so sincerely ministered, and forsooth for the good ministers ecclesiastical and civil, especially for our good and most holy king, and for our carnal and sinful life, "not knowing the time of our visitation." These things, and many other our misdeeds and evil life, methinks that thou dost object against us, as though we were not entreated otherwise now than we have deserved; yea, that great mercy thou shewest to us in not dealing with us as we have deserved, being, as we be yet, so far from true repentance, flattering ourselves in many evils; so that thou knowest not what to do with us or "strike us any further," as Esay witnesseth.

O Lord God and dear Father, we do not excuse us, we do not extenuate our sins, wherethrough we have provoked thee to wrath, so that thou mayest most justly "cast us away for ever," for we are very miserable sinners. "But if thou wilt mark what is done amiss, O Lord, who shall be able to abide it?" None certainly. Therefore "with thee is pro- [Ps. cxxx. 4 see Vulgate. pitiation" and mercy, "that thou mayest be worshipped."

Now to the end that we poor misers[3] may worship and serve thee, dear Father, have mercy upon us for thy name's sake; and through Christ Jesus thy dearly beloved Son, for his sake, grant that we may find mercy, grace, and help before thee, as thy people tofore us did when they cried as we now cry, "Remember not, O Lord, our old sins;" for "thou hast set our hid sins in th[y countenance:[4]"] for though we have forgotten our old transgressions, yet thou hast a counting book wherein every one are written, as we now feel; so justly art thou angry: but "in thine anger" thou art wont to "remember thy mercy."

For thy glory's sake therefore "remember not our old" nor new "sins:" but speedily at such time as may best please thee, let thy mercies prevent us; for we are wonderful poor and brought into great miseries, (and greater are like to be, dear Father, unless thou do help us,) but yet, O Lord, not by our deserts in respect of them who thus sharply persecute us, and purpose utterly to destroy us. Indeed in respect of thee and of our doings towards thee, dear Father, we have deserved these horrible plagues, and much more: but not our impenitence, unthankfulness, and disobedience to thee, but thee our enemies, O Lord, do persecute in us.

[3 See p. 73, note 4, above.]   [4 MS. torn.]

Thine is now then our cause, and not ours simply.

In that therefore thou art merciful, and can so not but be affected at the miseries of them whom thou hast received into thy covenant, as thou hast done us; (even as a father cannot but be affected at the miseries of his children, although they have of themselves enwrapped themselves therein;) so canst not thou but have mercy upon us in our miseries: and therefore wouldest thou that we should conceive a sure hope of thy help always. But whence cometh this hope? cometh not other good things from thee, dear Lord? Therefore in that this, 'I hope in thy goodness,' is good, in that this cometh from thee, and in that thou art affected towards us as a father, we beseech thee, dear Father, give us this lively hope of thy help, and hear us crying with thy people:

"Help us, O God of our salvation, for the glory of thy name; O deliver us, and be merciful unto our sins for thy name's sake." Help us which feel and see now our own unableness, O thou which art not only 'the God of salvation,' "saving man and beast," "the Saviour of all men," which is general; but also the "God of OUR salvation," which is peculiar to thy people that look for help and salvation, neither from Peter nor Paul, James, Mary, nor John, nor from any other but only from thee through the name of Christ Jesus, than which "name there is none other given to men wherein they must be saved." "Help us" therefore, I say, "O God of our salvation" and salvation itself, which hast made us, and dearly redeemed us; which hitherto hast kept us, and dost so still most graciously, and that of thine own goodness; for the which thou dost presently in these evils shew much mercy upon us, not dealing with us as we deserve, but dost expect, and as it were "tarry to shew mercy upon us," holding thy hand ready lifted up to strike, that thou mightest spare us. Thee, as I said, thee, most merciful and gracious good Lord and our God, "rich in mercy" [and kindness "un][1] to all them that call upon thee," do we beseech and humbly pray, that thou wouldest send thy help from above unto us which are thine by creation, redemption, conservation, profession; and that not for our merits or deserts, which are none but to damnation-wards, but "for the glory of thy name," which cannot but be glorified, when thine enemies

[[1] MS. torn.]

the wicked shall know and see that thou art careful for thy word and people; and they that "call upon thy name" and hope in thy help shall feel and perceive that thou canst no more finally forget them than "a woman should forget the child of her womb:" yea, if she should "forget her child," yet thou hast promised that thou wilt never do so.

"For the glory of thy name" therefore "help us;" and not only so, but "deliver us" out of the evils we are fallen into, and out of thine anger which our sins have deserved and provoked against us. The which do thou put away, dear Father, we beseech in the bowels and blood of our Saviour Jesus Christ, and for thy holy name's sake; for the which we can but think that thou wilt do much for us, which didst so much for the old people's sake, and hast so often promised that thou wilt do still when we shall call upon thee: for thou art not "the God of Jews only, but of the gentiles also;" so that "whosoever shall call upon thy name, the same shall be saved." O then give us thy good Spirit of prayer, and hear us crying unto thee. We confess that our sins have deserved all kinds of misery. But what wilt thou to thy holy name? Is not the glory of it in some peril if, attending to our sins, thou wilt destroy thy poor people? Art not thou called "good and merciful and of great compassion," which also "dost pardon sins and put away iniquities?" For this thy name, O Lord, that thou mayest be well seen and known to be the same which thou art called, "be merciful unto our sins," old and new, and we shall praise thy name for ever.

But yet eftsoons[2], methinks, thou answerest me, and sayest that it cannot but be to "the glory of thy name," to punish and take vengeance on us by whom thy holy name hath been evil spoken of by our carnal gospelling and using thy gospel a cloak for covetousness and all kind of carnalities; that nothing may be spoken of our horrible ingratitude for so exceeding great mercy showered upon this realm in giving us so plentifully and purely thy gospel and religion, and so innocent and godly a sovereign to set forth the same.

O Lord God, we are "ashamed to lift up our faces," for indeed these are most true: we "have sinned in heaven [and]

[2 'Eftsoons': soon afterward.]

against [thee, and are no more]¹ worthy to be called [thy children." The reason]¹ why thou becamest our God, and madest us thy people, was thine own goodness and mercy in Christ. In that these still remain, we cannot but take some comfort that thou now wilt " in thine anger remember thy mercy:" for, if it was to the glory and praise of thy name so to adopt us, how should it be but " to the glory of thy name" now to look upon us and "help us?" The more we are now unworthy, the more it shall be "to the praise of thy grace and glory;" for unto none other we come but to thee. Help we look not for elsewhere, but only from thee, and that not of our deserts, or any thing we can do, but only of thy mercy. The which in that thine enemies begin to limit, as though it would not care for us, and therefore say, " Where is their God?" dear Father, accordingly consider it. They say not, 'Where is God?' but, " Where is their God?" that is, the God whom we have taught and preached; as though thou, Lord, wert not the true God; as though we had swerved from thy word in teaching and profession. Indeed, O Lord, we have swerved from thee in living, but yet not in teaching, as thou knowest; even as the Israelites, which were put to a flight before Ai, departed not from thee in profession and doctrine, but only in² living.

As Josue thereon said, so say we, 'What wilt thou do, good Lord, to thy holy name?' As when thy ark was taken of the Philistines, they did not attribute the cause why the Israelites were overcome to their sins, and the cause of their victory to thee the true God, but to their own Dagon and the Israelites' contempt of him; even so our Philistines and enemies do not attribute this thy vengeance fallen upon us to our carnal life (because they are as evil therein, I will not say worse), for then we could and would acknowledge no less most humbly and thankfully; neither do acknowledge their victory and upper hand over us to thy working, but to their popery, false religion, mass, god of bread, &c.: for the which, as they have shed much innocent blood, as of Tyndale[3], Frith, Barnes, Garret, Jerome, Lacells, Lambert[4], &c., and more are purposed to do if thou let not; as therefore thou didst

[1 MS. torn.]   [2 The original has 'and,' not 'in.']
[3 Vide Foxe, Acts, &c. 1583, p. 1079; or ed. 1843—8, v. 127.]
[4 See p. 283, note 2, above.]

amongst the Philistines declare thy power and glory by taking vengeance on them and their false god, so, dear Lord, in thy good time do now the like. "Let the vengeance of thy servants' blood that is already shed," and the tyrannical handling of thy people at this present, being of these Philistines cast into prison and into miserable exile, " be openly shewed upon them[5]" which are not to be converted, whom thou only [dost know: and so many of them as are to be converted, we beseech thee to shew thy mercy upon them, and to convert them, if it][6] be thy good will. So shalt thou be known to be the Defender of the church and such as would serve thee after thy word; which now thine enemies tread under foot, and would have us full with swillings[7] and draff[8], utterly haling and persecuting all them that would return from keeping pigs[9] to serve thee in thy house; which they detest and abhor, seeking what means possible they can it should never rise and be builded again.

How many have they driven into exile! How many have they perverted by their promises and promotions; how many by terror and threats do they draw deadly to displease thee by doing outwardly against their consciences! How many have they cast into prison, and taken all they have most unjustly from them, lest by any means thy house and temple might be builded, thou knowest. How miserably they handle thy bond-servants, keeping from them all worldly consolations, as company, pen, paper, ink, books, &c., the prisons of the King's Bench, Marshalsea, Fleet, Newgate, and in many other places, at Oxford and elsewhere, doth presently to all the world cry out. O let their groans and " sorrowful sighs come up into thy sight. According to the greatness of thy power," (which our enemies by reason of their success puft up do think thou wantest, as Pharaoh did, when he said, "What fellow is God[10]?") " according," I say,

---

[5 Two or three words are wanting here in the MS. which is torn.]

[6 MS. torn: the blank is supplied from a parallel passage, p. 201, above.]

[7 Vide p. 160, note 4, above.] [8 'Draff:' refuse.]

[9 Allusion to the parable of the prodigal son, Luke xv.]

[10 "lest, if I be too full, I deny thee, and say, What fellow is the Lord?"—Prov. xxx. 9, in Matthew's Bible, Hyll 1551. Compare p. 183, l. 12, 13, above.]

"to the greatness of thy power preserve thou them that are appointed to die" and become thy slaughter-sheep. Thou disappointedst Herod of Peter, the sworn conspirators of Paul, king Joas of Eliseus, Ahab and Jezebel of Heli and Micheas, Haman of Mordecai. Even so, dear Lord, break the dream of thy combined enemies with us, and save thy servants Latimer, Cranmer, Ridley, Hooper, Crome[1], Rogers[2], Saunders, Bradford, Philpot, Coverdale, Barlow[3], Cardmaker[3], Taylor, &c., "which are appointed to die," if thou by thy mighty power deliver them not.

[2 Kings xiii. 10—19. Ecclus. xlviii. 12.]

It is "the glory of thy name," O Lord, which moveth us thus to make our moan; for thou knowest how thine enemies take part against thee, thy verity and truth. Thou forbiddest the making and worshipping of images: they command it as a worship. Thou forbiddest prayer in a tongue that is not to the edifying of the hearers: they straitly enjoin and command it. Thou forbiddest us all kinds of idolatry and spiritual fornication: they utterly enforce men thereto, even "to commit fornication" with bread, wine, gold, silver, stocks and stones. Thou wouldest the remembrance of thy death by the using of thy holy supper: they take away not only all remembrance of thy death, but even the place thereof by their mass, transubstantiation, and popish pelf. Thou commandest the lay as the clergy to drink of thy cup: but they forbid it utterly. Thou wouldest have the people brought up in knowledge, not as infants: and they seek by all means that none should have any true knowledge of thee; and therefore they chase out scriptures out of all places, and may not abide thy holy Testament to be had for thy people to look upon. And therefore they persecute many a one,

[1 See the history of doctor Crome in Strype, Mem. III. i. 157—67.]

[2 See p. 282, note 1, above.]

[3 The names of 'Barlow' and 'Cardmaker' are scored across in the original, probably by Bradford, because of the supposed recantation of the latter and the actual submission of the former. Bp. Barlow, having escaped into exile, returned on the accession of Elizabeth, assisted at the consecration of Abp. Parker, and was translated to the see of Chichester. Cardmaker, canon of Wells, was martyred in Smithfield, May 30, 1555. Vide Strype, Mem. III. i. 241—3, 431—4; Foxe, Acts, &c. 1583, p. 1578—81, or ed. 1843—8, VII. 77—85.]

and whet their tongues against not men only, but also[4] making indeed thy Christ and all that confess him and[4]

And who doeth this, O Lord? Not foreigners and strangers, but such as are our neighbours and profess thee; such as thou hast given the regiment[5] unto, as *scilicet* [to wit] in both the states in this poor and wretched realm of England, especially the clergy and such as would be counted pillars of thy church.

Therefore in thy time "reward them this their blasphemy wherewith they have blasphemed," and do still blaspheme "thee, and that sevenfold into their bosom;" that is, most plentifully and abundantly recompense thy tarrying with good measure, and plentifully upheaping thy measure.

And we poor misers[6], which are yet "thy people and sheep of thy pasture," having none other help nor hope but only thee, our God and Pastor; we, I say, "shall praise thy name for ever:" we shall, with thy people delivered out of the hands of Pharoah, Sennacherib, Holofernes, Haman, &c., [Judith.] give thanks to thy lovely name; "we will always," day and night, "be telling out thy praises from generation to generation."

This is the end why we crave thy help. This is the end why we desire to live, that, as we have been negligent, we might become diligent, to serve, love, laud, and magnify thy holy name in all our thoughts, words, and deeds, publicly and privately, when we shall perceive and feel how good thou our God art; when we shall see how thou art merciful and mindful of goodness towards them that put their trust in thee. O dear Father, so be it, so be it, so be it, so be it.

[4 MS. torn.]
[5 'Regiment:' rule.]   [6 See p. 73, note 4, above.]

A VERY GODLY PRAYER

OF ONE STANDING AT THE STAKE READY TO BE BURNT FOR CHRIST'S GOSPEL'S SAKE.

<small>MS. 1. 2. 8. no. 92. and MS. 2. 2. 16. no. 6. Emman. Coll. Cambridge.

Bull, Christian Prayers, &c. Middleton, n. d. p. 404.

Foxe, Acts, &c. 1570, p. 2002.</small>

MERCIFUL God and Father, to whom our Saviour Christ approached in his fear and need by reason of death, and found comfort; gracious God and most bounteous Christ, on whom Stephen called in his extreme need, and received strength; most benign Holy Spirit, which in the midst of all crosses and deaths didst comfort the apostle St Paul with more "consolations in Christ" than he felt sorrows and terrors; "have mercy upon me" a miserable, most vile, and wretched sinner, which now draw nigh the gates of death, deserved both in soul and body eternally by reason of my manifold, horrible, old and new transgressions, which to thine eyes, O Lord God, are open and known.

O "be merciful unto me," and forgive me, for the bitter death and blood-shedding of thy only Son Jesus Christ. And, though thy justice do require in respect of my sins, that now thou shouldest not hear me, measuring me with the same measure that I have measured thy majesty in contemning thy daily calls; yet let thy mercy, I say, prevail towards me (which is "above all thy works," and "wherewith the earth is filled") through and for the mediation of Christ our Saviour. For whose sake, in that it pleaseth thee to bring me forth now as one of his witnesses and a recordbearer of thy verity and truth, taught by him to give my life therefor, (to which dignity I do acknowledge, dear God, that there was never any so unworthy and unmeet, no, not the thief that hanged with him on the cross;) I humbly therefore pray thee that thou wouldest accordingly aid, help, and assist me with thy strength and heavenly grace, that with Christ thy Son I may find comfort; with Stephen I may see thy presence and gracious power; with St Paul and all others, which for thy name sake have suffered afflictions and death, I may find so present with me thy gracious consolation, that I may by my death glorify thy holy name, propagate and ratify thy verity, comfort the hearts of the heavy, confirm thy church in truth, convert some that are to be converted; and so to depart out of this miserable world (where I do nothing but heap daily sin upon sin), and enter into the fruition of thy blessed mercy. Whereof now give and increase in me a lively trust, sense[1], and feeling, wherethrough the terrors of death, the torments of fire, the pangs of sin, the darts of Satan, and the dolors of hell may never depress me, but may be driven away through the working of that most gracious Spirit. Which now plenteously endow me withal, that through the same Spirit I may offer (as now I desire to do in Christ and by him) myself, wholly soul and body, to be "a lively sacrifice, holy and acceptable in thy sight," dear Father, whose I am and always have been "even from my mother's womb," yea, "even before the world was made." To whom I commend myself, soul and body, faith and name, family and friends, country and all thy whole church, yea, even[2] my very enemies, according to thy good pleasure; beseeching thee entirely to give once more to this realm of England the blessing of thy word again, with godly peace to the teaching and setting forth of the same.

O dear Father, give me now to come unto thee; purge me and so purify me by this fire in Christ's death and passion, through thy Spirit, that I may be a "burnt offering of sweet smell" in thy sight, which livest and reignest with thy Son and the Holy Ghost, now and evermore, world without end. Amen.

JOHN BRADFORD[3].

[[1] 'sense,' MS. 2. 2. 16., not in MS. 1. 2. 8.]
[[2] 'even,' MS. 2. 2. 16., not in MS. 1. 2. 8.]
[[3] 'John Bradford,' MS. 2. 2. 16., not in MS. 1. 2. 8.]

[The five ensuing Treatises are brought together from different sources.

The 'Comparison between the old man and the new' is found in part among the MS. remains of Bradford in Emmanuel College, Cambridge [1].

This Essay observes, in the first twenty-seven lines, the text of the volume of Meditations, &c. of Bradford, printed by Seres 1567 [2] (the title of which is given on p. 296): the remainder, as marked in the notes, observes the text of the Emmanuel MS., which has been collated with the printed edition of 1567.

The side-notes, not being supplied in the MS., are taken from the edition printed in 1567 by Seres.

The entire treatise has been compared with the 'Christian Prayers,' &c., collected by Bull, Middleton 1570 [3], reverse of signature Y vi—Z ii, where it was reprinted from the Meditations, &c. of Bradford, Seres 1567. It has been collated also with Foxe, Acts, &c. 1570 [4], p. 1837—8, where too it was republished (among the letters of Bradford), and from whence it reappeared in the after editions of the 'Acts and Monuments.'

The variations are only noted where a deviation respectively from the MS. or printed edition of 1567 is followed.

The treatise upon 'The flesh and the spirit' is now first printed from a MS. in Emmanuel College.

The sources from which the 'Defence of election,' the treatise 'Against the fear of death,' and that on 'The restoration of all things,' are derived, are stated in the prefatory notes, p. 305—6, 331, and 350.]

[1 A transcript, of comparatively recent date, is in the British Museum, MS. Bibl. Sloan. 3205.4.]

[2 See prefatory note, p. 112 above.]

[3 The treatise upon 'the old man and the new' was also reprinted in the 'Prayers,' &c. collected by Bull, Middleton, n. d. (qu. 1578), and Beale 1619.]

[4 The title of this treatise in Foxe is, 'A letter of Master Bradford, describing a comparison between the old man and the new, &c.'; before which it is observed, 'To these letters of Master Bradford above specified, here is also adjoined another letter of the said Bradford, written to certain of his faithful friends, worthy of all Christians to be read; wherein is described a lively comparison between the old man and the new, also between the law and the gospel, containing much fruitful matter of divinity, necessary for christian consciences to read and understand.']

FIVE TREATISES,

NAMELY,

I. THE OLD MAN AND THE NEW.
II. THE FLESH AND THE SPIRIT.
III. DEFENCE OF ELECTION.
IV. AGAINST THE FEAR OF DEATH.
V. THE RESTORATION OF ALL THINGS.

GODLY
Meditations vppon the
ten Commaunde-
mentes, the Articles of
**the fayth, and the
Lords prayer.**

Whervnto is ioyned a trea-
tife against the feare of
death: Also a compari-
son betweene **the old**
man and the new
the lawe and
the gofple.
&c.

**Made by Maister John
Bradford.**

Seene and allowed according to the
Queenes Iniunctions
1567.

Imprinted at London by
William Seres.

A COMPARISON BETWEEN

THE OLD MAN AND THE NEW,

ALSO BETWEEN THE LAW AND THE GOSPEL;

CONTAINING A SHORT SUM OF ALL THE DIVINITY NECESSARY FOR A CHRISTIAN CONSCIENCE.

A MAN that is regenerate and "born of God," (the which thing that every one of us be, our baptism, the sacrament of "regeneration," doth require under pain of damnation; and therefore let every one of us with the virgin Mary say, "Be it unto me, O Lord, according to thy word," according to thy sacrament of baptism, wherein thou hast declared our adoption; and let us lament the doubting hereof in us, striving against it as we shall be made able in the Lord;) a man, I say, that is regenerate, consisteth of two men (as a man may say), namely of "the old man," and of "the new man." "The old man" is like to a mighty giant, such a one as was Goliath; for his birth is now perfect. But "the new man" is like unto a little child, such a one as was David; for his birth is not perfect until the day of his general resurrection. *Meditations, &c. of Bradford, Seres 1567, signature M iv—viii.* *The old man.* *The new man.*

"The old man" therefore is more stronger, lusty, and stirring than is "the new man," because the birth of "the new man" is but begun now, and "the old man" is perfectly born. And as "the old man" is more stirring, lusty, and stronger than "the new man;" so is the nature of him clean contrary to the nature of "the new man," as being earthly and corrupt with Satan's seed; the nature of "the new man" being heavenly, and blessed with the celestial seed of God. So that one man, inasmuch as he is corrupt with the seed of the serpent, is an "old man;" and inasmuch as he is blessed with the seed of God from above, he is a "new man." And as, inasmuch as he is an "old man," he is a sinner and an enemy to God; so, inasmuch as he is regenerate, he is righteous and holy and a friend to God, the seed of God[1] preserving him from sin, so that he cannot sin as the seed of the serpent, wherewith he is corrupt even from his conception, inclineth him, yea, enforceth him to sin, and nothing else but to sin: *Why the old man is stronger than the new.* *In what respect one man is both an old man and also a new man.* *MS. 1. 2. 8. no. 82. Emman. Coll. Cambridge.* *Meditations, &c. of Bradford, Seres 1567. 1 John iii.*

[1 The Emmanuel MS., being imperfect, begins with the words, 'of God preserving him.']

so that the best part in man tofore regeneration, in God's sight, is not only an enemy, but "enmity" itself.

How one man may be called always sinful and always just.
One man therefore which is regenerate well may be called always just, and always sinful: just in respect of God's seed and his regeneration; sinful in respect of Satan's seed and his first birth. Betwixt these two men therefore there is continual conflict and war most deadly; "the flesh and the old man" fighting against "the Spirit and new man," and "the Spirit and new man" fighting against "the flesh and old man."

Why the old man oftentimes prevaileth against the new man. The old man so mightily prevaileth against the new in the children of God, that the Spirit and seed of God seemeth to be utterly taken from them: whereas indeed it is not so, as afterwards to their great comfort they find and feel.
Which "old man" by reason of his birth that is perfect doth often for a time prevail against "the new man," being but as a child in comparison; and that in such sort as not only others, but even the children of God themselves, think that they be nothing else but "old," and that the Spirit and seed of God is lost and gone away: where yet notwithstanding the truth is otherwise, the Spirit and seed of God at the length appearing again, and dispelling away the clouds which cover "the Sun" of God's seed from shining, as the clouds in the air do the corporal sun; so that sometime a man cannot tell by any sense that there is any sun, cloud and wind so hiding it from our sight: even so our cæcity or blindness and corrupt affections do often shadow the sight of God's seed in God's children, as though they were plain reprobates.

Whereof it cometh, that they praying according to their sense, but not according to the truth, desire of God to give them again his Spirit, as though they had lost it, and he had taken it away. Which thing God never doth in deed, although he make us to think so for a time; for always he holdeth his hand under his children in their falls, that they lie not still as other do which are not regenerate. And this is the difference betwixt God's children which are regenerate and elect before all time in Christ, and the wicked castaways, that the elect lie not still continually in their sin as do the wicked, but at the length do return again by reason of God's seed, which is in them hid as a sparkle of fire in the ashes; as we may see in Peter, David, Paul, Mary Magdalene, and others.

For these (I mean God's children) God hath made all things in Christ Jesu, to whom he hath given them this dignity that they should be "his inheritance" and spouses.

This our Inheritor and "Husband" Christ Jesus, God with God, 'Light of Light,' co-eternal and consubstantial with the Father and with the Holy Ghost, to the end that he might become our "Husband" (because the husband and the wife must become "one body and flesh"), hath taken our nature upon him, communicating with it and by it in his own person, to us all his children, his "divine majesty," as Peter saith; and so is become "flesh of our flesh and bone of our bones" substantially, as we are become "flesh of his flesh and bone of his bones" spiritually; all that ever we have pertaining to him, yea[1], even our sins, as all that ever he hath pertaineth[2] unto us, even his whole glory. So that if Satan shall summon us to answer for our debts or[3] sins, in that the wife is no suitable[4] person, but the husband, we may well bid him enter his action against our "Husband" Christ, and he will make him a sufficient answer.

_{2 Pet. i.}

For this end (I mean that we might be coupled and married thus to Christ, and so be certain of salvation, and at godly peace with God in our consciences,) God hath given his holy word, which hath two parts, as now the children of God consisteth of two men; one part of God's word being proper to "the old man," and the other part of God's word being proper to "the new man." The part properly pertaining to "the old man" is the law: the part properly pertaining to "the new man" is the gospel.

The law pertaineth to the old man, and the gospel to the new.

The law is a doctrine which commandeth and forbiddeth, requiring doing and avoiding: under it therefore are[5] contained all precepts, inhibitions, threats, promises upon conditions of our doing and avoiding, &c. The gospel is a doctrine which always offereth and giveth, requiring nothing on our behalf as of worthiness or as a cause, but as a certificate unto us: and therefore under it are[5] contained all the free and[6] sweet promises of God, as "I am the Lord thy God," &c.

What the law is.

What the gospel is.

In those that be of years of discretion it requireth "faith," not as a cause, but as an instrument whereby we ourselves may be certain of our good "Husband" Christ and of his glory: and therefore, when the conscience feeleth itself disquieted for fear of God's judgments against sin, she may in nowise look upon the doctrine pertaining to "the old man," but to[7] the

The conscience, feared and beaten down with the terror of

[1 'yea' 1567: not in MS.]
[2 'pertaining,' MS.: 'pertaineth' 1567.]
[3 'and,' MS.: 'or' 1567.]
[4 'Suitable:' against whom an action would lie.]
[5 'is,' MS.: 'are' 1567.]   [6 'and' 1567: not in MS.]
[7 'of' MS.: 'to' 1567.]

doctrine only that pertaineth to "the new man;" in it not looking on that which it requireth, that is "faith," because we never believe as we should; but only on it which it offereth, which it giveth, that is, on God's grace and eternal mercy and peace in Christ Jesu.

So shall she be in quiet, when she looketh for it altogether out of herself in God's mercy in Christ Jesu; in whose lap if she lay her head with John, then is she happy, and shall find quietness indeed. When she feeleth herself quiet, then a God's name let her look on the law, and upon such things as God requireth, thereby to bridle and keep down the old Adam, to slay that Goliath; from whom she must needs keep the sweet promises, being the bed wherein her sweet spouse Christ and she meet and lie together. As the wife will keep her bed only for her husband, although in other things she is contented to have fellowship with her servants and others, as to speak, sit, eat, drink, go, &c.; so our consciences, which are Christ's wives, must needs keep the bed, that is, God's sweet promises, alonely for ourselves and for our "Husband," there to meet together, to embrace together, to laugh together, and to be joyful together. If sin, the law, the devil, or any thing, would creep into the bed, and lie there, then complain to thy "Husband" Christ, and forthwith thou shalt see him play Phineas' part.

Thus, my dearly beloved, I have given you in few words a sum of all that divinity which a christian conscience cannot want.

Per Johannem Bradford.

THE FLESH AND THE SPIRIT[1].
A DECLARATION HOW THESE WORDS 'FLESH' AND 'SPIRIT' ARE TO BE UNDERSTAND IN THE SCRIPTURES.

JESUS EMMANUEL.

For your better understanding of the scriptures, especially of the new Testament; for the forearming you against errors, which, through the ignorance or diverse acception and taking of terms or words used and written of the holy

[1 This Treatise is now printed for the first time.]

apostles, might happen; and for your consolation in the conflicts you are cumbered with in this present life; I am purposed, my dearly beloved, to write unto you some things (as God shall lend me his grace, the which I ask for his Christ's sake now and for ever) hereabout. Take it in good part, I pray you, at least for my good will's sake towards you in Christ.

In reading the scriptures, and especially Paul's epistles, we very often do see these words, "flesh" and "spirit." When therefore this word "flesh" is set against "the spirit" by the way of contrary, as Gal. v. and almost everywhere, then must we know that it comprehendeth all and every of the natural powers, gifts, and qualities of man: yea, it comprehendeth all that ever is in man, whatsoever it be, (the "sanctification of the Spirit," which none have but the elect and justified, only excepted:) like as this word "spirit," when it is opposed or set against as a contrary to the "flesh," doth signify that which in man the Holy Ghost hath purged from evil and sanctified to righteousness. The which word sometime Paul calleth "the mind," sometime "the inward man," sometime "the new man," and sometime "a new creature;" as the word "flesh," taken as before I have said, is sometime called "the old man," sometime "the outward man," sometime "the body." All which words do appertain, as to the soul so to the body; that look inasmuch as it (the soul, I mean) is regenerate, it is called "the spirit," "the mind," "the new man," "the inward man," "a new creature;" inasmuch as it retaineth the natural affections of man, it is called "flesh," "the old man," "the outward man," "the body." So that you may see in these terms and in every of them is comprehended whole man, both soul and body, to be considered either according to regeneration and to the sanctifying of God's Spirit, or else according to all that ever he is or hath by nature or otherwise, by any means, inwardly or outwardly.

Whilst we live here, there is a fight and strife in us which are the elect and "children of God;" "the flesh," outward man, body, and "old man," striving against "the spirit," inward man, "new man," and "new creature[2]:" that is, so much

[[2] The MS. repeats, after 'new creature,' the words 'and the spirit, inward man, new man, and new creature.']

as we are regenerate and endued with God's Spirit, we do strive and fight against all the powers of our souls and bodies; retaining the natural and corrupt affections we have in us, and shall have so long as we live, to bring them as much as may be into obedience to the Spirit; at the least to bridle them, that they bear not dominion or rule in us.

This battle and strife none have but the elect "children of God:" and they that have it are the elect "children of God" "in Christ before the beginning of the world," whose salvation is as certain and sure as is God himself; for they are given to Christ, a faithful Shepherd, who hath so prayed for them lest they should perish, that we know his prayer is heard: yea, he promiseth so to keep them that "they shall not perish." And therefore they ought to rejoice, and herethrough to comfort themselves in their conflicts, which are testimonials, and most true, that they are the elect and dear "children of God;" for else they could not nor should not feel any such strife in them.

An objection. But perchance you will say, that the wicked have strife also in themselves, and oft are grieved with themselves because they have done such a sin; and therefore this is no such certain demonstration of election.

The answer. To this I answer, that indeed the wicked and reprobate
1 Sam. xxiv. xxvi. have sometimes, as you say, strifes and conflicts; as in Saul
2 Macc. ix. we may see it against David, and in Antiochus. But this strife in them is not a strife or battle betwixt "the spirit and the flesh;" as you shall see if you mark the differences to discern these battles, which now I will give unto you.

Differences between the conflict of the godly and the wicked. When man is displeased with himself for any thing done amiss, and striveth thereagainst, in respect that the fault displeaseth God his Father and Lord, in respect of Christ, &c., then is the same strife the strife of a good man, of one elected and that is the dear child of God: and the same man so displeased with himself may assure himself that he hath the "good Spirit" of God, which hath wrought in him that affection. Let him therefore call to God and cry, 'Abba, dear Father,' and ask grace and mercy, which assuredly he shall find.

But when one is displeased with himself, and striveth to amend any fault, in respect of civil honesty, of men, shame, beauty, bodily health, profit, hurt, friendship, &c., and not in respect of God's displeasure and favour; then is the same sorrow after the world, and not after God; then is the same strife or battle a battle between the flesh and the flesh, and not between "the spirit and the flesh." Such battles have the wicked, as Saul had, in respect of worldly honesty, shame, civil justice, &c. The wicked have not God's Spirit of sanctification and regeneration to sanctify and regenerate them, though they have it concerning other gifts: and therefore they want the affections of the holy elect "children of God" and regenerated, although they have other affections by the which they are not discerned from the ungodly, or taken for holy in God's sight.

I pray you, my dearly beloved, to weigh this that I have written: and then, besides that you shall have some candlelight to keep you out of the errors of them which do attribute perfection to some works done by men, and make "flesh and blood" the outward man, "the old man" but only this our body, and not the soul and the powers and affections thereof, so much as it laboureth and lusteth against God's Spirit and the powers and affections stirred up in man by him; besides this, I say, you shall see that the doctrine of election is not a casting of the bridle in the horse's neck, or an overstrait curbing of the horse; that is, neither occasioneth licentiousness nor despair, but provoketh to battle against sin; and that not hypocritically, but in God's sight and for God's sake, (for they feel not their election that so fight not;) but it comforteth also in the cross and battle most comfortably, with comforts that never can be taken away: for what a comfort is it to see my sorrow and fight to be a demonstration of mine election! Wherein is true rejoicing, as Christ said, "Rejoice in this, that your names are written in the book of life."

If any man would alter the natural course of any water to run a contrary way, he shall never be able to do it with dams: for a time he may well stop it; but when the dam is full, it will either burst down the dam or overflow it, and so with more rage run than ever it did before. I will not speak of the often weesing[1] out, mauger all the diligence that can be. Therefore the alteration must be from the head, by making other thoroughs[2] and devices. Even so, if any man

[1 'Weesing:' oozing, from the Anglo-Saxon *wœs*, 'water.' Vide Holloway, Provinc. Dict. 1838.]

[2 'Thoroughs:' passages, channels.]

would have the streams of his nature and will altered, to run after the will and nature of God, the same shall never be able to do it, nor all the world for him, by making of dams; that is, by telling and teaching us by the creatures, works, and word of God, how that we should do, speak, and think otherwise than we do naturally. For a time the streams of our affections may be stopped by telling and teaching, and other corporal exercise; howbeit so yet that they will weesel[1] out now and then, and at length break down all our dams and devices, or else so overflow them that "the latter end will be worse than the beginning." Therefore the alteration hereof must be at the head-spring by making other throughs and rivers of incorruption for nature and will to run in.

But who can do this? The spring itself? Nay, God him[self,] and that alonely and alone, which worketh this in whom, when, and howsoever, it pleaseth him for his own good will's sake. And they in whom he worketh this are his elect children "before the beginning of the world;" who may and should feel their election by loving the good and hating that which is evil, although in great imperfection: whereas the hypocrites have a thousand parts more shew of holiness, but in deed less love to God and hatred to evil, yea, in deed none at all as it is in God's sight.

Wherefore let us pray for the daily increase of "regeneration," which is nothing else but the alteration of our natural streams, that, as from Adam we have received them running naturally contrary to his will, so we may receive from Christ, the second Adam, his "good Spirit" to draw, deduce, and lead us in all things after the throughs and ways of his good will: which he grant to us for his mercy's sake! For, my dearly beloved, man of himself, tofore his "regeneration," is so far from helping himself hereunto of himself and of all that ever he hath by his birth, that not only he bringeth nothing hereunto, as he bringeth nothing at all to his first birth; but also he bringeth that letteth and is adversary against this good work: which God work daily in us and in all his children more and more, to our full certainty of his salvation, and joy everlasting, through Christ our Lord! Amen.

JOHN BRADFORD.

[[1] See note 1 in the preceding page.]

[The 'Defence of Election' observes throughout, except where otherwise noted, the text of a MS. in the Bodleian Library, Oxford, all the parts of which are now first brought together in one publication, and small portions of which have not hitherto been printed; namely the three lines of inscription to Mistress Joyce Hales[2] at p. 307 in the beginning, twenty-three lines at p. 309 in the Dedication, and the numerous marginal notes of Part II. p. 318—30.

The title of that MS. is as follows:

'A treatise of predestination with an answer to certain enormities calumniously gathered of one to slander God's truth; by John Bradford.—Romans xi. "Israel hath not obtained that he sought, but the elected have obtained it. The remnant are blinded, as it is written, God hath given them the spirit of unquietness, eyes that they should not see, and ears that they should not hear, even unto this day."'

Part I. of the 'Defence,' p. 310—18, was printed (without the Dedication or Part II.) among the 'Godly Meditations' of Bradford, Hall 1562, signature O iii to P iii;[3] and re-appeared in the after editions of that collection, 1578, 1604, 1607, 1614, 1622, and 1633; and in the 'Fathers of the English Church' 1810, VI. p. 373—83.

The chief portion of the Dedication, p. 307—10, was given with Part I. in Bishop Coverdale, (Letters of the martyrs 1564, p. 391—401;) which were republished in the 'British Reformers,' Bradford, 1829, p. 331—40, and in the Life of Bradford by Stevens, 1832, p. 80—9.

The 'Dedication,' as given by Bishop Coverdale (ibid. 391—3,) exists in MS. (2. 2. 15. no. 93.) in Emmanuel College, Cambridge.

Part II. p. 318—30, was first printed when edited by the late Archbishop Laurence with Part I. (but without the Dedication), in 'Authentic Documents,' &c. on Predestination, Oxford 1819; both parts being taken from the Bodley MS.

The text of that MS. has now been collated with the chief printed editions: but the variations are only noted in special cases.

The 'Defence of Election' here published is, in all probability, the document[4] to which Bradford makes the following reference in a letter addressed to Archbishop Cranmer, Bishop Ridley, and Bishop Latimer, which was signed by Bishop Ferrar, Rowland Taylor, Bradford, and Archdeacon Philpot, and appears from internal evidence to have been written about January 18, 1555:

"Herewithal I send unto you a little Treatise which I have made, that you might peruse the same, and not only you but also ye my other most dear and reverend fathers in the Lord for ever, to give to it your approbation as ye may think good. All the prisoners hereabouts in manner have seen it and read it: and as therein they agree with me, nay, rather with the truth, so they are ready and will be to signify it as

[2 See p. 248 above, and p. 350.]   [3 See p. 112—4, and 211, above.]
[4 So it is regarded by Abp. Laurence, 'Authentic Documents,' &c. 1819, p. xxi.]

they shall see you give them example. I have sent you here a writing of Harry Hart's own hand, whereby ye may see how Christ's glory and grace is like to lose much light, if that your sheep *quondam* be not something holpen by them which love God, and are able to prove that all good is to be attributed only and wholly to God's grace and mercy 'in Christ,' without other respect of worthiness than Christ's merits. The effects of salvation they so mingle with the cause, that, if it be not seen to, more hurt will come by them than ever came by the papists; inasmuch as their life commendeth them to the world more than the papists'. God is my witness, that I write not this but because I would God's glory and the good of his people. In free-will they are plain papists, yea, Pelagians: and ye know that *modicum fermenti totam massam corrumpit*. They utterly contemn all learning. But hereof shall this bringer [Augustin Bernhere] shew you more[1]."

Further information will be obtained from the various letters of Bradford referring to the subject[2], which will appear in the concluding volume of his Writings; from the letters of Bishop Ridley, Works, Parker Soc. p. 367—8, and 379, and suppl. p. 539—42; and from the publications and documents referred to below[3].

The 'Defence of election' can be compared with the treatise on 'election and free-will,' and 'brief sum of election,' p. 211—20 above.

See also note G.]

[1 Bp. Coverdale, Letters of the martyrs, 1564, p. 358—9.
The original of this letter in the autograph of Bradford, with the autograph signatures also of Bp. Ferrar, Rowland Taylor, and Adn. Philpot, is now in the very extensive collection of manuscripts belonging to Dawson Turner, Esq., Yarmouth.
A contemporary transcript or rough draft of this letter is in Emmanuel College, Cambridge, MS. 2. 2. 15. no. 69.]

[2 See letters of Bradford to Abp. Cranmer and Bp. R. and Bp. L., Careless, Adn. Philpot, Cole and Sheterden, Cole, to certain men, and to Trewe and Abyngton, in Bp. Coverdale, Letters of the martyrs 1564, p. 357—9, 373—4, 408—11, 470—6, 650—2; Foxe, Acts, &c. 1583, p. 1645, 1657, or ed. 1843—8, VII. 241—2, 267—8. Vide also letter of Bradford to a freewiller, in MS. 2. 2. 15. no. 74., Emman. College, Cambridge.]

[3 Harl. MSS. 421. 64. British Museum, Depositions of divers witnesses against some Kentish men, accused of holding erroneous tenets touching predestination, &c., about 1550.—Strype, Mem. II. i. 369—70, Parker, I. 54—5, Cranmer, I. 502—5. Trewe on 'The cause of contention,' Jan. 30, 1555, in Abp. Laurence, Authentic Documents, 37—70, with which compare Adn. Philpot, Writings, Parker Soc. 305—8. Strype, Mem. III. i. 413, and 586—8. Letter by a freewiller, Letter by one who had been a freewiller, Confession of faith by Clement, Faith of the prisoners at Stratford-le-Bow, in Strype, Mem. III. ii. 321—34, 446—67, 469—71. Exam. of Careless, in Foxe, Acts, &c. 1563, p. 1529—34, or ed. 1843—8, VIII. 163—70. Stow, Life of Rowland Taylor, 1833, ch. VI. p. 179—213. Also, in MS. 53, Bodleian Library, Oxford, Bernhere on election; Bernhere, Testimonies from God's book; Letter from Laurence and Barre to Bernhere; Bernhere, Answer to the Letter of Laurence and Barre. Also a letter by Henry Harte, MS. 2. 2. 15. no. 43., in Emmanuel College, Cambridge. These documents and statements have been carefully examined by the present editor.]

DEFENCE OF ELECTION[4].

[DEDICATION.]

To his entirely beloved sister in the Lord, Joyce Hales[5], John Bradford wisheth "grace, mercy, and peace, from God the Father" through our Saviour and Mediator, Jesus Christ.

<small>MS. Bodl. 53. Bodleian Library, Oxford.</small>

Faith of God's election (I mean, to believe that we be in very deed "the children of God" through Christ, and shall be for ever inheritors of everlasting life through the only grace of God our Father in the same Christ) is of all things which God requireth of us, not only most principal, but also the whole sum: so that "without this faith" there is nothing we do that can "please God." And therefore, as God first requireth it in saying, "I am the Lord thy God," &c. that is, 'I remit thee thy sins, I give thee my holy[6] Spirit, and for ever will I keep thee;' so our Saviour would have us to be persuaded when we come to pray, and therefore teacheth, yea, he commandeth us, to call God "our Father:" whose power were not infinite, as we profess in the first article of our belief, when we call him expressly our 'Almighty Father,' if we should doubt of his final favour.

<small>To be persuaded of God's election is most necessary.</small>

<small>Rom. xiv. Heb. xi.</small>

<small>Exod. xx.</small>

<small>Matt. vi.</small>

And therefore I cannot but much marvel at some men which seem godly, and yet are in this behalf too malicious both to God and man. For what is more seemly to God than mercy? which is most magnified of the elected children

[4 Vide title of the Bodley MS., p. 305 above.
The heading of Part I. of this Treatise, p. 310—18, in the Meditations of Bradford, 1562, (see p. 305 above), is, 'A short and pithy defence of the doctrine of the holy election and predestination of God, gathered out of the first chapter of St. Paul's epistle to the Ephesians, by J. Bradford.'
The inscription of the portions of the 'Defence' given in Bp. Coverdale, Letters, &c. 1564, (see p. 305 above), is, "A letter written to a dear friend of his, wherein he entreateth as briefly so most perfectly, godly, soundly and pithily, of God's holy election, free grace, and mercy in Jesus Christ."]

[5 See p. 248 above, and p. 350. These three lines are now first printed.]

[6 'whole,' MS.: 'holy' 1564.]

of God. And what is more seemly to man than humility? the which is not nor cannot be indeed but in "the elect of God;" for they alone attribute nothing at all to themselves continually but damnation, that in God only and for ever may be their whole glory.

<small>Jer. ix.</small>

<small>More commodities cometh of election than man can conceive.</small>

But this notwithstanding, there is that have gone about to gather, yea, to set abroad, 'enormities' out of the doctrine of God's most holy and comfortable election and predestination; where the same doctrine hath more commodities than all the whole world can be able to conceive, much less to express. For what destroyeth enormities so much as it doth? It overthroweth the most pestilent papistical poison of doubting of God's favour, which is the very dungeon of despair and of the contempt of God. It destroyeth the ethnic opinion of fortune. It comforteth most comfortably in the cross, and casteth down all cogitations that would else cover us with sorrow and dolour, in telling that "all things" shall turn to the best. It maketh us modest and putteth away pride in prosperity, by pulling from men meriting or deserving. It enforceth men to love and carefully to travail for their brethren, utterly impugning the contempt of any. It provoketh to piety, and is the greatest enemy to ungodliness that can be, by teaching us of what dignity we be, of what price even our bodies, "temples of the Holy Ghost," "members of Christ." It engendereth a true desire of our home in heaven, and so to despise this world, and the things this world hath in estimation. It maketh man wholly and continually to give over himself to be careful, not for himself, but for his brethren and for those things that make to God's glory. It helpeth very much to the true understanding of the scriptures, and preserveth from errors, by knowing what is to be attributed to the law, the gospel, to the ministry, to the vocal word, to the old testament, to the new covenant, to the sacraments, to faith, to works, to prayer, to penance, to God, to man, &c.; for by the Spirit of election we see and know "Christ, in whom dwelleth all the riches or treasures of knowledge." It setteth up Christ's kingdom, and utterly overthroweth the wisdom, power, ableness, and choice of man, that all glory may be given only unto God.

<small>Rom. viii.</small>
<small>1 Cor. i.</small>
<small>1 John ii.</small>
<small>1 Cor. vi. iii.</small>
<small>Col. ii.</small>

But what go I about to recount the commodities coming out of the doctrine of God's election, in that they be innumerable? This is a sum, that, where a christian man's life hath respect to God, to man, and to himself, to "live godly, justly, and soberly," all is grounded in predestination in Christ. For who liveth "godly," but he that believeth? and who believeth but such as are "ordained to eternal life?" Who liveth "justly," but such as love their neighbours? and whence springeth this love, but of God's election "before the beginning of the world, that we might be blameless by love?" Who liveth "soberly" but such as be holy? and who are they but only those that be endued with the Spirit of sanctification? which is the "seal" of our election, which by election do believe. *Titus ii. Acts ii. xiii. Ephes. i. Ephes. i. 2 Cor. i.*

Therefore, as I said, I much marvel to see any man so blinded as one is especially, which is not ashamed to put forth in writing such horrible 'enormities' as he maliciously gathereth to proceed out of the doctrine of predestination: as you, my good sister, in this book following shall perceive and see immediately after the true doctrine of election, which I briefly first set forth, and then do particularly answer every part worthy the answering; not leaving out one tittle of every word as he hath put it abroad, so far as the bill that was sent to me from him, I think; for it was subscribed with his name, and the superscription was to me by name as truly written. If I shall seem to you in answering him more sharp than my wont is, you must consider the weightiness of the matter and the horrible slandering of the same cannot but require much more sharp writing than I have written.

Now because I know you are like hereafter to have something to do with some hereabouts in this thing, because by your means I was first brought in talk or debating of this matter; in that I am thus drawn to wade in it, I thought good even to dedicate this, which I have done herein, unto you, as well to be a help to you in this matter, joining to it the explications of the places, (which places and the explications I have sent to you at divers times,)[1] as also to be a

[[1] The last twenty-three lines, "Therefore, as I said, I much marvel . sent to you at divers times,)" are now first printed from the Bodleian MS. The printed edition of 1564 has instead, "Wherefore, my dearly beloved in the Lord, I have taken in hand at this present, something to write to you, and for your sake in this matter, which herewithal I have sent unto you, as well to be a help to you herein,"]

pledge of my careful love and hearty desire I have for your continuance in the truth: wherein I trust you stand presently when I shall be dead and burned; as I look for none other so soon as God shall give leave to his enemies for my weal and endless joy in Christ. To whom, as to a most faithful Pastor, I from the bottom of my very heart do commend and bequeath you, my most dearly beloved in the Lord, beseeching him to watch over you both night and day, as over one of his poor lambs, to keep you out of the claws of the lion and mouth of the wolves, to the comfort of his children and good bringing up of your poor babes, specially of the youngest my godson; to whom I wish the blessing of God the Father, the Son, and the Holy Ghost, now and for ever[1]. Amen.

The 11th of October, *anno* 1554.

[PART I].

JESUS EMMANUEL.

All things must be esteemed after God's will. [1562—4.]

THERE is neither virtue nor vice to be considered according to any outward action, nor according to the will and wisdom of man; but according to the will of God. Whatsoever is conformable thereto, the same is virtue, and the action that springeth thereof is laudable and good, howsoever it appear otherwise to the eyes and reason of man; as

Gen. xxii.

was "the lifting up of Abraham's hands to have slain his son." Whatsoever is not conformable to the will of God, that same is vice, and the action springing thereof is to be disallowed and taken for evil; and that so much the more and greater evil, by how much it is not consonant and agreeing to God's will, although it seem far otherwise to man's wisdom: as was

Matt. xvii.
Luke ix.

Peter's wish of "making three tabernacles," and the request of some which would have had "fire to have come down from heaven" upon a zeal to God, &c.

God's will must be sought for in his word. [1562—4.]

Now the will of God is not so known as in his word. Therefore according to it must vice and virtue, good and evil, be judged; and not according to the judgment, wisdom,

[[1] The last four lines, "the comfort of his children ..... ever." are now first printed from the Bodleian MS. The printed edition of 1564 has instead, "his glory and your eternal joy and comfort in him."]

reason, and collection of any man, or of all the whole world, if all the angels in heaven should take their part.

But this word of God, which is written in the canonical books of the Bible, doth plainly set forth unto us, that God hath of his own mercy and good will, and "to the praise of his glory" in Christ, elected some, and not all; whom he hath predestinate unto everlasting life in the same Christ, and in his time "calleth them, justifieth them, and glorifieth them," so that "they shall never perish" and err to damnation finally. *God's word is written in the Bible. [1562—4.] In the Bible is predestination published. [1562—4.]*

Therefore to affirm, teach, and preach this, hath in it no hurt, no vice, no evil, much less then no enormities[2], to the eyes and spirit of them which are guided and will be by the word of God. *No enormity is therefore in it. [1562—4.]*

That God the eternal "Father of mercies," "before the beginning of the world," hath of his own mercies and good will, "and to the praise of his grace and glory," "elected in Christ" some, and not all the posterities of Adam, whom he hath predestinate unto eternal life, and "calleth them" in his time, "justifieth them, and glorifieth them," so that "they shall never perish" or err to damnation finally; that this proposition is true, and according to God's plain and manifest word; by the help of his holy Spirit, (which in the name of Jesus Christ I humbly beseech his mercy plentifully to give to me at this present and for ever, to the sanctification of his holy name in myself and in many others[3],) by the help, I say, of his holy Spirit, I trust so evidently to demonstrate, that no man of God shall be able by the word of God ever to impugn it, much less to confute it. *The proposition that sheweth what is meant by election and predestination: [1562—4.] which he after proveth by the parts out of the text of St Paul immediately following. [1564.]*

In the first chapter of the Epistle to the Ephesians the example saith thus:

"Blessed be God the Father of our Lord Jesus Christ, which hath blessed us with all manner of spiritual blessings in heavenly things by Christ; according as he hath elect (or chosen) us in him before the foundation of the world was laid, that we should be holy and without blame before him through love; and hath predestinate us (or ordained us before) through *Ephes. i.*

[2 So the MS.: 'much less then hath it any enormities (as some do affirm),' 1562, 1564.]

[3 'in myself and in many others,' MS.: not in 1562 or 1564.]

Jesus Christ to be heirs unto himself, according to the good pleasure of his will, to the praise of the glory of his grace; wherewith he hath made us accepted in the Beloved: by whom we have received redemption through his blood, even the forgiveness of sins, according to the riches of his grace; which grace he hath shed on us abundantly in all wisdom and prudence, and hath opened unto us the mystery of his will, according to his good pleasure, which he purposed in himself to have it declared when the time was full come; that he might gather together all things by (or in) Christ, as well the things that be in heaven as the things that be in earth, even in (or by) him: by (or in) whom we are made heirs, being thereto predestinate according to the purpose of him that worketh all things according to the decree (or counsel) of his own will, that we which hoped before you in Christ should be to the praise of his glory: in whom you also hoped after you heard the word of truth, the gospel of your salvation; wherein you also believing were sealed with the Holy Spirit of promise, which is the earnest of your inheritance, until the redemption (or full fruition) of the purchased possession, unto the laud of his glory."

These be the words of Paul, which I have faithfully translated according to the very text in the Greek, as by the judgment of all that be learned I desire herein to be tried: out of the which words of Paul we may well perceive every thing affirmed in my proposition, as I will give occasion plainly to them that will to see it.

The cause of election is his grace and good will.

First, that the cause of God's election is of his good will, the apostle sheweth first in saying that it is "through his love," whereby we are "holy and without blame;" secondarily in saying that it is "according to the good pleasure of his will;" thirdly in saying, "according to his good pleasure purposed in himself;" fourthly in saying, "according to his purpose, which worketh all the counsel of his own will."

1.
2.
3.
4.

The time of God's election was from the beginning.

Secondly, that election was "before the beginning of the world," the apostle plainly sheweth in saying, that we were "chosen before the foundation of the world was laid;" and afterwards in calling it "the mystery of his will purposed with himself, in time to be declared."

Election is in Christ.

Thirdly, that election is "in Christ," the apostle doth so

flatly and plainly set it forth, that I need not here to repeat it. We, saith he, are "chosen in him": we are "accepted by him": we are "gathered together in him," &c.

Fourthly, that election is of some of Adam's posterity and not of all, we may plainly see it, if we consider that he maketh the true demonstration of it "believing," "hoping," and having "the earnest" of the Spirit. "In whom you hoped," saith he, "after you heard," &c.: "in whom you believing were sealed up," &c. Again, in attributing to the elect forgiveness of sins, holiness, blameless living, being in Christ, &c., "That we should be holy," saith he, &c.; "we have received forgiveness of sins," &c. Who seeth not that these are not common to all men? "All men have not faith," saith Paul elsewhere. None "believed," saith Luke, but "such as were ordained to eternal life." None "believe" but such as are "born of God." None believeth truly but such as have "good hearts," and keep good seed to "bring forth fruits by patience." *Election not of all men. [1562—4.]* *2 Thess. iii. Acts xiii. 1 John v. Matt. xiii. [Luke viii.]*

So that it is plain (faith being a demonstration of God's election to them that be of years of discretion,) that all men are not elect, because all men believe not; for "he that believeth in the Lord shall be as mount Sion," that is, he shall "never be removed;" for, if he be removed, that is, finally perish, surely he never truly believed. *Faith is the demonstration of election to such as be of years of discretion. Psal. cxxv.*

But what go I about to light a candle in the clear sunlight, when our Saviour plainly saith that all be not chosen, but "few?" "Many be called," saith he, "but few be chosen." And in the second chapter following, the apostle plainly saith that the great riches of God's "mercy through his exceeding great love" hath saved them[1] before their parents and many other gentiles, which were excluded from Christ, and strangers from the promise, hopeless, godless, &c. Wherethrough we may be occasioned to cry, 'O the depth of the judgments of God, which "is just in all his doings, and holy in all his works," extending his mercy after his good pleasure and will above all his works!' *Matt. xxii. Ephes. ii. Rom. xi. Psal. cxlv.*

Fifthly, that God hath predestinated these thus elect unto everlasting life "in Christ," the apostle doth also in the words before written declare, in saying, "And hath predestinate us through Jesus Christ to be heirs unto himself." Again, "By *Election is to eternal life.*

[1 'them' 1562, 1564: not in MS.]

him," saith he, "you are made heirs and predestinate to the praise of his glory." So saith the apostle elsewhere, "Them whom he hath predestinate, he hath predestinate them to be like-fashioned unto the shape of his Son." And Christ therefore saith, "Rejoice in this, that your names are written in heaven."

Rom. viii.

Luke x.

Sixthly, that the end of election is "the praise of God's glory and grace," the apostle sheweth here in saying, We are predestinate to "be holy and without blame before God," &c.; in saying, We are "predestinate to the glory of his grace;" and in saying also, "To the laud of his glory:" so that nothing can be more manifest.

The end of election is the praise and glory of God.

Seventhly, that predestination is not without vocation in God's time and justification, the apostle here doth teach it, in bringing us to the consideration of hearing the word of truth, believing and receiving the Holy Spirit, of remission of sins, &c. "In whom," saith he, "you have hoped, after that you had heard the word of truth," &c.: again, "by whom you have redemption, that is, remission of sins through the shedding of his blood," &c.: item, he hath in his full time "declared the mystery of his will," &c. Unto the Romans the apostle there sheweth it most manifestly, in saying, "Whom he hath predestinate, them he calleth; whom he calleth, them he justifieth:" whereby we may see that predestination nor election is not universal of all, for all be not justified.

Election is not without vocation and justification in time.

Rom. viii.

Eighthly and last of all, that election is so certain that the elect and predestinate to eternal life shall never finally perish or err to damnation finally, the apostle doth here also very plainly shew, in saying that they are "predestinate to the praise of God's grace." He saith not, to the praise of his justice, to the praise of his wisdom, to the praise of his power, although he might most truly say so; but he saith, "to the praise of his grace:" which were "not grace if there were respect at all of works" on our behalf, for then "were grace no grace."

Election is certain for ever.

Rom. xi.

If there should be any condemnation of the elect and predestinate to eternal life, it must needs be because of their sins: but where were "the praise of God's grace" then, which is the end of God's election? Shall we not by this means make God's election without an end, and so without a

Note.

head, and so no election at all (as[1] some would have) further than[1] they elect themselves? Let such fear they shall not find the benefit of God's election, because they seek it as the Israelites sought it, and not as the elect, which not only found it but also obtained it. The other are blinded, as it is written, "God hath given them the spirit of unquietness, ears that they should not hear, eyes that they should not see, even unto this day," &c.

Rom. xi.
[Isai. xxix. 10.]
Psal. lxix.

Again he sheweth the certainty of salvation to them that be elected, in saying that they be "accepted in the Beloved;" once accepted and beloved in Christ, and ever beloved: so whom he loveth, "he loveth to the end," and "God's gifts are such that he cannot repent him of them." And therefore saith Christ, "I know whom I have chosen," attributing to election the cause of final perseverance. By which thing Judas was seen not to be elected to eternal life, although he was elected to the office of an apostle, as Saul was elected to the office of a king: which kind of election is to be discerned in reading the scriptures from this kind of election I speak of now, that is, from election to eternal life "in Christ."

Note.

John xiii.
Rom. xi.

John xiii.

Two kinds of election.

Thirdly he sheweth the certainty of the salvation of the elected, by calling them "heirs[2] with Christ," to be both afflicted and glorified with Christ; and therefore saith, "according to the decree of his own will." Lo, he calleth it a[3] decree or counsel, which shall stand, as Esay saith, "The counsel of the Lord shall stand."

Rom. viii.

Isai. xlvi.

Fourthly he sheweth this certainty, by saying that they are "elect and predestinate to the praise of God's glory:" which we should more care for, than for the salvation of all the whole world. This "glory of the Lord" is set forth, as well in them that perish and are reprobates, as in the elect. And therefore St John, bringing in the place of Esay, speaking of the reprobate[4], saith that "Esay spake that, when he saw the glory of the Lord." This "glory of the Lord" to be set forth by us is a great mercy and benefit of God. I am assured, that if the very devils and reprobates did not repine

Note well.

John xii.
Isai. vi.

[1 'and,' 'that,' MS.: 'as,' 'than,' 1562, 1564.]
[2 'heirs,' and 'fellow-heirs,' 1562, 1564. 'heirs. For if we be heirs of God, then are we fellow-heirs with Christ,' 1562.]
[3 'a' 1562, 1564, not in MS.]
[4 'speaking of the reprobate' 1562, 1564: not in MS.]

thereat, but were thankful that they might be ministers in any point to set forth God's glory; I am assured, I say, that they should find no hell nor torments: their hell and torments cometh of the love they have to themselves, and of the malice, envy, and hatred they have against God and his glory.

Let them tremble and shake, that may not away with[1] the glory of the Lord in election and reprobation. Let not their eyes be evil, because God is good, and doth good to whom it pleaseth him: wrong he doth to no man, nor can do; for then were he not righteous, and so no God. He cannot condemn the just, for then were he untrue, because his word is contrary. He cannot condemn the penitent and believer, for that were against his promise.

Let us therefore labour, study, cry, and pray for[2] repentance and faith; and then cannot we be damned, because we are the "blessed of the Father" before all worlds: and therefore we believe, therefore we repent[3]. This, I say, let us do, and not be too busy-bodies in searching the majesty and glory of God, or in nourishing doubting of salvation: whereto we all are ready enough, and the devil goeth about nothing else so much as that; for by it we are dull to do good to others, we are so careful for ourselves that by it we are more dull to do good to ourselves, because we stand in

Matt. xx. Exod. xxxii.

Rom. ix.

Matt. xxv.

Whereabout the devil laboureth most.

[1 'Away with:' bear. So in the authorised version of Isai. i. 13, "the calling of assemblies I cannot away with."]

[2 'for the,' MS.: 'for' 1562, 1564.]

[3 The following passage occurs in this place in the editions of 1562 and 1564, but in the Bodley MS. not here, but in the second part of this Treatise at p. 327, l. 35, and p. 324, l. 16, having evidently been transferred thither (with a few slight alterations) by Bradford.

"And forasmuch as it pertaineth to us 'which be within' to see and to speak of those things which are 'given unto us of God' in Christ; let us labour hereabouts, and leave 'them that be without' to the Lord which will 'judge them' in his time. The apostle prayeth for the Ephesians for none other 'wisdom and revelation' from God than whereby they might 'know God,' and have their 'minds illumined to see what they should hope for by their vocation, and how rich the glory of his inheritance is upon his saints.' Further than this, I think, is unseemly for us to search, until we have sought out how rich God's goodness is and will be to us his children: the which we can never do; but the more we go thereabouts, and the more we taste his goodness, the more we shall love him, and loath all things that displease him."]

1 Cor. v.

1 Cor. ii.

Ephes. i.
Col. ii.

doubt whether it profiteth us or not. By it we dishonour God, either making him as though he were not true, or else as though our salvation came not only from him and altogether, hanging partly on ourselves. By it the devil will bring men at the length to despair and hatred of God. Doubt once of thy salvation, and continue therein, and surely he then will ask no more. It was the first thing wherewith he tempted Christ: "If thou be the Son of God," &c. It is the first and principallest shaft he shooteth at "God's elect." Matt. iv.

But, as he prevailed not against Christ, no more sha'l he do against any of his members; for they have "the shield of faith, which quencheth his fiery darts." They "pray to God night and day:" how then should they perish? "The angels of the Lord pitch their tents round about them:" how then should Satan prevail? They are "borne in the hands of the angels, lest they should hurt their foot at any stone:" God hath given commandment to his angels over them: "the angels are ministers unto them." Their names are "written in the book of life:" and therefore Christ bade them "rejoice," as Paul doth the Philippians: for "nothing shall separate them from the love wherewith God loved them in Christ Jesu;" who saith that it is impossible for them to err finally to damnation, for he "is their Light" to "illumine their darkness." They are "given to him" to keep, and he is faithful over all God's church: he saith, he will keep them so that "they shall never perish." After they believe, they are entered into "everlasting life." Christ hath set them there already: he hath committed them into his Father's hands by prayer, which we know is sure. And therefore death, hell, devils, nor all power, sins, nor mischief, shall never pull us out of our Head's hands, whose "members" we are: and therefore "receiving of this Spirit," as we do, we cannot but "bring forth the fruits thereof," though now and then the flesh fail us. Ephes. vi. Luke xviii. Psal. xxxiv. Psal. xci. Heb. i. Luke x. Phil. iv. Rom. viii. Matt. xxiv. Psal. xviii. John vi. John x. Heb. ii. John v. vi. Eph. ii. John xvii. Hebr. v. Rom. viii. John x. 1 Cor. vi. 1 Cor. ii.

But the Lord our Lord be praised, which is "more strong in us than he which is in the world." He always putteth under his hands, that we lie not still, nor shall do as the reprobate whose piety is "as the morning dew," soon comen[4] and soon gone; and therefore they cannot continue to the end. Cannot? No, they will not if they could, because they hate 1 John iv. Psal. lxvi. Hos. vi. xiii.

[4 'Comen:' an old form of the participle, 'come.']

God and his glory, and therefore all them that seek it or set it forth: whereas the elect love all men, and seek to do all men good in God, suspending their judgments of others, that they may "stand or[1] fall" to the Lord, and not to them.

<small>Rom. xiv.</small>

Hitherto out of this one place to the Ephesians, if the matter of election and predestination be so fully set forth to God's glory and to the comfort of his church, how may we suppose is this matter set forth in the whole body and books of the canonical scripture? Whereto I had rather send thee, good reader, with this candle-light I have now given thee, than in a matter so manifest to make more ado than needeth.

[PART II.]

<small>Answer to the enormities gathered of election.</small>

Now will I go about to answer a calumnious calumniator which hath whet his tooths against the Lord and his grace set forth in predestination, as appeareth by a certain bill and libel he hath set abroad, entitled, "The enormities proceeding of the opinion, that predestination, calling, and election, is absolute in man as it is in God[2]."

<small>The words of the title of the libel.</small>

<small>The author of the libel is ignorant and malicious.</small>

In which his title he declareth his ignorance and malice: ignorance in ordering the cart before the horse; for else would he not have put calling before election, if he knew whereof he spake; but he is one of them, that Paul did prophesy of, that "would be doctors of the law, and yet they knew not whereof they affirm:" malicious[ness] in saying that which never man I think did affirm, namely, that election and predestination, which is in God, should be in man.

As for this word 'absolute,' I dare well say, if he were apposed to declare the signification thereof, he would either by silence seem to be sage, or else be speaking under his ignorance.

[1 'and,' MS.: 'or,' 1562.]

[2 It is not unlikely that this controversial piece, of which Bradford observes at p. 309 above, that he has 'not left out one tittle of every word' as the author 'had put it abroad,' may have been written by Henry Hart, then a leader among those called 'free-willers.' It must have been penned before October 11, 1554, the date of Bradford's reply. The statement of Trewe (which also recounts many 'enormities') was written, January 1, 1555. See prefatory note, p. 305—6, and p. 310, l. 14, above.]

But let us look on the enormities that he reciteth.

"The first is," saith he, "that God's justice is general over all men, but his mercy is not so: and yet the Holy Ghost saith, 'The Lord is loving to every man, and his mercy over all his works;' and again by St. John, that Christ is 'the true Light that lighteneth every man that cometh into the world.'" *The first gathered and set forth in the libel.*

These be the words: wherein a man may easily see he hath not learned his A B C concerning the scriptures, or else his judgment could not be so base. For either he would have all men saved and none damned, by extending so God's mercy; or else he must put some degrees in God's mercy concerning his being, and concerning that he is God's creature; so that God's justice is not so general as his mercy, taking justice for that justice wherewith he is just himself, and punisheth that correspondeth not thereto. For this the elect of God feel not finally, because Christ felt it, bare it, and satisfied it, for us; as the devil and damned felt not the mercy and justice of God wherewith he justifieth his children and elect: to whom he "sheweth his mercy" because it pleaseth him, and "hardeneth the heart of others whom he will," as saith Paul. Which "will of God" were good for no creature to call into account. *That is not our part to dispute whether God's mercy or justice be greater: it is enough to know that he sheweth mercy to whom he will, and that it is righteous, whatsoever he willeth. Whether God condemn more through his justice, or save more through his mercy, pertaineth little to us to search; and much less to set him a limit, as this man doth, lest he seem more righteous than merciful, or contrariwise. Rom. i.*

As for that other text of Christ "lightening all men that cometh into the world," if he do understand it of the general lightening of men, that is, of so much light as may make men "excuseless," then it agreeth with Paul; and this all good men affirm: but if he understand it of the peculiar light given only to the elect, then it is against Christ, which "thanketh his Father for hiding it" from many, and telleth his disciples, that "it was given to them and not to others." *Matt. xi.*

Matt. xiii.

So that a man may see all blindness and lack of light in him; or else would he have written either more substantially, or else have kept silence till he had been better learned.

"The second," saith he, "is, that the virtue of Christ's blood doth not, neither can, extend to all people: and yet the Holy Ghost saith, that Christ 'by the grace of God should taste of death for all men;' and by St. John he saith, he came 'not for our sins only, but for the sins of all the world.' Likewise saith Christ, 'The bread that I will give for the life of the world;' and again by St. John, 'God sent not his Son into the world to condemn the world, but that the world through him might be saved.'" *The second enormity. Heb. ii. 1 John ii. John vi. John iii. Rom. xi. John iv. 1 Pet. ii. iii. 1 Tim. ii. 1 Cor. viii.*

These be the words as he hath written, word for word; *The answer.*

wherein he hath done untruly to recite St John's words, which be that Christ obtained grace "for the sins of the whole world," and not 'came for the sins of the world.' By this his untruth in reciting the word a man may see, that he goeth about to slander the doctrine of God's election, which crampeth not in Christ's blood, but extendeth it to the whole "church" and to every "member" thereof: but he would have it to devils also, and to all his bastards; for the devil, being "prince and god of this world," is one of the world, as the king of a realm is one of the realm. Now I ween he will be ashamed (however he thinketh) to extend the virtue of Christ's death to the devil, except he will admit the schoolmen's distinction of 'sufficiently' and 'effectually;' that is, that Christ's death is sufficient for all, but effectual to none but to the elect only: which distinction I desire him to admit. For I take "the whole world" there, as St John the Baptist doth in calling Christ "the Lamb of God which taketh away the sins of the world;" and as Paul doth in saying that "God hath reconciled the world in Christ:" which is to be discerned from that "world" for which Christ "prayed not;" for look, for whom he "prayed not," for them he died not.

This, I trust, is sufficient for the opening of the places in the second enormity he thought to have found out.

"The third is," saith he, "that there is no sin in man; for, if man have no choice, then the evil man doth that which God would have him to do, as well as the good man. But this is very false and ungodly, as the holy scripture doth declare. First, God said unto Cain, before he slew his brother, 'Why art thou angry, or wrathful, and why is thy countenance changed? Dost thou not know, if thou doest well thou shalt receive it; but if thou doest evil, lieth not the sin in the door? Unto thee pertaineth the lust thereof, that thou rule it, or have the dominion over it, &c.' Likewise Moses saith, 'I set before thee life and death, blessing and cursing:' therefore he saith to the people, 'Choose ye life, that thou and thy son may live, &c.'"

These be the words of his third enormity, wherein he writeth he wotteth not what. For, if the cause why there is no sin in man be want of choice, as he maketh it, then children have no sin: and so this man "returneth to his old vomit," to deny original sin in very deed, although in words he will seem to say otherwise. Again, he playeth the papist in attributing free-will and choice, which utterly destroyeth the justification by faith only, by God's own mercy and goodness. Thirdly, he maketh no difference in doing God's will, howsoever it be done: and therefore saith he, that 'the wicked man doth that which God will have done as well as the good man.'

But perchance he will say this word 'as well' is not comparatively, but by the way of a similitude, spoken. Well, I am content to admit it at his hands; because ignorance maketh him to speak improperly. This would I ask him, whether that David said truth, namely, that "God doeth all things in heaven and earth as pleaseth him." If this be true, I would advise him to be less curious to know the working of God, farther than he hath given us a light to see the same. God useth the wicked to work his will in working their own, as Nebuchodonosar in destroying Jerusalem, the devils in running "into the herd of swine:" and yet God is not the author and cause of sin. To be the author of any act, is not to be the author of the evil will that doth the act; as the magistrate may be the author that an executor putteth to death one justly condemned: and yet the executor may put the condemned person to death of a desire of vengeance, wherein he sinneth; and the magistrate which causeth the fact is not to be blamed of the sin committed of the executor. *[Psal. cxv.]* *[God worketh not sins in us, but uttereth[1] the sins which we have by the corruption of our nature, and which lie hidden in us, when and where and how it pleaseth God.]*

As for the testimonies of the scriptures, which he bringeth for free-will, a child of two years reading in the scriptures may see that they be legal sentences, and prove not that man can do as they require, but telleth man as the law doth, what he ought to do: as when Christ saith, "If thou wilt enter into life, keep the commandments;" teaching hereby not what man can do, (for then we had no need of Christ,) but what man ought to do; that by this means, in seeing his own penury and inability, he might be desirous of "the grace of God," and the free promise of God's gospel offered and given unto him.

"The fourth enormity is," saith he, "that God's power and omnipotence is thereby denied, in that it is said, that he cannot know first, predestinate, and elect all men in Christ Jesu to salvation, and also to give the choice during this life, as he hath said. And yet, as saith St. John, he is 'Almighty:' and Paul saith likewise, he is 'King of kings, and Lord of lords, which only hath immortality, and dwelleth in light that no man can attain unto,' &c.: and again to the Romans he saith, 'O the depth of the abundant wisdom and knowledge of God: how unsearchable are his judgments, and his ways past finding out!'" *[The fourth enormity.]* *[Rev. xvi. 1 Tim. vi. Ephes. iii.]* *[Rom. xi.]*

These be the words he reciteth for 'the fourth enormity,' *[An answer.]*

[[1] 'Uttereth:' maketh manifest, bringeth out.]

The author of the libel playeth like a papist.

even as he reciteth them; wherein he playeth even as the papists do concerning transubstantiation. For [the] question is there, whether God will transubstantiate the bread into his body, and not whether he can: so here the question is, whether God would elect all men, (where Christ saith, 'few be but elect,') or no. But, as the papists say, 'God can do this, and therefore ye deny God's power;' so doth this man reason papistically, as a mongrel papist in heart, that because God could have chosen all in Christ, therefore he did so.

Matt. xx.

God cannot save Satan, because he will not.

Again he maketh no difference between knowledge, foresight, predestination, and election: and so belike the angels that fell, whose fall God did foresee, were "elect angels;" where Paul seemeth to attribute to the angels not fallen election, as the cause why they fell not. If any will dispute with God, why he would do so to those and not to the other, I will say nothing but as Paul saith, "O man, what art thou that disputest with God?"

1 Tim. v.

Rom. ix.

Thirdly, in saying God hath given Christ to man, as he hath said, and telleth not where, nor what, a man may perceive the subtle kind of speech smelleth of sophistry and deceitfulness; and therefore his scriptures brought forth they are as hosen for no leg to put them on, making for no purpose except to prove God to be almighty, which no man denieth, except it be himself, as far as I know: except he dream that God knoweth a thing and knoweth it not, seeth a thing and seeth it not, by attributing of the choice to man, whereupon God's knowledge and sight, God's election and predestination, doth depend, lest it should come of God's own good will or be "to the glory of his grace;" and so salvation not to come from God only, yea, to be no God!

The author of the libel writeth sophistically. See, good reader, how this man may not abide God to have any determination in himself, but must have all in suspense till he see what we will do: and could he determine nothing before the beginning of the world, nor at this present, certainly, but conditionally, for he must discern of our wills.

O the deepness of man's foolishness, which will go about to comprehend "God's unsearchable ways" and wisdom!

The fifth enormity.

"The fifth enormity is," saith he, "that it thus putteth away the covenant between God and man; yea, partly on God's part, in that Christ is denied to be a general Saviour to all men; but wholly and altogether on man's part; for it taketh all the power and ableness, which God hath before given, from him. Nevertheless the Holy Ghost saith that 'God called Adam,' in whom then were all men; and they were then called in him, and came also to God; and he then made the covenant to us, as well as to him, in Christ, and gave him likewise unto us in promise also, saying 'that the seed of the woman,' which was Christ,

Gen. iii.

'should tread down the head of the serpent.' And afterwards God renewed the same covenant again to Abraham, saying, 'In thy seed shall all the generations of the earth be blessed.' Likewise Paul proveth the same, saying, 'Not in thy seeds, as in many; but in thy seed, as in one, which is Christ.' That no man is lost of God, as the Holy Ghost approveth, if they come to destruction wholly and clearly ignorant, the conditional promise made of the Lord to the people by Moses doth declare. Likewise was the covenant made by God to Jeroboam, as to David; and also the parable of the 'talents' 'delivered to the servants to every man after his ability:' and St. Luke saith that they were bidden to 'occupy the same, until the Lord come;' but if there be some that have nothing, &c., small occupying will serve them, and their account will soon be made. But our Saviour Christ hath taught, not only before the people, but also before the scribes and Pharisees, that every man should answer for that they have received, and render a just account; and that, by the parable of the lost sheep and the groat, they ought as well to have sought that which was lost, as to save that which was not lost: and by the 'two sons unto whom the father gave his goods,' he taught them also, though they judged of themselves to be right, yet they ought to have 'rejoiced, and to be glad for their brother, which was lost, and is found, was dead, and is alive.'"

Gal. iii.
Psal. civ.
Deut. xxviii.
1 Kings xi.
Matt. xxv.
Luke xix. xvi.

These be the words which he recited in 'the fifth enormity,' whereunto in the margin is put this note, that 'the dead was made alive, the lost was found;' whereby he thinketh he toucheth the quick, as though any body doth deny that all that be born of the seed of man are not "dead in sin," and "conceived in iniquity;" only he excepted, which denieth the original sin otherwise than Adam's offence simply considered, without any guiltiness in ourselves: and all this is to establish his doctrine of free-will, wherein he fully consenteth with the Jews, Mahomets, and papists.

Psal. li.

The author of the libel agreeth in free-will with the Jews, Turks, and papists.

But let us see his reasons: first see an impudent lie. 'Christ is denied,' saith he, 'to be a general Saviour to all men.' Who denieth this? 'Marry that do you,' will he say, 'because none shall be saved but the elect.' *Ergo* you mean by 'a general Saviour' to have all men saved. I pray you, take the devil also; and then a man shall more plainly perceive what you go about. For, rather than you will have them that be saved to be saved only of "the goodness of God," "freely of his grace," without man's work, you will go about with your generalities to save devils and all: such absurdities must need spring when men be offended at "the grace of God."

The author of the libel is found to be a liar.

The author of the libel seemeth by the stretching out of God's mercy generally to save the devil and all.

21—2

But perchance he will say, that he meaneth by 'a general Saviour' such a Saviour as is able to save "all men," and "would have all men saved," so that the cause of damnation is of themselves. If his meaning be this, let him shew, if he can, that any man hath spoken otherwise, but that the Lord himself "would have all men saved;" and that damnation cometh of ourselves, as the prophet saith.

'Why then' will he say, 'if God "will have all men saved," and damnation cometh of ourselves, then God hath not reprobate any or predestinate them to be damned: and where is election then of some, and not of all?'

To this I answer, that if we "have Christ's Spirit," we have received it to this end, that we should see what is "given to us of God" in Christ, as saith the apostle, and not what is given to the devil and to the reprobate: "these things," saith he, "we speak;" wherefore let us do the like. He prayeth for the Ephesians for none other "wisdom and revelation" from God, than whereby they might "know God," and have "their minds illumined to see what they shall hope by their vocation, and how rich the glory of his inheritance is to his saints." As for reprobation, and what mercy God offereth to them and their sire Satan, I think is unseemly for us to seek out, until we have sought out how rich God's goodness is and will be to us his children; the which we can never do, but the more we go thereabouts, and the more we taste his goodness, the more we shall love him, and loath all things that displeaseth him: whereas to dispute of Satan and the reprobate pertaineth nothing unto us, and therefore is to be omitted of us.

Again, how it is that God "would have all men saved," and yet "whom he will he maketh hard-hearted," and also "sheweth mercy on whom he will," I will be content to leave it till I shall see it in another life; where no contradiction shall be seen to be in God's will, which "would have all men saved," and yet "worketh all that he will both in heaven and in earth." As no man can "resist his will," so let no man search it further than he revealeth it: and God is but partly known of man in this life; so is his will in some things but partly known: in some things, I say, out of the which I except election, for the certainty thereof; for there is almost not two leaves in all the Testament, that doth not most sweetly insinuate or plainly shew the same. Yea, faith that is not certain of salvation from God, and that for ever, but doubteth of it, is either a weak faith, or else but a shew of faith.

"Lord, increase our faith."

If therefore we cannot tie these two together, that God "would have all men saved," and yet "his will is done," and cannot be withstood, but unto reason there must be some contradiction; yet let faith honour God, that his will is "just" and not mutable, (though his works are now and then altered,) how far soever otherwise it seem to "the flesh:" albeit to him that is not curious and contentious, the place how " God would have all men saved," and how God "will not the death of a sinner," is and may be well understand of penitent men and sinners; for else they that be impenitent God will damn. *Yea, when the scripture saith that God will have all men saved, it speaketh either of all the elects, or of men of all sorts, states, and conditions.*

Then now to know whose gift repentance is, I trust the scripture is so plain to shew it to be "God's gift," that no man will deny it. Again, that this repentance God giveth to whom he will, I need not to declare. Who they be that have this gift, are easily seen to be none others but such as be God's elect children and sons: as the parable telleth of the "lost son" that returned, not the lost servant; the "lost sheep" was found, not the lost swine; the "lost groat," wherein was printed the image and inscription of the prince, was found, not the lost plate. *Acts v. xi. xx. 2 Tim. ii.*

As for the argument which might be gathered of the contraries, 'If there be not reprobation, *ergo* there is no election,' a man of God may see it is not firm. For, though we may well say, and most justly say, that damnation is for our sins; yet can we not say that for our virtue we are saved: even so, because God hath elected some whom it pleaseth him, (as Christ saith, "few be chosen,") it doth not well follow that therefore he hath reprobated others, but to our reasons, except the scriptures do teach it. And in that the scriptures speak little thereof, (I mean of reprobation,) in that the next cause (that is sin) may well be seen to be the cause of condemnation, and in that also it pertaineth to us to see and speak of that which is given of Christ to us "that be within;" let us labour hereabouts, and leave "them that be without" to the Lord which will "judge them" in his time. *Arguments of contraries are not all very firm. A man may slay himself, but he cannot quicken himself. 1 Cor. v.*

Thus much I thought good to write hereabouts, that all *They that travail the* men might see that it is but curiosity that causeth men to travail the sweet doctrine of God's election; and that men might see how unjustly these 'enormities' are gathered of him that gathered them.

doctrine of election are curious.

Note.

God open his eyes according to his pleasure, and send him the same "good Spirit" in Christ I wish to myself! For I am sorry to write so sore against him as I do, if that the matter might suffer to do otherwise.

But to come again to his 'enormities.' 'It putteth away,' saith he, 'the covenant of God, partly on God's part, but wholly on man's part: on God's part,' saith he, 'because Christ is denied to be a general Saviour.' But here you see he hath spoken, and slandered the doctrine, untruly.

Let us see therefore, secondly, how truly he writeth that election putteth away the covenant on man's behalf wholly; 'for it taketh away,' saith he, 'the power and holiness[1], which God hath before given, from him.' This is the reason he maketh: wherein he is dark in these words 'from him,' to whom this 'him' is to be referred. Truth is plain and simple, but untruth must be obscured with ambiguous phrases, lest it should be espied.

The author of the libel is obscure.

But to let it pass, let 'him' be referred to whom it pleaseth him, God or man. This would I have him to do, namely, to set forth the power man hath now in this state to do God's will as God would have it done. Paul taketh from man the "thought," which is the best part of any good work: as for the "consent and deed," elsewhere he taketh it from man and giveth it to God. But this man will both give and take: I mean, he will both give it to God and to man also. In which doing I purpose to leave him, and to follow Paul, giving all to God, "thought," "will, and deed," in all that good is.

2 Cor. iii.

Phil. ii.

But, to confirm his doctrine, he thirdly saith, that 'as God called in Adam all men, so all men came in Adam unto him, whereupon he made the covenant.' First, here you must prove that 'all men came in Adam.' Yea, I read not that, Adam being called, he himself did come, much less all in him. Again, God's covenant, whose ground is his "mercy and truth," he maketh now our coming: so greatly doth he impugn

[[1] 'holiness,' MS. This seems an error of the early transcriber, for 'ableness;' see line 4 of the extract, p. 322 above.]

the mercy and "goodness of God." I pray God he do it of ignorance, for else greater is his sin. Moreover he discerneth not between the free promise and covenant; for else he would not call the free promise a 'covenant,' but on God's behalf only. For what is required here on man's behalf, if he have respect to infants and children which cannot believe? Besides this he confoundeth the covenants, as appeareth by his testimonies and examples. The covenant to David and Jeroboam were not alike, as a child can tell, that readeth the books of the Kings.

As for this that he writeth, that no man is 'lost' of God, I think it should be read 'left' of God, for else there were no reason in it; as there is little godly reason in it, being so taken, that is, 'left of God,' if any man discern between the promise of the law and the promise of the gospel, or if any man doth know wherefore the law is given. Whereof in that he is ignorant the reason, he heapeth up testimony upon testimony without rhyme or reason: and therefore I will do as Solomon willeth me, "not to answer a fool according to his foolishness, lest I should be like him." For godly wisdom and spiritual eyes would see, that as God's pure image at the first was given to Adam and in him unto us, so as he was guilty of the loss and corruption of the same, so we are in like manner until we be regenerate: and therefore God is not unjust in calling us all to account even therefor. Howbeit, who is he that in this life hath not, yea, daily doth not receive great gifts of God? For the which all shall render an account but such as shall not come into judgment, even true believers in Christ: which only are the 'lost and dead children found again,' through God's own mercy "in Christ." *Prov. xxvi.*

"The sixth enormity is this," saith he, "that it colourably denieth excommunication to be had and used in the congregation of Christ; for such as they call good they say are predestinate, and those that they call evil may (some say of them) be called: now how they be, nor when they shall be called, say they, that it cannot be known. For, although they say that predestination is absolute as well towards man, as it is in God himself, which indeed is not true; yet it is not known to any other, but only to them that can so think, or rather imagine: which indeed is called a strong faith in many; but, when the inward eyes of them are truly opened, it will appear either here, or in another place, where it will not be so easy to help a very vain and naughty opinion." *The sixth enormity.*

These be the words of the last 'enormity,' which words are so either ignorantly or untruly written, or both, (for I have written them word for word after the copy delivered to me, as God knoweth I lie not,) that the sentences hang not together, or else there wanteth words to make sentences.

The author of the libel is used to lie.

Howbeit, this is easy to be seen, that as before, so now, the truth is belied; for predestination denieth not 'excommunication,' or hindereth the good use thereof. Yea, this withal I say, that no man can use more godly discipline towards themselves, and to the correcting and chastening of "the old man," than those do which have truly tasted of the Spirit of God's election: for to such the corruption of our nature is felt a more horrible thing than hypocrites are able to think; and therefore they are more rough and severe to others which are fallen, than the elect be, who have "put on them bowels of mercies," and cannot but take other men's faults to heart as their own. And therefore, so soon as any lively sign of repentance ensueth, they seek with Paul that "charity" might prevail, where hypocrites are haut[1] and contemn the poor publicans, as did the proud Pharisee.

Nothing letteth the predestinate to be punished of us as sinners, when they sin; for God useth often this mean to bring them to repentance.

Col. iii.

Again, indeed we say, that none is good but such as be predestinate; and also we say, that of those which be now in our sight evil many may be called hereafter, and as God's dear elect declare themselves to the world and wicked, if they would see it.

2 Tim. ii.

As for who be the elect and who be not, because it is God's privilege to know who be his, God's people are not curious in others: but, as in themselves they feel "the earnest" of the Lord, and have God's Spirit in possession by faith, (I speak of those which be of years of discretion;) so do they judge of others by their works, and not further do they enter with God's office.

2 Cor. i. Ephes. i.

Moreover where he saith, 'predestination is not absolute,' if he meaneth it is not infallible, or it is not so certain but it may alter, then when he hath proved it by scripture, a man may something be moved to mark better his words: but till that time, which will never be, I will say that, if God predestinate any to life, they shall never be undone.

As for his surmised imagination of election in the elect,

[1 See p. 183, note 1, above.]

whereby he taunts their faith, I will speak nothing but, God *The author of the libel is a taunter.* increase his and all our faith, and open our eyes to see what true faith is! Whereof for my part I acknowledge a great weakness, and much more imagination than true faith: but yet, be it never so little, I hope the Lord alloweth it and will increase it for his name's sake, which I humbly crave at his hands 'for the love of our only blessed Saviour Jesus Christ,' "the Light of the world:" who "lighten all our darkness" to *John i. Psal. xviii.* see his "true light," and inflame our hearts and wills to ap- *Psal. xxvii.* prove and love the same unfeignedly! Amen.

Then will taunting not tarry, but charitable admonition and sorrowful sighing to see any professing God with us, entangled with such errors as nourish such 'enormities,' as here he maketh this most comfortable and profitable doctrine of God's holy election: for the which God's holy name be praised and magnified for ever, through Jesus Christ our blessed Lord and Saviour. Amen.

Now, to conclude, he writeth this:

"Whether these be good matters to be had, taught, and holden of *The conclusion of the libel.* such as think themselves not only true and right Christians, and the very 'sons of God,' but also to be masters and teachers in the church of Christ; I appeal to the judgment of the Spirit of God, and to all men that have true judgment."

These words I will not otherwise traverse, but that all *An answer to the conclusion.* men may see that every 'enormity' gathered by this man is of "a zeal not according to knowledge," (I will say no worse;) as thou mayest well perceive, if thou wilt mark well what I have written briefly concerning the doctrine of God's election, by the scriptures: to the which (the scriptures, I mean) I with *The author writeth anabaptistically, in applying to the Spirit without the scriptures.* Christ and his apostles do appeal, and not anabaptistically to the Spirit without the scriptures, as he doth.

By the scriptures, I say, there I have briefly and sufficiently so proved the doctrine of election taught and holden by me, that doing right to God's word he cannot be able to improve[2] it, if he shall take to help him herein the Jew's talmud, the Mahomet's alcoran, and the papist's decretals to help him, (for with them he plainly agreeth in this matter of election and free-will,) after that he hath put his name[3] to his

[2 'Improve:' disprove.]
[3 See p. 318, note 2, above.]

libel: which I suppress yet, because I have hope he shall see his own ignorance and blind zeal and arrogancy. Which God grant for his mercies sake!

There is one which hath written this that followeth:

<small>*An addition to the libel.*</small> "Other some would be satisfied, how that God's elect people are so 'elected from the beginning' in Christ that they cannot utterly fall away, and yet all men, they say, fell to damnation in Adam; and how that his mercy in saving his, and his justice in condemning his, could be at one instant with God."

<small>*An answer to the addition. The author of the addition is curious and very ignorant. All men were damned in Adam; and yet God chose some of that damned mass to be saved. What absurdity is herein! for no men say that all men were so damned that none might be saved through God's goodness: and the author of this addition taketh every damnation for final damnation. If they cannot imagine how God can do these things at once, they will deny him either to be God, or to be perfect, or to do any thing perfectly.*</small> These words first shew curious heads, as you may perceive by their 'hows:' secondly they shew ignorant persons, as may appear by their style and words improperly placed: therefore I stand in a doubt whether they understand what they demand. For they make variety of time with God, and will have instants with him, with whom there is no time but eternity. Again, they follow not God's word, but will look upon that first which hath his occasion of that which followeth: that is to say, they will look upon election afore they look on Adam's fall: and yet God did not open it to us but sithen the fall. Which order we should follow, and be no more offended therewith than we are at Christ, which was, and is called, "the Lamb slain from the beginning of the world," and tofore Adam's fall; and yet he had not died but in respect of the fall.

But they, because they cannot by their curious reason see how election should be before with God, and yet follow Adam's fall to us, therefore they come with their witless, unreasonable, arrogant, and very detestable 'hows.' I marvel they ask not how God did before he had any creature: else would they leave their witless, unreasonable, arrogant, and very detestable 'hows,' and come to know that the scripture descendeth to our capacities as much as may be in many things, that we might rest by faith to the consideration and admiration of God his power, wisdom, and glory.

Which he make us all careful for, as his dear children, and to live accordingly now and for ever. Amen.

J. B.

[The Treatise 'Against the fear of death' observes the text of the Meditations, &c. of Bradford, Seres 1567[1], except where otherwise noted.

It is to be found also in MS. Bodl. 53. in the Bodleian Library, Oxford; with which the printed edition of 1567 has been collated throughout: but the variations are only noted where a deviation from 1567 is followed.

It would seem likely from the words at the third line of this Treatise, p. 332, 'at whose door [that is, of death] though I have stand a great while, yet never so near (to man's judgment) as I do now;' that Bradford wrote it shortly after his condemnation, which took place January 31, 1555; after which his martyrdom was daily expected. The actual date of his death was July 1, 1555[2].

A Latin translation of this Treatise exists in MS. (119. article 14.) in the Lansdown collection in the British Museum. It is entitled, *Institutio divina et vere consolatoria contra vim mortis, Johanne Bradfordo Anglo authore, ex vernacula lingua in Latinum sermonem conversa.* This MS. formerly belonged to the church-historian, Strype, who supposed that the 'Treatise on death' was rendered into Latin by some of the English divines when abroad, during the reign of Mary, for their use and comfort[3].

Portions of this Latin version are supplied in the Appendix to this volume.]

[1] See p. 112 and 294, and black letter title, p. 296 above.]

[2] Vide Foxe, Acts, &c. 1583, calendar, July; or ed. 1843—8, vol. I. ibid.; Diary of Henry Machyn, under July 1, 1555, p. 90—1, Camden Soc. 1848; Strype, Mem. III. i. 355.]

[3] Strype, Mem. III. i. 364.]

A FRUITFUL TREATISE,

AND FULL OF HEAVENLY CONSOLATION,

AGAINST THE FEAR OF DEATH.

[See Vulgate.] "Make no tarrying to turn unto the Lord, and put not off from day to day; for suddenly shall his wrath come, and in the day of vengeance he shall destroy thee. Stand fast in the way of the Lord, be stedfast in thine understanding, and follow the word of peace and righteousness." Ecclesiasticus v.[1]

2 Tim. i.

John v.

BEING minded through the help of God, for mine own comfort and encouraging of others, to speak something of Death, (at whose door though I have stand a great while, yet never so near, to man's judgment, as I do now[2],) I think it most requisite to call and cry for thy help, O blessed Saviour Jesus Christ, "which hast destroyed death" by thy death, and brought in place thereof "life and immortality," as by the gospel it appeareth. Grant to me true and lively faith, wherethrough men pass from death to "eternal life;" that of practice, and not of naked speculation, I may something now write concerning Death, (which is dreadful out of thee, and in itself,) to the glory of thy holy name, to mine own comfort in thee, and to the edifying of all them to whom this my writing shall come to be read or heard. Amen.

Four kinds of death.

There be four kinds of death; one which is natural, another which is spiritual, a third which is temporal, and a fourth which is eternal. Concerning the first and the last, what they be I need not to declare: but the second and the third perchance of the simple (for whose sake especially I write) are not so soon espied.

Spiritual death, what it is.

By a 'spiritual death' therefore, I mean such a death as,

[1 The title of the Bodley MS. is, "*De morte.* A treatise not to fear death, J. B."]

[2 Vide prefatory note in the preceding page.]

the body living, the soul is "dead:" whereof the apostle maketh mention in speaking of widows, which "living daintily," being alive in body, "are dead" in soul. Thus you see what I mean by the 'spiritual death.'   1 Tim. v.

Now by a 'temporal death' I mean such a death, wherethrough the body and affections thereof are "mortified," that the spirit may live: of which kind of death the apostle speaketh in exhorting us to "kill our members."   Temporal death.

Col. iii.

And thus much of the kinds of death, wherein the judgment of the world is not to be approved: for it careth less for 'spiritual death' than for a 'natural death,' it esteemeth less 'eternal death' than 'temporal death;' or else would men leave sin, (which procureth both the one and the other, I mean 'spiritual and eternal death,') and choose temporally to die, that by 'natural death' they might enter into the full fruition and possession[3] of "eternal life:" which none can enjoy nor enter into, that here will not temporally die, that is, mortify their affections, and "crucify their lusts" and concupiscences; for by obeying them at the first "came death," as we may read, Genesis iii. If Eve had not obeyed her desire in eating the forbidden fruit, whereby she died spiritually, none of these kinds of death had ever come unto man, nor been known of us. Therefore (as I said) we must needs here temporally die, that is, mortify our affections, to escape the 'spiritual death,' and by 'natural death' not only escape 'eternal death' of soul and body, but also by it as by a door enter into "eternal life;" which Christ Jesus our Saviour hath procured and purchased to and for all that be "in him," translating 'eternal death' into a "sleep," or rather into a deliverance of soul and body from all kind of misery and sin.   The judgment of the world concerning the kinds of death is naught. [MS.]

Sin is the cause of death.

By what means death came into the world.

By reason whereof we may see, that to those that be "in Christ," that is, to such as do believe, which (believers, I mean) are discerned from others by "not walking after the flesh, but after the Spirit;" to those, I say, death is no damage but an advantage[4]; no dreadful thing but rather desirable, and of all messengers most merry, whiles he is looked upon with the eyes of faith in the gospel. But more of this hereafter.   Rom. viii.

[3 'and possession,' MS.: not in 1567.]
[4 'a vantage' 1567: 'an advantage,' MS.]

Thus have I briefly shewed thee the kinds of death, what they be, whence they come, and what remedy for them. But now, forasmuch as I am purposed hereafter to entreat only of the first kind of death, that is, of 'natural death,' something to comfort myself and others against the dread and pains of the same; I will speak of it as God shall instruct me, and as I accustom with myself to muse on it now and then, the better to be prepared against the hour of temptation.

Natural death.

I have shewed how that this 'natural death' came by 'spiritual death,' that is, by obeying our affections in the transgressions of God's precepts: but through the benefit of Christ, to such as be in him and die temporally, that is, to such believers as labour to mortify their affections, it is no destruction, but a plain dissolution both of soul and body from all kind of perils, dangers, and miseries; and therefore to such is not to be dread but to be desired, as we see in the apostle which "desired to be dissolved," and in Simeon which desired to be loosed, saying, "Dismiss (or loose) me, O Lord." By which words he seemeth plainly to teach that this life is a bondage, and nothing to be desired; as now I will something shew.

Death, what it is to Christians.

Phil. i.

Luke ii.

First, consider the pleasures of this life what they be, how long they last, how painfully we come by them, what they leave behind them; and thou shalt even in them see nothing but vanity. As for example, how long lasteth the pleasure that man hath in sensual gratification[1]? How painfully do men behave themselves before they attain it; how doth it leave behind it a certain loathsomeness and fulness! I will speak nothing of the sting of conscience, if it be come by unlawfully. Who, well seeing this and forecasting it aforehand, would not forego the pleasures willingly, as far as need will permit and suffer? If then in this one, whereunto nature is most prone, and hath most pleasure in, it be thus, alas! how can we but think so of other pleasures?

This life is not to be loved in respect of the pleasures thereof, being nothing else but vanity.

Put the case, that the pleasures of this life were permanent during this life: yet, in that this life itself is nothing in comparison, and therefore is full well compared to a candle-

[1 Two or three words of the original are changed.]

light which is soon blown out, to a flower which fadeth away, to a smoke, to a shadow, to a sleep, to a running water, to a day, to an hour, to a moment, and to vanity itself; who would esteem these pleasures and commodities, which last so little a while? Before they be begun, they are gone and past away. How much of our time spend we in sleeping, in eating, in drinking, and in talking! Infancy is not perceived, youth is shortly overblown, middle age is nothing, old age is not long. And therefore, as I said, this life, through the considerations of the pleasures and commodities of it, should little move us to love it, but rather to loath it. God open our eyes to see these things, and to weigh them accordingly! *What this life is, mark here and learn.*

Secondly, consider the miseries of this life, that, if so be the pleasures and commodities in it should move us to love it, yet the miseries might countervail, and make us to take it as we should do; I mean, rather to "desire to be loosed" and dismissed hence, than otherwise. Look upon your bodies, and see in how many perils and dangers you are: your eyes are in danger of blindness and blearedness; your ears in danger of deafness; your mouth and tongue of cankers, toothache, and dumbness; your head in danger of rheums and megrims; your throat in danger of hoarseness; your hands in danger of gouts and palsies, &c. But who is able to express the number of diseases whereto man's body is in danger, seeing that some have written that more than three hundred diseases may happen unto man? I speak nothing of the hurt that may come unto our bodies by prisons, venomous beasts, water, fire, horses, men, &c. *This life is more to be loathed for the miseries, than loved for the pleasures thereof. The miseries of this life concerning the body.*

Again, look upon your soul: see how many vices you are in danger of, as heresy, hypocrisy, idolatry, covetousness, idleness, security, envy, ambition, pride, &c. How many temptations may you fall into! But this shall you better see by looking on your old falls, folly, and temptations, and by looking on other men's faults; for no man hath done any thing so evil, but you may do the same. Moreover, look upon your name, and see how it is in danger to slanders and false reports; look upon your goods, see what danger they are in for thieves, for fire, &c.; look upon your wife, children, parents, brethren, sisters, kinsfolks, servants, friends, *The miseries of this life concerning the soul. By looking on our old falls and temptations, and other men's faults, we may see what danger we are always ready to fall into.*

Great and weighty causes for us to be sad and heavy, and little to joy in the pleasures of this life.

and neighbours, and behold how they also are in danger, both soul, body, name, and goods, as you are; look upon the commonweal and country; look upon the church, upon the ministers and magistrates, and see what great dangers they are in: so that, if you love them, you cannot but for the evil which may come to them be heavy and sad. You know it is not in your power, nor in the power of any man, to hinder all evil that may come. How many perils is infancy in danger of; what danger is youth subject unto! Man's state is full of cares: age is full of diseases and sores. If thou be rich, thy care is the greater: if thou be in honour, thy perils are the more: if thou be poor, thou art the more in danger to oppression. But, alas! what tongue is able to express the miserableness of this life? The which considered should make us little to love it.

An apt comparison between a ship on the sea and the life of man; for what dangers are so great; what so like?

I can compare our life to nothing so fitly as to a ship in the midst of the sea. In what danger is the ship and they that be in it! Here are they in danger of tempests, there of quicksands; on this side of pirates, on that side of rocks: now may it leak, now may the mast break, now may the master fall sick, now may diseases come among the mariners, now may there dissension fall among themselves. I speak nothing of want of fresh water, meat, drink, and such other necessaries.

Behold the great miseries and mischiefs that this life is in danger of on every side.

Even such another thing is this life. Here is the devil, there is the world: on this side is the flesh, on that side is sin which throughly cleaveth unto our ribs, and will do so long as we be in this flesh and natural life. So that none but blind men can see this life to be so much and so greatly to be desired: but rather, as the men that sail are most glad when they approach to the haven, even so should we be most glad when we approach to the haven, that is, death;

1 Cor. ii.

which setteth us a land whose commodities "no eye hath seen," no tongue can tell, no heart can conceive, in any point as it should. Happy, O happy were we, if we saw these things accordingly! God open our eyes to see them. Amen.

If any man would desire testimonies of these things, (although experience, a sufficient mistress, is to be credited,) yet will I here mark certain places whereunto the reader may resort, and find no less than I say, but rather much more, if that with diligence he read and weigh the places.

Job calleth this life "a warfare:" in the eighth chapter he painteth it out something lively, under divers similitudes. St James compareth it to "a vapour." All the book of Ecclesiastes teacheth it to be but "vanity." St John saith it is altogether "put in evil." David saith, the best thing in this life is but vanity, "labour, and sorrow." But what go I here about? seeing that almost every leaf in the scripture is full of the brevity and misery of this life. So that I think, as St Austin doth write, that there is no man that hath lived so happily in this world that would be content, when death cometh, to go back again by the same steps whereby he hath come into the world and lived[1]; except the same be in despair, and look for nothing after this life but confusion.

Job vii. [l. margin.]
James iv.
1 John v.
Psal. xc.
How short, transitory, and miserable, the life of man is, the scriptures do every where declare.

Thus I trust you see, that though the commodities of this life were such as could cause us to love it, yet the brevity, vanity, and misery of it is such as should make us little to regard it, which believe and know death to be the end of all miseries to them that are "in Christ:" as we all ought to take ourselves to be, being baptized in his name, (for our baptism requireth this faith under pain of damnation,) although we have not observed our profession as we should have done; if so be we now repent, and come to amendment. To such, I say, as are "in Christ," death is to be desired, even in respect of this, that it delivereth us from so miserable a life and so dangerous a state as we now be in. So that I may well say, they are senseless, without wit, void of love to God, void of all hatred and sense of sin (wherewith this life floweth), that rather desire not to depart hence out of all these miseries, than here still to remain to their continual grief; if that they have, as I said, any wisdom, any love to God or man, or any sense of sin[2].

The brevity, vanity, and misery, of this life should cause us little to regard it.

But if these things will not move us, I would yet we beheld the commodities whereunto death bringeth us. If we be not moved to leave this life in respect of the miseries whereof it is full, yet we should be moved to leave it in

1 Pet i.
Rev. vii.

[1 Quis autem non exhorreat, et mori eligat, si ei proponatur aut mors perpetienda, aut rursus infantia?—August. De Civit. Dei, XXI. xiv. Op. VII. col. 634, ed. Bened. Par. 1679—1700.]

[2 The last twenty words are in the MS., but not in 1567.]

[BRADFORD.]

respect of the infinite goodness which the other life, whereto death bringeth us, hath most plentifully. Men, though they love things, yet for things which are better can be content to forego them: even so we now, for the good things in the life to come (if we consider them), shall and will be content to forego the most commodious things in this present life.

Here we have great pleasure in the beauty of the world, and of the pleasures, honours, and dignities of the same; also in the company of our friends, parents, wife, children, subjects; also in plenty of riches, cattle, &c.: and yet we know that never a one of these is without his discommodity, which God sendeth, lest we should love them too much; as, if you will weigh things, you shall easily perceive. The sun, though it be fair and cheerful, yet it burneth sometimes too hot. The air, though it be light and pleasant, yet sometimes it is dark and troublous: and so of other things. But be it so that there were no discommodities mingled with the commodities; yet, as before I have said, the brevity and short time that we have to use them should assuage their dulcetness[1].

But if this were not also but that the pleasures of this life were without discommodity, permanent, and without peril (whereof they be full); yet are they nothing at all to be compared to the commodities of the life to come.

What is this earth, heaven, and shape of the world, wherein beasts have place, and wicked men, God's enemies, have abiding and liberty, in comparison of the "new heaven and earth wherein righteousness shall dwell?" in comparison of that place where angels and archangels, and all God's people, yea, God himself, hath his abiding and dwelling? What is the company of wife, children, &c., in comparison to the company of Abraham, Isaac, and Jacob, the patriarchs, prophets, apostles, martyrs, confessors, virgins, and all the saints of God[2]? What is the company of any in this world, in comparison to the company of the angels, archangels, cherubim, seraphim, powers, thrones, dominations; yea, of God the Father, God the Son, and God the Holy Ghost? What

[1 'Dulcetness:' sweetness.]

[2 Compare the eloquent passage often quoted from Cyprian. De Mortalit. Op. 166, Oxon. 1682: "Illic apostolorum transtulerunt."]

are the riches and pleasures of this life, in comparison of the felicity of everlasting life, which is without all discommodities, perpetual, without all peril and jeopardy, without all grief and molestation?

O the mirth and melody! O the honour and glory! O the riches and beauty! O the power and majesty! O the sweetness and dignity of the life to come! "The eye hath not seen, the ear hath not heard, nor the heart of man is not able to conceive" in any thing any part of the eternal felicity and happy state of heaven. Therefore the saints of God have desired so earnestly and so heartily to be there. *The blessed state of the life to come.* 1 Cor. ii.

"O how amiable are thy tabernacles!" saith David: "my soul hath a desire to enter into the courts of the Lord: my heart and my soul rejoice in the living God." "Blessed are those that dwell in thy house, that they may always be praising thee;" "for one day in thy courts is better than a thousand elsewhere. I had rather be a door-keeper in the house of my God, than to dwell in the tents of ungodliness; for the Lord God is a light and defence." And again, "As the hart desireth the water-brooks, so longeth my soul after thee, O God. My soul is athirst for God, yea, even for the living God: when shall I come to appear before the presence of God?" And, "My soul thirsteth for thee, my flesh also longeth after thee, in a barren and dry land, where no water is." *Psal. lxxxiv. The vehement desire and longing of God's saints to be dissolved and to be with God.* Psal. xlii. Psal. lxiii.

They (God's people I mean) desire the day of "their redemption:" and they still cry, "Let thy kingdom come:" they cry, "Come, Lord Jesus, come." They "lift up their heads," looking for his appearing, which will "make their vile bodies like to his own glorious (and immortal) body;" for, "when he shall appear, they shall be like unto him." *Rom. viii. Rev. xxii. Phil. iii.*

"The angels will gather them together;" and they "shall meet him in the clouds, and be always with him." They shall hear this joyful voice, "Come, ye blessed of my Father, possess the kingdom prepared for you from the beginning." *Matt. xxiv. 1 Thess. iv. Matt. xxv.*

Then shall they be "like unto his angels." Then shall they "shine like the sun in the kingdom." Then shall they have "crowns of glory," and be "endued with white garments" of innocency and righteousness, and "palms" of victory "in their hands." O happy, happy is he that may with *Rev. vii. The glory and felicity of God's* them see that immortal and incorruptible inheritance which then we shall enjoy for ever!

children in the kingdom of God.

Thus you see, I hope, sufficiently that in respect of heaven and eternal bliss, whereunto by the haven of death we land, this life, though there were no evil in it, is not to be loved; but rather we that be pilgrims in it should desire with Paul and Simeon to be "loosed and dissolved," that we might be with God.

Death the haven of eternal life.

Here our bodies (as before is spoken) are in danger of innumerable evils: but there our bodies shall be, not only without all danger, but also be "like the glorious (and immortal) body of the Lord Jesus Christ." Now our bodies be dark: then shall they be most clear and light, as we see Christ's "face did shine in his transfiguration, like to the sun." Now our bodies be vile, miserable, mortal, and corruptible: but then shall they be glorious, happy, immortal, and incorruptible. We shall be like unto Christ our Saviour: even "as he is," so shall we be. "As we have borne the image of the earthly, so shall we bear the image of the heavenly."

The miseries and dangers we pass, and the felicity we obtain by death. Phil. iii.

Matt. xiii. Dan. xii. Matt. xvii.

1 Cor. xv.

1 John iii.

1 Cor. xv.

Here our souls are in great darkness and dangers of many evils: but there they shall be in great light, safe security, and secure felicity. "We shall see God face to face:" where now we "see him but as in a glass through a dark speaking," there "shall we behold him even as he is," and be satisfied without loathsomeness of his presence. Yea, we shall be endued with most perfect knowledge: where "now we know but partly, there shall we know as we be known."

How foolish and senseless are they, which in respect of so glorious a state will not gladly forsake so miserable a life.

Here our commodities are measurable, short, uncertain, and mingled with many incommodities: but there is mirth without measure, all liberty, all light, all joy, rejoicing, pleasure, health, wealth, riches, glory, power, treasure, honour, triumph, comfort, solace, love, unity, peace, concord, wisdom, virtue, melody, meekness, felicity, beatitude, and all that ever can be wished or desired; and that in most security and perpetuity that may be conceived or thought, not only of men, but also of angels; as witnesseth he that saw it, I mean Paul, who was "carried up into the third heaven." "The eye hath not seen," saith he, "the ear hath not heard, neither hath entered into the heart of man, the felicity that God hath prepared for them that love him."

1 Cor. ii.

There the archangels, angels, powers, thrones, dominions, cherubim, seraphim, patriarchs, prophets, apostles, martyrs, virgins, confessors, and righteous spirits, cease not to sing night and day, "Holy, holy, holy Lord God of hosts!" *Rev. iv.* 'Honour, majesty, glory, impery, and dominion, be unto thee, O Lord God the Creator, O Lord Jesu the Redeemer, O Holy Spirit the Comforter[1]!' For "the light of the moon shall be as the light of the sun, and the light of the sun shall be seven-fold, even as the light of seven days," in his blessed kingdom, where and when he "will bind up the wounds of his people, and heal their plagues." *Isai. xxx.*

The clarity and brightness of God's children in his kingdom above the seven-fold brightness of the sun.

O that we might have some lively sight hereof, that we might rejoice over the "undefiled and immortal inheritance," whereunto God hath called us, and which he doth keep for us in heaven! that we might hear the sweet song of his saved people, crying, "Salvation be unto him that sitteth on the throne of our God, and unto the Lamb!" that we might with the elders and angels sing and say, "Praise, and glory, and wisdom, and thanksgiving, and honour, and power, and might, be to thee our God for evermore!" that we might be "covered with a white stole[2], and have a palm in our hands," to "stand before God's throne night and day, to serve him in his temple, and to have him dwell in us!" that we might "hear the great voice saying from heaven, Behold the tabernacle of the Lord is with men, and he will dwell with them, and they shall be his people, and God himself will be with them, their God!" O happy were they that now might have a little shew of that "holy city, new Jerusalem, descending from heaven, prepared of God as a bride decked for her husband," which he shewed to his servant John! Truly this should we see, if we were with him "in the Spirit:" but this cannot be, so long as we are "in the flesh." *Rev. xxi.* *Rev. xxi.*

Alas then and welaway[3], that we love this life as we do! It is a sign we have "little faith;" for else how could we but night and day desire the messenger of the Lord (death I

Lack of faith is the cause why we do so little desire to be out of this sinful life.

[[1] The last two pages occur, in part, in the meditation on the 'felicity of the life to come,' p. 273—5 above.]

[[2] See 'prayer for the presence of God,' p. 264—6 above, and p. 266, note 1.]

[[3] Vide p. 39, note 5 above.]

mean) to deliver us out of all miseries, that we might enter into the fruition of eternal felicity?

An objection proceeding of the sense of sin and reason which is an adversary to faith.

But here will some man say, 'O sir, if I were certain that I should depart from this miserable life into that so great felicity, then could I be right glad and rejoice as you will me, and bid death welcome: but I am a sinner, I have grievously transgressed and broken God's will; and therefore I am afraid I shall be sent into eternal woe, perdition, and misery.'

Answer. [MS.]

Here, my brother, thou doest well that thou dost acknowledge thyself a sinner, and to have deserved eternal death;

1 John i.

for doubtless, "if we say we have no sin, we are liars, and

Job xxv.

the truth is not in us." A child of a night's birth is not pure in God's sight. In sin were we born, and "by birth (or nature) we are the children of wrath," and firebrands of hell: therefore confess ourselves to be sinners we needs

Psal. cxxx.

must. For, "if the Lord will observe any man's iniquities, none shall be able to abide it:" yea, we must needs all cry,

Ps. cxliii.

"Enter not into judgment, O Lord; for in thy sight no flesh nor man living can be saved." In this point therefore thou hast done well, to confess that thou art a sinner.

But now where thou standest in doubt of pardon of thy sins, and thereby art afraid of damnation, my dear brother,

Three things whereby the afflicted conscience may be assured of pardon and forgiveness.

I would have thee answer me one question, that is, 'Whether thou desirest pardon or no; whether thou dost repent or no; whether thou dost unfeignedly purpose, if thou shouldest live, to amend thy life, or no?' If thou dost even before God so purpose, and desirest his mercy, then hearken, my good brother, what the Lord saith unto thee:

Isai. xliii.

"'I am he, I am he, that for my own sake will do away

Isai. i.

thine offences.' 'If thy sins be as red as scarlet, they shall

Ezek. xxxiii.

be made as white as snow;' for 'I have no pleasure in the death of a sinner. As surely as I live, I will not thy death, but rather that thou shouldest live, and be converted.' I

John iii.

have 'so loved the world,' that I would not spare my dearly beloved Son, 'the image of my substance and brightness of my glory,' 'by whom all things are made[1],' by whom all

---

[1 'by whom all things are made,' MS.: not in 1567]

things were given; but gave him for thee, not only to be man, but also to take thy nature, and to purge it from mortality, sin, and all corruption, and to adorn and endue it with immortality and eternal glory, not only in his own person, but also in thee and for thee: whereof now by faith I would have thee certain, as in very deed thou shalt at length feel and fully enjoy for ever. This my Son I have given to the death, and that a most shameful death, 'even of the cross,' for thee to 'destroy death,' to satisfy Phil. ii. my justice for thy sins: therefore 'believe,' and 'according to thy faith, so be it unto thee.'

"Hearken what my Son himself saith unto thee, ' Come Matt. xi. unto me all ye that labour and are laden, and I will refresh you:' 'I came not into the world to damn the world, but to John iii. save it:' 'I came not to call the righteous, but sinners to Luke v. repentance.' 'I pray not,' saith he, 'for these mine apostles John xvii. only, but also for all them that by their preaching shall believe in me.' Now what prayed he for such? 'Father,' saith he, 'I will that where I am they may also be, that they may see and enjoy the glory I have, and always had with thee. Father, save them, and keep them in thy truth. Father,' saith he, 'I sanctify myself, and offer up myself for them.' Lo, thus thou hearest how my Son prayeth for thee.

"Mark now what my apostle Paul saith: We know, saith he, that our Saviour Christ's prayers were 'heard:' also 'this Heb. v. is a true saying, that Jesus Christ came into the world to 1 Tim. i. save sinners.' Hearken what he saith to the jailer, 'Believe Acts xvi. in the Lord Jesus, and thou shalt be saved;' for he by his own self hath 'made purgation for our sins.' 'To him,' saith Heb. [i. 3.] Peter, 'beareth all the prophets witness, that whosoever Acts x. believeth in his name shall receive remission of their sins.' 'Believe,' man. Pray, 'Lord, help mine unbelief:' 'Lord, Mark ix. increase my faith.' 'Ask, and thou shalt have.' Hearken Luke xvii. what St John saith, 'If we confess our sins, God is righteous 1 John i. to forgive us all our iniquities; and the blood of our Lord Jesus Christ shall wash us from all our sins:' for, 'if we 1 John ii. sin, we have an Advocate,' saith he, 'with the Father, Jesus Christ the righteous, and he is the propitiation for our sins.' Hearken what Christ is called: 'Call his name Jesus, saith the angel, 'for he shall save his people from their sins.' Luke i.

344 AGAINST THE FEAR OF DEATH.

<small>Rom. v.</small> So that, 'where abundance of sin is, there is abundance of grace.'

<small>Rom. viii.</small> "Say therefore, 'Who shall lay any thing to my charge? It is God that absolveth me. Who then shall condemn me? It is Christ which is dead for my sins, yea, which is risen for my righteousness, and sitteth on the right hand of the Father, and prayeth for me.' Be certain therefore, and sure of pardon of thy sins; be certain and sure of everlasting life.

<small>Rom. x.</small> Do not now say in thy heart, 'Who shall descend into the deep?' that is, doubt not of pardon of thy sins, for that is to fetch up Christ. Neither say thou, 'Who shall ascend up into heaven?' that is, doubt not of eternal bliss, for that is to put Christ out of heaven. But mark what the Lord saith unto thee, 'The word is nigh thee, even in thy mouth, and in thy heart; and this is the word of faith which we preach: If thou confess with thy mouth that Jesus Christ is the Lord, and believe with thy heart, that God raised him up from the

<small>1 Thess. iv.</small> dead, thou shalt be safe.' If thou 'believe that Jesus Christ died and rose again,' even so shalt thou be assured, saith the Lord God, that 'dying with Christ I will bring thee again with him.'"

Thus, dear brother, I thought good to write to thee in the name of the Lord, that thou, fearing death for nothing else but because of thy sins, mightest be assured of pardon of them; and so embrace death as a dear friend, and insult

<small>1 Cor. xv.</small> against his terror, sting, and power, saying, "Death, where

<small>The greatest dishonour to God is to doubt of his mercy.</small> is thy sting? Hell, where is thy victory?" Nothing in all the world so displeaseth the Lord, as to doubt of his mercy. In the mouth of two or three witnesses we should be content: therefore, in that thou hast heard so many witnesses, how

<small>None rejected that desire mercy.</small> that indeed desiring mercy with the Lord thou art not sent empty away, give credit thereto; and say with the good

<small>Luke i.</small> virgin Mary, "Behold thy servant, O Lord: be it unto me according to thy word."

<small>In the word only we behold God's love and favour towards us: and therefore we should give credit to it against all</small> Upon the which word see thou set thine eye only and wholly. For otherwise here thou seest not God thy Father but in his word, which is the "glass" wherein now we behold his grace and fatherly love towards us in Christ: and therefore herewith we should be content, and give more credit to

it than to all our senses, and to all the world besides. "The word," saith our Saviour, "shall judge." According to it therefore, and not according to any exterior or interior shew, judge both of thyself, of all other and things else.

<small>our sense, reason, and judgment.
John xii.</small>

Concerning thyself, if thou desire indeed God's mercy, and lamentest that thou hast offended, lo, it pronounceth that "there is mercy with the Lord for thee, and plenteous redemption." It telleth thee which wouldest have mercy at the Lord's hand, that the Lord willeth the same: and therefore thou art happy, for he "would not thy death." It telleth thee, that if thou acknowledge thy faults unto the Lord, he will cover them in his mercy.

<small>Psal. cxxx.</small>

Again, concerning death it telleth thee, that it is but a "sleep," that it is but a passing unto thy Father, that it is but a deliverance out of misery, that it is but a putting off of mortality and corruption, that it is a "putting on of immortality and incorruption;" that it is a putting away of an "earthly tabernacle," that thou mayest receive an "heavenly house" or "mansion;" that this is but a calling of thee home from the watching and standing in the "warfare" of this miserable life. According to this (the word I mean) do thou judge of death: and thou shalt thus[1] not be afraid of it, but desire it as a most wholesome medicine, and a friendly messenger of the Lord's justice and mercy. Embrace him therefore, make him good cheer; for of all enemies he is the least. 'An enemy,' quoth I? Nay, rather of all friends he is the best; for he bringeth thee out of all danger of enemies, into that most sure and safe place of thy unfeigned "Friend" for ever.

<small>Death what it is by the word of God.</small>

<small>2 Cor. v.</small>

Let these things be often thought upon. Let death be premeditated, not only because he cometh uncertainly (I mean for the time, for else he is most certain), but also because he helpeth much to the contempt of this world, out of the which as nothing will go with thee, so nothing canst thou take with thee; because it helpeth to the mortifying of the flesh, which when thou feedest, thou dost nothing else but feed worms; because it helpeth to the well disposing and due ordering of the things thou hast in this life; because it helpeth to repentance, to bring thee unto the knowledge of thyself that

<small>Why death ought to be premeditate and often thought upon.</small>

[1 'thus,' MS.: not in 1567.]

thou art but "earth and ashes," and to bring thee the more better to "know God."

But who is able to tell the commodities that come by the often and true consideration of death? Whose time is therefore left unto us uncertain and unknown (although to God it be certain, and the "bounds thereof" not only known but "appointed of the Lord, over the which none can pass)," because we should not prolong and put off from day to day the amendment of our life, as did the "rich man" under hope of long life.

Job xiv.

Luke xii.

And seeing it is the ordinance of God, and cometh not but "by the will of God" even unto a sparrow, much more then unto us which are incomparably much "more dear than many sparrows;" and in that this will of God is not only just, but also good (for he is our Father); let us, if there were nothing else but this, submit ourselves, our senses, and judgments, unto the pleasure of him, being content to come out of the room of our soldiership whensoever he shall send for us by his pursuivant, Death. Let us render to him that which he hath lent us so long (I mean life), lest we be counted unthankful. And in that death cometh not but "by sin," forasmuch as we have sinned so often, and yet the Lord hath ceased from exacting this tribute and punishment of us until this present, let us with thankfulness praise his patience, and pay our debt; not doubting but that he, being our Father and our almighty Father, can and will, if death were evil unto us (as God knoweth it is a chief benefit unto us by Christ), convert and turn it into good.

But death being, as before I have shewed, not to be dread but to be desired, let us "lift up our heads" in thinking on it, and know that our "redemption draweth nigh." Let our minds be occupied in the consideration or often contemplation of the four last articles of our belief; that is, 'the communion of saints' or 'the holy catholic church,' 'remission of sins, resurrection of the flesh, and the life everlasting.'

Luke xxi.

The four last articles of the faith often to be meditate and thought upon.

The Lord doth not break the bruised reed, and the smoking flax he doth not quench. Isai. xlii.

By faith in Christ, be it never so faint, little, or cold, we are members in very deed of the catholic and holy church of Christ; that is, we have communion or fellowship with all the saints of God that ever were, be, or shall be. Whereby we may receive great comfort: for, though our faith be feeble, yet the church's faith (whereof our Saviour Christ is "the Head") is mighty enough; though our repentance be little, yet the repentance of the church, wherewith we have communion, is sufficient; though our love be languishing, yet the love of the church and of the Spouse of the church is ardent: and so of all other things we want. Not that I mean this, as though any man should think that our faith should be in any or upon any other than only upon God the Father, the Son, and the Holy Ghost; neither that any should think I mean thereby any other merits or mean to salvation, than only the merits and name of the Lord Jesus: but that I would the poor christian conscience, which by baptism is brought into God's church, and made a member of the same "through faith," should not for his sin's sake, or for the want of any thing he hath not, despair; but rather should know that he is a member of Christ's church and mystical body, and therefore cannot but have communion and fellowship of both; that is, of Christ himself, being the "Lord," "Husband," and "Head" thereof, and of all that ever hath been, be, or shall be, members of it, in all good things that ever they have had, have, or shall have. Still doth the church pray for us by Christ's commandment, "Forgive us our sins, lead us not into temptation, deliver us from evil:" yea, Christ himself doth pray for us, being "members of his body," as we be indeed if that we believe, though it be never so little. God grant this faith unto us all, and increase it in us. Amen. *No sin or want of any thing whatsoever it be should cause us to despair of God's final favour and mercy.*

Out of this church no pope nor prelate can cast us, or excommunicate us indeed, although exteriorly they segregate us from the society of God's saints. But enough of this.

As I would have us often to muse upon 'the catholic church' or 'communion of saints,' (whereof we may not doubt, in what state soever we be, under pain of damnation, being baptized "in the name of the Father, the Son, and the Holy Ghost;") so would I have us to meditate upon the other articles following, that is, 'remission of sins, resurrection of the flesh, and life everlasting.' *That we are partakers of this communion and fellowship we may not doubt, being received thereunto by baptism.*

It is an article of our faith to believe, that is, to be certain, that our sins are pardoned: therefore doubt not thereof, lest thou become an infidel. Though thou have sinned never so sore, yet now despair not: but be certain that "God is thy God," that is, that he "forgiveth thee thy sin." Therefore, as I said, doubt not thereof; for in so doing thou puttest a sallet[1] on the head of thy soul, that the "dew" of God's grace cannot indeed drop into it, but slip by as fast as it droppeth. Therefore, without that sallet or soul night-cap, be bareheaded; that is, "hope still in the mercy of the Lord," and so "mercy shall compass thee on every side."

In like manner, the article of 'the resurrection of the flesh' have often in thy mind, being assured by this, that thy carcass and body "shall be raised up again in the last day," when "the Lord shall come to judgment;" and shall be made incorruptible, immortal, glorious, spiritual, perfect, light, and even "like to the glorious body" of our Saviour Jesu Christ. For he is "the first-fruits of the dead;" and as God is "all in all," so shall he be unto thee "in Christ." Look therefore upon thine own estate; for "as he is," so shalt thou be. As thou hast "borne the image of the earthly Adam, so shalt thou bear the image of the heavenly:" therefore glorify thou now God, both in soul and body. Wait and look for this "day of the Lord" with groaning and sighing. Gather together testimonies of this, which I do omit for time's sake.

Last of all, have often in thy mind 'life everlasting,' whereunto thou art even landing. Death is the haven that carrieth thee unto this "land," where is all that can be wished, yea, above all wishes and desires; for in it we shall "see God" "face to face:" which thing now we can in no wise do, but must cover our faces with Moses and Elias, till the "face" or fore-parts of the Lord be "gone by." Now must we look on his "back-parts," beholding him in his word, and in his creatures, and in "the face of Jesus Christ" our Mediator: but then we shall see him "face to face," and "we shall know as we are known."

Therefore let us often think on these things, that we may have faith lustily and cheerfully to arrive at the happy haven of death: which you see is to be desired, and not to be dread,

[1 'Sallet:' a helmet, a covering for the head. Vide Richardson, Dict.; Nares, Glossary.]

to all those that are "in Christ," that is, to such as do believe indeed; which are discerned from those that only say they do believe, by dying temporally, that is, by labouring to mortify through God's Spirit the affections of the flesh; not that they should not be in them, but that they should "not reign in them, that is, in their mortal bodies," to give over themselves to "serve sin:" whose "servants" we are not, but "are made servants unto righteousness," "being now under grace, and not under the law;" and therefore hath God mercifully promised that "sin shall not reign in us." Rom. vi.

The which he continually grant for his truth, power, and mercy's sake.

Amen. Amen. Amen[1].

JOHN BRADFORD[2].

[1 'Amen' 1567: 'Amen. Amen. Amen.', MS.]
[2 'John Bradford,' MS.: not in 1567.]

[The treatise on the 'Restoration of all things' follows the text of the 'Letters of the martyrs' edited by Bishop Coverdale, 1564, p. 478—89, with the single exception of the first two lines.

This remarkable Essay, addressed as a letter to Mistress Joyce Hales[1], was evidently written about the same time and under the same circumstances with that 'Against the fear of death[2],' as Bradford states at the beginning, "Because this morning I had some knowledge how that my life stood in great danger, and that even this week,. I thought good. to go about something which might be on my behalf, as it were, *cygnea cantio*, 'a swan's song.'"

It was therefore penned, in all probability, not long after the condemnation of Bradford, January 31, 1555.

It is, through almost the whole, translated from the commentaries of the very learned Reformer Martin Bucer[3], with whom Bradford was on terms of close intimacy[4] in 1549—51, when Bucer was Regius Professor of Divinity at Cambridge. An extract from the original is given at p. 355—6, in connexion with a passage where Bradford specially refers to Bucer.]

[1 See the opposite page, line 1; and p. 248 and 307 above.]

[2 See prefatory note, p. 331 above.]

[3 Bucer. Metaph. et Enarr. epist. Paul. In Rom. viii. I. 339—46, Argentorat. 1536 : dedicated to Abp. Cranmer. Copy, Cathedral Library, Bristol.]

[4 Vide Preface of Sampson, p. 31 above ; Foxe, Acts &c. 1583, p. 1603, or ed. 1843—8, VII. 143 ; Letter of Car, in Hist. de Vit. Bucer. &c. 1562, fol. 20, 21, and in Bucer. Script. Angl. 1577, p. 874—5 ; Heylin, Quinq. Hist. 1681, p. 558 ; Fuller, Abel rediv. life, Bucer, 1651, p. 160 ; Strype, Mem. II. i. 383—4, Cranmer I. 356, Parker, I. 55—6, Annals, II. i. 394.]

THE RESTORATION OF ALL THINGS.

JESUS EMMANUEL.

To my dearest sister in the Lord, Joyce Hales, J. Bradford wisheth increase of all godliness in Christ[1].

Because this morning I had some knowledge, more than before I had, how that my life stood in great danger, and that even this week, so far as men might, both by the doings and sayings of such as be in authority attempted and spoken concerning me, judge and perceive[2]; I thought good, my right dearly beloved in the Lord, to go about something which might be on my behalf, as it were, *cygnea cantio*, 'a swan's song;' and towards you, both a monument of the kind of my love, and also a help, or at the least an occasion for you to profit in that which, I bear you record, you most desire; I mean, everlasting life and the state thereof. And this will I attempt, upon the last talk we had betwixt us, when you were here with me.

That is, which might be a special comfort to him being then ready to be burned, as the swan's song is sweetest a little before his death. [Bp. Coverdale.]

I know you have not forgotten that we talked together of the place of St Paul to the Romans, chapter viii., concerning the "groanings of the creature," and his "desire of the revelation of the children of God." You demand whether this word "creature" was to be understand of man, or no: and I told you, that though some did take "creature" there for man, because there is no kind of creature which may not be

[1 "Jesus Emmanuel . . godliness in Christ" is from the original MS. in the autograph of Bradford, in the possession of Dawson Turner, Esq. of Yarmouth. The Treatise, as given by Bp. Coverdale, ('Letters of the martyrs' 1564, p. 478,) begins, "Grace and peace, with increase of all godliness in Christ, I wish unto you, my dearly beloved." Its heading in Bp. C. is, "To a faithful and dear friend of his, entreating of this place of St. Paul to the Romans, 'The fervent desire of the creature waiteth when the children of God shall be delivered.'"]

[2 Vide prefatory notes in the last page and p. 331 above.]

acknowledged in man; yet, said I, the text itself, considered with that which the apostle writeth of Christ, the Restorer and Reformer of "all things that be both in heaven and earth," and with the argument which St Paul presently hath in hand there, doth enforce a godly mind to take "every creature" there, as also St Chrysostom[1] and St Ambrose[2] do, for the whole world and every creature both heavenly and earthly.

Eph. i. Col. i.

All things, I told you, were made for man: and according to man's state, so are they. When man was without sin and in God's favour, there was no malediction, curse, or corruption: but when man by sin was cast out of favour, then was the earth cursed. "For the wickedness of the inhabitants fruitful lands are turned into salt ground;" as, for their piety, barren countries are made fruitful. The angels themselves do "rejoice over one sinner that repenteth;" thereby giving us notice that in their kind they lament over the impenitent.

Psal. cvii.

In reading the prophets, you may see how all things do depend of man. When they prophesy any great blessing or plague to come to God's people, they do communicate the same both to heaven and earth, and to every thing else. As for example, when the prophets do foreshew the overthrows of realms and peoples, how do they say that the whole shape of the world shall be moved thereat! Look upon Esay, how he, when he prophesieth the fall of Babylon, doth say that "the stars shall not shine from heaven, the sun shall be darkened in his rising, the moon shall not give her light."

Isai. xiii.

[1 Ὅτι καὶ αὐτὴ ἡ κτίσις ἐλευθερωθήσεται. Τί ἐστι καὶ αὐτή; οὐχὶ σὺ μόνος, ἀλλὰ καὶ ὅ σου ἐστὶ καταδεέστερον, καὶ ὃ οὐ μετέχει λογισμοῦ οὐδὲ αἰσθήσεως, καὶ τοῦτό σοι κοινωνήσει τῶν ἀγαθῶν. Ἐλευθερωθήσεται γάρ, φησίν, ἀπὸ τῆς δουλείας τῆς φθορᾶς· τουτέστιν, οὐκέτι ἔσται φθαρτή, ἀλλὰ ἀκολουθήσει τῇ τοῦ σώματος εὐμορφίᾳ τοῦ σοῦ. ὥσπερ γὰρ γενομένου φθαρτοῦ γέγονε φθαρτὴ καὶ αὐτή· οὕτως ἀφθάρτου καταστάντος καὶ αὐτὴ ἀκολουθήσει, καὶ ἕψεται πάλιν. ὅπερ οὖν καὶ δεικνὺς ἐπήγαγεν, Εἰς τὴν ἐλευθερίαν τῆς δόξης τῶν τέκνων τοῦ Θεοῦ.—Chrysost. In Epist. ad. Rom. Homil. xiv. Op. ix. 582, ed. Bened. Par. 1718—38.]

[2 Ipsa elementa cum sollicitudine operas suas exhibent, quia et sol et luna non sine labore statuta sibi implent spatia; et spiritus animalium magno gemitu artatur ad exhibenda servitia: nam videmus illa gementia cogi invita ad laborem. Hæc ergo omnia exspectant requiem, ut a servili opere liberentur.—Ambros. In Ep. ad Rom. cap. viii. Op. II. Append. col. 75, ed. Bened. Par. 1686-90. This commentary is printed by the Benedictine editors as spurious.]

And afterwards he saith, "I will shake the heavens, and the earth shall be moved out of his place."

But the histories do witness that there are wonderful changes of all creatures, both heavenly and earthly, in the overthrows and destructions of realms and people.

Again, when Esay doth prophesy of the kingdom of Christ, he doth promise "new heavens and new earth;" and that so excellent and new, that he sheweth "the former heavens and earth to be utterly forgotten:" whereto the apostle agreeth, making Christ the Repairer of "all things in heaven and in earth." <small>Isai. lxv.</small> <small>Ephes. i. Col. i.</small>

How did both heaven and earth give their service to the Israelites coming forth of Egypt, as well in preserving them, as in destroying their enemies! How did the sun shine longer than it was wont to do, for Josue to overcome his enemies! How did the very angels fight for Hezekias against the Assyrians! Read the thirtieth chapter of Esay.

And behold the history of Christ: consider how the angels rejoiced; how the star brought the wise men to Christ; how the angels were ministers unto him in the wilderness; how the devils confessed him. In his death, how did all the whole world shew compassion! "The sun was darkened;" "the earth did quake; the rocks clave asunder; the veil of the temple rent asunder." When he arose, both heaven (for the angels with great heavenly brightness appeared), and earth which was moved, did rejoice: the angels were preachers of it. In his ascension also, did not a bright cloud "receive him and take him up?" Did not the angels testify of his return? When he sent the Holy Ghost, and made his "new covenant" of grace, did not all the whole world serve thereto, by thunder, smoke, fire, earthquake?

Now, how wonderfully they will do their service to Christ coming to judgment, is more plain than I need to rehearse. And inasmuch as we are "the members of Christ," he being our "Head," we may soon see how that all things have a certain compassion with man, and do after their kind (as the apostle writeth) look for a deliverance from vanity, which they shall obtain in their "restoration."

I therefore told you, how that I do take the apostle to mean, by "every creature" simply, even all the whole shape and creatures in the world. He doth attribute unto them,

[BRADFORD.]

how that they look for the perfection of our salvation; how that they are "subject to vanity;" how that they are "subject in hope;" how that they "groan and travail;" attributing these things unto the senseless creature by translation from man, to signify the society, cognation, and consent, which all and "every creature" hath with man; that, as every and all things were made for man, so by the man Christ all and "every thing both earthly and heavenly" shall be "restored."

[Eph. i. 10.]

These things, you know, in effect I spake unto you, to stir up both myself and you to a deeper consideration of our blessed state, which now we enjoy "in hope," which will never deceive us, the more to occasion us to desire the full fruition of the same.

But I do remember that you were something troubled with some doubtfulness hereabout. Therefore I purpose now to write of this matter more at large, thereby to occasion us both to see better, through the help of God's Spirit, that which we desire, and I pray God grant unto us both, for his mercy's sake; I mean the felicity of his children, and the happy state which one day in very deed, my dear heart, we shall fully possess, and both together praise the Lord with all his saints world without end. Amen, Amen.

This was your doubt. If so be that St Paul did mean by "all creatures" simply, as I have spoken, that they "shall be delivered from corruption" into such a state as shall adorn the freedom of God's children; whether that plants, beasts, and other things having life, shall be restored? If yea, then you would know, whether all things that have been shall be restored also? And after this, you will perchance ask in what place they shall be, what they shall do, and so forth.

As I think upon this matter, and as I am accustomed to answer such questions coming to me, I will here write for an answer unto you also; not doubting but that therewith you will be satisfied, because I know your heart is satisfied with godly and sufficient answers.

Thus I think. All and "every creature groaneth and travaileth" as yet, hoping and looking for my restoration: for they be subject to corruption for my sin's sake; but they all shall be delivered by my Christ "from the bondage of corruption" then, when he shall restore us his members. This will I muse on and weigh with myself, that I may duly know, both in me and in all other things, the atrocity and bitterness of sin which dwelleth in me; and so may the more heartily give over myself wholly to the Lord Christ, my Saviour; that he may, with what cross soever shall please him, slay sin in me, and bring me after his own will and way to "newness of life." Whereunto, that I for my part may faithfully and with all my whole heart do my diligence in mortifying the desires of my flesh, and in labouring to obey the desires of the Spirit to live a life acceptable to him, I beseech him of his grace. And that I may do this cheerfully, and continue in this purpose and diligence, I will fasten my mind, as much as the Lord shall enable me, to consider this my so great happiness, whereunto I shall be restored "in the resurrection:" the which "resurrection" doubtless shall be adorned by the whole shape of the world "delivered from corruption[1]."

These things will I think on, these things will I pause on: herein will I, as it were, drown myself, being careless of this, I mean, what parts of the world the Lord Christ will restore with me, or how he will do it, or what state or condition he will give it. It is enough and enough for me, that I, and all the whole world with me, shall be much more happy than now I can by any means conceive.

By reason hereof I will praise and glorify my Lord; and by his grace I will study to please him with all my heart, with all my soul, with all my strength; singing unto him that he both doth well, and hath done and made "all things well." To him be eternal glory for ever.

This is my cogitation in this matter, and not mine only, but the cogitation of one who was my father in the Lord[2], *He meaneth that most godly and learned father, M. Martin Bucer — [Bp. Coverdale.]*

[1 Compare the 'Catechismus brevis,' published by royal authority 1553, Liturgies, &c. of Edward VI., Parker Soc., p. 510—1, 558—9; and the 'Catechism' by Nowell, ('the larger Catechism heretofore by public authority set forth,' canon LXXIX, 1604,) p. 97—8, ed. Jacobson, Oxon. 1835.]

[2 Tota creatura congemiscit et parturit, adhuc exspectans et expetens meam restitutionem; nam corruptioni propter meum peccatum invita subjecta est. Hæc tota liberabitur per Christum meum a servitute corruptionis, cum ille nos sua membra restituerit. Istuc cogitabo et perpendam, ut in me et rebus omnibus atrocitatem peccati, quod in me inhabitat, rite agnoscam, indeque Christo Domino et Servatori meo me

and now, I am assured, with the Lord at home; where we yet are from home by reason of these our corruptible habitacles[1], wherein we abide the Lord's leisure.

If you would know the reason that moveth me to answer, as I have done, to the foresaid doubts or questions, it is this. You see that the apostle, in this place to the Romans, speaketh of the "deliverance of every creature from the bondage of corruption;" and that to the beautifying of the glory of God's children. This is so manifest that no man can well deny it. It is but a simple shift to say that the apostle doth mean in this place, by "every creature," man only: he is not wont to speak on that sort. Neither dare I say that the apostle speaketh here hyperbolically or excessively, although some think so. But as I said, I say again, that the apostle doth here simply affirm that there shall be a renovation and a "deliverance from corruption," not only of man, but also of all and of every part of the whole world: of every part, I say, meaning parts indeed, and not such as be rather vices and added for plagues, than for parts; for by reason of sin many spots and corruptions are come into the world, as is all that is hurtful and filthy in the creatures, also all that cometh of corruption, as perchance fleas, vermin, and such like.

[Acts iii. 21.] This "renovation of all things" the prophets do seem to promise, when they promise "new heavens and new earth;"

totum addicam, consecrem, permittam, quacunque is cruce peccatum in me conficere, et quacunque via ac vocatione me ad vitæ novitatem adducere velit: ad quod ei toto pectore inserviam mortificando studia carnis meæ, et enitendo ad studia Spiritus, ad vitam Dei. Utque huic vitæ alacriter insistam, et in eo conatu et studio infractus pergam, defigam mentem meam, quoad ejus ipse mihi Dominus dederit, in considerationem hujus tantæ felicitatis meæ, ad quam in resurrectione restituar; quam nimirum exornatura etiam est liberata a corruptione fabrica mundi universa. Ista cogitabo, in ista animum meum demergam, securus de eo, quasnam mundi partes mecum Christus Dominus restituturus sit, aut quo modo, et quam illis daturus conditionem. Satis superque mihi est, me et mecum totam creaturam habituros felicius, quam mens mea nunc queat cogitatione consequi. Hinc prædicabo et glorificabo Dominum meum, eique ipso donante studebo toto corde, tota anima, totis viribus, cantans illi, Et bene fecit, et bene faciet omnia; ipsi æterna gloria in secula. Amen.—Bucer. Metaph. et Enarr. Epist. Paul. In Rom. viii. I. 343, Argentorat. 1536.]

[1 'Habitacles:' habitations, dwelling-places.]

for "a new earth" seemeth to require no less renovation of earthly things than "new heavens" do of heavenly things. But these things the apostle doth plainly affirm that Christ will "restore, even whatsoever be in heaven and in earth." Col. i.
[Eph. i. 10.]

Therefore methinks it is the duty of a godly mind simply to acknowledge, and thereof to brag in the Lord, that in our resurrection "all things" shall be so repaired to eternity, as for our sin they were made subject to corruption.

The ancient writers, out of Peter, have, as it were, agreed to this sentence, that "the shape of this world shall pass away through the burning of earthly fire, as it was drowned with the flowing of earthly waters[2]." These be St Augustine's words, whereto I will add these which he here writeth: "The qualities," saith he, "of the corruptible elements, which agreed with our corruptible bodies, shall utterly be burned with that same worldly conflagration and burning, as I said: but the substance itself shall have those qualities which do agree by a marvellous change to our bodies, that the world, changing into the better, may openly be made meet to man, returned even in the flesh into the better[3]." 2 Peter iii.

August. de Civitate Dei.
Lib. xx. cap. xvi.

These be his words, whereby it is plain that this good man did believe that the elements should be renewed: but of other things he meddleth not, except it be of "the sea," by the occasion of that which is in the Apocalypse; howbeit, so he speaketh, that he "cannot well tell whether it also shall be changed into the better," adding these words, "But we read that there shall be a new heaven and a new earth[4]." For he did understand the place of Esay, concerning the "new

[2 figura hujus mundi mundanorum ignium conflagratione præteribit, sicut factum est mundanarum aquarum inundatione diluvium. —August. De Civit. Dei. xx. cap. xvi. Op. VII. coll. 593, 4, ed. Bened. Par. 1679—1700.]

[3 Illa itaque, ut dixi, conflagratione mundana elementorum corruptibilium qualitates, quæ corporibus nostris corruptibilibus congruebant, ardendo penitus interibunt; atque ipsa substantia eas qualitates habebit, quæ corporibus immortalibus mirabili mutatione conveniant: ut scilicet mundus, in melius innovatus, apte accommodetur hominibus etiam carne in melius innovatis.—Id. ibid.]

[4 Quod autem ait, 'Et mare jam non est;' utrum maximo illo ardore siccetur, an et ipsum vertatur in melius, non facile dixerim. 'Cœlum quippe novum et terram novam futuram' legimus.—Id. ibid.]

heaven and new earth" simply: of other things he expresseth nothing.

But Thomas Aquinas entreateth this question more exactly, or rather curiously, affirming the celestial bodies, the elements, and mankind to be renewed; but in no wise beasts, plants, &c. to be so [1]: and this is his principal reason: " The renovation of the world shall be for man: therefore such shall be the renovation, as shall be conformable to the renovation of man. But the renovation of man shall be from corruption to incorruption, from moving to rest:...the things therefore that shall be renewed with man must be brought also to incorruption. Now the celestial bodies and the elements were made to incorruption; the one wholly and in every part, the other, that is, the elements, though in part they are corruptible, yet concerning the whole they are incorruptible; as man...is incorruptible concerning part, that is, the soul...But beasts, plants, &c. are corruptible both wholly and in every part: therefore they were not made to incorruption;...and so are they not conformable to the renewing, that is, they are not receivable of incorruption: and therefore they shall not be restored[2]."

[1 .. fatendum est resurrectionem esse futuram. Corpora coelestia majorem claritatem accipient in illa innovatione. elementa induentur claritate quadam, non tamen æqualiter plantæ et animalia. non remanebunt in illa mundi innovatione.—Thom. Aquin. Summ. Theol. Partis III. Suppl. Quæst. LXXV. Art. i., Quæst. XCI. Art. iii. iv. v., p. 113, 142, 143, Colon. 1622. See also Aquin. Quæst. Disput. Quæst. v. Artic. vii. ix. p. 81—3—5, Venet. 1598.]

[2 RESPONDEO dicendum, quod cum innovatio mundi propter hominem fiat, oportet quod innovationi hominis conformetur. Homo autem innovatus de statu corruptionis in incorruptionem transibit et perpetuæ quietis; unde dicitur primæ ad Cor. 15. 'Oportet corruptibile hoc induere incorruptionem, mortale hoc induere immortalitatem'. Unde ad illam innovationem nihil ordinari poterit, nisi quod habet ordinem ad incorruptionem: hujusmodi autem sunt corpora coelestia, elementa, et homines. Corpora nunc coelestia secundum sui naturam incorruptibilia sunt, et secundum totum et secundum partes: elementa vero sunt quidem corruptibilia secundum partes, sed incorruptibilia secundum totum: homines vero corrumpuntur.. ex parte materiæ, non ex partæ formæ, scilicet animæ rationalis. . Animalia vero bruta, et plantæ, et mineralia, et omnia corpora mixta corrumpuntur et secundum totum et secundum partes; et sic nullo modo habent ordinem ad incorruptionem; unde in illa innovatione non manebunt . —Id. ibid. Quæst. XCI. Art. v. p. 144.]

This reason is true in this part, that it affirmeth 'things shall be restored with man, and with him shall be brought to perpetuity;' and, as the apostle saith, to be "delivered from the bondage of corruption." Again, his reason is true herein also, that man's reason may sooner be persuaded, that things now 'partly incorruptible' shall be restored altogether to incorruption.

But now to say, that by no reason those things may be brought to perpetuity, which now both wholly and partly be temporal and momentary, how can he prove it? in that the nature and being of all things dependeth on the omnipotency of God, which, after his own pleasure, doth give to things which he hath made their being: and all is one to him, to make a thing temporal, and to make it eternal. For he made all things of nothing: and therefore heaven and the celestial bodies have no more of themselves that they be perpetual, than have those things that last but a day. Wherefore this reason which Thomas maketh is not firm, in that it wholly leaneth to that which now seemeth and appeareth in things.

Indeed, as I said, it hath some shew or probability, that these things shall be renewed to eternity for the glory of God's children, which now something are partakers of the same. But now, seeing that both it which they now have, and also shall have, dependeth upon the beck and pleasure of God; whom hath God made of counsel with him concerning the renovation of the world and of all things, that he can tell what parts of things and what kinds of things he will renew?

Yea, even Aristotle did acknowledge that *physice* or 'natural knowledge,' because it bringeth his reasons from the disposition and nature of things, hath not full necessity of his reasons[3]. For nature is nothing else than the ordinary and wonted will of God, as a miracle, portent, or monster is the rare and unwonted will of God[4]. We say that the nature

[3 τὴν δ' ἀκριβολογίαν τὴν μαθηματικὴν οὐκ ἐν ἅπασιν ἀπαιτητέον, ἀλλ' ἐν τοῖς μὴ ἔχουσιν ὕλην. διόπερ οὐ φυσικὸς ὁ τρόπος. ἅπασα γὰρ ἴσως ἡ φύσις ἔχει ὕλην. διὸ σκεπτέον πρῶτον τί ἐστιν ἡ φύσις. οὕτω γὰρ καὶ περὶ τίνος ἡ φυσικὴ, δῆλον ἔσται.... Arist. Metaphys. II. iii. Op. II. 858, Lut. Par. 1629.]

[4 Etenim natura rerum nihil aliud est, ut pie sanctus ille vir Johannes Wesselus scripsit, quam voluntas Dei ordinata: ut miraculum,

of stones and all heavy things is to sink downward, which is nothing else but the pleasure of God so depelling them and putting them down; for else of themselves nothing is either heavy or light, all is alike to be carried downwards or upwards. Who may make God subject to his work? Cannot he, that made all things of nothing, give hereafter to the things that he hath made that whereof now in themselves they have no capacity?

These things I do therefore rehearse, to the end I might declare, that when we dispute what God will do concerning his works, how that it is not seemly for us to conclude according to that which seemeth and appeareth to us in things; but rather, as godliness requireth, to refer all things to the "will of God." This "will" if it be expressed in holy scripture, then may we simply determine that which we read expressed there. But if it be not so, then ought we freely to confess our ignorance, and not prescribe to God what he ought to do of his works, by that which already he hath done. God is of power infinite: and of nothing did he not only make all things, but also will "do what pleaseth him both in heaven and in earth," saith David.

The foresaid Thomas bringeth forth also other reasons, but which he himself counteth not for invincible. One is: "If beasts and plants shall be restored, either all or some shall be restored. If all shall be restored, then must the resurrection be communicate unto them, that the same in number be restored; which is not convenient. If some shall be restored, there appeareth no reason why these should be

---

voluntas Dei insolens.—Bucer. Metaph. et Enarr. Epist. Paul. In Rom. viii. I. 344, Argentorat. 1536.

vere dictum per prophetam, 'Quoniam gloria virtutis eorum tu es', quasi dicat, Virtus eorum creata non haberet gloriam, nisi tua immobilis voluntas accederet, et præciperes. . Jam facile liquet verbum Platonis, volentis 'naturam nihil aliud esse quam voluntatem;' et miraculum, opus divinæ voluntatis, non regulariter ita volentis.— Wessel. (qui olim lux mundi vulg. dict. fuit,) De orat. III. xiv. Op. 78, Groning. 1614.

ὧν ἐγὼ δημιουργὸς πατήρ τε ἔργων, ἃ δι' ἐμοῦ γενόμενα ἄλυτα, ἐμοῦ γε θέλοντος.—Plat. Timæ., Op. III. 41, ed. Serran. Paris. 1578. Vide annot. Stephan. et Bekker. in loc.: and see August. De Civit. Dei, XXI. viii. 2. Op. VII. col. 628, ed. Bened. Par. 1679—1700.]

restored more than other: therefore," saith he, "they shall not be restored[1]." But here what would he answer, if one should ask him, how he knoweth it is not convenient that either 'all' in number be restored (as man shall arise), either only 'some?' in that this thing wholly resteth in the hand and will of God.

Another reason he maketh out of Aristotle, and out of a ground which is uncertain. Aristotle affirmeth "the perpetuity of things to hang on the continual moving of heaven[2]." Thomas now hereto gathereth thus: "But the moving of heaven shall cease;" therefore he concludeth that "in these inferior things no perpetuity may be looked for[3]." But here what answer will he make, if a man shall say that all things hang at the beck and pleasure of God, who now for the conservation of his creatures, which now arise and spring, and now die and fall down, useth 'the moving of heaven,' and can afterwards not use it for this purpose? This is a truth, that all things of themselves are nothing: much more then can they not do any thing. Now men may conjecture that 'the moving of heaven shall cease;' but yet by the certain word of God they cannot prove it.

In like manner is his last reason, which he maketh of the "end" of beasts and plants; but which 'end' he knoweth not: "Beasts and plants," saith he, "were made for the sustenta-

[1 Si plantæ et animalia remanebunt, aut omnia, aut quædam. Si omnia, oportebit etiam animalia bruta quæ prius fuerunt mortua, resurgere, sicut et homines resurgent; quod dici non potest, quia cum forma eorum in nihilum cedat, non potest eadem numero resumi. Si autem non omnia, sed quædam, cum non sit major ratio de uno quam de alio, quod in perpetuum maneat, videtur, quod nullum eorum in perpetuum remanebit.—Thom. Aquin. Summ. Theol. Partis III. Suppl. Quæst. XCI. Art. v. p. 143, Colon. 1622.]

[2 ἀνάγκη . . εἴ γε ἀεὶ ἔσται συνεχὴς γένεσις καὶ φθορά, ἀεὶ μέν τοι κινεῖσθαι, ἵνα μὴ ἐπιλείπωσιν αὗται αἱ μεταβολαί· δύο δέ, ὅπως μὴ θάτερον συμβαίνῃ μόνον. τῆς μὲν οὖν συνεχείας ἡ τοῦ ὅλου φορὰ αἰτία.—Arist. De Gen. et Corr. II. x. Op. I. 524, Lut. Par. 1629: and vide De cœlo, II. iii. I. 456.]

[3 Secundum philosophum in 2 de Generatione, in animalibus et plantis et hujusmodi corruptibilibus speciei perpetuitas non conservatur, nisi ex continuatione motus cœlestis: sed tunc ille cessabit: ergo non poterit perpetuitas in illis speciebus conservari.—Thom. Aquin. ibid.]

tion of the mutual life of man: but this life shall cease, therefore shall they also[1]." But here hath he no answer, if a man should demand, Who knoweth whether God have made them to none other 'end' or use?

Seeing therefore these things be as you see, I suppose it not to pertain to a godly man to deny the beasts and plants to be restored, in that the apostle doth here expressly say that "every creature, which is now subject to vanity, shall be delivered from the bondage of corruption into the glorious liberty of the children of God." In that the Holy Ghost doth affirm this of "every creature," by what reason dare a godly mind exempt any part from this deliverance to come? Howbeit, neither will the godly mind contend whether every creature shall be renewed; for the Holy Ghost spake of "the creature" generally, and not particularly: and therefore we may not otherwise affirm, because we must not speak but God's word.

Therefore it is the part of a godly man, and of one that hangeth in all things upon the word of God, to learn out of this place that whatsoever corruption, death, or grief, he seeth in any thing wheresoever it be, that, I say, he ascribe that wholly unto his sins, and thereby provoke himself to true repentance. Now as soon as that repentance compelleth him to go to Christ, let him think thus: 'But this my Saviour, and my Head Jesus Christ, died for my sins; and therewith, as he took away death, so hath he taken away all the corruption and labour of all things, and will restore them in his time, whether soever they be in heaven or in earth. Now "every creature travaileth and groaneth" with us; but we being restored, they also shall be restored. There shall be "new heavens," "new earth," and "all things new."'

Thus I wish that our minds might stay in this generality of the renovation of the world; and not curiously to search what parts of the world shall be restored, and what shall not; or how all things shall be restored: much more then I would not have us curious nor inquisitive of their place, where they

[1 Cessante fine, cessare debet id quod est ad finem: sed animalia et plantæ facta sunt ad animalem vitam hominis sustentandam: sed post illam innovationem animalis vita in homine non erit: ergo nec plantæ nec animalia remanere debent.—Id. ibid.]

shall be; of their action, what they shall do; or of their properties, and such like. For if to have foreknown these things would have made much to godliness, surely the Holy Ghost would most plainly have told them; for, according to Christ's promise, "he bringeth us into all truth;" "all truth," I say, such as the knowledge of it would profit us.

"All the scripture is given to us for this purpose, that the man of God might be made perfect, and instructed to all good works:" and truly that can be no "good work" which we do, except God teach us the same. He "hath prepared the good works wherein we walk." But the certain and bottomless fountain of these "good works" is, in all things to hang on the beck and pleasure of God; and through our Lord Jesus Christ, to look for, with 'remission of sins,' 'life everlasting,' and the glory of 'the resurrection.' [Ephes. ii.]

To the end therefore that we may more fully know our sins, and more make of our redemption from them by Christ, let us set before our eyes death, the hire of sin; and that not only in ourselves, but also in "every creature" of the world. Howbeit, this let us do with a hope of so ample a "restoration," and never enough to be marvelled at; which shall be even in all things for our renovation by our Lord Jesus Christ, the Renewer of "all things whatsoever be in heaven or in earth." [Acts iii. 21.]

He that with true faith weigheth and considereth these things will be, as it were, swallowed up in the admiration of so exceeding great "benevolence and love of God" our heavenly Father, that he can never admit to yield to this curiosity of searching what kind of things shall be renewed, and how they shall be renewed, or what state or condition they shall be in when they are renewed.

These be things of the life to come, whereof this foreknowledge is sufficient, that all these things shall be more perfect and happy than the reach of reason is able to look upon the glory of them. For "the eye hath not seen, nor the ear heard, nor it cannot ascend into man's heart, that God hath prepared for them that love him;" for concerning our resurrection what other thing do we know beforehand, but that we shall be most happy? Even so therefore let us not doubt, but that there shall be a "deliverance of the creature from the servitude of corruption."

And let us consider these things so, that we may wholly bend ourselves to put away all "the oldness" of our flesh, whence indeed corruption and death doth come; and that we may provoke ourselves to the "newness of the Spirit" and "the life of Christ," wherein is all incorruption, and the true taste of the resurrection: for to this end the Holy Ghost did write this by the apostle. That therefore this Spirit might lead us hereunto, let us pray: and then we shall understand this place of Paul with profit.

If perchance it will move you, that the apostle speaketh not of this "deliverance of the creature from corruption" in any other place but here, neither any other holy writer; I would you would think, that the mystery of the "restoration of Israel," also of antichrist, is not expounded but in the apostle's writings, and that but in one place: yea, the manner of our resurrection is not written but in two places. We ought to know that they are the words of the Lord, whatsoever the apostle hath left to us written. Again the simplicity of this place, Romans viii., is plain.

And thus, my dearly beloved, I have written to you so much as I think is sufficient about this matter; and therefore need not to tarry herein any longer, or to spend any more time about the answering of that which is but curiosity.

God our Father give us now his holy Spirit, to lead us into this and all other necessary truth, in such sort that we may have a lively feeling of "eternal life" begun in us; that we may become first "new," and so "look for new heaven and earth, wherein righteousness dwelleth."

Which God impute to us and begin in us, for his Christ's sake. Amen, Amen.

Your own for ever in the Lord,

JOHN BRADFORD.

TEN

DECLARATIONS AND ADDRESSES

BY

JOHN BRADFORD.

[The ten following 'Declarations and Addresses' were written during the imprisonment of Bradford, which commenced on August 16, 1553, and ended with his martyrdom on July 1, 1555.

The 'Declaration concerning Religion,' p. 367—74, is reprinted from the scarce first edition of Foxe, Acts, &c. 1563, where it was originally published.

The 'Exhortation to patience,' and 'Letter to men who relieved the prisoners,' p. 375—84, that on ˙the mass, to Hopkins and others at Coventry,' p. 389—99, the 'Letter to the queen and parliament,' p. 401—3, and the 'Admonition to lovers of the Gospel,' p. 407—11, are reprinted from the 'Letters of the martyrs' edited by Bishop Coverdale 1564, where they were first published.

The 'Address on constancy,' p. 385—8, is now first printed from a MS. in Gonville and Caius College, Cambridge. It is attributed to Bradford by Bishop Tanner, Bibliotheca Britann. Hibern. 1748.

The 'Declaration on the Reformation,' p. 399—401, and the 'Remarks on a memorable trial,' (probably of Sir Nicholas Throgmorton, see p. 405, note 2,) follow the text of MSS. in Emmanuel College, Cambridge; the 'Remarks' being now printed for the first time.

The 'Supplication to the king, queen, and parliament,' p. 403—5, observes the text of the second edition of Foxe, Acts, &c. 1570, where it first appeared in print.

Three of the above-mentioned documents, which are of considerable importance and interest, are placed among the Writings of Bradford on the following grounds:

The 'Declaration concerning Religion' is printed in this volume, p. 367—74, because of the title given to it by Foxe[1]; and because it certainly expresses the opinions of Bradford, having received his signature.

The 'Declaration on the Reformation' is given in this collection, because of the conjecture of Strype, quoted, p. 399, note 2.

The 'Supplication to the king, queen, and parliament,' is printed in this volume, p. 403—5, because it represents the sentiments of Bradford, from whom among others it proceeded. It has also been supposed[2], with much probability, to be the document mentioned in the title of the 'Letter to the queen and parliament,' p. 401, to accompany which that 'Letter' was written: and it appears in no wise unlikely to have been penned by Bradford.]

[1 See the opposite page. Vide also Fathers of the English Church, 1810, IV. 271; Matthias on the Reformation, 1814, II. 112; 'English Hexapla,' 1841, Introduction, p. 125.]

[2 Life of Bradford by Stevens, 1832, p. 153.]

A COPY[3] OF A CERTAIN DECLARATION,

DRAWN AND SENT OUT OF PRISON BY MASTER BRADFORD, MASTER SAUNDERS, AND DIVERS OTHER GODLY PREACHERS, CONCERNING THEIR DISPUTATION AND DOCTRINE OF THEIR RELIGION, AS FOLLOWETH[4].

[May 8, 1554.]

BECAUSE we hear that it is determined of the magistrates, and such as be in authority, especially of the clergy, to send us speedily out of the prisons of the King's Bench, the Fleet, the Marshalsea, and Newgate, (where presently we are, and of long time some of us hath been; not as rebels, traitors, seditious persons, thieves, or transgressors of any laws of this realm, inhibitions, proclamations, or commandments of the queen's highness, or of any of the council's, God's name be praised therefor; but alonely for the conscience we have to God and his most holy word and truth, upon most certain knowledge;) because, we say, we hear that it is determined we shall be sent to one of the universities of Cambridge or Oxford, there to dispute with such as are appointed in that behalf; in that we purpose not to dispute otherwise than by writing, except it may be before the queen's highness and her council, or before the parliament houses; and therefore perchance it will be bruited abroad that we are not able to maintain by the truth of God's word, and the consent of the true and catholic church of Christ, the doctrine we have generally and severally taught, and some of us hath written and set forth; (wherethrough the godly and simple may be offended, and sometime weakened;) we have thought it our bounden duty now, whilst we may, by writing to publish and notify the causes why we will not dispute otherwise than

Foxe, Acts, &c. 1563, p. 1001—3, and after editions.

[3 Title in Foxe, Acts, &c. 1570, p. 1640, and in the after editions.]
[4 See Bp. Ridley, Letter to Bradford, Works, Parker Soc. 364—5; Bp. Hooper, Letter to Bp. Ferrar, Taylor, Bradford, and Philpot, in Foxe, Acts, &c. 1583, p. 1513, or ed. 1843—8, VI. 664—5; Strype, Mem. III. i. 221—3; Soames, Hist. Reform. IV 207—15, Lond. 1826—8.]

is above said, to prevent the offences which might come thereby.

First, because it is evidently known unto the whole world, that the determinations of both the universities in matters of religion, especially wherein we should dispute, are directly against God's word, yea, against their own determinations in the time of our late sovereign lord and most godly prince, king Edward: and further it is known they be our open enemies, and have already condemned our causes, before any disputation had of the same.

Secondly, because the prelates, and clergy do not seek either us or the verity, but our destruction and their glory. For if they had sought us as charity requireth, then would they have called us forth hereabouts tofore their laws were so made, that frankly and without peril we might have spoken our consciences. Again, if they had sought for the verity, they would not have concluded of controversies tofore they had been disputed: so that it easily appeareth that they seek their own glory and our destruction, and not us and the verity: and therefore we have good cause to refuse disputation, as a thing which shall not further prevail than to the setting forth of their glory, and the suppression of the verity.

Thirdly, because the censors and judges, as we hear who they be, are manifest enemies to the truth, and, that which worse is, obstinate enemies, "before whom pearls are not to be cast," by the commandment of our Saviour Jesus Christ, and by his own example. That they be such, their doings of late at Oxford[1], and in the Convocation-house in October last past[2], do most evidently declare.

Fourthly, because some of us have been in prison these eight or nine months, where we have had no books, no paper, no pen, no ink, or convenient place for study, we think we should do evil thus suddenly to descend into disputation with them, which may allege, as they list, the fathers and their testimonies; because our memories have not that which we have read, so readily as to reprove when they shall report and wrest

[1 Vide Foxe, Acts, &c. 1583, p. 1441—54, or ed. 1843—8, VI. 469—500; and Works of Bp. Ridley, Parker Soc. p. 189—252.]

[2 Vide Foxe, Acts, &c. 1583, p. 1410—7, or ed. 1843—8, VI. 395—411, and Works of Adn. Philpot, Parker Soc. p. 179—214.]

the authors to their purpose, or to bring forth that we may have there for our advantage.

Fifthly, because in disputation we shall not be permitted to prosecute our arguments, but be stopped when we would speak; one saying thus, another that, the third his mind, &c.: as was done to the godly-learned fathers, especially Doctor Ridley at Oxford, who could not be permitted to declare his mind and meaning of the propositions, and had oftentimes half a dozen at once speaking against him, always letting him to prosecute his argument, and to answer accordingly: we will not speak of the hissing, scoffing, and taunting which wonderfully then was used. If on this sort and much worse they handled these fathers thus, much more will they be shameless bold with us, if we should enter into disputation with them.

Sixthly, because the notaries that shall receive and write the disputations shall be of their appointment, and such as either do not or dare not favour the truth; and therefore must write either to please them, or else they themselves (the censors and judges we mean) at their pleasure will put to and take from that which is written by the notaries, who cannot nor must not have in their custody that which they write, longer than the disputation endureth, as their doings at Oxford declareth. No copy or scroll could any man have by their good will; for the censors and judges will have all delivered into their hands: yea, if any man was seen there to write, (as the report is,) the same man was sent for and his writings taken from him. So must the disputation serve only for the glory, not of God, but of the enemies of his truth.

For these causes, we all think it so necessary not to dispute with them, as, if we did dispute, we should do that which they desire and purposely purpose, to promote the kingdom of antichrist, and to suppress, as much as may be, the truth. We will not speak of the offence that might come to the godly, when they should hear, by the report of our enemies, our answers and arguments (you may be sure) framed for their fantasies, to the slandering of the verity.

Therefore we publish, and by this writing notify unto the whole congregation and church of England, that for these aforesaid causes we will not dispute with them otherwise than with the pen; unless it be before the queen's highness and her council, or before the houses of the parliament, as is above said.

If they will write, we will answer, and by writing confirm and prove out of the infallible verity, even the very word of God, and by the testimony of the good and most ancient fathers in Christ his church, this our faith and every piece thereof; which hereafter we in a sum do write and send abroad, purposely that our good brethren and sistern in the Lord may know it: and, to seal up the same, we are ready, through God's help and grace, to give our lives to the halter or stake[1], or otherwise as God shall appoint; humbly requiring, and in the bowels of our Saviour Jesus Christ beseeching, all that fear God to behave themselves as obedient subjects to the queen's highness and "the superior powers which are ordained of God" under her; rather after our example to give their heads to the block, than in any point to rebel, or once to mutter against "the Lord's anointed;" we mean our sovereign lady queen Mary: into whose heart we beseech the Lord of mercy plentifully to pour the wisdom and grace of his holy Spirit, now and for ever. Amen.

First, we confess and believe all the canonical books of the old Testament, and all the books of the new Testament, to be the very true "word of God," and to be written by the inspiration of the Holy Ghost; and therefore to be heard accordingly, as the judge in all controversies and matters of religion.

Secondly, we confess and believe the catholic church, which is the spouse of Christ, as a most obedient and loving wife to embrace and follow the doctrine of these books in all matters of religion; and therefore is she to be heard accordingly[2]: so that those which will not hear this church, thus following and obeying the word of her "Husband," we account as heretics and schismatics, according to this saying, "If he will not hear the church, let him be unto thee as a heathen."

Thirdly, we believe and confess all the articles of faith and doctrine set forth in the symbol of the apostles, which we commonly call the Creed, and in the symbols of the councils

[1 'stake,' Foxe, Acts, &c. 1563: 'fire' 1570, 1576, 1583.]

[2 'according,' Foxe, Acts, &c. 1563: 'accordingly' 1570, 1576, 1583.]

of Nice, kept in A.D. 324[3]; of Constantinople kept in A.D. 384[4]; of Ephesus kept in A.D. 432[5]; of Chalcedony kept in A.D. 454[6]; of Toletum the first[7] and the fourth[8]; also the symbols of Athanasius[9], Irenæus[10], Tertullian[11], and of Damasus[12], which was about the year of our Lord 376. We confess and believe, we say, the doctrine of these symbols generally and particularly; so that, whosoever doth otherwise, we hold the same to err from the truth.

Fourthly, we believe and confess concerning justification, that, as it cometh only from God's mercy through Christ, so it is perceived and had of none which be of years of discretion otherwise than by faith only. Which faith is not an opinion, but a certain persuasion wrought by the Holy Ghost in the mind and heart of man; wherethrough, as the mind is illumined, so the heart is suppled to submit itself to the will

[3 The first General Council of Nice, A.D. 325. Symb. Nicæn. Concil. in Concil. stud. Labb. et Cossart. II. col. 27—8, Lut. Par. 1671—2; and in Routh, Script. Eccles. Opusc. I. 367, Oxon. 1840.]

[4 The second General Council of Constantinople, A.D. 381. Symb. Concil. Constantinop. in Concil. II. 951—4; and in Routh, ibid. I. 398—9.]

[5 The third General Council of Ephesus, A.D. 431. Nicæn. fid. exposit. in Act. VI. Concil. Ephes. in Concil. III. col. 671—2.]

[6 The fourth General Council of Chalcedon, A.D. 451. Defin. fidei in Act. V. Concil. Chalc. in Concil. IV col. 561—8; and in Routh, ibid. II. 75—80.]

[7 The Council of Toledo, A.D. 400. Regula fidei in Concil. Tolet. I. in Concil. II. col. 1227—8.]

[8 The Council of Toledo, A.D. 633. Concil. Tolet. IV. capit. i. De evid. cathol. fid. verit. in Concil. V col. 1703.]

[9 Athanas. Exposit. fidei in Op. I. 99, ed. Bened. Par. 1698; and in Routh, ibid. II. 221—8. Athanas. Symb. de fid. cathol. Op. II. (inter spur.) 728—35; and in Concil. Rom. II. in Concil. II. col. 599—602. Vide Waterland, Crit. hist. Athan. Creed, Cambr. 1728, who refers the creed to Hilary, Abp. of Arles, A.D. 430.]

[10 Exposit. prædic. verit. apud Iren. Cont. Hær. Lib. Quinq. I. x. Op. I. 48—51, ed. Bened. Venet. 1734; and in Routh, ibid. II. 211—6.]

[11 Regula fidei apud Tertull. De Præscript. Hæret. xiii. Op. 206—7, Lut. Par. 1675; and in Routh, ibid. I. 132—3. Also Tertull. De Virgin. veland. i. p. 173; and Advers. Prax. ii. p. 501.]

[12 Symb. Damasi Papæ I. apud Hieron. Op. XI. col. 145—6, stud. Vallars. Veron. 1734—42: see Vallars. Admonit. Profess. fidei ex epist. Damasi in Concil. Rom. III. in Concil. II. col. 900—4: and Damasi epist. I. ad Paulin. Antioch. episc. De fide, &c. ibid. col. 864—5.]

of God unfeignedly, and so sheweth forth an inherent righteousness; which is to be discerned in the article of justification from the righteousness which God endueth us withal in justifying us, although inseparably they go together. And this we do, not for curiosity or contention sake, but for conscience sake, that it might be quiet; which it can never be, if we confound without distinction forgiveness of sins and Christ's justice imputed to us with regeneration and inherent righteousness.

By this we disallow papistical doctrine of free-will, of works of supererogation, of merits, of the necessity of auricular confession, and satisfaction to God-wards.

Fifthly, we confess and believe, concerning the exterior service of God, that it ought to be according to the word of God: and therefore in the congregation all things public ought to be done in such a tongue as may be most to edify, and not in Latin, where the people understand not the same.

Sixthly, we confess and believe that God only by Christ Jesus is to be prayed unto and called upon: and therefore we disallow invocation or prayer to saints departed this life.

Seventhly, we confess and believe that, as a man departeth this life, so shall he be judged in the last day generally, and in the mean season is entered either into the state of the blessed for ever, or damned for ever; and therefore is either past all help, or else needeth no help of any in this life. By reason whereof we affirm purgatory, masses of *scala cœli*[1], trentals[2], and such suffrages as the popish church doth obtrude as necessary, to be the doctrine of antichrist.

Eighthly, we confess and believe the sacraments of Christ, which be baptism and the Lord's supper, that they ought to be ministered according to the institution of Christ, concerning the substantial parts of them; and that they be no longer

[1 "Every brother and sister that will say any Wednesday, Friday, or Saturday, one *Pater noster*, one *Ave Maria*, and a *Credo* in any church or chapel where they do dwell, and put to their helping hand to the sustentation and maintenance of the charges of the said guild, as often as they so do, shall have clean remission *a pœna et culpa*, and the same remission as if they had visited the chapel of *Scala cœli* of Rome, and the church of St John Lateranense, when the stations there be celebrated for quick and dead."—Becon, Relics of Rome 1563, signature D d ii. Vide Bp. Latimer, Works, I. p. 97, note 2, Parker Soc.]

[2 Vide p. 49, note 5, above.]

sacraments than they be had in use, and used to the end for the which they were instituted.

And here we plainly confess that the mutilation of the Lord's supper, and the subtraction of one kind from the lay people, is antichristian. And so is the doctrine of transubstantiation of the sacramental bread and wine, after the words of consecration as they be called; item, the adoration of the sacrament with honour due unto God, the reservation and carrying about[3] of the same; item, the mass to be a propitiatory sacrifice for the quick and dead, or a work that pleaseth God. All these we confess and believe to be antichrist's doctrine: as is the inhibition of marriage as unlawful to any state.

And we doubt not by God's grace, but we shall be able to prove all our confessions here to be most true by the verity of God's word, and consent of the catholic church, which followeth and hath followed the governance of God's Spirit and the judgment of his word. And this through the Lord's help we will do, either in disputation by word before the queen's highness and her council, either before the parliament houses, (of whom we doubt not but to be indifferently heard,) either with our pens, whensoever we shall be thereto by them that have authority required and commanded.

In the mean season, as obedient subjects we shall behave ourselves towards all that be in authority; and not cease to pray to God for them that he would govern them all, generally and particularly, with "the Spirit of wisdom" and grace. And so we heartily desire, and humbly pray all men to do, in no point consenting to any kind of rebellion or sedition against our sovereign lady the queen's highness; but, where they cannot obey but they must disobey God, there to submit themselves, with all patience and humility, to suffer as the will and pleasure of the higher powers shall adjudge: as we are ready, through the goodness of the Lord, to suffer whatsoever they shall adjudge us unto, rather than we will consent to any contrary doctrine than this we here confess, unless we shall be justly convinced thereof, either by writing or by word, before such judges as the queen's highness and her council, or the parliament houses[4]. For the universities and

[3 'confirmation' 1563: 'carrying about' 1570, 1576, 1583.]

[4 So Foxe, Acts, &c. 1563. The words 'shall appoint' are added in 1570 and after editions, which seems to be an error, being against repeated statements in this 'Declaration.']

clergy have condemned our causes already by the bigger and not by the better part, without all disputation of the same: and therefore most justly we may and do appeal from them to be our judges in this behalf, except it may be in writing, that to all men the matter may appear.

The Lord of mercy endue us all with the Spirit of his truth and grace of perseverance therein unto the end. Amen. The 8th of May, A.D. 1554.

    ROBERT MENEVEN. alias ROBERT FERRAR.
    ROWLAND TAYLOR.
    JOHN PHILPOT.
    JOHN BRADFORD.
    JOANNES WIGORN. ET GLOUC. EPISCOPUS,
     alias JOANNES HOPER.
    EDWARD CROME.[1]
    JOHN ROGERS.
    LAURENTIUS SAUNDERS.
    EDMUND LAWRENCE.
    I. P.[2]
    T. M.[3]

To these things above said do I, MILES COVERDALE, late of Exon, consent and agree with these my afflicted brethren being prisoners, with mine own hand.

[1 See p. 290, note 1, above.]

[2 The initials 'J. P.' might possibly represent either 'James Pilkington,' afterward Bp. of Durham; or 'John Parkhurst,' afterward Bp. of Norwich; who severally were in exile at Zurich in the course of 1554. See 'Orig. Letters,' Parker Soc. II. 752; 'Troubles of Frankfort,' 1575, p. xvi.]

[3 The initials 'T. M.' might possibly stand, either for 'Tho. Matthew,' or 'Tho. Massye,' or 'Tho. Moor,' who were among the thirty-nine members of Parliament who absented themselves from the House of Commons, from Jan. 12, 1555, because of the measures then being carried against the Protestant faith.—Coke, Instit. Part IV. p. 17, Lond. 1797; Strype, Mem. III. i. 262—3.]

TO CERTAIN GODLY MEN,

WHOM HE EXHORTETH TO BE PATIENT UNDER THE CROSS AND CONSTANT IN THE TRUE DOCTRINE WHICH THEY HAD PROFESSED.

My dearly beloved in the Lord, as in him I wish you well to fare, so I pray God I and you may continue in his true service, that perpetually we may enjoy the same welfare, as here in hope, so in heaven indeed and eternally.

Bp. Coverdale, Letters of the Martyrs, 1564, p. 419—22. Foxe, Acts, &c. 1570, p. 1832—3; and after editions.

You know this world is not your home, but a pilgrimage and place wherein God trieth his children: and therefore, as it knoweth you not, nor can know you, so I trust you know not it; that is, you allow it not, nor in any point will seem so to do, although by many you be occasioned thereto. For this hot sun, which now shineth, burneth so sore that the corn which is sown upon sand and "stony ground" beginneth to wither: that is, many which before times we took for hearty gospellers begin now, for the fear of afflictions, to relent, yea, to "turn to their vomit again;" thereby declaring, that though "they go from amongst us, yet were they never of us; for else they would have still tarried with us," and neither for gain nor loss have left us either in word or deed. [1 John ii.]

As for their heart (which undoubtedly is double, and therefore in danger to God's curse,) we have as much with us as the papists have with them, and more too by their own judgment; for they, playing wily-beguile[4] themselves, think it enough inwardly to favour the truth, though outwardly they curry favour. 'What though with my body,' say they, 'I do this or that? God knoweth my heart is whole with him.' Ah brother! if thy 'heart be whole with God,' why dost not thou confess and declare thyself accordingly, by word and fact? Either that which thou sayest thou believest in thy 'heart' is good, or no. If it be good, why art thou ashamed of it? If it be evil, why dost thou keep it in thy 'heart?' Is not God able to defend thee, adventuring thyself

[4 'Playing wily-beguile:' deceiving. A proverbial expression. Vide Ray, Proverbs, p. 46, ed. 1817.]

for his cause? Or will not he defend his worshippers? Doth not the scripture say that "the eyes of the Lord are on them that fear him, and trust in his mercy?" And whereto? Forsooth, "to deliver their souls from death, and to feed them in the time of hunger."

If this be true, as it is most true, why are we afraid of death, as though God could not comfort or deliver us, or would not, contrary to his promise? Why are we afraid of the loss of our goods, as though God would leave them that fear him destitute of all good things, and so do against his most ample promises? Ah, faith, faith, how few feel thee now-a-days! Full truly said Christ, that he should scarcely "find faith when he came on earth:" for if men believed these promises, they would never do any thing outwardly which inwardly they disallow. No example of men, how many soever they be, or how learned soever they be, can prevail in this behalf; for the pattern which we must follow is Christ himself, and not the more company, or custom. His "word is the lantern to lighten our steps," and not learned men. Company and custom are to be considered according to the thing they allow. Learned men are to be listened to and followed according to God's lore and law; for else the more part goeth to the devil. As custom causeth error and blindness, so learning, if it be not according to the light of God's word, is poison, and learned men most pernicious. The devil is called 'demon' for his cunning[1]; and "the children of this world are much wiser than the children of light in their generation:" and I know the devil and his dearlings have always, for the most part, more helps in this life than Christ's church and her children.

They (the devil and his synagogue I mean) have custom, multitude, unity, antiquity, learning, power, riches, honour, dignity, and promotions plenty; as always they have had, and shall have commonly and for the most part until Christ's coming, much more than the true church have presently, heretofore have had, or hereafter shall have: for her glory,

[1 The word δαίμων, 'a divine being,' according to Plato, was derived from δαήμων, prudent, knowing. ὅτι φρόνιμοι καὶ δαήμονες ἦσαν, δαίμονας αὐτοὺς ['Ησίοδος] ὠνόμασε. καὶ ἔν γε τῇ ἀρχαίᾳ τῇ ἡμετέρᾳ φωνῇ αὐτὸ συμβαίνει τὸ ὄνομα.—Plat. Cratyl. Op. I. 398, ed. Serran. Paris. 1578.]

riches, and honour is not here; her trial, cross, and warfare is here.

And therefore, my dear hearts in the Lord, consider these things accordingly. Consider what you be, not worldlings, but God's children. Consider where you be, not at home, but in a strange country. Consider among whom you are conversant, even in the midst of your enemies and of a wicked generation: and then, I trust, you will not much muse at affliction, which you cannot be without, being as you be God's children, in a strange country, and in the midst of your enemies; except you would leave your Captain Christ, and follow Satan, for the muck of this mould, rest, and quietness, which he may promise you; and you indeed think you shall receive it, by doing as he would have you to do: but, my sweet hearts, he is not able to pay that he promiseth.

Peace and war come from God, riches and poverty, wealth and woe. The devil hath no power but by God's permission. If then God permit him a little on your goods, body, or life, I pray you tell me, "what can much hurt you," 1 Pet. iii. as Peter saith, "you being followers of godliness?" Think you that God will not remember you in his time, as most shall be to your comfort? "Can a woman forget the child of her Isai. xlix. womb? And if she should, yet will not I forget thee," saith the Lord. Look upon Abraham in his exile and misery; look upon Jacob, Joseph, Moses, David, the prophets, apostles, and all the godly from the beginning: and, my good brethren, is not God the same God? is he a changeling? "You have heard of the patience of Job," saith St James v. James, "and you have seen the end, how that God is merciful, patient, and long-suffering:" even so say I unto you that you shall find accordingly, if so be you be patient, that is, if so be you fear him, set his word before you, serve him thereafter; and, if he lay his cross on you, you bear it with patience: the which you shall do, when you consider it not according to the present sense, but according to the end. Heb. xii. 2 Cor. iv.

Therefore I heartily beseech you, and out of my bonds which I suffer for your sake pray you, mine own sweet hearts in the Lord, that you would cleave in heart and humble obedience to the doctrine taught you by me and many other my brethren. For we have taught you no fables, nor tales of men, or our own fantasies, but the very word of God, which we are ready with our lives, God so enabling us, as we trust he will, to confirm; and by the shedding of our bloods, in all patience and humble obedience to the superior powers, to testify and seal up; as well that you might be more certain of the doctrine, as that you might be ready to confess the same before this wicked world; knowing that, "if we confess Christ" and his truth "before men, he will confess us before his Father in heaven." "If so be we be ashamed hereof" for loss of life, friends, or goods, "he will be ashamed of us before his Father and his holy angels in heaven."

Therefore take heed for the Lord's sake, take heed, take heed, and defile not your bodies or souls with this Romish and antichristian religion, set up amongst us again; but "come away," "come away," as the angel crieth, "from amongst them," in their idolatrous service, "lest you be partakers of their iniquity."

<small>Rev. xviii.</small>

Hearken to your preachers, as the Thessalonians did to Paul: that is, confer their sayings with the scriptures; and, if they sound not thereafter, "the morning light shall not shine upon them." Use much and hearty prayer for "the Spirit of wisdom," knowledge, humbleness, meekness, sobriety, and repentance; which we have great need of, because our sins have thus "provoked the Lord's anger" against us. But let us "bear his anger," and acknowledge our faults with bitter tears and sorrowful sighs: and doubtless he will be merciful to us after his wonted mercy.

<small>Isai. viii. [20: see margin, and Vulgate.]</small>

The which thing he vouchsafe to do, for his holy name's sake, in Christ Jesu our Lord: to whom, with the Father and the Holy Ghost, be all honour, glory, praise, and everlasting thanks, from this time forth, for evermore. Amen.

Out of prison, by yours in the Lord to command,

JOHN BRADFORD.

A LETTER

TO CERTAIN GODLY MEN,

RELIEVERS AND HELPERS OF HIM AND OTHERS IN THEIR IMPRISONMENT.

THE peace of Christ, which passeth all pleasure and worldly felicity, be daily more and more felt in your hearts, my right dearly beloved in the Lord, by the inward working of the Holy Spirit, "the earnest of our inheritance," and guider of God's elect: with the which God our dear Father more and more endue us all unto the end, for his beloved Son's sake, our Lord Jesus Christ. Amen.

Bp. Coverdale, Letters of the Martyrs, 1564, p. 460—5.

MS. 2. 2. 15. no. 112. Emman. Coll. Cambridge.

Praised be God, "the Father of our Lord Jesus Christ," which is a "Father of mercy and a God of all consolation," that hath blessed you with the knowledge and love of his truth, not only to your own comforts, but also to[1] the great ease and comfort of many, which, without the help of God by you hitherto, had been in much more misery. By your relieving the Lord's prisoners I am brought to see the root whereof the work doth spring, even the knowledge and love of God's truth, wherefor we are in bonds. The which knowledge and love in that it is a blessing of all blessings the greatest, (for it is even "eternal life,") I cannot but praise God for you on this behalf, that it hath pleased him to vouch you worthy so excellent and singular a benefit, which is more to be esteemed, desired, and cared for, than any thing else.

John xvii.

The world, for all that ever it hath, cannot attain by any means to this blessing, which God our Father hath given you freely of his own good will through Christ, even before ye were purposed to desire it. Therefore I beseech you all to be thankful with me, and to "rejoice in the Lord:" for, if he have given us such a gift unasked, undesired, yea, unthought upon, how can it be that he will deny us any good thing now, which may be necessary for us? Will he, trow ye, "sow his seed" in the ground of your hearts, and not keep away "the fowls" from picking it up? Would he so bestow his seed in you as he hath, if that he would not hedge in your hearts,

[1 'to,' MS.: not in 1564.]

his field, from common paths, and from breaking in of beasts to destroy it? Will he be more careless than a good husbandman to weed out the weeds which are in us, lest they should overgrow the corn of his word? Will not he bestow muck and marl upon us, "that we may bring forth more fruit?" If in a good husbandman this be not lacking, alas! how should we think then but that the Lord God, a good husbandman, and nothing but good, and only good; how, I say, should it be, but that he is most careful to keep his seed already sown in your hearts by the ministry of us and other his preachers; and that to the bringing forth of just and full fruits? "He that hath begun with you," doubt not, my dearly beloved, but that he will happily make an end with you. He hath begun to sow his seed in you, as I dare say ye feel it.

Be sure then that all this will follow: first he will have scarecrows in your hearts; I mean, such sparkles of his fear will he drop, yea, already he hath dropped into you, that "the birds of the air," vain and evil cogitations, shall not be cherished of you, but expelled by crying to the Lord for his help. Secondly, he will make such hedges, as shall keep you as well from by-paths of all evil customs and usages, as also preserve you from the power of evil and "dominion of sin," which would have the upper hand on you. Thirdly, he will doubtless pour such showers upon you to supple you, so weed you, so muck and marl you by temptation and other exercises, that the sunshine of persecution shall make more to the ripening of his seed in you, than to the withering of it away.

These things, my dearly beloved, the Lord God, which hath begun them in you and for you, will continue with you, that in the end you may be brought into his barn, there to rest with him in eternal felicity. For God's sake therefore wait and look for no less than I have told you at his hands: a greater service can you not give him. If God keep not the order I have told you, but perchance begin to muck and marl you, to pour his showers upon you, to nip you with his weeding tongs, &c.; "rejoice and be glad" that God will do that in you and with you at once, which a long time he hath been a working in and for others.

Now undoubtedly great showers are fallen to supple our

hearts, that God's word might enter therein and take root. Now the Lord goeth a weeding, to weed out of us our carnality, security, covetousness, self-love, forgetfulness of God, love of this world. Now the Lord doth muck and marl us, loading us with heaps and burdens of crosses, that our hearts might be made "good ground," to "bring forth fruit" to God's glory "by patience;" as well in suffering inward temptations and griefs, whereof we must complain to the Lord for his scarecrows to drive them forth of us; as also in suffering outward assaults, for the which we must cry to our Master for his hedges and defence: which hath two parts, the one concerning us, to help and deliver us; and the other concerning our, or rather his, obstinate adversaries, to take vengeance upon them, which he will do in his time.

Therefore let us "by patience possess our souls," knowing that they "which persevere to the end shall be saved." "Let us not be weary of well-doing, for in our time we shall reap the fruits thereof." But rather, "whiles we have time," let us redeem it in " doing well to all men, but specially to the household of faith:" which thing hitherto you have done; (the Lord therefor be praised, and in the day of his coming he recompense you;) and in the rest I hope well; I mean that you have declared no less in confessing the truth planted in your hearts, by your words and works after your vocation, to the glory of God.

I hope you have godly behaved yourselves, not being as too many be now-a-days, even mongrels, giving half to God and half to the world, halting on both knees, going two ways: I mean it of the mass-gospellers, which are worse than any papists. In this point I hope well of you, my dearly beloved, that you have not contaminated yourselves; that you have both confessed the truth as often as need hath required, and also have refrained from coming to church now, where is nothing but idolatrous service. I hope you have glorified God both in soul and body. I hope you have "gathered with Christ," and not "scattered abroad." I hope you have drawn no "yoke with unbelievers," nor "communicated with other men's sins," but have "abstained from all appearance of evil;" confessing in heart, confessing in tongue, confessing in deed and act, the true knowledge of God, which he hath of his great mercy given unto you, "not to be as a candle under a bushel, but upon the candlestick, to give light that men may see your good works, and glorify your Father which is in heaven." All this I hope of you, my beloved, and also of all purity of life and godly conversation; not doubting but in this behalf also you have declared God's verity in your heart, and for the Lord's sake do so still in all points: that is, in your vocations be diligent and righteous, towards yourselves be sober and pure, towards your neighbours be charitable and just, towards God be faithful and thankful, loving and obedient.

Use earnest and often hearty prayer. Meditate much upon, and often hearken to, the word of God. If you be called, "give with modesty an account of the hope which is in you." Be not ashamed of God's true service; allow not that with your presence, which is contrary to God's will. Make not the members of Christ's church, that is, yourselves, members of antichrist's church. Be not ashamed of the gospel, or of such as be bound therefor, but rather be partakers thereof; first inwardly, by compassion, prayer, &c.; then outwardly, by giving according to that the Lord hath lent you to that end; and last of all by suffering with us, if God so will, and if it be needful for you. For, my dearly beloved, be certain that no man can touch you, or lay hands upon you, but by the will of God, which is all good towards you; even as the will of a most dear father which cannot always be angry, or otherwise use his rod than only to chastise and correct, not to destroy his children.

Again, be certain that no cross shall come unto you before you need it: for God is our "Physician;" and when he seeth our souls in peril, he preventeth the peril by purgation and ministering physic, which is the cross. As therefore for the body we follow the advice of the physicians for the health thereof, thankfully using their counsel and obeying their precepts; so, for God's sake, let us for our souls, being sick, thankfully receive the heavenly "Physician's" physic and diet. So shall we wax "strong men" in God and in his Christ: which thing I beseech thee, O Holy Spirit, to work in us all. Amen.

Phil. iv.

My dearly beloved, this have I briefly written unto you, not as one that "seeketh any gifts," as Paul saith, but as one that "seeketh abundant fruits on your behalf," and to your commodity. For "it is better to give than to receive," saith Christ by his apostle St Paul, who testifieth that "according to that we sow, so shall we reap." "He that soweth little shall reap little; he that soweth much shall reap much." Never should we forget how that "the Lord Jesus, being rich, for our sakes became poor, that we might be made rich by him." Again, never should we forget that we are "dead to sin and alive to righteousness." 2 Cor. ix.

Therefore should we live wholly unto God and for God, and not for ourselves. In all things therefore we must avoid the seeking of ourselves, as well in doing, as in leaving things undone. If the cross come upon us therefor, then "are we happy; for the Spirit of God and glory of God resteth upon us." Therefore "rejoice," saith Christ, "for your reward is great in heaven." In this we are made like to Christ here: therefore we shall be so elsewhere, even in eternal joy and endless glory. Matt. v.

The highway to heaven, you know, is affliction; so that "all that will live godly in Christ Jesu must suffer persecution." "If we were of the world, the world would love us: but we are not of the world," but bear witness against the world, and therefore "the world doth hate us." But let us "rejoice," our Lord "hath overcome the world." John xv.

"He suffered out of the city," bearing our rebuke, saith the apostle. "Let us then go out of our tents, and bear his rebuke;" that is, let us "deny ourselves, take up our cross (which is his also), and follow him." Let us know and esteem this "more riches than all the treasures of the world," as Moses did. Let us know that "he that saveth his life shall lose it." Let us know that the way to salvation is a "strait way," and a way wherein we cannot carry our bags and chests with us. Let us know that no excuse of wife, farm, house, or children, will excuse us. Let us know that in this case we must be so far from "loving father, mother, wife, and children," that we must "hate them, and our own selves also." Heb. xiii.

Luke xiv.

Though this be a hard saying, yet we must not leave our lodesman[1] for a little foul way. Yea, rather we should know indeed that it is but hard to the flesh, which, if she be handled daintily, will be imperious: under must she be kept, that the spirit, which is a precious thing in God's sight, may have her

[1 See p. 235, note 1, above.]

commodities. If we should follow the fancy of the flesh, we could not please God. Against it we have made a solemn profession, as also against the devil and the world, in our baptism. And shall we now look for easy things of our enemies? Shall we not look rather to be hardly entreated of them[1]? Shall not hard gear be more seemly for them[2]?

O that we considered often and indeed what we have professed in baptism! Then the cross and we should be well acquainted together; for we are "baptized into Christ's death;" that is, as to be partakers of the benefit of his death, which is remission of sins, so to be made like thereunto continually, by dying to sin.

O that we considered what we be, where we be, whither we are going, who calleth us, how he calleth us, to what felicity he calleth us, whereby he calleth us! Then, my dear hearts in the Lord, we should say to all worldly persuasions and persuaders, "Follow me, Satan, thou savourest not those things that be of God, but the things that be of men." "Shall we not drink the cup which our heavenly Father hath appointed for us?"

[Matt. xvi. 23. 'Come after me,' Tyndale 1534.]

O Lord God, "open thou our eyes," that we may see the hope whereunto thou hast called us. Give us eyes of seeing, ears of hearing, and hearts of understanding. "In the favour thou bearest to thy people remember us; visit us with thy saving health, that we may see the good" things thou hast prepared for thy elect children, that we may have some sight of thy "heavenly Jerusalem," and have some taste of the sweetness of thy house. O dear Father, kindle in us an earnest desire to be with thee in soul and body, to praise thy name for ever, with all thy saints, in thy eternal glory. Amen.

Your brother in bonds for the testimony of the Lord Jesus[3],

JOHN BRADFORD.

[1 The last eleven words are in 1564, but not in the MS.]
[2 The last nine words are in the MS., but not in 1564.]
[3 The last eleven words are in the MS., but not in 1564.]

ADDRESS ON CONSTANCY[4].

J. B.

PEACE be multiplied to you, dear brethren, in our Lord and Saviour Jesus Christ, that ye may be able through his holy Spirit, to be strong against all temptations in these present days of trouble. So be it. MS. 218, fol. 3—13. Gonv. and Caius Coll. Cambridge.

The time is even at hand, my dear brethren, that our Saviour Jesus Christ gave us warning of in divers places of his holy doctrine; who, tendering our infirmities, admonished us we should not fear, but with constant faith boldly follow, that his word should not be spoken to us in vain, and like valiant soldiers prepare ourselves to the battle that should be set before our eyes: so that, as I say, that time unawares do not happen, but a foreknowledge to us is premonished by our Saviour Christ.

Now all ye therefore, that be in Christ Jesu, "watch and pray," and be ye ready to "put on the armour" of Christ: for "flesh and blood" cannot attain to this conflict but through the mighty operation of God's holy Spirit; which we must desire of God our Father for his dear Son's sake, Jesus Christ, that we may be able to abide the storms and brunts of this present time.

My dear brethren, let not the cares of worldly things quail and quench the inheritance of our felicity. Let not princes and rulers by unlawful laws draw us from the unmoveable word of God: and let not fire, gallows, halter, imprisonment, famine, pain, wife, children, riches, father, mother, house, lands, friends, honours, nor all things worldly, separate us from the love that we have to God; but patiently to abide God's good will, whatsoever it please him to try us withal: for assured we be that "through many tribulations we must enter into the kingdom of Christ:" such is the promise of holy scripture. And should not we with joyful hearts give over ourselves and follow him, who hath made our entrance by the like sufferance, to the loss of his life and shedding of his most precious blood? Let us be strong and not faint, when that we shall be tried. And yet let us not

[4 This Address is now printed for the first time.]

[BRADFORD.]

think the afflictions of this life are worthy of the joys to come (but patiently abiding the same, that declareth in us our faithfulness to God) to purchase his favour, constantly believing that we be his sons "and coheirs with Christ:" for he "hath suffered for us," and we must suffer for his sake and our brethren; not that our suffering doth advantage his glory, but through his suffering that did advantage our glory in him: and so did he glorify us.

If we will glory in Christ, let it be "in the cross of Christ:" let our rejoicing be in persecutions, death, imprisonings, with all ignominies, for Christ's sake.

O my dear brethren, taste now how sweet the Lord is, according to his holy promise; for in your troubles he will so assist you, that hell and death shall not prevail against you: the sharp storms of death shall become pleasant and nothing troublesome to you: "your sorrow shall be turned into joy." Your death is most pleasant in his sight: "when you suffer for righteousness' sake, blessed are you."

Now God for his dear Son's sake, Jesus Christ, assist us in the time of temptation; and that it be not said to us, as the holy apostle Paul said to the Galatians: '"O ye foolish Galatians, who hath bewitched you? You began in the Spirit, and end in the flesh." Ye professed Christ Jesus, ye confessed him to be your only Saviour, ye were as men that sought all his honour and glory, and none other to have it but only God. But "who hath bewitched you, ye foolish Galatians," that ye be now [fallen] from that Spirit of grace, and now to take you to your old customs again?'

O far be it from us to hear those words laid to our charge, 'O ye foolish Englishmen, "who hath bewitched you?" Ye professed the gospel of Jesus Christ: ye could pronounce and declare every part thereof: your books were never out of your hands, and your houses replenished with the Bible, books, and Testaments. Your kings and governors were content to hear and set forth the same, maintaining God's prophets; and to command that universally in the kingdom to be set forth, willing all true subjects reverently to embrace the same, and to frame their lives accordingly: so that to all other realms God hath willed you to be a blazing star. But now, O thou foolish Englishman,' (it may be said,) '"who hath bewitched you?" that so suddenly hast forsaken the sweet gospel of thy Saviour Jesus Christ, renouncing the effects of his death and passion, girding[1] on the sweet and joyful promise that he made to you in his precious blood, and hast left the true saying as he commanded: whereas he would be known and worshipped to be thy Lord God and Saviour only. And now, thou foolish Englishman, thou art bewitched, so that all thy doings is become abominable in the sight of God: thy rulers and governors do stand up "against the Lord's anointed," oppressing the prophets and messengers of God, prisoning and pining[2] them of wilful malice for Christ's sake, destroying the holy library of God's holy word, setting up the traditions and dreams of men, and exalting "the abomination to stand in the holy place," honouring dead and dumb gods in the stead of the everlasting God who is a "living God," "turning to thy vomit again." O thou foolish Englishman, "who hath bewitched you?"'

Now, my dear brethren, be not bewitched by the persuasions of wicked men: let not their threats fear you, be not ye deceived with their vain speech, look not back with Lot's wife to Sodom again. Better it is "to obey God than man." Afflictions and trouble is the cognisance of God, declaring whose soldiers we be: it is the just promise of God, to "be hated of all men for his name's sake." Our example in the scriptures we may see from Abel from time to time, and last to Christ, who is the very mark we must look unto. We are not better than other men. If we account ourselves to be his servants, "if they called our Master Beelzebub, what will they then call us?" "If they hated me," saith Christ, "so will they do you."

Wherefore then should God's elect look to live in pleasures and felicities in this world? But rather look to the celestial joys, where "neither thieves shall steal, nor moths corrupt, nor rust or canker fret;" so that "we have no abiding here."

Wherefore the time draweth nigh, and "is even at hand," that God will try his people: he hath taken "his fan in his hand." And as for vain excuses before him, [they] must be

[1 'Girding': casting reproach. Nares, Glossary.]
[2 'Pining:' wearing out, making to languish. Todd's Johnson, Dict.]

laid apart. It may not be said, 'God knoweth my heart: I am not mortified; my wife and children should perish: I have not set my business at a stay with too many worldly ceremonies;' and so think they may please God in going to the church with a safe conscience (being there as the Lord God is blasphemed), yea, and can defend themselves with scriptures. But beware what you do: howsoever you take the scriptures for your purpose, you know this, that "no idolaters shall enter into the kingdom of God."

What difference is there between the thief that stealeth the goods and him that receiveth? The lawyers do call such accessories to the felony. Ye know that God is robbed of his honour; and ye be content to consent to the thief, with being present at their devilish doings. Jumble not up the scriptures after such manner, but rather look that ye fall not into God's vengeance: "it is a fearful thing to fall into the hands of the living God."

Therefore be "hot or cold, or else the Lord will spew you out of his mouth." His word doth condemn you; and the prophet doth cry out on such double-hearted men, saying, 'How long will ye halt on both knees?' The scripture of God willeth all men they should "draw nigh unto God," and not to go from him. "If ye deny me before men," saith our Saviour Christ, "I will deny you before my Father which is in heaven."

O Lord God, if thou deny us, to whom shall we flee?

Beware therefore, my dear brethren, dissemble not with God: he doth desire a sincere and a pure heart. He is called 'the Searcher of the heart:' all things is open unto him. Go through with him with a pure faith, and ye shall be rewarded accordingly.

Let us therefore walk circumspectly in the vocation that we are called unto, as it becometh saints; and as his dear children patiently abide our Father's correction, that at his coming we may be found sons, and not bastards; living in pureness of life all the days of our times, as he hath commanded: so that we may receive the joys of heaven through Jesus Christ our Lord: to whom, with the Father and the Holy Ghost, be all honour and glory, world without end. Amen.

Anno Domini 1554.

LETTER ON THE MASS,

TO HOPKINS AND OTHERS, AT COVENTRY[1].

[Sept. 2, 1554.]

To my dear brother in the Lord, Master Richard Hopkins and his wife dwelling in Coventry, and other his faithful brethren and sisters, professors of God's holy gospel, there and thereabouts.

Bp Coverdale, Letters of the Martyrs, 1564, p. 345—54.

MS. 2. 2. 15. no. 1. Emman. Coll. Cambridge.

The peace which Christ left to his church and to every true member of the same, the Holy Spirit, the Guide of God's children, so engraft in your heart, and in the heart of your good wife and of all my good brethren and sisters about you, that unfeignedly ye may in respect thereof contemn all worldly peace; which is contrary to that peace that I speak of, and driveth it utterly out of the hearts of all those which would patch them both together. For "we cannot serve two masters: no man can serve God and mammon:" Christ's peace cannot be kept with this world's peace. God therefore of his mercy do I beseech to give unto you his "peace which passeth all understanding," and so "keep your hearts and minds," that they may be pure habitacles and mansions for

MS. Lansd. 389. fol. 291 —5. British Museum.

Bp. Ridley on Sacram., and Letter by Bradford, Oxford, 1688. John xiv. Rom. viii.

Matt. vi.

Phil. iv.

[[1] The title of this letter in the Cambridge MS. is, 'An epistle of the godly man Master John Bradford, prisoner of the Lord in the King's Bench, for the testimony of his truth, unto his brother in Christ Richard Hopkyngs of Coventry, grocer.' Another letter to Hopkins is given in Bp. Coverdale, Letters of the Martyrs 1564, p. 354—7, and in Foxe, Acts, &c. 1583, p. 1648—9, or ed. 1843-8, VII. 249—50, which will appear hereafter in this collection of the Writings of Bradford.

Hopkins, who was sheriff of Coventry at the time, was afterward committed to the Fleet prison for some "matter pertaining to religion," and "being at length delivered . . and minding to keep his conscience pure from idolatry was driven with his wife and eight young children to avoid the realm; and so went into high Germany, where he continued in the city of Basil till the death of queen Mary; being like a good Tobias, to his power a friendly helper and a comfortable reliever of other English exiles there about him; God's holy blessing so working with him therefor, that in those far countries neither he fell in any great decay, neither any one of all his household during all that time there miscarried, but so many as he brought out, so many he recarried home again, yea, and that with advantage, and God's plenty withal upon him."—Foxe, ibid.]

the Holy Spirit, yea, for the blessed Trinity, who hath promised to come and dwell in all them that love Christ and keep his sayings.

<small>John xiv.</small>

My dearly beloved, the time is now come, wherein trial is made of men that have professed to love Christ, and would have been counted keepers of his testimonies. But, welaway[1]! the tenth person persevereth not: the more part do part stakes with the papists and protestants, so that they are become mangy mongrels, to the infecting of all that company with them, and to their no small peril; for they pretend outwardly popery, going to mass with the papists, and tarrying with them personally at their antichristian and idolatrous service; but 'with their hearts,' say they, 'and with their spirits' they serve the Lord. And so by this means, as they save their pigs, which they would not lose, (I mean their worldly pelf,) so they would please the protestants, and be counted with them for gospellers, yea, marry, would they.

<small>The mongrels' excuse.</small>

<small>Matt. viii.</small>

But, mine own beloved in the Lord, flee from such persons as from men most perilous and pernicious, both before God and man; for they are false to both, and true to neither. To the magistrates they are false, pretending one thing and meaning clean contrary. To God they are most untrue, giving him but a piece, which should have the whole.

<small>Company not with mongrels.</small>

<small>Mongrels are false both to God and man.</small>

I would they would tell me, who made their bodies? Did not God, as well as their spirits and souls? And who keepeth both? Doth not he still? And, alas! shall not he have the service of the body, but it must be given to serve the new-found god of antichrist's invention? Did not Christ buy both our souls and bodies? And wherewith? With any less price than with his precious blood?

<small>God will have the whole service of soul and body. He made both; he keepeth both; he redeemed both.</small>

Ah, wretches then that we be, if we will defile either part with the rose-coloured whore of Babylon's filthy mass-abomination! It had been better for us never to have been washed, than so to wallow ourselves in the filthy puddle of popery: it had been better never to have known the truth, than thus to betray it. Surely, surely, let such men fear, that their "latter end be not worse than the beginning."

<small>Rev. xviii.</small>

<small>2 Pet. ii.</small>

<small>Heb. vi. x.
Matt. xii.
Luke xi.</small>

Their own conscience now accuseth them before God (if so be they have any conscience), that they are but dissemblers and hypocrites to God and man: for all the cloaks they make,

<small>Mongrels sin against their own consciences.</small>

[¹ Vide p. 39, note 5, above.]

they cannot avoid this, but that their going to church and to mass is of self-love; that is, they go thither because they would avoid the cross, they go thither because they would be out of trouble. They seek neither the queen's highness, nor her laws, which in this point cannot bind the conscience to obey, because they are contrary to God's laws, which bid us often to "flee idolatry" and worshipping him after men's devices. They seek neither (I say) the laws, if there were any, neither their brethren's commodity; for none cometh thereby, neither godliness or good example, (for there can be none found in going to mass, &c.,) but horrible "offences and woe to them that give them:" but they seek their own selves, their own ease, their escaping the cross, &c. When they have made all the excuses they can, their own conscience will accuse them of this, that their going to church is only because they seek themselves: for, if there would no trouble ensue for tarrying away, I appeal to their conscience, would they come thither? Never, I dare say.

The only cause why mongrels go to mass is to avoid the cross.

Acts v.
1 Cor. x.
Deut. xii.

Matt xviii.

Therefore, as I said, they seek themselves; they would not carry the cross. And hereof their own conscience, if they have any conscience, doth accuse them. Now if their conscience accuse them at this present, what will it do before the judgment-seat of Christ? Who will then excuse it, when Christ shall appear in judgment, and shall begin to be "ashamed of them then, which now here are ashamed of him?" Who then, I say, will excuse these mass-gospellers' consciences? Will the queen's highness? She shall then have more to do for herself than, without hearty and speedy repentance, she can ever be able to answer; though Peter, Paul, Mary, James, John, the pope, and all his prelates take her part, with all the singing sir Johns[2] that ever were, are, and shall be. Will the lord chancellor and prelates of the realm excuse them there? Nay, nay, they are like then to smart for it so sore, as I would not be in their places for all the whole world. Will the laws of the realm, the nobility, gentlemen, justices of peace, &c. excuse our gospel-massmongers' consciences then? Nay, God knoweth they can do little there but quake and fear for the heavy vengeance of God, like to fall upon them. Will their goods, lands, and possessions, the which they by their dissembling have saved, will these serve to excuse them? No, no, God is no merchant, as our mass-priests

Luke ix. xii.
Mark viii.

[[2] See note E.]

be. Will masses or trentals[1] and such trash serve? No, verily, the haunters of this gear then shall be horribly ashamed. Will the catholic church excuse them? Nay, it will most of all accuse them; as will all the good fathers, patriarchs, apostles, prophets, martyrs, confessors, and saints, with all the good doctors, and good general councils.

All these already condemn the mass, and all that ever useth it as it is now, being of all idols that ever was the most abominable, and blasphemous to Christ, and his priesthood, manhood, and sacrifice; for it maketh the priest that saith mass God's fellow and better than Christ, for the offerer is always better or equivalent to the thing offered. If therefore the priest take upon him there to offer up Christ, as they boldly affirm they do, then must he needs be better, or equal with Christ[2]. O that they would shew but one iota of the scripture of God calling them to this dignity, or of their authority to offer up Christ for the quick and dead, and to apply the benefit and virtue of his death and passion to whom they will!

The most abomination on earth is the mass.
The mass-priest is Christ's fellow.

Heb. v.

Surely if this were true, as it is most false and blasphemous, prate they at their pleasure to the contrary, then it made no matter at all whether Christ were our friend or no, if so be the mass-priest were our friend: for he can apply us Christ's merits by his mass if he will, and when he will; and therefore we need little to care for Christ's friendship. They can make him when they will, and where they will. "Lo, here he is, there he is!" say they: but, "believe them not," saith Christ, "believe them not," "believe them not," saith he. For in his human nature and body, (which was made of the substance of the virgin's body, and not of bread,) in this body, I say, he is, and 'sitteth on the right hand of God the Father Almighty' in heaven, 'from whence' (and not from the pyx[3]) 'shall he come to judge both the quick and dead[4].'

The mass-priest's friendship is better than Christ's.
The mass-priest is above God, for he can make God. Matt. xxiv.
St Augustine. [Emman. MS.]

Acts iii.

In the mean season "heaven," saith St Peter, " must re-

[1 Vide p. 49, note 5, above.]   [2 Compare p. 6—8, above.]
[3 Vide p. 88, note 2, above.]
[4 Noli itaque dubitare ibi nunc esse hominem Christum Jesum, unde venturus est; memoriterque recole, et fideliter tene Christianam confessionem, quoniam resurrexit a mortuis, adscendit in cœlum, sedet ad dexteram Patris, nec aliunde quam inde venturus est ad vivos mortuosque judicandos.—August. Lib. ad Dardan. seu Epist. clxxxvii. 10. Op. II. col. 681, ed. Bened. Par. 1679—1700.]

ceive him;" and, as Paul saith, he "prayeth for us," and now is not seen elsewhere, or otherwise seen than by faith there, until he shall be "seen as he is," "to the salvation of them that look for his coming:" which I trust be not far off; for, if "the day of the Lord" drew near in the apostle's time, which is now above fifteen hundred years past, it cannot be, I trust, long hence now; I trust our Redeemer's "coming" is at hand. Then these mass-sayers and seers shall shake, and cry to the hills, "Hide us from the fierce wrath of the Lamb," if they repent not in time. Then will neither gold, nor goods, friendship nor fellowship, lordship nor authority, power nor pleasure, unity nor antiquity, custom nor council, doctors, devils, nor any man's device serve. "The word which the Lord hath spoken in that day shall judge;" "the word," I say, of God "in that day shall judge." Rom. viii. Heb. vii.
Heb. ix.
1 Thess. v.
Luke xxi.
Rev. vi.
John xii. The word of God shall be our judge.

And what saith it of idolatry and idolaters? Saith it not, "Flee from it?" and further, that "they shall be damned?" O terrible sentence to all mass-mongers, and worshippers of things made with the hands of bakers, carpenters, &c.! This word of God knoweth no moe oblations or sacrifices for sin, but one only, which Christ himself offered, never more to be re-offered; but in remembrance thereof his supper to be eaten sacramentally and spiritually, according to Christ's institution; which is so perverted now that there is nothing in it simply according to the judge, I mean the word of God. It were good for men to "agree with their adversary," the word of God, now "whilst they be in the way with it;" lest, if they linger, it will deliver them to the Judge Christ, who will "commit them to the jailer, and so they shall be cast into prison, and never come out thence till they have paid the uttermost farthing," that is, never. 1 Cor. x.
1 Cor. vi.
Heb. vii. ix. x.
Matt. v.

My dearly beloved, therefore mark the word, hearken to the word: it alloweth no massing, no such sacrificing, nor worshipping of Christ with tapers, candles, copes[5], canopies, &c. It alloweth no Latin service, no images in the temples, no praying to saints dead, no praying for the dead. It alloweth no such dissimulation as a great many use now outwardly. "If any withdraw himself, my soul," saith the In all things hearken to the word of God as did the Thessalonians, [qu. Bereans.] Acts xvii.
Heb. x.

[5 'Cope:' an ecclesiastical vestment, a cloak worn in public ministration; from the Anglo-Saxon *cæppe*. Vide Palmer, Orig. Liturg. II. append. sect. iii. and plates.]

Holy Ghost, "shall have no pleasure in him." It alloweth not the love of this world, which maketh men to do many times against their consciences; for "in them that love the world the love of God abideth not." It alloweth not gatherers elsewhere than with Christ, but saith, they "scatter abroad." It alloweth no lukewarm gentlemen: but, "if God be God, then follow him;" "if Baal (and a piece of bread) be God, then follow it." It alloweth not "faith in the heart," that hath not "confession in the mouth." It alloweth no disciples that will not "deny themselves," that will not "take up their cross and follow Christ." It alloweth not the "seeking of ourselves," or of our own ease and commodity. It alloweth not the more part, but the better part. It alloweth not unity, except it be in verity. It alloweth no obedience to any, which cannot be done without disobedience to God. It alloweth no church that is not the spouse of Christ, and hearkeneth not to his voice only. It alloweth no doctor that speaketh against it. It alloweth no general council that followeth not it[1] in all things. *Summa*, it alloweth no "angel," much more then any such as would teach any other thing than Moses, the prophets, Christ Jesus, and his apostles have taught and left us to look upon in the written word of God, the holy books of the Bible; but curseth all that teach, not only contrary, but also any other doctrine. It saith they are fools, unwise, proud, that will not consent to the sound word and doctrine of Christ and his apostles; and biddeth and commandeth us to flee from such.

Therefore obey this commandment. Company not with them, specially in their church-service, but flee from them; for in what thing consent they to Christ's doctrine? He biddeth us pray in a tongue to edify: they command contrary. He biddeth us call upon his Father in his name, when we pray: they bid us run to Mary, Peter, &c. He biddeth us use his supper in the remembrance of his death and passion, preaching it out "till he[2] come;" whereby he doth us to wit that corporally he is not there in the form of bread: therefore saith Paul, "till he come." He willeth us to "eat of the bread" (calling it 'bread' after consecration) and "drink of that cup" "all," making no exception, so that we do it worthily; that is, take it as the sacrament of his body and

[1 'it' Emman. MS., Lansd. MS., and 1688: not in 1564.]
[2 'it' 1564: 'he,' Emman. MS., Lansd. MS., and 1688.]

blood, "broken and shed for our sins," and not as the body itself, and blood itself, without bread, without wine; but as the sacrament of his body and blood, whereby he doth represent, and unto our faith give and obsign[3] unto us himself wholly, with all the merits and glory of his body and blood. But they forbid utterly the use of the supper to all but to their shavelings, except it be once in the year[4], and then also the cup they take from us: they never preach forth the Lord's death but in mockery and mows[5]. They take away all the sacrament by their transubstantiation; for they take away the element, and so the sacrament[6]. To be short, they most horribly abuse this holy ordinance of the Lord, by adoration, reservation, oblation, ostentation, &c.

The fruits that follow the worthy receiving of the Lord's supper.

Transubstantiation taketh away the sacrament

In nothing they are contented with the simplicity of God's word. They add to and take from at their pleasure: and therefore the plagues of God will fall upon them at the length, and upon all that will take their part. They seek not Christ, nor his glory; for you see they utterly have cast away his word: and therefore, as the prophet saith, "there is no wisdom in them." They follow the strumpet church and[7] spouse of antichrist, which they call the catholic church, whose foundation and pillars is the devil and his daughter the mass, with his children the pope and his prelates. Their laws are craft and cruelty; their weapons are lying and murder; their end and study is their own glory, fame, wealth, rest, and possessions.

Rev. xxii. John v.

Jer. viii. Deut. iv. Rev. x

For if a man speak nor do nothing against these, though he be a sodomite, an adulterer, an usurer, &c., it forceth not, he shall be quiet enough, no man shall trouble him. But if any one speak anything to God's glory, which cannot stand without the overthrow of man's glory, then shall he be disquieted, imprisoned, and troubled, except he will play mum,

[3 'Obsign:' seal, ratify.]

[4 The 'fifth article' of the Devonshire rebels, 1549, contained the demand, 'We will have the sacrament of the altar but at Easter delivered to the lay-people.' . Abp. Cranmer, Answ. to the rebels, Works, II. 173—4. Parker Soc. Vide Becon, Catechism, v. Works, II. 257—60, Parker Soc.; and Bingham, Orig. Eccl. xv. ix. Works, I. 824 —31, Lond. 1726.]

[5 'Mows:' grimaces, looks assumed in derision.]

[6 Compare p. 87 above.]

[7 A word of the original is omitted.]

and put his finger upon his mouth, although the same be a most quiet and godly man. So that easily a man may see, how that they be antichrist's church, and sworn soldiers to the pope and his spouse, and not to Christ and his church: for then would they not cast away God's word; then would they be no more adversaries to his glory, which chiefly consisteth in obedience to his word.

Therefore, my dear hearts in the Lord, seem not to allow this, or any part of the pelf of this Romish church and "synagogue of Satan." Halt not on both knees, for halting will "bring you out of the way;" but, like valiant champions of the Lord, confess, confess, I say, with your mouth, as occasion serveth, and as your vocation requireth, the hope and faith you have and feel in your heart.

But you will say that so to do is perilous; you shall by that means lose your liberty, your lands, your goods, your friends, your name, your life, &c.; and so shall your children be left in miserable state, &c. To this I answer, my good brethren, that you have professed in baptism to fight under the standard of your Captain Christ: and will you now, for peril's sake, leave your Lord? You made a solemn vow that you would forsake the world: and will you be forsworn, and run to embrace it now? You sware and promised to "leave all and follow Christ:" and will you now leave him for your "father, your mother, your children, your lands, your life," &c.? "He that hateth not these," saith Christ, "is not worthy of me." "He that forsaketh not these and himself also, and withal taketh not up his cross and followeth him, the same shall be none of his disciples."

Therefore either bid Christ adieu, be forsworn, and run to the devil quick; or else say, as a Christian should say, that wife, children, goods, life, &c. are not to be dear unto you in respect of Christ, who is your portion and inheritance. Let the worldlings, which have no hope of eternal life, fear perils of loss of lands, goods, life, &c. Here is not our home, we are here but "pilgrims and strangers;" this life is but the desert and wilderness to the land of rest. "We look for a city, whose workman is God" himself. We are now "dwellers in the tents of Kedar." We are now in "warfare," in "travail and labour," whereto we were born, as the bird to fly.

We sorrow and sigh, desiring the dissolution of our bodies and the putting off of corruption, that we might "put on incorruption." 2 Cor. v.
Rom. viii.
Phil. i.

The way we walk in is "strait and narrow," and therefore not easy to our enemy, the corrupt flesh: but yet we must walk on; for if we hearken to our enemy, we shall be served not friendly. Let them walk "the wide way," that are ruled by their enemies: let us be ruled by our friends, and walk "the strait way," whose end is weal, as the other is woe. The time of our suffering is but short, as the time of their ease is not long: but the time of our rejoicing shall be endless, as the time of their torments shall be ever and intolerable. Our breakfast is sharp, but our supper is sweet. "The afflictions of this life may not be compared" in any part "to the glory that shall be revealed unto us." Matt. vii.
Luke xiii.
2 Cor. iv.
John xvi.
Matt. xxv.
Rom. viii.

This is certain, "if we suffer with Christ, we shall reign with him;" "if we confess him, he will confess us, and that before his Father in heaven," and all his angels and saints, saying, "Come, ye blessed of my Father, possess the kingdom prepared for you from the beginning." There shall be joy, mirth, pleasure, pastime and[1] solace, melody, and all kind of beatitude and felicity, such as "the eye hath not seen, the ear heard, nor the heart of man is able in any point to conceive it" as it is. 2 Tim. ii.
Matt. x.
Matt. xxv.
Rev. vii. xiv.
xix. xx. xxi.
1 Cor. ii.
Isai. lxiv.

In respect of this, and of "the joy set before us," should not we run our race, though it be something rough? Did not Moses so, the prophets so, Christ so, the apostles so, the martyrs so, and the confessors so? They were drunken with the sweetness of this gear: and therefore they contemned all that man and devils could do to them. Their "souls thirsted after the Lord and his tabernacles:" and therefore their lives and goods were not too dear to them. Read the eleventh to the Hebrews, and the second of the Maccabees, the seventh chapter; and let us go the same way, that is, "by many tribulations." Let us labour to enter into the kingdom of heaven; for "all that will live godly in Christ Jesu must suffer persecution." Heb. xii.
Psal. xxxvi.
Psal. lxxxiv.
xlii. lxiii.
Acts xiv.
2 Tim. iii.

Think therefore the cross, if it come for confession of Christ, no strange thing to God's children; but rather take it as the Lord's medicine, by the which he helpeth our in- 1 Pet. iv.

[1 'pastime and,' Emman. MS.: not in 1564.]

firmities, and setteth forth his glory. Our sins have deserved cross upon cross. Now if God give us his cross, to suffer for his truth and confessing him, as he doth by it bury our sins, so doth he glorify us, making us like to Christ here, that we may be like unto him elsewhere: for "if we be partakers of the affliction, we shall be partakers of the consolation;" if we be like in ignominy, we shall be like in glory. Great cause we have to give thanks to God for lending us liberty, lands, goods, wife, children, life, &c. thus long: so that we shall be guilty of ingratitude, if he now shall come and take the same away, except we be cheerful and content.

"God hath given, and God hath taken away," saith Job; as it pleaseth the Lord, so be it done. And should not we do this, especially when the Lord taketh these away of love, to try us, and "prove us," whether we be faithful lovers or strumpets; that is, whether we love him better than his gifts, or otherwise? This is a truth of all truths to be laid up in our hearts, that that is not lost which seemeth so to be for the confession of Christ. In this life your children shall find God's plentiful blessing upon them, when you are gone, and all your goods taken away. God is so good, that he helpeth "the young ravens" before they can fly, and "feedeth them" when their dams have most unkindly left them. And trow ye that God, which is the God "of the widows and fatherless children," will not specially have a care for the babes of his dear saints which die or lose any thing for conscience to him?

O my dearly beloved, therefore look up with the eyes of faith. Consider not "things present," but rather "things to come." Be content now to go whither God "shall gird and lead us."

Let us now cast ourselves wholly into his hands, with our wives, children, and all that ever we have. Let us be sure[1] "the hairs of our head are numbered," so that "one hair shall not perish" without the good will of our dear Father; who hath commanded his angels to "pitch their tents about us," and "in their hands to take and hold us up, that we shall not hurt as much as our foot against a stone." Let us use earnest prayer, let us heartily repent, let us hearken diligently to God's word; "let us keep ourselves pure from all uncleanness both of spirit and body;" let us flee from all evil and " all

[¹ The Emmanuel MS. ends here, being imperfect.]

appearance of evil." Let us be diligent in our vocation, and in "doing good to all men, especially to them that be of the household of faith." Let us "live in peace with all men as much as is in us." And "the Lord of peace give us his peace," and that for evermore. Amen.

_{Matt. xxv.}
_{1 Tim. v.}
_{Rom. xii.}
_{Rom. xvi.}

I pray you remember me, your poor afflicted brother, in your hearty prayers to God.

This second of September.

JOHN BRADFORD.

THE PRISONERS FOR THE GOSPEL,

THEIR DECLARATION CONCERNING KING EDWARD HIS REFORMATION[2].

To the king and queen's most excellent and gracious majesties, with their most honourable high court of parliament.

MS. 2. 2. 15. nu. 111. Emman. Coll. Cambridge.

We, poor prisoners for Christ's religion, require your honours, in our dear Saviour Christ's name, earnestly now to repent, for that you have consented of late to the unplacing of so many godly laws set forth touching the true religion of Christ before by two most noble kings, being father and brother to the queen's highness, and agreed upon by all your consents, not without your great and many deliberations, free and open disputations, costs and pains-taking in that behalf; neither without great consultations and conclusions had by the greatest learned men in the realm, at Windsor, Cambridge,

MS. Lansd. 389. fol. 289. British Museum. Strype, Cranmer, Append. lxxxiv. 1693, p. 196—7, and after editions.

[2 "By whom this remarkable... Declaration was drawn up, unless by John Bradford, I know not: for I meet with it in a MS.* which contains divers pieces of that good man. This now is the second time a public challenge was made to justify king Edward's Reformation; the former the last year by Cranmer, the latter now by divers of the learned men in prison."—Strype, Cranmer, Oxf. I. 506.

This 'Declaration,' being addressed to both the king and queen, must have been penned after the marriage of queen Mary, July 25, 1554: and from the words in the fifth paragraph, "at this your assembly," it was probably written after the meeting of the third parliament of her reign, which took place, November 12 in that year. See Strype, Mem. III. i. 205, 321.]

[* Now in the British Museum, Lansd. 389.]

and Oxford; neither without the most willing consent and allowing of the same by the whole realm throughly: so that there was not one parish in all England that ever desired again to have the Romish, superstitious, vain service, which now by the popish, proud, covetous clergy is placed again, in contempt not only of God, all heaven, and all the Holy Ghost's lessons in the blessed Bible, but also against the honours of the said two most famous kings; against your own country, fore-agreements, and against all the godly consciences within this realm of England and elsewhere. By reason whereof God's great plagues must need follow, and great unquietness of consciences: besides other persecutions and vexations in bodies and goods must needs ensue.

Moreover we certify your honours, that since your said unplacing of Christ's true religion and true service, and placing in the room thereof antichrist's Romish superstition, heresy, and idolatry, all the true preachers have been removed and punished; and that with such open robbery and cruelty, as in Turkey was never used, either to their own countrymen, or to other their mortal enemies.

This therefore our humble suit is now to your honourable estates, to desire the same, for all the mercy's sake of our dear and only Saviour Jesus Christ, and for the duty you owe to God, to your native country, and to your own souls, earnestly to consider from what light to what darkness this realm is now brought; and that in the weightiest, chief, and principal matter of salvation of all our souls and bodies everlastingly and for evermore. And even so we desire you at this your assembly to seek some effectual reformation for the fore-written most horrible deformation in this church of England.

And touching ourselves, we desire you in like manner, that we may be called before your honours; and if we be not able both to prove and approve, by the catholic and canonical rules of Christ's true religion, the church Homilies and Service set forth in the most innocent king Edward's days; and also to disallow and reprove, by the same authorities, the Service now set forth since his departing; then we offer our bodies, either to be immediately burned, or else to suffer any other painful and shameful death, whatsoever it shall please the king and queen's majesties to appoint. And we think this trial and probation may be now best, either in the plain English tongue by writing, or otherwise by disputation in the same tongue.

Our Lord, for his great mercy's sake, grant unto you all the continual assistance of his good and holy Spirit. Amen.

A LETTER

SENT WITH A SUPPLICATION TO QUEEN MARY, HER COUNCIL, AND THE WHOLE PARLIAMENT[1]

IN most humble wise complaineth unto your majesty and honours a poor subject persecuted for the confession of Christ's verity; the which verity deserveth at your hands to be maintained and defended, as the thing by the which you reign, and have your honour and authorities.

Bp. Coverdale, Letters of the Martyrs, 1564, p. 476—8.

Foxe, Acts, &c. 1570, p. 1839, and after editions.

Although we that be professors, and through the grace of God the constant confessors of the same, are, as it were, the out-sweepings of the world; yet, I say, the verity itself is a thing not unworthy for your ears to hear, for your eyes to see, and for your hands to handle, help, and succour; according to that the Lord hath made you able, and placed you where you are, for the same purpose. Your highness and honours ought to know that there is no innocency in words or deeds, where it is enough and sufficeth only to accuse.

It behoveth kings, queens, and all that be in authority, to know that in the administration of their kingdoms "they are God's ministers." It behoveth them to know that they are no kings, but plain tyrants, which reign not to this end, that they may serve and set forth God's glory after true knowledge. And therefore it is required of them that they would "be wise," and

[1] If the 'Supplication' mentioned in the title of this Letter is the document which is printed next in this volume, the date of the Letter would be about November or December 1554: see p. 403, note 2; and prefatory note, p. 366 above.

The title in Bp. Coverdale, Letters of the martyrs, 1564, is 'A letter which he set as a preface before a supplication sent to queen Mary, her council, and the whole parliament; which supplication cometh not yet to our hands.' The heading given above is taken from Foxe, Acts, &c. 1570.]

[BRADFORD.]

suffer themselves to be taught; to submit themselves to the Lord's discipline, and to kiss their sovereign, "lest they perish:" as all those potentates with their principalities and dominions cannot long prosper, but perish indeed, if they and their kingdoms be not ruled with the sceptre of God, that is, with his word: which whoso honoureth not honoureth not God; and they that honour not the Lord, the Lord will not honour them, but bring them into contempt, and at the length take his own cause, which he hath most chiefly committed unto them to care for, into his own hands, and so overthrow them, and set up his truth gloriously; the people also perishing with the princes, where the word of prophecy is wanting, much more is suppressed, as it is now in this realm of England: over which the eyes of the Lord are set to destroy it, your highness, and all your honours, if in time you look not better to your office and duties herein, and not suffer yourselves to be slaves and hangmen to antichrist and his prelates, which have brought your highness and honours already to let Barabbas loose, and to hang up Christ: as by the grace and help of God I shall make apparent, if first it would please your excellent majesty, and all your honours, to take to heart God's doctrine, which rather through the malice of the Pharisees (I mean the bishops and prelates), than your consciences, is oppressed; and not for our contemptible and execrable state in the sight of the world to pass[1] the less of it.

For it (the doctrine I mean) is higher and of more honour and majesty than all the whole world. It standeth invincible above all power, being not our doctrine, but the doctrine of the everliving God, and of his Christ, whom the Father hath ordained King, to "have dominion from sea to sea, and from the river unto the ends of the world." And truly so doth he and will he reign, that he will shake all the whole earth with his iron and brasen power, with his golden and silvery brightness, only "by the rod of his mouth," to shivers, in such sort as though they were pots of clay, according to that which the prophets do write of the magnificence of his kingdom. And thus much for the thing, I mean the doctrine, and your duties to hearken, to propagate, and defend the same.

But now will our adversaries mainly cry out against us,

[[1] 'Pass:' care.]

Ps. lxxii.

because no man may be admitted once to whist against them, that we pretend falsely the doctrine and word of God, calling us the most wicked contemners of it, and heretics, schismatics, traitors, &c. All which their sayings, how malicious and false they are, though I might make report to that which is written by those men whose works they have condemned, and all that retain any of them, publicly by proclamation; yet here will I occasion your majesty and honours, by this my writing, to see that it is far otherwise than they report of us.

God our Father, for his holy name's sake, direct my pen to be his instrument to put into your eyes, ears, and hearts, that which most may make to his glory, to the safeguard of your souls and bodies, and preservation of the whole realm. Amen.

JOHN BRADFORD.

A SUPPLICATION

UNTO THE KING AND QUEEN'S MOST EXCELLENT MAJESTIES, AND TO THEIR MOST HONOURABLE AND HIGH COURT OF PARLIAMENT[2].

A supplication of the persecuted preachers to the king and queen.

IN most humble and lamentable wise complain unto your majesties, and to your high court of parliament, your poor desolate and obedient subjects, H[ooper], F[errar], T[aylor], B[radford], P[hilpot], R[ogers], S[aunders], &c., that whereas your said subjects, living under the laws of God and of this realm in the days of the late most noble king Edward VI. did in all things shew themselves true, faithful, and diligent subjects, according to their vocation; (as well in the sincere ministering of God's holy word, as in due obedience "to the higher powers," and in the daily practice of such virtues and good demeanour as the laws of God at all times, and the statutes of the realm did then allow;) your said subjects nevertheless, contrary to all laws of justice, equity, and right, are in very extreme manner not only cast into prison,

Foxe, Acts, &c. 1570, p. 1656, and after editions.

[2 This Supplication probably was addressed to the king, queen, and parliament, about November or December 1554, from the allusion in the fifteenth line to the memorialists having been in prison 'these fifteen or sixteen months.']

where they have remained now these fifteen or sixteen months; but their livings also, their houses and possessions, their goods and books taken from them, and they slandered to be most heinous heretics, their enemies themselves being both witnesses, accusers, and judges, belying, slandering, and misreporting your said subjects at their pleasure: whereas your said subjects, being straitly kept in prison, cannot yet be suffered to come forth, and make answer accordingly.

The long imprisonment of the Christian preachers.

Unorderly proceeding of the adversaries against God's people.

In consideration whereof, it may please your most excellent majesties, and this your high court of parliament, graciously to tender[1] the present calamity of your said poor subjects, and to call them before your presence, granting them liberty, either by mouth or writing in the plain English tongue, to answer before you, or before indifferent arbiters to be appointed by your majesties, unto such articles of controversy in religion as their said adversaries have already condemned them of, as of heinous heresies: provided that all things may be done with such moderation and quiet behaviour as becometh subjects and children of peace, and that your said subjects may have the free use of all their own books, and conference together among themselves.

Request of the preachers to stand to the trial of their doctrine before indifferent judges.

Which thing being granted, your said subjects doubt not but it shall plainly appear that your said subjects are true and faithful Christians, and neither heretics, neither teachers of heresy, nor cut off from the true catholic universal church of Christ; yea, that rather their adversaries themselves be unto your majesties, as were the charmers of Egypt unto Pharoah, Zedekias and his adherents unto the king of Israel, and Bar-jesu to the proconsul, Sergius Paulus. And if your said subjects be not able by the testimony of Christ, his prophets, apostles, and godly fathers of his church, to prove that the doctrine of the church Homilies and Service, taught and set forth in the time of our late most godly prince and king, Edward VI., is the true doctrine of Christ's catholic church, and most agreeable to the articles of the christian faith; your said subjects offer themselves then to the most heavy punishment that it shall please your majesties to appoint.

Acts xiii.

Wherefore, for the tender mercy of God in Christ, which you look for at the day of judgment, your said poor subjects in bonds most humbly beseech your excellent majesties, and

[1 See p. 103, note 7, above.]

this your high court of parliament, benignly and graciously to hear and grant this their petition, tending so greatly to the glory of God, to the edifying of his church, to the honour of your majesties, and to the commendation and maintenance of justice, right, and equity, both before God and man. And your said subjects, according to their bounden duty, shall not cease to pray unto Almighty God for the gracious preservation of your most excellent majesties long to endure.

REMARKS ON A MEMORABLE TRIAL[2]

1555. This Preface was made in *anno Domini* 1555.

To the reader John Bradford wisheth grace, mercy, peace, and increase of all godly knowledge and life.

MS. 2. 2. 15. no. 98. Emman. Coll. Cambridge.

After this book came to my hands, as I was in prison for the testimony of the Lord, I could not but read the same to see how the Lord assisted his servant that put his trust in him: which thing I thank God I did so see, that I could not but think myself bound to help what I could by my testimony, to allure all others by this book thereunto. And therefore I, being a poor man of vile state and condition concerning this world, and of learning unmeet of place in any book for my name, have presumed by a godly presumption, tending to do good to all men and hurt to no man, to write thus much in the behalf of this book, that it is worthy to be had in print, and diligently read of all men, but especially of the nobility and gentlemen of England: whose houses and names could not but continue, if that yet now they would begin to take this gentleman a sampler to ensue, and a pattern to press after. For here thou, good reader, shalt perceive a gentleman in deed, and not in name only: his trust was in the

[[2] These Remarks are now printed for the first time.
They were written by Bradford probably to accompany an account of the remarkable trial of Sir Nicholas Throgmorton, April 17, 1554: the expressions used by B. exactly describe the able defence of Sir N. T., and the proceedings of the judges and of the government upon the occasion. See the details of the trial in Holinshed, 1587, III. 1104; also in State Trials, London 1816, 1. 869—902; and in Criminal Trials, Jardine, 1832, 1. 62—120.]

Lord, and not in man, and therefore he was not confounded: he honoured God, and therefore God hath honoured him accordingly. His study was in God's word, and therefore found he comfort: by it he found more wisdom and had more knowledge than all his enemies, which were not few nor foolish to the judgment of the world. They came to him as Goliah the mighty giant, harnessed and armed a cap-a-pie: he came as a little David with his sling, and had the victory. In this weak man thou mayest see God's power, presence, wisdom, and goodness, to occasion thee to put thy trust in the Lord, and to hang altogether upon him, who in the evil day will deliver them that fear him. What wisdom, what grace, what audacity, did God give to him in his need! What could all the learned lawyers, which better might be termed lewd losels[1] of the realm, do against him? what could all the power of the queen's highness prevail? Such a thing it is to trust in the Lord, to fear him, and to be a godly student of his word, as doubtless it appeareth this good man was. Who would not serve such a God, as can in despite of all his enemies triumph over them by his simple servant?

Read the book, and thou shalt see what knowledge this gentleman had in the statutes, laws, and chronicles of the realm, to teach the nobility and gentlemen, which are and would be magistrates and rulers of the realm, to spend more time to attain wisdom and knowledge to execute their offices than they now do. Read this book, and thou shalt see what false packing there is against the simple and plain truth. Read this book, and thou shalt see how unrighteousness sitteth in place of justice. Read this book, and thou shalt see how truth is defaced, and falsehood maintained. Read this book, and thou shalt see how perilous a thing it is to testify the truth.

The good men empaneled of the quest shall tell the same. A greater honour never came to the city of London than by those twelve men. What said I, to the city of London? Nay, to the whole realm of England: for, alas! if they had not had more conscience and truth than king, queen, lords, councillors, judges, serjeants, attornies, solicitors, lawyers, &c., England had been guilty of innocent blood; as, alas, alas! it is to be feared too much thereof crieth for vengeance. Lord, spare us, and have mercy upon us.

[1 'Losels:' worthless persons, lost to all goodness. Nares, Glossary.]

But what reward had this good jury? Well, I pass over that: a papistical reward. What is that? Forsooth, such as Julianus Apostata gave to the faithful Christians[2].

God our Father look better on this gear in his good time, which in respect of his enemies is at hand; "for they have scattered abroad his law." O that amongst us, who pretend to be God's friends, were true repentance! Then might we say: *Tempus est ut miserearis, Domine:* 'It is time, O Lord, to shew mercy upon us.' God do so for his holy name's sake! Amen. [Psal. cxix. 126. Vulgate.]

Thus much I was so bold to scribble in this book, being lent unto me, because I would occasion some men of authority and learning to commend it, as it is most worthy.

E carcere, [From prison]

JOHN BRADFORD.

AN ADMONITION

TO LOVERS OF THE GOSPEL[3].

THE peace of Christ, which is the true effect of God's gospel believed, my dearly beloved, be more and more plentifully perceived of you, through the grace of our dear Father, by the mighty working of the Holy Spirit, our Comforter. Amen. [Bp. Coverdale, Letters of the Martyrs, 1564, p. 379—83. Foxe, Acts, &c. 1570. p. 1826, and after editions.]

Though I have many lets presently to hinder me from writing unto you, yet being desired I could not but something signify my ready good-will in this behalf, so much as I may, when I cannot so much as I would. You hear and

[2 Vide Mosheim, Eccl. Hist. cent. IV. 1. i. 12.]

[3 This 'Admonition' must have been written between February 9 and March 30, 1555, as it appears from p. 410, that it was penned after the martyrdoms of Bp. Hooper and Taylor, and before that of Bp. Ferrar.—Foxe, Acts, &c., 1583, p. 1510—27—55.

Its title in Bp. Coverdale, Letters of the martyrs, 1564, is, 'An admonition to certain professors and lovers of the Gospel, to beware they fall not from it, in consenting to the Romish religion, by the example of the shrinking, halting, and double-faced gospellers.']

see how Satan bestirreth him, raging "as a roaring lion to devour us." You see and feel partly what storms he hath raised up to drown the poor boat of Christ, I mean his church. You see how terribly he traineth his soldiers to give a fierce onset on the vaward[1] of God's battle. You see how he hath received power of God to molest God's children, and to begin at his house.

By reason whereof, consider two things; one, the cause on our behalf; the other, what will be the sequel on strangers.

For the first, if we be not blind, we cannot but well see, that our sins are the cause of all this misery: our sins, I say, which I would that every one of us would apply to ourselves after the example of Jonas and David; turning over the wallet, that other men's offences might lie behind, and our own before.

Not that I would excuse other men, which exteriorly have walked much more grossly than many of you have done; but that I would provoke you all, as myself, to more hearty repentance and prayer. Let us more and more increase to know and lament our doubting of God, of his presence, power, anger, mercy, &c. Let us better feel and hate our self-love, security, negligence, unthankfulness, unbelief, impatience, &c.: and then doubtless the cross shall be less careful, yea, it shall be comfortable, and Christ most dear and pleasant. Death then shall be desired as the despatcher of us out of all misery, and entrance into eternal felicity and joy unspeakable: the which is so much the more longed for, by how much we feel indeed the serpent's bites wherewith he woundeth our heels, that is, our outward Adam and senses.

If we had, I say, a lively and true feeling of his poison, we could not but, as rejoice over our Captain that hath "bruised his head," so be desirous to follow his example, that is, to give our lives with him and for him; and so to "fill up his passions," that he might conquer and overcome in us and by us, to his glory and comfort of his children.

Col. i.

Now the second (I mean the sequel, or that which will follow, on the strangers), my dearly beloved, let us well look upon. For if so be that God justly do thus give to Satan

[1 'Vaward:' forepart.]

and his seed to vex and molest Christ and his penitent people, O what and how justly may he and will he give to Satan to entreat the retchless[2] and impenitent sinners! "If judgment begin thus at God's house," what will follow on them that be without, if they repent not? Certainly for them is reserved the dross of God's cup, that is, "brimstone, fire, and tempest" intolerable.

Now are they unwilling to drink of God's cup of afflictions, which he offereth common with his Son Christ our Lord, lest they should lose their pigs with the Gergesites. They are unwilling to come into the way that bringeth to heaven, even afflictions; they in their hearts cry, "Let us cast his yoke from us;" they walk two ways, that is, they seek to "serve God and mammon," which is impossible. They will not come nigh "the strait way that bringeth to life;" they open their eyes to behold present things only; they judge of religion after reason, and not after God's word; they follow the more part, and not the better; they profess God with their mouths, but "in their hearts they deny him," or else they would "sanctify him" by serving him more than men. They part stake with God which would have all, giving part to the world, to the Romish rout, and antichristian idolatry now set abroad amongst us publicly. They will have Christ, but none of his cross; which will not be: they will be counted to "live godly in Christ," but yet they "will suffer no persecution;" they love this world, wherethrough the love of God is driven forth of them; they "savour those things that be of men, and not that be of God." *Summa*, they love God in their lips, but in their hearts, yea, and in their deeds deny him, as well by not repenting their evils past, as by continuing in evil still, by doing as the world, the flesh, and the devil willeth: and yet still perchance they will pray or rather prate, "Thy will be done in earth;" which is generally, that every one should "take up his cross and follow Christ."

Matt. viii.

But this is a hard sermon: "who is able to abide it?" Therefore Christ must be prayed to depart, lest all their pigs be drowned. The devil shall have his dwelling again in themselves, rather than in their pigs: and therefore to the devil shall they go, and dwell with him in eternal perdition

[2 'Retchless:' careless.]

and damnation, even in hell-fire, and torment endless, and above all cogitations incomprehensible, if they repent not.

Wherefore by them, my dearly beloved, be admonished to remember your profession, how that in baptism you made a solemn vow to renounce the devil, the world, &c. You promised to fight under Christ's standard. You learned Christ's cross, afore you began with A. B. C.[1] Go to then, pay your vow to the Lord; fight like men and valiant men under Christ's standard; "take up your cross" and follow your Master, as your brethren, M. Hooper, Rogers, Taylor[2], and Saunders have done; and as now your brethren, M. Cranmer, Latimer, Ridley, Ferrar[2], Bradford, Hawkes, &c. be ready to do.

The ice is broken before you; therefore be not afraid, but be content to die for the Lord. You have no cause to waver or doubt of the doctrine thus declared by the blood of the pastors. Remember that Christ saith, "He that will save his life shall lose it." And "what should it profit you to win the whole world," much less a little quietness, your goods, &c., and "to lose your own souls?" Render to the Lord that he hath lent you, by such means as he would have you render it, and not as you would. Forget not, Christ's disciples must "deny themselves," as well concerning their will, as concerning their wisdom. Have in mind that, as it is no small mercy to believe in the Lord, so it is no small kindness of God towards you, to suffer any thing, much more death, for the Lord. If they be "blessed that die in the Lord," how shall they be that die for the Lord!

O what a blessing is it to have death, due for our sins, diverted into a demonstration and testification of the Lord's truth! O that we had a little of Moses' faith, to look upon the end of the cross, to look upon the reward, to see continually with Christ and his people "greater riches than the riches of Egypt!" O let us pray that God would open our eyes to see his "hid manna," "heavenly Jerusalem, the congregation of the first-born," the melody of the saints, "the tabernacle of God dwelling with men." Then should we run

[1 Vide p. 264, note 1, above.]
[2 Vide p. 407, note 3, above.]

and become violent men, and so "take the kingdom of heaven," as it were, "by force."

God our Father give us, for his Christ's sake, to see a little what and how great joy he hath prepared for us, he hath called us unto, and most assuredly giveth us, for his own goodness and truth's sake. Amen.

My dearly beloved, repent, "be sober, and watch in prayer;" be obedient, and after your vocations shew your obedience to "the higher powers" in all things that are not against God's word. Therein acknowledge the sovereign power of the Lord: howbeit, so that ye be no rebels or rebellers for no cause; but, because with good conscience you cannot obey, be patient sufferers, and the "glory and good Spirit of God shall dwell upon us." I pray you remember us your afflicted brethren, being in the Lord's bonds for the testimony of Christ, and abiding the gracious hour of our dear and most merciful Father.

The Lord for Christ's sake give us merry hearts to drink lustily of his sweet cup; which daily we groan and sigh for, lamenting that the time is thus prolonged. The Lord Jesus give us grace to be thankful, and to abide patiently the provident hour of his most gracious good will. Amen, Amen.

From the Compter in the Poultry.

Yours in Christ,

JOHN BRADFORD.

[The following 'Exhortation' from Bradford to his 'dearly beloved brethren and sisters throughout the realm of England' was printed among his letters, and with his signature, in the 'Letters of the martyrs,' edited by Bishop Coverdale, 1564, p. 427—46.

It also forms a part of a very rare 'Exhortation to the carrying of Christ's cross,' without any date, or name of the author or printer[1]; of which there is a copy in the library of George Offor, Esq., Hackney.

The 'Exhortation' given in this volume is that portion of the treatise without date, which is attributed by Bishop Coverdale, as stated above, to the authorship of Bradford. It follows, in this reprint, the text of the 'Letters of the martyrs,' 1564, except where otherwise noted.

This address appears to have been written between November 1554 and June 1555, from the allusion at p. 425, to God having blessed queen Mary 'with fruit of the womb,' the unfounded rumour to that effect having prevailed during that period[2]. It will be remembered that Bradford was imprisoned, August 16, 1553, and was martyred July 1, 1555.

The Farewell Letters or Addresses to London, Cambridge, Lancashire and Cheshire, and Walden, observe the text of the first edition of the 'Acts and monuments' of Foxe 1563, where they were originally printed. The text of 1563 has been collated with MSS. in Emmanuel College, Cambridge. It has also been compared with the 'Letters of the martyrs' 1564, and occasionally with the after editions of the 'Acts and monuments' printed during the life of Foxe, 1570, 1576, 1583. The 'Farewell to Cambridge' has also been compared with an early transcript in the Library of that University.

The variations are only noted where a deviation from Foxe 1563 is followed.

The 'Farewells' were written by Bradford from prison, February 11 and 12, 1555, shortly after his condemnation, which had taken place on the preceding January 31.]

[1 The 'Exhortation' without date, being in the same type, and apparently issued at the same time, with a translation executed by Bp. Coverdale, was supposed by Strype to be by Bp. C. (Ecc. Mem. III. i. 239—40); and has appeared in the Works of Bp. C., Parker Soc. Vol. II. p. 230—77.]

[2 Foxe, Acts, &c. 1583, p. 1475—81, 1596—7, or ed. 1843—8, VI. 567—84, VII. 123—7; Strype, Cranmer, I. 526—8, II. 968—9, Doc. lxxxvii.]

AN

EXHORTATION

TO THE BRETHREN IN ENGLAND,

AND

FOUR FAREWELLS

TO

LONDON, CAMBRIDGE, LANCASHIRE AND
CHESHIRE, AND WALDEN.

BY

JOHN BRADFORD.

AN EXHORTATION
TO THE BRETHREN THROUGHOUT THE REALM OF ENGLAND[1].

<small>Bp. Coverdale, Letters of the martyrs, 1564, p. 427—46.</small>

THE Holy Spirit of God, which is "the earnest" and pledge of God given to his people for their comfort and consolation, be poured into our hearts, by the mighty power and merits of our alone Saviour Jesus Christ, now and for ever. Amen.

<small>Gen. xv.</small>
<small>Luke ix.</small>
<small>Gen. xix.</small>

Because I perceive plainly, that to the evils fallen upon us which profess Christ's gospel greater are most like to ensue, and after them greater, till the measure of iniquity be up-heaped, (except we shrink, and "having put our hands to the plough do look back," and so with Lot's wife and the Israelites desiring to return into Egypt fall into God's heavy displeasure incurably, all which God forbid;) and because I am persuaded of you, my dearly beloved brethren and sisters throughout the realm of England, which have professed unfeignedly the gospel of our Lord and Saviour Jesus Christ (for unto such do I write this epistle), that, as ye have begun to take part with God's gospel and truth, so through his grace ye will persevere and go on forwards, notwithstanding the storms risen and to arise; I cannot but write something unto you lustily to go on forwards in the way of the Lord, and not to become faint-hearted or "fearful" (whose place St John appointeth with the "unbelievers, murderers, and idolaters," in eternal perdition), but cheerfully to take "the Lord's cup," and drink of it afore it draw towards "the dregs" and bottom: whereof at the length they shall drink with the wicked, to eternal destruction, which will not receive it at the first with God's children; with whom God "beginneth his judgment," that, as the wicked world "rejoiceth when they lament," so they may "rejoice" when the wicked world shall mourn, and without end find woe intolerable.

<small>Rev. xxi.</small>

<small>Psal. lxxv.</small>

<small>1 Pet. iv.</small>
<small>John xvi.</small>

First therefore, my dearly beloved in the world, I beseech you to consider, that though ye be "in the world," yet ye

<small>John xvii.</small>

[1 The title in Bp. Coverdale, Letters of the martyrs, 1564, is 'An exhortation to the patient suffering of trouble and afflictions for Christ's cause, written to all the unfeigned professors of the Gospel throughout the realm of England, at the beginning of his imprisonment, and here placed as it came to our hands.']

are "not of the world." Ye are not of them which look for their "portion in this life," whose captain is "the god of this world," even Satan, who now ruffleth it apace as he were wood[2], because his time on earth is not long. Psal. xvii.
2 Cor. iv.

Rev. xii.

But ye are of them that look for a city of God's own blessing. Ye are of them that know yourselves to be here but "pilgrims and strangers;" for here ye have no dwelling-place. Ye are of them whose "portion is the Lord," and which have their hope "in heaven;" whose Captain is Christ Jesus, the Son of God, and Governor of heaven and earth. "Unto him is given all power;" yea, he is God Almighty, with the Father and the Holy Ghost, praiseworthy for ever. Heb. xi.

1 Pet. ii.
Heb. xiii.
Psal. cxix.

Heb. xii.
Matt. xxviii.
Rom. ix.
1 John v.

Ye are not of them which receive "the beast's mark," which here rejoice, "laugh," and have their hearts' ease, joy, paradise, and pleasure: but ye are of them which have received the angel's mark, yea, God's mark; which here lament, "mourn," sigh, sob, weep, and have your wilderness to wander in, your purgatory, and even hell, to purge and burn up your sins. Ye are not of them which cry, "Let us eat and drink, for to-morrow we shall die." Ye are not of that number which say, "they have made a covenant with death and hell," for hurting of them. Ye are not of them which take it for a "vain thing to serve the Lord." Ye are not of them which are lulled and rocked asleep in Jezebel's bed, a bed of security. Ye are not of the number of them which say, 'Tush, God is in heaven, and seeth us not, nor much passeth what we do.' Ye are not of the number of them which will "fall down," for the muck of the world, to worship the fiend; or for displeasing of men, to "worship the golden image." Finally, ye are not of the number of them which set more by your pigs than by Christ; which, for ease and rest in this life, will say and do as Antiochus biddeth you do or say; and will "follow the multitude to do evil," with Zedekias and the three hundred false prophets, yea, Ahab, Jezebel, and the whole court and country. Rev. xiii.
Luke vi.

Ezek. ix.
Matt. v.

Isai. xxii.
1 Cor. xv.

Isai. xxviii.

Mal. iii.
Rev. ii.

Ezek. viii.
Psal. lxxiii.
Matt. iv.

Dan. iii.
Matt. viii.

1 Mac. i. ii.
Exod. xxiii.
1 Kings xxii.

But ye are of the number of them which are dead already, or at least be in dying daily to yourselves and to this world. Ye are of them which have made a covenant with God to forsake yourselves in this world and Satan also. Ye are of them which say, Nay, the Lord hath all things "written in his memorial book, for such as fear him and re- Rom. vi. vii.
Col. iii.

Luke xii.

Mal. iii.

[[2] 'Wood:' mad, furious, from the Anglo-Saxon *wod*, 'rabidus.']

member his name." Ye are of them which have "their loins girded about, and their lights burning in their hands, like unto men that wait for their Lord's coming." Ye are in the number of them that say, "The Lord looketh down from heaven, and beholdeth the children of men: from the habitation of his dwelling he considereth all them that dwell upon the earth." Ye are of the number of them which "will worship the only Lord God," and will not worship "the works of men's hands," though the oven burn never so hot. Ye are in the number of them to whom "Christ is precious" and dear; which cry out rather because your habitation is prolonged here, as David did. Ye are of them which follow Mattathias and the godly Jews; which know the way to life to be a "strait way," and "few to go through it;" which will not stick to follow poor Micheas, although he be racked and cast into prison, having the sun, moon, seven stars, and all against him.

Thus therefore, dearly beloved, remember first that, as I said, ye "are not of this world;" that Satan is not your captain; your joy and paradise is not here; your companions are not the multitude of worldlings, and such as seek to please men, and live here at ease in the service of Satan. But ye are of another world: Christ is your Captain; your joy is "in heaven, where your conversation is;" your companions are the fathers, patriarchs, prophets, apostles, martyrs, virgins, confessors, and the dear saints of God, which "follow the Lamb whithersoever he goeth," dipping their garments in his blood; knowing this life and world to be full of evil, "a warfare," "a smoke," "a shadow," "a vapour;" and as replenished, so environed with all kind of miseries.

This is the first thing which I would have you often and diligently with yourselves to consider, and to muse well upon; namely, what ye be, and where ye be.

Now, secondly, forget not to call to mind that ye ought not to think it any "strange thing," if misery, trouble, adversity, persecution, and displeasure, come upon you. For how can it otherwise be, but that trouble and persecution must come upon you? Can the world love you, which are none of his? Can worldly men regard you, which are your chief enemy's soldiers? Can Satan suffer you to be in rest, which will do no homage unto him? Can this way be chosen of any that make it so narrow and strait as they do? Will ye look to travel, and to have no foul way or rain? Will shipmen shrink, or sailors on the sea give over, if storms arise? Do they not look for such?

And, dearly beloved, did not we enter into God's ship and ark of baptism at the first? Will ye then count it strange, if perils come or tempests blow? Are not ye travelling to your heavenly city of Jerusalem, where is all joy and felicity; and will ye now tarry by the way for storms or showers? The mart and fair will then be past; the night will so come upon you, that ye cannot travel; "the door will be sparred[1]," and the bride will be at supper. 1 Pet. iii.
John ix.
Matt. xxv.

Therefore away with dainty niceness. Will ye think the Father of heaven will deal more gently with you in this age, than he hath done with others, his dearest friends, in other ages? What way, yea, what storms and tempests, what troubles and disquietness found Abel, Noe, Abraham, Isaac, Jacob, and good Joseph? Which of these had so fair a life and restful times as we have had? Moses, Aaron, Samuel, David the king, and all the good kings, priests, prophets, in the old Testament, at one time or other, if not throughout their life, did feel a thousand parts more misery than we have felt hitherto. Gen. iv. vi.
vii. viii. ix.
&c.
Exod. ii. iii.
iv. v. &c.

As for the new Testament, Lord God, how great was the affliction of Mary, of Joseph, of Zachary, of Elizabeth, of John Baptist, of all the apostles and evangelists, yea, of Jesus Christ our Lord, the dear Son and darling of God! And since the time of the apostles, how many and great are the number of martyrs, confessors, and such as have suffered the shedding of their blood in this life, rather than they would be stayed in their journey, or lodge in any of Satan's inns, lest the storms or winds which fell in their travellings might have touched them! And, dearly beloved, let us think what we are, and how far unmeet to be matched with these; with whom yet we look to be placed in heaven. Matt. ii.
Euseb. Eccl.
Hist.
Tripart. Hist.

But with what face can we look for this, that are so fearful, unwilling, and backward[2] to leave that which, will we, nill[3] we, we must leave; and that so shortly, as we know not the time when? Where is our abrenouncing and forsaking of the world and the flesh, which we solemnly took upon Psal. xlix.

[1 'Sparred:' barred, shut, from the Anglo-Saxon *sparran*.]
[2 This word is changed.]   [3 'Nill:' be unwilling.]

[BRADFORD.]

us in baptism? Ah, shameless cowards that we be, which will not follow the trace of so many fathers, patriarchs, kings, priests, prophets, apostles, evangelists, and saints of God, yea, even of the very Son of God!

How many now go with you lustily, as I and all your brethren in bonds and exile for the gospel! "Pray for us;" for, God willing, we will not leave you now, we will go before you. Ye shall see in us, by God's grace, that we preached no lies nor tales of tubs[1], but even the very true word of God; for the confirmation whereof we, by God's grace and the help of your prayers, will willingly and joyfully give our blood to be shed, as already we have given our livings, goods, friends, and natural country: for now be we certain that we be in the highway to heaven's bliss; as St Paul saith, "By many tribulations and persecutions we must enter into God's kingdom." And because we would go thither ourselves, and bring you thither also, therefore the devil stirreth up the coals. And forasmuch as we all loitered in the way, he hath therefore received power of God to overcast the weather, and to stir up storms, that we, God's children, might more speedily go on forwards, and make more haste: as the counterfeits and hypocrites will tarry and linger till the storms be past, and so when they come, the market will be done, and the doors sparred, as it is to be feared. Read Matthew xxv.

This wind will blow God's children forwards, and the devil's darlings backward. Therefore, like God's children, let us go on forward apace: the wind is on our backs; hoist up the sails; "lift up your hearts and hands unto God" in prayer, and keep your anchor of faith to cast out in time of trouble on the rock of God's word and mercy in Christ by the cable of God's verity; and I warrant you.

And thus much for you secondly to consider; that affliction, persecution, and trouble, is no strange thing to God's children, and therefore it should not dismay, discourage, or discomfort us; for it is none other thing than all God's dear friends have tasted in their journey to heaven-wards.

As I would, in this troublesome time, that ye would con-

[1 'Tale of a tub:' a trifling or fabulous story. Todd's Johnson, Dict.]

sider what ye be by the goodness of God in Christ, even citizens of heaven, though ye be presently in the flesh, even in a strange region, on every side full of fierce enemies; and what weather and way the dearest friends of God have found; even so would I have you, thirdly, to consider for your further comfort, that if ye shrink not, but go on forwards, "pressing to the mark appointed," all the power of your enemies shall not overcome you, nor in any point hurt you. Phil. iii.

But this must not you consider according to the judgment of reason, and the sense of old Adam; but according to the judgment of God's word, and the experience of faith and "the new man;" for else you mar all. For to reason, and to the experience of our sense, or of the outward man, we poor souls which stick to God's word, to serve him as he requireth only, are counted to be vanquished and to be overcome, in that we are cast into prison, lose our livings, friends, goods, country, and life also at the length, concerning this world.

But, dearly beloved, God's word teacheth otherwise, and faith feeleth accordingly. Is it not written, "Who shall separate us from the love of God? Shall tribulation, or anguish, or persecution, either hunger, either nakedness, either peril, either sword? As it is written, For thy sake are we killed all day long, and are counted as sheep appointed to be slain. Nevertheless in all these things we overcome through him that loved us. For I am sure that neither death, neither life, neither angels, nor rule, neither power, neither things present, neither things to come, neither high, nor low, neither any creature, shall be able to part us from that love wherewith God loveth us in Christ Jesu our Lord." Thus spake one which was in affliction, as I am, for the Lord's gospel's sake; his holy name be praised therefor, and he grant me grace with the same to continue in like suffering unto the end. This, I say, one spake which was in affliction for the gospel, but yet so far from being overcome, that he rejoiced rather of the victory which the gospel had; for though he was bound, "yet the gospel was not bound." And therefore giveth he "thanks unto God, which alway giveth the victory in Christ, and openeth the savour of his knowledge by us" and such as suffer for his truth; although they shut us up never so much, and drive us never so far out of our own natural country in every place. Rom. viii. Psal. xliv. 2 Tim. ii. 2 Cor. ii.

27—2

The world for a time may deceive itself, thinking it hath the victory; but yet the end will try the contrary. Did not Cain think he had the victory, when Abel was slain? But how say you now? Is it not found otherwise? Thought not the old world and men then living, that they were wise and well, and Noe a fool, which would creep into an ark, leaving his house, lands, and[1] possessions? for I think he was in an honest state for the world: but, I pray you, who was wise when the flood came? Abraham, I trow, was counted a fool to leave his own country and friends, kith and kin, because of God's word: but, dearly beloved, we know it proved otherwise.

I will leave all the patriarchs, and come to Moses and the children of Israel. Tell me, were not they thought to be overcome and stark mad, when for fear of Pharaoh, at God's word, they ran into the Red Sea? Did not Pharaoh and the Egyptians think themselves sure of the victory? But, I trow, it proved clean contrary. Saul was thought well, and David in an evil case and most miserable, because he had no hole to hide him in: but yet at the length Saul's misery was seen, and David's felicity began to appear.

The prophet Micheas, being cast into prison for telling Ahab the truth, was thought to be overcome of Zedekias and the other false prophets: but, my good brethren and sisters, the holy history telleth otherwise. Who did not think the prophets unhappy in their time? for they were slain, prisoned, laughed to scorn, and jested at of every man. And so were all the apostles, yea, the dearly beloved "friend of God," "than whom among the children of women none arose greater;" I mean John Baptist, who was beheaded, and that in prison, even for a dancing damsel's desire. As all these to the judgment of reason were then counted heretics, runagates, unlearned, fools, fishers, publicans, &c.; so now unhappy and overcome in deed, if God's word and faith did not shew the contrary.

But what speak I of these? Look upon Jesus Christ, to whom we must be like fashioned here, if we will be like him elsewhere. How say ye? was not he taken for a most fool, a seditious person, a new fellow, an heretic, and one overcome

[1 'and,' only in the edition without date: see prefatory note, p. 412 above.]

of every body; yea, even forsaken both of God and men? But the end told them and telleth us another tale; for now is he in majesty and glory unspeakable. When he was led to Pilate or Herod, or when he was in prison in Caiphas' house, did not their reason think that he was overcome? When he was beaten, buffeted, scourged, crowned with thorns, hanged upon the cross, and utterly left of all his disciples; taunted of the high priests and holy fathers, cursed of the commons, railed on of the magistrates, and laughed to scorn of the lewd heathen; would not a man then have thought that he had been out of the way, and his disciples fools to follow him and believe him?

Think ye that, whilst he did lie in his grave, men did not point with their fingers, when they saw any that had followed and loved him, or believed in him and his doctrine, saying, 'Where is their master and teacher now? What, is he gone? Forsooth, if they had not been fools, they might well have known that this learning he taught could not long continue. Our doctors and Pharisees are no fools, now they may see.' On this sort either men spake, or might have spoken, against all such as loved Christ or his doctrine: but yet at the length they and all such were proved fools and wicked wretches. For our Saviour arose maugre their beards, and published his gospel plentifully spite of their heads and the heads of all the wicked world, with the great powers of the same; always overcoming, and then most of all, when he and his doctrine were thought to have the greatest fall: as now, dearly beloved, the wicked world rejoiceth, the papists are puffed up against poor Christ and his people.

After their old kind now cry they out, 'Where are these new-found preachers? Are they not in the Tower, Marshalsea, Fleet, and beyond the seas? Who would have thought that our old bishops, doctors, and deans were fools? as they would have made us to believe, and indeed have persuaded some already which are not of the wisest, especially if they come not home again to the holy church.' These and such like words they have to cast in our teeth, as triumphers and conquerors.

But, dearly beloved, short is their joy; they beguile themselves. This is but a lightning before their death. As God, after he had given the Jews a time to repent, visited them by Vespasian and Titus most horribly to their utter subver- Euseb. Eccl. Hist. Lib. iii. cap. v. vi. vii. viii. ix.

sion, delivering first all his people from among them; even so, my dear brethren, will he do with this age. When he hath tried his children from amongst them, as now he beginneth, and by suffering hath made us like to his Christ; and, by being overcome, to overcome indeed to our eternal comfort; then will he, if not otherwise, come himself in the clouds; I mean our dear Lord whom we confess, preach, and believe on. He will come, I say, "with the blast of a trump and shout of an archangel," and so "shall we be caught up in the clouds to meet him in the air;" the angels gathering together the wicked wretches which now walter[1] and wallow as the world and wind bloweth, to be "tied in bundles," and cast into the fire which burneth for ever most painfully. There and then shall they see who hath the victory, they or we, when they shall see us "afar off in Abraham's bosom." Then will they say, "Oh, we thought these folks fools, and had them in derision; we thought their life madness, and their end to be without honour: but look how they are counted among the children of God, and their portion is with the saints. Oh, we have gone amiss, and would not hearken." Such words as these shall the wicked say one day in hell; whereas now they triumph as conquerors.

marginalia: 1 Thess. iv.; Matt. xiii.; Luke xvi.; Wisd. v.

And thus much for you thirdly to look often upon; namely, that whatsoever is done unto you, yea, even very death itself, shall not dash or hurt you no more than it did Abel, David, Daniel, John Baptist, Jesus Christ our Lord, with other the dear saints of God which suffered for his name's sake.

Let not reason therefore be judge in this matter, nor present sense, but faith and God's word, as I have shewed. In the which if we set before our eyes the shortness of this present time wherein we suffer, and consider the eternity to come; as our enemies and persecutors shall be in intolerable pains helpless, and we, if we persevere to the end, in such felicity and joys dangerless, as the very heart of man in no point is able to conceive; if we consider this, I say, we cannot but even contemn and set nothing by the sorrows and griefs of the cross, and lustily go through thick and thin with good courage.

marginalia: 1 Cor. ii.; Isai. lxiv.

Thus have I declared unto you three things necessary to

[¹ 'Walter:' lie grovelling.]

be mused on of every one which will abide by Christ and his gospel in this troublesome time, as I trust you all will: namely, first, to consider that we are not of this world, nor of the number of the worldlings or retainers to Satan; that we are not at home in our own country; but of another world, of the congregation of the saints and retainers to Christ, although in a region replete and full of untractable enemies. Secondly, that we may not think it a strange thing to be persecuted for God's gospel, from the which the dearest friends of God were in no age free: as indeed it is impossible that they should any long time be, their enemies being always about them to destroy them if they could. And thirdly, that the assaults of our enemies, be they never so many and fierce, in no point shall be able to prevail against our faith, albeit to reason it seemeth otherwise: wherethrough we ought to conceive a good courage and comfort; for who will be affeared, when he knoweth the enemies cannot prevail? *Heb. xii.*

Now will I, for the more encouraging you to the cross, give you a further memorandum; namely, of the commodities and profits which come by the trouble and afflictions now risen and to arise to us, which be God's children elect through Jesus Christ. But here look not to have a rehearsal of all the commodities which come by the cross to such as are exercised well therein; for that were more than I can do: I will only speak of a few, thereby to occasion you to gather, and at the length to feel and perceive, more.

First, in that there is no cross which cometh upon any of us without the counsel of our heavenly Father, (for as for the fancy of fortune it is wicked, as many places of the scripture do teach,) we must needs, to the commendation of God's justice (for in all his doings he is just,) acknowledge in ourselves that we have deserved at the hands of our heavenly Father this his cross or rod fallen upon us. We have deserved it, if not by our unthankfulness, slothfulness, negligence, intemperance, uncleanness, and other sins committed often by us, (whereof our consciences can and will accuse us, if we call them to counsel with the examination of our former life,) yet at least by our original and birth sin; as by doubting of the greatness of God's anger and mercy, by self-love, concupiscence, and such like sins; which as we brought *Amos iii. Lam. iii. Matt. x. Isai. xlv.* *Psal. li. Heb. xii.*

with us into this world, so do the same alway abide in us, and even as a spring do always bring something forth in act with us, notwithstanding the continual fight of God's Spirit in us against it.

<small>Gal. v.</small>

The first commodity therefore that the cross bringeth is knowledge, and that double, of God and of ourselves: of God, that he is just, pure, and hateth sin; of ourselves, that we are "born in sin," and are from top to toe defiled with concupiscence and corruption, out of the which hath sprung all the evils that ever at any time we have spoken and done: the greatest and most special whereof, by the cross, we are occasioned to call to mind; as did the brethren of Joseph their evil fact against him, when the cross once came upon them. And so by it we come to the first step to get health for our souls; that is, we are driven to know our sins original and actual by God's justice declared in the cross.

<small>Psal. li.
Gen. viii.
Jer. xvii.
Eph. ii.
1 Kings viii.</small>

<small>Gen. xlii.</small>

Secondly, the end wherefor God declareth his justice against our sin original and actual, and would by his cross have us to consider the same, and to call to mind our former evil deeds; the end hereof, I say, is this, that we might lament, be sorry, sigh, and pray for pardon, that so doing we might obtain the same by the means of faith in the merits of Jesus Christ his dear Son; and further that we, being humbled because of the evil that dwelleth in us, might become thankful for God's goodness and love, in continual watching and wariness to suppress the evil which lieth in us, that it "bring not forth fruits to death" at any time. This second commodity of the cross therefore must we not count to be a simple knowledge only, but a great gain of God's mercy, with wonderful rich and precious virtues of faith, repentance, remission of sins, humility, thankfulness, mortification, and diligence in doing good. Not that properly the cross worketh these things of itself; but because the cross is the mean and way by the which God worketh the knowledge and feeling of these things in his children: as many both testimonies and examples in [the] scriptures are easily found of them that diligently weigh what therein they read.

<small>James i.</small>

To these two commodities of the cross join the third, of God's singular wisdom, that it may be coupled with his justice and mercy. On this sort therefore let us conceive, when we see the gospel of God and his church persecuted and troubled, as now with us it is, that, because the great, learned, and wise men of the world use not their wisdom to love and serve God, as to natural wisdom and reason he openeth himself mani- Rom. i. festly by his visible creatures; therefore doth God justly infatuate and make them foolish, giving them up to unsensibleness, especially herein. For on this manner reason they concerning the affliction which cometh for the gospel:

'If,' say they, 'this were God's word, if these people were God's children, surely God would then bless and prosper them and their doctrine. But now, in that there is no doctrine so much hated, no people so much persecuted as they be, therefore it cannot be of God.—Rather this is of God, which our queen and old bishops have professed; for how hath God preserved them and kept them! What a notable victory hath God given unto her, where it was impossible that things should so have come to pass as they have done! —And did not the great captain[1] confess his fault, that he was out of the way, and not of the faith which these gospellers profess? How many are come again from that which they professed to be God's word!—The most part of this realm, notwithstanding the diligence of preachers to persuade them concerning this new learning which now is persecuted, never consented to it in heart, as experience teacheth.—And what plagues have come upon this realm sithen this gospel, as they call it, came in amongst us! Afore we had plenty; but now there is nothing like as it was.—Moreover all the houses of the parliament have overthrown the laws made for the stablishing of this gospel and religion; and new laws are erected for the continuance of the contrary.—How miraculously doth God confound their doctrine and confirm ours! For how was Wyat overthrown[2]! How prosperously came in our king[2]! How hath God blessed our queen with fruit of womb[3]! How is the pope's holiness restored again to his right[4]! All these do teach plainly, that this their doctrine is not God's word.'

[[1] The duke of Northumberland, who, at his execution, August, 1553, professed himself to hold the doctrines of Rome. See Strype, Cranmer, I. 450—4, and append. no. lxxiii. Vol. II. 917—8.]

[[2] See Strype, Mem. III. i. 125—39, 200—9.]

[[3] See prefatory note, p. 412 above.]

[[4] The last five lines, 'How miraculously to his right,' do not occur in the edition without date.]

Thus reason the worldly-wise, which see not God's wisdom. For else, if they considered that there was with us unthankfulness for the gospel, no amendment of life, but all kind of contempt of God, all kind of shameless sinning ensued the preaching of the gospel, they must needs see that God could not but chastise and correct; and, as he let Satan loose, after he had bound him a certain time, for unthankfulness of men, so to let these champions of Satan run abroad, by them to plague us for our unthankfulness. Great was God's anger against Ahab, because he saved Ben-hadad, king of Syria, after he had given him into his hands; and afterward it turned to his own destruction. God would that double sorrow should have been repaid to them, because of the sorrow they did to the saints of God. Read the eighteenth of the Revelation.

Rev. xx.

1 Kings xx.

As for the victory given to the queen's highness, if men had any godly wit, they might see many things in it. First God hath done it to win her heart to the gospel. Again he hath done it, as well because they that went against her put their trust in horses and power of men, and not in God, as because in their doing they sought not the propagation of God's gospel. Which thing is now plainly seen by the confession of the captain[1]: his heart loved popery, and hated the gospel. Besides this, men may easily see he was purposed never to have furthered the gospel, but so to have handled the livings of ministers, that there should never have been any ministry in manner hereafter. And what one of the councillors, which would have been taken as gospellers in our good king's days, declare now that even they loved the gospel[2]? Therefore no marvel why God fought against them. They were hypocrites, and under the cloak of the gospel would have debarred the queen's highness of her right: but God would not so cloak them.

Now for the relenting, returning, and recanting of some from that which they once professed or preached, alas! who would wonder at it? For they never came to the gospel but for commodity and gain's sake; and now for gain they leave it.

The multitude is no good argument to move a wise man: for who knoweth not more to love this world better than

[1 See note 1 in the preceding page.]

[2 The last eight lines, 'by the confession . loved the gospel,' are taken from the 'Exhortation' without date, and do not occur in the 'Letters of the martyrs,' 1564.]

heaven, themselves better than their neighbours? "Wide is the gate," saith Christ, "and broad is the way that leadeth to destruction, and many there be that go in thereat: but strait is the gate, and narrow is the way, which leadeth unto life; and few there be that find it." All the whole multitude cry out upon Jesus, "Crucify him," truss him up: but, I trow, not because they were the bigger part, therefore they were to be believed. All Chaldee followed still their false gods: only Abraham followed the true God. *Matt. vii.* *Gen. xii.*

And where they say that greater plagues are fallen upon the realm in poverty and such other things than before, is no argument to move others than such as love their swine better than Christ. For the devil chiefly desireth his seat to be in religion: if it be there, then he will meddle with nothing we have; all shall be quiet enough: but if he be raised thence, then will he beg leave to have at our pigs. Read Matthew viii. of the Gergesites. As long as with us he had the ruling of religion, which now he hath gotten again, then was he Robin Good-fellow[3]; he would do no hurt: but when he was tumbled out of his throne by preaching of the gospel, then ranged he about as he hath done, but secretly. *Matt. viii.*

Finally, effectual he hath not been but in "the children of unbelief." Them indeed hath he stirred up to be covetous, oppressors, blasphemers, usurers, whoremongers, thieves, murderers, tyrants: and yet perchance he suffered them to profess the gospel, the more thereby to hinder it, and cause it to be slandered. How many now do appear to have been true gospellers? *Eph. ii.*

As for the parliament and statutes thereof, no man of wisdom can think otherwise but that, look what the rulers will, the same must there be enacted; for it goeth not in those houses by the better part, but by the bigger part. And it is a common saying, and no less true, *Major pars vincit meliorem,* 'The greater part overcometh the better.' So they did in condemning Christ, not regarding the counsel of Nicodemus: so they did also in many general councils. But all wise men know that acts of parliament are not for God's law in respect of God's law, but in respect of the people. *John vii.*

[3 'Robin Good-fellow:' an imaginary being, a domestic goblin, supposed to be of use to farm-servants. Vide Nares, Glossary; and Warton on Milton, L'Allegro, Vol. vi. p. 95—7, ed. Todd, 1809.]

Now what we are, God knoweth, and all the world seeth; more meet a great deal to have the devil's decrees, than God's religion, so great is our contempt of it. And therefore justly for our sins, as Job saith, God hath set "hypocrites to reign over us," which can no more abide God's true religion than the owl the light, or bleared eyes the bright sun; for it will have them to do their duties, and walk in diligent doing of the works of their vocation. If God's word, I mean, had place, bishops could not play chancellors and idle prelates as they do, priests should be otherwise known than by their shaven crowns and tippets. But enough of this.

Job xxxiv.

As for miracles of success against Wyat and other, of the king's coming in, &c., I would to God men would consider two kinds of miracles: one to confirm and prepare men in the doctrine which they have received; and another to prove and try men how they have received it, and how they will stick unto it. Of the former these miracles be not, but of the second. Now, by this success given to the queen, God trieth whether we will stick to his truth simply for his truth sake or no. This is a mighty illusion which God sendeth to prove his people, and to deceive the hypocrites which receive not God's truth simply, but in respect of gain, praise, estimation. Read how Ahab was deceived[1].

2 Thess. ii. Deut. xiii.

But I will now return to the third commodity coming by the cross. Here let us see "the wisdom of God" in "making the wisdom of the world foolish," which knoweth little of man's corruption, how foul it is in the sight of God, and displeaseth him; which knoweth little the portion of God's people to be in another world; which knoweth little the Patron of Christians, Christ Jesus; which knoweth little the general judgment of God, the great malice of Satan to God's people, the price and estimation of the gospel; and therefore in the cross seeth not as God's wisdom would we should see, namely, that God in punishing them which sin least would have his anger against sin seen most, and to be better considered and feared.

Luke xii.

In punishing his people here, he kindleth their desire towards their restful home. In punishing his servants in this life, he doth conform and make them like to Christ; that as

Phil. iii.

[1 This paragraph does not occur in the edition without date.]

they be like in suffering, so shall they be in reigning. In punishing his church in the world, he doth give a demonstration of his judgment which shall come on all men, when the godly shall there find rest, though now they be afflicted; and the wicked now wallowing in wealth shall be wrapped in woe and smart. In punishing the professors of his gospel on earth, he setteth forth the malice of Satan against the gospel and his people, for the more confirming of their faith, and the gospel to be God's word indeed, and they to[2] be God's people; for else the devil would let them alone. In punishing the lovers of his truth more than others which care not for it, he putteth them in mind how they have not had in price, as they should have had, the jewel of his word and gospel. Before such trial and experience came, perchance they thought they had believed and had had faith; which now they see was but a lip-faith, a mock faith, or an opinion. All which things we see are occasions for us to take better heed by mean of the cross. Acts xvi.

Psal. cxix.

Therefore, thirdly, let us consider the cross to be commodious for us to learn God's wisdom, and what is man's foolishness, God's displeasure at sin, a desire to be with God, the conformity with Christ, the general judgment, the malice of Satan, hatred of sin, the gospel to be God's word, and how it is to be esteemed, &c. Thus much for this.

Now will I, fourthly, briefly shew you the cross or trouble to be profitable for us to learn and behold better the providence, presence, and power of God, that all these may be coupled together as in a chain to hang about our necks; I mean God's justice, mercy, wisdom, power, presence, and providence.

When all things be in rest, and men be not in trouble, then they are forgetful of God commonly, and attribute too much to their own wisdom, policies, providence, diligence; as though they were the procurers of their own fortune, and workers of their own weal. But when the cross cometh, and that in such sort as their wits, policies, and friends cannot help; though the wicked despair, run from God to saints and such other unlawful means; yet do the godly therein behold the presence, the providence, and power of God. For the scripture teacheth all things to come from God, weal and

[2 'to,' edition without date: not in 1564.]

woe; and that the same should be looked upon as God's work, although Satan, the devil, be often an instrument by whom God worketh justly and mercifully; justly to the wicked, and mercifully to the godly: as by the examples of wicked Saul and godly Job easily we may see God's work by Satan his instrument in them both.

<small>Amos iii.
Lam. iii.
Isai. xlv.
Matt. x.</small>

The children of God therefore, which before forgat God in prosperity, now in adversity are awaked to see God in his work, and no more to hang on their own forecasts, power, friends, wisdom, riches, &c.; but learn to cast themselves on God's providence and power, whereby they are so preserved and governed, and very often miraculously delivered, that the very wicked cannot but see God's providence, presence, and power, in the cross and affliction of his children; as they (his children I mean) to their joy do feel it, thereby learning to know God to be the Governor of all things.

<small>Isai. xlv.
Hos. i.
Luke i.
1 Sam. ii.
Psal. cxxxix.
1 Pet. v.
2 Cor. iv.</small>

He it is that giveth peace; he it is that sendeth war; he giveth plenty and poverty; he setteth up and casteth down; "he bringeth to death, and after giveth life." His presence is everywhere; his providence is within and without; his power is the pillar whereby the godly stand, and to it they lean, as to the thing no less able to set up than to cast down. Which thing full well the apostle saw in his afflictions, and therefore greatly rejoiced in them, that *eminentia virtutis Dei*, 'God's power,' might singularly be seen therein.

Concerning this thing I might bring forth innumerable examples of the affliction of God's children, both in the old and new Testament, wherein we may see how they felt God's presence, providence, and power plentifully. But I will omit examples, because every one of us that have been or be in trouble cannot but, by the same, remember God's presence, which we feel by his hand upon us; his providence which leaveth us not unprovided for, without any of our own provision; and his power which both preserveth us from many other evils which else would come upon us, and also maketh us able to bear more than we thought we could have done. So very often doth he deliver us by such means as have been thought most foolish, and little to have been regarded: and therefore we shake off our sleep of security and forgetting of God, our trust and shift in our own policies, our hanging on men or on our own power.

So that the cross you see is commodious, fourthly, for to see God's presence, providence, and power, and our negligence, forgetfulness of God, security, self-love, trust and confidence in ourselves; and things in this life to be cast off, as the other are to be taken hold on.

And this shall suffice for the commodities which come by the cross; wherethrough we may be in love with it for the commodities' sake, which at length we shall find, though presently in sense we feel them not. 'No castigation or punish- Heb. xii. ment is sweet for the present instant,' saith the apostle, 'but afterwards the end and work of the thing is otherwise:' as we see in medicines, the more wholesome that they be, the more unpleasant is the taste thereof, as in pills, potions, and such like bitter stuff; yet we will, on the physician's word, drink them gladly for the profit which cometh of them. And, dearly beloved, although to lose life and goods, or friends, for God's gospel sake, it seem a bitter and sour thing; yet in that our "Physician" which cannot lie (Jesus Christ I mean) doth tell us that it is very wholesome, howsoever it be [un]-toothsome, let us with good cheer take the cup at his hand, and drink it merrily. If the cup seem unpleasant, and the drink too bitter, let us put some sugar therein, even a piece of that which Moses cast into the bitter water, and made the Exod. xv. same pleasant; I mean an ounce, yea, a dram of Christ's 1 Pet. iv. afflictions and cross which he suffered for us. If we call this to mind, and cast of them into our cup, (considering what he was, what he suffered, of whom, for whom, to what end, and what came thereof,) surely we cannot loath our medicine, but wink, and drink it lustily.

Lustily therefore drink the cup which Christ giveth, and will give unto you, my good brethren and sisters; I mean, prepare yourselves to suffer whatsoever God will lay upon you for the confessing of his holy name. If not because of these three things, that ye are not of the world, ye suffer not alone, your trouble shall not hurt you; yet, for the commodities which come of the cross, I beseech you heartily to embrace it[1].

The fight is but short, the joy is exceeding great. *Opor-* Luke xviii.

[1 The 'Exhortation' without date supplies, after this paragraph, a confutation of 'four pillars of the mass,' transubstantiation, the sacrifice, praying for the dead, and praying to the dead.]

tet semper orare: "We must pray alway." Then shall we undoubtedly be directed in all things by God's holy Spirit, which Christ hath promised to be our doctor, teacher, and Comforter: and therefore we need not to fear what man or devil can do unto us either by false teaching or cruel persecution; for our Pastor is such a one that "none can take his sheep out of his hands." To him be praise for ever. Amen[1].

<small>John xiv. xv. xvi.</small>

Thus much, my dear brethren and sisters in our dear Lord and Saviour Jesus Christ, I thought good to write unto you for your comfort in these troublesome days, and for the confirmation of the truth that ye have already received[2]: from the which if ye for fear of man, loss of goods, friends, or life, do swerve or depart, then ye depart and swerve from Christ, and so snarl[3] yourselves in Satan's sophistry to your utter subversion. Therefore, as St Peter saith, "watch and be sober, for as a roaring lion he seeketh to devour you." "Be strong in faith," that is, mammer[4] not, nor waver not, in God's promises, but believe certainly that they pertain to you, that God "is with you in trouble, that he will deliver you and glorify you." But yet see that ye call upon him specially "that ye enter not into temptation," as he taught his disciples, even at such time as he saw Satan "desire to sift them," as now he hath done to sift us.

<small>Psal. xxvii. Heb. xiii. 1 Pet. ii. John x.</small>

<small>1 Pet. v.</small>

<small>Acts ii. Exod. xx. Psal. xci.</small>

<small>Matt. xxvi. Luke xxii.</small>

O dear Saviour, prevent him now, as thou didst then with thy prayer, I beseech thee; and grant that our "faith faint not;" but strengthen us to confirm the weak that they deny not thee and thy gospel, that they "return not to their vomit" and puddle of mire in popery and superstition; as massing, praying to saints, praying for the dead, or worshipping the work of men's hands, instead of thee their Saviour. Oh, let us not so run down headlong into perdition[5], stumbling on those sins from the which there is no recovery, causing thee to "deny them before thy Father," making "their latter

<small>2 Pet. ii.</small>

<small>Heb. vi. x.</small>

<small>Matt. x. Mark viii. Luke xii.</small>

[1 The last seven words occur only in the edition without date.]
[2 The last sixteen words occur only in the edition without date.]
[3 'Snarl:' entangle. Vide Nares, Glossary.]
[4 'Mammer:' hesitate.]
[5 The last four lines, 'and puddle. . into perdition,' occur only in the edition without date.]

end worse than the beginning:" as it chanced to Lot's wife, Judas Iscariot, Francis Spira[6], and to many others. But rather strengthen them and us all in thy grace, and in those things which thy word teacheth, that we may here hazard our life for thy sake; and so shall we be sure to save it; as, if we seek to "save it, we cannot but lose it:" and that being lost, "what profit can we have, if we win the whole world?" O set thou always before our eyes, not as reason doth, this life, the pleasure of the same, death of the body, and prisonment, &c.; but everlasting life, and those unspeakable joys which undoubtedly they shall have, which "take up the cross and follow thee." Set ever before us also the[7] eternal hell-fire and destruction of soul and body for evermore, which they must needs at length fall into, the which are afraid for the hoar frost of adversity that man or the devil stirreth up to stop or hinder us from[8] going forward in[9] our journey to heaven's bliss. To the which do thou bring us for thy name's sake. Amen.

Matt. xvi.

Pray for all your brethren which be in prison and exile, and so absent from you in body, but yet present with you in spirit: and heartily pray God once to prove us, and trust us again with his holy word and gospel; that we may be suffered to speak, and you to hear his voice, as heretofore we and you have done, but unthankfully and negligently, I may say, yea, very unworthily and carnally. And therefore is his most just anger fallen now upon us.

He remember his mercy towards us in his time, we beseech him. Amen[10].

Your own in the Lord,

JOHN BRADFORD.

[[6] An eminent lawyer of Citadella near Venice, who, having denied the Protestant faith, died in despair in 1548. His most affecting history has often been printed in a separate form, as for instance, 'Relation,' &c. by Nath. Bacon, Lond. 1681. Vide Sleidan. Comm. de stat. relig. XXI. p. 474—5, Francof. 1568; and Seckendorf. Hist. Lutheran. III. cxxix. Vol. II. 601, Francof. et Lips. 1692.]

[[7] 'and' 1564: 'set ever before us also the,' edition without date.]
[[8] 'for' 1564: 'from,' edition without date.]
[[9] 'in,' edition without date: not in 1564.]
[[10] The last two paragraphs are taken from the 'Exhortation' without date, and do not occur in the 'Letters of the martyrs,' 1564.]

FAREWELL TO THE CITY OF LONDON[1].

Foxe, Acts, &c. 1563, p. 1176–8, and after editions.
Bp. Coverdale, Letters of the martyrs, 1564, p. 251—6.
MS. 1. 2. 8. no. 51.[2] and MS. 1. 2. 8. no. 66. Emman. Coll. Camb.

To all that profess the gospel and true doctrine of our Lord and Saviour Jesus Christ in the city of London, John Bradford, a most unworthy servant of the Lord, now not only in prison, but also excommunicated and condemned to be burned for the same true doctrine, wisheth "mercy, grace, and peace," with increase of all godly knowledge and piety, from God "the Father of mercy," through the merits of our alone and omnisufficient Redeemer Jesus Christ, by the operation of the Holy Spirit, for ever. Amen.

My dearly beloved brethren in our Saviour Christ, although the time I have to live is very little, (for hourly I look when I should be had hence to be conveyed into Lancashire, there to be burned, and to render my life by the providence of God where I first received it by the same providence;) and although the charge is great to keep me from all things whereby I might signify any thing to the world of my state; yet, having as now I have pen and ink through God's working, maugre the head of Satan and his soldiers, I thought good to write a short confession of my faith, and thereto join a little exhortation unto you all to live according to your profession.

This my faith I would gladly particularly declare and expound to the confirmation and comfort of the simple; but, alas! by starts and stealth I write in manner that that I write,

[1 "After the time that Master Bradford was condemned, and sent to the Compter, it was purposed of his adversaries. that he should be had to Manchester where he was born, and there be burned: whereupon he writeth to the city of London, thinking to take his last *vale* of them in this letter.—Foxe, Acts, &c. 1583, p. 1625, or ed. 1843—8, VII. 198.]

[2 MS. 1. 2. 8. no. 51. has on it the name, 'Cuthbert Symson.' C. Symson was 'deacon of the Christian congregation in London in queen Mary's days;' and, after most severe torture on the rack, underwent martyrdom, March 28, 1558.—Foxe, Acts, &c. 1583, p. 2031—4, or ed. 1843—8, VIII. 454—61.]

and therefore I shall desire you all to take this brevity in good part[3].

First for my faith, I do confess and pray all the whole congregation of Christ to bear witness with me of the same, that I do believe constantly, through the gift and goodness of God (for "faith is God's only gift"), all the twelve articles of the symbol or creed commonly attributed to the collection of the apostles; not because of the creed itself, but because of the word of God, the which teacheth and confirmeth every article accordingly[4].

This word of God, written by the prophets and apostles, left and contained in the canonical books of the holy[5] Bible, I do believe to contain plentifully 'all things necessary to salvation[6];' so that nothing, as necessary to salvation, ought to be added thereto: and therefore the church of Christ, nor none of his congregation, ought to be burdened with any other doctrine than which hereout hath his foundation and ground. In testimony of this faith I render and give my life, being condemned, as well for not acknowledging the antichrist of Rome to be Christ's vicar-general and supreme head of his catholic and universal church, here and[7] elsewhere, upon earth; as for denying the horrible and idolatrous doctrine of transubstantiation, and Christ's real, corporal, and carnal presence in his supper, under the forms and accidents of bread and wine.

To believe Christ our Saviour to be "the Head of his church," and kings in their realms to be "the supreme powers" to whom every soul oweth obedience; and to believe that in the supper of Christ (which 'the sacrament of the altar,' as the papists call it and use it, doth utterly overthrow) is a true and very presence of whole Christ, God and man, to the faith of the receiver, (but not to the stander by and looker upon,)

[3 This last paragraph is written on the margin of MS. 1. 2. 8. no. 66., and is printed in the margin of Foxe, Acts, &c. 1563, and of Bp. Coverdale, Lett. of mart. 1564, but is given as above in the text of MS. 1. 2. 8. no. 51., and forms part of the ensuing paragraph in Foxe 1570 and after editions.]

[4 See Article VIII. Ch. of Eng.]

[5 'hole' 1563: 'holye,' Emman. MSS.: 'holy' 1564: 'whole' 1570, 1576, 1583.]

[6 Article VI. Ch. of Eng.]

[7 'or' 1563: 'and,' Emman. MSS., and 1564.]

as it is a true and very presence of bread and wine to the senses of men; to believe this, I say[1], will not serve; and therefore as an heretic I am condemned and shall be burned. Whereof I ask God heartily mercy that I do no more rejoice than I do, having so great cause as to be an instrument wherein it may please my dear Lord God and Saviour to suffer.

For, albeit my manifold sins even sithen I came into prison have deserved at the hands of God not only this temporal, but also eternal fire in hell, (much more then my former sinful life, which the Lord pardon for his Christ's sake, as I know he of his mercy hath done, and never will lay mine iniquities to my charge to condemnation, so great is his goodness, praised therefor be his holy name!) although, I say, my manifold and grievous late sins have deserved most justly all the tyranny that man or devil can do unto me; and therefore I confess that the Lord is "just, and that his judgments be true," and deserved on my behalf; yet the bishops and prelates do not persecute them in me, but Christ himself, his word, his truth, and religion. And therefore I have great cause, yea, most great cause, to rejoice that ever I was born and hitherto kept of the Lord; that by my death, which is deserved for my sins, it pleaseth the heavenly Father to glorify his name, to testify his truth, to confirm his verity, to repugn his adversaries.

O good God and merciful Father, forgive me my great unthankfulness, especially herein.

And you, my dearly beloved, for the Lord Jesu Christ's sake, I humbly and heartily in his bowels and blood do now, for my last *vale* and 'farewell' in this present life, beseech you and every of you, that you will consider this work of the Lord accordingly; first by me to be admonished to beware of hypocrisy and carnal security: profess not the gospel with tongue and lips only, but in heart and verity; frame and fashion your lives accordingly. Beware God's name be not evil spoken of, and the gospel less regarded, by your conversation. God forgive me that I have not so heartily professed it as I should have done, but have sought much myself therein!

Hypocrisy and carnal security.

[1 'I say' 1564, 1570, and the after editions of Foxe; not in 1563, nor in Emman. MSS.]

The gospel is a new doctrine to the "old man:" it is "new wine," and therefore cannot be "put in old bottles" without more great hurt than good to "the bottles." If we will talk with the Lord, we must "put off our shoes" and carnal affections: if we will hear the voice of the[2] Lord, we must "wash our garments," and be holy: if we will be Christ's disciples, we must "deny ourselves, take up our cross, and follow Christ." We "cannot serve two masters:" if we seek Christ's kingdom, we must also seek for "the righteousness thereof." To the petition of, "Let thy kingdom come," we must join, "Thy will be done," done, done "on earth as it is in heaven." If we will "not be doers of the word but hearers of it only, we sore deceive ourselves." If we hear the gospel and love it not, we declare ourselves to be but fools and "builders upon the sand." The Lord's Spirit hateth feigning; deceitfulness the Lord abhorreth. If we come to him, we must beware we come not to him "with a double heart;" for then it[3] may chance that God will answer us according to the block which is in our heart, and so we shall deceive ourselves and others. To faith see that we couple "a good conscience," lest we "make a shipwreck." To the Lord we must come "with fear and reverence." If we will be gospellers, we must be Christ's: if we "be Christ's, we must crucify our flesh, with the lusts and concupiscences thereof." If we will "be under grace, sin must not bear rule in us." We may not come to the Lord, and "draw nigh[4] to him with our[5] lips, and leave our hearts elsewhere;" lest the Lord's wrath wax hot, and he take from us the good remaining. In no case can the kingdom of Christ approach to them that repent not.

Good conscience.

Therefore, my dearly beloved, let us repent and be heartily sorry that we have so carnally, so hypocritically, so covetously, so vain-gloriously professed the gospel. For all these I confess of myself, to the glory of God and mine own confusion here[6], that he may "cover mine offences" in the day of judg-

Psal. xxxii.
1 John i.

[2 'the,' Emman. MSS., 1564, 1570, and after editions: not in 1563.]

[3 'it' 1564: not in 1563.]

[4 'high' 1563, a misprint for 'nigh.']

[5 'our' 1564, 1570, and after editions: not in 1563 or Emman. MSS.]

[6 The last five words are in the Emman. MSS. and 1564, but not in 1563.]

ment. Let the anger and plagues of God, most justly fallen upon us, be applied to every one of our deserts, that from the bottom of our hearts every of us may say:

'It is I, Lord, that have sinned against thee: it is mine hypocrisy, my vain-glory, my covetousness, uncleanness, carnality, security, idleness, unthankfulness, self-love, and such like, which have deserved the taking away of our good king, of thy word and true religion, of thy good ministers by exile, prisonment, and death: it is my wickedness that causeth success and increase of authority and peace to thine enemies. O "be merciful, be merciful, unto us." "Turn to us again," O Lord of hosts, and "turn us unto thee." "Correct us, but not in thy fury, lest we be consumed." "In thine anger chastise us not." "In thy wrathful displeasure reprove us not," but "in the midst of thine anger remember thy mercy;" for, "if thou wilt mark what is done amiss, who shall be able to abide it? But with thee is mercifulness, that thou mightest be worshipped." O then be merciful unto us, that we might truly worship thee. "Help us for the glory of thy name;" "be merciful unto our sins, for they are great." O heal us and help us for thine honour: let not the wicked people say, "Where is their God?"' &c.

Prayer: hearing and reading the holy scriptures.

On this sort, my right dearly beloved, let us heartily bewail our sins, repent us of our former evil life, heartily and earnestly purpose to amend our lives in all things, continually "watch in prayer," diligently and reverently attend, hear, and read the holy scriptures, labour after our vocation to amend our brethren. Let us "reprove the works of darkness;" let us "fly from all idolatry;" let us abhor the antichristian and Romish rotten service, detest the popish mass, abrenounce[1]

Obedience to magistrates in all that is not against God's word.

their Romish god, prepare ourselves to the cross; be obedient to all that be in authority in all things that be not against God and his word: for then answer with the apostles, "It is more meet to obey God than man."

Howbeit, never for any thing resist or rise against the magistrates; "avenge not yourselves," but "commit your cause to the Lord," "to whom vengeance pertaineth;" and he in his time will reward it. If ye feel in yourselves an hope and trust in God that he "will never tempt you above that he will

---

[1 'abrenounce' 1563 and after editions, and Emman. MSS.: 'forsake' 1564.]

make you able to bear," be assured the Lord will be true to you, and you shall be able to bear all brunts. But if you want this hope, flee and get you hence, rather than by your tarrying God's name should be dishonoured.

In sum, "cast your care upon the Lord, knowing for most certain that he is careful for you." With him "are all the hairs of your head numbered," so that "not one of them shall perish" without his good pleasure and will; much more then nothing shall happen to your bodies which shall not be profitable, howsoever for a time it seem otherwise to your senses. Hang on the providence of God, not only when you have means to help you, but also when you have no means, yea, when all means be against you. Give him this honour, which of all other things he most chiefly requireth at your hands, namely, believe that you are his children through Christ; that he is your Father and God through him; that he loveth you, pardoneth you all your offences; that[2] "he is with you in trouble," and will be with you for ever. When you fall, he will put under his hand; you shall not lie still. "Tofore you call upon him, he heareth you:" "out of evil he will finally bring you, and deliver you to his eternal kingdom." Doubt not, my dearly beloved, hereof; doubt not, I say, this will God your Father do for you in respect not of yourselves, but in respect of Christ your Captain, your Pastor, your Keeper, "out of whose hands none shall be able to catch you." In him be quiet, and often consider your dignity; namely, how that you be God's children, the saints of God, citizens of heaven, "temples of the Holy Ghost," the thrones of God, "members of Christ," and lords over all.

We ought to depend upon God's providence always.

Therefore be ashamed to think, speak, or do any thing that should be unseemly for God's children, God's saints, Christ's members, &c. "Marvel not though" the devil and "the world hate you," though ye be persecuted here; for "the servant is not greater nor[3] above his Master." Covet not earthly riches, fear not the power of man, "love not this world, nor things that be in this world;" but long for the Lord Jesus his coming, at which time your "bodies shall be made like unto his glorious body." "When he appeareth, you shall be like unto him." When your life thus shall be

[2 'that,' only in 1564.]
[3 'greater nor,' only in MS. 1. 2. 8. no. 51.]

revealed, "then shall ye appear with him in glory." In the mean season live in hope thereof.

<small>We must live in the faith of Christ.</small>

Let the life you lead be in "the faith of the Son of God:" for "the just doth live by faith;" which faith flieth from all evil, and followeth the word of God as "a lantern to her feet

<small>The property of faith.</small>

and a light to her steps." Her eyes be above where Christ is; she beholdeth not the "things present," but rather "things to come;" she "glorieth in afflictions," she knoweth that "the afflictions of this life are not like to be compared to the glory which God will reveal to us and in us."

Of this glory God grant us here a lively taste! Then shall we run after the scent it sendeth forth; it will make us valiant men to take to us the kingdom of God: whither the Lord of mercy bring us in his good time, through Christ our Lord; to whom with the Father, and the Holy Ghost, three Persons and one God, be all honour and glory, world without end. Amen.

My dearly beloved, I would gladly have given here my body to have been burned for the confirmation of the true doctrine I have taught here unto you; but that my country must have: therefore, I pray you, take in good part this signification of my good-will towards every of you; impute the want herein to time and trouble. Pardon me mine offensive and negligent behaviour when I was amongst you.

With me repent, and labour to amend; continue in the truth which I have truly taught unto you by preaching, in all places where I have come, God's name therefor be praised. "Confess Christ" when you are called, whatsoever cometh thereof: and "the God of peace be with us all. Amen."

This eleventh of February, *anno* 1555.

Your brother in bonds for the Lord's sake.

JOHN BRADFORD.

FAREWELL TO THE UNIVERSITY AND TOWN OF CAMBRIDGE.

To all "that love the Lord Jesus" and his true doctrine, being in the university and town of Cambridge, John Bradford, a most unworthy servant of the Lord, now not only prisoned but also condemned for the same true doctrine, wisheth "grace, peace, and mercy," with increase of all godliness, from God "the Father of all mercy," through the bloody passion of our alone full[2] Saviour Jesus Christ, by the lively working of the Holy Spirit, for ever. Amen.

Although I look hourly when I should be had to the stake, my right dearly beloved in the Lord, and although the charge over me is great and strait; yet, having by the providence of God secretly pen and ink, I could not but something signify unto you my solicitude which I have for you and every of you in the Lord, though not as I would, yet as I may.

You have often and openly heard the truth, especially in this matter wherein I am condemned, disputed and preached, that it is needless to do any more but only to put you in remembrance of the same: but hitherto you have not heard it confirmed, and as it were sealed up, as now you do and shall hear by me, that is, by my death and burning. For, albeit I have deserved through my uncleanness, hypocrisy, avarice, vain-glory, idleness, unthankfulness, and carnality, (whereof I accuse myself to my confusion before the world, that before God through Christ I might, as my assured hope is I shall, "find mercy,") eternal death and hell-fire, much more then this affliction and fire prepared for me; yet, my dearly beloved, it is not these or any of these things wherefor the prelates do persecute me: but God's verity and truth, yea, even Christ himself, is the only cause and thing wherefor I now am condemned and shall be burned as an heretic. For, because I will not grant the antichrist of Rome to be Christ's vicar-general and supreme head of his church

[1 The Emmanuel MS. 2. 2. 15. no. 3. is in the autograph of Bradford.]

[2 'alonely' 1563, 1564: 'alone full,' Emman. MSS.]

here and every where upon earth, by God's ordinance; and because I will not grant such corporal, real, and carnal presence of Christ's body and blood in the sacrament, as doth transubstantiate the substance of bread and wine, and is received of the wicked, yea, of dogs and mice also; I am excommunicated, and counted as a dead member of Christ's church, as a rotten branch, and therefore shall be cast into the fire.

Therefore ye ought heartily to "rejoice with me" and to give thanks for me, that God the eternal Father hath vouchedsafe our mother[1] to bring up any child in whom it would please him thus[2] to magnify his holy name, as he doth, and I hope for his mercy and truth's sake will do, in me and by me. O what such like[2] benefit upon earth can it be, as that that which deserved death by reason of my sins should be diverted to a demonstration, a testification, and confirmation of God's verity and truth?

Thou, my mother, the university, hast not only had the truth of God's word plainly manifested unto thee by reading, disputing, and preaching, publicly and privately; but now (to make thee altogether excuseless, and as it were almost to sin "against the Holy Ghost," if thou put to thy helping hand with the Romish rout to suppress the verity, and set out the contrary) thou hast my life and blood as a seal to confirm thee, if thou wilt be confirmed, or else to confound thee and bear witness against thee, if thou wilt take part with the prelates and clergy; which now "fill up the measure of their fathers which slew the prophets" and apostles, "that all the[3] righteous blood from Abel" to Bradford "shed upon the earth" may be required at their hands.

Of this therefore I thought good tofore my death, as time and liberty would suffer me, for the[4] love and duty I bear unto thee, to admonish thee, good mother, and my sister the town, that you would call to mind from whence you are fallen, and study to "do the first works." Ye know, if you will, these matters of the Romish supremacy, and the antichristian transubstantiation, whereby Christ's supper is over-

[1 i. e. the University of Cambridge.]
[2 'thus,' 'like,' only in autograph MS.]
[3 'the,' Emman. MSS. and Univ. MS.: not in 1563 or 1564.]
[4 'the,' Emman. MSS., Univ. MS., and 1564: not in 1563.]

thrown, his priesthood evacuate, his sacrifice frustrate, the ministry of his word unplaced, repentance repelled, faith fainted, godliness extinguished, the mass maintained, idolatry supported, and all impiety cherished; you know, I say, if you will, that these opinions are not only besides God's word, but even directly against God's word[5]: and therefore to take part with them is to take part against God, against whom you cannot prevail.

Therefore, for the tender mercy of Christ in his bowels and blood, I beseech you to take Christ's *collyrium* and "eye-salve to anoint your eyes, that you may see" what you do and have done in admitting (as I hear you have admitted, yea, alas! authorised and by consent confirmed) the Romish rotten rags which once you utterly expelled. O be not *canis reversus ad vomitum*, ["the dog returned to his vomit;"] be not *sus lota, reversa ad volutabrum cœni*, ["the washed sow returned to her rolling in the mire."] Beware lest old Satan "enter in with seven other spirits," and then *postrema* "the last[6] shall be worse than the first." It had been better ye had never known the truth, than after knowledge to run from it. Ah, woe to this world and the things therein, which hath now so wrought with you! O that ever this dirt of the devil should daub up the eye of the realm! For thou, O mother, art as it were the eye of the realm. If thou be light and give shine, all the body shall fare the better; but if thou, "the light, be darkness," alas, "how great will the darkness be!" "What is man whose breath is in his nostrils, that thou shouldest thus be afraid of him?"

Oh, what is honour and life here, but plain[7] bubbles? What is glory in this world, and of this world, but plain[8] shame? Why art thou afraid "to carry Christ's cross?" Wilt thou come into his kingdom, and not "drink of his cup?" Dost thou not know Rome to be Babylon? Dost thou not know that as the old Babylon had the children of Judah in captivity, so hath this true Judah, that is, the

[5 'it' 1563, 1564, MS. 1. 2. 8. and Univ. MS.: 'God's word,' autogr. MS.]

[6 *postrema* 1563 and Emman. MSS.: 'the last' 1564.]

[7 'but plain,' Emman. MSS. and 1564: not in 1563, or Univ. MS.]

[8 'but' 1563, 1564, and Univ. MS.: 'and of this world, but plain,' Emman. MSS.]

confessors of Christ? Dost thou not know that, as destruction happened unto it, so shall it do unto this? And trowest thou that God will not deliver his people now, when the time is come, as he did then? Hath not God commanded his people to "come out from her;" and wilt thou give ensample to the whole realm to run into her? Hast thou forgotten the woe that Christ threateneth to offence-givers? Wilt thou not remember that "it were better a millstone were hanged about thy neck, and thou thrown into the sea, than that thou shouldest offend the little ones?" And, alas, how hast thou offended; yea, how dost thou still offend! Wilt thou consider things according to the outward shew? Was not the synagogue more seemly and like to the true church, than the simple flock of Christ's disciples? Hath not the whore of Babylon more costly array and rich apparel externally to set forth herself, than the homely housewife of Christ? Where is the beauty of "the king's daughter," the church of Christ, without or within? Doth not David say, "within?" O remember that as "they are happy which are not offended at Christ," so are they happy which are not offended at his poor church.

Can the pope and his prelates mean honestly, which make so much of the wife, and so little of the "Husband?" The church they magnify, but Christ they contemn. If this church were an honest woman, that is, Christ's wife, except they would make much of her "Husband" Christ and his word, she would not be made much of of[1] them. When Christ and his apostles were upon earth, who was more like to be the true church; they, or the prelates, bishops, and synagogue? If a man should have followed custom, unity, antiquity, or the more part, should not Christ and his company have been cast out of the doors? Therefore bade Christ, "Search the scriptures." And, good mother, shall "the servant be above his master?" Shall we look for other entertainment at the hands of the world, than Christ and his dear disciples found?

Who was taken in Noe's time for the church, poor Noe and his family, or others? Who was taken for God's church in Sodom, Lot or others? And doth not Christ say, "As it went then, so shall it go now towards the coming of the Son

[1 'of them' 1563, autogr. MS. and Univ. MS.: 'of of them' MS. 1. 2. 8. and 1564.]

of man?" What meaneth Christ, when he saith, "Iniquity shall have the upper hand?" Doth not he tell that "charity shall wax cold?" And who seeth not a wonderful great lack of charity in those, which would now be taken for Christ's church? All that fear God in this realm truly can tell more of this than I can write.

Therefore, dear mother, receive some admonition of one of thy poor children now going to be burned for the testimony of Jesus. Come again to God's truth; "come out of Babylon;" "confess Christ" and his true doctrine; repent that which is past; make amends by declaring thy repentance by the fruits. Remember the readings and preachings of God's prophet and true preacher, Martin Bucer. Call to mind the threatenings of God now something seen by thy children, Lever and others. Let the exile of Lever, Pilkington, Grindal, Haddon, Horne, Scory, Ponet, &c., something awake thee. Let the imprisonment of thy dear sons, Cranmer, Ridley, and Latimer, move thee. Consider the martyrdom of thy chickens, Rogers, Saunders, Taylor: and now cast not away the poor admonition of me going to be burned also, and to receive the like crown of glory with my fellows. Take to heart God's calling by us. Be not as Pharaoh was; for then will it[2] happen unto thee as it[2] did unto him. What is that? "Hardness of heart." And what then? Destruction eternally both of body and soul.

Ah, therefore, good mother, awake, awake, repent, repent; buskel[3] thyself, and make thee bowne[4] to turn to the Lord; for else "it shall be more easy for Sodom and Gomorrah in the day of judgment, than for thee." O "harden not your hearts." O stop not your ears to-day in hearing God's voice, though it be by me a most unworthy messenger. O fear the Lord, for his anger is begun to kindle. "Even now the axe is laid to the root of the tree."

You know I prophesied truly to you before the sweat[5] came, what would come if you repented not your carnal gospel-

Martin Bucer's preaching.

Lever, Pilkington, Grindal, Haddon, Horne, Scory, Ponet, Rogers, Saunders, Taylor.

Bradford prophesieth in the sweat time what would follow of carnal gospelling, if repentance did not come.

[2 'it' 1564 and Univ. MS.: not in 1563 or Emman. MSS.]

[3 'Buskel:' prepare.]

[4 'Bowne:' ready, prepared. Jamieson, Scotch. Dict. 'Haste' 1563, 1564, and Univ. MS.: 'thee bowne,' autogr. MS.: 'thyself bowne' MS. 1. 2. 8.]

[5 See p. 61, note 3, above.]

ling[1]: and now I tell you before I depart hence, that the ears of men will tingle to hear of the vengeance of God that will fall upon you all, both town and university, if you repent not, if you leave not your idolatry, if you turn not speedily to the Lord, if ye still be ashamed of Christ's truth, which you know.

Perne. Thomson. O Perne[2], repent; O Thomson[3], repent; O ye doctors, bachelors, and masters, repent; O mayor, aldermen, and town-dwellers, repent, repent, repent, that you may escape the near vengeance of the Lord. "Rend your hearts," and come apace, calling on the Lord. Let us all say, '*Peccavimus*, "we have sinned, we have done wickedly, we have not hearkened to thy voice, O Lord. Deal not with us after our deserts, but be merciful to our iniquities, for they are great." O pardon us our offences. "In thine anger remember thy mercy." Turn us unto thee, O Lord God of hosts, for the glory of thy name's sake. Spare us, and be merciful unto us. Let not the wicked people say, "Where is now their God?" Oh, for thine own sake, for thy name's sake, deal mercifully with us. "Turn thyself unto us," and us unto thee: and "we shall praise thy name for ever."'

If in this sort, my dearly beloved, in heart and mouth we come unto God[4] our Father, and prostrate ourselves before "the throne of his grace," then surely, surely, we shall "find mercy;" then shall the Lord look merrily upon us for his mercy's sake in Christ; then shall we hear him "speak peace unto his people:" for he "is gracious and merciful, of great pity and compassion;" "he cannot be chiding for ever, his anger cannot last long" to the penitent. Though we weep in the morning, yet at night we shall have our sorrow to cease; for he is exorable, and "hath no pleasure in the death of a sinner:" he "rather would our conversion and turning."

[1 Compare the conclusion of Abp. Parker's sermon on the death of Bucer, 1551, 'Prospice tibi, Cantabrigia, cui Deus misit prophetas suos,' &c. in Bucer, Script. Angl. p. 898, Basil. 1577.]

[2 See account of Perne in Wood, Fasti Oxon. I. p. 141, ed. Bliss, Lond. 1815—20; and in 'Exam.' &c. of Philpot, p. 169, Parker Soc.: and see index to Oxford ed. of Strype.]

[3 Possibly the same as 'Edmund Thompson,' ordained by Bp. Ridley, Nov. 9, 1550.—Strype, Mem. II. i. 403.]

[4 'God,' Emman. MSS.: not in 1563, or 1564, or Univ. MS.]

O "turn you now and convert," yet once again I humbly beseech you; and then "the kingdom of heaven" shall "draw nigh." "The eye hath not seen, the ear hath not heard, nor the heart of man is able to conceive" the joys prepared for us, if we repent, amend our lives, and heartily turn to the Lord. But if you repent not, but be as you were, and go on forwards with the wicked, following the fashion of the world, "the Lord will lead you on with wicked doers," you shall perish in your wickedness, "your blood will be upon your own heads;" your part shall be with hypocrites, "where shall be weeping and gnashing of teeth;" ye shall be cast "from the face of the Lord" for ever and ever; eternal shame, sorrow, woe, and misery, shall be both in body and soul to you, "world without end."

O therefore, right dear to me in the Lord, "turn you, turn you;" repent you, repent you; amend, amend your lives, "depart from evil, do good," "follow peace and pursue it." "Come out from Babylon," "cast off the works of darkness," "put on Christ," confess his truth, be not ashamed of his gospel, prepare yourselves to the cross, drink of God's cup before it come to "the dregs:" and then shall I with you and for you "rejoice" in the day of judgment, which "is at hand:" and therefore prepare yourselves thereto, I heartily beseech you.

And thus I take my *vale in æternum* [farewell for ever] with you in this present life, mine own dear hearts in the Lord. The Lord of mercy be with us all, and give us a joyful and sure meeting in his kingdom! Amen, Amen.

Out of prison, ready to the stake[5], the 11th of February, *anno* 1555.

Your own in the Lord for ever,

JOHN BRADFORD.

[[5] 'Ready to the stake,' only in the autograph Emmanuel MS. 2. 2. 15.]

FAREWELL TO LANCASHIRE AND CHESHIRE.

<small>*Lancashire, Cheshire, and Manchester.*</small>

<small>*Foxe, Acts, &c. 1563, p. 1180—2, and after editions.*</small>

<small>*Bp. Coverdale, Letters of the martyrs, 1564, p. 263—9.*</small>

<small>*MS. 2. 2. 15. no. 109.¹ and MS. 1. 2. 8. no. 68. Emman. Coll. Camb.*</small>

To all those that profess the name and true religion of our Saviour Jesus Christ in Lancashire and Cheshire, and specially abiding in Manchester and thereabout, John Bradford, a most unworthy servant of the Lord, now not only in bonds, but also condemned for the same true religion, wisheth " mercy and grace, peace" and increase of all godliness, from God the Father of all pity, through the deserts of our Lord Jesus Christ, by the worklng of the most mighty and lively Spirit the Comforter, for ever. Amen.

<small>*The enemies had appointed to burn him at Manchester, but the Lord altered their purpose. [1564.]*</small>

I hear² it reported credibly, my dearly beloved in the Lord, that my heavenly Father hath thought it good to provide that, as I have preached his true gospel and doctrine amongst you by word, so I shall testify and confirm the same by deed; that is, I shall with you leave my life, which by his providence I first received there, (for in Manchester was I born,) for a seal to the doctrine I have taught with you and amongst you: so that, if from henceforth you waver in the same, you have none excuse at all.

I know the enemies of Christ which exercise this cruelty upon me (I speak it in respect of mine offence which is none to them-wards) think, by killing of me amongst you, to affray you and others, lest they should attempt to teach Christ truly, or believe his doctrine hereafter. But I doubt not but my heavenly Father will by my death more confirm you in his truth for ever. And therefore I greatly rejoice to see Satan and his soldiers supplanted in their own sapience, which is plain "foolishness" amongst the wise indeed, that is, amongst such as have heard God's word, and do follow it; for they only are counted "wise" of the wisdom "of God our Saviour."

<small>Matt. vii.</small>

Indeed, if I should simply consider my life with that which it ought to have been, and as God in his law requireth, then could I not but cry as I do, *Justus es, Domine, et omnia judicia tua vera:* " Righteous art thou, O Lord, and all

[¹ The Emmanuel MS. 2. 2. 15. no. 109. is in the autograph of Bradford.]

[² 'heard' 1563: 'hear' 1564 and Emman. MSS.]

thy judgments are true;" for I have much grieved thee, and transgressed thy holy precepts, not only before my professing the gospel, but sithen also, yea, even sithen my coming into prison. I do not excuse, but accuse myself before God and all his church, that I have grievously offended my Lord God. I have not lived his gospel as I should have done; I have sought myself, and not simply and only his glory, and my brethren's commodity; I have been too unthankful, secure, carnal, hypocritical, vain-glorious, &c. All which my evils the Lord of mercy pardon me for his Christ's sake, as I hope and certainly believe he hath done for his great mercy in Christ our Redeemer.

But when I consider the cause of my condemnation, I cannot but lament that I do no more rejoice than I do: for it is God's verity and truth; so that the condemnation is not a condemnation of Bradford simply, but rather a condemnation of Christ and his truth: Bradford is nothing else but an instrument, in whom Christ and his doctrine are condemned. *The papists condemn not Bradford, but Christ.* And therefore, my dearly beloved, rejoice, rejoice, and give thanks, with me and for me, that ever God did vouchsafe so great a benefit to our country, as to choose the most unworthy (I mean myself) to be one in whom it would please him to suffer any kind of affliction, much more this violent kind of death, which I perceive is prepared for me with you for his sake. All glory and praise be given unto God our Father, for this[3] his exceeding great mercy towards me, through Jesus Christ our Lord. Amen.

But perchance you will say unto me, 'What is the cause for the which you are condemned? We hear say that ye deny all presence of Christ in his holy supper, and so make it a bare sign and common bread, and nothing else.' My dearly beloved, what is said of me and will be, I cannot tell. It is told me that Master Pendleton is gone down to preach with you, not as he once recanted (for you all know how he hath preached contrary to that he was wont to preach afore I came amongst you), but to recant that which he hath recanted. How he will speak of me and report[4] tofore I come, when I am come, and when I am burned, I much pass not; *Doctor Pendleton.*

[3 'this,' only in autogr. MS.]
[4 'report of' 1563: 'report,' Emman. MSS. and 1564.]

for he that is so uncertain and will speak so often against himself, I cannot think he will speak well of me except it make for his purpose and profit: but of this enough.

The causes why Bradford was condemned.

Indeed the chief thing which I am condemned for as an heretic is, because I deny the sacrament of the altar; which is not Christ's supper[1], but a plain perverting of it, (being used as the papists now use it to be a real, natural, and corporal presence of Christ's body and blood under the forms and accidents of bread and wine;) that is, because I deny transubstantiation, which is the darling of the devil, and daughter and heir to antichrist's religion, whereby the mass is maintained, Christ's supper perverted, his sacrifice and cross imperfited, his priesthood destroyed, the ministry taken away, repentance repelled, and all true godliness abandoned.

In the supper of our Lord or sacrament of Christ's body and blood I confess and believe that there is a true and very presence of whole Christ, God and man, to the faith of the receiver, (but not of the stander-by or[2] looker-on,) as there is a very true presence of bread and wine to the senses of him that is partaker thereof. This faith, this doctrine, which consenteth with the word of God, and[3] with the true testimony of Christ's church, which the popish church doth persecute, will I not forsake: and therefore am I condemned as an heretic, and shall be burned.

But, my dearly beloved, this truth (which I have taught and you have received, I believed and do believe, and therein give my life) I hope in God shall never be burned, bound, nor overcome; but shall triumph, have victory, and be at liberty, maugre the head of all God's adversaries. For there is no counsel against the Lord, nor no device of man can be able to defeat the verity in any other than in[4] such as be "children of unbelief," which have no "love to the truth," and therefore are given up to "believe lies." From which plague the Lord of mercies deliver you and all this realm, my dear hearts in the Lord, I humbly beseech his mercy. Amen.

And to the end you might be delivered from this plague, right dear to me in the Lord, I shall, for my farewell with

[1 'supper' 1564 and Emman. MSS.: not in 1563.]
[2 'and' 1563: 'or' 1564 and Emman. MSS.]
[3 'and' 1564 and Emman. MSS.: not in 1563.]
[4 'in,' only in 1564.]

you for ever in this present life, heartily desire you all, in the bowels and blood of our most merciful Saviour Jesus Christ, to attend unto these things which I now shall shortly write unto you out of the holy scriptures of the Lord.

You know an heavy plague, or rather plagues, of God is fallen upon us, in taking away our good king, God's true religion, God's true prophets and ministers, &c., and setting over us such as seek not the Lord after knowledge; whose endeavours God prospereth wonderfully to the trial of many, that his people may both better know themselves, and be known. Now the cause hereof is our iniquities and grievous sins. We "did not know the time of our visitation," we were unthankful unto God, we contemned the gospel, and carnally abused it to serve our hypocrisy, our vain-glory, our viciousness, avarice, idleness, security, &c. Long did the Lord linger and "tarry to have shewn mercy upon us;" but we were ever the longer the worse. Therefore most justly hath God dealt with us, and dealeth with us. Yea, yet we may see that his justice is tempered with much mercy: whereto let us attribute "that we are not utterly consumed;" for if the Lord should deal with us after our deserts, alas! "how could we abide it?"

In his anger therefore, seeing he doth "remember his mercy" undeserved, yea, undesired on our behalf, let us take occasion the more speedily to go out to meet him, not with force and arms, (for we are not so able to withstand him, much less to prevail against him,) but to beseech him to "be merciful unto us," and according to his wonted mercy to deal with us. Let us arise with David and say, *Ne intres in judicium cum servo tuo, &c.*: "Enter not into judgment, O Lord, with thy servant, for in thy sight no flesh living shall be justified." Let us send ambassadors with the centurion, and say, "Lord, we are not worthy to come ourselves unto thee; speak the word, and we shall have peace." Let us penitently with the publican look down on the earth, knock our hard hearts to burst them, and cry out, 'O God, be merciful unto us wretched sinners.' Let us with the lost son return and say, 'O Father, we have sinned against heaven and earth, and before thee; we are unworthy to be called thy children.' Let us, I say, do on this sort; that is, heartily repent us of our former evil life and unthankful gospelling past, convert and "turn to God" with our whole hearts, hoping in his great mercy through Christ, and heartily calling upon his holy name: and then undoubtedly we shall find and feel otherwise than yet we feel, both inwardly and outwardly. Inwardly we shall feel peace of conscience between God and us, "which peace passeth all understanding;" and outwardly we shall feel much mitigation of these miseries, if not an utter taking of them away.

Bradford's Farewell.

Therefore, my dearly beloved in the Lord, I your poorest brother now departing to the Lord, for my *vale in æternum* [farewell for ever] for this present life, pray you, beseech you, and even from the very bottom of my heart, for all the mercies of God in Christ shewed unto you, most earnestly beg and crave of you out of prison, (as often out of your pulpits I have done,) that you will repent you, leave off[1] your wicked and evil life, be sorry for your offences, and turn to the Lord, whose arms are wide open to receive and embrace you; whose stretched out hand to strike to death stayeth that he might shew mercy upon you. For he is the Lord of mercy and "God of all comfort;" he "will not the death of a sinner, but rather that he should return," convert, and amend; he hath no pleasure in the destruction of men; his "long suffering draweth us[1] to repentance" tofore the time of vengeance and the day of wrath, which is at hand, doth come.

"Now is the axe laid to the root of the tree," utterly to destroy the impenitent. Now is the fire gone out before the face of the Lord: and who is able to quench it? O therefore repent you, repent you. It is enough to have lived as we have done; it is enough to have played the wanton gospellers, the proud protestants, hypocritical and false Christians, as, alas! we have done. Now the Lord speaketh to us in mercy and grace: O turn tofore he speak in wrath. Yet is there "mercy with the Lord and plenteous redemption;" yet he hath not forgotten to shew mercy to them that call upon him. O then "call upon him while he may be found;" for "he is rich in mercy and plentiful to all them that call upon him, so that he that calleth on the name of the Lord shall be saved." "If your sins be as red as scarlet," the Lord saith, he "will make them as white as snow." He hath sworn, and never will repent him thereof, that he will "never

[1 'off,' 'us,' only in the autograph MS.]

remember our iniquities;" but as he is good, faithful, and true, so "will he be our God, and we shall be his people; his law will he write in our hearts, and engraft it in our minds, and never will he have in mind our unrighteousness."

Therefore, my dear hearts in the Lord, turn you, turn you to the Lord your Father, to the Lord your Saviour, to the Lord your Comforter. Oh, why do you stop your ears and "harden your hearts" to-day, when you hear his voice by me your poorest brother? O forget not how that the Lord hath shewed himself true, and me his true preacher, by bringing to pass these plagues which at my mouth you oft heard me preach of[2] before they came; specially when I treated of Noe's flood, and when I preached of the 23rd chapter of St Matthew's Gospel on St Stephen's day[3], the last time that I was with you.

And now by me the same Lord sendeth you word, dear countrymen, that if you will[4] go on forwards in your impenitency, carnality, hypocrisy, idolatry, covetousness, swearing, gluttony, drunkenness, whoredom, &c., wherewith, alas, alas! our country floweth; if, I say, you will not turn and leave off, seeing me now burned amongst you, to assure you on all sides how God seeketh you, and is sorry to do you hurt, to plague you, to destroy you, to take vengeance upon you; Oh, your blood will be upon your own heads; you have been warned and warned again by me in preaching, by me in burning.

As I said therefore, I say again, my dear hearts and dearlings in the Lord, turn you, turn you, repent you, repent you; "cease from doing evil, study to do well." Away with idolatry, flee the Romish god and service, leave off from swearing, cut off carnality, abandon avarice, drive away drunkenness, flee from fornication and flattery, from[5] murder and malice; destroy deceitfulness, and "cast away all the works of darkness." Put on piety and godliness, serve God after his word and not after custom, use your tongues to

[2 'of,' only in the autograph MS.]

[3 Matt. xxiii. 34 to the end is, in the second Book of Edward 1552, as before and since, the Gospel appointed for St Stephen's day, Dec. 26.]

[4 The autograph MS. 2. 2. 15. no. 109. ends with the words, 'if you will,' being imperfect.]

[5 'from' 1564: not in 1563.]

glorify God by prayer, thanksgiving, and confession of his truth, &c. Be spiritual, and by the Spirit mortify carnal affections; be sober, holy, true, loving, gentle, merciful: and then shall the Lord's wrath cease, not for this your[1] doing's sake, but for his mercies' sake.

Go to therefore, good countrymen, take this counsel of the Lord by me now sent unto you as the Lord's counsel, and not as mine, that in the day of judgment I may rejoice with you and for you; the which thing I heartily desire, and not to be a witness against you. My blood will cry for vengeance, as against the papists, God's enemies, (whom I beseech God, if it be his good[2] will, heartily to forgive, yea, even them which put me to death, and are the causers thereof, "for they know not what they do;") so will my blood cry for vengeance against you, my dearly beloved in the Lord, if ye repent not, amend not, and turn not unto the Lord.

Turn unto the Lord, yet once more I heartily beseech thee, thou Manchester, thou Ashton-under-line, thou Bolton, Bury, Wigan, Liverpool, Mottrine, Stepport, Winsley, Eccles, Prestwich, Middleton, Radcliffe, and thou city of West-chester, where I have truly taught and preached the word of God. Turn, I say unto you all and to all the inhabitants thereabouts, unto the Lord our God, and he will turn unto you; he will say unto his angel, "It is enough, put up thy sword."

The which thing that he will do, I humbly beseech his goodness, for the precious blood's sake of his dear Son, our Saviour Jesus Christ.

Ah, good brethren, take in good part these my last words unto every one of you. Pardon me mine offences and negligences in behaviour amongst you. The Lord of mercy pardon us all our offences for our Saviour Jesus Christ's sake. Amen.

Out of prison, ready to come to you; the 11th of February, *anno* 1555.

JOHN BRADFORD[3].

[1 'our' 1563: 'your' 1564, and MS. 1. 2. 8.]
[2 'good' 1564: not in 1563.]
[3 'John Bradford' 1564, and MS. 1. 2. 8.: not in 1563.]

FAREWELL TO THE TOWN OF WALDEN.

JESUS EMMANUEL.

To the faithful and such as profess the true doctrine of our Saviour Jesus Christ, dwelling at Walden and thereabouts, John Bradford, a most unworthy servant of the Lord, now in bonds and condemned for the same true doctrine, wisheth "grace, mercy, and peace," with the increase of all godliness in knowledge and living, from God "the Father of all comfort," through the deserts of our alone and full Redeemer Jesus Christ, by the mighty working of the most Holy Spirit the Comforter, for ever. Amen.

Foxe, Acts, &c. 1563, p. 1182—4.
Bp. Coverdale, Letters of the martyrs, 1564, p. 269—74.
MS. 2. 2. 15. no. 11.[4]
MS. 2. 2. 15. no. 100. and MS. 1. 2. 8. no. 69.
Emman. Coll. Camb.

When I remember how that, by the providence and grace of God, I have been a man by whom it hath pleased him, through my ministry, to call you to repentance and amendment of life, something effectually as it seemed, and to sow amongst you his true doctrine and religion; lest that by my affliction, and the[5] storms now arisen to try the faithful, and to conform them like to the image of the Son of God into whose company we are called, you might be faint-hearted, I could not but out of prison secretly (for my keepers may not know that I have pen and ink) to write unto you a signification of the desire I have that you should not only be more confirmed in the doctrine I have taught amongst you, (which I take on my death, as I shall answer at the day of doom, I am persuaded to be God's assured, infallible, and plain truth,) but also should after your vocation avow the same by confession, profession, and living.

Rom. viii.
2 Cor. iii.

I have not taught you, my dearly beloved in the Lord, fables, tales, or untruth; but I have taught you the verity, as now by my blood gladly (praised be God therefor) I do seal the same. Indeed, to confess the truth unto you and to all the church of Christ, I do not think of myself but that I have most justly deserved not only this kind but also all kinds of death, and that eternally, for mine hypocrisy, vain-

[4 The Emmanuel MS. 2. 2. 15. no. 11. is in the autograph of Bradford.]

[5 'the' 1564: not in 1563.]

glory, uncleanness, self-love, covetousness, idleness, unthankfulness, and carnal professing of God's holy gospel, living therein not so purely, lovingly, and painfully, as I should have done. The Lord of mercy for the blood of Christ pardon me, as I hope, yea, I certainly believe he hath done, for his holy name's sake through Christ. But, my dearly beloved, you and all the whole world may see and easily perceive, that the prelates persecute in me another thing than mine iniquities, even Christ himself, Christ's verity and truth, because I cannot, dare not, nor will not confess transubstantiation; and how that wicked men, yea, mice and dogs, eating the sacrament which they term of the altar, (thereby overthrowing Christ's holy supper utterly,) do eat Christ's natural and real body born of the virgin Mary.

To believe and confess, as God's word teacheth, the primitive church believed, and all the catholic and good holy fathers taught for[1] five hundred years at the least after Christ, that in the supper of the Lord (which the mass overthroweth, as it doth Christ's priesthood, sacrifice, death and passion, the ministry of his word, true faith, repentance, and all godliness,) whole Christ, God and man, is[2] present by grace to the faith of the receiver (but not of the standers-by and lookers-on), as bread and wine is to their senses, will not serve: and therefore I am condemned, and shall be burned out of hand as an heretic. Wherefore I heartily thank my Lord God, that will and doth vouch me worthy to be an instrument in whom he himself doth suffer: for you see my affliction and death is not simply because I have deserved no less, but much more, at his hands and justice; but rather because I confess his verity and truth, and am not afraid through his gift that to do, that you also might be confirmed in his truth.

Therefore, my dearly beloved, I heartily do pray you, and so many as unfeignedly love me in God, to give with me and for me most hearty thanks to our heavenly Father, through our sweet Saviour Jesus Christ, for this his exceeding great mercy towards me and you also, that your faith waver not from the doctrine I have taught, and ye have received. For what can you desire more to assure your con-

[1 'for' 1564: not in 1563: 'of,' Emman. MSS.]
[2 'is' 1564, and Emman. MSS.: not in 1563.]

sciences of the verity taught by your preachers, than their own lives?

Go to therefore, my dear hearts in the Lord, waver not in Christ's religion truly taught you and set forth in king Edward's days. Never shall the enemies be able to burn it, to prison it, and keep it in bonds. Us they may prison, they may bind, and burn, as they do, and will do so long as shall please the Lord: but our cause, religion, and doctrine, which we confess, they shall never be able to vanquish and put away. Their idolatry and popish religion shall never be built in the consciences of men that love God's truth. As for those that love not God's truth, that have no pleasure to walk in the ways of the Lord, in those, I say, the devil shall prevail; for "God will give them strong illusion to believe lies." *God's truth can never be kept under by the adversaries.*

Therefore, dear brethren and sisters in the Lord, I humbly beseech you and pray you in the bowels and blood of our Lord and Saviour Jesus Christ, now going to the death for the testimony of Jesus, as oftentimes I have done before this present out of your pulpit, that you would love[3] the Lord's truth, love, I say, to live it and frame your lives thereafter.

Alas! you know, the cause of all these plagues fallen upon us, and of the success which God's adversaries have daily, is for our not living God's word. You know how that we were but gospellers in lips, and not in life. We were carnal, concupiscentious, idle, unthankful, unclean, covetous, arrogant, dissemblers, crafty, subtle, malicious, false, backbiters, &c., and even glutted with God's word; yea, we loathed it, as did the Israelites the manna in the wilderness: and therefore, as to them the Lord's wrath waxed hot, so doth it unto us. So that there is no remedy but that (for it is better late to turn than never to turn) we confess our faults even from the bottom of our hearts, and with hearty repentance (which God work in us all, for his mercy's sake) we run unto the Lord our God, which is exorable, merciful, and sorry for the evil poured out upon us; and cry out unto him with Daniel, saying:

'We have sinned, we have sinned grievously, O Lord God, against thy majesty. We have heaped iniquity upon iniquity; the measure of our transgressions floweth over: so

[3 'live' 1563: 'love' 1564 and Emman. MSS.]

that just is thy vengeance and wrath fallen upon us: for we are very miserable, we have contemned thy long-suffering, we have not hearkened to thy voice. When thou hast called us by thy preachers, we hardened our hearts; and therefore now deserve that thou send thy curse hereupon to "harden our hearts" also, that we should henceforth "have eyes and see not, ears and hear not, hearts and understand not, lest we should be converted and saved." O be merciful unto us; spare us, good Lord, and all thy people, whom thou hast dearly bought. Let not thine enemies triumph altogether and always against thee; for then will they be puft up. "Look down, and behold the pitiful complaints of the poor;" "let the sorrowful sighing of the simple come in thy sight, and be not angry with us for ever." "Turn us," O Lord God of hosts, "unto thee," and turn thee unto us, "that thou mayest be justified" in thy sweet sentences, and "overcome when thou art judged," as now thou art of our adversaries; for they say, '"Where is their God?" Can God deliver them now? Can their gospel save[1] them?' O Lord, how long? For the glory of thy name, and for thy honour's sake, in the bowels and blood of Jesus Christ, we humbly beseech thee, come and help us; for we are very miserable.

On this sort, I say, dearly beloved, let us publicly and privately bewail our sins; but so that hereto we join ceasing from wilfulness and sin of purpose: for else "the Lord heareth not our prayers" as David saith; and in St John it is written, The impenitent "sinners God heareth not." Now impenitent are they which purpose not to amend their lives: as for example, not only such which follow still their pleasures in covetousness[2], uncleanness, carnality; but those also which for fear or favour of man do against their conscience consent to the Romish rags, and resort to the rotten religion, communicating in service and ceremonies with the papists; thereby declaring themselves to love more the world than God, to fear man more than Christ, to dread more the loss of temporal things than of eternal; in whom it is evident "the love of God abideth not," for "he that loveth the world hath not God's love abiding in him," saith St John.

Therefore, my dear hearts, and dear again in the Lord,

[1 'serve' 1563 and 1564: 'save,' Emman. MSS.]
[2 'in covetousness' 1564 and Emman. MSS.: not in 1563.]

remember what you have professed, Christ's religion and name, and the renouncing of the devil, sin, and the world. Remember that tofore ye learned A. B. C.[3], your lesson was Christ's cross. Forget not that Christ will have no disciples but such as will promise "to deny themselves, to take up their cross (mark, they must[4] take it up) and follow him," and not the multitude, custom, and use[5].

Consider for God's sake, that "if we gather not with Christ, we scatter abroad." "What should it profit a man to win the whole world, and lose his own soul?" We must not forget that this life is a wilderness, and not a paradise. Here is not our home; we are now in warfare; we must needs fight, or else be taken prisoners. Of all things we have in this life we shall carry nothing with us. If Christ be our Captain, we must follow him as good[6] soldiers. If we keep company with him in affliction, we shall be sure of his society in glory. If we forsake not him, he will never forsake us. " If we confess him, he will confess us: but if we deny him, he will deny us:" if we be ashamed of him, he will be ashamed of us. Wherefore, as he forsook Father, and heaven, and all things, to come to us; so let us forsake all things and come to him, being sure and most certain that we shall not lose thereby. Your children shall find and feel it double, yea, treble, whatsoever you lose for the Lord's sake: and you shall find and feel peace of conscience and friendship with God, which is more worth than all the goods of the world.

My dearly beloved, therefore, for the Lord's sake consider these things, which now I write unto you of love, for my *vale* and last 'farewell' for ever, in this present life. Turn to the Lord, repent you your evil and unthankful life, declare repentance by the fruits. Take time while you have it; come to the Lord whiles he calleth you; run into his lap whiles his arms be open to embrace you; " seek him whiles he may be found;" "call upon him" whiles time is convenient. Forsake and "flee from all evil," both in religion, and in the

Matt. xii.

[[3] See p. 264, note 1, above.]

[[4] 'they must' 1564 and autograph MS.: not in 1563, or MS. 2. 2. 15. no. 100., or MS. 1. 2. 8.]

[[5] '&c.' 1563, autograph MS., and MS. 2. 2. 15. no. 100.: 'and use' 1564 and MS. 1. 2. 8.]

[[6] 'good' 1564: not in 1563, or Emman. MSS.]

rest of your life and conversation. "Let your light so shine before men, that they may see your good works, and praise God in the day of his visitation."

"O come again, come again, you strange children, and I will receive you," saith the Lord. "Convert and turn to me, and I will turn unto you." "Why will ye needs perish? As sure as I live," sweareth the Lord, "I will not your death; turn therefore unto me." "Can a woman forget the child of her womb? If she should, yet will not I forget you, saith the Lord your God." "I am he, I am he which put away your sins for mine own sake."

O then, dear friends, turn, I say, unto your dearest Father. Cast not these his sweet and loving words to the ground, and at your tail; for the Lord watcheth on his word to perform it, which is in two sorts: to them that lay it[1] up in their hearts and believe it, will he pay all and eternal joy and comfort; but to them that cast it at their backs and wilfully forget it, to them, I say, will he pour out indignation and eternal shame.

Wherefore I heartily yet once more beseech and pray you and every of you not to contemn this poor and simple exhortation, which now out of prison I make unto you, or rather the Lord by me. Loth would I be to be a witness against you in the last day; as of truth I must be if ye repent not, if ye love not God's gospel, yea, if ye live it not.

Therefore to conclude, repent, love God's gospel, live it in all your conversation: so shall God's name be praised, his plagues mitigated, his people comforted, and his enemies ashamed.

Grant all this, thou gracious Lord God, to every of us for thy dear Son's sake, our Saviour Jesus Christ: to whom, with thee and the Holy Ghost, be eternal glory, for ever and and ever, Amen. The[2] 12th of February, 1555.

By the bondman of the Lord, your afflicted poor brother,

J. BRADFORD.

[[1] 'it' 1564 and Emman. MSS.: not in 1563.]
[[2] 'the' 1564: not in 1563.]

EXAMINATIONS

AND

PRISON-CONFERENCES,

1555.

¶ All the examinacions of the Constante Martir of GOD M. Iohn Bradforde, before the Lorde Chauncellour, B. of Winchester the B. of London, & other cōmissioners: wherbnto ar annexed his priuate talk & conflictes in prison after his condemnacion, with the Archbishop of york, the B. of Chichester, Alfonsus, and King Philips confessour, two Spanishe freers, and sundry others. With his modest learned and godly answeres. Anno. Domini. 1561.

¶ Cum Priuilegio ad imprimendum solum.

[See the colophon at p. 556 of this volume.]

[The 'Examinations' of Bradford were forwarded in MS. by Archbishop Grindal from Strasburgh, November 28, 1557, to Foxe the martyrologist. The archbishop wrote: 'I now send to you the examinations of Bradford, and some of his other writings, that you may employ yourself as you please in translating them.' To this Foxe replied: 'I have received the narrative of Bradford, with various letters of his, which had been sent to different persons. I perceive in this matter, my Edmond, how faithful you are to your promise, and without fault, as they say. Would that we had all other remains of the martyrs brought together with equal care[1]!'

The 'examinations' and a large portion of the 'conferences' appeared in Latin, in the edition of the 'Acts and monuments' of Foxe printed in that language, the *Rerum in ecclesia gestarum commentarii, Basil.* 1559; and nearly the whole is given in the first English impression, 1563, of the 'Acts' of Foxe, and in all subsequent editions.

The 'Examinations and conferences,' printed separately by Griffith 1561, alone supply the 'conferences,' p. 493—552, in the form in which they were penned, at least for the most part, by Bradford himself; for that impression supplies words and phrases throughout, sentences occasionally, and in one place (515—8[2]) three pages not given in any edition of Foxe. The 'Prison-conferences' are also written throughout in the edition of 1561 in the first person; and sometimes convey the feelings of Bradford in that edition in brief colloquialisms, which could scarcely have been employed by any one else[3].

The present follows the text (unless where otherwise noted) of a copy of the exceedingly scarce edition of Griffith, 1561, in the possession of the editor[4].

The 'Reasons against transubstantiation,' p. 544—6, are printed from the 'Acts,' &c. of Foxe, 1563; see p. 544, note 3: and the 'Colloquy between Bradford and a gentlewoman's servant,' p. 553—6, is taken from the 'Acts,' &c. of Foxe, 1570, where it was first published.

[1 Abp. Grindal, Remains, p. 228—30, Parker Soc. The originals of these letters are in Latin.]
[2 See p. 518, note 1.]
[3 As for instance, p. 495, line 3 of text; and p. 534, lines 1 and 2 of fourth paragraph.
It should be observed that the various editions of the 'Acts and monuments' present the 'examinations and conferences' faithfully; the omissions in most instances not affecting the dialogues, but being either merely verbal, or connected with the change from the first to the third person, or referring to the personal history or character of Bradford.]
[4 The short headings of the various 'Conferences' (as for instance, 'Talk between Dr Harpsfield, archdeacon, and Master Bradford,' p. 502, not being supplied in the 'Examinations and conferences' 1561, are taken from the 'Acts and monuments' 1583.]

The text of the 'Examinations and conferences,' Griffith 1561, has been compared throughout with the Latin edition of Foxe, 1559, and with the English editions of 1563 and 1583. The 'first examination,' the conferences with Harpsfield, and part of that with Archbishop Heath and Bishop Day, have also been compared with early transcripts in the British Museum and Emmanuel College, Cambridge: and nine lines are now first printed at p. 472. A few of the most important differences are mentioned in the notes; and the minutest variations are specified whenever the text of 1561 is not followed.

It deserves to be recorded, that the line which Bradford pursued in his three Examinations obtained the most cordial approbation from his illustrious friend and patron, Bishop Ridley. That prelate, on receiving the documents, while in prison at Oxford, wrote to Bradford as follows:

"Blessed be the Holy Trinity, the Father, the Son, and the Holy Ghost, for your threefold confession. I have read all three with great comfort and joy, and thanksgiving unto God for his manifold gifts of grace, wherewith it is manifest to the godly reader that God did assist you mightily. And blessed be God again and again, which gave you so good a mind and remembrance of your oath, once made against the bishop of Rome; (lest you should be partaker of the common perjury, which all men almost are now fallen into, in bringing in again that wicked usurped power of his:) which oath was made according to the prophet in judgment, in righteousness, and in truth; and therefore cannot without perjury be revoked, let Satan roar and rage, and practise all the cruelty he can.

"O good Lord, that they are so busy with you about the church! It is no new thing, brother, that is happened unto you; for that was always the clamour of the wicked bishops and priests against God's true prophets, 'The temple of the Lord,' 'the temple of the Lord,' 'the temple of the Lord:' and they said, 'The law shall not depart from the priest, nor wisdom from the elder;' and yet in them whom they only esteemed for their priests and sages, there was neither God's law, nor godly wisdom[1]."]

[[1] Bp. Coverdale, Letters of the martyrs, 1564, p. 65—6; Bp. Ridley, Works, p. 369—70. Parker Soc.]

THE EFFECT OF
MASTER JOHN BRADFORD'S EXAMINATION
BEFORE THE LORD CHANCELLOR BISHOP OF WINCHESTER, THE BISHOP OF LONDON, AND OTHERS IN COMMISSION, THE 22nd OF JANUARY[1],
ANNO DOMINI 1555.

AFTER the lord chancellor, and the residue of the queen's council in commission with him, had ended their talk with master Ferrar, late bishop of St David's, the under-marshal of the King's Bench was commanded to bring in master Bradford; who, being come into the presence of the council sitting at a table, he kneeling down on his knee, but immediately by my lord chancellor was bidden to stand up; and so he did.

Examinations, &c. of Bradford, Griffith, 1561.
Foxe, Acts, &c. 1563, and after editions.
MS. Lansd. no. 389. two early transcripts. British Museum.
MS. I. 2. 8. no. 59. Emman. Coll. Cambridge.

When he was risen, the lord chancellor earnestly looked upon him, to have, belike, over-faced him: but he gave no place; that is, he ceased not in like manner to look on the lord chancellor still and continually, save that once he cast his eyes to heaven-ward, sighing for God's help, and so out-faced him, as they say.

Then the lord chancellor, as it were amazed and something troubled, spake thus to him in effect: "Thou hast been a long time imprisoned justly for thy behaviour at Paul's Cross, the 13th of August, *anno* 1553, for thy false preaching and arrogance, taking upon thee to preach without authority[2]. But now," quoth he, "the time of mercy is come: and therefore the queen's highness, minding to offer unto you mercy, hath by us sent for you, to declare and give the same, if so be ye will with us return: and," quoth he, "if you will do as we have done, you shall find as we have found, I warrant you." These were the sum, and even in manner the words which he spake. To these words master Bradford spake (after reverent obeisance made) in this manner:

"My lord and lords all, I confess that I have been long prisoned, and (with humble reverence be it spoken) unjustly;

[1 'April,' the edition of 1561, a misprint or error: 'January,' Foxe, Acts, &c. 1563.]

[2 'Thou hast been . authority,' Emman. MS.: 'that of long time he had been,' &c. in the third person, . . 'without authority,' 1561.]

[BRADFORD.]

for that I did nothing seditiously, falsely, or arrogantly, in word or fact, by preaching or otherwise; but rather sought peace and all godly quietness, as an obedient and faithful subject, both in going about to save the bishop of Bath that now is[1], then master Bourn, the preacher at the Cross, and in preaching for quietness accordingly."

At these words, or rather before he had fully finished them, the lord chancellor something snuffed, and spake with an admiration, that "there was a loud lie; for," quoth he, "the fact was seditious, as you my lord of London can bear witness."

"You say true, my lord," quoth the bishop of London, "I saw him with mine own eyes, when he took upon him to rule and lead the people malapertly; thereby declaring that he was the author of the sedition."

Here John Bradford replied, and said that, "notwithstanding my lord bishop's seeing and saying, that he had told was the truth: as one day," quoth he, "my Lord God almighty shall reveal to all the world, when we all shall come and appear before him. In the mean season, because I cannot be believed of you, I must and am ready to suffer, as now your sayings, so whatsoever God shall license you to do unto me."

"I know," quoth my lord chancellor then, "thou hast a glorious tongue, and goodly shews thou makest; but all is lies thou speakest[2]. And again, I have not forgotten how stubborn thou wert when thou wert before us in the Tower, whither thou wast committed to prison concerning religion: I have not forgotten thy behaviour and talk, wherethrough worthily thou hast been kept in prison, as one that would have done more hurt than I will speak of."

[This talk of Bradford first in the Tower came not to our hands.[Foxe, Acts, &c. 1570, and after editions.]

"My lord," quoth Bradford, "as I said I say again, that I stand, as before you, so before God; and one day we shall all stand before him: the truth then will be the truth, though you will not now so take it. Yea, my lord," quoth he, "I dare say that my lord of Bath, master Bourn, will witness with me that I sought his safeguard with the peril of mine own life; I thank God therefor."

"That is not true," quoth the bishop of London; "for I myself did see thee take upon thee too much."

"No," quoth Bradford, "I took nothing upon me un-

[1 'now' 1561: 'that now is,' Emman. MS.]
[2 'that thou doest' 1561: 'thou speakest' 1563.]

desired, and that of master Bourn himself, as, if he were here present, I dare say he would affirm it; for he desired me both to help him to pacify the people, and not to leave him till he was in safety. And as for my behaviour in the Tower, and talk before your honours, if I did or said anything that did not beseem me, if wherein your lordships would tell me, I should and would shortly make you answer."

"Well," quoth my lord chancellor, "to leave this matter; how sayest thou now? Wilt thou return again, and do as we have done? and thou shalt receive the queen's mercy and pardon."

"My lord," quoth Bradford, "I desire mercy with God's mercy; but mercy with God's wrath, God keep me from! although (I thank God therefor) my conscience doth not accuse me that I did or spake any thing wherefor I should need to receive the queen's[3] mercy or pardon, but rather reward and praise[4]. For all that ever I did or spake was both[5] agreeing to God's laws, and the laws of the realm at that present, and did make much to[5] quietness."

"Well," quoth my lord chancellor, "if thou make this babbling rolling in thy eloquent tongue, being altogether ignorant and vain-glorious, and will not receive mercy offered to thee, know for truth that the queen is minded to make a purgation of all such as thou art."

"The Lord," quoth Bradford, "tofore whom I stand as well as before you, knoweth what vain-glory I have sought and seek in this behalf: his mercy I desire, and also would be glad of the queen's favour, to live as a subject without clog of conscience: but otherwise the Lord's mercy is to me better than life. And I know," quoth he, "to whom I have committed my life, even to his hands which will keep it, so that no man may take it away before it be his pleasure. There are twelve hours in the day; and as long as they last, so long shall no man have power thereon: therefore his good will be done. Life in his displeasure is worse than death; and death in his true favour is true life."

"I knew well enough," quoth my lord chancellor, "that we should have glorious talk enough of thee: be sure there-

[3 'the queen's' 1563: not in 1561.]
[4 'but rather reward and praise,' Emman. MS.: not in 1561.]
[5 'both,' 'to,' 1563: not in 1561.]

fore that, as thou hast deceived the people with false and devilish doctrine, so shalt thou receive."

"I have not deceived," quod[1] Bradford, "the people, nor taught any other doctrine than by God's grace I am, and hope shall be, ready to confirm with my life. And as for devilishness and falseness in the doctrine, I would be sorry you could so prove it."

[Cuthbert Tonstal.] "Why," quoth the bishop of Duresme, "tell me what you say by the ministration of the communion as you now know it is?"

"My lord," saith Bradford, "here must I desire of your lordship and of all your honours a question, tofore I do make answer to any interrogatory or question wherewith you now begin. I have been six times sworn, that I should in no case consent to the practising of any jurisdiction, or any authority, on the bishop of Rome's behalf within this realm of England. Now therefore, before God, I humbly pray your honours to tell me, whether you ask me this question by his authority, or not? If you do, I dare not, nor may not answer you any thing in his authority you shall demand of me, except I would be forsworn; which God forbid."

"Hast thou been sworn six times?" quoth master secretary Bourn: "what offices hast thou borne?"

"Here is another lie," quoth my lord chancellor.

"Forsooth," quoth Bradford, "I was thrice sworn in Cambridge; when I was admitted master of art, when I was elected[2] fellow in Pembroke hall, and when I was there the visitors came thither and sware the university. Again I was sworn when I entered into the ministry, when I had a prebend given me, and when I was sworn to serve the king a little before his death[3]."

"Tush," quoth my lord chancellor, "Herod's oaths a man should make no conscience at."

"But," quoth Bradford, "my lord, these oaths were no Herod's oaths, nor no unlawful oaths, but oaths according to

[1 'Quod:' quoth, saith, or said. Vide Nares, Glossary.]
[2 'admitted' 1561: 'elected,' Emman. MS.]
[3 The Latin edition of Foxe, Acts, &c., 1559, has 'sub mortem rursus regis, quando hoc idem jusjurandum promiscue a nobis omnibus est repetitum.'—Fox. Rerum in eccles. gestar. comm. p. 468, Basil. 1559.]

God's word; as you yourself have well affirmed in your book, *De vera obedientia*[4]."

"My lords," quoth another of the council that stood by the table (master Rochester, I ween), " I never knew wherefor this man was in prison before now; but I see well that it had not been good that this man had been abroad. Whatsoever was the cause he was laid in prison, I know not; but I now see well that not without cause he was and is to be kept in prison."

"Yea," quoth secretary Bourn, "it was reported this parliament time by the earl of Derby, that he hath done more hurt by letters, and exhorting those that have come to him in religion, than ever he did when he was abroad by preaching. In his letters he curseth all that teacheth false doctrine (for so he calleth that which is not according to that he taught), and most heartily exhorteth them to whom he writeth to continue still in that they have received by him, and such like as he is." All which words divers others of the council affirmed. Whereunto the said master Bourn added, saying, "How say you, sirrah?" speaking to Bradford, " have you not thus seditiously written and exhorted the people?"

"I have not[5]," quoth Bradford, " written, nor spoken any thing seditiously; and (I thank God therefor) I have not admitted any seditious cogitation, nor I trust never shall do."

"Yea, but thou hast written letters," quoth master secretary Bourn.

"Why speakest thou not?" quoth my lord chancellor: "hast thou not written as he saith?"

"That," quoth Bradford, " I have written, I have written."

[4 Et æquum cuiquam videbitur, quia veritati pareo, appellari mendacem? quia in obediendo principi Deo inservio, sacrorum contemptorem dici aut jurisjurandi violatorem? Et quod ridicule objicitur marito post divortium, qui fidem non præstitit, quam dare non debuit; id mihi in hac causa graviter et serio objicietur, qui gravissimo quidem veritatis judicio ab illa Romana ecclesia, quam mihi retinere non licuit, divulsus, sponsam veritatem tandem postliminio redeuntem cogor agnoscere, atque illi firmiter adhærere? Secundum quam rationem fit, ut ne in civilibus quidem legibus ulla sit turpium obligatio: videlicet ne in criminibus perseverantiam potius quam resipiscentiam probasse videantur. In ecclesiasticis vero sanctionibus, nullo eum teneri nexu, qui illicita juraverit, diffinitum est, cum juramentum non sit vinculum iniquitatis.—Steph. Winton. De vera obed. signat. I. 3—4, Lond. 1535. Copy, Bodl. Libr. Oxford. See note H.]

[5 'not' 1563: omitted in 1561.]

"Lord God," quoth master Southwell, "what an arrogant and stubborn boy is this, that thus stoutly and dallyingly behaveth[1] himself before the queen's council!" Whereat one looked upon another with disdainful countenance.

"My lords and masters," quoth Bradford, "the Lord God which is, and will judge us all, knoweth that as I am certain I stand now before his Majesty, so with reverence in his sight I stand before you: and unto you[2] accordingly in words and gesture I desire to behave myself. If you otherwise take it, I doubt not but God in his time will reveal it. In the mean season I shall suffer with all due obedience your sayings and deeds too, I hope."

"These be gay glorious words," quoth my lord chancellor, "of reverence; but, as in all other things, so herein thou dost nothing but lie."

"Well," quoth Bradford, "I would God, the Author of truth, and abhorrer of lies, would pull my tongue out of my head before you all, and shew a terrible judgment on me here presently, if I have purposed or do purpose to lie before you, whatsoever you shall ask me."

"Why then," quoth my lord chancellor, "dost thou not answer? Hast thou written such letters as here is objected against thee?"

"As I said, my lord," quod Bradford, "that I have written, I have written. I stand now before you, which either can lay my letters to my charge or not. If you lay any thing to my charge that I have written, if I deny it, I am then a liar."

"We shall never have done with thee, I perceive now," saith my lord chancellor. "Be short, be short: wilt thou have mercy?"

"I pray God," quoth Bradford, "give me his mercy; and if therewith you will extend yours, I will not refuse it; but otherwise I will not."

Here was now much ado, one speaking this, and other speaking that, of his arrogancy in refusing the queen's pardon, which she so lovingly did offer unto him: whereto Bradford answered thus:

"My lords, if I may live as a quiet subject without clog of conscience, I shall heartily thank you for your pardon: if

[1 'behave' 1561: 'behaveth' 1563.]
[2 'unto your and' 1561: 'and unto you' 1563.]

otherwise I behave myself, then I am in danger of the law[3]. In the mean season I ask no more but the benefit of a subject, till I be convinced of transgression. If I cannot have this, as hitherto I have not had, God's good will be done."

Upon these words, my lord chancellor began a long process of the false doctrine wherewith people were deceived in the days of king Edward; and so turned the end of his talk to Bradford, saying, "How sayest thou?"

"My lord," quoth Bradford, "the doctrine taught in king Edward's days was God's pure religion, the which as I then believed, so do I now more believe than ever I did: and therein I am more confirmed, and ready to declare it, by God's grace even as he will, to the world, than I was when I first came into prison."

"What religion mean you," quoth the bishop of Duresme, "in king Edward's days? What year of his reign[4]?"

"Forsooth," quoth Bradford, "even that same year of his reign, my lord, that the king died, and I was a[5] preacher."

Here wrote master secretary Bourn I wot not what.

Now after a little pausing, my lord chancellor beginneth again to declare that the doctrine taught in king Edward's days was heresy, using for probation and demonstration thereof no scripture nor reason but this, that it ended with treason and rebellion: "so that," quoth he, "the very end were enough to improve that doctrine to be naught."

"Ah, my lord!" quoth Bradford, "that you would enter into God's sanctuary, and mark the end of this present doctrine you now so magnify!"

"What meanest thou by that?" quoth he: "I ween we shall have a snatch of rebellion even now."

[3 'faute' 1561: 'law' 1563, and Emman. MS.]

[4 The Latin edition of Foxe, Acts, &c., 1559, has: 'Erant temporibus Edouardi librorum ad sacrum ecclesiæ cultum ac ritus attinentium plures editiones: qui etsi omnes reformandæ serviebant religioni, tamen quia sic visum erat illis, quorum id interfuit, ecclesiæ statum paulatim ac temporibus quasique intervallis quibusdam emendare, semel atque iterum mutabantur, vel potius corrigebantur codices. Eam varietatem exprobrans evangelicis Tonstallus episcopus Dunelmensis, velutique eos levitatis et inconstantiæ insimulans, rogat illico Bradfordum, Quamnam religionis sub Edouardo formulam sentiret, quotoque in anno regni illius editam?'—Fox. Rerum &c. comm. p. 469, Basil. 1559.]

[5 'a' 1563: not in 1561.]

"No," quoth Bradford, "my lord, I mean no such end as you would gather: I mean an end which none seeth but they that enter into God's sanctuary. If a man look but on present things, he will soon deceive himself."

Here now did my lord chancellor offer again mercy; and Bradford answered, as before, "Mercy with God's mercy should be welcome; but otherwise he would none." Whereupon the said lord chancellor did ring a little bell, belike to call in somebody; for there was present none in manner but only those before named, and the bishop of Worcester. Now when one was come in, "It is best," quoth master secretary Bourn, "that you give the keeper a charge of this fellow." So was the under-marshal called in.

"You shall take this man to you," quoth my lord chancellor, "and keep him close without conference with any man but by your knowledge; and suffer him not to write any letters, &c.; for he is of another manner of charge unto you now than he was before."

And so, after humble obeisance to the council, [I] went with my keeper; and, as God knoweth, with as merry a heart and so quiet a conscience and ever I had in all my life; rejoicing that it had pleased the goodness of God, through his mercy, to call me, most wretched sinner, to such an office as to be a witness-bearer of his truth.

This is the sum of my first examination. God of his mercy deliver his people from evil. Amen.

By me, JOHN BRADFORD[1].

(And so they departed, the said Bradford looking as cheerfully as any man could do, declaring thereby even a desire to give his life for confirmation of that he hath taught and written: and surely, if he do so, his death will destroy more of the Philistines, as Sampson did, than ever he did in his life. God Almighty keep him, and all his fellows bound for the Lord's sake. Amen[2].)

[[1] The last nine lines are now first printed from the Lansdowne MS. no. 389. fol. 10.]

[[2] The second transcript of this 'Examination' in the Lansd. MS. no. 389. and a fragment of an early transcript in Emman. Coll. Cambridge, MS. 1. 2. 8. no. 14. 3. add here: 'Thus have I written unto you the effect and order of the talk, as I heard it reported of a credible person that was not far off when the examination was made.']

THE EFFECT OF THE
SECOND EXAMINATION OF JOHN BRADFORD

IN THE TEMPLE OF ST MARY OVERY'S, BEFORE THE LORD CHANCELLOR, AND DIVERS OTHER BISHOPS, THE 29TH DAY OF JANUARY, 1555.

AFTER the excommunication of John Rogers, John Bradford was called in; and standing before the lord chancellor and other bishops set with him, the said lord chancellor spake thus in effect, that where tofore, the 22nd of January, they called the said Bradford before them, and offered unto him the queen's pardon, although he had contemned the same, and further he said that he would stiffly and stoutly maintain and defend the erroneous doctrine holden in the days of king Edward the sixth; yet, in consideration that the queen's highness is wonderful merciful, they thought good eftsoons to offer the same mercy again, before it be too late. "Therefore," quoth my lord chancellor, "now advise you well; there is yet space and grace tofore we so proceed that you be committed to the secular power, as we must do and will do, if you will not follow the example of master Barlow and Cardmaker[3]:" whom he there commended, adding oratoriously amplifications, to move the said Bradford to yield to the religion presently set forth.

Examinations, &c. of Bradford, Griffith, 1561. Foxe, Acts, &c. 1563, and after editions.

After the lord chancellor's long talk, Bradford began on this sort to speak:

"My lord," quoth he, "and my lords all, as now I stand in your sight before you, so I humbly beseech your honours to consider that you sit in the sight[4] of the Lord, who, as David doth witness, 'is in the congregations of judges,' and sits in the midst of them judging: and as you would your place to be now of us taken as God's place, so demonstrate yourselves to follow him in your sitting; that is, seek no guiltless blood, nor hunt not by questions to bring into the

[Ps. lxxxii. 1.]

[3 See p. 290, note 3, above.]
[4 'sight' 1561: 'seat' 1563.]

snare them which are out of the same. At this present I stand before you guilty or guiltless: if guilty, then proceed and give sentence accordingly; if guiltless, then give me the benefit of a subject, which hitherto I could not have."

Here the lord chancellor replied, and said that the said Bradford began with a true sentence, *Deus stetit in synagoga*, ["God hath stood in the congregation,"] &c.: "but," quoth he, "this and all thy gesture declareth but hypocrisy and vain-glory." And further he made much ado to purge himself, that he sought no guiltless blood; and so began a long process how that Bradford's fact at Paul's Cross was presumptuous, arrogant, and declared a taking upon him to lead the people; "which could not but turn to much disquietness," quoth he, "in that thou" (speaking to Bradford) "wast so prefract[1] and stout in religion at that present. For the which, as thou wast then committed to prison, so hitherto hast thou been kept in prison, where thou hast written letters to no little hurt to the queen's people, as by the report of the earl of Derby in the parliament-house was credibly reported." And to this he added, that the said Bradford did stubbornly behave himself the last time he was before them: "and therefore not for any other thing now I demand thee of," quoth he, "but of and for thy doctrine and religion."

"My lord," quoth Bradford, "where you accuse me of hypocrisy and vain-glory, I must and will leave it to the Lord's declaration, which one day will open yours and my truth and hearty dealings. In the mean season I will content myself with the testimony of mine own conscience; which, if it yielded to hypocrisy, could not but have God my foe also; and so both God and man were against me. As for my fact at Paul's Cross, and behaviour before you at the Tower, I doubt not but God will reveal it to my comfort: for if ever I did any thing which God used to public benefit, I think that that my deed was one; and yet for it I have been and am kept of long time in prison. And as for letters and religion, I answer," quoth Bradford, "as I did the last time I was before you."

"There didst thou say," quoth my lord chancellor, "that thou wouldest stubbornly and manly maintain the erroneous doctrine in king Edward's days."

Si illum objurges, vitæ qui auxilium tulit; quid facias illi qui dederit damnum aut malum? [Terent. Andr. Act. i. Scen. i. 115—6.] [Foxe, 1563, and after editions.]

[1 'Prefract:' obstinate, from the Latin 'præfractus.']

"My lord," quoth Bradford, "I said the last time I was before you, that I had six times taken an oath that I should never consent to the practising of any jurisdiction on the bishop of Rome his behalf; and therefore durst not answer to any thing that[2] should be demanded so, lest I should be forsworn; which God forbid. Howbeit, saving mine oath, I said that I was more confirmed in the doctrine set forth public in king Edward's days, than ever I was before I was put in prison: and so I thought I should be, and think yet still I shall be, found more ready to give my life as God will, for the confirmation of the same."

"I remember well," quoth my lord chancellor, "that thou madest much ado about a needless matter, as though the oath against the bishop of Rome were so great a matter. So others have done before thee, but yet not in such sort as thou hast done; for thou pretendest a conscience in it, which is nothing else but mere hypocrisy."

"My conscience," quoth Bradford, "is known to the Lord: and whether I deal herein hypocritically or no, he knoweth. As I said therefore then, my lord," quoth he, "so say I again now, that, for fear lest I should be perjured, I dare not make answer to any thing you shall demand of me, if my answering should consent to the practising of any jurisdiction for the bishop of Rome here in England."

"Why," quoth my lord chancellor, "didst thou not begin to tell that we are *dii* [gods] and sit in God's place; and now wilt thou not make us answer?"

"My lord," quoth Bradford, "I said you would have your place taken of us now as God's place; and therefore I brought forth that piece of scripture, that ye might be the more admonished to follow God and his ways at this present; who seeth us all, and well perceiveth whether of conscience I pretend this matter of the oath or no."

"No," quoth my lord chancellor, "all men may see thine hypocrisy: for if for thine oath's sake thou dost not answer, then wouldest thou not have spoken as thou didst, and have answered me at the first: but now men may well perceive that this is but a starting-hole to hide thyself in, because thou darest not answer, and so wouldest escape,

[2 'that' 1570: not in 1561 or 1563.]

blinding the simple people's eyes, as though of conscience you did all you do."

"That which I spake at the first," quoth Bradford, "was not a replication or an answer to that you spake to me; and therefore I needed[1] not to lay for me mine oath: for I thought perchance you would have more weighed what I did speak, than you did. But when I perceived you did not consider it, but came to ask matter, whereto by answering I should consent to the practising of jurisdiction on the bishop of Rome his behalf here in England, and so be forsworn; then of conscience and simplicity I spake, as I do yet again speak, that I dare not for conscience' sake answer you: and therefore I seek no starting-holes, nor go about to blind the people, as God knoweth. For if you of your honour shall tell me that you do not ask me any thing whereby my answering should consent to the practising of[2] the bishop of Rome's jurisdiction, ask me wherein you will, and you shall hear that I will answer you as flatly as ever any did that came before you. I am not afraid of death, I thank God; for I look and have looked for nothing else at your hands of long time: but I am afraid, when death cometh, I should have matter to trouble my conscience by the guiltiness of perjury; and therefore do answer as I do."

"These be but gay glorious words," quoth my lord chancellor, "full of hypocrisy and vain-glory: and yet dost not thou know," quoth he, speaking to Bradford, "that I sit here as bishop of Winchester in mine own diocese, and therefore may do this which I do, and more too?"

"My lord," quoth Bradford, "give me leave to ask you this question, that my conscience may be out of doubt in this matter. Tell me here *coram Deo*, 'before God,' all this audience being witness, that you demand me nothing whereby my answering should consent to and confirm the practice of jurisdiction for the bishop of Rome here in England; and your honour shall hear me give you as flat and as plain answers briefly to whatsoever you shall demand me, as ever any did."

Here the lord chancellor was wonderfully offended, and spake much how that the bishop of Rome's authority needed no

[1 'need' 1561: 'needed' 1563.]
[2 'to' 1561: 'of' 1563.]

confirmation of Bradford's answering, nor no such as he was; and turned his talk to the people, how that Bradford followed crafty covetous merchants, which, because they would lend no money to their neighbours when they were in need, would say that they had sworn oft they would never lend any more money, because their debtors[3] had so oft deceived them. "Even so thou," quoth he to Bradford, "dost at this present, to cast a mist in the people's eyes, to blear them with an heresy, (which is greater, and more hurtful to the commonwealth,) pretend thine oath, whereby the people might make a conscience, where as they should not. Why speakest thou not?" quoth he.

"My lord," quoth Bradford, "as I said, I say again: I dare not answer you for fear of perjury, from which God defend me; or else I could tell you that there is a difference between oaths. Some be according to faith and charity, as the oath against the bishop of Rome: some be against faith and charity, as this, to deny my help to my brother in his need."

Here again the lord chancellor was much offended, still saying that Bradford durst not answer; and further made much ado to prove that the oath against[4] the bishop of Rome was against charity.

But Bradford answered, that howsoever his honour took him, yet was he assured of his meaning, that no fear but the fear of perjury made him affeared to answer. "For as for death, my lord," quoth he, "as I know there are twelve hours in the day, so with the Lord my time is appointed; and when it shall be his good time, then shall I depart hence: but in the mean season," quoth he, "I am safe enough, though all the world had sworn my death. Into his hands I have committed it: his good will be done! And," quoth Bradford, "saving mine oath, I will answer you in this behalf, that the oath against the bishop of Rome was not, nor is not, against charity."

"How prove you that?" quoth my lord chancellor.

"Forsooth," quoth Bradford, "I prove it thus: That is not against charity, which is not against God's word; but this oath against the bishop of Rome's authority in Eng-

[3 'creditors' 1561: 'debtors' 1563.]
[4 'to' 1561: 'against' 1563.]

land is not against God's word: therefore it is not against charity[1]."

"Is it not against God's word," quoth my lord chancellor, "that a man should take a king to be supreme head of the church in his realm?"

"No," quoth Bradford, "saving still mine oath, it is not against God's word, but with it, being taken in such sense as it may be well taken; that is, attributing to the king's power the sovereignty in all his dominions."

"I pray you," quoth the lord chancellor, "where find you that?"

"I find it in many places," quoth Bradford, "but specially in the thirteenth to the Romans, where St Paul writeth, 'every soul to be obedient to the superior power:' but what power? *Quæ gladium gestat*, 'The power verily which beareth the sword;' which is not the spiritual, but the temporal power: as Chrysostom full well noteth," quoth Bradford, "upon the same place, which your honour knoweth better than I. He (Chrysostom I mean) there plainly sheweth that bishops, prophets, and apostles, owe obedience to the temporal magistrates[2]."

Here yet more the lord chancellor was stirred, and said how that Bradford went about to deny all obedience to the queen for his oath; "and so," quoth he, "this man would make God's word a warrant of disobedience: for he will answer the queen on this sort, that, when she saith, 'Now swear to the bishop of Rome, or obey his authority;' 'No,' will he say, 'for I am then forsworn;' and so make the queen no queen."

[1 Foxe, Acts, &c. 1570, p. 1785, and the after editions, give the reasoning of Bradford in the following form:

Argument.

Fe- Nothing is against charity, which is with God's word, and not against it.

sti- The oath against the bishop of Rome's authority in England is with God's word, and not against it.

no. *Ergo* the oath against the bishop of Rome's authority in England is not against charity.]

[2 καὶ δεικνὺς ὅτι πᾶσι ταῦτα διατάττεται, καὶ ἱερεῦσι, καὶ μοναχοῖς, οὐχὶ τοῖς βιωτικοῖς μόνον, ἐκ προοιμίων αὐτὸ δῆλον ἐποίησεν, οὕτω λέγων· πᾶσα ψυχὴ ἐξουσίαις ὑπερεχούσαις ὑποτασσέσθω.—Chrysost. In Epist. ad Rom. Hom. xxiii. Op. ix. 686, ed. Bened. Par. 1718—38.]

"No," quoth Bradford, "I go not about to deny all obedience to the queen's highness by denying obedience in this part, if she should demand it. For I was sworn to king Edward, not simply (that is, not only concerning his own person), but also concerning his successors: and therefore in denying to do the queen's request herein, I deny not her authority, nor become disobedient."

"Yes, that doest thou," quoth my lord chancellor: and so he began to tell a long tale, how, if a man should make an oath to pay a hundred pounds by such a day, and the man to whom it was due would forgive the debt, the debtor would say, 'No, you cannot do it; for I am forsworn then,' &c.

Here Bradford desired my lord chancellor not to trifle it, saying that he wondered his honour would make solemn oaths made to God trifles in that sort; and make so great a matter concerning vows (as they call it) made to the bishop for marriage of priests.

At these words the lord chancellor was much offended, and said, he did not trifle; "but," quoth he, "thou goest about to deny obedience to the queen, which now requireth obedience to the bishop of Rome."

"No, my lord," quoth Bradford, "I do not deny obedience to the queen, if you would discern between *genus* and *species*. Because I may not obey in this, to reason, *ergo* I may not obey in the other, is not firm: as if a man let or sell a piece of his inheritance, yet, this notwithstanding, all his inheritance is not let or sold; and so in this case, all obedience I deny not, because I deny obedience in this branch."

"I will none of those similitudes," said the lord chancellor.

"I would not use them," quoth Bradford, "if that you went not about to persuade the people I mean that which I never meant: for I myself not only mean obedience, but will give ensample of all most humble obedience to the queen's highness, so long as she requireth not obedience against God."

"No, no," quoth my lord chancellor, "all men may perceive well enough your meaning. There is no man, though he be sworn to the king, doth therefore break his oath, if afterwards he be sworn to the French king and to the emperor."

"It is true, my lord," quoth Bradford: "but the cases be

not like; for here is an exception, 'Thou shalt not swear to the bishop of Rome at any time.' If in like manner we were sworn, 'Thou shalt not serve the emperor,' &c., you see there were some alteration and more doubt. But," quoth Bradford, "I beseech your honour remember what ye yourself have written, answering the objections hereagainst in your book, *De vera obedientia*[1]. *Vincat modo Domini verbi veritas:* 'Let God's word and the reasons thereof bear the bell away'[2]."

Here the lord chancellor was thoroughly moved, and said still how that Bradford had written seditious letters, and perverted the people thereby, and did stoutly stand as though he would defend the erroneous doctrine in king Edward's time against all men: " and now," quoth he, " he saith he dare not answer."

"I have written no seditious letters," quoth Bradford, "I have not perverted the people: but that which I have written and spoken, that will I never deny, by God's grace. And where your lordship saith, I dare not answer you; that all men may know I am not afraid, saving mine oath, ask me what you will, and I will plainly make you answer, by God's grace, although I now see my life lieth thereon. But, O Lord!" quoth he, "into thy hands I commit it, come what come will: only sanctify thy name in me, as in an instrument of thy grace. Amen.

"Now ask what you will," quoth Bradford, "and you shall see I am not afraid, by God's grace, flatly to answer."

"Well then," quoth my lord chancellor, "how say you to the blessed sacrament? Do you not believe there Christ to be present concerning his natural body?"

"My lord," quoth Bradford, "I do believe Christ to be corporally present in his sacrament duly used: corporally I say, that is, in such sort as he would: I mean, Christ is there corporally present unto faith."

"Unto faith," quoth my lord chancellor: "we must have many more words to make it more plain."

"You shall so," quoth Bradford; "but first give me leave to speak two words."

[1 See p. 469, note 4, above, and note H.]
[2 A proverbial expression, from winning a bell, the prize at a race. Vide Nares, Glossary.]

"Speak on," quoth my lord chancellor.

"I have been now a year and almost three quarters in prison," quoth Bradford; "and of all this time you never questioned with me hereabouts, when I might have spoken my conscience frankly without peril: but now you have a law to hang up and put to death, if a man answer freely, and not to your appetite; and so you now come to demand this question. Ah, my lord," quoth Bradford, "Christ used not this way to bring men to faith: no more did the prophets or the apostles. Remember what Bernard writeth to Eugenius the pope: *Apostolos lego stetisse judicandos; sedisse judicantes non lego. Hoc erit, illud fuit*[3], *&c.*: 'I read that the apostles stood to be judged; but I read not that they sat to judge. This shall be, that was[4],'" &c.

Here the chancellor was appeased[5], as it seemed, and spake most gently that he used not this means. "It was not my doing, although some there be," quoth he, "that think this to be the best way. I, for my part," quoth he, "have been challenged for being too gentle oftentimes." The which thing the bishop of London confirmed, and so did almost all the audience, that he "had been ever too mild and too gentle."

At which words Bradford spake thus: "My lord," quoth he, "I pray you stretch out your gentleness, that I may feel it; for hitherto I never felt it."

As soon as he had spoken thus, the lord chancellor (belike thinking Bradford would have had mercy and pardon, as Cardmaker and Barlow[6] had) said that with all his heart not only he, but the queen's highness, would stretch out mercy, if with them he would return.

"Return! my lord," quoth Bradford: "God save me from that going back; I mean it not so: but I mean," quoth he, "that I was three quarters of a year in the Tower without paper, pen, or ink; and never in all that time nor sithen did I feel any gentleness from you. I have rather looked for, as I have hitherto found, extremity. And," quoth he,

---

[3 Bernard. De Consid. I. vi. Op. I. col. 412, ed. Bened. Par. 1690, where, "Stetisse denique lego apostolos judicandos, sedisse judicantes non lego. Erit illud, non fuit."]

[4 'I read. that was, &c.' 1563: not in 1561.]

[5 'appeased' 1561: 'appalled' 1563.]

[6 See p. 290, note 3, above.]

"I thank God I perceive now you have kept me in prison thus long, not for any matter you had, but for matter you would have. God's good will be done."

Here was now divers telling my lord it was dinner-time: and so he rose up, leaving Bradford speaking, and saying that in the afternoon they would speak more with him. And so was he had into the vestry, and was there all that day till dark night; and so was conveyed again to prison, declaring by his countenance great joy in God; the which God increase in him[1]!

THE EFFECT
AND SUM OF THE LAST EXAMINATION
OF THAT FAITHFUL INSTRUMENT OF GOD, JOHN BRADFORD, IN THE CHURCH OF ST MARY OVERY'S, THE 30TH[2] DAY OF JANUARY, 1555.

AFTER the excommunication of Lawrence Saunders, John Bradford was called in; and, being brought before the lord chancellor and other bishops there sitting, the lord chancellor began to speak thus in effect, that Bradford, being now eftsoons come before them, would answer with modesty and humility, and conform himself to the catholic church with them; and so yet might he find mercy, because they would be loth to use extremity. Therefore he concluded with an exhortation that Bradford would recant his doctrine.

After the lord chancellor had ended his long oration, Bradford began to speak thus:

"As yesterday I besought your honour to set in your

[1] The 'Talk with Hussey and Seton,' which is placed the first in order of the 'prison-conferences,' in the edition printed by Griffith, 1561, (p. 493—6 of this volume,) is printed after the second Examination of Bradford in all the editions of Foxe.]

[2 '29th' 1561, a misprint for 30th.]

sight the majesty and presence of God, to follow him which seeketh not to subvert the simple by subtle questions; so," quoth he, " I humbly beseech every one of you to-day ; for that you know that guiltless blood will cry vengeance. And this," quoth he, " I pray not your lordship to do, as one that taketh upon me to condemn you utterly herein, but that you might be the more admonished to do that, which none doth so much as he should do; for our nature is so much corrupt, that we are very oblivious and forgetful of God. Again," quoth Bradford, " as yesterday I pretended my oath and oaths against the bishop of Rome, that I should never consent to the practising of any jurisdiction for him or in his behalf in the realm of England; so do I[3] again this day, lest I should be perjured. And last of all, as yesterday the answer I made was by protestation and saving my oath, so would I your honours should know that mine answers[3] shall be this day : and this I do, that when death (which I look for at your hands) shall come, I shall not be troubled with the guiltiness of perjury."

At these words the lord chancellor was wroth, and said that they had given him respite to deliberate until this day, whether he would recant the heresies of the blessed sacrament, " which yesterday," quoth the lord chancellor, " before us you uttered."

" My lord," quoth Bradford, " you gave me no time of any such deliberation, neither did I speak[3] any thing of the sacrament, which you did disallow; for when I had declared a presence of Christ to be there to the faithful, you went from the matter to purge yourself that you were not cruel, and so went to dinner."

" What! I perceive," quoth my lord chancellor, " we must begin all again with thee. Did I not yesterday tell thee plainly, that thou madest a conscience where none should be? Did I not make it plain, that the oath against the bishop of Rome was an unlawful oath ?"

" No," quoth Bradford: " indeed, my lord, you said so," quoth he; "but you proved it not yet[4], nor never can do."

" O Lord God," quoth the lord chancellor, " what a fellow art thou ! Thou wouldest go about to bring into the people's heads, that we, all the lords of the parliament-house, the

[3 'do I,' 'answers,' 'speak,' 1563: omitted in 1561.]
[4 So 1563: 'but proved is not' 1561.]

knights, burgesses, and all the whole realm[1], is perjured. O what an heresy is this! Here, good people, ye may see what a churlish heretic this fellow is. If I should make an oath I would never help my brother, or lend him money in his need, were this a good answer to tell my neighbour desiring my help, that I had made an oath to the contrary, I could not do it?"

Bradford. "O my lord, discern betwixt oaths that be against charity and faith, and oaths that be according to faith and charity, as this is against the bishop of Rome[2]."

Here the lord chancellor made much ado; and a long time was spent about oaths, which were good and which were evil; he captiously asking of Bradford often answer of things concerning oaths, which Bradford would not give simply, but with distinction: whereat the lord chancellor was sore offended. But Bradford still kept him at the bay, that the oath against the bishop of Rome was a lawful[3] oath, using thereto the chancellor's own book, *De vera obedientia*[4], for confirmation.

At the length they came to this issue, who should be[1] judge of the lawfulness of the oaths?

And Bradford said, "The word of God, according to Christ's own words, John xii., saying, 'My word shall judge;' and according to the testimony of Isaiah ii., and Micah iv., that God's word, coming out of Jerusalem, shall give sentence amongst the Gentiles. By these words, my lord," quoth he, "I will prove the oath against the bishop of Rome's authority to be a good, a godly, and a lawful oath."

So thereof the lord chancellor left his hold, saying that as the other day he pretended denial of the queen's authority and obedience to her highness, so did he now.

But Bradford, as the day before, proved that obedience in this point or particular to the queen's highness, if she should demand an oath to the bishop of Rome, being denied, it was a general denial of her authority and obedience to her "no more," quoth he, "than the sale[1], gift, or lease of a sole piece of a man's inheritance proveth a sale, gift, or lease of the whole inheritance."

[1 'realm,' 'be,' 'sale,' 1563: omitted in 1561.]
[2 The last three lines are in 1563, but not in 1561.]
[3 'an unlawful' 1561: 'a lawful' 1563.]
[4 See p. 469, note 4, above, and note H.]

And thus much ado was made about the matter; the lord chancellor talking much, and using many examples of debt, of going out of the town to-morrow by oath, yet tarrying till Friday, and such like: which trifling talk Bradford did touch, saying that it was a wonder that his honour did weigh conscience no more in this, and would be so earnest in vows for marriage of priests made to bishops, and be careless for solemn oaths made to God and the prince.

Summa, this was the end: the lord chancellor said, "the queen might dispense with it, and did it to all the whole realm:" but Bradford said, "the queen's highness could do no more but remit her right: and as for the oath made to God, she could never remit, forasmuch as it was made to God."

At which words the lord chancellor chafed wonderfully, and said that in plain sentence he slandered the whole realm of perjury: "and therefore," quoth he to the people, "you may see how this fellow taketh upon him to have more knowledge and conscience than all the wise men of England; and yet," quoth he, "he hath no conscience at all."

"Well," quoth Bradford, "my lord, let all the standers-by see who hath conscience. I have been a year and a half in prison: now, before all this people, declare wherefor I was prisoned, or what cause you had to punish me. You said the other day in your own house, my lord of London witnessing with you, that I took upon me to speak to the people undesired. There he sitteth by your lordship, (I mean my lord bishop of Bath,) which desired me himself, for the passion of Christ, I would speak to the people: upon whose words I, coming into the pulpit, had like to have been slain with a naked dagger, which was hurled at him[5], I think; for it touched my sleeve. He eftsoons prayed me I would not leave him; and I promised him[6], as long as I lived, I would take hurt that day before him; and so went out of the pulpit and entreated with the people[6], and at length brought him safe to a house. Besides this, in the afternoon I preached at Bow-church; and there[6], going up into the pulpit, one willed me not to reprove the people; 'for,' quoth he, 'you shall never come down alive, if you do it.' And yet," quoth Bradford, "notwithstanding, I did in that sermon reprove their fact, and called it sedition at the least twenty times. For all

[5 'at me' 1561: omitted in 1563: 'at him' 1570.]
[6 'him,' 'and entreated with the people,' 'there,' 1563: not in 1561.]

which my doing I have received this recompence, prison a year and a half and more, and death now which you go about. Let all men," quoth Bradford, "now judge where conscience is."

In speaking of these words, there was that endeavoured to have letted[1] it; but Bradford still spake on, and gave no place till he had made an end, speak what they would[2]. And then[3] the lord chancellor said, that for all his fair talk his fact at the Cross was naught.

"No," quoth Bradford, "my fact was good, as you yourself did bear witness with me: for when I was first before you in the Tower, you youself did say that the fact was good; 'but,' quoth you, 'the mind was evil.' 'Well then,' quoth I, 'my lord, in that you allow my facts and condemn my mind in it, I cannot otherwise declare my mind to man than by saying and doing: God, I trust, one day will open to my comfort what my mind was, and what yours is.'"

Here the lord chancellor was offended, and said that he never said so. "I," quoth he, "had not so little wit, I trow, as to[4] discern betwixt meaning and doing;" and so brought forth, little to the purpose, many examples that men construe things by the meanings of men, and not by their doings[5]. But when this could not serve, then cometh he to another matter; and said, he was put in prison at the first, because he would not yield, nor be conformable to the queen's religion.

"Why," quoth Bradford, "your honour knoweth that you would not then reason with me in religion; but you said, a time should afterward be found out, when I should be talked withal. But," quoth Bradford, "if it were, as your lordship saith, that I was put in prison[3] for religion, in that my religion was then authorised by the public laws of the realm, could conscience punish me, or cast me in prison therefor? Wherefore let all men judge, in whom conscience wanteth."

Here came forth master Chamberlain of Woodstock, and said to the lord chancellor that Bradford had been a serving man, and was with master Harrington[6].

[1 'Letted:' hindered.]
[2 So 1563: 'spake on, and let them speak what they would,' 1561.]
[3 'then,' 'prison,' 1563: not in 1561.]
[4 'not to' 1561: 'to' 1563.]
[5 So 1563: 'not by the meaning of men, but by their doings' 1561.]
[6 Bradford was a paymaster under Sir John Harrington of Exton

"True," quoth the lord chancellor, "and did deceive his master of twenty-seven[7] pounds; and because of this, he went to be a gospeller and a preacher, good people: and yet you see how he pretendeth conscience."

"My lord," quoth Bradford, "I set my foot to his foot, whosoever he be, that can come forth, and justly vouch to my face that ever I deceived my master. And as you are chief justicer[8] by office in England, I desire justice upon them that so slander me, because they cannot prove it[9]."

Here my lord chancellor and master Chamberlain were struck blank, and said they heard it. "But," quoth the lord chancellor, "we[8] have another manner of matter than this against you[10]; for you are a heretic." "Yea," quoth the bishop of London, "he did write letters to master Pendleton, which knoweth his hand as well as his own: your honour," quoth the bishop to the lord chancellor, "did see them."

"That is not true," quoth Bradford; "I never did write to Pendleton sith I came into prison: therefore I am not justly spoken of."

"Yea, but you indited it," quoth the bishop of London.

"I did not," quoth Bradford, "nor know not what you mean; and that I offer to prove."

Here cometh another (I trow they call him master Allen, one of the clerks of the council) putting my lord in remembrance of letters sent into Lancashire.

"It is true," quoth the lord chancellor unto him, "for we have his hand to shew."

"I deny," quoth Bradford, "that you have my hand to shew of letters sent into Lancashire, otherwise than before you all I will stand up and prove them to be good and lawful."

Here was all answered: and therefore the lord chancellor began a new matter.

"Sir," quoth he, "in my house the other day you did most contemptuously contemn the queen's mercy, and further

in Rutlandshire, when Sir J. H. was treasurer of the camp of Henry VIII., at Boulogne, A.D. 1544. Vide p. 32, note 3, above, and p. 493.]

[7 'twenty-seven' 1561: 'seven score' 1563.]

[8 'justices,' 'you,' 1561: 'justicer,' 'we,' 1563.]

[9 Various letters of Bradford (chiefly addressed to Traves) refer to this subject, which will receive further notice in the concluding volume of his Writings.]

[10 'against you' 1563: not in 1561.]

said you would maintain the erroneous doctrine in king Edward's days against all men: and this you did most stoutly."

"Well," quoth Bradford, "I am glad that all men see now[1] you had no matter to imprison me afore that day justly. Now say I that I did not contemptuously contemn the queen's mercy, but would have had it, (though if justice might take place, I need it not,) so that I might have had it[2] with God's mercy; that is, without saying and doing any thing against God and his truth. And as for maintenance of doctrine, because I cannot tell how you will stretch this word 'maintenance,' I will repeat again that which I spake. I said I was more confirmed in the religion set forth in king Edward's days than ever I was: and if God so would, I trust I should declare it by giving my life for the confirmation and testification thereof. So I said then, and so I say again now," quoth Bradford. "As for otherwise to maintain it, than pertaineth to a private person by confession, I thought not nor think."

"Well," quoth the lord chancellor, "yesterday thou didst maintain false heresy concerning the blessed sacrament: and therefore we gave thee respite till this day to deliberate."

"My lord," quoth Bradford, "as I said at the first, I spake nothing of the sacrament, but that which you allowed; and therefore you[1] reproved it not, nor gave me no time to deliberate."

"Why," quoth he, "didst thou not deny Christ's presence in the sacrament?"

"No," quoth Bradford, "I never denied nor taught, but that to faith[3] whole Christ's body and blood was as present as bread and wine to the due receiver."

"Yea, but dost thou not believe that Christ's body naturally and really is there[1], under the form of bread and wine?"

"My lord," quoth Bradford, "I believe Christ is present there to the[4] faith of the due receiver: as for transubstantiation, I plainly and flatly tell you, I believe it not."

Here was Bradford called *diabolus*, 'a slanderer[5];' "for

[1 'now,' 'you,' 'there,' 1563: omitted in 1561.]
[2 'though if. had it' 1563: omitted in 1561.]
[3 'the faith' 1561: 'faith' 1563.]
[4 'the' 1563: not in 1561.]
[5 So 1563: 'a devil or slanderer' 1561.]

we ask no question," quoth the lord chancellor, "of transubstantiation, but of Christ's bodily presence."

"Why," quoth Bradford, "I deny not his presence to the faith of the receiver, but deny that he is included in the bread, or that the bread is transubstantiated."

"If he be not included," quoth the bishop of Worcester[6], "how is he then present?"

"Forsooth," quoth Bradford, "my faith knoweth how, though my tongue cannot express it, nor you otherwise than by faith hear it, or understand it."

Here was much ado now, one doctor starting up and speaking this, another that, and the lord chancellor talking much of Luther, Zuinglius, and Œcolampadius: but still Bradford kept them at this point, that Christ is present to faith, and that there is no transubstantiation nor including of Christ in the bread: but all this would not serve them.

Therefore another bishop asked this question, whether the wicked man received Christ's very body or no? And Bradford answered plainly, "No." Whereat[7] the lord chancellor made a long oration, how that it could not be that Christ was present, except that the evil man receive him.

But Bradford put his oration away in few words, that grace was at that present offered to his lordship, although he received it not: "So that," quoth he, "the receiving maketh not the presence, as your lordship would affirm; but God's grace, truth, and power, is the cause of the presence, the which the wicked that lacketh faith cannot receive." And here Bradford prayed him not to divorce that which God hath coupled together. "He hath coupled all this together, 'Take, eat, this is my body:' he saith not, 'See, peep, this is my body;' but, 'Take, eat.' So that it appeareth, this is a promise depending upon condition, if we take and eat[8]."

Here the lord chancellor and the rest of the bishops made a great ado, that Bradford had found out a toy that no man else ever did, of the conditions; and the lord chancellor made many words to the people hereabout.

But Bradford said this: "My lord," quoth he, "are not these words, 'Take, eat,' a commandment? And are not these words, 'This is my body,' a promise? If you will

[6 Richard Pates.]
[7 'where' 1561: 'whereat' 1563.]
[8 This last sentence is in 1563, not in 1561.]

challenge the promise, and do not the commandment, may you not deceive yourself?"

Here the lord chancellor denied Christ to have commanded any thing in the sacrament, or the use of it.

"Why," quoth Bradford, "my lord, I pray you tell the people what mood, *Accipite, manducate*, [Take, eat,] is: it is plain to children that Christ, in so saying, commandeth."

At these words the lord chancellor made a great toying and trifling at the imperative mood, and fell to parsing[1] or examining, as though he should teach a child; and so concluded that it was no commandment, but "such a phrase as this, 'I pray you give me drink,' which," quod he[2], "is no commandment, I trow."

But Bradford prayed him to leave toying and trifling, and said thus: "My lord," quoth he, "if it be not a commandment of Christ to take and to eat the sacrament, why do any take upon them to command and make of necessity that which God leaveth free? as you do in making it a necessary commandment, once[3] a year[4], for all that be of lawful discretion to receive the sacrament."

1 Cor. xi.

Here the lord chancellor calleth him again *diabolus* or 'slanderer;' and so began out of these words, "Let a man prove himself, and so eat of the bread," ("the bread," quoth Bradford,) "and drink of the cup," to prove[5] that it was no commandment to receive the sacrament[6]: "for then," quoth he, "if it were a commandment, it should bind all men, in all places, and at all times."

"O my lord," quoth Bradford, "discern between commandments: some be general, as the ten commandments[7], that they bind always, in all places, and all persons; some be not so general; as this is of the supper, the sacrament of baptism, of the thrice[8] appearing before the Lord yearly[8] at Jerusalem, Abraham's offering Isaac."

[1 'proposing' 1561 : 'parsing' 1563.]
[2 'quod he' 1563 : not in 1561.]
[3 'that once' 1561 : 'once' 1563.]
[4 See p. 395, note 4, above; and Concil. Lateran. IV. cap. xxi. in Concil. stud. Labb. et Cossart. XI. I. col. 171—4, Lut. Par. 1671—2.]
[5 'to prove' 1570 : not in 1561 or 1563.]
[6 'was no commandment' 1561: 'it was no commandment to receive the sacrament' 1563.]
[7 'as the ten commandments' 1563; not in 1561.]
[8 'thrice,' 'yearly,' 'that,' 'quod he,' 1563 : not in 1561.]

Here my lord chancellor denied the cup to be commanded of Christ; "for then," quoth he[9], "we shall have eleven commandments."

"Indeed," quoth Bradford, "I think you think as you speak; for else you would not take the cup from the people, seeing that Christ saith, 'Drink of it all.' But how say you, my lord?" quoth Bradford; "Christ saith to you bishops specially, *Ite, prædicate evangelium:* 'Go and preach the gospel:' 'Feed Christ's flock.' Is this a commandment, or not?"

Here was the lord chancellor in a great chafe, and said as pleased him. Another (I ween the bishop of Durham) asked him when Christ began to be present in the sacrament, whether before the receiver received it, or no?

Bradford answered that the question was curious, and not necessary; and further said that[8], as the cup was the new testament, so the bread was Christ's body to him that receiveth it duly, but yet so that bread is bread; "for," quod he[8], "in all the scripture ye shall not find this proposition, *Non est panis,* 'There is no bread:'" and so he brought forth St Chrysostom, *Si in corpore [non] essemus*[10]: ["If we were not in the body."]

Summa, much ado was hereabout, they calling Bradford heretic; and he desired them to proceed a God's name; he looked for that which God appointed them to do.

"Lo," quoth the lord chancellor, "this fellow is now in another heresy of fatal destiny, as though all things were so tied together that of mere necessity all things must come to pass."

But Bradford prayed him to take things as they were spoken, and not wrest them into a contrary sense. "Your lordship," quoth he, "doth discern betwixt God and man. Things are not by fortune to God at any time, though to man they seem so sometimes. I," quoth Bradford, "spake but as the apostles spake: 'Lord,' quoth they[11], 'see how   Acts iv.

[9 So 1570. 'Here the lord chancellor said, What say you that baptism is commanded? Then, quoth he,' 1561.]

[10 Εἰ μὲν γὰρ ἀσώματος εἶ, γυμνὰ ἄν αὐτά σοι τὰ ἀσώματα παρέδωκε δῶρα· ἐπεὶ δὲ σώματι συμπέπλεκται ἡ ψυχή, ἐν αἰσθητοῖς τὰ νοητά σοι παραδίδωσι.—Chrysost. In Matt. Hom. LXXXII. (al. LXXXIII) Op. VII. 787, ed. Bened. Par. 1718—38.]

[11 'he' 1561: 'they' 1563.]

Herod and Pontius Pilate with the prelates are gathered together against thy Christ, to do that which thy hand and counsel hath before ordained them to do.'"

Here began the lord chancellor to read the excommunication[1]: and in the excommunication, when he came to the name of Bradford, *laicus*, 'layman,' "Why," quoth he, "are you no priest?"

"No," quoth Bradford, "nor never was either priest, either beneficed, either married, either any preacher, afore public authority had established religion, but preached after public authority had established religion[2]: and yet," quoth he, "I am thus handled at your hands: but God, I doubt not, will give his blessing where you curse." And so he fell down on his knees, and heartily thanked God that he counted him worthy to suffer for his sake; and so prayed God to give them repentance and a good mind.

After the excommunication was read, he was delivered to the sheriffs of London, and so had to the Clink, from thence to the Compter in the Poultry[3]; where he remaineth close, without all company, books, paper, pen or ink, looking for the dissolution of his body: in the which God grant to him his sweet mercy through Christ our Lord. Amen.

[1 The 'officium' and 'sententia contra Johannem Bradford' are printed from the original MS., Harl. 421., British Museum, in the Appendix to this volume.]

[2 Bradford was ordained deacon by Bp. Ridley, at Fulham, August 10, 1550.—Vide Bp. Ridley, Register MS., fol. 319 b; Strype, Mem. II. i. 403.]

[3 After the words 'in the Poultry," Foxe (Acts, &c. 1563, p. 1199) proceeds, 'in the same city of London; this being then purposed of his murderers, that he should be delivered from thence to the earl of Derby to be conveyed into Lancashire, and there to be burned in the town of Manchester, where he was born: but their purpose concerning the place was afterward altered, for they burned him in London.'

The Latin version of Foxe, 1559, after, 'eo rursus mutato consilio,' has, 'episcopi, sive occulto metu amicorum Bradfordi (erat enim apud suos gratiosus Bradfordus) sive occultiori aliqua fiducia ejus expugnandi sententiam, Londini apud se retinent menses aliquot, crebris interim colloquiis et legationibus eum adorientes.'—Fox. Rerum in eccles. gestar. comm. p. 484, Basil. 1559.]

THE SUM OF THE PRIVATE TALK HAD WITH MASTER JOHN BRADFORD, SITHEN THE 29TH DAY OF JANUARY, BY SUCH AS THE PRELATES HAVE SENT UNTO HIM.

AFTER my first arraignment in the church of St Mary Overy's, the twenty-ninth day of January, about four of the clock in the evening, there came into the revestry, whither I was had after my arraignment, and tarried there all day, a gentleman called master Thomas Hussey of Lincolnshire, (which was once an officer in the duke of Norfolk's house,) to inquire for one Stoning: and when it was answered him by the under-marshal's officers of the king's bench, which were there with doctor Taylor and me, that there was none such, he came forthwith into the house, and took acquaintance of me, saying further that he would commune and speak with me in the morning for old acquaintance sake: for I was at Muttrel journey[4] a paymaster, in which he was, and had often received money at my hands.

Now in the morning, about seven of the clock, he came into the chamber wherein I lay; and being alone with me, and set down, he began a long talk how that of love and old acquaintance he came unto me, to speak unto me that which he would further utter; the effect whereof was that I did so wonderfully (quod he) behave myself before the lord chancellor and the other bishops the other day, that even the veriest enemies I had did see how that they had no matter against me: therefore [he] advised me (as though it came of his own goodwill, without making any other man privy, or any other procuring him, as he said) that I would this day ("for," quoth he, "anon you shall be called before them again,") desire therefor time, and men to confer withal. By reason whereof he thought that all men would think a wonderful wisdom, gravity, and goodness in me: and by this mean I should

[4 'Muttrel': Montreuil, in Picardy, on the north east of France. 'Journey': a battle, or day of battle, from the French *journée*. The siege of Montreuil was conducted by the English army under the duke of Norfolk, at the same period with that of Boulogne, A.D. 1544. Vide references in p. 32, note 3, above.]

"escape the danger, which is nearer than you be ware of," quoth he.

But I answered briefly, and said that "I could not, nor would not, make any such request: for then," quod I, "occasion should I give to the people, and to all other, to think[1] that I stood in doubting of the doctrine; the which thing," I told him, "I did not, but thereof was most assured: and therefore I would give no such offence."

As we were thus talking, the chamber-door was unlocked; and who should come in at the door, but one doctor Seyton? When he saw master Hussey, "What, sir," quoth he, "are you come before me?"

"Yea," thought I, "goeth the matter thus? and he told me, no man knew of his coming." "Well, Lord," quoth I to myself, "give me grace to remember thy lesson, *Cavete ab hominibus istis*, 'Beware of those men,' &c. 'Cast not your pearls before dogs;' for I see these men be come to hunt the matter, that the one may bear witness with the other."

Matt. x.
Matt. vii.

This doctor Seyton, after some by-talk of my age, of my country, and such like, he began a gay and long sermon of my lord of Canterbury, master Latimer, and master Ridley, and how at Oxford they were not able to answer any thing at all; and therefore my lord of Canterbury desired to confer with the bishop of Duresme and others: all which talk tended to this end, that I should make the like suit, being in nothing to be compared in learning to my lord of Canterbury; which thing is most true.

But I briefly answered as before I did to master Hussey; wherewith they were neither of them both contented: and therefore they used many persuasions; and master doctor said how that he had heard much good talk of me, telling how that yesternight master Runcorn had made report of me at my lord chancellor's table at supper, how that I was able to persuade as much as any that he knew. "And I myself," quoth he, "though I never heard you preach, nor to my knowledge never saw you before yesterday, yet methought your modesty was such, your behaviour and talk so without malice and impatiency, that I would be sorry you should do worse than myself. And I tell you," quoth he, "further, I do perceive that my lord chancellor hath a favour toward

[1 'to think' 1563: not in 1561.]

you. Wherefore be not obstinate, but desire respite, and sue to some learned men to confer withal."

But still I kept me to my cuckoo[2]: "I could not, nor would not so offend God's people: I stood in no wavering, but was most certain of the doctrine I had taught."

Here master doctor waxed hot, and called me "arrogant, proud, vain-glorious, and spoke like a prelate;" having no other answer of me but that he should beware of judging, Matt. vii. lest he condemned himself. Howbeit this would not serve; but still he urged me, shewing how merciful my lord chancellor was, and how charitably they entertained me.

Unto which words I briefly shewed him, that "I never found any justice, much less charity, (I speak it for my part," quoth I[3],) "in my lord chancellor;" and so shewed how I had been in prison, how I had been handled, and how they had "no matter now against me but such as they should have by mine own confession."

But nothing of this talk moved master doctor, who went from matter to matter, from this point to that point: and I gave him still the hearing and answered not; because he came to have had something whereby my lord chancellor might have seemed[4] to have kept me in prison not causeless. When all their talk took no such effect as they would and looked for, master Hussey began to ask me whether I would not admit conference, if my lord chancellor should offer it me publicly?

To whom I answered this in effect, that "conference, if it had been offered before the law had been made, or conference if it were offered so that I might be at liberty to confer, and as free as he with whom I should confer, then," quoth I, "it were something: but else I see not to what purpose conference should be offered, but to defer that which will come at the length; and the lingering may give more offence, than do good. Howbeit," quoth I, "if my lord shall make such an offer of his own voluntariness, I will not refuse to confer with whomsoever shall come."

Master doctor hearing this called me arrogant still, proud,

[2 These words only occur in 1561. Foxe reads, 'But John Bradford kept still one answer.'—Acts, &c., 1563, and after editions.]

[3 'he' 1561, a misprint for 'I.']

[4 'have had seemed' 1561.]

and whatsoever pleased him: so that I besought them both (because I perceived by them I should shortly be called for) to "give me leave to talk with God, and to beg wisdom and grace of him; for," quoth I, "otherwise I am helpless."

And so they with much ado departed: and I went to God, and made my prayer accordingly, which of his goodness he did graciously accept, and did help me in my need: praised therefore be his holy name.

Shortly after they were gone, I was had to St Mary Overy's, and there tarried uncalled for till eleven of the clock; that is, till master Saunders was excommunicated.

Upon the fourth[1] of February, the bishop of London came to the Compter in the Poultry, to disgrade master doctor Taylor, about one of the clock at afternoon: but before he spake to master Taylor, I was called forth unto him. When he saw me, off went his cap, and outstretched he his hand; and on this sort he spake to me, that because he perceived I was desirous to confer with some learned man, therefore he had brought master archdeacon Harpsfield to me: "And," quoth he, "I tell you, you do like a wise man; but I pray you go roundly to work, for the time is but short."

"My lord," quoth I, "as roundly as I can I will go to work with you: I never desired to confer with any man, nor yet do. Howbeit if you will have any to talk with me, I am ready to hear and answer him."

"What," quoth my lord of London, in a fume to the keeper, "did not you tell me that this man desired conference?"

"No, my lord," quoth he, "I told you that he would not refuse to confer with any; but I did not shew to any that it was his desire."

"Well," quoth my lord of London, "master Bradford, you are well beloved: I pray you consider yourself, and refuse not charity when it is offered."

"Indeed, my lord," quoth I, "this is small charity to condemn a man as you have condemned me, which never brake the laws. In Turkey a man may have charity[2]; but in England I could not find it; for I am condemned for my

[1 'third' 1561: 'fourth' 1563.]
[2 'charity' 1563: 'tought free' 1561.]

faith, so soon as I uttered it at your request, before I had committed any thing against the laws. As for conference, I am not afraid," quoth I, "to talk with whom you will; but to say that I desire to confer, that do I not."

"Well, well," quoth my lord of London, and so called for master Taylor; and I went my way.

Upon the fourth of February came one of my lord chancellor's gentlemen, sent as he said from my lord, as then being come from the court. This was about eight of the clock [in] the evening. The effect and end of his talk and message was, that my lord his master did love me well, and therefore he offered me time to confer if I would desire it.

But as I had answered others in this matter, so I answered him, that "I would never make that suit; but," quoth I, "to confer with any I will never refuse, because I am certain and able, I thank God, to defend by godly learning my faith."

Thus with much ado we shook hands, and departed, he to his master, and I to my prison[3].

ANOTHER PRIVATE MATTER OF TALK BETWEEN MASTER BRADFORD AND WILLERTON.

Upon the seventh of February came one master Willerton, a chaplain to the bishop of London, to confer with me; who, when he perceived that I desired not his coming, being as one most certain of my doctrine, and therefore wished rather his departing than abiding; "Well, master Bradford," quoth he, "yet I pray you let us confer a little: perchance you may do me good, if I can do you none." Upon which words I was content to talk. He spake much of the doctors and fathers, of the bread in the sixth chapter of John; and so would prove transubstantiation, and how that wicked men do receive Christ's body.

[3 The last three paragraphs occur in 1561 only.]

[BRADFORD.]

And I, on the contrary part, improved[1] his authors, with much by-talk betwixt us both and the keeper, who took his part, little to the purpose.

Summa, to this issue we came, that he should draw out of the scriptures and doctors his reasons, and I would peruse them; and if I could not answer them, I would give place: and so I desired him to do my reasons which I would make; and so departed for that day.

The next day following, in the morning, he sent me half a sheet of paper written on both sides, with no reasons how he gathered his doctrine, but only the bare sentence, *Panis quem ego dabo:* "The bread which I will give is my flesh;" and the places in the twenty-sixth of Matthew, fourteenth of Mark, twenty-second of Luke, and the tenth and eleventh [of the first epistle] to the Corinthians, with some sentences of the doctors, all which made as much against him as with him, alonely one of Theophylactus[2] except.

In the afternoon he came himself, and then we had a long babbling to none effect; and at the length he came to the church, and how that I swerved from the church.

"No," quoth I, "that do I not, but you do. For the church is Christ's spouse, and Christ's obedient spouse; which[3] your church is not, which robbeth the people of the Lord's cup, and of service in the English tongue."

"Why," quoth he, "it is not profitable to have the service in English:" and so he brought forth this sentence to prove it, *Labia sacerdotis custodiunt legem;* "The lips of the priest should keep the law, and out of his mouth men must look for knowledge."

[Mal. ii. 7.]

"Why," quoth I, "should not the people then have the scriptures? Wherefor serveth this saying[4] of Christ, 'Search the scriptures?'"

John v.

[1 'Improved:' disproved.]

[2 μεταποιεῖται γὰρ ἀπορρήτοις λόγοις ὁ ἄρτος οὗτος διὰ τῆς μυστικῆς εὐλογίας, καὶ ἐπιφοιτήσεως τοῦ ἁγίου πνεύματος εἰς σάρκα τοῦ Κυρίου.—Theoph. In Joann. Comm. cap. vi. Op. I. 594. Venet. 1754—63: and vide In Matt. Comm. cap. xxvi. Op. I. 146; and In Marc. Comm. cap. xiv. Op. I. 249. See Becon, Works, Parker Soc. II. 289, and III. 388; Abp. Cranmer, Works, I. 188, et seq. Parker Soc., or Works, III. 292, et seq., Oxford, 1833; and Bp. Jewel, Reply to Harding, Art. XI. div. vi. Parker Soc. 574—7.]

[3 'as' 1561: 'which' 1563.]   [4 'saying' 1563: not in 1561.]

"This," quoth he, "was not spoken to the people, but to the scribes and learned men."

"Well," quoth I, "then the people must not have the scriptures:" which he affirmed, bringing forth this, *Et erunt docti a Deo;* "They shall be all taught of God."

"But must we," quoth I, "learn all at the priests?"

"Yea," quoth he.

"Well then," said I, "I see you would bring the people to hang up Christ, and let Barabbas go; as the priests then did persuade the people." Luke xxiii.

At which words he was so offended, that he had no lust to talk any more. *Summa*, I gave him the reasons I had gathered against transubstantiation[5], and prayed him to frame his in the form of reasons, and I would answer them.

"Well," quoth he, "I will do so; but first I will answer yours." The which thing he hath not done hitherto, nor will not; for I hear that he is ridden into the country.

Upon the 12th of February, there came one of the earl of Derby his men, called Stephen Beiche, one of old acquaintance to me; who shewed me that my lord sent him to me, and willed me to tender myself, and he would be good lord unto me: when I answered, that I thanked his "lordship for his good-will towards me; but," quoth I, "in this case I cannot tender myself more than God's honour."

Then he set before me my mother, my sisters, friends, kinsfolks, and country: "What a great discomfort it would be unto them to see you[6] die as a heretic!"

"Well, sir," quoth I, "I have learned to forsake father, mother, brother, sisters, friends, and all that ever I have, and mine own self; or else I cannot be Christ's disciple."

And so he telling me that my death would do much hurt, and such like talk, we shook hands. Howbeit, now I remember that in our talk he asked me, "if my lord should obtain for me that I might depart the realm, whether I would not be content to be at the queen's appointment, where she would appoint me beyond the sea."

[5 The 'reasons against transubstantiation' are printed, p. 544—6. in this volume.]

[6 'see you' 1563: not in 1561.]

"No," quoth I, "I had rather be burned in England, than be burned beyond the sea; for I know," quoth I, "that if she should send me to Paris, to Louvain, &c., forthwith they would burn me."

TALK BETWEEN MASTER BRADFORD AND ONE PERCIVAL CRESSWELL; AND AFTER THAT WITH DR HARDING.

Upon the 14th of February there came to me Percival Cresswell, one of my old acquaintance, and one that loveth my body well, and my soul also after his religion, bringing with him (as[1] I learn) a kinsman of master Feckenham; who after much ado prayed me that he might make labour for me, a God's name.

Quod I, "Do: you may do what you will."

"Yea, but," quoth he, "tell me what suit I should make for you[2]."

"Forsooth," said I, "that that you will do, do it not at my request; for I desire nothing at your hands. If the queen will give me life, I will thank her. If she will banish me, I will thank her. If she will condemn me to perpetual prisonment, I will thank her. If she will burn me, I will thank her."

Hereupon Cresswell[3] went away; and about an eleven of the clock he and the other man came again, and brought a book of master More's making, to read over; the which book I took.

"But," quoth I, "good Percival, I am too sure settled for being moved in these matters."

"O," quoth he, "if ever you loved me, do one thing for me."

"What is that?" quoth I.

At the length (for I would not promise) saith he, "To desire and name what learned men or man you will have to come unto you: my lord of York, my lord of Lincoln, my lord of Bath, my lord of Chichester, &c. will gladly come to you."

[1 '& as' 1561.]
[2 'for you' 1563: not in 1561.]
[3 'he' 1561: 'Cresswell' 1563.]

"No," quoth I, "never will I desire them, or any others, to come to confer with me; for I am as certain of my doctrine as I am of any thing. But for your pleasure," quoth I, "and that all men may know I am not ashamed to have my faith sifted and tried, bring whom you will, and I will talk with them."

So they went their way: and about three of the clock in the afternoon cometh master doctor Harding[4], the bishop of Lincoln's chaplain; and after a great and solemn protestation, (when he knew I desired not his coming,) how that he had prayed to God, before he came forth, to turn his talk to my good, he began to tell of the good opinion he had of me, "and may God give you good even;" so that our talk was to none effect or purpose, save that I prayed him to consider from whence he was fallen, and not to follow the world, or love it; because the love of God is not where the world[5] is.

Summa, he counted me in a damnable estate, as one being out of the church; and therefore willed me to take heed to myself, and not to die in such an opinion.

"What, master Harding!" quoth I, "I have heard you with these ears maintain this that I stand[6] in."

"I have," quoth he, "preached that the doctrine of transubstantiation was a subtle doctrine; but otherwise I never taught it."

And so inveighing against marriages of priests, and much against Peter Martyr, Martin Bucer, Luther, and such[7], "which for breaking their vows were justly given up into heresies," quod he; I, seeing him altogether given up into popery, after admonishment thereof, bade him farewell.

[4 The reader will find accounts, severally, of Harding, Harpsfield, Pendleton, Cole, and Weston; and of Bps. Bonner, Tonstal, Bourn, and Abp. Heath, in Wood, Athenæ, Oxon. Bliss, I. 402—4, 491—3, 325—6, 450—4, 295—7, 368—73, 303—7, II. 805—7, 817—20; and in the 'Examinations,' &c. of Philpot, p. xxv—xxx, 167, Parker Soc.]

[5 'it' 1561: 'the world' 1570.]

[6 'stood' 1561: 'stand' 1563.]

[7 'and Luther' 1561: 'Luther and such' 1563.]

TALK BETWEEN DR HARPSFIELD[1], ARCHDEACON, AND MASTER BRADFORD[2].

Upon the 15th of February, about four of the clock in the afternoon, cometh Percival Cresswell and the other man, waiting upon master Harpsfield, archdeacon of London; who, after gentle salutation and many formalities, began a long oration, how that all men, even the infidels, Turks, Jews, anabaptists, and libertines, desire felicity as well as the Christians; and how that every man thinketh they shall attain to it by their religion.

To the which long oration I answered briefly, that he spake not far amiss.

Then goeth he on: "Yea, but the way," quoth he, "thither is not all alike:" and so he set forth how infidels by Jupiter, Juno, the Turk[2] by his alcoran, the Jew by his talmud, believed to come to heaven. "For so many I speak," saith he, "as believe the immortality of the soul."

And this long oration I as briefly answered, and said he had spoken truly.

"Well, then," quoth he, "here is the matter, the way to this heaven: we may not invent any new way."

"There is but one way," quoth I, "and that is Jesus Christ, as he himself doth witness: 'I am the way.'"

Here master Harpsfield affirmed and denied, and further said that I meant " by Christ, believing in Christ."

"I have learned," quoth I, "to discern betwixt faith and Christ; albeit I confess, that whosoever believeth in Christ, the same shall be saved."

"No," quoth he, "not all that believe in Christ; for some will say, 'Lord, Lord, have not we cast out devils?' &c. But Christ will say in the day of judgment to those, 'Depart from me, I know you not.'"

"Yea, sir," quoth I, "you must make a difference betwixt believing, and saying I believe: as for example, if one should say and swear he loved you, for all his saying you

[1 This and nearly the whole of the following conference exist in an early transcript in MS. 1. 2. 8. no. 26. Emman. Coll. Cambridge.]

[2 'Mahomet' 1561: 'Turk' 1563.]

will not believe him, when you see he goeth about to utter and do all evil things against you."

"Well," quoth he, "this is not much material. There is but one way, Christ. How come we to know him? Where shall we seek to find him?"

"Forsooth," quoth I, "we must seek him by his word, and in his word, and after his word."

"Very good," quoth master Harpsfield; "but tell me now how first we come into the company of them that could tell us this, but by baptism?"

"True," quoth I: "baptism is the sacrament, by the which outwardly[3] we are insert and engraft into Christ: I say outwardly, because[4] I dare not," quoth I, "exclude out of Christ all that die without baptism. I will not tie God, where he is not bound. Some infants die, whose parents desire baptism for them, and may not have it."

"To those," quoth he, "we may think perchance some mercy God will shew."

"Yea," quoth I, "those infants whose parents do contemn baptism will not I contemn utterly, because the child shall not bear the father's offence."

"Well," quoth he, "we agree that by baptism then we are brought, and, as one would say, begotten of Christ; for Christ is our Father, and the church his spouse is our mother. As all men naturally have Adam for their father and Eve for their mother, so all spiritual men have Christ for their Father and the church for their mother; which church, as Eve was taken out of Adam's side, so was she out of Christ's side, whereout flowed blood for satisfaction and purging of our sins."

"All this is true," quoth I, "and godly spoken."

"Now then," quoth he, "tell me whether this church of Christ hath not been always?"

"Yes," quoth I, "sithen the creation of man, and shall be for ever."

"Very good," quoth he; "but yet tell me whether this church is not a visible church, or no?"

"Yes," quoth I, "that it is, howbeit none otherwise visible than Christ was here on earth; that is, no exterior pomp

[3 'exteriorly' 1561: 'outwardly' 1563.]
[4 'for' 1561: 'I say outwardly, because' 1563.]

or shew setteth her forth commonly: and therefore to see her we must put on such eyes, as good men put on to see and know Christ when he walked here on earth: for as Eve was of the same substance Adam was of, so is the church of the same substance Christ is of; I mean 'flesh of his[1] flesh, and bone of his bones,' as Paul saith, Ephes. v. Look therefore, how Christ was visibly known to be Christ when he was on earth, (that is, by considering him after the word of God,) so is the church known."

"I do not come to reason," saith he, "at this present; and therefore I will go on forward. Is not this church[2] a multitude?"

"Yes," quoth I, "that it is. Howbeit, *latet*[3] *anguis in herba*, [a snake lurks in the grass,] as the proverb is[4]: you mean a subtlety in the word. What visible multitude was there in Elias' time, or when Moses was on the mount, Aaron and all Israel worshipping the calf?"

Virgil. [Ecl. iii. 93.]

"You go from the matter," quoth he.

"No, nothing at all," said I, "for I do but prevent[5] you, knowing well whereabout you go: and therefore fewer words might serve, if that you so would."

"Well," quoth he, "I perceive you have knowledge, and by a little perceive the more. Tell me yet more, whether this multitude have not the ministry or preaching of God's word?"

"Here, sir," quoth I, "you go about the bush. If you understand preaching for confessing the gospel, I will go with you: or else, if you will, you may know that persecution often letteth preaching."

"Well, I mean it so," quoth he. "Tell me yet more: hath it not the sacraments duly[6] administered?"

"It hath the sacraments[7]," quoth I; "howbeit the ministry thereof is often letted. But I will put you off your purpose, because I see whereabout you go. If heretics have baptized and do baptize, as they did in St Cyprian's

[1 'his' 1563: not in 1561.]
[2 'church' 1563: not in 1561.]
[3 *quod latet* 1561: *latet* 1563.]
[4 'as the proverb is' 1563: not in 1561.]
[5 'Prevent:' anticipate.]
[6 'duly,' Emman. MS.: not in 1561, or 1563.]
[7 'administered? It hath the sacraments,' 1563, and Emman. MS.: not in 1561.]

time[8], you know this baptism is baptism, and not to be reiterated."

This I spake, that the standers-by might see that, though the popish church have baptism which we have received[9] of them, yet therefore is it not the true church, nor never need we to be baptized again: which thing he saw well enough; and therefore he said I went from the matter, adding that I had more errors than one or two.

"So ye say," quoth I; "but that is not enough till you prove them."

"Well," quoth he, "this church is a multitude, hath the preaching of the gospel, and the ministration of the sacraments: and yet more, hath it not the power of jurisdiction?"

"O sir," quoth I, "whither go you? You walk not wilily enough; you cannot deceive me, I thank God: what jurisdiction is exercised in time of persecution and[10] affliction?"

"I mean," quoth he, "by jurisdiction, admonishing one another, and so forth."

"Well, go to," said I, "what then?"

"It hath also," quoth he, "succession of bishops." And here he made much ado to prove that this was an essential point.

"You say as you would have it[11]," quoth I; "for if this point fail you, all the church you go about to set forth will fall down. You shall not find in all the scripture this your[12] essential point of succession of bishops," quoth I. "In Christ's church antichrist will sit. And Peter telleth us, as it went in the old church afore Christ's coming, so will it be in the new church sithen Christ's coming: that is, as there were false prophets, and such as bare rule were adversaries to the true prophets; so shall there be, sithen Christ's coming, false teachers, even of[13] such as be bishops, and bear rule amongst the people."

"You always go out of the matter," quoth he: "but I will prove," saith he, "the succession of bishops."

[8 See p. 524, further on.]
[9 'receive' 1561: 'have received' 1583.]
[10 'in' 1561: 'and' 1563.]
[11 'true' 1561: 'as you would have it' 1563.]
[12 'is' 1561: 'your' 1563.]
[13 'as of' 1561: 'of' 1563.]

"Do so," quoth I.

"Tell me," quoth he, "were not the apostles bishops?"

"No," quoth I, "except you will make a new definition of bishops; that is, give him[1] no certain place."

"Indeed," saith he, "the apostles' office was more than bishops', for it was universal; but yet Christ instituted bishops in his church, as Paul saith, 'He hath given pastors, prophets:' so that I trow it be proved by the scriptures the succession of bishops to be an essential point."

Eph. iv.

To this I answered that "the ministry of God's word and ministers is an essential point; but to translate this to bishops and their succession," quoth I, "is a plain subtlety: and therefore," quoth I, "that it may be plain, I will ask you a question, Tell me whether the scripture know any difference between bishops and ministers, which you call priests?"

"No,[2]" saith he.

"Well, then, go on forwards," quoth I, "and let us see what you shall get now by the succession of bishops, that is, of ministers; which cannot be understand of such bishops as minister not, but lord it."

"I perceive," quoth he, "that you are far out of the way. By[3] your doctrine you can never shew in your church[4] this, a multitude which ministereth God's word and his sacraments, which hath jurisdiction and succession of bishops, which hath[5] from time to time believed as you believe; beginning now, and so going[6] upwards, as I will do," quod he, "of our doctrine: and therefore you are out of the church, and so may not be

[1 'him,' Emman. MS., and 1563: not in 1561.]

[2 "The Romanists, apparently in order to exalt the pope as the sole fountain of ecclesiastical power, did much to depress the authority and office of bishops. Sometimes in enumerations of the orders of the church, bishops seem hardly admitted to be a distinct order. Discussions upon this point occurred at the Council of Trent; when those who held that all the apostles, and by consequence all bishops, derived their authority from Christ, were told that they took away the due authority of the pope. See Fra. Paolo. Hist. Conc. Tr. Lib. VII."—Ayre on Becon, Catechism, Works, Parker Soc. II. 319.]

[3 'For' 1561: 'By' 1563.]

[4 'in your church' 1563: not in 1561.]

[5 'to have' 1561, and Emman. MS.: 'which hath' 1563.]

[6 'go' 1561: 'going' 1563.]

saved. Perchance you will bring me downwards a shew to blear the people's eyes; but to go upwards, that can you never do; and this is the true trial."

To this I answered, that he ought to give me leave to follow the scripture and examples of good men.

Then [he] said, "Yea."

"Well, then," quoth I, "Stephen was accused and condemned, as I am, that he taught new and false doctrine, before the fathers of the church then, as they were taken. Now what doth Stephen for his purgation, but improved their accusations? But how doth he it? by going upwards? No, but by coming[7] downwards, beginning at Abraham, and continuing still till Esaias' time, and the people's captivity; from whence he maketh a great leap until that time he was in, which was, I think, upon a four hundred[8] years; and called them by their right name hell-hounds, rather than heaven-hounds. On this sort, sir," quoth I, "will I prove my faith; and that you can never do yours."

"Yea, sir," quoth he, "if we did know you had the Holy Ghost, then could we believe you."

Here might have been answered, that Stephen's enemies would not believe he had the Holy Ghost, and therefore they did as they did: but in speaking he rose up; and the keeper talked[9], and others that stood by, to take his part all against me; howbeit gently, without any taunting or railing, only praying me to take heed to that master Harpsfield spake; who still said I was out of the church, and did contemn it, spit against it, and I cannot tell what.

But I still affirmed that I was most certain I was in Christ's church, and could shew a demonstration of my religion from time to time continually.

And so we made an end, he[10] saying that in the morning he would come again unto me.

God our Father, for the name and blood of his Christ, be merciful unto us, and unto all his people, and deliver[11] them *Prayer of master Bradford's.*

[7 'going' 1561: 'coming' 1563.]
[8 'four years' 1561: 'four hundred' 1563.]
[9 'talked,' Emman. MS.: 'called' 1561.]
[10 'he,' Emman. MS.: not in 1561.]
[11 'keep' 1561: 'deliver' 1563.]

from all false teachers and blind guides, through whom[1], alas! I fear me, much hurt will come to this realm of England. God our Father bless us, and keep us in his truth and poor church for ever. Amen.

THE NEXT DAY'S TALK BETWEEN DR HARPSFIELD AND MASTER BRADFORD.

Upon the sixteenth of February, in the morning, about nine of the clock, there came again the said master Harpsfield and the other two with him.

Now, after a few words spoken, we sat down: and master Harpsfield began[2] a very long oration, almost three quarters of an hour long, first repeating what we had said, and how far we had gone over-night[3]; and therewith did begin[4] to prove upwards succession of bishops here in England for eight hundred years, in France at Lyons for twelve hundred years, in Spain at Hispalen[5] for eight hundred years, in Italy at Milan for twelve hundred years, labouring by this[6] to prove his church; whereto he used also succession of bishops in the east church for the more confirmation of his words, and so concluded with an exhortation and an interrogation: the exhortation, that I would obey this church; the interrogation, whether I could shew any such succession for the demonstration of my church (for so he called it), which I followed.

Unto this his long oration I made a short answer, how that my memory was evil for to answer particularly his long oration; therefore I would generally do it, thinking that because his oration was rather to persuade than to prove, that a general answer would serve. So I told him, that if

[1 'whereby' 1561: 'through whom' 1563.]
[2 'beginning' 1561: 'began' 1563.]
[3 'what and how far we have gone astray' (misprint for 'yesterday') 1561: 'what we had said, and how far we had gone over-night' 1563.]
[4 'beginning' 1561: 'therewith did begin' 1563.]
[5 'Hispalen:' the town of Seville.]
[6 'going by that' 1561: 'labouring by this' 1563.]

Christ or his apostles, being here on earth, had been[7] demanded of the prelates of the church then to have made a demonstration of the church by succession of high priests which had approved the doctrine he taught; "I think," quoth I, "that Christ here would have done as I do; that is, have brought forth that which upholdeth the church, even the verity of the word of God taught and believed, not of the high priests (which of long time had persecuted it), but by the prophets and other good simple men which perchance were counted for heretics with the church, that is, with them that were ordained high priests in the church; to whom the true church was not then tied by any succession, but the word of God. And thus to think," quoth I, "St Peter giveth an occasion, when he saith that, as it went in the church before Christ's coming, so shall it go in the church after his coming: but then the pillars of the church were persecutors of it: therefore the like we must look for now." 2 Pet. ii.

"Why," quoth he, "I can gather and prove you succession in Jerusalem of the high priests from Aaron's time."

"I grant," quoth I[8], "but not such succession as allowed the truth."

"Why," quoth he, "did they not all allow Moses's law?"

"Yes," quoth I, "and kept it for the books thereof, as you do the Bible and holy scripture. But the interpretation and meaning of it they did corrupt, as I take it you have done: and therefore the persecutions they stirred up against the prophets and Christ was not for the law, but for the interpretation of it; as you say now, that we must fetch[9] the interpretation of the scriptures at your hands. But to make an end," quoth I, "death I do look daily for, yea, hourly; and I think my time be but very short. Therefore I had need to spend in prayer as much time with God as I can (whilst I have it), for his help and comfort: and therefore I pray you bear with me, that I do not now particularly[10], and in more words, answer your long talk. If I saw death not so near me as it is, I would then weigh every piece of your oration, if you would give me the sum of them, and I would answer them accordingly, I hope: but because I dare not, nor

[7 'hath him' 1561: 'had been' 1563.]
[8 'he' misprint for 'I' 1561.]   [9 'have' 1561: 'fetch' 1563.]
[10 'more plainly' 1561: 'now particularly' 1563.]

I will not, leave off looking and providing for that which is at hand, I shall desire you to hold me excused because I do as I do; and I heartily thank you for your gentle good-will: I shall heartily pray God our Father to give you the same light and life as I wish to myself."

And so I began to[1] rise up. But then master Harpsfield began to tell me, that I was in a very perilous case; and he was sorry to see me so settled; telling further that indeed he could tell me nothing whether death were far off, or near: "but that forceth not," quoth he, "so that you did die well."

"Well?" quoth I, "yes, for I doubt not in this case but to die well; for as I hope and am certain my death shall please the Lord, so I trust I shall die cheerfully, to the comfort of his children."

"Yea, but what if you be deceived?" quoth he.

"What," quoth I, "if you did say the sun did not shine now?" Then it did shine through the window where we sat.

"Well," quoth he, "I am sorry to see you so secure and careless."

"Indeed I am more carnally secure and careless[2] than I should be: God make me more vigilant! But in this case," quoth I, "I cannot be too secure, for I am most assured I am in the truth."

"That are ye not," quoth he, "for you are not of the catholic church."

"No," quoth I, "though you have excommunicate me, yet am I in the catholic church of Christ, and am, and by God's grace shall be[3], a child of it, and an obedient child for ever. I hope Christ will have no less care for me, than he had for the blind man excommunicate of the synagogue. And," quoth I, "further, I am certain that the necessary articles of the faith (I mean the twelve articles of the Creed) I confess and believe with that which you call the holy church: so that even your church hath taken something too much upon her to excommunicate me for that which, by the testimony of my lord of Duresme in his book of the sacra-

[1 'as to' 1561: 'to' 1563.]
[2 So 1563: 'careless and secure carnally' 1561.]
[3 'will be' 1561: 'am and by God's grace shall be' 1563.]

ment lately put forth, was free of many an hundred[4] years after Christ, to believe or not believe[5]."

"What is that?" quoth he.

"Transubstantiation," said I.

"Why, you are not condemned therefor only," quod he.

"Yes," quoth I, "that am I, and because I deny that wicked men do receive Christ's body."

"No," quoth he, "you agree not with us in the presence, nor in nothing else."

"How you believe," quoth I, "you know: for my part I confess a presence of whole Christ, God and man, to the faith of the receiver."

"No," quoth he, "you must believe a real presence in the sacrament."

"In the sacrament?" quoth I. "No, I will not shut him up, nor tie him to it, otherwise than faith seeth and permitteth. If I should[6] include Christ's real presence in the sacrament, or tie him to it otherwise than to the faith of the receiver, then the wicked man should receive him; which I do not, nor will not believe by God's grace."

"More pity," quoth he; "but a man may easily see you make no presence at all, and therefore you agree not therein with us."

"I confess[7] a presence," quoth I, "and a true presence, but to the faith of the receiver."

"What," quoth one that stood by, "of Christ's very body which died for us?"

"Yea," quoth I, "even of whole Christ, God and man, to the faith of him that receiveth it."

[4 'an' 1561: 'an hundred' 1563.]

[5 .... ante Innocentium tertium Romanum episcopum, qui in Lateranensi concilio præsedit, tribus modis id posse fieri curiosius scrutantibus visum est: aliis existimantibus una cum pane, vel in pane Christi corpus adesse, veluti ignem in ferri massa, quem modum Lutherus secutus videtur; aliis panem in nihilum redigi vel corrumpi; aliis substantiam panis transmutari in substantiam corporis Christi, quem modum secutus Innocentius reliquos modos in eo concilio rejecit.—Tonstal. De verit. corp. et sang. Christ. in Euchar. Lib. I. p. 46, Lutet. 1554. Vide also p. 545 of this volume. The council of Lateran was held A. D. 1215.]

[6 'would' 1561: 'should' 1563.]

[7 'make' 1561: 'confess' 1563.]

"Why," quoth master Harpsfield, "this is nothing else but to exclude the omnipotency of God and all kind of miracle in the sacrament."

"No," quoth I, "I do not exclude his omnipotency, but you rather do it: for I believe that Christ can accomplish his promise, the substance of bread and wine being there still, as well as the accidents; which you believe not[1]. And," quoth I, "I count it a great miracle that common bread should be made a spiritual bread, that is, a bread ordained of God not for the food of the body, but rather for the food of the soul: for when we come to the sacrament, we come not to[2] feed our bodies, and therefore we have but a little piece of bread; but we come to feed our souls with Christ[3] by faith, which the wicked want; and therefore they receive nothing but *panem Domini*, [the bread of the Lord,] as Judas did, and not[4] *panem Dominum*[5], [the bread the Lord,] as the other apostles did."

"The wicked," saith master Harpsfield, "do receive the very body of Christ, but not the grace of his body."

"No," quoth I, "they receive not the body; for Christ's body[6] is no dead carcass: he that receiveth it receiveth the Spirit, which is not without grace, I ween."

"Well," quoth he, "you have very many errors. You count the mass for abomination; and yet St Ambrose said mass:" and so he[7] read, out of a book written, a sentence of St Ambrose[8] to prove it.

"Why sir," quod I, "the mass as it is now was nothing

[1 'which you believe not' 1563: not in 1561.]
[2 'to' 1563, and Emman. MS.: not in 1561.]
[3 'with Christ' 1563: not in 1561.]
[4 'and' 1561: 'and not' 1563.]
[5 Illi manducabant panem Dominum, ille panem Domini contra Dominum; illi vitam, ille pœnam.—August. In Johan. Evang. cap. xiii. Tractat. LIX. 1. Op. III. Pars II. col. 663, ed. Bened. Par. 1679—1700.]
[6 'it' 1561: 'Christ's body' 1563.]
[7 'he' 1563: not in 1561.]
[8 Omni.. hebdomada offerendum est, etiam si non quotidie peregrinis, incolis tamen vel bis in hebdomada.—Ambros. Comm. in I. Epist. ad Tim. cap. iii. Op. II. Append. col. 295, ed. Bened. Par. 1686—90. These commentaries are spurious: vide Cave, Hist. Liter. I. 263, Oxon. 1740—3; and see the 'Admonitio' of the Benedictine editors.]

so in St Ambrose' time. Was not the most part of the canon made sithen by Gregorius[9] and Scholasticus[10] and others?"

"Indeed," quoth he, "a great piece of it was made, as ye say, by Gregorius[9]: but Scholasticus was before St Ambrose' time[11]."

"I ween not[11]," quoth I; "howbeit I will not contend. St Gregory saith that the apostles said mass without the canon[12], only with the Lord's prayer[13]."

"You say true," quoth he; "for the canon is not the greatest part of the mass: the greatest part is the sacrifice, elevation, transubstantiation, and adoration."

"I can away with none of those," quoth I.

"No, I think the same," quoth he: "but yet *Hoc facite* [Do this] telleth plainly the sacrifice of the church."

"You consider not well," quoth I, "this word 'sacrifice,' not discerning betwixt the sacrifice of the church, and the sacrifice for the church. The sacrifice of the church is no propitiatory sacrifice, but a gratulatory sacrifice. The sacrifice Christ himself offered is the propitiatory sacrifice: and as for

[9 Gelasianum codicem de missarum solemniis, multa subtrahens, pauca convertens, nonnulla vero superadjiciens, pro exponendis evangelicis lectionibus in unius libri volumine coarctavit. In canone apposuit, 'Diesque nostros in tua pace dispone, atque ab æterna damnatione nos eripi, et in electorum tuorum jubeas grege numerari.'—Gregor. Magni Papæ I. Vita, auct. Johann. Diacono, II. xvii. in Gregor. Op. IV col. 50, ed. Bened. Par. 1705. Vide also Bedæ Hist. Eccl. II. i. ed. Smith. p. 77—8, Cantabr. 1722.]

[10 precem quam scholasticus [id est, vir aliquis doctus et eruditus, *annot. ed. Bened.*] composuerat. .—Id. Registr. Epist. Lib. IX. Indict. Ad Joann. Syracus. Epist. xii. (al. lxiv.) Op. II. col. 940.]

[11 Gavantus observes,... 'putant esse Gelasium doctrina clarissimum, Innoc. III. [Op. I. 370, Col. 1575, Myster. Miss.] Lib. III. c. x. et Honor. in Gemma an. Lib. I. cap. xc.'—Gavant. Thesaur. sacr. rit. cum addit. Merati, I. xii. 5. Tom. I. p. 67, Venet. 1769. Gelasius flourished A.D. 492. It is not however known who the scholastic or learned man mentioned by Gregory was. Vide note of Merati in loc. Gavant.; Bona, Rer. Liturg. libr. duo, II. xi. 2. stud. Sala, Tom. III. p. 245—7, August. Taur. 1747—53; and Palmer, Orig. Liturg. 1846. ch. 'Liturgy of Rome.']

[12 'canons' 1561: 'the canon' 1570.]

[13 Orationem Dominicam idcirco mox post precem dicimus, quia mos apostolorum fuit, ut ad ipsam solummodo orationem oblationis hostiam consecrarent.—Gregor. Magn. ibid.]

[BRADFORD.]

your *Hoc facite* [Do this, it] is not referred to any sacrificing, but to the whole action of[1] taking, eating, &c.[1]"

"You speak now," quoth he, "not learnedly; for Christ made his supper only to the twelve apostles[1], not admitting his mother or any of the seventy disciples to it: now the apostles do signify the priests."

"I think," quoth I, "that you speak as you would men should understand it; for else you would not keep the cup away from the laity. We have great cause to thank you, that you will give us the bread; for I perceive you make it, as though Christ had not commanded it to his whole church."

From this talk he went to shew me elevation[2], bringing out a place of St Basilius *De Spiritu*[3].

And I told him that "I had read the place, which seemeth to make nothing for[4] elevation: but," quoth I, "be it as it is, this is no time for me to scan the doubtful places of the doctors with you[1]. I have been in prison long without books and all necessaries for study; and therefore I must omit these things: death draweth nigh, and I by your leave must not leave off to prepare for it."

"If I could do you good," quoth he, "I would be right glad, either in soul or body; for you are in a perilous case both ways."

"Sir," quoth I, "I thank you for your good-will. My case is as it is. I thank God, it was never so well with me; for death to me shall be life, I trust and hope in God."

"It were best for you to desire master Harpsfield," quoth master Cresswell, "that he might make suit for you, that ye might have[5] a time to confer." Unto which words, master

[1 'of,' '&c.', 'apostles', 'this is no...with you,' 1563: not in 1561.]
[2 i. e. of the host in the service of the mass.—Missal. ad us. Sar. Canon, fol. clviii, Londin. 1555.]
[3 Τὰ τῆς ἐπικλήσεως ῥήματα ἐπὶ τῇ ἀναδείξει τοῦ ἄρτου τῆς εὐχαριστίας καὶ τοῦ ποτηρίου τῆς εὐλογίας, τίς τῶν ἁγίων ἐγγράφως ἡμῖν καταλέλοιπεν;—Basil. Lib. de Spir. Sanct. cap. xxvii. Op. III. 54—5, ed. Bened. Paris. 1721—30. The Benedictine editors observe on this: "Non respicit Basilius ad ritum ostensionis eucharistiæ, ut multi existimarunt, sed potius ad verba Liturgiæ ipsi adscriptæ, cum petit sacerdos, ut veniat Spiritus sanctus ἁγιάσαι καὶ ἀναδεῖξαι τὸν μὲν ἄρτον τοῦτον αὐτὸ τὸ τίμιον σῶμα τοῦ Κυρίου."]
[4 'not to make of' 1561: 'to make nothing for' 1570.]
[5 'for' 1561: 'that ye might have' 1563.]

Harpsfield said that he would do the best he could, for he pitied my case very sore.

"Sir," quoth I, "to desire any body to sue for time for me, I never will do it by God's help; for I am not wavering, nor I would not that any body should think I were so. But if you have the charity and love towards me you pretend, and thereto do think that I am in an error, I think the same should move you to do as you would be done by. As you think of me, so do I of you, that you are far out of the way; and not only think it, but also am thereof assured."

In this and such like gentle talk we departed, he saying that he would pray for me, others willing me to desire him to sue for me, which I did not; but I wished him as much good as he did me. And as he was going and bade me farewell, he turneth again, and giveth me Irenæus, praying me to read over a certain place in it; which thing I told him I would, although I had read it before.

At the door the wife of the house met him, and asked him how he had done.

"Forsooth, mistress," quoth he, "I find always one manner of man of him; as I found him, so I leave him."

"I pray you, sir," quoth she, "do him no hurt."

"No," quoth he; "but if I can, I will do him good."

At after dinner the same day, master Clayden my keeper cometh unto me from the earl of Derby, with whom he had dined, being sent for purposely about me. Now after his coming home, this was the sum of his talk, that the earl would gladly have me not to die, and therefore he would make suit on my behalf to the queen's highness. "Wherefore," quoth my keeper, "you must tell me what you would have him to do, that to-morrow I may bring him word, as he hath required me."

"Marry," quoth I, "master Clayden, I hope I shall need little to make many words in telling you my suit: as I heartily thank his lordship for his good-will and zeal that he beareth unto me, so you know I cannot desire any to make suit for me. If of his own will he do sue for pardon, banishment, perpetual prison, or what his pleasure shall be for me, I were to blame if that I would take it unthankfully; albeit I know death and speedy despatch were most welcome unto me."

"Well," quoth he, " I will tell him to-morrow, that though you cannot nor will not make suit to any to sue for you, yet you will be content if he, on his lordship's good-will, will labour on your behalf."

"Yea," quod I, "and to tell you truth, where I perceive that others do sue for me," (meaning Percival Cresswell and master Harpsfield,) " I had rather my lord of Derby should do it, for that my friends and the country might less be offended at him, because he must have the burning of me."

After this talk with my keeper, master Clayden, there cometh one of the queen's servants and officers, whose name I will not rehearse, which after a little talk fell down on his knees, and with tears besought me for the passion of Christ, that I would a little look to myself to make some suit, &c.; "for," quoth he, swearing an oath, "it will not be long unto, before thou shalt be able to do more good than ever thou didst."

But I, shewing myself not unthankful for his good-will, departed from him, as one little lusting to hear such counsel. Of him I learned Tuesday following was the uttermost day I should tarry here.

Within an hour after this man's departure from me, the keeper, master Clayden, called me, saying that he perceived how that my friend Percival had told him that master Harpsfield had written to master doctor Martin, to be a means to the council for longer time for me: whereupon quoth he, " I think it were best to send my lord of Derby word of this to-night, lest he be prevented[1]."

And I answered thus, that as he thought good, so he might do: " but," quoth I, " beware, I heartily pray, that you do not tell my lord any thing that I desire this; for if you do, it will in the end be more against you than with you." And he promised the same, and so departed out of hand to the court.

Upon the 17th day, which was Sunday, in the afternoon, Percival Cresswell sent me word by him that came first with him, that if I would make any suit myself, or will any to do for me, I might speed; " but else," quoth he, " nothing will

[1 'Prevented:' anticipated.]

be done, as he presently hath received answer of my lord chancellor."

"Well," quoth I, "I am at a point;" and so took my leave, looking still when the sheriffs would come for me: for I had heard over night, that one of the guard which was appointed to convey me down into Lancashire had told one that they had warning against to-morrow for me.

Upon the 19th day, which was Tuesday, I heard that the writ for my execution was called in again, and the sheriff of Lancashire discharged of me for the present: and in the afternoon one of my lord of Derby's men brought me word, how that my lord had taken great pains for me, and had kneeled before the queen, and many more words, desiring me something to see to myself now. "But," quoth he, "what and how much is done for you, I cannot tell; but this much I think," saith he, "you shall have your books, and time enough to peruse them."

"Well," quoth I, "I pray you heartily thank my lord for his good-will towards me: I shall, as I have done, pray that God would give unto him as to myself; the which is all I can do. For doing for myself, as I would be sorry that my lord or you should think any wavering in me for my doctrine, so I would be loath but to do all for myself that I can do with a good conscience. And as for time," quoth I, "and books, although I see it is but a lingering of the time, yet I am glad of it in this respect, that my lord and others may know I hold no opinion but such as I dare sift, and abide the reasoning for with any man. I trust you and many others shall see that our doctrine is true, and therefore dare and desire to abide the light and all men's looking on; where perchance it is bruited abroad that we are altogether obstinate, and cannot defend it by learning."

After this talk there was a priest, called master Couppage, which began to exhort me "to take the injuries done unto me patiently; for," quoth he, "I doubt not but if you will come unto us, you should be more able to help many, and your friends also, than ever you were, both spiritually and corporally."

"If," quoth I, "you keep your master Christ, I will come unto you; but otherwise I know you not."

This and such like talk we had for that present, the earl

of Derby his man appointing master Clayden my keeper in the morning to come to my lord.

Upon the 20th day, which was Wednesday, master Clayden came from my lord, and in his name asked me whether I would be content to speak with the king's confessor and Alphonsus a friar, and to send him word.

"Sir," quoth I, "you know that as I desire conference with no man, so (I thank God) I am not afraid to speak with any man."

Whereupon he sent my lord word, as he said: and so I heard nothing till the day following, how that my lord of Derby had sent back again two of his men, which came to me, saying that they were sent to solicit my cause; but how or what way, I could not learn[1].

THE TALK OF DR HEATH ARCHBISHOP OF YORK, AND DAY BISHOP OF CHICHESTER, WITH MASTER BRADFORD[2].

Upon the 22nd day, which was Friday, the archbishop of York and the bishop of Chichester came to the Compter to speak with me. When I was come before them, they both, and specially my lord of York, used me very gently: they would have had me sit down; and because I would not, they also would not sit. So we all stood; and whether I would or no, they would needs I should put on, not only my night-cap, but my upper cap also, saying unto me, that "obedience was better than sacrifice."

Now thus standing together, my lord of York began to tell me, how that they were not sent to me: "but of love and charity we come to you; and I," quoth he, "of old acquaintance which I have had with you, more than my lord of

[1 The last three pages, from p. 515 above, third paragraph, 'he saying that he would pray for me,' &c., are taken from the 'Examinations,' &c. 1561; and do not occur in any edition of the 'Acts and monuments' of Foxe.]

[2 A fragment of this conference exists in an early transcript in MS. 1. 2. 8. no. 27. Emman. Coll. Cambridge.]

Chichester hath had;" and so commended me of a godly life, &c., concluding with a question, how I was certain of salvation, and of my religion?

"Marry," quod I, (omitting all formalities, save that I thanked them for their good-will,) "by the word of God, by the scriptures, I am certain of salvation, and of my religion."

"Very well said," quod my lord of York: "but how do you know the word of God and the scriptures, but by the church?"

"Indeed, my lord," quoth I, "the church was and is a mean to bring a man more speedily to know the scriptures and the word of God, as was the woman of Samaria[3] a mean that the Samaritans knew Christ: but as when they had heard him speak, they said, 'Now we know that he is Christ, not because of thy words, but because we ourselves have heard him;' so," quoth I, "after we come to the hearing and reading of the scriptures shewed to us, and discerned by the church, we do believe them and know them, not because the church saith they are the scriptures, but because they be so; being thereof assured by the same Spirit which wrote and spake them."

"Yea," quoth my lord of York, "but you know in the apostles' time, at the first, the word was not written."

"True," quoth I, "if you mean it for some books of the[3] new Testament; but else for the old Testament Peter telleth us that we have *firmiorem sermonem propheticum,* 'a more sure word of prophecy:' not," quod I, "that it is simply so, but in respect of the apostles' persons, which, being alive and compassed with infirmity, attributed to the word written more firmity, as wherewith no fault could be found; whereas for the infirmity of their persons men perchance might have found some fault at their preaching: albeit in very deed no less obedience and faith ought to have been given to the one than to the other, as being all of one 'Spirit of truth.'"

"That place of Peter," quoth my lord of York, "is not so to be understand of the word of God written."

"Yes, sir," quoth I, "that it is, and of none other."

"Yea, indeed," quoth my lord of Chichester, "master Bradford doth tell you the truth in that point."

[3 'was,' 'books of the,' repeated by misprints in 1561.]

"Well," quoth my lord of York, "you know that Irenæus and others do magnify much the church, and allege the church against the heretics, and not the scripture[1]."

"True," quoth I; "for they had to do with such heretics as did deny the scriptures, and yet did magnify the apostles[2]; so[3] that they were enforced to use the authority of[3] those churches wherein the apostles had taught, and which had still retained[4] the same doctrine."

"You speak the very truth," quoth my lord of Chichester; "for the heretics did refuse all scriptures, except it were a piece of Luke's gospel."

"Then," quoth I, "the alleging of the church cannot be primarily or principally used against me, which am so far from denying of the scriptures, that I appeal unto them utterly as to the only judge."

John xii.

"A pretty matter," quoth my lord of York, "that you will take upon you to judge the church: I pray you, where was your church these many years? For the church of Christ is catholic and visible hitherto."

"My lord," quoth I, "I do not judge the church, when I discern it from that congregation and those which be not the church[5]; and I never denied the church to be catholic and visible, although at some times it is more visible than at some."

"I pray you," quoth my lord of Chichester, "tell me

[1 Quid enim? Et si de aliqua modica quæstione disceptatio esset, nonne oporteret in antiquissimas recurrere ecclesias, in quibus apostoli conversati sunt, et ab eis de præsenti quæstione sumere quod certum et re liquidum est? Quid autem si neque apostoli quidem scripturas reliquissent nobis, nonne oportebat ordinem sequi traditionis, quam tradiderunt iis quibus committebant ecclesias?—Iren. Cont. Hær. Lib. III. cap. iv. 1. Op. I. 178, Venet. 1734. Vide Stillingfleet, Vindic. of Abp. Laud, Conf. part I. ch. ix. 4. 5. p. 268—72, ed. 1665; and Goode, Rule of Faith, 1842, II. p. 277—90, in connexion with this passage.]

[2 Cum enim ex scripturis arguuntur [hæretici], in accusationem convertuntur ipsarum scripturarum, quasi non recte habeant, neque sint ex auctoritate, et quia varie sint dictæ, et quia non possit ex his inveniri veritas ab his qui nesciant traditionem: non enim per literas traditam illam, sed per vivam vocem.—Id. ibid. ii. 1. p. 174.]

[3 'so,' 'the authority of,' 1563: not in 1561.]

[4 'that church still had received' 1561: 'which had still retained' 1563.]

[5 'in it' 1561: 'the church' 1570.]

where the church, which allowed your doctrine, was these four hundred years."

"I will tell you, my lord," quoth I; "or rather you shall tell it yourself, if you will tell me this one thing[6], where the church was in Elias' time, when Elias said that he was left alone."

"That is no answer," quoth my lord of Chichester.

"I am sorry that[7] you say so: but this will I tell your lordship, that, if you had the same eyes wherewith a man might have espied the church then[8], you would not say, it were no answer. The fault why the church is not seen of you is, not because the church is not visible, but because your eyes are not clear enough to see it."

"You are much deceived," quoth he, "to make such a collation betwixt the church then and now."

"Very well spoken, my lord," quoth the bishop of York; "for Christ said, *Ædificabo ecclesiam*, 'I will build my church;' and not 'I do,' or 'have built it;' but 'I will build it.'"

"My lords[9]," quoth I, "Peter taught me to make this collation, saying, 'As in the people there was false prophets,' which were much in estimation afore Christ's coming, so 'shall there be false teachers now, and very many shall follow them.' And as for your future tense, I hope your grace," quod I, "will not thereby conclude[10] Christ's church not to have been before, but rather that there is no building in the church but by Christ's work only; for Paul and Apollos be but waterers."

"In good faith, master Bradford," quoth my lord of Chichester, "I am sorry to see you so little to mind the church."

"He taketh upon him, as they all do, to judge the church," quod my lord of York. "A man shall never come to certainty that doth as they do."

"My lords[9]," quoth I, "take me, beseech you, in good part. I speak simply what I think; and I desire reason to answer my objections: your affections and sorrows cannot be my[9] rules. If that you consider the end and cause of my con-

[6 'this one thing' 1570: not in 1561 or 1563.]
[7 'more sorry' 1561: 'sorry that' 1563.]
[8 So 1570: 'that the same. then if you now had them' 1561.]
[9 'lord,' 'by,' a misprint, 1561: 'lords,' 'be my,' 1563.]
[10 'exclude thereby' 1561: 'thereby conclude' 1563.]

demnation, I cannot think but that it should something move your honours. You know it well enough, for you heard it: no matter was laid against me, but what was gathered upon mine own confession. Because I denied transubstantiation, and the wicked to receive Christ's body in the sacrament, therefore I was condemned and excommunicate, but not of the church, although the pillars of the same, as they be taken, did it."

"No," quoth my lord of Chichester, "I heard say that the cause of your prisonment was, for that you exhorted the people to take the sword in the one hand, and the mattock in the other."

"I never meant any such thing, nor spake any thing in that sort, my lord," quoth I.

"Yea," quoth my lord of York, "you behaved yourself before the council so stoutly at the first, that you would defend the religion then; and therefore worthily were you punished."

"Your grace," quoth I, "did hear me answer my lord chancellor in that point. But put the case I had been so stout as they and your grace make it: was not the laws of the realm on my side then? Wherefore unjustly I was punished. Only transubstantiation, which was had on mine own confession, was the thing on which my lord chancellor proceeded."

"You deny the presence," quoth my lord of York.

"I do not," quoth I, "to the faith of the worthy receiver."

"Why," quoth he, "what is that than to say that Christ lieth not on the altar?"

"No, my lord," quoth I, "indeed I believe not such a presence."

"It seemeth," quoth my lord of Chichester, "that you have not read Chrysostom; for he proveth it[2]."

"Of truth, my lord," quoth I, "hitherto I have been kept well enough without books: howbeit this I remember of Chrysostom, that he saith that Christ[1] lieth upon the altar, as the seraphim with their tongs[1] do touch our lips with the coals of the altar in heaven[2]; which is an hyperbolical locution, as you know Chrysostom floweth with them."

[[1] 'saith that Christ,' 'with their tongs,' 1563: not in 1561.]
[[2] Μὴ ὅτι ἄρτος ἐστὶν ἴδῃς, μηδ' ὅτι οἶνός ἐστι νομίσῃς· οὐ γὰρ ὡς αἱ

"It is too evident," quoth my lord of York, "that you are gone too far: but let us come again to the church, out of the which you are excommunicated."

"I am not excommunicate out of Christ's church[3], my lord, although they which seem to be in the church, and of the church, have excommunicate me, as the poor blind man was (John ix.): I hope Christ receiveth me."

"You deceive yourself," quoth he: and here much was spoken of excommunication.

At the last I said: "My lord, I pray you bear with me that which I shall simply speak before you. Assuredly," quoth I, "as I think you did well to depart from the Romish church, so I think you have done wickedly to couple yourselves[4] to it again; for you can never prove it, which you call[4] the mother church, to be Christ's church."

"O master Bradford," quoth my lord of Chichester, "you were but a child when this matter began. I was a young man then coming from the university, [and] went with the world; but I tell you, it was always against my conscience[4]"

"I was but a child then," quoth I: "howbeit, as I told you, I think you have done evil: for now ye are come, and have brought others[5], to 'the wicked man which sitteth in the temple of God,' that is, in the church; for it cannot be understand of Mahomet[6], or any out of the church, but of such as bear rule in the church."

"See," quoth my lord of York, "how you build your faith upon such places of scripture as are most obscure, to deceive yourself, as though you were in the church, where you are not."

"Well, my lord," quoth I, "though I might by your

λοιπαὶ βρώσεις εἰς ἀφεδρῶνα χωρεῖ· ἄπαγε, μὴ τοῦτο νόει· ἀλλ' ὥσπερ κηρὸς πυρὶ προσομιλήσας οὐδὲν ἀπουσιάζει, οὐδὲν περισσεύει· οὕτω καὶ ὧδε νόμιζε συναναλίσκεσθαι τὰ μυστήρια τῇ τοῦ σώματος οὐσίᾳ. διὸ καὶ προσερχόμενοι, μὴ ὡς ἐξ ἀνθρώπου νομίσητε μεταλαμβάνειν τοῦ θείου σώματος, ἀλλ' ὡς ἐξ αὐτῶν τῶν σεραφὶμ τῇ λαβίδι τοῦ πυρός, ἥνπερ Ἡσαΐας εἶδε, τοῦ θείου σώματος μεταλαμβάνειν νομίζετε.... Chrysost. De Pœnit. Hom. ix. Op. II. 350, ed. Bened. Par. 1718—38.]

[3 'excommunicate out of Christ's church' 1563: not in 1561.]

[4 'us,' 'make,' 'stomach,' 1561: 'yourselves,' 'call,' 'conscience,' 1563.]

[5 'we are come' 1561: 'ye are come and have brought others' 1563.]

[6 'the Mahomet' 1561: 'Mahomet' 1563.]

fruits judge of you and others, yet will not I utterly exclude you[1] out of the church; for perchance you sin of ignorance. And if I were in your case, I think not," quoth I, "that I should not condemn him utterly that is of my faith in the sacrament, knowing, as you know, that at the least eight hundred years after Christ, as my lord of Duresme writeth, it was free to believe or not to believe transubstantiation[2]."

"This is a toy," quoth he, "that you have found out of your own brain; as though a man not believing as the church doth (that is, transubstantiation) were of the church."

"He is an heretic, and so none of the church," quoth my lord of Chichester, "that doth hold any doctrine against the definition of the church; as now you do hold against transubstantiation." And he brought forth Cyprian, "which was no heretic, though he believed re-baptizing of them which were baptized of heretics[3], because he held it before the church had defined it: whereas if he had holden it after, then had he been a heretic."

"Oh, my lord," quod I, "will you condemn to the devil any man that believeth truly the twelve articles of the faith (wherein I take the unity of Christ's church to consist), although in some points he believe not the definitions of that which you call the church? If I shall speak to you frankly, I doubt not but he that holdeth firmly[4] the articles of our belief, though in other things he dissent from your definitions, yet he shall be saved."

"Yea," quod they both, "this is your doctrine."

"No," quoth I, "it is Paul's, which saith that if they hold the foundation Christ, though they 'build upon him hay, straw, and stubble,' yet they shall be saved."

"Lord God!" quoth my lord of York, "how you delight to lean to so hard and dark places of scripture!"

[1 'condemn you for ever' 1561: 'exclude you' 1563.]

[2 Vide p. 511, note 5, above.]

[3 Meam sententiam plenissime exprimit epistola quæ ad Jubaianum collegam nostrum scripta est; hæreticos secundum evangelicam et apostolicam contestationem adversarios Christi et antichristos appellatos, quando ad ecclesiam venerint, unico ecclesiæ baptismo baptizandos esse, ut possint fieri de adversariis amici et de antichristis christiani.—Cypr. Concil. Carthag. Op. p. 243, Oxon. 1682: and vide annot. Fell. Episc. Oxon. in loco.]

[4 'sincerely' 1561: 'firmly' 1563.]

"Yea," quoth my lord of Chichester, "I will shew you how that Luther doth excommunicate Zuinglius for this matter:" and so he[5] read a place of Luther making for his purpose[6].

"My lord," quoth I, "what Luther writeth, as you much pass[7] not of, no more do[8] I in this case. My faith is not builded on[8] Luther, Zuinglius, or Œcolampadius, in this point: and indeed, to tell you truly, I never read any of their works in this matter. As for their persons, whatsoever their sayings were, yet do I think assuredly that they were and are God's children and saints with him."

"Well," quoth my lord of York, "you are out of the communion of the church."

"I am not," quoth I, "for it consisteth and is in faith."

"Lo," quoth he, "how you make your church invisible, that would have the communion of it to consist in faith."

"Yea, and like your grace," quoth I; "for to have communion with the church needeth not visibleness of it: communion consisteth, as I said, in faith, and not in exterior ceremonies: as appeareth both by Paul, which would have *unam fidem*, 'one faith;' and by Irenæus to Victor, for the observation of Easter, saying that *dissonantiam jejunii*, 'disagreeing of fasting,' should not *rumpere consonantiam fidei*[9], 'break the agreeing of faith[10]'"

"That same place," quoth my lord of Chichester, "hath often even wounded my conscience, because we dissevered ourselves from the see of Rome."

"Well," quoth I, "God forgive you; for I think you have done evil to bring England thither again. Your honours know I am plain; and therefore I beseech you bear with me."

[5 'so' 1560: 'and so he' 1563.]

[6 Vide Luth. Defens. verb. cœn. accip. comed. Op. VII. fol. 379-417, Witeberg. 1550-7. Luther observes: 'Deus novit, quod his crassis similitudinibus non studeam deformare Zuinglium, multo minus Œcolampadium. neque in ejusmodi verbis stylum in illos stringo, sed potius adversus Diabolum superbe et acerbe nobis illudentem, qui eos circumvenit et seduxit; ut animi mei contra ipsum explcam libidinem, in Dei honorem, et vicissim ei insultem.' . Ibid. fol. 384-5.]

[7 'Pass:' care.]

[8 'so do,' 'built of,' 1561: 'no more do,' 'builded on,' 1563.]

[9 . ἡ διαφωνία τῆς νηστείας τὴν ὁμόνοιαν τῆς πίστεως συνίστησι.— Iren. Frag. Ep. ad Victor. Op. I. 340, Venet. 1734.]

[10 The rendering of the Latin is in 1563, not in 1561.]

Here my lord of York took a book of paper of common places out of his bosom, and read a piece of St Augustine, *Contra epistolam Fundamenti*, how that there were many things that did hold St Augustine in the bosom of the church; "consent of people and nations, authority confirmed with miracles, nourished with hope, increased with charity, established with antiquity: besides this there holdeth me in the church," saith St Augustine still, "the succession of priests from Peter's seat until this present bishop: last of all, the very name of catholic[1] doth hold me," &c.[2] "Lo," quoth he, "how say you to this of St Augustine? Point me out your church thus."

"My lord," quoth I, "this of St Augustine maketh as much for me as for you: although I might answer that all these, if they had been so[3] firm as you make them, they might have been alleged against Christ and his apostles; for there was the law and ceremonies consented in by the whole[4] people, confirmed with miracles, antiquity, and continual succession of bishops from Aaron's time until that present."

"In good faith," quod my lord of Chichester, "master Bradford, you make too much of the state of the church before Christ's coming."

"Sir," quod I, "therein I do but as St Peter teacheth, 2 Pet. ii., and Paul very often. You would gladly have your church here very glorious, and as a most pleasant lady: but as Christ saith, *Beatus est quicunque non fuerit offensus per me;* so may his church say, 'Blessed are they that are not offended at me.'"

"Yea," quoth my lord[5], "you think none is of the church, but such as suffer persecution."

"What I think," quod I, "God knoweth: I pray your

[1 'catholic doctrine' 1561: 'catholic' 1563.]

[2 Tenet consensio populorum atque gentium: tenet auctoritas miraculis inchoata, spe nutrita, caritate aucta, vetustate firmata: tenet ab ipsa sede Petri apostoli, cui pascendas oves suas post resurrectionem Dominus commendavit, usque ad præsentem episcopatum successio sacerdotum: tenet postremo ipsum catholicæ nomen.—August. Cont. epist. Manich. quam vocant Fundamenti, 5. Op. VIII. col. 153, ed. Bened. Par. 1679-1700.]

[3 'alleged to be so' 1561: 'so' 1563.]

[4 'whole' 1563: not in 1561.]

[5 'quoth I my lord' 1561, a misprint.]

grace, judge me by my words and speaking; and mark what Paul saith, *Omnes qui volunt,* ' All that will live godly in Christ Jesu must suffer persecutions.' Sometime Christ's church hath rest here; but commonly," quoth I, " it is not so, and specially towards the end her form will be more unseemly."

" But what say you to St Augustine?" quoth he: "where is your church that hath the consent of people and nations?"

" Marry," quod I, " all people and nations that be God's people have consented with me, and I with them, in the doctrine of faith."

" Lo," quoth he, " how you go about to shift off all things."

" No, my lord," quoth I; "I mean simply, and so speak, God knoweth."

" St Augustine," quoth he, " doth here talk of succession, even from Peter's see."

" Yea, and like your grace," quoth I, " that see then was nothing so much corrupt as it is now."

" Well," quod he, " you always judge the church."

" No, my lord," quod I: " as Christ's sheep discern Christ's voice, but they judge it not[6]; so they discern the church, but not judge her."

" Yes, that you do," saith he.

" No, and like your grace," quoth I: " full well may a man doubt of the Romish church; for she obeyeth not Christ's voice, as Christ's true church doth."

" Wherein?" quod he.

" In Latin service," quoth I, " and robbeth the laity of Christ's cup in the sacrament; and in many other things, in which it committeth most horrible sacrilege[7]."

" Why," quoth my lord of Chichester, " Latin service was in England when the pope was gone."

" True," quoth I, " the[7] time was in England[7] when the pope was away, but not all popery, as in king Henry's days."

" Latin service," quoth my lord of York, " was appointed to be sung and had in the choir, where only were *clerici,* that is, such as understand Latin; the people sitting in the body of

[6 'judged not it' 1561: 'judge it not' 1563.]
[7 'and in. sacrilege', 'the,' 'in England,' 1563: not in 1561.]

the church, praying their own private prayers: and this," quoth he, "may well be yet seen by making of the chancel and choir, so as the people could not come in, or hear them."

"Yea, but, my lord," quoth I, "both in Chrysostom's time[1], and also in the Latin church in St Jerome's time, as he writeth in the preface, I trow, to the Galatians, all the church, saith he, *reboat Amen*[2]; that is, 'answereth[3] again mightily, Amen:' whereby we may see that the prayers were made so that[4] both the people heard them and understood them."

"You are to blame," quoth my lord of Chichester, "to say that the church robbeth the people of the cup."

"Well, my lord," quod I, "term[4] it as it[5] please you; all men know that the laity hath none of it."

"Indeed," quoth he[6], "I would wish the church would define again, that they might have it, for my part."

"If God make it free," quoth I, "who can define to make it bound[7]?"

"Well," quoth my lord of York, "master Bradford, we leese our[8] labour; for you seek to put away all things that be told you to your good: your church no man can know."

"Yes, that you may well," quoth I.

"I pray you, whereby?" said he.

"Forsooth, Chrysostom sheweth it *tantummodo per scripturas*[9], 'only by the scriptures:' and thus speaketh he very oftentimes together[9], as you well know," quod I.

[1 κοιναὶ καὶ παρὰ τοῦ ἱερέως καὶ παρ' αὐτῶν γίνονται αἱ εὐχαί· καὶ πάντες μίαν λέγουσιν εὐχήν. Ἐπ' αὐτῶν πάλιν τῶν φρικωδεστάτων μυστηρίων ἐπεύχεται ὁ ἱερεὺς τῷ λαῷ, ἐπεύχεται καὶ ὁ λαὸς τῷ ἱερεῖ.—Chrysost. In Epist. II. ad. Cor. Hom. XVIII. Op. X. 568, ed. Bened. Par. 1718-38.]

[2 Ubi sic ad similitudinem coelestis tonitrui *Amen* reboat?—Hieron. Comm. Lib. II. in Epist. ad Gal. Præf. Op. VII. col. 427-8, stud. Vallars. Veron. 1734-42.]

[3 So 1563: 'saith Amen, answering' 1561.]

[4 'that,' 'turn,' 1561: 'so that,' 'term,' 1563.]

[5 'as' 1561, 1563, 1570, 1576: 'as it' 1583.]

[6 'I,' 1561: a misprint for 'he.']

[7 So 1563: 'make free . make bound generally' 1561.]

[8 'but' 1561, 1563, 1570, 1576: 'our' 1583.]

[9 Nunc nullo modo cognoscitur,.. quæ sit vera ecclesia Christi, nisi tantummodo per scripturas.—Chrysost. Op. Imp. in Matt. Hom. xlix. ex cap. xxiv. Op. VI. p. cciv, ed. Bened. Par. 1718-38. The words

"Indeed," quod he, "that is of Chrysostom *in opere imperfecto*, which may be doubted of: the thing whereby the church may be known best is succession of bishops."

"No, my lord," quod I; "Lyra full well writeth upon Matthew, that *ecclesia non consistit in hominibus ratione potestatis secularis aut ecclesiasticæ, sed in hominibus in quibus est notitia vera et confessio fidei et veritatis*[10]: that is, 'The church consisteth not in men, by reason either of secular or temporal power; but in men endued with true knowledge, and confession of faith, and of verity[11].' And in Hilarius' time, you know, he writeth to Auxentius, that the church did rather *delitescere in cavernis*, than *eminere in primariis sedibus*[12]; that is, 'was hidden rather in caves and holes,' than 'did glister and shine in thrones of pre-eminence[11]'"

Here cometh one of their servants, and told them that my lord of Duresme tarried for them at master York's house: for indeed it was past twelve of the clock; upon a four hours they tarried with me. And after that their man was come, they put up their written books of common places, and said, they lamented my case; and so wishing me to read over a book "which did Dr Crome good," as my lord of Chichester said, and wishing me good in words, they went their ways, and I to my prison.

"nisi tantummodo per scripturas" occur again twice in the immediate context.—This Treatise is considered not to be by Chrysostom: see Cave, Hist. Liter. I. 312, Oxon. 1740-3. See also Goode, Rule of Faith, vol. II. p. 127—9, 439—41.]

[10 Bibl. cum Gloss. Ord. et Expos. N. de Lyra, Matt. cap. xvi. Pars V. fol. 52, Basil, 1502, where... 'ecclesia,' &c... 'potestatis, vel dignitatis ecclesiasticæ, vel secularis, quia multi principes et summi pontifices et alii inferiores inventi sunt apostatasse a fide: propter quod ecclesia consistit in illis personis in quibus,' &c.]

[11 The rendering of the Latin is in 1570, not in 1561.]

[12 Unum moneo, cavete antichristum: male enim vos parietum amor cepit, male ecclesiam Dei in tectis ædificiisque veneramini, male sub his pacis nomen ingeritis. An ne ambiguum est, in his antichristum esse sessurum? Montes mihi, et silvæ, et lacus, et carceres, et voragines sunt tutiores: in his enim prophetæ aut manentes aut demersi Dei Spiritu prophetabant.—Hilar. Lib. cont. Auxent. 12. Op. col. 1269, ed. Bened. Par. 1693.]

TALK BETWEEN MASTER BRADFORD AND TWO SPANISH FRIARS.

UPON Monday which was the twenty-fifth of February, about eight of the clock in the morning, which was an hour sooner than was appointed, there came to the Compter where I was in prison two Spanish friars, Alphonsus and the king's confessor, as they said, and with them two priests which were Englishmen, as I ween: and when the house was voided of other company, I was called down; and being come before them, a stool was pulled out, and I bidden sit down, which thing I did, after a sign of civility given to them.

Now thus sitting, beginneth the confessor to speak in Latin and ask in Latin (for all our talk was in Latin), whether I had not seen nor heard of one Alphonsus, that had written against heresies[1]?

And I answered that I did not know him.

"Well," quoth he, "this man," pointing to Alphonsus, "is he."

"Very good," quoth I.

After this he beginneth to tell me how that of love and charity, by the means of the earl of Derby, they come to me because I desired to confer with them.

And I answered that I never desired their coming, nor to confer with them or any other; "but," quoth I, "seeing you are come of charity, as you say, I cannot but thankfully acknowledge it; and as for conference, though I desire it not, yet," quoth I, "I will not refuse to talk with you, if you will."

Then began Alphonsus to tell me that it were requisite I did pray unto God, that I might follow the direction of God's Spirit, and as he should inspire me, not being addict to mine own self-will and wit.

Whereupon I made a prayer, and besought God to "direct all our wills, words, and works, as the wills, words, and works of his children for ever."

"Yea," quoth Alphonsus, "you must pray with your

[1 Alfons. de Castro Adv. Hær. Colon. 1539. Copy, British Museum.
This Romish divine died at Brussels, February 1558, having been appointed Archbishop of Compostella.]

heart; for if you speak but with tongue only, God will not give you his grace."

"Sir," quoth I, "'do not judge, lest you be judged.' You have heard my words: now charity would have you to leave the judgment of the heart to God."

"You must," quoth Alphonsus, "be as it were a neuter, and not wedded to your sentence: but as one standing in doubt, pray, and believe, and be ready to receive what God shall inspire; for," quoth he, "in vain laboureth our tongue to speak else."

"Sir," quoth I, "my sentence, if you mean it for religion, must not be in a doubting, or uncertain, as I thank God it is not even for that wherein I am condemned: I have no cause to doubt, but rather to be most certain of it; and therefore I pray God to confirm me more in it, for it is his truth. And therefore, because it is so certain and true that[2] it may abide the light, I dare be bold to have it looked on, and confer it with you, or any man: in respect whereof I am glad of your coming, and thank you for your coming; although, as I said, I desired not your coming, nor was willing of your coming, or could be content of it otherwise."

"Why," quod he, "what is the matter wherefor you were condemned? for we know not."

"Sir," quod I, "in prison have I been almost two years: I never transgressed any of the laws wherefor I might justly be punished: but now am I condemned, only[2] because I frankly confessed (whereof I repent not) my faith concerning the sacrament, being demanded in these two points; one that there is no transubstantiation, the other that the wicked do not receive Christ's body."

"Let us," quoth he, "look a little on the first. Do you not believe Christ's presence really and corporally in the form of bread?"

"No," quoth I, "I do believe that there Christ is present to the faith of the worthy receiver, as there is present bread and wine to the senses and outward man. As for any such presence of including and placing Christ, I believe not, nor dare not do."

"Why," quoth he, "I am sure you believe Christ's natural body is circumscriptible."

[2 'it is   that,' 'now am. . only,' 1563: not in 1561.]

And here he made much ado of the[1] two natures of Christ, how that the one is every where, and the other is in his proper place; demanding questions hereabout which I answered with *etiam*, that is, 'affirmatively,' because they were such as no wise man would have spent any such time about as he did; for I never heard of any that would have denied them.

Now then cometh he to this conclusion, (which I prayed him he would make, for else he had forgotten,) how that "because Christ's body was circumscriptible concerning the humanity in heaven, therefore it was so in the bread."

"This hangs not together," quod I; for to reason thus[1], Because you are here, *ergo* you are at Rome, is far[2] out of frame[2]. Even so reason you[1], 'Because Christ's body is in heaven, *ergo* it is in the sacrament under the form of bread:' no wise man will grant it," quoth I.

"Why," quoth he, "you will believe nothing but that which is expressly spoken in the scriptures."

"Yes, sir," quoth I, "I will believe whatsoever you shall by demonstrations out of the scriptures declare unto me."

"He is obstinate," quod Alphonsus[2] to his fellow. "But," quoth he to me, "is not God able to do it?"

"Yes, sir," quoth I; "but here the question is of God's will, and not of his power."

"Why," quoth he, "doth he not say plainly, 'This is my body'?"

"Yes," quod I; "and I deny it not but that it is so[3] to the faith of the worthy receiver."

"To faith?" quoth he, "how is that?"

"Forsooth, sir," quoth I, "as I have no tongue to express it, so I know you have no ears to hear and understand it; for faith seeth more than man can utter."

"Yea, but," quoth he, "I can tell all that I believe."

"You believe not much then," quoth I; "for if you believe the joys of heaven, and[4] believe no more thereof[3] than

[1 'the,' 'for to reason thus,' 'even so reason you,' 1563: not in 1561.]

[2 'it is,' 'France,' 'saith he,' 1561: 'is far,' 'frame,' 'quod Alphonsus,' 1563.]

[3 'so,' 'thereof,' 1563: not in 1561.]

[4 'if you' 1561: 'and' 1563.]

you can tell, you will not much desire to come thither: for as the mind is more capable and receivable than the mouth, so it conceiveth more than the tongue can express."

"Christ saith, it is his body," quoth he.

"And so say I, after a certain manner," quoth I.

"After a certain manner?" quoth he; "that is, after another manner than it is in heaven."

"St Augustine," quoth I, "telleth it more plainly, that it is Christ's body after the same manner that[5] circumcision was the covenant of God, and the sacrament of faith is faith; or, to make it more plain, as baptism and the water of baptism is regeneration[6]."

"Very well said," quoth he: "baptism and the water thereof is a sacrament of God's grace and Spirit in the water, cleansing the baptized[7]."

"No, sir," quoth I, "away with your inclosing: but this I grant, that after[8] the same sort Christ's body is in the bread, on which sort the grace and Spirit of God is in the water."

"In the water," quod he, "is God's grace, by signification."

"So is the body in the bread," quoth I, "in the sacrament."

"You are much deceived," quoth he, "in that you[9] make no difference between the sacraments that be standers, and the sacraments that are *transeuntes*, 'transitory[5],' and passers-by: as for example, the sacrament of orders, which you deny,

[5 'that,' 'transitory,' 1563: not in 1561.]

[6 Sicut secundum quemdam modum sacramentum corporis Christi corpus Christi est, sacramentum sanguinis Christi sanguis Christi est, ita sacramentum fidei fides est. Ac per hoc cum respondetur parvulus credere, qui fidei nondum habet affectum, respondetur fidem habere propter fidei sacramentum, et convertere se ad Deum propter conversionis sacramentum, quia et ipsa responsio ad celebrationem pertinet sacramenti.—August. Epist. xcviii. 9. Ad Bonifac. Op. II. col. 267-8, ed. Bened. Par. 1679—1700.]

[7 'closing the baptism' 1561: 'cleansing the baptized' 1563. 'Baptismi lavacrum sacramentum fit divinæ gratiæ, et Spiritus in unda inclusi, quo perpurgantur hi qui baptismo abluuntur.'—Fox. Rerum in eccles. gestar. comm. p. 500, Basil. 1559.]

[8 'on' 1561: 'but this I grant that after' 1563.]

[9 'that' 1561: 'in that you,' 1563.]

though St Augustine affirm it[1], is a[2] standard, although the ceremony be past. But in baptism, so soon as the body is washen, the water ceaseth to be a sacrament."

"True, good sir," quoth I, "and so it is in the Lord's supper: no longer than it is in use, is it Christ's sacrament."

Here was master Alphonsus wonderfully chafed, and spake, as often he had done before, so that the whole house did ring again with an echo. He hath a great name of learning; but surely he hath little patience. If I had been any thing hot, one house could not have kept us both. At the length he cometh to this[3] point, that I could not find in the scripture baptism and the Lord's supper to have any like similitude together. And here, Lord God! what array he made, how that we would receive nothing but scripture, and yet were[3] able to prove nothing by the scripture.

"Father," quoth I, (for so I called him, God forgive me if I did amiss,) "be patient, and you shall see that by the scripture I will find baptism and the Lord's supper coupled together."

"No," quoth he, "that canst thou never do: let me see one text of it." And a great ado he made.

1 Cor. xii.

At the length, "Sir," quoth I, "Paul saith that as 'we are baptized into one body,' so we are *potati in uno Spiritu*, 'we have drunken of one Spirit,' meaning it of the cup in the Lord's supper."

"Paul hath no such words," quod he.

"Yes, that he hath," quoth I.

"I trow he hath not," quoth the king's confessor.

"Give me a Testament," quoth I, "and I will shew it to you."

So a priest that sat by them gave me his Testament, and I shewed them the plain text. Here was now looking one upon another. Finally this simple shift was found, that Paul spake not of the sacrament.

[[1] Utrumque enim sacramentum est, et quadam consecratione utrumque homini datur, illud cum baptizatur, istud cum ordinatur: ideoque in catholica utrumque non licet iterari.—August. Cont. Epist. Parmenian. Lib. II. cap. xiii. Op. IX. col. 44, ed. Bened. Par. 1679-1700. See Bp. Jewel on this passage in the Defence of the Apology of the Church of Eng., Part II. chap. xi. Divis. 2.]

[[2] 'a' 1563: not in 1561.]

[[3] 'that,' 'we are,' 1561: 'this,' 'were,' 1563.]

"Well, sir," quoth I, "though the text be plain, yet I ween the fathers do expound it so: especially, except my memory fail me, Chrysostom[4] doth it."

Here I seeing them blank, I began to tell them how I had been handled in prison, without book, paper, pen, ink, and how unjustly I had been handled; and prayed them that as they told me their coming was to do me good, so they would do it, and not to do me hurt: which thing they much marked not, because of the foil they had, which I would have suppressed.

Alphonsus therefore, which had the Testament in his hand, and turned over leaf by leaf, at the length he cometh to the eleventh [of the first epistle] to the Corinthians, and there read how that he was guilty which made no difference of the Lord's body.

"Yea, sir," quoth I, "but therewith he saith, 'He that eateth of the bread;' calling it bread still, and that after consecration, as you call it: and so [I] brought forth the sentence of the tenth [of the first epistle] to the Corinthians, 'The bread which we break,'" &c.

"O," quoth he, "how ignorant are you, which know not that things retain the names they had before[5], after their conversion, as Moses' rod!"

And here they called for a Bible; and so [he] was almost a quarter of an hour before he could find out the place, finding fault at the Bible because it was Vatable's Bible[6]. At the length when he had found it, Lord God, how he triumphed!

But I cooled the heat forthwith; for, "Sir," quoth I, "there is mention made of the conversion, as well as that[7] the same appeared to the sense: but," quoth I, "here you cannot find it so. Find me one word how the bread is converted, and I will then say, you bring some matter that maketh for you."

At these words he was troubled; and at the length he said, how that I hanged on mine own sense.

[4 Vide p. 88, note 4, above.]

[5 'before' 1563: not in 1561.]

[6 Biblia veteris ac novi Testamenti summa fide ac studio singulari, cum aliorum doctissimorum interpretum, tum vero in primis S. Pagnini ac Fr. Vatabli opera... ex Hebræis Græcisque fontibus expressa, et latinitate donata.... Basil. per Thom. Guarin. 1564.]

[7 'that' 1563: not in 1561.]

"No," quoth I, "that do I not; for I will bring you forth, for eight hundred years after Christ, the fathers of the church to confirm this which I spake."

"No," quoth he, "you have the church against you."

"I have not," quoth I, "Christ's church against me."

"Yes, that you have," saith he; and so asked me, what the church was.

"Marry," quoth I, "Christ's wife, the chair and seat of verity."

"Is she visible?" quoth he.

"Yea, that she is," quoth I, "if that you will put on the spectacles of God's word to look on her."

"This church," quoth he, "hath defined the contrary; and that will I prove by all the good fathers continually from Christ's ascension, even for fifteen hundred years at the least, continually."

"What will you prove so," quoth I, "transubstantiation?"

"Yea," quoth he, "that the bread is turned into Christ's body."

"You speak more than you can do," quod I.

"That do I not," quod he.

"Then," quod I, "I will give place."

"Will you believe?" quod he.

"Belief," quoth I, "is God's gift; therefore cannot I promise: but I tell you," quod I, "that I will give place; and I hope I[1] shall believe God's truth always, so good is he to me in Christ my Saviour[1]."

Here he found a great fault with me, that I would not discern betwixt *habitum* and *actum*; as though *actus*, which he called 'credulity,' had been in our power. But this he let pass, and cometh again, asking me, if he could prove it as he said, whether that I would give place?

"Yea," quoth I, "that I will."

Here was called for paper, pen, and ink, to write: and then I said, "What and if that I prove it you, continually for eight hundred years after Christ at the least, the substance of bread to remain in the sacrament, by the testimony of the fathers; what will you do?" quod I.

"I will give place," quod he. With this, paper came in.

"Then," said I, "write you how that you will give place,

[[1] 'I,' 'to me in Christ my Saviour,' 1563: not in 1561.]

if I so prove; and I will write that I will give place, if you so prove: because you are the ancient, you shall have the pre-eminence."

Lord God, how angry he was now, and said that he came not to learn at me; and so said, "Here is two witnesses," meaning it of the two priests; "and they be sufficient." And so hereabout we had much ado, to none effect but to a plain scolding, if I had not given place to the furor of Alphonsus; for he was very testy and hasty: and here he dispraised Bucer and all that praised him, with much other talk.

At the length the king's[2] confessor asked me of the second question, what it was.

"Sir," quoth I, "that the wicked men receive not Christ's body in the sacrament; as St Augustine speaketh of Judas, that he received *panem Domini* [the bread of the Lord,] but not *panem Dominum*[3] [the bread the Lord.]"

"St Augustine saith not so," quoth Alphonsus.

"Yes, that doth he," quoth I.

And so they rose up, and talked no more of that matter; but asked me how they should get me all the fathers and old authors, that prove and affirm the bread to be turned into Christ's body.

"Sir," quoth I, "you may soon do it: howbeit, because you shall not trouble yourself, if I may have my books, I need no more but notes of the places."

Thus they went their ways: how they brooked my talk, I cannot tell; for they bade me not farewell.

After they were gone, cometh one of the priests, and willed me "not to be so obstinate."

"Sir," quoth I, "be not you so wavering: in all the scripture cannot you find me, *non est panis*, [it is not bread.]"

"Yes, that I can," quoth he, "in five places."

"Then will I eat your book," quoth I.

So the book was opened, but no place found; and he went his way smiling. God help us.

[2 'king's' 1563: not in 1561.]
[3 Vide p. 512, note 5, above.]

TALK BETWEEN MASTER BRADFORD AND DR WESTON AND OTHERS[1].

Upon the twenty-first of March, by the means of one of the earl of Derby his men, left behind my lord his master for the soliciting of my cause, as he said to me, there came to the Compter to dinner one master Collier, once warden of Manchester, and the said servant of the earl of Derby; of whom I learned that master doctor Weston, dean of Westminster, would be with him in the afternoon, about two of the clock or before. At dinner therefore (when the said warden did discommend king Edward, and went about to set forth the authority of the pope, which I withstood, defending the king's faith, that it was catholic, and that the authority of the bishop of Rome his supremacy was usurped, bringing forth the testimony of Gregory, which affirmeth[2] the name of supreme head to be a title of the forerunner to antichrist[3],) a woman prisoner was brought in: whereupon I took occasion to rise from the table, and so went to my prison-chamber to beg of God grace and help therein, continuing there still until I was called down to speak with master Weston.

So soon as I came into the hall, master Weston very gently took me by the hand, and asked me how I did, with such other talk. At the length he willed avoidance of the chamber: so they all went out save master Weston himself, master Collier, the earl of Derby his servant, the subdean of Westminster, the keeper master Clayden, and the parson of the church where the Compter is.

Now then he beginneth to tell me how that he was often minded to have come unto me, being thereto desired of the earl of Derby: "and," quod he, "after that I perceived by

[1 This conference with Weston on March 21, 1555, is omitted in the first English edition of Foxe's Acts, &c. 1563, but is supplied in 1570 and the after editions from the 'Examinations and conferences' of Bradford, printed by Griffith, 1561. The conference with Weston on March 28, p. 544—9, is also misplaced in the Acts, &c. 1563, which is corrected in the subsequent impressions of that work.]

[2 'calleth' 1561: 'affirmeth' 1570.]

[3 Ego . fidenter dico quia quisquis se universalem sacerdotem vocat, vel vocari desiderat, in elatione sua antichristum præcurrit, quia superbiendo se ceteris præponit.—Gregor. Magni Papæ I. Epist. Lib. vii. Indict. xv. Ad Mauric. August. Epist. xxxiii. Op. II. col. 881 ed. Bened. Par. 1705.]

his man, that you could be contented rather to speak with me than any others, I could not but come to do you good, if I can; for hurt you[4], be sure, I will not."

"Sir," quoth I, "when I perceived by the report of my lord's servant, that you did bear me good-will, more (as he said) than any other of your sort, I told him then, that therefore I could be better content and more willing to talk with you, if you should come unto me. This did I say," quoth I; "otherwise I desired not your coming."

"Well," quoth he, "now I am come to talk with you: but before we shall enter into any talk, certain principles we must agree upon, which shall be this day's work. First," quoth he, "I shall desire you to put away all vain-glory, and not to hold any thing for the praise of the world."

"Sir," quoth I, "Augustine maketh that indeed a piece of the definition of an heretic[5]; which if I cannot put away clean, (for I think there will a spice of it remain in us, as long as this flesh liveth,) yet I promise you, by the grace of God, that I purpose not to yield to it. God I hope will never suffer it to bear rule in them that strive thereagainst, and desire all the dregs of it utterly to be[6] driven out of us."

"I am glad," quoth he, "to hear you say so, although indeed," quoth he, "I think you do not so much esteem it as others do. Secondly I would desire you that you will put away singularity in your judgment and opinions."

"Sir," quod I, "God forbid that I should stick to any singularity or private judgment in God's religion. Hitherto I have not desired it, neither do, nor mind at any time to hold any other doctrine than is public and catholic; understanding catholic as good men do, according to God's word."

"Very well," quod he, "this is a good day's work; I hope to do you good: and therefore now, thirdly, I shall pray you to write me *capita* [the heads] of those things whereupon you stand in the sacrament, and to send them to me betwixt this and Wednesday next; until which time, yea, until I come to you again, be assured that you are without

[4 'you' 1570: not in 1561.]
[5 hæreticus est, ut mea fert opinio, qui alicujus temporalis commodi, et maxime gloriæ principatusque sui gratia, falsas ac novas opiniones vel gignit vel sequitur. — August. lib. de Util. Credend. cap. i. Op. VIII. col. 45, ed. Bened. Par. 1679-1700.]
[6 'to be' 1570: not in 1561.]

all peril of death. Of my fidelity I warrant you: therefore away with all dubitations, &c."

"Sir," quod I, "I will write to you the grounds I lean to in this matter. As for death, if it come, welcome be it: this which you require of me shall be no great let to me therein."

"You know," saith he, "that St Augustine was a Manichean, yet was he converted at the length: so I have good hope of you."

"Sir," quod I, "because I will not flatter you, I would you should flatly know that I am even settled in the religion wherefor I am condemned."

"Yea, but," quod he, "if it be not the truth, and if you see evident matter to the contrary, will not you then give place?"

"God forbid," quod I, "but that I should always give place to the truth."

"I would have you to pray so," quod he.

"So I do," quoth I, "and that he will more and more confirm me in it; as I thank God he hath done and doth."

"Yea, but," quoth he, "pray with a condition, if you be in it."

"No, sir," quod I, "I cannot pray so, because I am settled and assured of his truth."

"Well," quoth he, "as the learned bishop answered St Augustine's mother, that though he was obstinate, yet the tears of such a mother could not but win her son[1]; so," quod he, "I hope your prayers" (for mine eyes did shew that I had wept in prayer) "cannot but be heard of God, though not as you would, yet as best shall please God. Do you not," quod he, "remember the history hereof?"

"Yes, sir," quoth I, "I think it to be of St Ambrose[2]."

"No," quod he, "that it is not." And here he would have laid a wager, and began to triumph, saying, "As you are overseen herein, so you are in the other things."

[1 Vade, inquit, a me; ita vivas: fieri non potest, ut filius istarum lacrymarum pereat.—August. Confess. Lib. III. cap. xii. Op. I. col. 96.]

[2 The answer to Monica in the last note is stated by Augustine *in loco* to have been given "per sacerdotem tuum, quemdam episcopum nutritum in ecclesia, et exercitatum in libris tuis:" but Ambrose was the means of turning Augustine from Manichæism.—August. Confess. Lib. v. cap. xiii. xiv. Op. I. col. 117, 118; and De Util. Credend. cap. viii. Op. VIII. col. 58.]

"Well, sir," quoth I, "I will not contend with you for the name. This, I remember, St Augustine writeth in his Confessions."

After this talk he began to tell how that the people were by me procured to withstand the queen; but I bade him hang me up as a traitor and a thief, if ever I encouraged any to rebellion: which thing my keeper, and others that were there of the priests, affirmed on my behalf. So much talk there was *ad Ephesios*[3] [to the Ephesians], how he had saved men going in the cart to be hanged, and[4] such like. The end was this, that I should send unto him *capita doctrinæ* [the heads of the doctrine] of the supper; and after Wednesday he would come unto me again.

And thus departed he, after that he had drunken to me in beer and wine. I omit here talk of Oxford, of books of German writers, of the fear of death, and such other talk, which are to no purpose.

DISPUTATION OR TALK BETWEEN MASTER BRADFORD AND DR PENDLETON.

UPON the 28th of March came to the Compter doctor Pendleton, and with him master Collier, once warden of Manchester, and Stephen Beiche. After salutations master Pendleton began to speak to me, that he was sorry for my trouble: "and further," quod he, "after that I did know you could be content to talk with me, I made the more speed, being as ready to do you the good and pleasure that I can, as you would wish," &c.

"Sir," quod I, "the manner how I was content to speak with you was on this sort: master Beiche was often in hand with me whom he should bring unto me, and named you amongst other; and," quod I, "I remember that I said I had rather speak with you than with any of all other. Now the cause I so would I will briefly tell you. I remember that once you were, as far as a man might judge, of the religion that I am of at this present; and I remember that you have set forth the same earnestly. Gladly therefore would I learn of you, what thing it was that moved your conscience to alter;

[3 See note I.]   [4 'and' 1570: not in 1561.]

and gladly would I see what thing it is or was that you have seen sithen, which you saw not before."

Here master Pendleton was something abashed, as appeareth by his fumbling in his speech. "Master Bradford," quod he, "I do not know wherefor you are condemned."

"Marry," quod I, "transubstantiation is the thing whereof I am condemned, and also the denial of wicked men to receive Christ's body: wherein I would desire you to shew me what reasons, which before you knew not, did move your conscience to alter; for once, as I said, you were as I am in religion."

Here again master Pendleton, half amazed, began to excuse himself, if it would have been, as though he had not denied fully transubstantiation in deed, "although the word," quod he, "I said was not in scripture:" and so he made an endless tale of the thing that moved him to alter. As far as I could perceive, it was because he had looked too much, and given too much diligence and estimation to Luther and Melancthon. "But," quod he, "I will gather to you the places, and send them." And here he desired me that he might see a copy of that which I had sent master Weston; the which I did promise him.

Pendleton belike would study out the reasons that moved him to alter; for he had none ready to shew.
[Foxe, Acts, &c. 1570.]

This is a sum of the effectual talk we had; besides which talk we had a reasoning a little, whether evil men did receive Christ's body; I no, and he yea.

I said, "they received not the Spirit, *ergo* not the body; for it is no carcass," quoth I. Hereto I brought out St Augustine, how Judas received *panem Domini*, [the bread of the Lord,] and not *panem Dominum*[1], [the bread the Lord;] and[2] how that he must be in *corpore Christi*, [in Christ's body,] that must receive *corpus Christi*[3], [the body of Christ:] which he went about to put away with *idem*, and not *ad idem*, out of St Jerome[4]; and how that "*in corpore Christi*[3], [in the body of Christ,] was to be understand of all that be in the visible church, although they be not in the invisible church with God:" which I denied to be St Augustine's meaning, and said also that St Jerome's allegations[4] could not make for that purpose.

[1 Vide p. 512, note 5, above.]
[2 'and' 1563: not in 1561.]
[3 Vide p. 91, note 7, above.]
[4 Vide August. Cont. Lit. Petil. Lib. II. cap. xlvii. Op. IX. col. 246,

Again we had talk of transubstantiation: he bringeth forth Cyprian, *Panis quem dedit Dominus natura mutatus*[5] [The bread which the Lord gave, changed in nature.]

And I expounded *natura* not for the substance: "as," quod I, "the nature of an herb is not the substance of it, so the bread changed in nature is not to be taken for changed in substance; for now it is ordained, not for the food of the body simply, but rather for the food of the soul." And here I brought forth Gelasius[6], who he said was a pope.

"Yea, marry," quod I; "but his faith is my faith," quod I, "for the sacrament, if you would receive it."

From this talk we went to talk whether *accidentia* were *res*, or no. "If they be properly *res*," quod I, "then be they substance; and if they be substance, in that we must have *terrestrem rem*, 'an earthly substance,' in the sacrament, as Irenæus saith[7]; then must we not deny bread," quod I.

But he said that colour was the earthly thing, and called it "an accidental substance:" and so hereabouts we had much babbling to none effect.

I omit the talk we had of my lord of Canterbury, of Peter Martyr's book, of his[8] letter laid to my charge when I[9] was condemned, with other talk more[10] of the church, whether *Dic ecclesiæ*, &c. [Tell it unto the church] was spoken[11] of the universal church, or of a particular church, which at the length he granted; of vain-glory, which he willed me to beware of at his coming forth of the Compter; and such like talk.

A little before his departing I said this: "Master doctor,"

'ipsa [mensa] utrique fuit una, sed non utrique valuit ad unum;' and Hieron. Comm. in Mal. cap. I. et cap. II. Op. VI. col. 949—65, stud. Vallars. Veron. 1734—42: and see Abp. Cranmer, Works, I. p. 57—8, 223—5, Parker. Soc.]

[5 Panis iste quem Dominus discipulis porrigebat, non effigie sed natura mutatus, omnipotentia verbi factus est caro.—Arnold. Abbat. Bonæ-vall. De cœn. Dom. in Cypr. Op. Append. p. 40, Oxon. 1682. Arnoldus flourished A.D. 1162. See Bp Jewel, Reply to Harding, Art. X. div. ii. Parker Soc. p. 565, on the passage in question.]

[6 ... esse non desinit substantia vel natura panis et vini.—Gelas. Episc. Rom. adv. Eutych. et Nestor. in Mag. Biblioth. Vet. Patr. IV. I. 423, Paris. 1634: also in Routh, Script. Eccl. Opusc. II. 139, Oxon. 1840.]

[7 Vide p. 87, note 5, above.]
[8 i. e. Pendleton's. See before, p. 487.]
[9 'he' 1561, a misprint for 'I.']
[10 'with other talk more' 1570: not in 1561.]
[11 'spoken' 1563: not in 1561.]

quod I, "as I said to master Weston the last day, so say I unto you again, that I am the same man in religion against transubstantiation still, which I was when I came into prison; for," quod I, "hitherto I have seen nothing in any point to infirm[1] me."

At which words he was something moved, and said that "that was not catholic."

"Yes," quod I, "and I trust so to prove it even by the testimony of the catholic fathers until *concilium Lateranense*[2], and thereabouts."

The keeper, master Clayden, desired him to tarry dinner; which thing he denied, because [he] had elsewhere promised: and so went his way, saying that he would come oftener to me.

God our Father be with us all, and give us the Spirit of his truth for ever. Amen.

In the afternoon, about five of the clock, cometh master Weston, which sent word to the keeper that he would have been with me by two of the clock. Now when I was come down out of my prison-chamber unto him, he very gently saluted me, desired the company every man to depart; and so sat down, and I beside him. And after that he had thanked me for my writing unto him, he pulled out of his bosom the same writing which I had sent him. The writing is this that followeth[3]:

'CERTAIN REASONS AGAINST TRANSUBSTANTIATION, GATHERED BY JOHN BRADFORD, AND GIVEN TO DOCTOR WESTON AND OTHERS.

'1. "THAT which is former," saith Tertullian, "is true: that which is later is false[4]." But the doctrine of transub-

[1 'Infirm:' weaken.]

[2 See p. 511, note 5, above; and note 5 in the next page.]

[3 So 1563. 'The copy whereof in English (for I did write it in Latin) shall immediately follow this communication' 1561. The paper on transubstantiation does not however appear in the 'Examinations,' &c. of Bradford, 1561: it is therefore reprinted above from the first English edition of the Acts, &c. of Foxe, 1563. There is an early transcript of this document in MS. 1. 2. 8. (no. 12.) Emman. Coll. Cambridge. An abstract of it is given in the Latin edition of Foxe, Acts, &c. *Rerum in ecclesia gestarum commentarii*, Basil. 1559.]

[4 Quo peræque adversus universas hæreses jam hinc præjudi-

stantiation is a late doctrine; for it was not defined generally afore the council of Lateran, about 1215 years after Christ's coming, under pope Innocentius, the third of that name[5]:" for before that time it was free for all men to believe it, or not believe it, as the bishop of Duresme doth witness in his book of the presence of Christ in his supper lately put forth[6]. *Ergo* the doctrine of transubstantiation is false.

'2. That the words of Christ's supper be figurative, the circumstances of the scripture, the analogy or proportion of the sacraments, and the sentences of all the holy fathers, which were and did write for the space of one thousand years after Christ's ascension, do teach. Whereupon it followeth that there is no transubstantiation.

'3. That the Lord gave to his disciples bread, and called it his "body," the very scriptures do witness. For he gave that, and called it his "body," which he took in his hands, whereon he gave thanks, which also he brake, and gave to his disciples; that is to say, bread: as the fathers Irenæus, Tertullian, Origen, Cyprian, Epiphanius, Augustine[7], and all the residue which are of antiquity, do affirm. But inasmuch as the substance of bread and wine is another thing than the substance of the body and blood of Christ, it plainly appeareth that there is no transubstantiation.

'4. The bread is no more transubstantiate than the wine: but that the wine is not transubstantiate, St Matthew and St Mark do teach us; for they witness that Christ said that he would "drink no more of the fruit of the vine;" which was not blood, but wine: and therefore it followeth that there

catum sit, id esse verum quodcumque primum; id esse adulterum quodcumque posterius.—Tertull. Adv. Prax. cap. ii. Op. 206-7, Lut. Par. 1675.]

[5 . idem ipse sacerdos et sacrificium Jesus Christus, cujus corpus et sanguis in sacramento altaris sub speciebus panis et vini veraciter continentur, transubstantiatis pane in corpus et vino in sanguinem potestate divina, ut ad perficiendum mysterium unitatis accipiamus ipsi de suo quod accepit ipse de nostro.—Innocent. III. Concil. Lat. Decr. De Trin. i. Op. I. 461, Col. 1575. See also Concil. Lateran. IV. in Concil. stud. Labb. et Cossart. XI. 1. col. 143, Lut. Par. 1671-2; and Corp. Jur. Canon. Decretal. Greg. IX. Lib. 1. De Summ. Trin. et Fid. Cath. Tit. i. cap. i. p. 460, Paris. 1618.]

[6 See p. 511, note 5, above.]

[7 See note F.]

is no transubstantiation. Chrysostom upon Matthew[1], and St Cyprian[2], do confirm this reason.

'5. As the bread in the Lord's supper is Christ's natural body, so is it his mystical body; for the same Spirit that spake of it, "This is my body," did say also, " For we many are one bread, one body," &c. But now it is not the mystical body by transubstantiation: and therefore it is not his natural body by transubstantiation.

'6. The words spoken over the cup in St Luke and St Paul are not so mighty and effectual as to transubstantiate it; for then it, or that which is in it, should be transubstantiate into the new Testament. Therefore the words spoken over the bread are not so mighty as to make transubstantiation.

'7. All that doctrine which agreeth with those churches which be apostolic mother churches, or original churches, is to be counted for truth, in that it holdeth that which these churches received of the apostles, the apostles of Christ, Christ of God. But it is manifest that the doctrine taught at this present of the church of Rome, concerning transubstantiation, doth not agree with the apostolic and mother churches in Greece, of Corinthus, of Philippos, Colossia, Thessalonica, Ephesus, which never taught transubstantiation: yea, it agreeth not with the doctrine of the church of Rome taught in time past; for Gelasius the pope, setting forth the doctrine which that see did then hold, doth manifestly confute the error of transubstantiation[3], and reproveth them of sacrilege, which divide the mystery, and keep from the laity the cup[4]. Therefore the doctrine of transubstantiation agreeth not with the truth.'

[1 καὶ τίνος ἕνεκεν οὐχ ὕδωρ ἔπιεν ἀναστάς, ἀλλ' οἶνον; ἄλλην αἵρεσιν πονηρὰν πρόρριζον ἀνασπῶν. ἐπειδὴ γάρ τινές εἰσιν ἐν τοῖς μυστηρίοις ὕδατι κεχρημένοι, δεικνὺς ὅτι ἡνίκα τὰ μυστήρια παρέδωκεν οἶνον παρέδωκε, καὶ ἡνίκα ἀναστὰς χωρὶς μυστηρίων ψιλὴν τράπεζαν παρετίθετο, οἴνῳ ἐκέχρητο ἐκ τοῦ γεννήματός, φησι, τῆς ἀμπέλου. ἄμπελος δὲ οἶνον, οὐχ ὕδωρ, γεννᾷ.—Chrysost. In Matt. Hom. LXXXII. Op. VII. 784, ed. Bened. Par. 1718-38.]

[2 'Dico vobis, non bibam a modo ex ista creatura vitis, usque in diem illum, quo vobiscum bibam novum vinum in regno Patris mei.' Qua in parte invenimus calicem mixtum fuisse quem Dominus obtulit, et vinum fuisse quod sanguinem suum dixit. Unde apparet sanguinem Christi non offerri, si desit vinum calici.—Cypr. Epist. lxiii. ad Cæcil. Op. 152, Oxon. 1682.] [3 See p. 543, note 6, above.]

[4 Comperimus autem, quod quidam sumpta tantummodo corporis sacri portione a calice sacri cruoris abstineant. Qui proculdubio (quoniam nescio qua superstitione docentur obstringi) aut integra sacra-

This is the writing which Weston pulled out of his bosom[5]; and before he began to read it, he shewed me that he asked of my conversation at Cambridge sithen his last[6] being with me. "And," quod he, "master Bradford, because you are a man not given to the glory of this world, I will speak it before your face: your life I have learned was such there always, as all men, even the greatest enemies you have, cannot but praise you and it; and therefore I love you," quod he, "much better than ever I did. Now," quod he, "I will read over your arguments, and so we will confer them. Such they are, that a man may well perceive you stand of conscience; and therefore I am glad, and the more ready to pity you."

So he began to read the first, and there began to tell how that, "though the word transubstantiation began but lately, yet the thing," quod he, "always[7] was and hath been sithen Christ's institution."

And I told him that "I did not contend or hang upon the word only, but upon the thing, which," quod I, "is as new as the word."

Then went he to the second, and there brought out St Augustine, how that if an evil man, going to the devil, did make his will, "his son and heir would not say his father did lie in it[8]," or speak tropically: "much more Christ," quod he, "going to God, did never lie, nor use any figurative speech in his last will and testament. Do you not remember this place of St Augustine?" quod he.

"Yes, sir," quod I; "but I remember not that St Augustine hath those words *tropice* or *figurative*, that is, 'figuratively spoken[9],' as you rehearse; for a man may speak a thing figuratively and lie not, as Christ did in his last supper.

menta percipiant, aut ab integris arceantur; quia divisio unius ejusdemque mysterii sine grandi sacrilegio non potest provenire.—Gelas. in Corp. Jur. Canon. Decret. Gratian. Decr. Tert. Pars, De Consecr. Dist. ii. can. 12. p. 417, Paris. 1618.]

[5 The last eleven words are in 1563, not in 1561.]
[6 'last' 1563: not in 1561.] [7 'always' 1563: not in 1561.]
[8 Puer dicit, Credatur patri meo, quia moriens mentiri non potuit.—August. Serm. CCCLV. (al. De diversis XLIX.) Op. V col. 1382, ed. Bened. Par. 1679-1700.]
[9 St Augustine expressly says, 'Quidquid autem figurate fit aut dicitur, non est mendacium.'—Id. De mendac. cap. v. Op. VI. col. 423: and vide Cont. mendac. ad Consent. cap. x. Op. VI. col. 460-2.]

After this he went to the third, and brought forth Cyprian, how that the nature of the bread is turned into flesh[1]. Here saith he, that my lord of Canterbury " expoundeth 'nature' for 'quality,' by Gelasius[2]; the which interpretation serveth for the answer of your third argument, that Christ called bread his body; that is, the quality, form, and appearance of bread. And further," quod he, " the scripture is wont to call things as they aver, by the same names which they had before[3], as Simon the leper, not which was so presently, but because he had been so."

"Sir," quod I, " Cyprian wrote before Gelasius: therefore Cyprian must not expound Gelasius, but Gelasius Cyprian: and so they both teach that bread remaineth still. As for things having still the names they had, maketh nothing to answer this, except you could shew that this now were not bread, as easily as[3] a man might have known and seen then Simon to have been healed and clean from his leprosy[4]."

After this he went to the fourth, of the cup, the which he did not fully read, but digressed into a long talk of Cyprian's epistles *De Aquariis*[5]; also of St Augustine expounding the breaking of bread by Christ to his two disciples going to Emmaus, to be the sacrament[6], with such other talk to no certain purpose: and therefore I prayed him, that inasmuch as I had written to him the reasons that stablished[7] my faith against transubstantiation, so he would do the like to me, that is, answer mine by writing, and shew me more reasons in writing to confirm transubstantiation: which he promised me to do, and said that he would send or bring it to me again within three days.

And so when he had overly[8] read my arguments, and

[1 See p. 543, note 5, above.]

[2 See the passage from Gelasius in p. 543, note 6, above: and see Abp. Cranmer on the passage in the pseudo-Cyprian referred to in the last note, Defence of the sacrament, II. xi. Works, I. 308, Parker Soc.]

[3 'which they had before,' 'as,' 1563: not in 1561.]

[4 Compare the Sermon on the Lord's supper, p. 86 above.]

[5 Cypr. Epist. lxiii. ad Cæcil. Op. 148-57, Oxon. 1682: and vide annot. Fell. Episc. Oxon. in Epist.]

[6 ..quia hospitalitatem sectati sunt, eum quem in ipsa expositione scripturarum non cognoverant, in panis fractione cognoscunt.—August. Quæst. Evang. Lib. II. Quæst. li. Op. III. II. col. 276, ed. Bened. Par. 1679-1700. Vide Bp. Jewel, Reply to Harding, Art. II. div. xii. p. 232, Parker Soc.]

[7 'stablished' 1563: 'stablish' 1561.] [8 'Overly:' over.]

here and there spake little to the purpose for avoiding of them, (and therefore I eftsoons prayed him to give me in writing his answers;) he began to tell me how and what he had done for Grimbold, and how that I needed[9] not to fear any reproach or slander I should sustain, belike meaning to have me secretly to have come to them, as Grimbold did; for he subscribed.

And therefore I spake on this sort unto him: "Master dean," quod I, "I would gladly that you should not conceive of me that I pass of shame of men simply in this matter: I rather would have you to think of me as the very truth is, that hitherto, as I have not[10] seen nor heard any thing[9] to infirm my faith against transubstantiation, so I am no less settled in it than I was at my first[10] coming hither. I love," quod I, "to be plain with you and to tell you at the first that you shall find at the last."

"In good faith, master Bradford," quod he, "I love you the better for your plainness: and do not think otherwise of me," quod he, "but that you shall find me plain in all my talk with you."

Here he began to ask me of my imprisonment and condemnation. So I began and told him how I had been handled; whereat he seemed to wonder: yea, in plain words he said I had been handled otherwise than I had given cause; and so shewed me how that my lord of Bath reported that I had deserved a benefit at the queen's hand, and at all the council's. In this kind of talk we spent an hour almost; and so as one weary I did arise up; and he called in the keeper, and before him bade me be of good comfort, and to be out of all peril of death.

"Marry, sir," quoth the keeper, "but it is in every man's mouth, that he shall die to-morrow." Whereat he seemed something half amazed, and said he would go before evensong before the queen, and speak to her on my behalf: and I think the queen had almost supped at that present, for it was past six of the clock.

Before the keeper, I told him again that still I was the same man I was at the first; and till I should see matter to touch conscience to the contrary, must needs so continue.

The keeper desired me to hearken to master doctor's counsel, and prayed master doctor to be good unto me: and

[9 'need,' 'nothing,' 1561: 'needed,' 'any thing,' 1563.]
[10 'not,' 'first,' 1563: omitted in 1561.]

so after we had drunk together, master doctor with most gentle words took his leave for three days.

Now when he was gone, the keeper told me how that master doctor spake openly how that he saw no cause why they should burn me: which sentence, for the ambiguity of the meaning, made me sorry, lest I had behaved myself in any thing, wherein he gathered any conformableness to them in their doctrine; which God knoweth I never as yet did so.

God our Father bless us as his children, and keep us from all evil for ever. Amen.

ANOTHER TALK OR CONFERENCE BETWEEN MASTER BRADFORD AND DR WESTON [1].

Upon the fifth day of April came master doctor Weston to the Compter, about two of the clock in the afternoon, who excused himself for being so long absent; partly by sickness, partly for that doctor Pendleton told him that he would come unto me; "and partly for that," quoth he, "I withstood certain monks, which would have come again into Westminster." After which talk he told me how that the pope was dead: and then he told me how he had spoken to the queen for me, and how that death was not near unto me. Last of all he excused himself for not answering mine arguments against transubstantiation; "because my coming to-day," quoth he, "was more by fortune, than of purpose."

"I would gladly," quoth I, omitting all other talk, "have seen an answer to my arguments."

"Why," quoth he, "you have remembered something what I spake to you, when I was last with you?"

"No, sir," quoth I, "I never called them in manner to mind sithen that time, as well because I hoped you would have written them, as also for that they seemed not to be so material."

"In good faith," quoth he, "I cannot see any other or

[1 This conference on April 5 is given in the 'Examinations,' &c. 1561, and in Foxe, Acts, &c. 1570 and after editions, but is omitted in 1563. The 'Talk with a servant,' p. 553-6, is reprinted from Foxe, Acts, &c. 1570, as it does not occur in the 'Examinations,' &c. 1561, or in Foxe 1563. That last 'colloquy' must have taken place after Febr. 25, the date of the conference with A Castro, to which Bradford refers, p. 554.]

better way for you, than for to submit yourself to the judgment of the church."

"Marry, so I will, sir," quoth I, "if so be by the church you understand Christ's church."

"Lo," quoth he, "you take upon you to judge the church."

"No, sir," quoth I, "that do I not: in taking upon me to discern, I do not judge the church."

"Yes, that you do," quoth he, "and make it[2] invisible."

"I do neither," quoth I.

"Why," saith he, "who can see your church?"

"Those, sir," quoth I, "that have spiritual eyes, wherewith they might have discerned Christ's visible conversation here upon earth."

"Nay," quoth he, "Christ's church hath three tokens, that all men may look well upon; namely unity, antiquity, and consent."

"These three," quoth I, "may be as well in evil as in good; as well in sin as in virtue; as well in the devil's church, as in God's church: as for ensample," quoth I, "idolatry among the Israelites had all those three. Chrysostom telleth plainly, as you well know," said I, "that the church is well known *tantummodo per scripturas*[3], 'alonely by the scriptures.'"

"In good faith," quoth he, "you make your church invisible, when you will have it 'known alonely by the scriptures.'"

"No, sir," quoth I, "the scriptures do plainly set forth to us the church, that all men may well enough thereby know her, if they list to look."

"The church," quoth he, "is like a tower or 'town upon a hill,' that all men may see."

"True, sir," quoth I, "all men that be not blind. Visible enough is the church; but men's blindness is great. Impute not therefore to the church that which is to be imputed to men's blindness."

"Where," quoth he, "was your church forty years ago? Or where is it now, except in a corner of Germany?"

"Forsooth, sir," quoth I, "the church of God is dispersed, and not tied to this or that place, but to the word of God; so that where it is, there is God's church, if it be truly taught."

"Lo," quoth he, "is not this to make the church invisible? Point me out a realm a hundred years past, which maintained your doctrine."

[2 'it' 1570: not in 1561.]   [3 Vide p. 528, note 9, above.]

"Sir," quoth I, "if you will, or would well mark the state of the church before Christ's coming with it now, (as St Paul and Peter willeth us,) I think you would not look for such shews of the church to be made, as to point it out by realms. You know," quoth I, "that in Elias' time, both in Israel and elsewhere, God's church was not pointable; and therefore cried he out that he was left alone."

"No, marry," quoth he, "did not God say that there was 'seven thousand which had not bowed their knees to Baal?' Lo, saith he, 'seven thousand.' Shew me seven thousand a hundred years ago of your religion."

"Sir," quoth I, "these seven thousand were not known to men; for then Elias would not have said that he had been before left alone. And this is plain enough by that which the text hath, namely, that God saith, *Reliqui mihi*[1], 'I have reserved to me seven thousand.' Mark that it saith, God had reserved to himself, to his own knowledge; as I doubt not but the hundred years ago God had his seven thousand in his proper places, though men knew not thereof."

"Well, master Bradford," saith he, "I will not make your case worse than for transubstantiation, although I know that we agree not in other matters. And I pray you," quoth he, "make you it yourself not worse. If I can do you good, I will: hurt you I will not. I am no prince, and therefore I cannot promise life, except you will submit yourself to the definition of the church."

"Sir," quoth I, "so that you will define me your church, that under it you bring not in a false church, you shall not see but that we shall soon be at a point."

"In good faith, master Bradford," quoth he, "I see no good will be done; and therefore I will wish you as much good as I can, and hereafter I will perchance come or send to you again." And so he sent for master Weal, and departed.

Now after his departing cometh the keeper, master Clayden, and Stephen Beiche; and they were very hot with me, and spake unto me in such sort that I should not look but to have them utter enemies unto me, notwithstanding the friendship they both have hitherto pretended.

God be with us; and what matter is it who be against us?

[1 'mihi' 1570: not in 1561.]

AMONG divers which came to master Bradford in prison, some to dispute and confer, some to give counsel, some to take comfort, and some to visit him, there was a certain gentlewoman's servant, which gentlewoman had been cruelly afflicted and miserably handled by her father and mother and all her kindred, in her father's house, for not coming to the mass, and like at length to have been pursued to death, had not the Lord delivered her out of her father's house, being put from all that ever she had. This gentlewoman's servant therefore, being sent to master Bradford with recommendations, had this talk with him, which I thought here not to over-slip:

Foxe, Acts, &c., 1570, p. 1802—3; and after editions.

This gentlewoman is yet alive, to whom Bradford wrote a Letter [2], which hereafter followeth. [Foxe, 1570.]

A COLLOQUY BETWEEN MASTER BRADFORD AND A GENTLEWOMAN'S SERVANT, BEING SENT TO VISIT HIM IN PRISON [3].

THIS servant or messenger of the foresaid gentlewoman, coming to master Bradford, and taking him by the hand, said, "God be thanked for you: how do you?"

Master Bradford answered: "Well, I thank God: for as men in sailing, which be near to the shore or haven where they would be, would be nearer; even so the nearer I am to God, the nearer I would be."

Servant. "Sir, I have never seen you so strong and healthsome of body, as methink you be now; God be thanked for it."

"Why," quoth he, "I have given over all care and study; and only do I covet to be talking with him, whom I have always studied to be withal."

Servant. "Well, God hath done much for you since the time that I first knew you, and hath wrought wondrously in you to his glory."

Bradford. "Truth it is; for he hath dealt favourably with me, in that he hath not punished me according to my sins, but hath suffered me to live, that I might seek repentance."

Servant. "Truly, we hear say, there is a rod made so grievous, out of the which I think no man shall pluck his head."

Bradford. "Well, let all that be of Christ's flock arm themselves to suffer: for I think verily, God will not have

[2 Foxe, Acts, &c. 1583, p. 1651-2, or ed. 1843-8, VII. 255-7. It will appear hereafter among the letters of Bradford.]

[3 See p. 550, note 1, above.]

one of his to escape untouched, if he love him; let them seek what means or ways they can."

Servant. "Well, sir, there goeth a talk of a friar that should preach before the king, and should tell him, that he should be guilty of the innocent blood that hath been shed of late[1]."

"Verily," quoth Bradford, "I had a book within these two days of his writing, and therein he saith that it is not meet nor convenient that the heretics should live[2]; and therefore I have marvel how that talk should rise, for I have heard of it also: and I have also talked with this friar (he is named friar Fons) and with divers other; and I praise God they have confirmed me; for they have nothing to say but that which is most vain."

Servant. "Sir, father Cardmaker hath him commended unto you."

Bradford. "How doth he? how doth he?"

Servant. "Well, God be thanked."

Bradford. "I am very glad thereof; for indeed my lord chancellor did cast him in my teeth: but, as David saith, 'God hath disappointed him.'"

[See p. 473, 481, above.]

Servant. "Forsooth, God's name be praised, he is very strong."

Bradford. "And, I trust, so are we. What else? Our quarrel is most just: therefore let us not be affeared."

Servant. "My mistress hath her recommended unto you."

Bradford. "How doth she?"

Servant. "Well, God be praised, but she hath been sorer afflicted with her own father and mother than ever you were with your imprisonment: and yet God hath preserved her, I trust, to his glory."

Bradford. "I pray you tell her, I read this day a goodly history, written by Basilius Magnus, of a virtuous woman which was a widow, and was named Julitta[3]. She had great lands and many children; and nigh her dwelled a cormorant, which

[1 Alphonsus a Castro preached before King Philip against religious persecution, Feb. 10, 1555: it was a political manœuvre. See Foxe, Acts, &c., 1583, p. 1529, or ed. 1843-8, VI. 704-5; Bp. Burnet, Hist. Ref.; Collier, Ecc. Hist.; Turner, Hist. III. 481-2, ed. 1829; Anderson, Annals, Eng. Bible, II. 289-92.]

[2 dico et firmissime teneo justum esse, ut hæreticus incorrigibilis occidatur.—Alfons. a Castro De just. hæret. punit. Lib. II. cap. xii. fol. 121, Salmant. 1547. Copy, British Museum.]

[3 Basil. Homil. in Martyr. Julitt. 1-3. Op. II. 33-5, ed. Bened. Paris. 1721-30.]

for her virtuousness and godly living had great indignation at her; and of very malice he took away her lands, so that she was constrained to go to the law with him: and in conclusion the matter came to the trial before the judge, who demanded of this tyrant, why he wrongfully withheld these lands from this woman? He made answer and said, he might do so: 'for,' saith he, 'this woman is disobedient to the king's proceedings; for she will in no wise worship his gods, nor offer sacrifice unto them.' Then the judge, hearing that, said unto her: 'Woman, if this be true, thou art not only like to lose thy land, but also thy life, unless that thou worship our gods, and do sacrifice unto them.' This godly woman, hearing that, stept[4] forth to the judge, and said: 'Is there no remedy but either to worship your false gods, or else to lose my lands and life? Then farewell suit, farewell lands, farewell children, farewell friends, yea, and farewell life too; and, in respect of the true honour of the everliving God, farewell all.' And with that saying did the judge commit her to prison; and afterward she suffered most cruel death. And being brought to the place of execution, she exhorted all women to be strong and constant: 'For,' saith she, 'ye were redeemed with as dear a price as men: for although ye were made of the rib of the man, yet be you also of his flesh; so that also, in the case and trial of your faith towards God, ye ought to be as strong.' And thus died she constantly, not fearing death. I pray you tell your mistress of this history."

Servant. "That shall I, sir, by God's grace: for she told me that she was with you and master Saunders, and received your gentle counsel."

Bradford. "We never gave her other counsel but the truth; and in witness thereof we have and will seal it with our bloods: for I thought this night that I had been sent for, because at an eleven of the clock there was such rapping at the door."

Then answered a maid, and said, "Why, then I perceive you were afraid."

Bradford. "Ye shall hear how fearful I was; for I considered that I had not slept, and I thought to take a nap before I went: and after I was asleep, these men came into the next chamber, and sang, as it was told me; and yet, for all my fearfulness, I heard them not: therefore belike I was not afraid, that slept so fast."

[4 'stept me' 1570, 1576, 1583.]

Servant. "Do you lack any thing toward your necessity?"

Bradford. "Nothing but your prayers; and I trust I have them, and you mine."

Servant. "I saw a priest come to you to-day in the morning."

Bradford. "Yea, he brought me a letter from a friar, and I am writing an answer."

Servant. "Then we let you; therefore the living God be with you."

Bradford. "And with you also, and bless you."

"Amen," said we; and gave him thanks, and departed.

Thus still in prison continued Bradford, until the month of July, in such labours and sufferings as he before always had sustained in prison. But when the time of his determined death was come, he was suddenly conveyed out of the Compter, where he was prisoner, in the night season to Newgate, as afore is declared: and from thence he was carried the next morning to Smithfield, where he, constantly abiding in the same truth of God which before he had confessed, earnestly exhorting the people to repent and to return to Christ, and sweetly comforting the godly young springal of nineteen or twenty years old, which was burned with him, cheerfully he ended his painful life, to live with Christ.

[The following is the colophon of the Examinations, &c. of Bradford, 1561.]

¶ **Imprinted at London,**
in Fleetstrete, at the Sign of
ye Faucon by William Griffith, and are to be sold at
the litle shop in Saincte
Dunstones churchyard. Anno. 1561.
The. xiii. daie
of Maye.

APPENDIX.

PREFACES,

&c.

[The two following Prefaces accompany a reprint of Bradford's Sermon on Repentance, which has the following title:

'The good old way, or an excellent and profitable treatise of Repentance, made by that precious man of God and faithful martyr of Jesus Christ, Mr John Bradford, in the year 1553. Now published with two prefaces, relating the life of the author, and the excellency of the work.—'Except ye repent, ye shall all likewise perish.' Luke xiii. 5. 'The times of this ignorance God winked at, but now commandeth all men every where to repent.' Acts xvii. 30. OXFORD, Printed by Leon. Lichfield, printer to the University, 1652.'

The Prefaces are followed respectively by the signatures 'H. W' and 'R. H.' in the edition of 1652: and they are referred to as being severally by Dr Wilkinson and Dr Harris, in the Preface to 'Capel's Remains,' Lond. 1658, by Valentine Marshall.

A copy also of Bradford's 'Sermon on Repentance,' 1652, belonging to the editor, has the autograph of its former possessor, 'Tho. Hall,' on the title. T. Hall has written in full, after each Preface, the names, 'Dr Henry Wilkinson,' and 'Dr Robert Harris.'

Thomas Hall was rector of King's Norton, 'a lover of books and learning,' 'a plain and profitable preacher,' and author of several works. He died 1665.—Wood, Athenæ Oxon. Bliss. III. 677—81.

Dr Henry Wilkinson was senior fellow of Magdalene College, and canon of Christ Church, Oxford: he was the author of several sermons, and died 1675.—Wood, Athenæ Oxon. III. 1038—40.

There was another 'Henry Wilkinson,' a bachelor of divinity, and principal of Magdalene Hall, Oxford, who died 1690.—Id. ibid. IV. 283—6.

Robert Harris was rector of Hanwell in Oxfordshire, and in 1648 president of Trinity College, Oxford. His works were collected and published in 1654: he died at Oxford, 1658, aged 80.—Wood, Athenæ Oxon. III. 458—60. Clarke, Lives of English Divines, p. 314—38, Lond. 1677.]

PREFACES TO BRADFORD ON REPENTANCE; OXFORD, 1652.

PREFACE BY DR WILKINSON.

TO all faithful Mnasons, old disciples, and all those who desire and endeavour to walk in the good old gospel way of faith and repentance, "grace, mercy, and peace from God our Father and from our Lord Jesus Christ."

It is a common proverb, that 'good wine needs no ivy-bush:' no more doth this good old wine, this excellent treatise of that saint of God Mr Bradford, need any letters of commendation. Yet it will be requisite to speak something: and I hope it will be interpreted a deed of charity, if I interpose as an advocate for the truth of this orphan tract, whose father was a saint on earth, and now reigns as a glorious saint in heaven. The work is legitimate, transcribed after an exact copy; and it is suitable to the style, and savours of the author's spirit. The many choice breathings in his letters, and this treatise, are all of a piece, good old gold, "more precious than that of Ophir."

Something I shall briefly speak of the author, and then of this tract. For the author, what his learning was is upon record: how solid and sinewous his disputations were with the popish prelates, Spanish friars, and others that visited him in prison; and how dexterously he managed all his disputations, with wisdom, judgment and zeal, you may read largely in Mr Foxe's Martyrology. He was a man of an acute wit, penetrating judgment, and had the approbation and advice of Martin Bucer[1] to enter into the ministry.

His piety was rare and eminent. As was the man, so was his communication, holy and useful. Whoso reads his spiritual breathings (I might almost call it a transcendant style) in his epistles, must needs confess that he was one of the holiest men that ever lived since the apostles' time. Take a taste of him in these few characters:

1. He was a zealous, plain, profitable preacher of God's word. He knew how "to divide the word aright," and "walk accord-
[2 Tim. ii. 15. Gal. ii. 14.] ingly:" he had those two rare qualifications of a preacher, ὀρθο-

[¹ See references, p. 350, note 4, above.]

τομεῖν καὶ ὀρθοποδεῖν. He was "a Boanerges, a son of thunder," to impenitent obdurate sinners; but "a Barnabas, a son of consolation," to the children of God.

2. He was of an humble self-denying spirit. I never read of any that had a meaner opinion of himself than he had. You shall find the subscription of his letters, *Miserrimus peccator*, ['A most miserable sinner;'] 'A very hypocrite, the most hard-hearted unthankful sinner, a very painted hypocrite, John Bradford[2]:' so cheap an esteem had he of himself. This humility is an adorning grace, next to the garment of Christ's righteousness, none like to it: wherefore the apostle's phrase is emphatical, 1 Pet. v., Τὴν ταπεινοφροσύνην ἐγκομβώσασθε· "Be ye clothed with humility;" let it be your uppermost garment. Cyprian saith: *Fundamentum sanctitatis est humilitas*: ["Humility is the groundwork of holiness."] This holy man's example is worthy of our imitation.

3. He was much acquainted with God, and enjoyed a holy communion and familiarity with him in prayer and meditation. He meditated much: and meditation is the spiritual digestion of the soul; it is a divine ruminating upon the word read or preached. When we meditate seriously on the promises, attributes, or such choice subjects, we are up in the mount with Moses, we soar aloft even to heaven, being carried by the wings of holy meditation. This meditation is an up-hill duty: Isaac, Moses, Paul, and other saints of God, have found sweet consolation flowing from it. And he joined prayer to meditation: he was frequently upon his knees; and he would not rise up, till he felt something coming in, some spiritual illapse darted upon his soul. His practice was suitable to Bernard's resolution, *Nunquam, Domine, discedam a te sine te*: ["Never will I depart from thee, O Lord, without thee."] He studied usually upon his knees, and prayed much in his study: and indeed he studies well who prays well. And he can take the most comfort of his study, who reaps the fruits of his pains as returns from his prayers.

4. He was of a melting tender heart. He wept much and mourned that he could not bring his dull heart to love Jesus Christ more. At table, as he sat at meat, he usually pulled his hat down before his eyes, and poured forth abundance of tears upon his trencher[3]. He had a tender heart, bowels opened to the prisoners; he had a tender care both of their bodies and souls. When he was in prison, he visited frequently his fellow-prisoners; and spent

[2 Bradford only describes himself thus in some of his earliest letters, addressed to Traves.—Foxe, Acts, &c. 1583, p. 1660—4, or ed. 1843—8, VII. 275—84.]

[3 See p. 35—6, above.]

much time in praying for them, exhorting of them, and contributing liberally out of his purse unto them.

I need add no more; for what I can say is too little and beneath the author's worth, "of whom the world was not worthy." He lived a saint, and died a martyr.

Now, for this work which I here present to the reader, I am assured that it is not spurious, but the genuine issue of this worthy author. Herein is handled the doctrine of Repentance, with many moving considerations thereunto. Perhaps his plain phrase may not suit this curious age, which is too too much given to affectation of words. *Sed distinguenda sunt tempora:* ['But we should distinguish between times:'] those times were not used to set forth or garnish their dishes as now they are; yet the food is wholesome, plain, and profitable. And if our palates cannot relish such food, I fear there is some distemper in them, and it is our duty to pray for the removal thereof.

I shall not make a panegyric on the treatise: the work will abundantly commend itself. Here is evangelical Repentance pressed home unto the conscience with many cogent convincing arguments. It was then spoken "in season;" and it is a doctrine that can never be pressed "out of season." These are gospel days: "the kingdom of heaven is at hand:" and of all times gospel times are peculiar times of repentance. The Lord calls upon all ranks of men, magistrates, ministers, people: "Repent," "repent." Various dispensations call on us to repent: sometimes God speaks in the thunder of judgment, sometimes in the music of mercy: both by mercies and judgments we are called to repentance. The last words of this holy martyr were, REPENT, ENGLAND: and truly the words of a dying man should be much set by, especially of a dying saint, who bequeaths this legacy to England in his last breath.

Now, whoever thou art that readest this book, and art hereby won to think on thy ways, and turn unto God, give God the glory, and look on it as a special hand of providence, in bringing this book to thy sight.

I will not detain thee longer from reading this ensuing treatise. Read it, and read it again with prayer and meditation: and the Lord teach thee to profit by it. And so I commend thee to the grace of God, and bid thee heartily farewell, entreating thy prayers for him who in love to thy soul hath revived this Treatise, and remains

Thy servant for Christ's sake,
H[ENRY] W[ILKINSON.]

PREFACE BY DR HARRIS.

TO THE READER.

BEING over-entreated to preface something to this piece, I crave a little patience, whilst I speak a little both to the work and workman.

In the work there is first the matter, secondly the frame or composure, considerable. The subject matter is Repentance: and that is a thing which will never be out of season, till sin, which never is in season, be out of men's hearts and lives. Some men indeed have thought (in temptation only, I hope) this a work (for some at least in these days) too legal, and below their gospel privileges. But if it be rightly stated and understood, it will be found a gospel both duty and privilege beyond the mercy of law, and never more seasonable than in times of grace; much pressed by the Lord of preachers Acts xvii. 30. and his forerunners, by his apostles and their successors down to our author's time, who frequented no one doctrine or duty more.

For the form and manner of handling this theme, we refer thereunto his method, his style or phrase. In the first we must allow a latitude to him, to others, according to each man's gift and genius, so long as curiosity and confusion be avoided, and the capacity of the hearer considered. Much I know is written about the method of preaching: and it must be granted that nothing contributes more to the memory both of the speaker and hearer, than method doth. Howbeit, the rule holds that the greatest art is to dissemble art[1]: and that preacher, who studies himself and his people most, usually speaks most to the heart, and to edification. A workman may fetch his stuff from another's shop; but if he will make the suit fit, he must apply himself to the party concerned, and take measure of him: I mean this, a teacher must fetch all his materials from the word, but his application from the auditory: and herein this good man was his craft's master.

Nor will his method, I am confident, be quarrelled by any true artist. He begins with a description of the term, of the thing; and that done, he casts it into the parts, vindicating them from false glosses and mistakes, and restoring them to their proper sense; and the way thus cleared, he bears down all before him with strength of argument and application, wherein lies the life of this, of any sermon.

For his phrase, that is suited to the times wherein he lived, and to the matter that lies before him: and whilst it is so, it was not

---

[1 Quinctil. De Instit. Orat. Lib. I. cap. xi.]

needful, either to alter a term, unless it were superannuated; or to add a word, unless it were to make up a gap where the copy seemed defective. It is confessed on all hands (his persecutors not gainsaying it), that the author was in those times a master of speech: but he had learned of his Master not to speak what he could speak, but what his hearers could hear: he knew that clearness of speech was the excellency of speech; and therefore resolved, with a good orator, to speak beneath himself rather than above his auditory, and with the nurse to speak broken words rather than obscure and doubtful[2] Otherwise his eloquence was confessedly great, that is, native, masculine, modest, in one, heavenly: for, if you mark him, he savours and breathes nothing but heaven; yea, he sparkles, thunders, lightens, pierces the soft, breaks only the stony heart.

Mark iv. 33. Lumen orationis perspicuitas.[1] Augustine, who would call a bone ossum to avoid the ambiguity in os. In Psal. cxxxviii. secundum Aug.[2]

The blessing of God hath been signally eminent upon this land in her preachers, I had almost said beyond all lands since the Reformation: the Lord make us sensible of it, and really thankful for it, to the encouragement of all such. Amongst these I have, in my time, met with four mighty men upon this very argument, now all with God; for I forbear to instance in the living: the men are, John Bradford, John Udal[3], Arthur Dent[3], Dan. Dyke[4]; and (if I might be pardoned for comparing dead men, which I do not practise towards the living) I should think that as Mr Bradford is before them all in time, so not behind any one of them in this way of preaching. He was of a most sweet, humble, and melting spirit, who (I know not how) will be in a man's bosom ere he be aware, and willingly win him from himself to Christ.

Many years are now passed since I first read this tract; and it is not to be stranged, if still I affect it. It is the first printed sermon that affected me to purpose: and I were to blame, if I should be unwilling to carve and convey it to others: which whilst I do, it is not to be expected that I should engage either for or against every punctilio in it. He shall shew little ingenuity and less charity, who cannot look upon such a brother dissenting in some opinion or expression, without some abatement of affection or respect. It was the frequent profession of my ever honoured predecessor[5]: 'Where I see most of Christ, there will I love most,

[[1] Id. ibid. Lib. I. cap. vi.: and vide Lib. II. cap. iii.; Lib. VIII. cap. ii.]

[[2] August. Enarr. in Psal. cxxxviii. Op. IV. col. 1545, ed. Bened. Par. 1679—1700: and De Doctr. Christ. Lib. IV. 24. Op. III. Pars I. col. 73.]

[[3] Vide Herbert, Typogr. Antiq. II. 1141, 1156.]

[[4] Vide Fuller, Worthies, Hertfordshire, Lond. 1662.]

[[5] John Dod, fellow of Jesus College, Cambridge, had preceded Dr Robert Harris in the rectory of Hanwell. He died 1645, aged 96.—Clarke, Lives, p. 168—78, Lond. 1677. Fuller, Worthies, Cheshire, Lond. 1662.]

whether the party be of my opinion or of a different judgment:' so he, so I.

But of the work enough: shall I speak a little of the workman? This blessed martyr, who beautified his sufferings with his meekness and humility, was doubtless one of a thousand; whether a better preacher or scholar, is to me a great question. After his conversion, his whole life was a continued sermon of repentance. In his addresses to the university, to the city, to his countrymen and kinsmen, he preached repentance: he lived repentance; and in his last farewell to this land he breathed out his last thus: "O ENGLAND, ENGLAND, REPENT, REPENT OF THY SINS."

I am much ashamed when I read his works and life penned by many, and cannot without sad reflections upon myself consider how far our means, helps, opportunities, are beyond his times, and how infinitely I (to censure none but myself) fall short of him in the practice of godliness and power of exhortation. Truly if Luther's three ingredients, first prayer, second meditation, third temptation, make up either preacher or Christian, you will find them all in him, who was a man of prayer, of meditation, of temptations; as his works speak him, and they found him who have made use of him in their temptations and desertions.

The man who most, in my mind, resembled him in preaching, conference, prayer, temptation, every way, was the man whose society I sometimes enjoyed[6]: this blessed man, now "with Christ," hath often told me, that he himself (whose ability and dexterity in settling and satisfying troubled spirits was certainly great) hath been at one time so overwhelmed with temptations, and at another so becalmed into a flatness and listlessness of spirit, that he hath been enforced to adopt Mr Bradford's meditations, ejaculations and expressions, and to spread them before God as his own, upon this account, because Mr Bradford had in his writings (as he thought) represented his case, said more for him, and done his errand better, than he could for himself.

This passage I the rather publish, because upon this occasion I would stir up men of parts and experience to impart their experiences and sufficiencies in this kind whilst they live, as little knowing how many drooping and desponding souls their surviving works may help, when themselves "sleep in the dust." It is a thing that long since I bewailed, that so little is this way done by able, orthodox, experienced casuists: but they who (for aught appears) know least of "the mystery of godliness," and methods of

[6 Evidently John Dod: see last note, and Clarke, ibid. p. 319.]

Satan, undertake the work. I do not mean such as Gerson[1], Parisiensis[2], Savonarola[3], &c. who speak as if they had met with something of God in their lives and consciences; but certain Jesuits and canonists, who resolve all into a blind and (upon the matter) an human credence, and shew more wit than grace (as it was once said of a rabbin) in their resolves. There be not, I believe, more able men for case divinity and all practicals in the world, than in this nation, would they apply themselves accordingly. Some yet living have given undeniable proofs of their ability in this errand: I forbear to name them, because I would decline the suspicion of flattery. I may more freely speak of our Greenhams, Dods, Perkins, Ameses, Baineses, as also of our Randalls, Boltons, Balls[4], &c., who are now out of hearing, but not out of memory. O that others, behind them in time, but not in abilities, would take up the work where they left, and carry it on; at least, that that brother who owes so much to God for temptations, and can say, out of his observations, so much for God in the case of temptation and desertion, would at last perfect his Tract of Temptations[5], so happily begun.

Mr R[ichard] Ca[pel] of Temptat.

But I have made the porch too wide: I conclude where I began, with humble (and when I say humble, I say all) Mr Bradford. I have had some other works of his: but war hath plundered me of many books[6]. This piece a godly brother (who is never weary of doing good) hath recovered out of the dust, and once more made public. Under God, thank him, reader, if thou be the better for it: and better thou mayest be, if thou wilt lay down pride and prejudice, and take this up in humility; and with purpose of amend-

[1 Mosheim. Eccl. Hist. cent. xv. ii. ii. 24. and iii. 9.]

[2 Possibly a reference to Peter 'Cantor Parisiensis,' who died 1197.—Id. ibid. cent. xii. ii. iii. 6: Apology for Lollard doctrines, p. 154, Camden Soc. 1842.]

[3 Mosheim. ibid. cent. xv. ii. ii. 24.: McCrie, Reform. Italy, p. 27—36, Edinb. 1833.]

[4 See accounts of these divines in Clarke, Lives, p. 12—5, 22—4, Lond. 1677; Fuller, Abel redivivus 1651, p. 431—40, 586—92; Mosheim, Eccl. Hist. cent. xvi. sect. iii. ii. ii. 37, and cent. xvii. sect. ii. ii. ii. 9; Wood, Athenæ Oxon. Bliss. II. col. 319—20, 514—7, 670—3.]

[5 Richard Capel, author of 'Temptations, their nature, danger, and cure,' 1650, published afterward a 'fourth part,' 1655: he was fellow of Magdalen College, Oxford, and rector of Eastington. After his death, 1656, were published his 'Remains, being an appendix to his treatise of Temptation,' &c., 1658.—Wood, ibid. III. 421—3; Clarke, ibid. p. 303—13; and account of his Life in Preface to his 'Remains,' by Valentine Marshall.]

[6 The battle of Edgehill, a few miles from Hanwell, was fought, Oct. 23, 1642, while Dr Harris was rector of the latter place: and soldiers were quartered in his house.—Clarke, Lives, p. 321, Lond. 1677.]

ment read it, think on it, pray for a blessing: and, if thou findest little at first, read again, pray again, apply again; and I miss my aim, if thou dost not meet with more at last than it seemed to promise at first.

I commend both it and thee to the blessing of the great God; and having answered the importunity of my friend in saying thus much, I rest

Thine in Christ,
R[OBERT] H[ARRIS].

PREFACE BY THOMAS LEVER[7] TO THE MEDITATIONS, &c., OF BRADFORD, 1567[8].

GOD, of his eternal wisdom and providence, hath assigned unto every man such time, place, and continuance in this world, as by giving a taste of his goodness unto man in every thing might and should best teach and move man to seek and find the fountain and head-spring of all goodness, which is even God himself. And this doth God, not for any lack or need that he hath of man; but for that of God's goodness every man might receive liberally and freely, as God seeth expedient for their lack and necessity.

Therefore in most expedient and best wise hath God ordained, that the taste of God's goodness in this mortal life should make man more desirous of the fulness of the same in eternal life; and the perceiving of God's goodness partly and covertly in his creatures should stir the mind of man more to see and enjoy God's goodness openly and perfectly in God himself.

Now seeing that man, having no goodness of his own, hath yet God's goodness at all times in every thing, by all means, thus offered unto him, he must needs either come with comfort freely to

[[7] Thomas Lever was ordained deacon and priest by Bp. Ridley, 1550, and was an eloquent preacher in the reign of Edward VI. He was appointed master of Sherborn Hospital, 1561; and died, 1577. He was the author of various Sermons and other pieces. Vide Strype, Mem. II. i. 403, 404—9, 427, Grindal, 253, Annals, II. ii. 156; and Bp. Ridley, Works, p. 59, Parker Soc.]

[[8] See p. 112 and 296 above.

The heading to this preface, in the 'Godly Meditations,' &c. 1567, is:

'A preface, shewing the true understanding of God's word, and the right use of God's works and benefits, evident and easy to be seen in the exercise of these Meditations.']

eternal life in God, if he proceed so far; or else worthily perish from God, if he turn, stay, and satisfy himself in any thing or things, afore he find, feel, and attain everlasting life in God.

And thus staying and sticking fast in any thing from God is damnable; yea, and the more near a man cometh to God, the more damnable it is then to stay and turn from God: as for example, evil is it for a man to stay and satisfy himself in worldly wealth, without any religion; and worse, in ceremonial religion of man's invention, without any word of God; and worst of all is it, having also the word of God, to be without any true comfortable knowledge and love of God.

And the beginning and cause of all such evil stays and turnings from God is the corrupt concupiscence and lust of our own hearts. And this corruption in man did begin and doth continue and increase by sin, shrinking from God's will revealed by his word: as contrariwise the remedy and recovery of man is only in God, calling and drawing man from deserved misery unto free mercy by his word. For the word of God doth, by the law and commandments, declare unto man his own sinful misery, threatening the terrible wrath and vengeance of God due for the same: and by the gospel and promise of God in Christ is opened and offered the well-spring of mercy and grace, to heal all man's sinful misery, and to call and draw man from wrath and damnation, deserved by sin in man, unto favour and salvation freely opened and offered unto man through Christ in God.

Therefore every man should use such hearing, reading, and meditation of God's word, as might make him to see, feel, and confess in himself sin and wretchedness, and in God mercy and grace, so as should most move the mind in prayer to desire and procure God's mercy and grace, to deliver and preserve man from corruption and perdition in himself, unto sanctification and everlasting life in God.

And for that every man cannot have all scriptures, and no man ought to be without the ten commandments, the articles of the belief, and the Lord's prayer, to meditate in his mind; therefore the meditation of them should be in such sort, as we might best find and feel the sickness and danger of our sin by the commandments; then see the remedy and salve for sin, which is the goodness of God confessed in the articles of the belief; and so, as followeth in the Lord's prayer, use the manner and form of desiring and joining the medicine and salve of God's merciful goodness unto the sickness and sores of man's sinful wretchedness.

And so, using these three things to cause and increase in us daily repentance, faith, and prayer, we shall learn better how to use the word and works of God, so as we may thereby be brought with comfort more near unto him; and not by abusing them be staid and drawn further from him. For when as we recite, read, speak, or hear any portion of God's word, without any desire, meditation or consideration of the meaning thereof to enter into our minds, then do we abuse "the letter which killeth," refusing or neglecting "the Spirit which quickeneth:" and that is no service by the which God is honoured and pleased, but rather a taking of the name and word of God in vain, for the which man so doing deserveth to be plagued. And it can be nothing else but a grievous sin and plague, so to be delighted and deluded with the vain sound, number, and order of words, that a man cannot or will not taste of the most comfortable matter and meaning contained in the same words. For so do many men in outward vanities stay, stick, and turn from "worshipping of God in spirit and truth:" so do hypocrites "worship God with their lips, having their hearts far from him:" and so do people coming to hear God's word, with the idols of men's imaginations in their hearts, and evident offences in their manners, desire and deserve such ministers and ministry of God's word, as have an outward form and fashion of godliness in words and rites, with refusing and slandering of the same in minds and manners.

But here note, that when there is any desire and diligence to have the mind moved and edified by the meaning of good words, that is profitable to man and acceptable to God. And where there is no regard to the meaning of good words, but a mere observation of outward fashion by custom or prescription, in speaking or hearing of good words, that is an ungodly abusing of those good words, yea, a dangerous taking of the name and word of God in the mouth, suffering Satan to feed and fill the heart with ignorance, negligence, superstition, and idolatry.

It is a dangerous thing so to feed thy affections with worldly vanities and fleshly lusts, that thou canst not or wilt not feed upon the food of God's word. And a more dangerous thing is it, in feeding upon God's word, to feed upon the only outward "letter which killeth," without any taste or desire of "the Spirit which quickeneth."

So, if the use of the benefits of God in other things do further thee unto the word of God, and the outward use of the letter of the word, unto the inward meaning and spirit of the same, then dost thou proceed aright and well, from death in thyself, unto life in God; not forsaking nor losing any goodness of God in any thing, but thankfully embracing and using the goodness of God in every thing, so as may allure, move, and draw thee most comfortably towards the fulness, pureness, and perfection of all goodness in God himself.

And for example, practice, and trial of this, thou hast here Master Bradford's Meditations upon the ten commandments, the articles of the Christian faith, and the Lord's prayer; which being well used of thee will ready thee much unto the right understanding of God's word, and to the right use of God's works. And the well using of these is, when thy leisure is but little, yet in the meditation of the commandments to consider thy sinful misery; and in the confession of the faith to consider God's merciful goodness; and in the Lord's prayer to consider the best way to procure and apply God's grace and mercy to heal and put away thy sinful misery: and when thou hast more leisure, thou mayest consider more of and in these three things, as the good example of godly Master Bradford will well teach thee.

And my advice is, that when thou comest to the perusing of Bradford's Meditations, then thou provide thee a quiet mind, time, and place, rather perusing one commandment, article, or petition, advisedly and well, than many with much haste and little consideration. So shalt thou find most sweetness in that thou readest, and best print and keep the effect and sum of it in thy memory, reading and considering one thing after another, as thou findest to thy time and capacity may best agree.

And whereas there lacked a meditation upon the last commandment, I have added my endeavour to supply that lack. But considering how deeply and well Master Bradford hath handled the others, and that this last doth descend more deeply into man than the others, I beseech thee take in good part my willing diligence, albeit thou seest many things to be lacking in my meditation, to make it meet to be joined unto Master Bradford's meditations, and more to teach thee duly to consider this commandment.

THOMAS LEVER.

MEDITATION ON THE TENTH COMMANDMENT, BY THOMAS LEVER, 1567[1].

THOU SHALT NOT COVET THY NEIGHBOUR'S HOUSE, NEITHER SHALT THOU COVET THY NEIGHBOUR'S WIFE, NOR HIS MAN-SERVANT, NOR HIS MAID, &c.

Now dost thou, O most gracious God, instruct me how I should use my heart and mind towards my neighbour. And albeit, in the other commandments concerning words and deeds, there be also doctrine and charge concerning will and purpose, (as Christ doth expound and declare the commandments of not killing nor committing adultery to be observed or transgressed, not only by word and deed, but also by will and purpose;) yet by this commandment thou dost further teach and charge me how to use the first motions of the heart and mind, which be desires and devices, whereof by consent proceed wills, purposes, words and deeds.

So that now by this commandment I am taught and forced with Paul to feel and confess, that "in me, that is to say, in my flesh, there is no goodness;" for, being not regenerate by thy "Spirit of grace," I did neither feel nor find how that all the thoughts, imaginations, devices, and desires of the heart of man, be always only evil. But now, by thy "Spirit of grace" in regeneration, I regarding aright this commandment do not only know and confess that man conceived and born in sin cannot afore regeneration do, say, or think any thing that is good; but also being regenerate, and thereby having a will to do good, yet by this lust "the law of sin in his members" is ever tempted and allured, and many times drawn and brought to do evil. *[marginal: Only they that be regenerate by the Spirit of grace regard this commandment. Gen. vi.]*

So that this thy law in forbidding lust, which is the corruption of heart and mind, word and deed, doth command "love of a pure heart, a good conscience, and an unfeigned faith," which is the fountain and pure spring of all good thoughts, words and deeds. Therefore by this commandment I am forbidden such lust of any thing, and commanded such love of my neighbour as should ever move and cause me not to desire, get, or keep any good thing to myself from my neighbour; but to will, give, communicate, and procure every good thing unto him.

[1 See p. 112, 296, above.]

By reason whereof I have great cause to be thankful and praise thee, for that thou wouldest have me not to have and utter[1] my own evil lusts to hurt, hinder or grieve others; but to have and use a pure love, to minister the gifts of thy good things unto mutual comfort and commodity, and commendation of me and of others.

O gracious good God, great is thy love towards me, which dost not only restrain and keep the evils rising and beginning in many men's hearts from hurting and destroying of me, but dost command all men, and causest very many, in thought, words, and deeds, to help, preserve, and prosper me.

If this thy commandment were not, I see, as I should have done (and do in not restraining and forbearing my lusts) much worse to others than is happened; so should I have found and felt of others towards me. If we consider how all evil thoughts, murders and adulteries, fornications, thefts, false witnessings, slanders, &c., do abundantly issue out of men's hearts, causing all manner of misery and mischief to come amongst men; easily may we see a wonderful benefit and providence of thee for us in this commandment.

But, O most gracious good God, as my unthankfulness, disobedience, and hypocrisy be wonderful great in every thing, so do the same most exceedingly abound in and by these lusts that lie secretly lurking in my heart: for I do so negligently suffer them to live and lurk in me, that at every occasion of any thing they are ready to arise, inflame, and corrupt my heart with covetousness, voluptuousness, pride, arrogancy, disdain, emulation, security, blind zeal, and many such other affections; and being discovered and reproved by this thy good law, they be not taken away and abolished, but through infirmity and corruption that is in me they increase sin and transgression. For I, finding thy law and commandment against my lusts, do feel them in me rebounding against this thy law with more strong rebellion: and so I of frailty (neither able to attain to the righteousness of thy law in fulfilling of it, nor to sustain and abide thy just severity for not fulfilling of it,) am carried away captive from thee and thy law to "the law of sin which is in my members."

Rom. vii.

"O miserable man that I am!" which now perceive, find, and feel that the pure goodness and just severity of thy law doth not reform and put away, but declare, irritate, augment, and condemn my corrupt sinful unthankfulness, disobedience, and hypocrisy.

[[1] See p. 321, note 1, above.]

But yet thou, O most merciful Father, dost by thy law thus declare sin, and work in thine elect a feeling and fear of thy deserved wrath, that they thereby may be learned, moved, and forced to know, desire, and embrace "the end of thy law," which is Christ thy Son our Saviour. For even as a good surgeon doth first make bare and open a grievous corrupt sore thoroughly, that then he may lay thereto a good plaister to heal the same effectually; so dost thou, O good God, by thy law declare and open our sores, full of sinful corruption, to cleanse and heal the same by the salve and plaister of "Christ crucified."

Wherefore we beseech thee now, O most gracious God and merciful Father, cause us, in mindful meditation of thy law, to find, feel and confess the sore grievous disease of sin in every member and part of us, and especially in the very bottom of our hearts; so that in the light of thy gospel, by the eyes of faith, we may see, desire, and feel the medicine of thy mercies in "Christ crucified;" daily more and more cleansing and healing our sinful sores; changing our hard stony hearts into fleshy soft hearts; scouring and washing out of our hearts our corrupt concupiscences and lusts, to write into our hearts thy law of pure love; and mortifying in us "the old man of sin," so that ever hereafter we may now not live in the flesh, but that "Christ may live in us," unto thy glory, our comfort, and the good example of others.

A PRAYER FOR THE FAITHFUL AFFLICTED IN FRANCE, FOR THE GOSPEL.

[The following prayer is printed at the end of the 'Godly Meditations of Bradford,' Hall, 1562, on the reverse of the table of 'faults escaped in the printing:' and it now follows the text of that publication. There is not any ground for attributing it to Bradford.

It was probably composed in the year 1562, when aid was afforded by England to the French Protestants against the Guisian faction. Vide Strype, Annals, I. i. 423—4, 545; and 'Liturgical Services of the reign of Elizabeth,' p. 458—9, 476—7, Parker Soc.

It was reprinted, with a few variations, in the 'Christian Prayers,' &c., collected by Bull, Powell, (see p. 118, note 1.) and Middleton 1570: vide Parker Soc. edition, p. 161—2, where it is entitled, 'A Prayer for the afflicted and persecuted under the tyranny of antichrist.']

O MERCIFUL Father, who never dost forsake such as put their trust in thee, stretch forth thy mighty arm to the defence of our brethren and neighbours in France, who in their extreme necessity cry for comfort unto thee. Prevent the cruel device of Haman, stay the rage of Holophernes, break off the counsel of Ahithophel. Let not the wicked say, "Where is now their God?" Let thy afflicted flock feel present aid and relief from thee, O Lord; look down upon them with thy pitiful eye from thy holy habitation. Send terror and trembling among their enemies; make an end of their outrageous tyranny; beat back their boldness in suppressing thy truth, in destroying thy true servants, in defacing thy glory, and in setting up antichrist. Let them not thus proudly advance themselves against thee and against thy Christ: but let them understand and feel that against thee they fight. Preserve and defend "the vine which thy right hand hath planted;" and let all nations see the glory of "thine Anointed." Amen.

JOANNIS LUDOVICI VIVIS VALENTINI PRECES ET MEDITATIONES DIURNÆ.

[See p. 223, and 230—42, above.]

QUUM EXPERGISCIMUR.

DEUS et Pater Domini nostri Jesu Christi, quem nemo nisi ex tuo ipsius munere cognoscit, effice, ut ad alia ingentia tua erga me beneficia accedat hoc quoque maximum, quod generi hominum præstari potest, ut quemadmodum corpus somno consopitum excitasti, sic et animum a somno peccatorum et tenebris mundi hujus liberes; quodque ex somno ad vigiliam revocasti, post mortem reddas vitæ: nam est somnus tibi, quæ nobis mors. Oramus atque obsecramus te, ut per benignitatem tuam socium sit corpus in vita hac atque administrum pietatis animæ; quo sit et in altera illa vita particeps beatitudinis sempiternæ. Per Jesum Christum Filium tuum Dominum nostrum, per quem omnia nobis tribuis bona et salutaria.

"Exsurge qui dormis, et surge a mortuis, et illuminabit te Christus."

Excursus ad meditandum.

Revocanda in mentem lætitia illa et beatitas resurrectionis æternæ; tum clarissimum et splendidissimum illud mane, et lux nova corporum post tenebras; quæ omnia plena sunt gaudiorum.

AD PRIMUM INTUITUM LUCIS.

Lux maxima et verissima, unde lux ista nascitur diei ac solis, quæ illuminas omnem hominem venientem in hunc mundum; Lux, cujus nulla est nox, nulla vespera, meridies clarus semper ac serenus, sine qua densissimæ sunt tenebræ, per quam sunt omnia lucidissima; Mens et Sapientia tanti Patris, illustra mentem meam, ut tua tantum videam, cæcus ad reliqua, et per tuas vias ingresso nihil præterea mihi luceat, aut sit gratum.

"Illumina, Domine, oculos meos, ne unquam obdormiam in morte; ne quando dicat inimicus meus, Prævalui adversus eum."

Excursio contemplationis.

Quanto potior lux animi, et præstabilior mentis oculus, quam corporis! quam convenit magis curare, ut acutius cernat mens, quam corpus! Oculum corporis bestiolæ habent, mentis autem soli homines, et quidem sapientes.

QUUM SURGIS.

Primus parens ex præclara et præcellenti sublimitate devolvit se in cœnum ignominiæ et abyssum flagitiorum ac scelerum; surrexit, manu abs te, Christe, sublatus. Ita et nos, nisi abs te sustollamur, in perpetuum jacebimus. Christe, generis humani Patrone indulgentissime, ut grave hoc onus beneficio tuo erigis, ita et animos nostros ad cognitionem amoremque evehe tuæ sublimitatis.

Excursus ad meditandum.

Quam acerbus casus Adæ propter peccatum, tum etiam cujusque nostrum a fastigio gratiæ Dei! Quantum beneficium Christi, cujus ope toties quotidie a casu surgimus!

QUUM INDUIMUR.

Indue me, Christe, te ipso, homine secundo, qui per justitiam factus es Deo Patri tuo adjuratissimus, ad exuendas concupiscentias omnes, et crucifigendum regnum carnis. Tu nobis adversus frigus hoc mundi esto indumentum, quo foveamur: qui si absis, omnia fiunt protinus torpida, infirma, mortua; sin adsis, vivida, tuta, fortia, vigentia. Et ut corpus amiculo hoc circumdo, ita tu me totum, sed animum potissimum, te ipso vestias.

Excursio.

Quomodo incorporamur Christo! ille nos induit, et regit, et fovet, ut sub alis ejus servemur, et regnemus.

INDUTUS PRO AUSPICIO DIEI.

DEUS et Domine Jesu Christe, tu scis, imo tu docuisti nos, quanta sit hominis imbecillitas, quam nihil possit absque tua ope. Si ipse sibi fidat et credat, necesse est ruat in mille exitia. Miserere, Pater, infirmitatis filii tui; adsis propitius et dexter, ut te illuminante vera bona videam, te hortante expetam, te ducente consequar. Mihi diffisus me cunctum tibi uni trado commendoque.

EGREDIENS DOMO.

INTER laqueos a dæmone et ministro ejus mundo extentos gradiendum est mihi, et circumfero stimulos carnis meæ.

Duc me, certissime Dux, ac tuere a plagis atque insidiis, ut quæcunque occurrent, non pluris faciam quam ipsa sint: in te unum aspiciens ac intentus sic pergam, ut unumquicque eatenus a me sumatur, quatenus ad te referendum est. "Vias tuas demonstra mihi, et semitas tuas edoce me."

Egressio ad contemplandum.

Quam vana est occupatio filiorum Adæ, quam varie distinetur ac distinguitur! quomodo mentes suas ad cogitationem[1] sui maximi boni tributas in tam diversa dissecant et dissipant, ut ejus quod primum et potissimum est obliviscatur, ut aliis sint offensio et Satan!

INGREDIENS ITER.

PEREGRINATIO est hæc vita nostra: a Domino discessimus, ad Dominum tendimus, sed inter voragines et præcipitia, quæ malus ille hostis per viam fabricatus est nobis, peccato exoculatis.

Porrige nobis manum, Christe, verus, certus, videns, amicus, et fidelis Dux. "Aperi oculos nostros," illustra regiam illam viam, quam tu primus ingressus ex hac corruptibilitate vitæ ad immortalitatem alterius munivisti. Tu es hæc "via;" duc nos ad Patrem per te ipsum, ut omnes simus unum cum illo, sicut tu et ille estis.

Altera.

Misericors Pater, tu sanctis hominibus, qui puro et simplici corde tibi placent, mittis angelos custodes, a quibus ducantur, tanquam imbecillioribus filiis filios natu grandiores ac magis validos: omnes enim, et angelos et homines, paterno affectu complecteris. Ita Tobiæ probi patris filio modestissimo, iter ingressuro, Raphaelem ministrum tuum misisti viæ comitem. Nobis virtute quidem Tobiæ longe inferioribus, sed bonitate tua confisis, mitte sanctum angelum tuum, qui nos et magno animo esse faciat, quoniam te fidimus, et per vias deducat tibi gratas.

[[1] The words 'et cogitationem' are added in the original.]

Digressio.

Quomodo peregrinamur a patria, a domo, a nostra origine, nempe Deo! quam libenter immoramur et intricamur in peregrinatione, hoc est, in miseria, immemores bonorum!

SUMPTURUS CIBUM.

ADMIRANDUM mysterium operis tui, Fabricator et Rector mundi, ut cibis istis hominum et animantium vitas sustentes. Profecto non est in pane atque obsoniis ea potentia, sed in voluntate et verbo tuo, quo uno vivunt et consistunt omnia. Tum et illud quantum est, te in annos singulos sufficere, unde tot animantibus alendis sit satis! quod sanctus propheta tuus, in enarratione laudum tuarum, dixit, "spectare ad te omnia, ut tu des sibi escam in tempore opportuno: aperis tu manum tuam, et imples omne animal benedictione." Hæc sunt mirabilia omnipotentiæ tuæ opera.

Rogamus te, Princeps et Pater munificentissime, ut qui vitam nostris corporibus subministras cibis per verbum tuum, animos quoque nostros gratia per idem verbum tuum vivifices, ut digni simus quos merito, tanquam pater carissimos filios, saluberrimis alimentis enutrias, donec ad perfectionem illam ventum sit Filii tui Jesu Christi, in qua "mortale hoc induet immortalitatem," nec amplius alimoniæ indigebimus, facti unum cum te ipso.

Digressio animi.

Quantæ potentiæ, condidisse nos; quantæ sapientiæ, tuerique ac conservare; quantæ bonitatis, immerentes! Quam multa data nostris usibus; quam admirabile, sustentari illis vitam; quanto admirabilius, animæ vitam ad immortalitatem propagare solo suo nutu!

IN CONVIVIO.

BENIGNISSIME munerum tuorum Distributor, qui donas bona omnia ad utendum, purus pura, sanctus sancta; fac adsit nobis auxilium tuum, ne prave abutamur iis, quæ tu ad nostros rectos usus condidisti. Non te amemus, quia illa das; sed illa diligamus, quia veniunt abs te, et ad tempus sunt nobis necessaria revertentibus ad te. Sobrie, pure, moderate, sancte versemur inter tua dona, qui es talis; ne, quæ tu largiris nobis tanquam medicinam vitæ corporeæ, nos in venenum convertamus mortis animæ: quin potius recte ea sumendo, et animo grato, fiant nobis corpori ac animo salutaria.

Egressio.

Ad usum data esse illa nobis, non ad abusum; ut prosint, non ut noceant; non nobis solis, sed aliis etiam per nos.

SUMPTO CIBO.

CORPORALIBUS cibis corporalem vitam fulcis ruentem. Grande hoc opus; sed illud utilius et sanctius, quod gratia tua, Christe Jesu, mortem nostrarum animarum arcet. Multum quidem pro ævo hoc debemus tibi; et quoniam id muneribus tuis prorogas, habemus atque agimus tibi gratias: sed hæc [vita] modo via est ad æternam illam, quam obsecramus te per mortem tuam ut beneficio quoque tuo immortali beatitudine dones. Hic pro re temporaria gratias quidem agimus, sed temporarias, videlicet ut possumus: illic pro æterna agemus æternas. Rogamus te, ut huic voto annuas, qui vivis cum Patre et Spiritu sancto, Deus in æternum.

REVERTENS DOMUM.

NIHIL est, Domine, tuæ illi sanctæ naturæ similius, quam animus in tranquillitate compositus. Tu nos ex mundi tumultibus in quietem illam et pacem tuam vocasti, ceu ex tempestatibus in portum; pacem qualem dare mundus non valet, "quæ omnem exuperat hominum sensum."

Domicilia nobis constituta sunt, in quæ confugeremus ab injuria cœli, a sævitia belluarum, a fluctibus turbæ, et mundi negotiis. Fiat, Pater indulgentissime, tuo maximo beneficio, ut in hæc se recipiat corpus nostrum ab externis actionibus, quo sese animo præbeat morigerum, nec reluctetur, quominus hic se in quietem illam tuam altissimam extollat; nihil obstrepat, nihil obturbet; omnia sint per pacem illam tuam placida et tranquilla.

Pax Christi huic domui, et omnibus habitantibus in ea.

Excursio animi.

Qualis et quam lætus erit reditus in domum illam sempiternam, quietissimam, beatissimam! Molestia omnis abest: si quid est hic lætum et jucundum, umbra est præ illis voluptatibus.

IN OCCASU SOLIS.

MISEROS, quibus sol tuus occidit, Domine! ille sol, qui sanctis tuis nunquam occiduus est, meridianus semper, serenus, ac fulgens. Gravius nox etiam in meridie incubat illorum mentes, qui abs te discedunt: at iis, qui tecum versantur, nunquam non est dies lucidissima. Habet sol hic vices suas: tu, si te vere diligamus, non habes. Utinam obicem hunc peccati a nobis removeas, quo sit semper in nostris pectoribus dies!

Digressio.

Non dolere nos quod sol occidat, quia rediturum scimus: ita non dolendum discedere animam e corpore, quam scimus esse reversuram.

QUUM ACCENDUNTUR LUCERNÆ.

Magnæ ac densissimæ animos nostros premunt tenebræ, nisi tua lux eas dispellat: fax est corporali mundo sol tuus, Artifex sapientissime; fax spiritali mundo sapientia tua, per quam animorum et corporum lux est orta. Post diem succedente nocte in remedium tenebrarum lucernas dedisti; post peccatum in remedium ignorantiæ doctrinam tuam, quam ad nos Filius tuus nostri amantissimus detulit. Fac nos, Auctor et Magister totius veritatis, utraque luce ea cernere, quibus caligo mentium depellatur.

"Signatum est super nos lumen vultus tui, Domine: dedisti lætitiam in corde meo." "Lucerna pedibus meis verbum tuum, et lumen semitis meis."

Excursio.

Lucernas hujus noctis esse scientiam et sapientiam a Deo hominibus traditam, quibus ea cernant in hac corporum nocte, quæ ipsis expediant: quantopere doctrinam hujusmodi optandam esse, et ubi contigerit, diligenter ac pie amplectendam.

QUUM EXUERIS.

Corpus hoc per peccatum fluxum et male cohærens sensim dissolvetur, ac reddetur terræ de qua sumptum est: ibi erit finis vanitatis hujus, quam nos stultitia nostra nobis confinximus. Sic dissolve me, Pater mitissime, qui et compegisti, ut dissolvi me sentiam, et a quo victus fuerim recorder; et quo eundum mihi sit considerem, ne imparatus rapiar ad tribunal tuum.

Excursio.

Non ponimus vestes gravate, quas sumus recepturi transacta nocte: sic corpus, post hanc noctem curriculi seculorum resumendum, ne posuerimus inviti.

CUM INTRAS LECTUM.

Peracto die, tradimus nos quieti [hac] nocte[1]: sic, vita hac finita, quiescemus in morte. Nihil vitæ similius quam quivis dies, nec morti quam somnus, nec sepulturæ quam lectus. Fac, Domine, Præses et Propugnator nostri, ut et nunc jacentes nos, ac nostri impotes, ab astu et incursibus crudelis hostis tueare; et tunc finito vitæ curriculo magis adhuc invalidos, non meritis nostris, sed clementia tua ad te voces, ut tecum semper vivamus, æternumque vigilemus. Nunc vero obdormiscamus in te: tu solus, tua illa bona ingentia, incredibilia, per visum nobis observentur, ut ne dor-

[[1] In the original, 'die nocte.']

mientes quidem a te absimus: quæ somnia tum cubicule ipsum et corpora nostra pura conservent, tum animos exhilarent beata illa tua lætitia.

"In pace in id ipsum obdormiam, et requiescam."

Excursio.

Peracto tumultuoso hoc die, succedit nox, et quies, et lectus, et somnus dulcissimus, qui summos reges et infimos servos pares facit: sic post tumultus et tempestates vitæ hujus, fidentibus Christo portum et quietem gratissimam esse paratam.

QUUM OBDORMISCIS.

Suscipe me tuendum, Jesu Christe, Præsidium nostrum. Fac ut sopito corpore animus in te meus vigilet, et felicem illam, lætissimamque cælestem vitam, lætus atque alacer contempletur, in qua tu es Princeps cum Patre et Spiritu Sancto; angeli vero et puri sanctique animi sunt cives ad æternitatem beatissimi.

A PRAYER COMPILED BY R. P.[1]

[See p. 242, note 1.— This Prayer follows the text of the Meditations of Bradford, printed by Copland, 1559, Bodleian Library, Oxford: see p. 222—3, above. It has also been compared with the reprints of that series, 1578, 1607, 1614. It was probably written in 1554, from the allusion to the marriage of queen Mary.

The initials 'R. P.' might possibly stand for 'Robert Pownall,' who was in exile, 1557, and was ordained by Abp. Grindal in 1560. Vide 'Original Letters,' p. 170, Parker Soc.; and Strype, Grindal, p. 59.]

Meditations of Bradford, Copland 1559, and after editions.

Strype, Mem. III. ii. p. 315—9.

O MOST omnipotent, magnificent, and glorious God, and Father of all consolation, we here assembled do not presume to present and prostrate ourselves before thy mercy-seat in the respect of our own worthiness and righteousness, which is altogether polluted and defiled; but in the merits, righteousness, and worthiness of thy only Son Jesus Christ, whom thou hast given unto us as a most pure and precious garment to cover our pollution and filthiness withal, to the end we might appear holy and justified in thy sight through him. Wherefore in the obedience of thy commandments, and in the confidence of thy promises contained in thy holy word, that thou shalt accept and grant our prayers presented unto thee in the favour of thy only Son our Saviour Jesu Christ, either for ourselves or for the necessity of thy saints and congregation, we here

[1 The heading of this prayer in the Meditations of Bradford, 1559, is: 'A most fruitful prayer for the dispersed church of Christ, very necessary to be used of the godly in these days of affliction, compiled by R. P.']

congregated together do with one mouth and mind most humbly beseech thee, not only to pardon and forgive us all our sins, negligences, ignorances, and iniquities, 'which we from time to time incessantly do commit against thy divine Majesty, in word, deed, and thought,' (such is the infirmity of our corrupted nature;) but also that it would please thee, O benign Father, to be favourable and merciful unto thy poor afflicted church and congregation, dispersed throughout the whole world, which in these days of iniquity are oppressed, injured, despised, persecuted, and afflicted for the testimony of thy word and for the obedience of thy laws.

And namely, O Lord and Father, we humbly beseech thee to extend thy mercy and favourable countenance upon all those that are imprisoned or condemned for the cause of thy gospel, whom thou hast chosen forth, and made worthy to glorify thy name; that either it may please thee to give them such constancy as thou hast given to thy saints and martyrs in time past, willingly to shed their blood for the testimony of thy word; or else mightily deliver them from the tyranny of their enemies, as thou deliveredst the condemned Daniel from the lions, and the persecuted Peter out of[2] prison, to the exaltation of thy glory, and the rejoicing of thy church.

Furthermore, most beneficial Father, we humbly beseech thee to stretch forth thy mighty arm into the protection and defence of all those that are exiled for the testimony of thy verity; (and that because they would not bend their backs and incline their necks under the yoke of antichrist, and be polluted with the execrable idolatries and blasphemous superstitions of the ungodly;) that it would please thee not only to feed them in strange countries, but also to prepare a resting-place for them, as thou hast done from time to time for thine elect in all ages, where as they may unite themselves together in the sincere ministration of thy holy word and sacraments, to their singular edification. And in due time restore them home again to their land, to celebrate thy praises, promote thy gospel, and edify thy desolate congregation.

Consequently, O Lord, thou that hast said that thou "wilt not break the bruised reed, nor quench the smoking flax," be merciful, we beseech thee, unto all those that through fear and weakness have denied thee by dissimulation and hypocrisy; that it may please thee to strengthen their "weak knees," thou that art the strength of them that stand[3], and "lift up their feeble hands," that their little smoke may increase into a great flame, and their "bruised reed" into a mighty oak, able to abide all the blustering blasts and

[2 'of' 1578, 1607, 1614: not in 1559.]
[3 'standeth' 1559: 'stand' 1578, 1607, 1614.]

stormy tempests of adversity; to the end that the ungodly do no longer triumph over their faith, which, as they think, they have utterly quenched and subdued. "Stir up thy strength" in them, O Lord, and behold them with that merciful eye wherewith thou beheldest Peter, that they, rising by repentance, may become the constant confessors of thy word, and the sanctified members of thy church; to the end, that when as by thy providence thou purposest to lay thy cross upon them, they do no more seek unlawful means to avoid the same, but most willingly to be contented with patience to take it up, and "follow thee," in what sort soever it shall please thee to lay the same upon their shoulders, either by death, imprisonment, or exile; and that it will please thee "not to tempt them above their powers," but give them grace utterly to despair of their own strength, and wholly to depend upon thy mercy.

On the other side, O Lord God, thou "righteous Judge," "let not the ungodly," the enemies of thy truth, continually "triumph over us," as they do at this day; let not "thine heritage" "become a reproach" and common laughing-stock unto the impudent and wicked papists, who by all possible means seek the utter destruction of thy "little flock," in shedding the blood of thy saints for the testimony of thy word, seeking by most devilish and damnable practices to subvert thy truth. Confound them, O God, and all their wicked counsels, and "in the same pit they have digged for other let them be taken," that it may be universally known, that "there is no counsel nor force that can prevail against the Lord" our God. Break, O Lord, the horns of those bloody "bulls of Basan;" pull down those high mountains that elevate themselves against thee; and root up the rotten race of the ungodly, to the end that, they being consumed in the fire of thine indignation, thine exiled church may in their own land find place of habitation.

O Lord, deliver our land, which thou hast given us for a portion to possess in this life, from the invasion and subduing of strangers. Truth it is, we cannot deny but that our sins hath justly deserved this great plague, now imminent and approaching, even to be given over into the hands and subjection of that proud and beastly nation that neither know thee nor fear thee, and to serve them in a bodily captivity that have refused to serve thee in a spiritual liberty[1]. Yet, Lord, forasmuch as we are assuredly persuaded by thy holy word, that thine anger doth not last for ever towards those that earnestly repent, but in the stead of vengeance dost

[1 An allusion to the marriage of queen Mary with Philip II. of Spain, July 25, 1554.—Strype, Mem. III. i. 196—210, 418—20.]

shew mercy; we most penitently beseech thee to remove this thy great indignation bent towards us; and give not over our land, our cities, towns and castles, our goods, possessions and riches, our wives, children, and our own lives, into the subjection of strangers: but rather, O Lord, expel them our land, subvert their counsels, dissipate their devices, and deliver us from their tyranny, as thou deliveredst Samaria from that cruel Ben-hadad, Jerusalem from that blasphemous Sennacherib, and Betulia from that proud Holophernes.

Give us, O Lord, such princes and rulers, such magistrates and governors, as will advance thy glory, erect up thy gospel, suppress idolatry, banish all papistry, and execute justice and equity. Water again, O Lord, thy vine of England with the moisture of thy holy word, lest it utterly perish and wither away. Build up again the decayed walls of thy ruined Jerusalem, thy congregation in this land, lest the ungodly do attribute our confusion not unto our sins (as the truth is), but unto our profession in religion.

Remember, O Lord, that we are a parcel of thy portion, "thy flock," the inheritors of thy kingdom, "the sheep of thy pasture," and the members of thy Son our Saviour Jesus Christ. Deal with us therefore "according to the multitude of thy mercies," that all nations, kindreds, and tongues may celebrate thy praises in the restoring of thy ruined church to perfection again; for it is thy work, O Lord, and not man's, and from thee do we with patience attend the same, and not from the fleshly arm of man. And therefore to thee only is due all dominion, power, and thanksgiving, now in our days and evermore. Amen.

INSTITUTIO DIVINA ET VERE CONSOLATORIA CONTRA VIM MORTIS, JOANNE BRADFORDO ANGLO AUTHORE, EX VERNACULA LINGUA IN LATINUM SERMONEM CONVERSA.

[Vide p. 331 et seq. above.]

Quum Dei auxilio fretus, meipsum non minus consolandi gratia quam alios excitandi causa, statuissem aliquid de Morte scribere, (cujus in limine quamvis diu versatus sim, nunquam tamen juxta aliorum judicium tam prope ejus foribus adstiti quam nunc;) maxime certe necessarium mihi et utile videbatur te, mi Jesu, invocare, tuumque implorare auxilium, qui moriendo mortem de-

MS. Lansd. no 119. 14. British Museum.

glutisti, vitamque ac immortalitatem in ejus locum substituisti, sicut per evangelium constat. Tu me vera ac indubitata fide imbue, qua statim a morte homines in æternam vitam transeunt; ut factis, non autem nuda speculatione, aliquid nunc scribam de morte (quæ extra te et in se ipsa formidabilis admodum et truculenta videtur) ad gloriam tui nominis, et ad meam ipsius in te consolationem, et ad omnes alios instruendos, ad quos hæc mea oratio vel legenda vel audienda venerit. Amen.

Quatuor mortis genera sunt, primum vero naturale est, aliud spirituale, tertium temporale, quartum æternum. De primo vero ac ultimo, qualia sunt, non est quod dicam. Secundum vero et tertium non ita fortasse rudi plebeculæ, quorum gratia hæc scribo, sunt manifesta.

Per spiritualem itaque mortem talem intelligo, qua factum est ut, corpore vivente intereat tamen anima; cujus mentionem facit apostolus, cum dicat "viduam, quæ in deliciis versatur, viventem quidem mortuam esse." Videtis ergo quid mihi volo per 'spiritualem mortem.'

1 Tim. v.

Quod ad 'temporale mortis genus' attinet, istiusmodi sentio, quo corpus et animi passiones ita mortificantur ut vivat spiritus. Hujus mortis mentionem facit apostolus, exhortans nos ut "mortificemus membra nostra."

Col. iii.

[The following is the conclusion of the MS.]

Item sæpe cogita de articulo, carnis scilicet resurrectione, certus hoc corpus "resurrecturum in ultimo die," quando "Dominus ad judicandum veniet," et incorruptibile, immortale, gloriosum, spirituale, purum, et lucidum futurum esse, "instar gloriosi corporis" Salvatoris nostri Jesu Christi. Nam is est "primitiæ mortuorum;" et ut Deus "omnia est in omnibus," sic tibi erit "in Christo." Contemplare ergo statum tuum; tu enim eris "ut is est:" nam "ut imaginem terreni Adam induisti, sic imaginem cœlestis indues." Glorificato igitur Deum cum animo tum corpore. Exspectes igitur "hunc diem Domini," et para tibi supellectilem copiosam scripturarum in illum diem, quam ego temporis angustia pressus omitto.

Phil. iii.

Postremo obversetur tibi sæpissime 'vita æterna,' ad quam jam appulisti pæne. Mors enim porta est quæ transportat nos in illam terram, ubi affatim sunt omnia quæ optes, imo omnia preciosissima longe antecellunt, siquidem illum "Deum videbimus facie ad faciem;" quod jam nulla ratione fieri potest, sed potius obvelandæ sunt facies nostrum cum Moyse et Helia, donec "vultus" et anteriores partes Domini "præterierunt." Nunc "posteriora"

Exod. iii. iv.

illius contemplanda sunt, ut illum in verbo suo, in creaturis, et in facie Mediatoris nostri Jesu Christi intueamur: ast tum ipsum "vultum ejus contemplabimur," et "cognoscemus ut cogniti sumus."

De his ergo sæpissime cogitemus, ut fidem habeamus, ut volentes ac cupidi ad felicem mortis portum appellamus: quam exoptandam videtis, et non reformidandam omnibus, præsertim suis qui "in Christo" sunt, id est, his qui indubitate credunt; qui sic discernuntur ab his qui ore tantum se credere dicunt, si de die in diem moriantur, id est, si totis viribus enituntur corpus crucifigere, et per Spiritum Dei carnis concupiscentias mortificare; non quidem ut illis prorsus destituantur, sed "ne regnet in illis, id est, in mortali hoc corpore," ut hoc pacto carnis et corporis illecebris inserviant, (cujus "servi" non sunt,) sed Deo potius ad justitiam, cujus servi sumus omnes, quandoquidem "nunc sub gratia sumus, et non sub lege;" ob quam quidem causam promisit Dominus "peccatum non regnaturum in nobis:" quod propter nominis sui gloriam, veritatem, potentiam, et misericordiam, in nobis perpetuo præstet et confirmet. Amen.

A PREFACE BY BISHOP IRONSIDE, WHEN VICE-CHANCELLOR OF OXFORD, 1688.

[This Preface accompanies a publication which has the following title:

'An account of a disputation at Oxford, *anno Dom.* 1554; with a Treatise of the blessed sacrament; both written by Bishop Ridley, martyr. To which is added a letter written by Mr. John Bradford[1], never before printed[1]. All taken out of an original manuscript. OXFORD, Printed at the Theatre, *anno Dom.* 1688.'

This publication is not referred to in the 'Catalogue of all the discourses published against Popery during the reign of James II. [228 in number] by members of the church of England...London, 1689.'

Bishop Ironside, writer of this Preface, had been elected Warden of Wadham college, Oxford, 1665, and was Vice-Chancellor of that university, 1687 and 1688. He became Bishop of Bristol, 1689, and of Hereford, 1691; and died 1701, aged 69.—Wood, Athenæ, Oxon. Bliss. IV. 896—7. Godwin. De præsul. Angl. p. 497, ed. Richardson, Cantab. 1743.]

THERE is no good Protestant but will be glad to meet with any relic, though never so small, (a finger or a tooth, if I may so speak,) of our blessed martyrs, especially such eminent ones as

[[1] The letter is that 'on the mass, to Hopkins and others at Coventry,' p. 389-99 above. It had been printed before by Bp. Coverdale, 'Letters of the martyrs' 1564, p. 345-54.]

Bishop Ridley and Mr Bradford: I mean, any of their writings that never yet were printed cannot but find a very hearty welcome amongst them; and such is a good part of what is now published.

Bishop Ridley's Treatise indeed hath been printed long since, and is in our libraries, and hath been again lately reprinted[1]: but any account of the Disputation with him at Oxford, in Latin, I have not met with but in this manuscript[2]; neither is the letter of Mr Bradford's, now published, in Foxe's History.

However there is no impartial reader will have reason to suspect either of them to be spurious: they are of the same spirit and temper, which we find from our histories to have animated and governed these great men: and what is now printed, I do assure the reader, is exactly according to the manuscripts I found in my father's study presently upon his death, 1671.

Our adversaries boast, the relics of their saints work miracles; (indeed as they have been, and, which is more, are still managed, they are full of wonders:) I hope these of ours will do some good, partly by shewing the world how consonant the church of England is, and always hath been, to her principles, particularly in that concerning the presence in the eucharist; (in managing of which she always walked after the scripture phrase with great fear and reverence, and expressed herself in the interpretation with so much nicety and caution, as to have given occasion perhaps to have been misunderstood by some weak, or to be artificially misrepresented by some evil men, to I know not what purposes;) partly by setting before us examples, not only of suffering, if it be the will of God, but also of all good and dutiful behaviour towards our superiors with meekness and fear; for whom we do and will always implore the throne of grace to support their authority over us, let the sceptre held out be what it will.

For these reasons I am content this manuscript be printed.

GILB. IRONSIDE, Vice-Chan.

Wadham Coll.
Oxford, Aug.
the 10th, 88.

[1 Bp. Ridley's Declaration of the Lord's supper was reprinted by the learned Henry Wharton, Lond. 1688. See Works of Bp. Ridley, p. xiv, 5—45.]

[2 The entire Disputation of Bp. Ridley had appeared in Latin in the edition of Foxe's 'Acts and Monuments,' printed in that language, the *Rerum in ecclesia gestarum commentarii, Basil.* 1559; and has lately been reprinted after collation with a MS. in the collection of Abp. Parker in Corpus Christi Coll. Cambridge) in Works of Bp. Ridley, p. 433—81, Parker Soc.]

OFFICIUM ET SENTENTIA CONTRA JOHANNEM BRADFORD.

ACTA die lunæ vicesimo octavo die Januarii, anno Domini juxta computationem ecclesiæ Anglicanæ millesimo quingentesimo quinquagesimo quarto, in ecclesia parochiali Sancti Salvatoris, nuncupata *Saynte Mary Overey*, in burgo de Southwark.

MS. Harl. 421. fol. 36, 42—4. British Museum. Original.

OFFICIUM DOMINI CONTRA JO. BRADFORD.

EISDEM die, hora, et loco productus fuit coram Domino Johannes Bradford, laicus, etc. Cui post exhortationem per Dominum factam, ut se reconciliaret et ad unitatem sanctæ ecclesiæ et catholicæ fidei rediret, dictus Dominus Episcopus, quia videbat eundem Bradford pertinaciter in sententia persistentem, objecit articulum sequentem; videlicet, quod ipse Johannes Bradford, tam intra diocesim suam Wintoniæ, quam aliis quamplurimis locis hujus regni, asseruit, dixit, prædicavit, et publicavit, et defendebat, sicque in præsenti asserit, dicit, credit, et defendit, quod in eucharistia sive altaris sacramento verum et naturale Christi corpus, ac verus et naturalis Christi sanguis, sub speciebus panis et vini vere non est; et quod ibi est materialis panis et materiale vinum tantum, absque veritate et præsentia corporis et sanguinis Christi. Cui articulo ipse Bradford respondendo dixit, *That Christ is present in the sacrament when the sacrament is duly ministered; and that Christ is present in the sacrament by faith, to faith, and in faith, and none otherwise; and saith that Christ is not in the sacrament by transubstantiation; and saith that simply he believeth no transubstantiation; also that it is not the body of Christ but to him that receiveth it; and that an evil man doth not receive it* in forma panis; *and that after and before the receipt there is the substance of bread.* Cui dictis perversis assertionibus inhærenti Dominus assignavit ad comparendum crastina die in hoc loco inter horas viii et x ante meridiem, ad videndum ulteriorem processum fieri.

30 Januarii.

Eisdem die et loco comparuit personaliter dictus Johannes Bradford. Qui licet fuerit per Dominum Episcopum multis argumentis et rationibus suasus et exhortatus ut se reconciliaret et rediret ad ecclesiæ catholicæ unitatem, Episcopo tamen pertinaci ac indurato animo persistat, nec valuit ullis rationibus flecti aut persuaderi. Et ideo Dominus Episcopus visa ejus pertinaci induritia tulit etiam contra eum condemnationis sententiam definitivam, pronuntiando

Officium Domini contra Bradford.

eum [pro] obstinato hæretico et excommunicato; et insequenter tradidit eum seculari manui, videlicet, dictis Vicecomitibus, etc. præsentibus de quibus in prioribus hujus diei actis habetur mentio.

SENTENTIA CONTRA JOHANNEM BRADFORD.

MS. Harl. 421.
fol. 46.
Original.

IN DEI NOMINE, AMEN. Nos Stephanus, permissione divina Wintoniensis Episcopus, judicialiter et pro tribunali sedentes; in quodam hæreticæ pravitatis negotio contra te Johannem Bradford laicum, coram nobis in judicio personaliter comparentem, et nobis super hæretica pravitate detectum, denunciatum, et delatum, ac in ea parte apud bonos et graves notorie et publice diffamatum, rite et legitime procedentes; auditis, visis, intellectis, rimatis, et matura deliberatione discussis et ponderatis dicti negotii meritis et circumstantiis; servatisque in omnibus et per omnia in eodem negotio de jure servandis, ac quomodo libet requisitis, Christi nomine invocato, ac ipsum solum Deum præ oculis nostris habentes: quia per acta inactitata, deducta, probata, confessata, et per te sæpius coram nobis in eodem negotio recognita, asserta, et confirmata, comperimus et invenimus te, tum per confessiones tuas varias, tum per recognitiones tuas judiciales coram nobis judicialiter factas, errores, hæreses, et falsas opiniones subscriptas, juri divino ac catholicæ, universalis, et apostolicæ ecclesiæ determinationi obviantes, contrarias, et repugnantes, tenuisse, credidisse, affirmasse, prædicasse, et dogmatizasse, videlicet[1], *that Christ is in the sacrament of the altar by and to faith, and none otherwise; also that in the sacrament of the altar is not the body of Christ, except it be taken, received, and eaten; also that transubstantiation is nothing:* quos quidem errores, hæreses, et falsas opiniones, juri divino ac catholicæ, universalis, et apostolicæ ecclesiæ determinationi obviantes, contrarias, et repugnantes, coram nobis tam in judicio quam extra, animo obstinato, pertinaci, et indurato, arroganter, pertinaciter, scienter, et obstinate, asseruisti, tenuisti, affirmasti, dixisti, pariter et defendisti, atque te sic credere, asserere, tenere, affirmare, et dicere velle paribus obstinatia, malitia, et cordis cæcitate, etiam prudens et sciens affirmasti: Idcirco nos Stephanus, Wintoniensis Episcopus, ordinarius et diocesanus antedictus, tam de venerabilium confratrum nostrorum Episcoporum præsentium et nobis assidentium consensu et assensu

---

[1 The following words are scored across in the original, 'Quod in eucharistiæ, sive altaris sacramento, verum et naturale Christi corpus et verus et naturalis Christi sanguis sub speciebus panis et vini vere non est; et quod ibi est et materialis panis et materiale vinum tantum, absque veritate et præsentia corporis et sanguinis Christi.']

expressis, quam etiam de et cum consilio et judicio jurisperitorum et sacrarum literarum professorum, cum quibus communicavimus in hac parte, TE Johannem Bradford de meritis, culpis, obstinatiis et contumaciis, per improbas et sceleratas tuas obstinatias et pertinacias multipliciter contractis, incursis, et aggravatis in detestabili, horrendo, et impio hæreticæ pravitatis reatu et execrabili dogmate comprehensum fuisse et esse, atque hujusmodi scelerata et impia dogmata coram nobis sæpe dixisse, asseruisse, atque scienter, voluntarie, et pertinaciter defendisse, et manutenuisse per varias tuas confessiones, assertiones, et recognitiones tuas judiciales, sæpe coram nobis repetitas ita asseruisse, affirmasse, et credidisse, declaramus et pronuntiamus, teque in hac parte rite et legitime confessum fuisse et esse decernimus. Idcoque te Johannem Bradford antedictum, hujusmodi tuos errores, hæreses, ac impias et damnatas opiniones refutare, retractare, recantare, et abjurare in forma ecclesiæ approbata nolentem, sed obstinate et pertinaciter dictis tuis sceleratis hæresibus et execratis opinionibus inhærentem, et ad unitatem sacrosanctæ ecclesiæ redire nolentem, præmissorum occasione, causa, et prætextu, hæreticum obstinatum et pertinacem fuisse et esse cum animi dolore et cordis amaritudine etiam declaramus, pronuntiamus, et decernimus. Teque tanquam hæreticum obstinatum et pertinacem exnunc judicio sive curiæ seculari, ut membrum putridum, a corpore sacrosanctæ ecclesiæ resecatum, ad omnem juris effectum exinde sequi valentem, relinquendum et tradendum fore decernimus et declaramus, atque de facto relinquimus et tradimus, teque Johannem Bradford, hæreticum obstinatum et pertinacem hujusmodi, majoris excommunicationis sententia præmissorum occasione innodatum et involutum, eaque ligatum fuisse et esse, sententialiter et diffinitive declaramus per hanc nostram sententiam finalem, quam in et contra te dolenter ferimus et promulgamus in his scriptis.

Lecta, lata, et promulgata fuit hæc sententia in Ecclesia parochiali Beatæ Mariæ Overy, alias nuncupata Sancti Salvatoris, in Burgo de Sowthwark, Wintoniæ Diocesi, die Mercurii, tricesimo die Januarii, Anno Domini juxta cursum ecclesiæ Anglorum, 1554, præsentibus testibus de quibus in actis illius diei fit mentio.

NOTES.

Note A, p. 45, 'Lady Psalters.'

Vide Horæ beat. Mar. V sec. us. Eccl. Sarisb., Rosarium aureum beat. Virg., signat. R 5, 1542: copy, British Museum. See too the Offic. b. Mar. Virg. Pii V jussu editum, Psalterium sive Rosarium beat. V Mariæ, p. 721—30, Antv. 1780.

The 'Rosary' or 'Lady's Psalter' was instituted by Dominick at the beginning of the 13th century; and consisted of 150 small beads, for each of which the 'Ave Maria,' and 15 large, for each of which the 'Pater noster,' was recited, to commemorate the fifteen mysteries of our Lord and Saviour, 'quorum consors fuit B. Virgo Maria.'—Du Cange, Gloss., v. 'psalterium' and 'rosarium.' Vide Fowns, Trisagion, p. 395, Lond. 1618.

The parody also on the book of Psalms, attributed to Bonaventure, (in which the supplications and praises, originally addressed to the Most High, are blasphemously transferred to the virgin,) was called the 'Lady's Psalter.' Herbert (Typogr. Antiq. III. 1789,) mentions ' Our Lady's Psalter, and Rosary, by Bonaventure, 1555,' printed by Wayland. Vide Foxe, Acts, &c. 1583, p. 1598—1601, or ed. 1843—8, VII. 131—6; Bonavent. Opusc. I. 504, Paris. 1647; Psalt. Virg. Mariæ, Bonavent. Paris. 1618; Critical inquiry as to the Psalter of Bonavent. by King, 1840.

Note B, p. 46, 'confession' and 'satisfaction.'

Vide Concil. Trident. Sess. IV. Jul. Tert. ann. 1551, cap. v. fol. 67, Antv. 1564; Id. ibid. canon XIII. fol. 72; Thom. Aquin. Summ. Partis III. Suppl. Quæst. VI. Art. i. p. 8, Colon. 1622.

Note C, p. 49, 'pardons,' and 'purgatory.'

Concil. Trident. Sess. IX. Pii Quart. ann. 1563, Decr. de Indulgent., Thom. Aquin. ibid. Quæst. XXV. Art. i. p. 32.

Concil. Florent. in Concil. stud. Labb. et Cossart. Tom. XIII. col. 515—6, Lut. Par. 1671—2; Concil. Trident. Sess. IX. Pii Quart. ann. 1563, Decr. de Purgat.; Catech. Concil. Trident. ad Par. De Symb. artic. descendit ad inferos, fol. 35, Paris. 1568.

Vide Willet, Synopsis Papismi, 1600, contr. XIV., and addit. to book v., contr. IX.; Field, Of the Church, book v. app. sect. 4, Lond. 1635; Fowns, Trisagion, p. 628—52, 329—44, Lond. 1619; Bp. Stillingfleet, Vindic. of Abp. Laud, Conf. part III. ch. vi. p. 636—54, Lond. 1665; Bp. Burnet on Art. XXII. Ch. of Eng.

Note D, p. 49—280, 'placebos' and 'diriges.'

'Placebo' or 'Dirige.' Vide Horæ beat. V Mar. ad leg. Sarisb. Eccl. rit. fol. cxxv, Paris. 1519. It was 'the Office of the dead:' there are various names given to it in the old books; sometimes the 'Placebo' from the antiphon [Ps. cxvi. 9, Vulgate] at the beginning; or the 'Placebo and Dirge,' the latter so called also from its first antiphon [Ps. v. 8, Vulgate]; sometimes the *Vigiliæ mortuorum*, or *Officium pro defunctis;* sometimes the 'Dirge' only.—Maskell on 'The Prymer in English,' in 'Monumenta Ritualia, 1846, II. 110 et seq., where the Office occurs.

P. 50, note 4, Comm. in Epist. ii. ad Cor. cap. vii. in Heiron. Op. V. col. 1025, ed. Bened. Par. 1693—1706.

P. 50, note 4, Comm. in Epist. ii. ad Cor. cap. vii. in Hieron. Op. V col. 1025, ed. Bened. Par. 1693—1706.

This commentary is considered by Vallarsius to be by Pelagius: vide Hieron. Op. XI. col. 835—6, stud. Vallars. Veron. 1734—42; and Oudin. Comm. de script. eccles. I. col. 845—6, 916, Lips. 1722.

Note E, on 'sir Johns,' p. 71, 391.

'A priest was the third of the three sirs, which only were in request of old, (no baron, viscount, earl, nor marquess, being then in use;) to wit, sir king, sir knight, and sir priest.'—Watson, Decacord. Quodlib. quest. 1602, p. 53. Hence a 'sir John' became a familiar name for a priest. Vide Bp. Bale, Image of both churches, part II. signat. K 4 ed. Jugge; Todd's Johnson, Dict.

Note F, p. 86, 545. Testimonies of Irenæus, Tertullian, Origen, Cyprian, Epiphanius, Jerome, Augustine, Theodoret, Cyril of Alexandria, and Bede, that what the Lord gave in the eucharist was "bread."

...τὸ ἀπὸ τῆς κτίσεως ποτήριον αἷμα ἴδιον ὡμολόγησε, ἐξ οὗ τὸ ἡμέτερον δένει αἷμα· καὶ τὸν ἀπὸ τῆς κτίσεως ἄρτον ἴδιον σῶμα διεβεβαιώσατο, ἀφ' οὗ τὰ ἡμέτερα αὔξει σώματα.—Iren. Cont. Hær. Lib. v. cap. ii. 2. Op. I. 294, ed. Bened. Venet. 1734.

...acceptum panem, et distributum discipulis, corpus illum suum fecit, Hoc est corpus meum dicendo, id est, figura corporis mei.—Tertull. Advers. Marcion. Lib. iv. 40. Op. 457—8, Lut. Par. 1675.

...τὸ ἁγιαζόμενον βρῶμα διὰ λόγου Θεοῦ καὶ ἐντεύξεως, κατ αὐτὸ μὲν τὸ ὑλικὸν εἰς τὴν κοιλίαν χωρεῖ, καὶ εἰς ἀφεδρῶνα ἐκβάλλεται· κατὰ δὲ τὴν ἐπιγενομένην αὐτῷ εὐχὴν, κατὰ τὴν ἀναλογίαν τῆς πίστεως, ὠφέλιμον γίνεται, καὶ τῆς τοῦ νοῦ αἴτιον διαβλέψεως, ὁρῶντος ἐπὶ τὸ ὠφελοῦν· καὶ οὐχ ἡ ὕλη τοῦ ἄρτου, ἀλλ' ὁ ἐπ' αὐτῷ εἰρημένος λόγος, ἐστὶν ὁ ὠφελῶν τὸν μὴ ἀναξίως τοῦ Κυρίου ἐσθίοντα αὐτόν.—Origen. Comm. in Matt. Tom. XI. cap. xiv. Op. III. 449, 500, ed. Bened. Par. 1733—59.

...quando Dominus corpus suum panem vocat de multorum granorum adunatione congestum; populum nostrum, quem portabat, indicat adunatum: et quando sanguinem suum vinum appellat, de botris atque acinis plurimis expressum atque in unum coactum; gregem item nostrum significat commixtione adunatæ multitudinis copulatum.—Cypr. Epist. LXIX. ad Magn. Op. 182, Oxon. 1682.

Ὁρῶμεν γὰρ ὅτι ἔλαβεν ὁ πατὴρ [Pro πατὴρ leg. σωτήρ, annot. *Petav.*] εἰς τὰς χεῖρας αὐτοῦ, ὡς ἔχει ἐν τῷ εὐαγγελίῳ, ὅτι ἀνέστη ἐν τῷ δείπνῳ, καὶ ἔλαβε τάδε· καὶ εὐχαριστήσας εἶπε, Τοῦτό μου ἐστὶ τόδε· καὶ ὁρῶμεν ὅτι οὐκ ἴσον ἐστιν, οὐδὲ ὅμοιον, οὐ τῇ ἐνσάρκῳ εἰκόνι, οὐ τῇ ἀοράτῳ θεότητι, οὐ τοῖς χαρακτῆρσι τῶν μελῶν. Τὸ μὲν γάρ ἐστι στρογγυλοειδὲς καὶ ἀναίσθητον, ὡς πρὸς τὴν δύναμιν· καὶ ἠθέλησεν χάριτι εἰπεῖν, Τοῦτό μου ἐστι τόδε....—Epiphan. Ancorat. 57. Op. II. 60, Par. 1622.

Postquam typicum pascha fuerat impletum, et agni carnes cum apostolis comederat, assumit panem qui confortat cor hominis, et ad verum paschæ transgreditur sacramentum; ut quomodo in præfiguratione ejus Melchisedec, summi Dei sacerdos, panem et vinum offerens fecerat, ipse quoque veritatem sui corporis et sanguinis repræsentaret.—Hieron. Comm. Lib. IV. in Matt. cap. xxvi. Op. VII. col. 216, stud. Vallars. Veron. 1734—42.

Non enim Dominus dubitavit dicere, 'Hoc est corpus meum,' cum signum daret corporis sui...Sic est...sanguis anima, quomodo petra erat Christus...nec tamen ait, Petra significabat Christum; sed ait, 'Petra erat Christus.'—August. Cont. Adimant. cap. xii. 3, 5. Op. VIII. col. 124—6, ed. Bened. Par. 1679—1700.

ΟΡΘ. Ὁ δέ γε σωτὴρ ὁ ἡμέτερος ἐνήλλαξε τὰ ὀνόματα· καὶ τῷ μὲν σώματι τὸ τοῦ συμβόλου τέθεικεν ὄνομα, τῷ δὲ συμβόλῳ τὸ τοῦ σώματος. οὕτως ἄμπελον ἑαυτὸν ὀνομάσας, αἷμα τὸ σύμβολον προσηγόρευσεν......ὁ γὰρ δὴ τὸ φύσει σῶμα σῖτον καὶ ἄρτον προσαγορεύσας, καὶ αὖ πάλιν ἑαυτὸν ἄμπελον ὀνομάσας, οὗτος τὰ ὁρώμενα σύμβολα τῇ τοῦ σώματος καὶ αἵματος προσηγορίᾳ τετίμηκεν, οὐ τὴν φύσιν μεταβαλών, ἀλλὰ τὴν χάριν τῇ φύσει προστεθεικώς.—Theod. Immut. Dial. I. Op. IV 17—8, Lut. Par. 1642.

Τοῖς γὰρ ἤδη πεπιστευκόσι διακλάσας τὸν ἄρτον ἐδίδου, λέγων· λάβετε, φάγετε· τοῦτό ἐστι τὸ σῶμά μου.—Cyril. Alex. In Joan. Evang. Lib. IV. cap. ii. Op. IV 360, Lut. 1638.

Frangit autem ipse panem quem porrigit, ut ostendat corporis sui fractionem non sine sua sponte futuram......'Similiter et calicem, postquam cænavit, dedit eis.' Quia ergo panis carnem confirmat, vinum vero sanguinem operatur in carne, hic ad corpus Christi mystice, illud refertur ad sanguinem.—Ven. Bed. In Luc. Evang. cap. xxii. Lib. VI. Op. V col. 424, Col. Agrip. 1688.

P. 91, line 3, and note 5, on August. In Johann. Evang. vii. Tract. xxx. 1. (Op. III. ii. col. 517, ed. Bened. Par. 1679—1700.) 'Oportet in uno loco esse.'

The Benedictine editors state that the various editions and MSS. of Augustine agree in the reading ' uno loco esse potest;' but that the words of that father are cited with the variation, 'oportet' instead of 'potest,' in Ivo, Gratian, Lombard, and Aquinas.

Vide August. in Ivon. Decr. Pars ii. cap. viii. p. 56, Lovan. 1561 : Id. in Corp. Jur. Canon. Decret. Gratian. Decr. Tert. Pars, De Consecr. Dist. ii. can. 44, p. 421, Paris. 1618: Id. in Lomb. Lib. Sentent. Lib. iv. Dist. x. fol. 351, Col. Agrip. 1576: Id. in Thom. Aquin. Summ. Pars III. Quæst. lxxv. Art. i. p. 164, Colon. 1622.

Note G, p. 306, 'Defence of election.'

Bradford mentions both the parts of this treatise, as follows, in a letter addressed " To his dearly beloved in the Lord, Henry Hart, John Barre, John Lidley, Robert Coole, Nicholas Shetterden, William Porrege, Roger Newman, William Lawrence, John Gibson, Richard Porrege, Humfrey Middleton, William Kempe, and to all other that fear the Lord and love his truth, abiding in Kent, Essex, Sussex, and thereabout[1]:" *[MS. 1. 2. 8. no. 34. Emman.Coll. Cambridge. Bp. Coverdale, Letters of the martyrs, 1564, p. 470—1.]*

"Although I look hourly for officers to come and have me to execution, yet can I not but attempt to write something unto you, my dearly beloved, (as always you have been, howsoever you have taken me,) to occasion you the more to weigh the things wherein some controversy hath been amongst us, especially the article and doctrine of predestination, whereof I have written a little Treatise, and direct it to our dear and godly sister Joyce Hales[2]; therein, as briefly shewing my faith, so answering the 'enormities' gathered of some to slander the same necessary and comfortable doctrine.

"That little piece of work I commend unto you, as a thing whereof I doubt not to answer to my comfort before the tribunal-seat of Jesus Christ: and therefore I heartily pray you and every of you, for the tender mercies of God in Christ, that you would not be rash to condemn things unknown, lest God's woe should fall upon you for calling[3] good evil, and evil good. For the great love of God in Christ, cavil not at things that be well spoken, nor construe not things to an evil part, when ye have occasion otherwise. Do not suppose that any man, by affirming predestination, (as in that book I have truly set it forth, according to God's word and the consent of Christ's church,) either to seek carnality, or to

---

[1] This heading is in the Emmanuel MS., but not in 1564.
[2] The last eleven words are in the Emmanuel MS., but not in 1564.
[3] 'call' MS.: 'calling' 1564.

set forth matter of desperation. Only by the doctrine of it I have sought[1], as to myself, so to others, a certainty of salvation, a setting up of Christ only, an exaltation of God's grace, mercy, righteousness, truth, wisdom, power, and glory, and a casting down of man and all his power; that he that glorieth may glory only and altogether, and continually, in the Lord."

Note H, p. 469, 480, 484, Bp. Gardiner *De vera obedientia.*

Shall any man think it indifferent that I shall be called a liar, because I obey the truth; because I serve God in obeying my prince, that I shall be reported to be a contemner of the sacraments, or an oath-breaker? And that that is fondly laid to the husband's charge after he is divorced, because he performed not his promise that he ought not to have made; shall that in this cause be grievously and earnestly trumped in my way, because I am by most grave judgment of the truth divorced from the church of Rome, (which it was not lawful for me to keep still,) and am compelled to take my wife truth to me?..... It is decreed that not so much as by the civil laws a man is bounden to perform unhonest or unlawful promises, lest it might be thought that those laws do rather commend perseverance in crimes, than repentance: and in the ecclesiastical decrees it is also established, that no man is bounden to perform an unlawful oath, seeing an oath cannot bind a man to wickedness.—Bp. Gardiner, De vera obedient., Translation, signature I v, vi, Roane, Oct. 26, 1553.

Note I, p. 541, 'So much talk there was *ad Ephesios.*'

'Talk *ad Ephesios:*' irrelevant or idle words. So Bp. Jewel: 'As for Marcus Ephesius, he seemeth well to brook his name, for his talk runneth altogether *ad Ephesios.*'—Bp. J. Reply to Harding, Art. x. div. vi. p. 579, Parker Soc. The phrase, Ἐφέσια γράμματα, had in ancient times been applied proverbially to those who 'spoke what was obscure and hard to be understood:' Δοκεῖ δέ τι πρὸς πονηρίαν τῷ τοιούτῳ Εὐρυβάτῃ συμβαλέσθαι καὶ ἡ πατρὶς Ἔφεσος· ἀφ' ἧς καὶ παροιμία τὸ Ἐφέσια γράμματα, ἐπὶ τῶν ἀσαφῆ τινα λαλούντων καὶ δυσπαρακολούθητα.—Eustath. Arch. Thessal. Comm. in Hom. Odyss. T. 247. p. 694, Basil. 1559. The Ἐφέσια γράμματα were enigmatical letters inscribed on the statue of Diana at Ephesus. Id. ibid. See also Hesych. Lex. col. 1544-5, Lugd. 1746; and Etymol. Magn. in voc.

---

[1] 'sought' MS.: 'taught.'

CPSIA information can be obtained
at www.ICGtesting.com
Printed in the USA
LVHW082304051222
734659LV00005B/141